Fromm

# South Africa

**Here's what the critics say about Frommer's:**

"Amazingly easy to use. Very portable, very complete."
—*Booklist*

♦

"The only mainstream guide to list specific prices. The Walter Cronkite of guidebooks—with all that implies."
—*Travel & Leisure*

♦

"Complete, concise, and filled with useful information."
—*New York Daily News*

♦

"Hotel information is close to encyclopedic."
—*Des Moines Sunday Register*

# South Africa

by Pippa de Bruyn

MACMILLAN • USA

## About the Authors

**Pippa de Bruyn** was born in Durban, schooled in Johannesburg and now lives in Cape Town. She is a freelance copywriter, journalist and copyeditor, and is passionate about her country. Covering over 18,000 kilometers in 3 months, Pippa was accompanied by her 3-month-old daughter and husband Tom, to whom she owes a huge debt of gratitude for his support and assistance.

## MACMILLAN TRAVEL

Macmillan General Reference USA, Inc.
1633 Broadway
New York, NY 10019

Find us online at **www.frommers.com**



ISBN 0-02-862642-7
ISSN 1520-9822

Editor: Margot Weiss
Production Editor: Suzanne Snyder
Photo Editor: Richard Fox
Design by Michele Laseau
Staff cartographers: John Decamillis, Roberta Stockwell
Page creation: Pete Lippincott and Julie Trippetti

## Special Sales



Manufactured in the United States of America

5 4 3 2 1

# Contents

# List of Maps

## An Invitation to the Reader

In researching this book, we discovered many wonderful places—hotels, restaurants, shops, and more. We're sure you'll find others. Please tell us about them, so we can share the information with your fellow travelers in upcoming editions. If you were disappointed with a recommendation, we'd love to know that, too. Please write to:


Pippa de Bruyn
*South Africa,* 1st Edition
Macmillan Travel
1633 Broadway
New York, NY 10019


## An Additional Note

Please be advised that travel information is subject to change at any time—and this is especially true of prices. We therefore suggest that you write or call ahead for confirmation when making your travel plans. The authors, editors, and publisher cannot be held responsible for the experiences of readers while traveling. Your safety is important to us, however, so we encourage you to stay alert and be aware of your surroundings. Keep a close eye on cameras, purses, and wallets, all favorite targets of thieves and pickpockets.

## What the Symbols Mean

### ✪ Frommer's Favorites

Our favorite places and experiences—outstanding for quality, value, or both.

The following abbreviations are used for credit cards:

- AE American Express
- CB Carte Blanche
- DC Diners Club
- DISC Discover
- ER EnRoute
- EURO Eurocard
- JCB Japan Credit Bank
- MC MasterCard
- V Visa

## Find Frommer's Online

**Arthur Frommer's Budget Travel Online** (www.frommers.com) offers more than 6,000 pages of up-to-the-minute travel information—including the latest bargains and candid, personal articles updated daily by Arthur Frommer himself. No other Web site offers such comprehensive and timely coverage of the world of travel.

# The Best of South Africa, Zimbabwe & Botswana

1

People come to southern Africa for its natural beauty, sunshine, and wildlife, and few leave disappointed. This immensely varied terrain supports a rich diversity of animals, birds, and plants, and offers a correspondingly diverse range of experiences. Whether you're here on safari or to enjoy the beaches, breathtaking drives, and unspoiled wilderness, this chapter will help you experience the very best southern Africa has to offer.

## 1 Unique Southern African Moments

- **Getting Caught Up in the Cape Minstrel Carnival** (Cape Town; ☎ **021/397-6429**): Every New Year, brightly dressed troupes of "coloured" men dance through the streets of Cape Town, singing to the quick-paced strum of banjos and the thump of drums. This tradition was inspired by American minstrels who came to the Cape in the late 1800s, but the celebration actually dates back to 1834 when slaves took to the streets to celebrate their liberation. See chapter 3.
- **Spotting Zebra from the Highway** (Cape Town): Zebra, wildebeest, and various antelope graze on Table Mountain's slopes literally minutes from the city center. Look out for them as you drive in from the airport. See chapter 3.
- **Enjoying the Sunset from Table Mountain** (Cape Town): From this great vantage point, you can watch the sun sink into the Atlantic Ocean, turning the Twelve Apostles a deep pink; then walk across the tabletop to the lip and watch the lights of the city start to twinkle and the dusky outline of the hinterland mountains. See chapter 3.
- **Feeling Humbled at Mandela's Prison Cell** (Cape Town; ☎ **021/419-2875**): Tours of Robben Island are pretty restrictive, but looking into the tiny cell where Nelson Mandela spent the majority of his time in prison leaves few emotionless. Further insight into the years spent here is provided by guides who were incarcerated at the same time as Mandela, in what came to be known as the University of Robben Island. See chapter 3.
- **Rolling Through Spectacular Scenery on the Blue Train** (☎ **011/773-7631** in Johannesburg or 021/405-2672 in Cape Town): There's no better way to pass the time and see the countryside than in the glorious luxury of the Blue Train. Relax in

your private car with a drink (delivered by your personal butler, of course), or venture down to one of the club cars to socialize with the other passengers while you watch the world outside zip by. Fabulous wine, five-star meals, and an incredibly accommodating staff make this a must for seeing South Africa and Zimbabwe in style. See chapters 2, 3, 4, 6, and 9 for descriptions of the various routes.

- **Watching Whales on the Western Cape:** The white dunes on De Hoop Nature Reserve's endless beaches stretch into the sea, turning its deep blue into a hypnotic turquoise, This is the perfect place to watch these gentle giants as they cavort off the Overberg Coast during their annual migration. See chapter 4.
- **Walking Through Carpets of Flowers** (Northern Cape): In this annual miracle of spiritual proportions, the semi-arid and seemingly barren West Coast bursts into life after the first spring rains. Over 2,600 species of flowers literally carpet the Namaqualand plains for a few weeks, before subsiding back into the soil for another year-long wait. See chapter 4.
- **Jiving with Jo'burg Jollers to the Sounds of Kwaito** (Gauteng): The best place to experience the melting pot of Rainbow Nation culture, and to celebrate the emergence of a cohesive national identity, is on the dance floors grooving to kwaito, South Africa's own homegrown version of house. Look out for performances by TKZee, Arthur, Bongo Maffin, and Boom Shaka. See chapter 6.
- **Seeing Game on an Early Morning Drive** (Northern Province, North-West, Mpumalanga, and Botswana): During winter (May to August), considered by some to be the best time of the year to go on safari as animals are the most visible, rangers set off in their open-topped vehicles before dawn. See chapters 4, 5, 6, 7, and 10.
- **Admiring Ancient Rock Art** (Western Cape, Northern Cape, Eastern Cape, and KwaZulu-Natal): Created by the San hunter-gatherers, an ancient civilization all but destroyed by the migrating Nguni and white settlers, these rock-art paintings date back between 100 and 20,000 years, and document the history and spiritual beliefs of these gentle people. Over 15,000 sites are scattered throughout the country, with some of the best and most easily accessed in the Drakensberg. See chapters 4, 5, and 8.
- **Soaking Up Victoria Falls** (Zimbabwe): The sight of over 500 million liters of water a minute thundering into the Batoka Gorge, creating soaring rainbows and a mist of drenching spray, will never leave you. See chapter 9.
- **Rafting the Churning Waters of the Zambezi** (Victoria Falls, Zimbabwe): There's absolutely nothing like hearing this mighty river pound past, drowning the guide's last-minute instructions as you plunge into such vividly named white waters as "the Muncher." See chapter 9.
- **Drinking the Waters of the Delta** (Okavango Delta, Botswana)**:** As you're poled along in your *mokoro* (dugout canoe), past palm-fringed islands and aquatic game, sample the life-giving waters of the delta. Simply scoop up a handful (keeping an eye out for crocs!) and sip. See chapter 10.

## 2 The Wildest Animal Encounters

- **Swimming with Penguins** (Boulders Beach, Cape Town): This is a beautiful place to swim; large boulders create natural swimming pools shared by the only land-breeding colony of jackass penguins. Watch them waddle and dive through the crystal-clear waters, which are slightly warmer than the Atlantic seaboard side—cold comfort considering how icy that is. See chapter 3.

- **Baiting Great White Sharks** (Dyer Island, Western Cape; ☎ **082455-2438** or 044/691-3796): Descend in a steel cage to meet Jaws up close and personal. Specialist tour operators offer controversial cage diving off Dyer Island in "Shark Alley" where Great Whites hunt the resident seal population. Sharks are attracted by fish bait and swim within spitting distance of cages—not that there's much to spit when your mouth is dry with fear. See chapters 3 and 4.
- **Staring Down a Roaring Lion** (private game reserves in Mpumalanga, Northern Province, North-West, and Botswana): Tourists are notoriously hungry for shots of big cats, and if you spend 2 nights at one of the top private game reserves you will certainly get close to lions and leopards; often on the first drive. If you're lucky enough to get close enough to have your vehicle shuddering from the powerful noise that erupts from the king of the jungle's gut, you are talking a truly wild animal encounter. See chapters 4, 6, 7, and 10.
- **Taking a Bush Bath with Elephants** (Mpumalanga; ☎ **011/327-0161**): You will find outdoor showers in most of the reserves and some coastal resorts, but very few alfresco baths, and only one where you could be disturbed by elephants. Garonga's bush bath, which is elevated on a hill, is best experienced at night, with candles, oils, champagne, and a guard walking the broad perimeter below. See chapter 7.
- **Waiting for a Leopard to Finish Its Dinner** (private game reserves, Mpumalanga): Holing up in your room while a leopard gnaws its dinner outside your door might happen at any of the private game reserve lodges that are set in the bush. Animals roam freely in this environment, and if dinner happens to be on your patio, celebrate the fact that you're not it and plunder the minibar. See chapter 7.
- **Stalking a Rhino on Foot** (Kruger National Park, ☎ **012/343-1991;** Hluhluwe-Umfolozi Reserve, ☎ **0331/845-1000;** Lapalala Wilderness Area, ☎ **011/453-7645**): You will almost definitely track white rhino on the Bushman, Wolhuter, and Napi Trails run by the Kruger National Park, as well as on the Umfolozi Trails run by the KwaZulu-Natal Nature Conservation Services (KN NCS), which boasts the highest concentration. Despite their appearance, these are relatively docile animals; it is the black rhino that is dangerous. They are also quite shy, and prefer to hide out in thickets, where hikers sometimes surprise them. Lapalala specializes in tracking black rhino. See chapters 7 and 8.
- **Watching Rare Turtles Nest** (KwaZulu-Natal; ☎ **0331/845-1000**): In December and January, the female leatherback and loggerhead turtles leave the safety of the sea at night to lay their eggs above the high-tide mark on the northern beaches of KwaZulu-Natal. Two months later, hatchlings scramble out of their nests and make a run for the ocean. Only one or two out of every thousand make it to maturity; those that do, return to the same beach to produce the next generation. See chapter 8.
- **Avoiding a Territorial Hippo** (Okavango Delta): The delta's watery channels are best explored by gliding along in a *mokoro,* but you're more than likely going to meet a hippo this way. Always treat them with respect—they are one of Africa's most dangerous mammals. See chapter 10.

## 3 The Best Private Game Lodges

- **Tshukudu** (North-West; ☎ **014/552-1610**): Set overlooking one of the grassy volcanic plains that make up the beautiful Pilanesberg, the six luxury chalets at

Tshukudu have some of the best views in South Africa. The lodge is reached via a private road, and game drives avoid the crush that arises from the Pilanesberg's proximity to the Sun City hotels. See chapter 6.

- **Madikwe River Lodge** (North-West; ☎ **011/788-1258**): In an industry that has very little tolerance for children, Madikwe deserves a standing ovation for its special innovation: game drives for kids. These take place after breakfast, and last as long as the children on board are interested. Besides this, the accommodation is comfortable, rates are reasonable, and game plentiful. See chapter 6.
- **Singita** (Mpumalanga; ☎ **011/234-0990**): This is the most expensive game lodge in South Africa, and with good reason. Modern design, organic materials, wraparound views of the Sand River, private timber decks and pools, a roving masseuse, exquisite food, and a choice of over 12,000 bottles of wine (hand-picked by well-known vintner Vaughn Johnson) ensure a fantastic stay. See chapter 7.
- **Londolozi** (Mpumalanga; ☎ **011/784-7077**): Londolozi is the flagship lodge of safari operator Conservation Corporation, known for setting the standards in luxury bush accommodation. (They also established Singita, Makalali, and Phinda.) Facilities are similar to Singita, though not as grand, and you feel more as if you're in the jungle than overlooking it. Londolozi's leopards are legendary. See chapter 7.
- **MalaMala** (Mpumalanga; ☎ **011/789-2677**): When it comes to providing guests with an outstanding game-viewing experience, no one can beat Mala-Mala. Upon departure guests are issued Big 5 certificates; these could almost be completed when you check in, as you will almost certainly tick them all off even if you're only here for 1 day. Hardly surprising, as MalaMala shares a 30-kilometer (19-mile) unfenced border with southern Kruger National Park and covers some 18,000 hectares (45,000 acres), none of which is traversed by neighbors. Main camp accommodations will suit the older traveler, while Kirkman's Kamp is a good value-for-money option. See chapter 7.
- **Honeyguide** (Mpumalanga; ☎ **011/880-3912**): If the thought of a luxury hotel in the bush leaves you cold, Honeyguide's tented camp delivers a more authentically *Out of Africa* experience—right down to the tin baths and cheeky local elephants. The lack of commercial activity in the Manyeleti Reserve, where Honeyguide is situated, is also a great plus. See chapter 7.
- **Lapalala Wilderness Area** (Northern Province; ☎ **011/453-7645**): Lapalala, the second biggest privately owned game reserve in southern Africa, is only 3½ hours from Johannesburg, yet it's a lot more remote than the Kruger. A minimum of roads and development mean that visitors can only explore the 35,382 hectares (88,455 acres) on horseback or foot. You'll truly feel as if you're the only person in the world, which for some is a lot more important than seeing lions or elephants, neither of which occurs here. See chapter 7.
- **Phinda** (KwaZulu-Natal; ☎ **011/784-7077**): This is Africa's most diverse wilderness experience: You can dive with tropical fish in the morning or go big-game fishing, visit a Zulu village in the afternoon, and follow a pride of lions in the evening. Phinda has four distinctly different camps, of which the ultra-luxurious Phinda Vlei and Rock have the most glorious settings. See chapter 8.
- **Ndumo** (KwaZulu-Natal; ☎ **011/883-0747**): Not only is this one of the top birding destinations in Africa (on a par with Mkuzi and often compared to the Okavango), it is also an incredibly beautiful reserve. More than 420 bird species are attracted to its diverse and lush vegetation—almost as many species as the

Kruger, which is 190 times its size. The 6-kilometer-long (almost 4-mile-long) Nyamithi Pan is generally considered to be one of the finest game drives in Africa. See chapter 8.

## 4 The Best National Parks & Provincial Nature Reserves

- **De Hoop Nature Reserve** (Western Cape; ☎ **028/542-1126**): A magnificent coastal reserve featuring deserted beaches, interesting rock pools, beautiful fynbos, a wetland with over 200 bird species, and number of small game. Limited accommodations ensure that the reserve is never crowded. See chapter 4.
- **Tsitsikamma National Park** (Western Cape; ☎ **042/391-0393**): Stretching from Storms River Mouth to Nature's Valley, this coastline is best explored on foot, via the 5-day Otter Trial. If you're pressed for time, or the trail is full, take the 1-kilometer (just more than a half mile) walk to the mouth, or complete the first day of the Otter Trial, which terminates at a beautiful waterfall. For an alternative viewsite of the coast, take the turn off to Harkerville (between Storms River Mouth and Nature's Valley) and have a picnic atop the craggy cliffs overlooking the ocean. See chapter 4.
- **Goegap Nature Reserve** (Northern Cape; ☎ **0251/21-880**): This is one of the best places in Namaqualand to witness the floral transformation after the first spring rains. A recommended way to explore the reserve is to hire a bike and complete the two trails that traverse the reserve. Grazing amidst the flowers you may see zebra, springbok, the stately gemsbok, or oryx. See chapter 4.
- **Kalahari Gemsbok National Park** (Northern Cape; ☎ **012/343-1991** in Pretoria or 021/22-2810 in Cape Town): This is one of the largest conservation areas in southern Africa (nearly a million hectares/more than 400,000 acres), yet because of the long distances traveled to reach it, this desert reserve is seldom included in the first visitor's itinerary. It is starkly beautiful, with red dunes, blonde grasses, and sculptural camelthorn trees contrasting with cobalt-blue skies; and despite its aridity, supports a number of predators, including the famed black-maned "Kalahari" lion, hyena, wild dog, and cheetah. See chapter 4.
- **Pilanesberg National Park** (North-West; ☎ **014/555-6135**): This reserve is South Africa's most accessible (it is just 2 hours from Johannesburg and minutes from Sun City), and is also remarkably attractive. Lying on the eroded remains of a 1.4 billion-year-old extinct volcanic crater—one of only three in the world—the 58,000-hectare (23,200-acre) reserve is the fourth largest national park south of the Limpopo and supports over 35 large mammal species, including the Big 5, cheetah, and brown hyena. See chapter 6.
- **Kruger National Park** (Mpumalanga and Northern Province; ☎ **012/343-1991**): One of the great game parks of Africa, with probably the best developed infrastructure, Kruger is the most cost-effective, do-it-yourself way to go on safari. Accommodations are pretty basic, but clean, functional, and affordable; and the park, particularly the southern section, teems with wildlife. There are over 147 mammals, 114 reptiles, and 500 bird species to spot. See chapter 7.
- **Mkuzi Game Reserve** (KwaZulu-Natal; ☎ **0331/845-1000**): This is one of the top birder's destinations in southern Africa (others are Ndumo, Okavango, and Kruger). Its varied vegetation ranges from wetland to dense thicket, from sycamore fig forest to open savannah, and supports some 400 bird species. Head straight for Nsumo Pan, known for the large diversity of its waterbirds. See chapter 8.

- **The Kosi Bay Coastal Forest Reserve** (KwaZulu-Natal; ☎/fax **0322/947-0538**): This chain of four lakes fringed by a lush and varied vegetation (marsh forests, mangroves, giant swamp figs, dune forests, raffia palm forest) is home to rare birds (Pels Fishing Owl and the Palm Nut Vulture) and tropical fish. Kosi Bay is a delight for hikers, birders, and canoeists alike, though it takes some commitment to get to this northeastern corner of South Africa. See chapter 8.
- **Natal Drakensberg Park and Royal Natal** (KwaZulu-Natal; ☎ **0331/845-1000**): The Drakensberg in its entirety is spectacular, but if you have time to visit only one region, head north for the Amphitheatre. One of the most magnificent rock formations in Africa, it is also the source of South Africa's major rivers, the Vaal, the Orange, and the Tugela. Rolling grasslands, breathtaking views, and crystal-clear streams can only be explored on foot or horseback. See chapter 8.
- **The Victoria Falls National Park** (Victoria Falls, Zimbabwe; ☎ **263/13-4202**): This World Heritage Site offers the most stupendous views of the 1,000-meter-wide (3,280-foot-wide) falls, and the constant spray, crowned by a permanent rainbow, sustains a lush and verdant rainforest. See chapter 9.
- **Moremi Game Reserve** (Botswana; ☎ **267/535-024** or 267/66-0492): No visit to Botswana would be complete without visiting Moremi. Covering an area of 487,200 hectares (194,880 acres), including waterways, islands, pans, and forests, this reserve is home to over 500 species of birds as well as lion, elephant, cheetah, wild dog, leopard, and buffalo. See chapter 10.

## 5 The Best Wilderness Trails

- **The Otter Trial** (Western Cape; ☎ **021/22-2810**): This 5-day trail between Storms River Mouth and Nature's Valley is the most popular trail in the country; book at least a year in advance. The coastline offers spectacular views of forested cliff faces plunging into the ocean, tea-colored rivers, tumbling waterfalls, deep pools, and deserted beaches. You need to be relatively fit to complete it without discomfort. (Note that the **Harkerville Hiking Trail, ☎ 044/382-5466,** also known as the mini-Otter, is a good 2-day alternative.) See chapter 4.
- **The Wild Coast** (Eastern Cape; ☎ **047/531-2711**): This spectacular coastline is mostly inaccessible by vehicle or boat, with kilometers of deserted beaches and estuaries best explored on foot. It takes at least 15 days to cover the full 169 kilometers (105 miles), but with no trail markers and virtually no facilities, shorter versions are recommended. This is a great way to meet rural Xhosa. See chapter 5.
- **Kruger Wilderness Trails** (Mpumalanga and Northern Province; ☎ **012/343-1991**): There are seven Kruger Wilderness Trails, each offering more or less the same experience but in differing ecozones. Groups are limited in number, are accommodated in rustic base camps, and go on day excursions accompanied by an armed ranger. They are definitely worth booking for, with the 2-day Wolhuter and Olifants the most popular. Once again, book at least a year in advance. See chapter 7.
- **Blyde River Canyon Trail Hiking Trail** (Mpumalanga; ☎ **013/758-1035**): A 5-day trail that takes you from the grassveld and forests of the Escarpment Lip, past the Bourke's Luck potholes and the Three Rondawel viewsites, to the tumbling waterfalls and deep pools of the Blyde River as it makes its sinuous way through the lowveld plains, this 65-kilometer (40-mile) route covers the best viewsites of the Panorama Route. Book well in advance. See chapter 7.

- **Umfolozi Trails** (Zululand, KwaZulu-Natal; ☎ **0331/845-1000**): Considered superior to even the Kruger Wilderness Trails, the Umfolozi Trails traverse a large wilderness area inaccessible by car. The subtropical vegetation, abundant wildlife, and the fact that you don't return to a base camp, are some of the reasons given for its top rating. The reserve also boasts the world's highest concentration of rhino. Once again, book early. See chapter 8.
- **The Giant's Cup Trail** (Drakensberg, KwaZulu-Natal; ☎ **0331/845-1000**): This 5-day, 59-kilometer (36½-mile) trail is considered the best introduction to the Drakensberg, and winds its way through mountain grasslands, past dramatic cliffs and eroded rock formations. See chapter 8.

## 6 The Best Beaches

- **Long Beach** (Cape Town): This 4-kilometer-long (2½ -mile-long) stretch of sand—almost as wide as it is long—is both the city's best walking beach and the best place to go horseback riding. Even if you don't have time to sample the waves, at least stop to admire it during your Chapman's Peak drive. See chapter 3.
- **Clifton** (Cape Town): A beautiful beach just minutes from the city center, this is where Cape Town's beautiful people like to parade. It's also the most wind-free area in Cape Town—handy when the southeaster, known locally as the Cape Doctor, is driving you mad. Divided by large boulders into First, Second, Third, and Fourth beaches, it is accessible only via steep steps. Other great Cape Town beaches include **Camps Bay** and **Llandudno.** See chapter 3.
- **De Hoop Nature Reserve** (Western Cape; ☎ **028/542-1126**): Tall white dunes sliding into the sea, coves, evocative limestone outcrops, an aquamarine sea, and picture-perfect rock pools make this reserve's beaches the most glorious in the Overberg, if not the entire Cape. See chapter 4.
- **Noezie** (Western Cape): One of the closest beaches to Knysna is also the most charming, not least because of the mini-castles overlooking it. If the sea's too wild, take a dip in the lagoon. See chapter 4.
- **Plettenberg Bay** (Western Cape): It's a toss-up between Lookout and Robberg Beach, but safe to say that "Plet," as the locals call it, has the best beaches on the Garden Route. Pity about the monstrous houses that overlook them. Head for Lookout for the view of the distant Outeniqua Mountains, and Robberg for whale watching. See chapter 4.
- **Port St Johns** (Eastern Cape): The entire Wild Coast is renowned for its magnificent, deserted coastline; but as Port St Johns is one of the more accessible points, you may wish to head straight here, and laze away the sultry days on Second Beach, a perfect crescent fringed with tropical vegetation. For total seclusion, head for Umngazi, a few kilometers south. See chapter 5.

## 7 The Best Golf Courses

- **Erinvale Country Estate** (Winelands; ☎ **021/847-1144**): The latest course to be designed by Gary Player, Erinvale is protected from the Cape's gale-force winds by the towering Helderberg and Hottentots' Holland Mountains—the very reason for the course's lovely views. And if you play over par, nevermind; the proximity to the Stellenbosch Wine Route offers welcome relief, and you may even wish to try your hand on the **Stellenbosch course** (☎ **021/880-0103**); having recently hosted the South African Open, it's in tip-top condition. See chapter 3.

- **Milnerton Golf Club** (Cape Town; ☎ **021/434-7808**): Golfers like this course, the only true links course in Cape Town, both for its layout and the classic post-card views of Table Mountain. During summer, the wind can be a real problem (in which case, head for Erinvale). See chapter 3.
- **Fancourt Country Club Estate** (Garden Route, Western Cape; ☎ **044/870-8282**): Rated by World Cup winner Ernie Els as the best in the country, this Gary Player–designed course features water on 27 of the 36 holes and exquisite views of the Outeniqua Mountains. Golf widows/widowers are well catered to in the luxurious hotel and health-and-beauty pavilion. Other courses worth considering on the Garden Route include the George Club (☎ **044/873-6116**), and the two courses at Plettenberg Bay (☎ **04457/32-132** and 044/533-5082). See chapter 4.
- **Gary Player Country Club** (Sun City, North-West; ☎ **014/557-1000**): Hosting the annual Million Dollar Challenge, this par-72 course has been played by most of the world's best golfers. Carved out of the crater of an extinct volcano, it has some interesting challenges, not least of which are the live crocodiles at the 13th hole. See chapter 6.
- **Leopard's Creek Country Club** (Malelane, Mpumalanga; ☎ **013/790-3322**): If the sight of animals in the rough doesn't put you off your game, play Leopard's Creek, adjoining Kruger in the south. Decked out in the finest examples of the Afro-colonial style, the clubhouse is probably the most exclusive in South Africa, and provides limited access to visitors. It's worth it though, not least because of the elusive leopard sometimes seen crossing the fairways. See chapter 7.
- **Hans Merensky Country Club** (Northern Province; ☎ **015/781-3931**): Bordering central Kruger and surrounded by its own game reserve, this par-72 course is arguably the wildest course in Africa, as the golfers who recently watched an elephant charge down a fellow player will no doubt agree. It has six water hazards that attract a variety of game, particularly during the dry winter months, as well as crocodile and hippo. See chapter 7.
- **Durban Country Club** (Durban, KwaZulu-Natal; ☎ **031/23-8282**): Players consistently rate this course, fashioned from the dunes along the Indian Ocean beachfront, as one of the top 50 in the world. It is often described as "a masterpiece of design," and has hosted the national championship 13 times, challenging local and foreign players alike. See chapter 8.
- **Wild Coast Country Club** (KwaZulu-Natal; ☎ **039/305-2799** or 03931/22-322): Designed by Robert Trent Jones II, in the style of an American seaside course, this par-70 winds through some spectacular ravines, waterfalls, and subtropical bush. It's a mere 90-minute drive south from Durban, and along the way you could try your hand at **San Lameer** (☎ **039/313-5141**), **Southbroom** (☎ **039/31-6051**), and **Selbourne** (☎ **0323/975-3564**), other highly rated courses on Durban's "Golf Coast." (For more information, see chapter 8.)

## 8 The Best Outdoor Adventures

- **Throwing Yourself Off Table Mountain** (Cape Town; ☎ **021/424-1580**): Attached to a rope, of course. At 100 meters (328 feet), this is the highest commercially run abseil in the world, and is the most exhilarating way to see the city and the Atlantic seaboard. See chapter 3.
- **Paragliding Off Lion's Head to Camps Bay Beach** (Cape Town; ☎ **021/424-1580**): It's a breathtaking ride hovering over the slopes of Table Mountain.

As you slowly glide toward the white sands of Camps Bay, lapped by an endless expanse of ocean, you'll have time to admire the craggy cliffs of the Twelve Apostles. See chapter 3.

- **Kayaking to Cape Point** (Cape Town; ☎ **082556-2520**): Kayaking is the most impressive way to view this towering outcrop, the southwesternmost point of Africa. It's also the ideal opportunity to explore the rugged cliffs that line the coastline, with numerous crevices and private coves to beach yourself on. See chapter 3.
- **Mountain Biking Through the Knysna Forests** (Western Cape; ☎ **044/382-7785**): Starting at the Garden of Eden, the 22-kilometer (14-mile) Harkerville Red Route is considered the most challenging in the country. Its steep, single-track slip paths take you past indigenous forests, silent plantations, and magnificent coastal fynbos. See chapter 4.
- **Bungee Jumping Off Bloukrans River Bridge** (Western Cape; ☎ **042/281-1450**): The real daredevils do the highest bungee jump in the world in just their birthday suits, leaping 216 meters (708 feet) and free falling (not to mention screaming) for close to 7 seconds. See chapter 4.
- **Surfing "Bruce's Beauties"** (Cape St Francis, Eastern Cape; ☎ **042/293-2588**): Bruce's Beauties, the waves featured in the 1960s cult classic *Endless Summer,* form an awesome right-point break. They need a massive swell, however, and don't work very often; the same goes for Supertubes, hailed the "perfect wave," in nearby Jeffrey's Bay. See chapter 5.
- **Tracking Big Game on Horseback** (Northern Province; ☎ **011/788-3923;** and in Okavango Delta, Botswana; ☎ **267/66-1671**): Experience Africa as the pioneers did. Equus Wilderness Horse Safaris offers relatively luxurious facilities and the chance to track rhino, giraffe, zebra, and many species of antelope in the Waterberg Conservancy; while Okavango Horse Safaris offers an alternative form of transport to the popular *mokoro* (dugout canoe). See chapters 7 and 10.
- **Surfing the Mighty Zambezi River** (Victoria Falls, Zimbabwe): Not content with rafting down the Zambezi, the latest adrenaline rush offered by river operators is plunging into the churning waters attached to nothing more than a boogie board, and riding the 2- to 3-meter-high (6- to 10-foot-high) waves. See chapter 9.
- **Riding an Elephant Through the African Wilderness** (Okavango Delta, Botswana; ☎ **267/66-1260**): This is a great way to explore the delta, not only because of the elevated view, and the proximity with which you can approach animals, but because you can't feel safer—no one in the jungle messes with an elephant. See chapter 10.

## 9 The Most Dramatic Drives

- **The Cape Peninsula Drive** (Cape Town): Cover the mountainous peninsula in a circular day drive that covers both seaboards, as well as Cape Point (Africa's southwesternmost point) and Chapman's Peak Drive. Chapman's Peak, scene of a hundred car commercials, is the corker, snaking along sheer cliffs as they plunge directly down into the ocean. See chapter 3.
- **Tulbagh via Du Toit's Kloof and Bain's Kloof Passes** (Winelands): You'll enjoy majestic mountain scenery should you choose to ignore the toll tunnel and traverse the Du Toit's Kloof Pass, built in 1942 by Italian prisoners of war. Travel via this and the Slanghoek Pass to Tulbagh, lunch at Paddagang, then return to

Cape Town or your Winelands base via Bain's Kloof Pass. Much older than Du Toit's Kloof, Bain's Kloof was built by Andrew Bain, who together with his son Thomas Bain, was the most prolific pass builder in South Africa. See chapter 3.

- **The Four Passes Route** (Winelands): This aptly named route traverses four mountain ranges and winds its way through the fruit-producing valleys of Elgin, Grabouw, and Villiersdorp (spectacular in spring) before returning to the vineyard valley of Franschhoek. A highly recommended day excursion if you don't mind spending the greater part of the day behind the wheel. See chapter 3.
- **Swartberg Pass and Meiringspoort** (Western Cape): For many, the most unforgettable drive in the country is the Swartberg Pass, a dirt road built in 1887 to link Oudtshoorn with Prince Albert. From the top, you have a magnificent view of the Klein Karoo, before slowly descending via numerous hairpin bends into the Great Karoo. Having lunched at the Victorian village of Prince Albert, return via Meiringspoort as it winds its way along the base of the mountains. See chapter 4.
- **The Lakes' Drive, George to Knysna** (Western Cape): The N2 takes you flying past the ocean on one side and the seven expanses of water that lie within the Wilderness National Park on the other. Pockets of indigenous forest are interspersed with dense plantations and backed by the Outeniqua Mountains. (The alternative, the Passes Route, is less busy and equally pretty, but you won't see the sea.) See chapter 4.
- **Panorama Route** (Mpumalanga): From the forestry town of Graskop, you head north to follow the Escarpment Lip where it overlooks the lowveld plains that stretch all the way to Mozambique. The descent to the lowveld is via the dramatic Abel Erasmus Pass; from here, you can either return to Graskop, take a boat or raft trip through the world's third highest canyon, or head to a game reserve. See chapter 7.
- **Sani Pass** (KwaZulu-Natal): This Drakensberg pass, connecting South Africa with the mountain kingdom of Lesotho, climbs more than 1,000 meters (3,280 feet) in 25 kilometers (15½ miles), finally reaching "the roof of Africa" at a breathtaking 2,874 meters (9,427 feet). See chapter 8.

## 10 The Most Spectacular Views

- **The Table Mountain Cable Car** (Cape Town; ☎ **021/424-5148**): It takes no more than 4 minutes to get to the top, but the cable car rotates a full 360 degrees, giving you superb views of Cape Town as it recedes into the distance, and close-ups of the mountain face. See chapter 3.
- **Robben Island and the Robben Island Ferry** (Cape Town; ☎ **021/419-2875**): As the ferry pulls out of the harbor, you can watch the city slowly diminish, dwarfed by the massive bulk of Table Mountain. Once on the island, yet another perspective emerges and remote Cape Town seems like a slim, fragile necklace draped at the base of the towering mountain. See chapter 3.
- **Sir Lowry's Pass** (Western Cape): You can see the whole of False Bay and the distant mountain chain as you ascend Sir Lowry's Pass. This is part of the Four Passes route on the N2 and is also the most direct way to get to the Garden Route. (Remember to stop for *padkos* (literally "road food") at Peregrine Farm Stall, opposite Grabouw. See chapter 4.
- **Swartberg Pass** (Western Cape): The massive, uninhabited vistas of the Klein Karoo, its fields reduced to a patchwork quilt, are as soothing as they are breathtaking. See chapter 4.

- **God's Window** (Mpumalanga): Aptly named, this is an easily accessed viewpoint along the Panorama Route, a fissure which provides an awesome view over the lip of the Escarpment to the lowveld plains shimmering thousands of meters below. On a clear day, you can see beyond the bushveld plains of the Kruger to the hills bordering Mozambique. See chapter 7.
- **The Three Rondawels** (Mpumalanga): If possible, this Escarpment view is even better than God's Window. The lookout point takes in Blyde River Canyon (the third largest in the world) as it snakes its way into the Blyde River Dam, and the three outcrops that do in fact bear a passing resemblance to rondawels (circular huts topped with thatch peaks). See chapter 7.
- **Olifants Rest Camp** (Kruger National Park, Northern Province; ☎ **013/735-6606**): This rest camp in central Kruger, has a most breathtaking view over the Olifants River. You can hear the cry of the fish eagle circling below while enjoying your own bird's-eye view of hippos cavorting, or a solitary lion padding down to the banks of the river. See chapter 7.
- **Kosi Bay Lookout Point** (KwaZulu-Natal): Look toward the sea, and you'll see the Tonga fish traps, looped like delicate chains. Beyond the estuary mouth, you'll find a host of tropical fish and the beaches where turtles come to nest. Look back and you'll see the Kosi Bay lake system, each linked via a narrow water channel, and fringed with palm nuts. Now you simply have to decide where to start. See chapter 8.
- **Devil's Cataract** (Victoria Falls, Zimbabwe): You'll find this viewpoint near the statue of David Livingstone (who incidentally only saw the falls from the Zambian side, from **Livingstone's Island,** another great viewsite), some 30 meters (97 feet) below the top of the falls. From here, you can see the greatest flow of the Zambezi as it plunges into the gorge. See chapter 9.

## 11 The Best Places to Discover South African Culture & History

- **Robben Island** (Cape Town; ☎ **021/419-2875**): A prison for political activists since the 17th century, including its most famous prisoner, Nelson Mandela, the island was commonly known as the Alcatraz of Africa. Today the island is a museum and a nature reserve, and a tangible symbol of South Africa's transformation. See chapter 3.
- **Bo-Kaap** (Cape Town; ☎ **021/240719**): This Cape Malay area, replete with cobbled streets and quaint historical homes, was one of the few "non-white" areas to escape destruction during the apartheid era, despite its proximity to the city. A walk or drive through the streets should be combined with a visit to the **District Six Museum** (☎ **021/424-3846**), which commemorates a less fortunate community. Visible today only as cleared land on the southern outskirts of town (opposite the Bo-Kaap), this once vibrant suburb was razed to the ground in the 1960s. See chapter 3.
- **Wuppertal Mission** (Western Cape; ☎ **027/482-3410**): Located at the end of a long, dusty road in the Cederberg Mountains, Wuppertal remains unchanged to this day, and is both architecturally and culturally a living legacy of the early missionaries. Other mission stations worth visiting are **Elim** and **Genandendal,** both in the Overberg. See chapter 4.
- **The Hector Peterson Memorial** (Soweto, Gauteng): When schoolchildren took to the streets on June 16, 1976 in a peaceful protest against the decision to use

Afrikaans as the sole means of instruction in schools, police opened fire, killing amongst others, young Hector Peterson. This was a turning point in the battle against apartheid. Widespread riots and international condemnation followed, and nothing would ever be the same. The Hector Peterson Memorial documents the anger, terror, and pain of these times. The best way to see the memorial is with a township tour. See chapter 6.

- **The Sterkfontein Caves** (Gauteng; ☎ **011/956-6342**): Having shot to fame in 1947 with the discovery of a 2½ million-year-old hominid skull, the caves produced a skull dating back 3½ million years in 1998. There are daily tours of the caves as well as a museum to introduce visitors to some of the most intriguing aspects of human evolution in southern Africa. See chapter 6.
- **Voortrekker Monument** (Pretoria, Gauteng; ☎ **012/323-0682**): This massive granite structure commemorates the Great Trek, in particular the Battle of Blood River (fought between Trekkers and Zulus on December 16, 1838), and remains hallowed ground for Afrikaner nationalists. Every year on December 16, at exactly noon, a hole in the top of the monument allows a ray of sunlight to light up a central plaque that celebrates the covenant the Trekkers made with God on this day. See chapter 6.
- **Rorke's Drift and Isandlwana** (the Battlefields, KwaZulu-Natal): These two Anglo-Zulu War battlefield sites, fought within walking distance of each other, encompass both the British Empire's most humiliating defeat, and its most heroic victory in the colonies. At the Battle of Isandlwana, over 1,300 armed men were wiped out by a "bunch of savages armed with sticks," as the mighty Zulu nation were then referred to. Hours later, 139 British soldiers (of which 35 were ill) warded off a force of 4,000 Zulus for 12 hours, for which an unprecedented 11 Victorian Crosses were awarded. See chapter 8.
- **Kwa Muhle Museum** (Durban; ☎ **031/300-6313**): Excellent user-friendly displays explain how the "Durban System" not only exploited the indigenous peoples, but made them pay for its administration. It is a good introduction to the discriminatory laws that preceded apartheid. See chapter 8.
- **The Vukani Collection Museum** (Eshowe, KwaZulu-Natal; ☎ **0354/41-254**): While most Westerners head for the cultural villages to gain some insight into Zulu tribal customs and culture, Vukani is where Zulu parents take their children. With the largest collection of Zulu artifacts in the world, and an informative curator/guide, this is a highly recommended excursion, particularly for those interested in crafts. The Vukani shop, associated with the museum, is also excellent. Note that if you aren't venturing this far afield, the **Killie Campbell Museum** (☎ **031/207-3432**) in Durban is an alternative. See chapter 8.
- **Victoria Street Market** (Durban, KwaZulu-Natal): The most culturally diverse city in southern Africa is Durban, and the best place to see this diversity is in the streets surrounding the Victoria Street Market. The number of shops selling anything from saris to spices is not surprising (Durban has the greatest Indian population outside of India); but woven into this dense and fragrant fabric are Zulu *sangomas* (healers) selling traditional medicines (*muti*) made of barks and animal parts, and street hawkers pawning everything from fresh fruit to haircuts. See chapter 8.

## 12 The Top Architectural Landmarks

- **The Castle of Good Hope** (Cape Town; ☎ **021/469-1249**): The oldest building in southern Africa, the castle was built between 1666 and 1679 by the

Dutch. Today it is still a military headquarters, but thankfully no shots have ever been fired from its ramparts. See chapter 3.

- **Cape Dutch Homesteads** (Winelands): You'll find one of the most elegant examples of the classic H-shaped and gabled Cape Dutch manor houses on the Helshoogte Pass to Franschhoek. **Boschendal** (☎ **021/870-4000**) was built between 1812 and 1818 and was fully restored in the 1970s. It is beautifully furnished, and authentically finished with original colors. Other Cape Dutch beauties worth visiting are **Groot Constantia** (Cape Town; ☎ **021/794-5067**) and **Vergelegen** (Somerset West, ☎ **021/847-1334**). See chapter 3.
- **Ostrich Palaces** (Oudtshoorn, Western Cape): Take a drive through the streets of Oudtshoorn and admire some of the elaborate ostrich palaces, built by rich farmers during the turn-of-the-century ostrich boom. You can visit the townhouses of the so-called ostrich barons (they're part of the **CP Nel Museum;** ☎ **044/272-7306**) to gain some idea of how much lucre the feathers of Africa's largest bird brought to this previously impoverished area. See chapter 4.
- **Union Building** (Pretoria, Gauteng; ☎ **012/325-2000**): This is the best example of the work of Sir Herbert Baker, South Africa's most prolific imperialist architect. The building houses the administrative headquarters of the South African government and was the scene of immense jubilation on May 10, 1994, when South Africa's first black president was inaugurated. See chapter 6.
- **Palace of the Lost City** (Sun City, North-West; ☎ **014/557-1000**): Southern Africa's most opulent hotel, and co-owned by Michael Jackson, the Palace of the Lost City takes its cue from the great themed hotels of Vegas. It's worth visiting to gape at the exquisite craftsmanship of the myriad carved animals and wander through the lush gardens: 1.6 million plants (of which 4,000 were fully grown trees) were transplanted into the bushveld plains, transforming the grounds surrounding the "city" into a man-made jungle. See chapter 6.
- **Pilgrim's Rest** (Mpumalanga; ☎ **013/768-1060**): Once a mecca for gold prospectors, this tiny Victorian Escarpment town remained almost unchanged for over a century, and eventually was declared a national monument. Despite being somewhat touristy, the corrugated iron buildings, most with broad verandahs to shake off the summer downpours, are charming. They're best admired by taking a leisurely stroll down the tree-shaded main street. See chapter 7.
- **Ondini Historical Reserve** (KwaZulu Natal; ☎ **0358/70-2050**): In 1873, Cetshwayo, the last king of the independent Zulu nation, built his royal kraal at Ondini, with some 1,500 huts housing 5,000 people. The *isigodlo* (royal enclosure) has been rebuilt on the original foundations uncovered by archeologists, and a model shows the full extent of the original village. See chapter 8.

## 13 The Most Authentic Culinary Experiences

- **Ordering a Cape Malay Dish** (Cape Town): Typified by mild, sweet curries and stews, this cuisine is easy on the uninitiated palate. The most authentic restaurant is **Biesmiellah** (☎ **021/23-0850**) located in the Bo-Kaap in Cape Town, but one of the loveliest environments is at **Paddagang** (☎ **0236/300-242**), in Tulbagh—their *waterblommetjie bredie* (waterlily stew) is arguably the best in the Cape. See chapter 3.
- **Picnicking at Kirstenbosch** (Cape Town; ☎ **021/762-9120**): Find out when the Cape Town Philharmonic Orchestra is playing, pick up a picnic from one of the recommended delis, and spread your blanket under one of the trees in this magnificent botanical garden. You can purchase picnic hampers during the

summer concert season. Alternatively, order a meal at the well-priced, no-frills Kirstenbosch restaurant. See chapter 3.

- **Lunching in the Vineyards** (Winelands): Set at least one afternoon aside to lunch in the Winelands overlooking vine-carpeted valleys. If you're based in Cape Town and pressed for time, try **Constantia Uitsig (☎ 021/794-4480)**, on the Constantia Wine Route. Great Winelands choices are the **Green Door (☎ 021/885-1756)** at Delaire, which overlooks the Helshoogte Pass and is on the Stellenbosch Wine Route, and **La Petite Ferme (☎ 021/876-3016)**, which overlooks the lush Franschhoek Valley. See chapter 3.
- **Braaing Fish on the Beach** (West Coast, Western Cape): These all-you-can-eat beach *braais* (barbecues) are legendary, giving you an opportunity to try a variety of local fish as well as local preparation styles. It's virtually impossible, but try not to fill up on the bread (just baked on the beach) and the farm-fresh butter. Your best bet is **Muisbosskerm (☎ 027/432-1017)**, near Lambert's Bay, and ideal if you want to combine a trip to the Cederberg. See chapter 4.
- **Eating with Your Fingers:** You'll find the African staple *pap* (maize-meal prepared as a stiff porridge that resembles polenta) best sampled by balling a bit in one hand and dipping the edge into a sauce or stew—try *umngqusho,* a stew made from maize kernels, sugar beans, chilies, and potatoes, and said to be one of Mandela's favorites. There are a number of restaurants in Gauteng serving traditional food; alternatively, visit a shebeen on a township tour. See chapter 6, in particular, or any restaurant that serves traditional cuisine.
- **Dining Under the Stars to the Sounds of the Bush** (private game reserves throughout South Africa and Botswana): There's nothing like fresh air to work up an appetite, unless it's the smell of sizzling food cooked over an open fire. Happily, dinners at private game reserves combine both more often than not. Weather permitting, meals are served in the *boma* (a reeded enclosure), or in the bush on tables placed in riverbeds or under massive trees. Armed rangers and massive fires keep the predators at bay. See chapters 5, 6, 7, 8, and 10.
- **Snacking on *Samoosas* in Victoria Street** (Durban, KwaZulu-Natal): Known as "samosas" in America, this Indian delicacy—curried and minced meat or vegetables wrapped in paper-thin pastry and deep fried—makes a delicious snack. If you're really hungry, try a *bunnychow,* a scooped out half-loaf of bread, stuffed with curry. See chapter 8.
- **Chewing *Biltong* on a Road Trip:** *Biltong,* strips of game, beef, or ostrich cured with spices and dried, are sold at farm stalls and butchers throughout the country. This popular local tradition that dates back to the Voortrekkers is something of an acquired taste, but almost addictive once you've started. See "South African Cuisine" in Appendix A, "South Africa in Depth," for more information.

# Planning Your Trip to Southern Africa

2

South Africa is a pretty developed country, though it has definite third-world elements—fear of crime is obviously a common complaint, and visitors expecting a high level of service are likely to be disappointed. While generally smaller than those in Europe and the States, South Africa's major cities offer all the same facilities and, combined with its many and varied attractions, this is one good reason to start your southern African trip here. Unless you're heading into really remote areas (which Botswana certainly constitutes), don't panic while planning your trip: anything you've forgotten can be purchased here, credit cards are an accepted form of payment, and you're unlikely to be affected by water or food-borne illnesses. You'll also find a reasonably efficient tourism infrastructure in South Africa and Victoria Falls, never more so than now, as southern Africa experiences an unprecedented boom in visitors. There are a great number of services, maps, and books designed to help you make the most of your trip. Start by browsing the Web and contacting your local travel agent. Or simply read this chapter.

## 1 The Regions in Brief

### SOUTH AFRICA

South Africa once consisted of four large provinces with borders created by the country's colonial past. These were where, by law, the white population resided. The black "tribes" were crammed into a number of shamefully small, quasi-independent homelands peppered throughout the country. After the 1994 elections (which finally saw Nelson Mandela the rightful leader of the New South Africa), the country had, at all costs, to be redivided, taking into account the economic hubs of every region. This was one of the first tasks the new government completed, and the country found itself with nine new provinces. The **Western Cape** stretches along the south coast to encompass most of the Garden Route at its eastern extreme, and to the north as far as Namaqualand and the Northern Cape. Farther east come the coastal provinces of the **Eastern Cape** and **KwaZulu-Natal. Mpumalanga** and the **Northern Province** together encompass the northeastern corner of South Africa, and west of these are the highveld provinces of **North-West, Gauteng** (*how*-teng), and **Free State.** See the following map of South Africa for more information, and for maps of Zimbabwe and Botswana, turn to chapters 9 and 10, respectively.

# South Africa

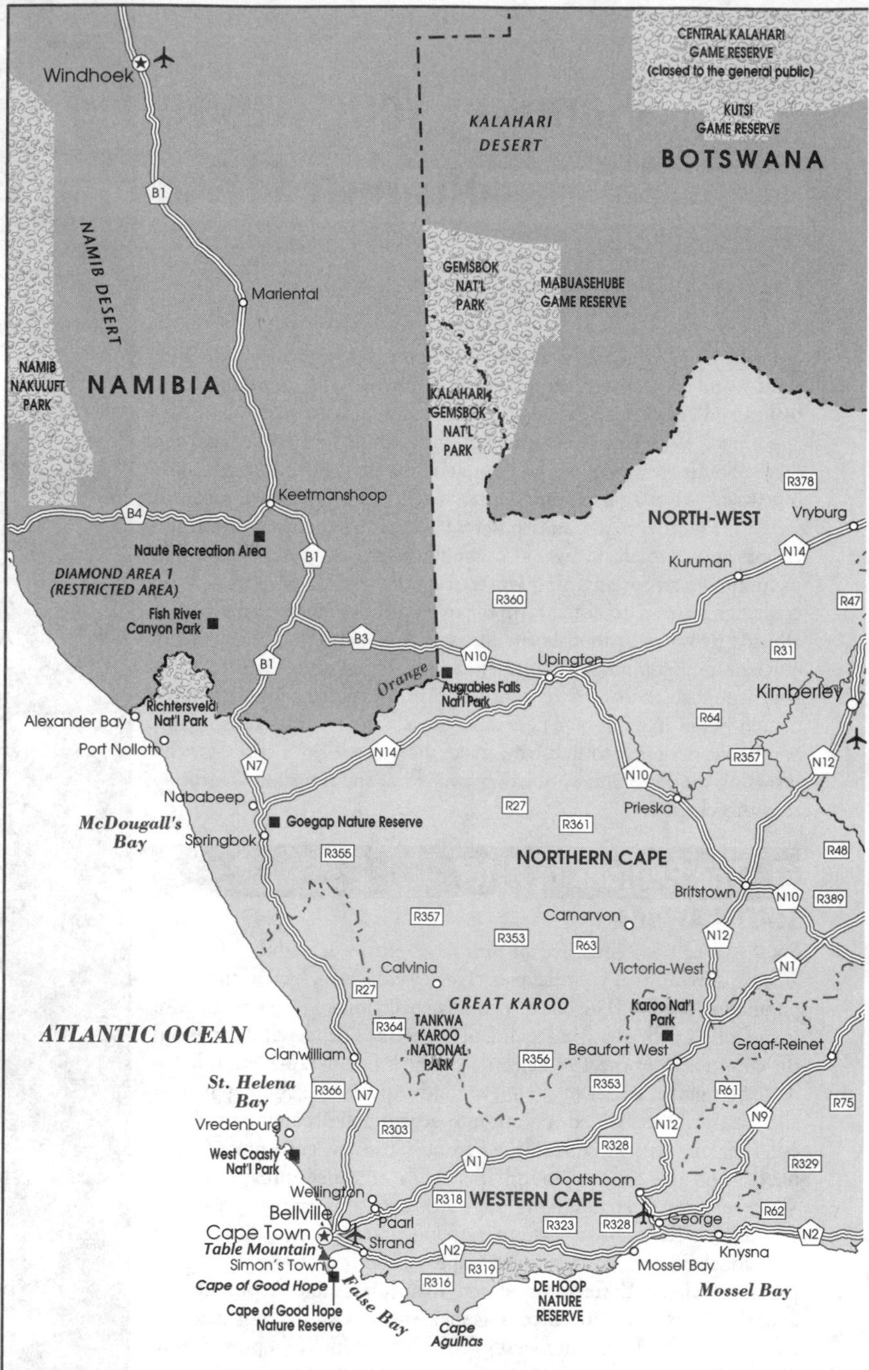

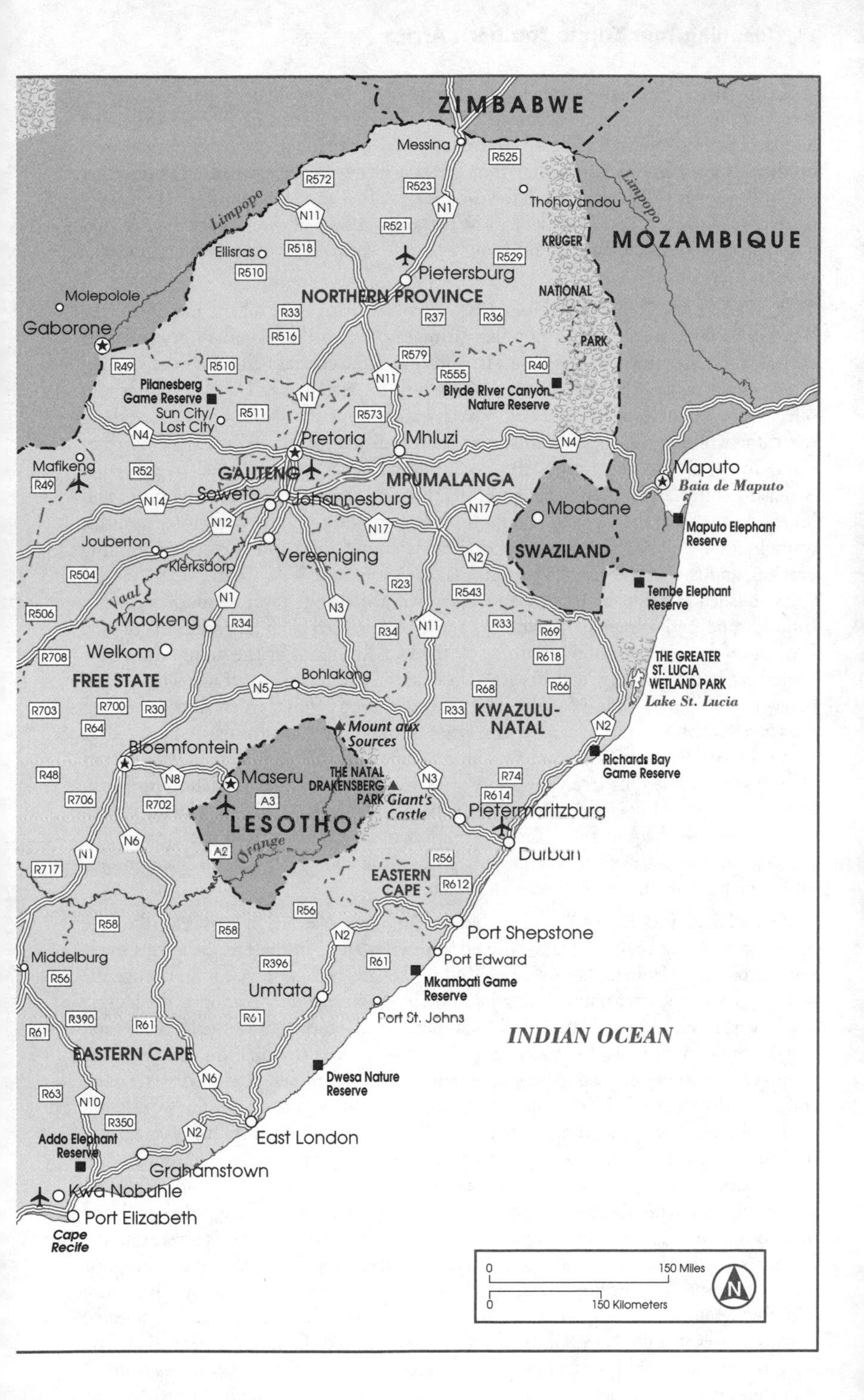

ZIMBABWE
MOZAMBIQUE
Messina
Thohoyandou
Limpopo
KRUGER
NATIONAL
PARK
Ellisras
Pietersburg
NORTHERN PROVINCE
Molepolole
Gaborone
Pilanesberg Game Reserve
Sun City/ Lost City
Blyde River Canyon Nature Reserve
Pretoria
Mhluzi
Mafikeng
GAUTENG
MPUMALANGA
Soweto
Johannesburg
Maputo
Baia de Maputo
Mbabane
Maputo Elephant Reserve
SWAZILAND
Jouberton
Klerksdorp
Vereeniging
Tembe Elephant Reserve
Vaal
Maokeng
Welkom
FREE STATE
THE GREATER ST. LUCIA WETLAND PARK
Lake St. Lucia
Bohlakong
KWAZULU-NATAL
Mount aux Sources
Bloemfontein
Maseru
THE NATAL DRAKENSBERG PARK
Giant's Castle
Richards Bay Game Reserve
LESOTHO
Orange
Pietermaritzburg
Durban
EASTERN CAPE
Port Shepstone
Port Edward
Middelburg
Mkambati Game Reserve
Umtata
Port St. Johns
INDIAN OCEAN
EASTERN CAPE
Dwesa Nature Reserve
Addo Elephant Reserve
East London
Grahamstown
Kwa Nobuhle
Port Elizabeth
Cape Recife
0 150 Miles
0 150 Kilometers
N

South Africa's tourism slogan has for years been "A World in One Country"—certainly during the years of sanctions during apartheid it became that for the many South Africans, who tired of being treated as pariahs, opted to travel within their own borders. It is an enormous country that offers a variety of experiences, and one that you will not get to know in a single visit. For the first-time visitor, there are usually three crucial stops: **Cape Town** and its **Winelands,** a tour of the **Garden Route,** and a trip to **Big-Game Country,** most of which is located in Mpumalanga and the Northern Province.

**THE WESTERN & EASTERN CAPE** The least African of all the provinces, the Western Cape is also the most popular, primarily due to the legendary beauty of its capital city, Cape Town, the Winelands, and the scenic coastal belt called the Garden Route which winds through South Africa's well-traveled Lakes District. But it also offers some of the best beach-based whale watching in the world on the Overberg coast; the world's most spectacular spring flowers display on the West Coast, north of Cape Town; and in the Karoo, the quaint *dorps* (small towns) which typify rural Afrikaans culture. The mountains and hills that trail the coastline are a botanist's and hiker's dream, with the Cape floral kingdom at its best during the wet winter months, from June to August. The Eastern Cape has some of the country's best swimming beaches, and two of the country's top trails: the Otter and Wild Coast.

Established as a port in 1652, **Cape Town** was the first gateway to southern Africa from Europe, and subsequently retains a more colonial feel than any other major city. It is cut off from the rest of the country by the Hex River and by the mountains of the Cederberg and Swartberg, and has its own distinctive climate—cool wet winters and hot windy summers—ideal for the wine and deciduous fruits which further cocoon the Cape's inhabitants from the harsh realties of the hinterland. Insularity has bred its own problems, however. Gang warfare in the Cape Flats, homelessness, and drug trafficking are all at serious levels. In a city this size, such problems are hardly unusual, but what is surprising is how cut off from them you'll feel as a visitor. Having driven past the endless shacks of the black townships on the way in from the airport, the problems of Cape Town are "conveniently" kept out of sight by the majestic mountains which divide much of the city into valleys.

**GAUTENG & FREE STATE** Situated on the inner plateau, or highveld, the Free State and Gauteng were originally covered with grasslands. In the Free State this made way for farming, while the discovery of gold in the late 19th century was to change the Gauteng landscape irreparably. Today Johannesburg International Airport is the biggest and busiest in sub-Saharan Africa; and Johannesburg, the capital of Gauteng, the busiest city. In the City of Gold (or Egoli, as it is known to locals), you'll find some of the country's best museums and galleries, as well as the gold mines of the Witwatersrand (ridge of white waters). Here miners dig deeper than anywhere else in the world; and while gold resources are starting to dwindle, all the country's major industries are based in Gauteng. The resulting urban sprawl covers most of the province and houses an estimated population of 5 to 7 million. **Downtown Johannesburg** is notoriously dangerous, but in the **northern suburbs** of Sandton, Rosebank, and Hyde Park, you'll find luxurious hotels and elegant shopping centers. Even farther north is **Pretoria,** the country's administrative capital. Pretoria is a great deal more laid back than Jo'burg. As it is equidistant from the airport, many use Pretoria as a base and bypass Johannesburg entirely. Certainly Gauteng is not a province to tarry in, unless you are really interested in the changes that the New South Africa has wrought. For Jo'burg is where you'll find the growing black middle class flexing its financial muscle and where Africans from all over the continent congregate to shop, party, and generally have a good time.

**MPUMALANGA AND THE NORTHERN PROVINCE** To the east of Gauteng and the Free State lies the Escarpment—the end of the Drakensberg mountain range which rises in the Eastern Cape, running up the western border of KwaZulu-Natal before dividing Mpumalanga and the Northern Province into the high- and lowveld. Traveling through the Escarpment to the lowveld's Big-Game Country, you will find some of the country's most gorgeous views, the world's third largest canyon, the largest man-made forests in the world, many spectacular waterfalls, and the country's first gold rush towns, one of which has been declared a living monument. Traveling east on scenic mountain passes, you will drop thousands of feet to the lowveld plains before reaching Big-Game Country. If you want to see Africa's wild animals on a budget, **Kruger National Park** offers the best deal on the continent—a high density of game combined with spotlessly clean, albeit spartan accommodations. Along its western flank lie the **private game lodges** in the Sabi Sand, Manyeleti, and Timbavati reserves, offering a variety of experiences—from over-the-top decadent luxury chalets to more authentic East-African safari tents or rough huts. There are also a number of budget options, and if you're not too hung up on ticking off the **Big 5** (lion, leopard, buffalo, elephant, and rhino), it's worth looking at the lodges in the Makalali Reserve, which emphasize spiritual rejuvenation as much as animal tracking, or at Lapalala, a true wilderness area.

**KWAZULU-NATAL** Hot and humid in summer, warm and balmy in winter, the KwaZulu-Natal coast offers excellent **beach holidays,** with temperatures never dropping below 16°C (61°F), and the Indian Ocean kept warm by the Mozambique current that washes past its subtropical shores. Unfortunately, this is no well-kept secret, and development along most of its south and much of its north coast (Durban being the center) has resulted in another paradise lost, and an endless string of ugly, indifferent holiday and timeshare resorts. There are exceptions, the best of which combine great beach and golf vacations. But even **St Lucia,** Africa's biggest estuary and home to large populations of Nile crocodile and hippo, has had its beautiful beaches largely ruined by the 4×4 tracks made by macho Gauteng vacationers and local fishermen using the beach as a road. Thankfully, **north of Mabibi** this practice is outlawed and the beaches are safe for the annual pilgrimage of loggerhead and leatherback turtles that heave themselves ashore at night to lay their eggs. There's good diving off this coast, though only scuba diving is allowed at the Kosi Bay Mouth, which borders the Mozambique border.

After Cape Town, **Durban** is the most enjoyable city to visit, with great museums, arts and crafts, restaurants, the busiest port in Africa, and an interesting blend of cultures besides the Zulu, the largest group in South Africa, the biggest population of Indians outside of India resides here. It is also well situated should you be interested in visiting malaria-free Big 5 game reserves, taking one of the historic battlefields tours, or hiking through the majestic Drakensberg.

**NORTH-WEST & THE NORTHERN CAPE** This is *Thelma and Louise* territory—perfect for people who like taking roadtrips through endless horizons with very little sign of human habitation. North-West is not as arid as the Northern Cape, and it is much more accessible—its most famous attraction—**Sun City** and its centerpiece, the **Palace of the Lost City**—can be visited as a day trip from Johannesburg or Pretoria. The region also has two excellent, malaria-free **Big 5 game reserves.** The Northern Cape is the least accessible and the least populated province in South Africa, and—perhaps as a consequence—has some of the most beautiful scenery in the world, though its starkness doesn't strike a chord in everyone. However, no one can remain unmoved in the spring when the first rains transform many of the vast arid plains into horizon-filled **fields of flowers.** For some, the distances from city centers to this

**Did You Know?**

- South Africa is the world's number one producer of gold, and its mine shafts forge some 4 kilometers (2½ miles) under the earth's surface—the deepest in the world.
- South Africa boasts 24,000 plant species, close to 10% of all the flowering plants on earth.
- South Africa is home to the largest collection of Stone Age art in the world.
- When a coelacanth, a species thought to be over 350 million years old, was caught off the Eastern Cape coast in 1938, it blew away theories that the fish became extinct some 65 million years ago. Several specimens have been caught off the South African coast since then.
- The white rhino was the first mammal to be removed from the endangered species list (in 1994), thanks to the efforts of South African conservation authorities.
- The British Empire suffered its most humiliating defeat at the Battle of Isandlwana, when over 1,300 armed men were wiped out by the Zulu army, led by "Africa's Napoleon," Shaka.
- The South African Constitution is the only one in the world that expressly forbids discrimination on the basis of sexual orientation.

region are tiresome; in this case, fly in—it's definitely worth visiting a desert reserve, particularly if you've only visited the bushveld before.

## ZIMBABWE

Zimbabwe is one of Africa's most popular tourist destinations, due mainly to its natural attractions, of which **Victoria Falls** is the highlight. A country of great natural beauty, Zimbabwe has a wide variety of habitats: In the west lie the expanses of the Kalahari sand; traveling east, you pass through woodland savannah and open grassland, until, in the east, you come up against the lush montane forests of the Eastern Highlands.

## BOTSWANA

Straddling the tropic of Capricorn in southern Africa, Botswana is one of the last true wilderness areas on the continent. Roughly the size of France and totally landlocked, it is bordered by Namibia to the west and north (its northern border with Namibia is the long, narrow, lushly vegetated panhandle of the Caprivi Strip), Zimbabwe to the east, and South Africa to the south.

A sparsely populated country of just over 1 million inhabitants, Botswana offers a varied wilderness experience, from forest to salt pan, from bushveld to rolling savannah, from ancient lake beds to palm-fringed islands. The waterless Kalahari covers two-thirds of its surface, so it is nothing short of incredible that this self-same country is home to one of the world's largest inland delta systems—the **Okavango Delta,** highlight of Botswana. This 15,000-square-kilometer (9,300-square-mile) inland flood plain fans out in the northwestern corner of the country, creating a paradise of palms, papyrus, and crystal-clear channels and backwaters. The life-giving waters provide a much-needed oasis for birds and animals, and consequently unparalleled opportunities for humans to view them.

In addition to the delta, Botswana has **Chobe National Park** to the northeast. This 12,000-square-kilometer (7,450-square-mile) park is home to some 35,000 elephants; and to the southeast are the spectacular wide-open spaces of **Makgadikgadi** and **Nxai Pans.**

## 2 Visitor Information

**SOUTH AFRICA** Contact **South African Tourist Offices (SATOUR). In the United States** 500 5th Ave, Suite 2040, New York, NY 10110 (☎ **800/822-5368**); 9841 Airport Blvd., Suite 1524, Los Angeles, CA 90045 (☎ 800/782-9772). SATOUR's Web site is www.satour.org. For specific information on game parks and safaris, visit www.africa.com/-venture/ntpks/npbhome.htm. To find out what's happening in South Africa, from politics to art exhibitions, visit www.mg.co.za/mg, the home page for the ***Mail & Guardian,*** South Africa's best national newspaper.

**In Canada** Contact SATOUR, 4117 Lawrence Ave. E., Suite 2, Ontario M1E 2S2 (☎ **416/283-0563**).

**In the United Kingdom** Contact SATOUR, Nos. 5–6 Alt Grove, Wimbledon SW19 4DZ (☎ **0181/944-8080**).

**In Australia** Contact SATOUR, 6/285 Clarence St., Sydney, NSW 2000 (☎ **02/9261-3424**). There is no office in New Zealand.

**ZIMBABWE In the United States,** the tourism office is at 1270 Avenue of the Americas, Suite 2315, New York, NY 10020 (☎ **212/332-1090**).

**In Canada** 332 Somerset St., West Ottawa, Ontario K2P OJ9 (☎ **613/237-4388**).

**In the United Kingdom** 429 Strand, London WC2R 05A (☎ **0171/240-6169**).

**In Australia** The High Commission is at 11 Culogoa Circuit, O'Malley, Canberra ACT 2606 (☎ **02/282700**), or check out the website www.australia.co.zw. There is no representation in New Zealand.

**BOTSWANA** The Republic of Botswana's Web site at www.gov.bw/home.html has a lot of practical information. Otherwise, **in the United States** contact the **Embassy of the Republic of Botswana,** Suite 7M, 3400 International Dr., NW., Washington, DC 20008 (☎ **202/244-4990**).

**In the United Kingdom** The embassy is at 6 Stratford Place, London W1N 9AE (☎ **0171/499-0031**).

**In Canada** Contact the **Honorary Consul of Botswana,** 14 South Dr., Toronto, Ontario M4W 1R1 (☎ **416/978-2495,** fax 416/324-8239). There is no representation in Australia or New Zealand.

## 3 Entry Requirements & Customs

Citizens of the United States, Canada, Australia, and New Zealand need only a valid passport for a 90-day stay in **South Africa, Zimbabwe,** and **Botswana.** European nationals can stay up to six months. For longer stays in southern Africa, visit the **Aliens Control Section** at the Department of Home Affairs at 56 Barrack St., Cape Town (☎ **27/21/462-4970**); or 77 Harrison St., Johannesburg (☎ **27/11/836-3228**). For visits to all southern African countries, visitors need a return ticket and may have to prove that they'll have sufficient funds during their stay.

If you plan on crossing the border to Zambia while in Zimbabwe (this gives you another spectacular view of Victoria Falls), be aware that members of

**Telephone Tips**

As this chapter contains telephone numbers for three African countries, **country codes precede the local numbers.** The country code for **South Africa** is **27;** the country code for **Zimbabwe** is **263;** the country code for **Botswana** is **267.** Numbers in the United States, United Kingdom, Ireland, Australia, and New Zealand have been written without their country codes. For more information, see "Telephoning" in "Fast Facts," later in this chapter.

---

non-Commonwealth countries need a visa. Day-pass visas are issued at the bridge for about $10. (If you intend moving between the two countries for a few days, a multiple entry visa will cost $65.)

For additional information on entry requirements, travelers may contact the embassies listed under "Visitor Information."

## PASSPORT INFORMATION

Safeguard your passport in an inconspicuous, inaccessible place like a money belt. If you lose it, visit the nearest consulate of your native country as soon as possible for a replacement. Passport applications are downloadable from the Internet sites listed below.

### FOR RESIDENTS OF THE UNITED STATES

If you're applying for a first-time passport, you need to do it in person at one of 13 passport offices throughout the United States; a federal, state, or probate court; or a major post office (though not all post offices accept applications; call the number below to find the ones that do). You need to present a certified birth certificate as proof of citizenship, and it's wise to bring along your driver's license, state or military ID, and social security card as well. You also need two identical passport-sized photos (2 in. by 2 in.), taken at any corner photo shop (not one of the strip photos, however, from a photo-vending machine).

For people over 15, a passport is valid for 10 years and costs $60 ($45 plus a $15 handling fee); for those 15 and under, it's valid for 5 years and costs $40. If you're over 15 and have a valid passport that was issued within the past 12 years, you can renew it by mail and bypass the $15 handling fee. Allow plenty of time before your trip to apply; processing normally takes 3 weeks but can take longer during busy periods (especially spring). For general information, call the **National Passport Agency** (☎ **202/647-0518**). To find your regional passport office, call the **National Passport Information Center** (☎ **900/225-5674;** travel.state.gov).

### FOR RESIDENTS OF CANADA

You can pick up a passport application at one of 28 regional passport offices or most travel agencies. The passport is valid for 5 years and costs $60. Children under 16 may be included on a parent's passport but need their own to travel unaccompanied by the parent. Applications, which must be accompanied by two identical passport-sized photographs and proof of Canadian citizenship, are available at travel agencies throughout Canada or from the central **Passport Office, Department of Foreign Affairs and International Trade,** Ottawa K1A 0G3 (☎ **800/567-6868;** www.dfait-maeci.gc.ca/passport). Processing takes 5 to 10 days if you apply in person, or about 3 weeks by mail.

### For Residents of the United Kingdom

To pick up an application for a regular 10-year passport (the Visitor's Passport has been abolished), visit your nearest passport office, major post office, or travel agency. You can also contact the London Passport Office at ☎ **0171/271-3000** or search its Web site at www.open.gov.uk/ukpass/ukpass.htm. Passports are £21 for adults and £11 for children under 16.

### For Residents of Ireland

You can apply for a 10-year passport, costing IR£45, at the Passport Office, Setanta Centre, Molesworth Street, Dublin 2 (☎ **01/671-1633;** www.irlgov.ie/iveagh/foreignaffairs/services). Those under age 18 and over 65 must apply for a IR£10 3-year passport. You can also apply at 1A South Mall, Cork (☎ **021/272-525**) or over the counter at most main post offices.

### For Residents of Australia

Apply at your local post office or passport office or search the government Web site at www.dfat.gov.au/passports/. Passports for adults are A$126 and for those under 18 A$63.

### For Residents of New Zealand

You can pick up a passport application at any travel agency or Link Centre. For more info, contact the Passport Office, P.O. Box 805, Wellington (☎ **0800/225-050**). Passports for adults are NZ$80, and for those under 16, NZ$40.

## Customs

Before leaving your home country, register your foreign-made electronic equipment with customs.

When entering **South Africa,** items for personal use are duty free; beyond this you may bring new or used goods of up to R500 ($83.35) into the country, 2 liters of wine, 1 liter of alcohol, 50ml of perfume, 250ml of eau de toilette, 400 cigarettes, 50 cigars or 250g of tobacco. Only prescription drugs are allowed into the country, and a permit is required for weapons (a 180-day permit can be obtained upon entry as long as you can prove ownership).

When entering **Zimbabwe,** personal items are duty free and you may bring in 5 liters of alcohol, but not more than 2 liters of spirits. Family members traveling together may aggregate allowances.

When entering **Botswana,** duty-free goods are 200 cigarettes, 50 cigars or 250g of tobacco; 2 liters of wine or 1 liter of spirits; 50ml of perfume and 250ml of eau de toilette.

### Import Restrictions

Returning **U.S. citizens** who have been away for 48 hours or more are allowed to bring back, once every 30 days, $400 worth of merchandise duty free. You'll be charged a flat rate of 10% duty on the next $1,000 worth of purchases. Be sure to have your receipts handy. On gifts, the duty-free limit is $100. You cannot bring fresh foodstuffs into the United States; tinned foods, however, are allowed. For more information, contact the **U.S. Customs Service,** 1301 Constitution Ave. (P.O. Box 7407), Washington, DC 20044 (☎ **202/927-6724**) and request the free pamphlet *Know Before You Go.* It's also available on the Web at www.customs.ustreas.gov/travel/kbygo.htm.

**U.K. citizens returning from a non-EC country** have a customs allowance of 200 cigarettes; 50 cigars; 250g of smoking tobacco; 2 liters of still table wine; 1 liter of spirits or strong liqueurs (over 22% volume); 2 liters of fortified wine, sparkling wine or other liqueurs; 60cc (ml) perfume; 250cc (ml) of toilet water; and £145 worth of all other goods, including gifts and souvenirs. People under 17 cannot have the tobacco or alcohol allowance. For more information, contact HM Customs & Excise, Passenger Enquiry Point, 2nd Floor Wayfarer House, Great South West Road, Feltham, Middlesex TW14 8NP (☎ **0181/910-3744;** from outside the United Kingdom, 44/181-910-3744), or consult their Web site at www.open.gov.uk.

For a clear summary of **Canadian** rules, write for the booklet *I Declare,* issued by **Revenue Canada,** 2265 St Laurent Blvd., Ottawa K1G 4KE (☎ **613/993-0534**). Canada allows its citizens a $500 exemption, and you're allowed to bring back duty free 200 cigarettes, 1 kilogram (2.2 pounds) of tobacco, 40 imperial ounces of liquor, and 50 cigars. In addition, you're allowed to mail gifts to Canada from abroad at the rate of Can$60 a day, provided they're unsolicited and don't contain alcohol or tobacco (write on the package "Unsolicited gift, under $60 value"). All valuables should be declared on the Y-38 form before departure from Canada, including serial numbers of valuables you already own, such as expensive foreign cameras. Note: The $500 exemption can only be used once a year and only after an absence of 7 days.

The duty-free allowance in **Australia** is A$400 or, for those under 18, A$200. Personal property mailed back should be marked "Australian goods returned" to avoid payment of duty. Upon returning to Australia, citizens can bring in 250 cigarettes or 250 grams of loose tobacco, and 1,125ml of alcohol. If you're returning with valuable goods you already own, such as foreign-made cameras, you should file form B263. A helpful brochure, available from Australian consulates or Customs offices, is *Know Before You Go.* For more information, contact **Australian Customs Services,** GPO Box 8, Sydney, NSW 2001 (☎ **02/9213-2000**).

The duty-free allowance for **New Zealand** is NZ$700. Citizens over 17 can bring in 200 cigarettes, or 50 cigars, or 250 grams of tobacco (or a mixture of all three if their combined weight doesn't exceed 250 grams); plus 4.5 liters of wine and beer, or 1.125 liters of liquor. New Zealand currency does not carry import or export restrictions. Fill out a certificate of export, listing the valuables you are taking out of the country; that way, you can bring them back without paying duty. Most questions are answered in a free pamphlet available at New Zealand consulates and Customs offices: *New Zealand Customs Guide for Travelers, Notice no. 4.* For more information, contact New Zealand Customs, 50 Anzac Ave., Box 29, Auckland (☎ **09/359-6655**).

## 4 Money

### CASH

For the most favorable rates, change money at banks. It's a good idea to get a small amount of the local currency before arriving at your destination.

The **South Africa currency** unit is the **rand** (R), with 100 cents making up R1. Notes (sometimes called "bucks") come in R10, R20, R50, R100, and R200. Minted coins come in 1, 2, and 5 rand denominations and 1, 2, 5, 10, 20, and 50 cents—small change doesn't buy much; add to tips. At press time, the exchange rates were R6 to the $1(U.S.); R10 to the British pound. The value of the rand against major foreign currencies keeps plummeting, however, and visitors will find costs considerably lower than at home. The exceptions to this are flights, international calls, private game reserves, and certain city hotels.

In **Zimbabwe** the monetary unit is the **Zimbabwe dollar,** abbreviated as Z$ and comprising 100 cents. Notes come in denominations of 2, 5, 10, 20, 50, and 100

**What Things Cost in South Africa**

| | South African Rand | British Pound | U.S. Dollar |
|---|---|---|---|
| A cup of coffee | R3–5 | 30–50p | 50–85¢ |
| A beer in a bar | R5–8 | 50–80p | 85¢–$1.35 |
| A main course in a restaurant | R18–65 | £1.80–£6.50 | $3–$11 |
| Taxi ride | R5/km | 50p/km | 85¢/km |
| Moderate accommodations | R400–800, double | £40–£80 | $66.65–$133.35 |
| Luxurious accommodations | R1,000 and up, double | £100 and up | $166.65 and up |
| One night at a game lodge (includes all meals) | R1,800–3, 900 double | £180–£390 | $300–$650 |
| A rental car per day | R150 | £15 | $25 |
| Liter of petrol (gas) | R2.50 | 25p | 42¢ |

dollars. Coins in 1, 5, 10, and 50 cents, and Z$1 and Z$2. The conversion rate used in this chapter was $1 = Z$38, or 1 British pound = Z$62. Note that travelers to Zimbabwe are usually required to pay for all lodging with credit cards or internationally convertible currency such as U.S. dollars or British pounds. Zimbabwe currency, even if obtained by exchanging foreign cash or traveler's checks in Zimbabwe, may not be accepted for payment of hotel bills.

The **pula** (which incidentally means "rain") is the official currency of **Botswana.** One pula (P) is divided into 100 thebe. Bills come in P1, P2, P5, P10, P20, and P50 and coins in 1t, 2t, 5t, 10t, 25t, 50t, and P1. This is by far the most expensive region in southern Africa; at press time, the exchange rates were P4.40 to $1, or P7 to 1 British pound.

## TRAVELER'S CHECKS

Traveler's checks are only useful in cities—always carry some cash when traveling in remote rural areas. Note that credit cards are generally accepted throughout southern Africa, particularly MasterCard and Visa, which means that traveler's checks are somewhat redundant.

You can get traveler's checks at almost any bank. **American Express** offers denominations of $10, $20, $50, $100, $500, and $1,000. You'll pay a service charge ranging from 1 to 4%. You can also get American Express traveler's checks over the phone by calling ☎ **800/221-7282;** by using this number, Amex gold and platinum cardholders are exempt from the 1% fee. AAA members can obtain checks without a fee at most AAA offices.

**Visa** offers traveler's checks at Citibank locations nationwide, as well as several other banks. The service charge ranges between 1.5 and 2%; checks come in denominations of $20, $50, $100, $500, and $1,000. **MasterCard** also offers traveler's checks. Call ☎ **800/223-9920** for a location near you.

### ATMS

ATMs offering 24-hour service are located throughout South Africa—your bank will be able to give you a list—though in small rural towns you'll have to rely on going into a bank. ATMs are linked to a national network that most likely includes your bank at home. **Cirrus** (☎ **800/424-7787;** www.mastercard.com/atm/) and **Plus** (☎ **800/843-7587;** www.visa.com/atms) are the two most popular networks; check the back of your ATM card to see which network your bank belongs to. Be sure to check the daily withdrawal limit before you depart, and ask whether you need a new personal ID number.

### CREDIT CARDS

American Express, Diner's Club, MasterCard, and Visa are accepted at most hotels, restaurants, and stores in **South Africa,** though the latter two are the most popular. Many lodges in **Botswana** do not accept credit cards (though in all likelihood you will be booking and paying for these ahead of time as part of a safari). For the most part, however, you'll find your credit cards invaluable when traveling. They are a safe way to carry money and provide a convenient record of all your expenses. You can also withdraw cash advances from your credit cards at any bank. At most banks, you don't even need to go to a teller; you can get a cash advance at the ATM if you know your PIN number. If you've forgotten your PIN number or didn't even know you had one, call the phone number on the back of your credit card and ask. It usually takes 5 to 7 business days, though some banks will provide the number over the phone if you tell them your mother's maiden name or pass some other security clearance.

## 5 When to Go

### SOUTH AFRICA

As southern Africa is such a large area, with each region offering different seasonal benefits, when you go should only affect where you go. Not surprisingly, the summer months (November to February) tend to attract the majority of visitors, though the region is big enough to absorb these increased numbers without causing the discomfort most people associate with the year's most crowded season—accommodation prices do increase though, some by as much as 80%; and you should try never to coincide with the South African busiest school holidays, which take place over December and Easter. Spring (September and October) and autumn (March and April) are considered by many to be the best time to visit, particularly in the Western Cape and KwaZulu-Natal when temperatures are not quite so harsh. Certainly it's well worth trying to time your trip so that it coincides with the 2- to 3-week spring flower displays that occur on the West Coast and Northern Cape, though this can be tricky, with flowers dependant on the fickle rainfall and often occurring as early as mid-August. July to November are the months when the Southern Right whales migrate to the Cape's southern coast, providing guaranteed sightings. May through August are considered the best months for sighting big game: foliage is less dense, malaria is a lower risk in the South African game reserves, and many of the private game reserves drop their prices substantially. This is also an ideal time to visit Botswana and Zimbabwe, though Victoria Falls will not be in full flood (Zimbabwe is a summer rainfall area) and malaria remains a high risk all year round in both these areas. Thanks to the year-round sunshine that the Garden Route and Karoo enjoy, any time is a good time to tour this region.

**Average Temperatures & Rainfall in Southern Africa**
**Minimum/Maximum Temperatures & Monthly Rainfall in Inches**

| Cape Town, South Africa | Jan | Feb | Mar | Apr | May | June | July | Aug | Sept | Oct | Nov | Dec |
|---|---|---|---|---|---|---|---|---|---|---|---|---|
| Avg. Temp in °F | 61/79 | 59/79 | 57/77 | 54/73 | 50/68 | 46/64 | 45/63 | 45/64 | 46/66 | 50/70 | 55/75 | 59/77 |
| Avg. Temp in °C | 16/26 | 15/26 | 14/25 | 12/23 | 10/20 | 8/18 | 7/17 | 7/18 | 8/19 | 10/21 | 13/24 | 15/25 |
| Rain in Inches | 0.6 | 0.7 | 0.7 | 2.0 | 3.5 | 3.3 | 3.5 | 3.1 | 2.0 | 1.4 | .5 | .6 |
| **Johannesburg, South Africa** | | | | | | | | | | | | |
| Avg. Temp in °F | 59/79 | 57/77 | 55/75 | 52/72 | 46/66 | 41/61 | 41/61 | 45/66 | 48/72 | 54/75 | 55/77 | 57/77 |
| Avg. Temp in °C | 15/26 | 14/25 | 13/24 | 11/22 | 8/19 | 5/16 | 5/16 | 7/19 | 9/22 | 12/24 | 13/25 | 14/25 |
| Rain in Inches | 4.5 | 3.8 | 2.9 | 2.5 | 0.9 | 0.3 | 0.3 | 0.2 | 0.1 | 2.7 | 4.6 | 4.3 |
| **Victoria Falls, Zimbabwe** | | | | | | | | | | | | |
| Avg. Temp in °F | 65/85 | 64/85 | 62/85 | 57/84 | 49/81 | 43/76 | 42/77 | 47/82 | 55/89 | 62/91 | 64/90 | 64/86 |
| Avg. Temp in °C | 18/30 | 18/30 | 17.30 | 14/29 | 9/27 | 6/24 | 6/24 | 8/28 | 13/32 | 17/33 | 18/32 | 18/30 |
| Rain in Inches | 6.6 | 5 | 2.8 | 1.0 | 0.1 | 0 | 0 | 0 | 0.7 | 1.1 | 2.5 | 6.8 |
| **Maun, Botswana** | | | | | | | | | | | | |
| Avg. Temp in °F | 66/90 | 66/88 | 64/88 | 57/88 | 48/82 | 43/77 | 43/77 | 48/82 | 55/91 | 64/95 | 66/93 | 66/90 |
| Avg. Temp in °C | 19/32 | 19/31 | 18/31 | 14/31 | 9/28 | 6/25 | 6/25 | 9/29 | 13/33 | 18/35 | 19/34 | 19/23 |
| Rain in Inches | 4.3 | 3.2 | 2.8 | 1.0 | 0.3 | 0.1 | 0 | 0 | 0 | 1.2 | 2.0 | 3.8 |

## The Climate

Depending on where you are, average maximum temperatures can vary from 80°F/27°C (Cape Town) to 90°F/32°C (Kruger National Park) in the summer, and from 69°F/21°C (Cape Town) to 77°F/25°C (Durban) in winter. While summer is most popular, it's worth mentioning that high humidity in KwaZulu-Natal can make for muggy days and cloying nights, and gale-force winds often occur in Cape Town and Port Elizabeth. Winter visitors would be well advised to pack warm clothes—despite higher average temperatures than in the United States or Europe, South Africa is simply not geared for the cold, and insulation and central heating are low on the priority list. Temperatures in the interior fluctuate wildly in winter; you're best off layering.

## Rainfall

South Africa is generally considered an arid region, with two-thirds of the country receiving less than 500mm of rain a year. In the interior, rain usually falls during summer, and spectacular thunderstorms and the smell of damp earth bring great relief from the searing heat. The Garden Route enjoys rain all year-round; while in Cape Town and surrounds, the rain falls mostly during winter, when the gray skies are a perfect foil for the burnt orange strelitzias, pink proteas, and fields of white arum lilies, not to mention the perfect accompaniment to crackling fires and fine red wines.

## Holidays

If you are traveling during the South African school holidays (check exact dates with SATOUR), make sure you book your accommodation well in advance. Flights can also be impossible, particularly over the Christmas holidays (usually December 5 to

January 20). Easter holidays (usually March 20 to April 15) can also be busy, while the Kruger is almost always packed during the winter vacation (approximately June 20 to July 20). There's another short school break in spring, from about September 20 to October 7.

**Public holidays in South Africa** include New Year's Day, March 21 (Human Rights Day), Good Friday, Easter Sunday and Monday, April 27 (Founders/Freedom Day), May 1 (Workers Day), June 16 (Soweto/Youth Day), August 9 (Women's Day), September 24 (Heritage Day), December 16 (Day of Reconciliation), Christmas Day, and December 26 (Boxing Day).

## ZIMBABWE

Zimbabwe's climate is similar to South Africa's, with a summer rainy season, and most of the rainfall occurring between December and mid-March. Summers are warm to hot, October and November being the hottest months, and winters are mild. Malaria is still a danger in many areas; there is tsetse fly in parts of the Zambezi Valley and in the southeast, and many of the country's rivers, lakes, and dams are infected with bilharzia. Victoria Falls are at their most impressive from January to April, and fullest in March, at the end of the rainy season. This is also, however, when malaria-carrying mosquitoes are at their most prolific and the mist created by the falling water may obscure the view. Temperatures are pleasant from April to October, and at this time some of the upmarket lodges raise their prices. Many consider that the best time to see the falls is from August to December, when the flow of the water is at its lowest and the view is clearer. White-water rafting is at its best during these months. It is, however, sometimes extremely hot and quite uncomfortable at this time of year, particularly toward November and December.

**Holidays in Zimbabwe** are New Years Day, January 1; Good Friday through Easter Monday; Independence Day, April 18; Workers Day, May 1; Africa Day, April 25; Heroes Day, August 11; Defense Forces Day, August 12; Christmas Day; and Boxing Day, December 26.

## BOTSWANA

Botswana has a pleasant subtropical climate with low humidity. Rain falls during the summer months, from November to March, when it can be very hot. From mid-May to mid-August, the days are mild to warm, but it can be cold at night and early in the morning, particularly around June and July. From mid-August to November the days are usually warm to hot, although it does cool down a little at night. The best time to visit the delta is during June and July, when the rain that falls on the Angolan bushveld plains seeps down to create what is locally referred to as the "flood." At this time, waterlilies bloom, countless aquatic creatures frolic in the water, and a huge diversity of game from the surrounding dry areas moves into the delta.

**Holidays in Botswana** are New Year's Day, January 2 (public holiday); July 1 (Sir Seretse Khama Day); third Monday and Tuesday in July (President's Day); September 30 (Independence Day); Christmas; Boxing Day; Good Friday, Easter Monday; May 1, Labour Day; and Ascension Day (40 days after Easter).

# Calendar of Events

Check exact dates with **Jane Bristow** at SATOUR, ☎ **27/12/347-0600** or fax 27/12/347-8753; e-mail: satour@is.co.za; or with your local SATOUR branch—see regional contact information in "Visitor Information," above.

### January

- **Cape Minstrels Carnival,** Cape Town. Cape Malay groups dressed in colorful outfits parade through the streets, singing and jiving to banjo beats. The event culminates in a competition held at Green Point Stadium. Call Mr. Hendricks, ☎ **27/21/397-6429.** 1, 2, and 9 January.
- **Spier Arts Festival,** Spier Estate, Stellenbosch, Winelands. The Western Cape's premier arts festival features local and international opera, classical music, comedy, and drama at the Spier Amphitheatre. Call ☎ **27/21/809-1100.** January to March; call for exact dates.
- **Maynardville Open Air Theatre,** Maynardville, Wynberg, Cape Town. Pack a picnic to enjoy this annual Shakespeare play performed in the Maynardville Gardens. Call ☎ **27/21/430-8010.** January to February; call for exact dates.
- **Duzi Canoe Race,** Pietermaritzburg, KwaZulu-Natal. The country's most prestigious canoeing event attracts some 1,600 entrants and covers the 115 kilometers (71 miles) between Pietermaritzburg and Durban. Call ☎ **27/331/94-9994.** January 21–23.
- **J&B Metropolitan Horse Race,** Kenilworth Race Course, Cape Town. The Western Cape's premier horse-racing event is Cape Town's excuse to party, and attracts as many of the city's socialites—all decked out in designer gear—as it does real punters. Call ☎ **27/21/762-7777.** Last Saturday in January.

### February

- **FNB Vita Dance Umbrella,** Wits Theatre, Johannesburg. This is the oldest of the Vita Dance festivals, which provide a platform for contemporary choreography and dance. Keep an eye out for African dance events. Call ☎ **27/11/442-8435.** February 21 to March 18.

### March

- **Cape Argus Cycle Tour,** Cape Town. The largest of its kind in the world, this race attracts 25,000 cyclists and covers 105 kilometers (65 miles) of Cape Town's most scenic routes. Call ☎ **27/21/689-8420.** Second Sunday of every March.
- **Dunhill Symphony of Fire,** V&A Waterfront, Cape Town and Kyalami, Johannesburg. A breathtaking fireworks competition, with displays syncopated with live orchestras, showcasing the top pyro-musical teams in the world. (The 1999 competitors were China, Spain, Germany, Canada, and South Africa.) Call ☎ **27/21/421-1111.** Tickets can be purchased through **Ticketweb,** ☎ **27/860/40-0500.** March 27 to April 11.
- **Klein Karoo National Arts Festival,** Oudtshoorn, Western Cape. This is the best selection of Afrikaans drama, as well as excellent dance and music acts. Call ☎ **27/44/272-7771.** March 25 to 31.

### April

- **Two Oceans Marathon,** Cape Town. This 56-kilometer (35-mile) scenic route attracts some 12,000 athletes. ☎ **27/21/61-9407.** Easter Saturday.
- **FNB Vita Dance Umdudo,** Rhodes Theatre, Grahamstown, Eastern Cape. This is a venue for contemporary choreography and dance in the Eastern Cape. Call ☎ **27/11/442-8435.** April 19 to 24.

### June

- **Whale Season,** Western Cape coast. In whale season, migrating whales move into the bays along the coast, particularly Hermanus, to court, mate, and calve. Call the Whale Hotline at ☎ **27/800/22-8222** or see chapter 4 for more information. June to November.

- **Comrades Marathon,** Pietermaritzburg, KwaZulu-Natal. Over 13,000 runners participate in this 89-kilometer (55-mile) race, which started in 1921. Call ☎ **27/331/94-3512.** June 16.
- **Standard Bank National Arts Festival,** Grahamstown, Eastern Cape. The largest arts festival in the southern hemisphere has performances that range from cutting-edge to classical. Call ☎ **27/466/22-7115.** June 26 to July 11.

### July

- **Knysna Oyster Festival,** Knysna, Garden Route, Western Cape. The festival encompasses the Forest Marathon, a mountain-bike cycling tour, a regatta, a golf championship, and flea markets. Call ☎ **27/44/382-5510.** First Friday to second Saturday of every July.
- **Rothmans July Handicap,** Greyville Racecourse, Durban. This horseracing event has stakes of 1 million rand. Call ☎ **27/31/309-4545.** First Saturday of every July.
- **Ocean Action,** Durban beachfront. This world-class watersports and beach-related tournament includes the **Gunston 500,** one of the world's premier surfing events. Call ☎ **27/31/332-0111.** July 13 to 18.
- **FNB Vita Dance Indaba,** Baxter Theatre, Rondebosch, Cape Town. This dance festival features contemporary choreography and dance acts by professional and amateur individuals and groups based in the Western Cape. Call ☎ **27/11/442-8435.** July 21 to 25.

### August

✪ **Namaqualand Wild Flower Season,** Western and Northern Cape. From mid-August (depending on rain), the semi-arid West Coast is transformed into a floral paradise with over 2,600 species in bloom. Call ☎ **27/21/418-3705.** August to October.

### September

- **Haenertsburg and Magoebaskloof Spring Festival,** Northern Province. Flowering azaleas, cherry blossoms, and crab apples are celebrated with a craft market, carnival, exhibitions, and evening events. Call ☎ **27/15/276-4297** for exact dates.
- **Arts Alive International Festival,** Johannesburg. This excellent urban arts festival features the best local talent and international stars. Includes the **Jazz on the Lake Concert** held at Zoo Lake. Call ☎ **27/11/838-5639** or 27/11/838-4563 for exact dates.
- **Whale Festival,** Hermanus, Western Cape. The Whale Festival includes drama performances, an arts ramble, a craft market, and whale-route lectures and tours. Call ☎ **27/283/21-785.** September 23 to October 4.
- **Darling Wildflower and Orchid Show and Hello Darling Arts Festival,** Arcadia Street, Darling, West Coast. Combine a trip to see the flowers, call ☎ **27/22/492-3361,** with a show at Evita se Perron (☎ **27/22/492-3145**) hosted by Pieter Dirk Uys, South Africa's most famous female impersonator. End-September; call for exact dates.
- **International Eisteddfod of South Africa,** Roodepoort, Gauteng. This competitive international music and dance festival features entrants from some 30 countries. Call ☎ **27/11/472-2820.** September 24 to October 2.
- **Xhosa Cultural Dress Competition,** Grahamstown, Eastern Cape. A few Xhosa still dress in traditional gear daily, but most only do so for special events—this is one of them. Call ☎ **27/46/622-2312.** September 24.

**October**

- **Johannesburg Biennial,** Newtown Cultural Precinct, Johannesburg. This exhibition of contemporary South African and foreign art, much of it performance-based, is internationally curated. The event takes place every odd-numbered year. Call ☎ **27/11/838-6407.** October 1999 to January 2000; call for exact dates.
- **Anglo-Boer War Centenary Commemoration,** Durban and Dundee, KwaZulu-Natal. There is an emphasis on reenacting many of the battles, and various special tour packages include participation in these events. Call ☎ **27/31/307-3800.** October 16, 1999 to May 31, 2000.
- **FNB Vita Dance Shongololo,** Playhouse Theatre, Durban. A dance and choreography festival featuring the best of KwaZulu-Natal's considerable talent. Call ☎ **27/11/442-8435.** October 18 to 24.

**December**

- ✪ **Mother City Queer Project,** Cape Town. This masked costume ball features 10 different dance zones and various teams decked out in their interpretation of the annual theme. All are celebrating Cape Town's vibrant and creative queer culture. Call ☎ 27/83/309-1553. Early December; call for exact dates.
- **Million Dollar Golf Challenge,** Sun City, North-West Province. This high-stakes tournament attracts the world's best golfers. Call ☎ **27/11/780-7444.** December 4 to 6.

## 6 Safaris & Other Active Vacations

Surrounded by oceans and with a diverse landscape that includes forests, rivers, mountains, and large tracts of pristine wilderness, southern Africa is the ideal destination for outdoor adventures and safaris. For more on enjoying the outdoors, see the "Staying Active" sections in specific chapters, or purchase *Adventure Travel in Southern Africa* by Jennifer Stern (Menasha Ridge).

**Where & When to See Game**

**E = Excellent, G = Good, F = Fair, P = Poor**

| | Jan | Feb | Mar | Apr | May | June | July | Aug | Sept | Oct | Nov | Dec |
|---|---|---|---|---|---|---|---|---|---|---|---|---|
| Kruger National Park | P | P | P | F | F | G | E | E | E | E | G | F |
| Private Game Reserves | G | G | G | G | G | E | E | E | E | E | E | G |
| Moremi & Okavango Delta | G | G | G | G | E | E | E | E | E | E | E | G |
| Chobe | F | F | F | G | G | E | E | E | E | E | E | G |
| Makgadikgadi & Nxai Pan | E | E | E | E | G | F | F | P | P | P | F | G |

### GOING ON SAFARI

As wildlife viewing is the reason most set their sights on southern Africa, a number of ways to experience the bush have developed. You can opt for a self-drive safari or head straight for a luxurious lodge in a private game reserve. The more adventurous take their chances on a specialist safari and go on foot, horseback, bike, or houseboat; or in dugout canoes, hot-air balloons, or even on the back of an elephant. South Africa has the best-managed national parks in Africa, as well as some of the most luxurious private reserves; but if you're looking for the original untamed Eden, you're best off visiting Botswana. This is largely due to a government policy aimed at low-density, high-cost tourism. So be warned: Little comes cheap.

For **recommended safari operators** that include the cost of a flight to southern Africa, see "Package Tours" in "Getting There," below, and also see regional chapters.

### SELF-DRIVE SAFARIS

By far the best budget option is to rent a car and drive yourself around the reserves in South Africa, making use of their self-catering facilities. There are a number of advantages besides cost: You can set your own pace, take in more than one environment (many, for instance, combine a trip to Kruger with a few of KwaZulu-Natal's reserves), and bring the kids (most private game reserves don't accept children). Accommodation is in semi-serviced rondawels (pronounced ron-*da*-vels; these are round, thatch-roofed cottages with kitchens and en-suite bathrooms) that offer excellent value for money. Cheaper units won't have their own kitchen, but all feature a fridge, tea-making facilities, and a barbecue area. Linen and towels are also provided. In some of the rest camps in the KwaZulu-Natal parks, you must give your food to the camp chef who prepares your meals and washes up for no additional cost. Most rest camps have a shop selling supplies, including basics like dishwashing liquid, wood, firelighters, tinned foods, frozen meat, toiletries, and aspirin; you can also purchase field guides here. Most also have a restaurant serving breakfast, lunch, and dinner, which mostly consist of a starter (for example, avocado), main course (meat and two vegetables) and pudding (a.k.a. a dessert consisting of ice cream or fruit salad).

### PRIVATE RESERVES & LODGES

With all game-viewing activities organized for you, this is the way to do your safari in style. A typical day starts with a 3-hour, early-morning game drive—8 (or fewer, at the more expensive lodges) guests accompanied by a game ranger and tracker in an open-topped vehicle—followed by a large cooked breakfast, possibly in the bush. Generally a guided walk is offered before lunch, and afternoons are spent relaxing at the pool or overlooking the standard waterhole; night drives take place during the sunset/early-evening hours, with drinks (sundowners) served in the bush. Dinners are large, often buffet, and served under the stars by firelight. It's worth mentioning that some of the larger lodges simply feel like plush hotels. These have the advantage of amenities like air-conditioning and electricity, and are good if you are the type who craves creature comforts after a long, hot drive. However, if you want to get a real feel for the bush, consider tented bush camps, where you are very unlikely to find a creepy crawly sharing your bed (hot water, plunge pools, and en-suite bathrooms are standard features), but a real attempt is made to connect you with the outdoors. Alternatively, opt for a private lodge that takes no more than 10 to 12 guests per camp—this means you are given very personal service, with knowledgeable rangers available to answer the most detailed of questions, and the peace to absorb your surrounds. If you don't mind living out of a suitcase, moving from camp to camp is the ideal way to see different environments as well as plentiful game; and nowhere does it get as good as Botswana—see chapter 10 for safari operators specializing in this area, as well as for a detailed description of the type of accommodations available.

### ALTERNATIVE SAFARIS

If you can think of it, there's probably a safari where you can do it. The following is just a brief listing of what's available. For details, see the specific chapters referenced below.

If you're keen to walk the wilderness, accompanied by an experienced, armed game ranger, the **Umfolozi Wilderness Trail** is rated by experienced hikers as South Africa's best. For information, contact the **Natal Parks Board.** For more details, see chapter 8. **Kruger National Park** also offers excellent walking safaris with a choice of seven separate wilderness trails. For more information, see chapter 7.

For game spotting on **horseback** and from a **hot-air balloon,** see chapter 6, "Gauteng & North-West Province." Accompanied by a Botswana guide, gliding along in a *mokoro* (dugout canoe) is one of the best ways to get around the Okavango Delta, particularly when it's flooded during June to September; the back of an elephant is another. For **elephant, mokoro,** and many other specialized safaris, see chapter 10.

## What to Pack

Keep in mind that you will need to pack light, particularly if you are taking a charter plane to Botswana, which only allows one soft-sided bag weighing 10 to 12 kilograms (22–26 lbs.). Choose colors that blend in with the bush (gray, brown/beige, khaki). Green clothes are best, but camouflage clothing is forbidden. Loose cotton clothing tends to be the most comfortable. If you're walking, you'll need long pants to protect you from prickly vegetation and ticks, and comfortable hiking boots. A warm sweater, coat, long pants, scarf, and gloves are recommended during evening game drives in winter (June to August); you'll also need warm sleepwear. A fitted broad-brimmed hat, swimwear, sunglasses, and sunscreen are essential in summer. (Don't forget the sunscreen, especially for children, as the African sun can be brutally strong.) Your feet will be happiest in comfortable walking shoes and socks, and also rubber slip-on sandals. Though many lodges supply insect repellent, you'll also want to bring your own, as well as malaria precautions (see "Health, Safety & Insurance," below).

And, of course, don't forget binoculars and a camera (a telephoto lens is ideal) and also plenty of film, budget two to three rolls a day. If you bring a video camera, bring a 12-volt adapter for charging the batteries (although remember that electricity isn't always supplied on safaris).

## Wilderness Etiquette

If you aren't using your own water, check that you don't need to ask permission to draw water or swim from the local source—water rights are sensitive issues in semi-arid countries. As southern Africa is constantly afflicted by drought, and tap water is not recycled, try to use as little water as possible, even in cities. Never use detergents (including so-called biodegradable ones) in rivers or dams (this includes brushing your teeth). Defecate at least 50 meters (160 feet) from water sources, and bury feces at least 25 centimeters (10 inches) deep. Burn rather than bury toilet paper or tampons, and never bury litter: Burn it or carry it with you. Do not make open fires except where permitted. Do not stray from paths, as this leads to erosion. If you're in a 4×4, do not thunder along unspoiled dunes or bush. If you smoke, be sure to extinguish matches and cigarettes and carry butts with you as they take over 20 years to biodegrade. Never touch, scratch, or wet rock art. Never approach wildlife if they appear in any way disturbed by your presence—rules regarding marine animals are particularly strict. Finally, clichéd, but true: Take nothing but photographs; leave nothing but footprints.

# OTHER OUTDOOR ADVENTURES

For a complete list of **specialist nationwide operators** offering some 40 different activities, contact the **Council of Adventure Travel Associations of Southern Africa** (☎ **27/11/705-3201**). Otherwise, some recommended operators include **Adventure Safaris & Sports Tours** (☎ **27/21/438-5201**); **African Routes** (☎ **27/31/**

**304-6358**); **Southern African Adventure Tours** (☎ **27/11/396-1860**); and **Specialized Tours** (☎ **27/21/25-3259**).

**ABSEILING** With numerous mountainsides to drop off, and a number of rivers to drop into, the Western Cape offers the most scenic abseiling options in South Africa; see the Cape Town and Western Cape chapters for details, If you go with a recommended operator, no previous experience is necessary. More serious climbers should check out the "Mountaineering" entry, below.

**BALLOONING** For the best hot-air balloon views, head for the Pilanesberg and Madikwe game reserves in the North-West and drift over the savannah looking for big game. A close second is to sample a glass of wine while soaring over its source in the Winelands of the Western Cape. For ballooning operators, check the relevant chapters, or contact the **Aero Club of South Africa** (☎ **27/11/805-0366**).

**BIRD WATCHING** Situated on one of the world's biggest continents, with a range of totally different environments, the southern African region offers hours of rewarding bird watching, and many species occur nowhere else but here. The best areas are Ndumo and Mkuzi in KwaZulu-Natal, with the bush savannah of Mpumalanga and the Northern Province, or the Okavango Delta in Botswana (see chapter 10), also extremely rewarding. For the best bird-watching safaris in southern Africa, contact **Peter Lawson** (see chapter 8). Good identification books include *Robert's Birds of Southern Africa* by Gordon Lindsey Maclean (Struik) and *Newman's Birds of Southern Africa,* by Ken Newman (Menasha Ridge).

**BOARDSAILING (WINDSURFING)** The most exhilarating windsurfing spots are in the Scarborough and Kommetjie area on Cape Town's western seaboard, off the Cape Point coast, and at Langebaan on the West Coast, where the wind comes up almost every afternoon (see chapter 3).

**BUNGEE/BRIDGE-JUMPING** No experience necessary, just a need for speed. You can take the highest bungee jump in the world at Bloukrans River Bridge—216 meters (708 feet), which rather makes the 65 meters (213 feet) from the Gouritz River Bridge seem like child's play. Both these jumps are on the Garden Route, Western Cape. At 104 meters (341 feet), the world's second-highest bungee jump is off the Victoria Falls Bridge (see chapter 9). **Kiwi Extreme** (☎ **27/42/281-1450**) offers bungee jumping in the Western Cape; **Africa Extreme** (☎ **260/332-4156**) runs the Victoria Falls jumps.

**CANOEING AND KAYAKING** Canoes can usually be hired wherever there's water—check the regional chapters or with the local tourism bureaus. This is certainly a great way to explore South Africa's Lakes District in the Garden Route; you can book a canoe and canoe trail through the Wilderness National Park (see chapter 4, "Western Cape"). Major canoeing events are held in KwaZulu-Natal in the summer and the Cape in the winter. See relevant chapters or contact the **South African Canoe Federation** (☎ **27/331/94-0509**) for further information. Kayaking is offered on the coast as well as on certain rivers, but takes considerably more practice. Before attempting anything on a kayak, make sure you know how to get out of it. Gliding through the waters in a dugout canoe (called a *mokoro*) in the delta is one of the highlights of a trip to Botswana (see chapter 10).

**DIVING** You'll need to take a recognized dive course before taking the plunge and meeting some of the 2,000 species that live off the African shores. If you're doing it here (and this is one of the cheapest places in the world to do so), make sure the organization is part of **South African Underwater Union (SAUU),** which is affiliated with agencies worldwide. Sodwana Bay in northern KwaZulu-Natal is the most popular dive destination, and March is considered the best diving month in South Africa. Even farther north, Kosi Bay offers the most rewarding snorkeling. The Cape coast is good for wreck-diving. For more information, contact **SAUU** (☎ **27/21/930-6549**).

**FISHING** With over 2,500 kilometers (some 1,860 miles) of coastline, rock, and surf, anglers are spoilt for choice. June through November are particularly popular months on the KwaZulu-Natal coast, for which you require no license. Permits are required in certain areas along the Cape coast; for information, contact the **South African Federation of Sea Angling** at ☎ **27/12/46-1912.** The confluence of the warm Indian Ocean and cold Atlantic is responsible for one of the highest concentrations of game fish in the world, including marlin. For more information, contact the **South African Marlin and Tuna Club** at ☎ **27/21/786-2762.** Nor will spear fishermen leave disappointed; the area between Umhlanga Rocks and Salt Rock in KwaZulu-Natal is particularly recommended; for more information, contact **SAUU** (see "Diving," above). Trout fishing is also extremely popular, particularly in the Dullstroom area (Mpumulanga), the Drakensberg (KwaZulu-Natal), and the mountains of the Western Cape. For organized fly-fishing holidays, contact **Trout Adventures Africa** (☎ **27/21/26-1057**).

**GOLFING** There are over 300 golf courses registered throughout the country, and almost every province features at least one of South Africa's best. Courses in KwaZulu-Natal and the Western Cape are usually very beautiful, and incorporate the natural environment. Those in the Western Cape often have views of the surrounding mountains. Unique to Africa are the courses that feature wild animals (in Mpumalanga and the Northern Province). Many of the best courses have been designed by world champion Gary Player. See "The Best Golf Courses" in chapter 1 for specific recommendations, or call the **South African Golf Union** (☎ **27/21/461-7585**) for more information.

**HANG- AND PARAGLIDING** This is a popular activity in the northern areas of South Africa due to good weather and huge thermals; but to combine flights with beautiful scenery, head for Wilderness in the Western Cape, which is considered the best area for coastal flying, or dive off Lion's Head for a bird's eye view of Cape Town. To fly alone, you'll need to complete a course here, or ensure that your license is recognized. If you've never flown before, simply do a tandem flight with an instructor. The **South African Hang and Paragliding Association** (☎ **27/11/805-5429**) will provide names of schools or clubs in the various regions.

**HIKING** South Africa has the most comprehensive trails network in Africa, with short rambles to tough 2-week hikes covering everything from fragrant botanical gardens, indigenous forests, savannah, fynbos-clad mountains, or uninhabited coastlines. Unique to Africa are trails in game reserves where you may encounter big game on foot. Also keep an eye out for **"kloofing"** trails, on which you follow a river through a mountain gorge (kloof), swimming and clambering your way out. Most of the best hiking trails are in the Western Cape and KwaZulu-Natal, as well as Mpumalanga and the Northern Province. As capacity is usually limited, advance planning for the most popular trails is essential, and many require reservations up to a year in advance. For more information, see chapter 1, "The Best Wilderness Trails"; contact SATOUR for a copy of *Follow the Footprints;* contact the **Hiking Federation of South Africa** at ☎ **27/11/886-6524;** or purchase *The Complete Guide to Walks and Trails in Southern Africa* by Jaynee Levy (Struik). **Cape Union Mart** (☎ **27/21/465-7611**) sells a wide range of hiking equipment in branches throughout Cape Town and Johannesburg.

**MOUNTAIN BIKING** This is not as established as hiking in South Africa, but it's catching up fast, with a range of trails suitable for novices and the more experienced. Mpumalanga and Northern Province are great areas for mountain biking, but you'll find even better trails in the Western Cape: Explore the Cape's Winelands, Table Mountain, Cape Point, or the indigenous forests and superb coastline of the Garden Route. Bikes can be hired wherever there are trails. For more information, read *Guide to Mountain Bike Trails in the Western Cape* by Paul Leger (Red Mill Publications) or contact **AFTRAC** (☎ **27/11/794-1713,** aftrac@global.co.za), a helpful source on all aspects of the sport.

**MOUNTAINEERING** The most challenging and popular mountains are in KwaZulu-Natal (Drakensberg) and the Western Cape (Table Mountain, Cederberg, Du Toit's Kloof). Table Mountain alone offers over 500 routes. Some of the best mountains are privately owned, but local climbing clubs can provide permits. For more information, contact the **Mountain Club of South Africa** at ☎ **27/21/465-3412.**

**PARACHUTING (SKYDIVING)** You need no previous experience to do a same-day jump—simply complete an accelerated free-fall course or try a tandem jump. For the best views, leap into the skies above Stellenbosch in the Western Cape; contact the **Cape Parachute Club** (☎ **27/21/58-8514** or 27/082800-6290). Also highly recommended is dropping over magnificent Victoria Falls; call **Safari par Excellence** (☎ **263/13-4424** in Zimbabwe).

**RIDING** There are horse trails throughout southern Africa, ranging from 2-hour excursions around town surrounds (Noordhoek Beach in Cape Town is particularly recommended) to week-long expeditions. One of the best wilderness trails—involving tracking black rhino—is found in Lapalala, Northern Province. Another area perfect for exploring on horseback is the Drakensberg. If horses aren't your bag, you can mount an ostrich in Oudtshoorn (Western Cape), a camel in the Northern Cape, or an elephant in Botswana.

**SAILING** Should you decide to sail these shores, you'll find the yacht facilities in South Africa excellent, with winds averaging 15 to 25 knots. Offshore sailing requires that you belong to a recognized yacht club; to find out more about local harbor regulations, contact **The Cruising Association of South Africa** (☎ **27/21/439-1147**).

**SHARK-CAGE DIVING** Unlike scuba diving, this needs no experience. Great White sharks are baited by operators who lower cages (usually containing two persons) into the water to view this protected species feeding from close up. This activity is offered in the Western Cape—off Dyer Island, near Hermanus; and Mossel Bay, Garden Route—but there are considerable environmental and safety concerns. See chapter 4 for details.

**SURFING** For many, Jeffrey's Bay in the Eastern Cape represents the surf mecca of South Africa; but KwaZulu-Natal's Durban, with its all-year-round warm weather and water, and consistently good waves, is South Africa's real surfing center. Boards are relatively cheap, and a number of shops sell secondhand gear. The major surfing event of the year—the Gunston 500—takes place here in July. For weather and swell forecasts, visit http://os2.iafrica.com/weather. For advanced and beginner surf training, contact **Ocean Sports Centre** (☎ **27/31/368-5318**) or **Pro Surf Coaching** (☎ **27/31/368-5488**) in Durban, or **Charlie Moir** (☎ **27/21/701-2727**) in Cape Town. **Replay Sports** (☎ **27/21/25-1056**) in Cape Town and **Secondhand Surf Shop** (☎ **27/31/332-1875**) in Durban buy and sell secondhand gear.

**WHITE-WATER RAFTING** Commercial river running is a well-developed industry, and no experience is necessary if you're escorted by a reputable outfit (that is, registered with **South African Rafting Association [SARA]**). But be warned: Certain rivers can be fatal. One of the most dangerous, the Zambezi below Victoria Falls, offers one of the greatest adrenaline trips on water, with grade 3 to 4 rapids. The biggest wildwater after this is the Tugela River in KwaZulu-Natal, which is only runnable in the summer. Other rivers worth rafting are the Blyde in Mpumalanga, an 8-kilometer (5-mile) descent with grade 3 to 5 rapids, the Doring (late August/September) and Palmiet in the Western Cape, and the Orange in the Northern Cape. For the most part, the latter offers the most relaxing raft. Ask what you should wear or bring when making a booking. For more information or reservations, contact **River Rafters** in Cape Town at ☎ **27/21/712-5094;** or **Felix Unite River Adventures** (☎ **27/21/683-6433**), considered South Africa's leading river operator. **Shearwater** (☎ **27/11/804-6537** in Jo'burg, or ☎ **263/13-4471** in Zimbabwe) covers the Zambezi River. (See chapter 9 for a list of other operators in Zimbabwe.)

## 7 Health, Safety & Insurance

### STAYING HEALTHY & SAFE

Visiting Southern Africa should pose no serious threat to your health: Dental care is on a par with the best, hospitals are generally efficient (though in an emergency you'd be better off going to a private hospital to avoid a lengthy wait), hygiene is rarely a problem, tap water is safe, stomach upsets from food are rare, there are no weird tropical viruses, and medical aid is generally always within a 2-hour drive. That said, there are a few things to watch out for: Malaria in certain areas is problematic; AIDS/HIV is rampant; bilharzia and tick-bite fever can be unpleasant; and precautions against the summer sun are essential. If you're used to civilized, law-abiding drivers, you'll find South African manners leave a lot to be desired, and drunk driving can be a problem.

Unless you're already covered by a health plan, it's a good idea to take out **medical travel insurance,** particularly if you're going to participate in adventure activities (see the section on travel insurance later in this chapter). In most cases, however, your existing health plan will provide all the coverage you need. Be sure to carry your identification card in your wallet.

If you suffer from a chronic illness, consult your doctor before your departure. For conditions like epilepsy, diabetes, or heart problems, wear a **Medic Alert Identification Tag** (☎ **800/825-3785;** www.medicalert.org), which will immediately alert doctors to your condition and give them access to your records through Medic Alert's 24-hour hotline. Membership is $35, plus a $15 annual fee.

Pack prescription medications in your carry-on luggage. Carry written prescriptions in generic, not brand-name form, and dispense all prescription medications from their original labeled vials. Also bring along copies of your prescriptions in case you lose your pills or run out.

If you wear contact lenses, pack an extra pair in case you lose one.

Contact the **International Association for Medical Assistance to Travelers (IAMAT)** (☎ **716/754-4883** or 416/652-0137; www.sentex.net/~iamat). This organization offers tips on travel and health concerns in the countries you'll be visiting. The United States **Centers for Disease Control and Prevention** (☎ **404/332-4559;** www.cdc.gov) provides up-to-date information on necessary vaccines and health hazards by region or country. (By mail, their booklet is $20; on the Internet, it's free.)

For up-to-date travel advisories, log on to the **State Department** Web site at travel.state.gov/ or www.fco.gov.uk/, the **Foreign & Commonwealth Office.**

Note that children under the age of 12 are generally not allowed in game lodges unless special arrangements have been made with the management.

## Of Special Concern

**AIDS** Africa's AIDS population has reached epidemic proportions. If you're entering into sexual relations, use a condom. There's no real risk that you'll contract the virus from medical treatment.

**BILHARZIA** Do not swim in dams, ponds, or rivers unless they are recommended as bilharzia free. Symptoms are at first difficult to detect—tiredness followed by abdominal pain and blood in the urine or stools—but are effectively treated by praziquantel.

**CREEPY CRAWLIES** You are unlikely to encounter snakes as they are shy and, with the exception of puff adders, tend to move off when sensing humans approaching. If you get bitten, stay calm—very few are fatal—and get to a hospital. Scorpions and spiders are similarly timid and most are totally harmless. To avoid them, shake out clothing that's been lying on the ground and be careful when gathering firewood. If you're hiking through the bush, keep an eye out for ticks; tick-bite fever is unpleasant, though you should recover in 4 days—to remove ticks, smear Vaseline over them.

**INOCULATIONS** No shots necessary, unless you're from a country where yellow fever is endemic, in which case you'll need a vaccination certificate. Ensure that your polio and tetanus shots are up to date, and ask your doctor or a travel-health specialist about vaccinations for hepatitis.

**MALARIA** A course of anti-malarial tablets should be started 2 weeks prior to entering northern KwaZulu-Natal, the Kruger National Park and surrounding reserves, the Mozambican border, Zimbabwe, and Botswana. Anti-malarial drugs containing chloroquine and proguanil are recommended for southern Africa by the World Health Organization; contact your physician or a travel-health specialist to see what is currently prescribed in your country. Keep in mind that no prophylactic is totally effective, however, and your best protection is to avoid being bitten. Sleep under a mosquito net if possible, burn mosquito coils (available at most pharmacies and supermarkets), plug in mosquito destroyers if you have electricity, wear loose full-length clothing, cover exposed skin with repellent, and make sure to take your full course of tablets even after you've left a malarial zone. The flu-like symptoms—fever, diarrhea, and joint pains—can take up to 3 months to develop. Consult a doctor immediately, as a delay in treatment can be fatal. Certain areas have low- and high-risk times; to find out where and when, contact the **Malaria Hotline** (☎ **27/11/403-3586**). (Note that prophylactics are not really recommended for children under the age of 5, so it's best to choose a malaria-free reserve if you're traveling with young children.)

**SAFETY** The rules are the same all over the world, though the high incidence of muggings and street crime warrant extra caution in southern African cities. Try not to look like a tourist, or lost; if you're using a map, walk into a shop. Don't wear flashy jewelry or cameras; wear handbag straps across the neck and keep a good grip on items. Don't walk the city streets after dark, especially if you're alone. If confronted by an assailant, keep calm, and don't resist in any way. Keep your doors locked at all times, particularly in Johannesburg. Avoid no-go areas and unless there are great attractions, don't visit city centers—find out from your hotel how to get where you're going and what's been happening on the streets recently.

With such widespread poverty, you will inevitably have to deal with **beggars,** some of them children. Money is often spent on alcohol or drugs, and many argue that donating to a relevant charity, such as a street shelter, is a more effective way to combat the problem. Some beggars offer services, such as washing or cleaning your car. There's no need to feel intimidated, and the decision to give is entirely personal.

**SUN** Getting sunstroke can ruin your holiday, and skin cancer should be a major deterrent to irresponsible exposure. Remember that the sun doesn't have to be shining for you to burn—wear a broad-brimmed hat at all times, and apply a high-factor screen or total block—at least initially. Wear sunglasses that reduce both UVA and UVB substantially, and stay out of the sun entirely between 11am and 3pm. Children should be kept well covered at the beach; it can take as little as 15 minutes for an infant's skin to develop third-degree burns.

## INSURANCE

There are three kinds of travel insurance: trip cancellation, medical, and lost-luggage coverage. **Trip cancellation insurance** is a good idea if you have paid a large portion of your vacation expenses up front. The other two types of insurance, however, don't make sense for most travelers. Rule number one: Check your existing policies before you buy any additional coverage.

Your existing **health insurance** should cover you if you get sick while on vacation (though if you belong to an HMO, you should check to see whether you are fully covered when away from home). If you need hospital treatment, most health-insurance plans and HMOs will cover out-of-country hospital visits and procedures, at least to some extent. Before you go, contact your insurance provider to make sure you understand details like whether medical costs are paid up front or reimbursed after you've returned and filed the paperwork.

Members of **Blue Cross/Blue Shield** can now use their cards at select hospitals in most major cities worldwide (☎ **800/810-BLUE** or www.bluecares.com/blue/bluecard/wwn for a list of hospitals). For independent travel health-insurance providers, see below. Your homeowner's insurance should cover **stolen luggage.**

Among the reputable issuers of travel insurance are:

- **Access America,** 6600 W. Broad St., Richmond, VA 23230 (☎ **800/284-8300**)
- **Travel Guard International,** 1145 Clark St., Stevens Point, WI 54481 (☎ **800/826-1300**)
- **Travel Insured International, Inc.,** PO Box 280568, East Hartford, CT 06128 (☎ **800/243-3174**)
- **Columbus Travel Insurance,** 279 High St., Croydon CR0 1QH (☎ **0171/375-0011** in London; www2.columbusdirect.com/columbusdirect)
- **International SOS Assistance,** PO Box 11568, Philadelphia, PA 11916 (☎ **800/523-8930** or 215/244-1500) (strictly an assistance company)
- **Travelex Insurance Services,** PO Box 9408, Garden City, NY 11530-9408 (☎ **800/228-9792**)

Medicare only covers U.S. citizens traveling in Mexico and Canada. For Blue Cross/Blue Shield coverage abroad, see above. Companies specializing in accident and medical care include:

- **MEDEX International,** PO Box 5375, Timonium, MD 21094-5375 (☎ **888/MEDEX-00** or 410/453-6300; fax 410/453-6301; www.medexassist.com).
- **Travel Assistance International** (Worldwide Assistance Services, Inc.), 1133 15th St. NW, Suite 400, Washington, DC 20005 (☎ **800/821-2828** or 202/828-5894; fax 202/828-5896).
- **The Divers Alert Network** (DAN) (☎ **800/446-2671** or 919/684-2948) insures scuba divers.

## 8 Tips for Travelers with Special Needs

### TIPS FOR TRAVELERS WITH DISABILITIES

While not as sophisticated as those in first-world countries, facilities are generally satisfactory, with a growing number of tourist attractions designed to be disability-friendly. All major airlines can provide assistance, and Avis and Budget offer cars with automatic transmissions and hand controls. **SATOUR** publishes an accommodation guide, which includes up-to-date information about disability-friendly establishments. Note that the Kruger and Karoo Parks, and a number of the Natal Parks Board camps have specially adapted huts; the Natal Parks Board has also created a 4-kilometer (2½-mile) wheelchair trail near Kamberg in the southern Drakensberg. Contact their offices in KwaZulu-Natal for more information. For adventure-oriented tours of South Africa, contact **Roll-A-Venture** at **☎ 27/83/625-6021. Wilderness Wheels Africa** (**☎ 27/11/648-5753**) specializes in safaris to Kruger National Park, Botswana, and Zimbabwe, and has a Land Cruiser with a lift for wheelchairs, as well as accessible tents, toilets, and showers. **Southern Africa Tours and Safaris** (**☎ 27/12/342-2246**) can provide tours, guides, and physiotherapists for wheelchair users and their families in groups of 6 to 8. **Titch Travel Agency** (**☎ 27/21/689-4151;** e-mail: **titcheve@iafrica.com**) can make arrangements for the visually impaired. **Eco-Access** (**☎ 27/11/673-4533**) will provide information for self-drive safaris and travel, as will Carol Schafer at the **Disabled Adventurers' Association** (**☎ 27/21/686-7330**).

In the United States, *A World of Options,* a 658-page book of resources for travelers with disabilities, covers everything from biking trips to scuba outfitters. It costs $35 ($30 for members) and is available from **Mobility International USA,** PO Box 10767, Eugene, OR 97440 (**☎ 541/343-1284,** voice and TDD; www.miusa.org). Annual membership for Mobility International is $35, which includes their quarterly newsletter, *Over the Rainbow.* In addition, **Twin Peaks Press,** PO Box 129, Vancouver, WA 98666 (**☎ 360/694-2462**), publishes travel-related books for persons with disabilities.

You can join **The Society for the Advancement of Travel for the Handicapped (SATH),** 347 Fifth Ave., Suite 610, New York, NY 10016 (**☎ 212/447-7284,** fax 212-725-8253; www.sath.org) for $45 annually, $30 for seniors and students, to gain access to their vast network of connections in the travel industry.

### FOR GAY & LESBIAN TRAVELERS

You'll find the most developed infrastructure in South Africa, where the new constitution outlaws any discrimination on the basis of sexual orientation, making it the most progressive gay policy in the world. Cities are gay-friendly, and Cape Town, often called "the gateway to Africa" has been dubbed in recent years "the gayway to Africa," or simply "the gay capital of Africa." (See "The Great Gay EsCape" in chapter 3 for details on gay-friendly destinations.) Good sources of information include local press (*Exit, Outright,* or *Gay Pages*), Web sites (www.q.co.za or www.queer.co.za), and the **Pink Map,** a free guide to gay-friendly establishments and events, published by the Western Cape tourism authority. Especially recommended is the annual **Mother City Queer Project** party, a costume ball held every December in Cape Town.

Rural areas may be less accepting, with both blacks and whites tending to be very conservative, so take care when venturing off the beaten tourist track. Note also that Zimbabwean president Robert Mugabe is virulently anti-gay, though establishments at Victoria Falls are safe to visit as a couple. To ensure that bookings are made at gay-friendly establishments, or gay-only places, contact specialist travel agent **Gay EsCape** at **☎ 27/21/23-9001** (e-mail: gayesc@cis-co.za; www.icafe.co.za/gayes).

In the United States, contact **The International Gay & Lesbian Travel Association** (IGLTA) (☎ **800/448-8550** or 954/776-2626; fax 954/776-3303; www.iglta.org), which links travelers up with the appropriate gay-friendly service organizations or tour specialists.

## TIPS FOR SENIORS

Admission prices are often substantially reduced for senior citizens (known as pensioners in South Africa), as are transport prices. For instance, **Spoornet** (the national railway company) discounts prices by 25% for people aged 60 and over. Don't be shy about asking for discounts, but always carry some kind of identification, such as a driver's license, that shows your date of birth. Also, mention the fact that you're a senior citizen when you first make your travel reservations. Accommodation discounts are unusual, but check anyway; national parks may offer discounts, but these tend to be for South African nationals only.

Members of the **American Association of Retired Persons (AARP),** 601 E St. NW, Washington, DC 20049 (☎ **800/424-3410** or 202/434-2277), get discounts not only on hotels but on airfares and car rentals, too. AARP offers members a wide range of special benefits, including *Modern Maturity* magazine and a monthly newsletter.

The **National Council of Senior Citizens,** 8403 Colesville Rd., Suite 1200, Silver Spring, MD 20910 (☎ **301/578-8800**), a nonprofit organization, offers a newsletter six times a year (partly devoted to travel tips) and discounts on hotel and auto rentals; annual dues are $13 per person or couple.

**Mature Outlook,** P.O. Box 9390, Des Moines, IA 50306 (☎ **800/336-6330**), began as a travel organization for people over 50, though it now caters to people of all ages. Members receive discounts on hotels and receive a bimonthly magazine. Annual membership is $19.95, which entitles members to discounts.

**Golden Companions,** P.O. Box 5249, Reno, NV 89513 (☎ **702/324-2227**), helps travelers 45-plus find compatible companions through a personal voice-mail service. Contact them for more information.

**Grand Circle Travel** is also one of the hundreds of travel agencies specializing in vacations for seniors (347 Congress St., Suite 3A, Boston, MA 02210 (☎ **800/221-2610** or 617/350-7500). Many of these packages, however, are of the tour-bus variety, with free trips thrown in for those who organize groups of 10 or more. Seniors seeking more independent travel should probably consult a regular travel agent. **SAGA International Holidays,** 222 Berkeley St., Boston, MA 02116 (☎ **800/343-0273**), offers inclusive tours and cruises for those 50 and older. SAGA also sponsors the more substantial "Road Scholar Tours" (☎ **800/621-2151**), which are fun-loving but with an educational bent.

If you want something more than the average vacation or guided tour, try **Elderhostel** (☎ **877/426-8056;** www.elderhostel.org) or the University of New Hampshire's **Interhostel** (☎ **800/733-9753**), both variations on the same theme: educational travel for senior citizens. On these escorted tours, the days are packed with seminars, lectures, and field trips, and the sightseeing is all led by academic experts.

## TIPS FOR FAMILIES

South Africa is regarded as the most child-friendly country in Africa, with plenty of family accommodation options, well-stocked shops, and pizzas and burgers on tap. Hotels usually provide discounts to children under 12 years, and children under 2 sharing with parents are usually allowed to stay for free. Ages and discounts vary considerably, however, so it's best to check beforehand. South Africa also has a number of excellent self-catering hotels and guest lodges. Bear in mind that most private game reserves will not accept children under 12, and since prophylactics are not recommended for those under 5, choose a malaria-free area. Children are particularly vulnerable to sunburn and should avoid the fierce midday sun (10:30am to 3pm).

### TIPS FOR STUDENTS

South Africa has a large number of lodges and activities catering for the growing backpacker market—once here, contact **Africa Travel Centre** at ☎ **27/21/23-4530** in Cape Town or e-mail them at backpack@gem.co.za. Alternatively, become a member of **Hostelling International** before you leave and contact the South African branch for bookings (☎ **27/21/419 1853**).

In the United States, the best resource for students is the **Council on International Educational Exchange** (CIEE) (www.ciee.org). They can set you up with an ID card (see below), and their travel branch, **Council Travel Service** (☎ **800/226-8624;** www.counciltravel.com), is the biggest student travel agency operation in the world. It can get you discounts on plane tickets, rail passes, and the like. Ask them for a list of CTS offices in major cities so that you can keep the discounts flowing (and aid lines open) as you travel.

From CIEE you can obtain the student traveler's best friend, the $18 **International Student Identity Card** (ISIC). It's the only officially acceptable form of student identification, good for cut rates on rail passes, plane tickets, and other discounts. It also provides you with basic health and life insurance and a 24-hour help line. If you're no longer a student but are still under 26, you can get a GO 25 card from the same people, which will get you the insurance and some of the discounts (but not student admission prices in museums).

In Canada, **Travel CUTS,** 200 Ronson St., Suite 320, Toronto, Ont M9W 5Z9 (☎ **800/667-2887** or 416/614-2887; www.travelcuts.com), offers similar services. **Campus Travel,** 52 Grosvenor Gardens, London SW1W 0AG (☎ **0171/730-3402;** www.campustravel.co.uk), opposite Victoria Station, is Britain's leading specialist in student and youth travel.

## 9 Getting There

For information about overland travel to Zimbabwe and Botswana from South Africa, see chapters 9 and 10, respectively.

### BY PLANE

#### TO SOUTH AFRICA

The major airport hubs in South Africa are Johannesburg, Cape Town, and Durban, with Cape Town and Johannesburg receiving direct international flights. To visit Kruger National Park or surrounding private game reserves in Mpumalanga and the Northern Province, fly from Johannesburg to Hoedspruit or Skukuza, or direct from Cape Town to Hoedspruit.

**From North America** your best bet is to fly with **South African Airways (SAA)** (☎ **800/722-9675,** www.saa.co.za), the only carrier to offer non-stop flights to South Africa. **SAA** flies daily from New York to Johannesburg (at 17 hours, this is the longest non-stop commercial flight in the world), and from Miami to Cape Town, with continuing service to Johannesburg. From the United Kingdom, both **SAA** (☎ **0171/312-5005**) and **British Airways** (☎ **0181/897-4000,** www.british-airways.com) have direct flights.

British Airways (☎ **800/AIRWAYS**) also operates a number of flights from New York to South Africa **via London.** Connection time is usually no longer than an hour, and flights continue on to Johannesburg, Cape Town, and Durban. **Delta** (☎ **800/221-1212,** www.delta-air.com) will take you to Europe and connect you with a partner airline that flies to South Africa. **Virgin Atlantic Airways** (☎ **800/862-8621** in the United States or ☎ **0293/747-747** in Britain, www.fly.virgin.com) flies daily from New York to Johannesburg via London, and **KLM** (☎ **800/447-4747** in the United States; **08705/074074** in the United Kingdom; **800/505-747** in Australia; www.klm.com) flies from New York to Johannesburg via Amsterdam Sunday to Friday.

To get to South Africa **from Australia and New Zealand:** Contact **SAA** (☎ **02/9223-4448**) or **QANTAS** (☎ **13-13-13;** www.qantas.com.au/).

### To Zimbabwe

Most flights to **Victoria Falls International Airport** (☎ **263/13/4250**) go via Johannesburg. **SAA** (☎ **27/11/978-1763** in Johannesburg); **Zimbabwe Express** (☎ **27/ 11/442-3740** in Johannesburg; ☎ **263/13/5992** in Victoria Falls, or ☎ **267/4/706-602** in Harare); and **Air Zimbabwe** (☎ **27/11/331-1541** in Johannesburg or ☎ **263/13/4316** in Victoria Falls) all fly direct between Johannesburg and Victoria Falls. **Sun Air** (☎ **27/11/397-2233**) and **Comair/British Airways** (☎ **27/11/921-0222**) both fly to Victoria Falls from Johannesburg three times weekly. **Air Botswana** (☎ **263/14/733-836**) has connections to Gaborone and Maun.

You could also choose to fly to the main gateway airport in Harare, **Harare International Airport** (☎ **263/14/575-528**), and then make a connection to Victoria Falls. Scheduled airlines flying to and from Harare include **Air Botswana** with connections to Gaborone; **Air Zimbabwe** with connections to Gaborone, Johannesburg, Perth, and Sydney; **British Airways** with connections to London; **QANTAS** with connections to Perth and Sydney; and **South African Airways** with connections to Johannesburg.

### To Botswana

No matter where you're coming from, you'll probably have to make a connection in Johannesburg. The main gateway airport is **Sir Seretse Khama International** (☎ **267/314-518** in Gaborone). **Air Botswana** (☎ **267/66-0391**) flies between Johannesburg and Victoria Falls and Harare in Zimbabwe. **Air Zimbabwe** has connections with Harare, and **British Airways** flies from London to Gabarone via Johannesburg.

To fly to Maun, the airport just south of the Okavango Delta in Botswana, contact **Air Botswana,** the only international carrier that flies here from Johannesburg. Flights leave daily at 10am and arrive at 12.30pm. You can also charter light aircraft from **Lanseria Airport** or **Grand Central Airport** outside of Johannesburg.

To fly directly into the **Okavango Delta,** contact an **air-charter company** that operates small planes from Maun to all the delta camps. Note that strict luggage restrictions apply: 10 to 12 kilograms (22–25 lbs.), preferably packed in soft bags. Charter prices vary, so be sure to compare the following companies' prices for the best deal: **Northern Air** (☎ **267/66-0385**); **Aer Kavango** (☎ **267/66-0393**); **Merlin Services** (☎ **267/66-0635**); **Swamp Air** (☎ **267/66-0569,** fax 267/66-0040); and **Synergy Seating/Delta Air** (☎ **267/66-0044,** fax 267/66-1703).

### Finding the Best Airfare

When using the tips below to shop for your ticket, keep in mind that high-season for southern Africa is June to August for Americans, and mid-December to mid-January for Europeans. A great way to see the country is to travel overland, say from Johannesburg to Cape Town, or from Port Elizabeth to Cape Town; purchasing an "open-jaw" ticket will allow you to arrive in one city and depart from another.

Passengers within the same airplane cabin rarely pay the same fare for their seats. Here are some easy ways to save.

1. Periodically airlines lower prices on their most popular routes. Check your newspaper for advertised discounts or call the airlines directly and ask if any **promotional rates** or special fares are available. If your schedule is flexible, ask if you can secure a cheaper fare by staying an extra day or by flying midweek. (Many airlines won't volunteer this information.) If you already hold a ticket when a sale breaks, it may even pay to exchange your ticket, which usually incurs a $50 to $75 charge.

   Note, however, that the lowest-priced fares are often nonrefundable, require advance purchase of 1 to 3 weeks and a certain length of stay, and carry penalties for changing dates of travel.
2. **Consolidators,** also known as bucket shops, are a good place to find low fares. Consolidators buy seats in bulk from the airlines and then sell them back to the public at prices below even the airlines' discounted rates. Their small boxed ads usually run in the Sunday travel section at the bottom of the page. Before you pay, however, ask for a confirmation number from the consolidator and then call the airline itself to confirm your seat. Be prepared to book your ticket with a different consolidator—there are many to choose from—if the airline can't confirm your reservation. Also be aware that bucket shop tickets are usually non-refundable or rigged with stiff cancellation penalties, often as high as 50 to 75% of the ticket price.

   **Council Travel** (☎ **800/226-8624;** www.counciltravel.com) and **STA Travel** (☎ **800/781-4040;** www.sta.travel.com) cater especially to young travelers, but their bargain-basement prices are available to people of all ages. **Travel Bargains** (☎ **800/AIR-FARE;** www.1800airfare.com) was formerly owned by TWA but now offers the deepest discounts on many other airlines, with a 4-day advance purchase. Other reliable consolidators include **1-800-FLY-CHEAP** (www.1800flycheap.com); **TFI Tours International** (☎ **800-745-8000** or 212/736-1140), which serves as a clearinghouse for unused seats; or "rebators" such as **Travel Avenue** (☎ **800/333-3335** or 312/876-1116) and the **Smart Traveller** (☎ **800/448-3338** in the United States), which rebate part of their commissions to you.
3. Book a seat on a **charter flight.** Discounted fares have pared the number available, but they can still be found. Most charter operators advertise and sell their seats through travel agents, thus making these local professionals your best source of information for available flights. Before deciding to take a charter flight, however, check the restrictions on the ticket: You may be asked to purchase a tour package, to pay in advance, to be amenable if the day of departure is changed, to pay a service charge, to fly on an airline you're not familiar with (this usually is not the case), and to pay harsh penalties if you cancel—but be understanding if the charter doesn't fill up and is canceled up to 10 days before departure. Summer charters fill up more quickly than others and are almost sure to fly, but if you decide on a charter flight, seriously consider cancellation and baggage insurance.
4. Look into **courier flights.** Companies that hire couriers use your luggage allowance for their business baggage; in return, you get a deeply discounted ticket. Flights are often offered at the last minute, and you may have to arrange a pretrip interview to make sure you're right for the job. **Now Voyager,** open Monday to Friday from 10am to 5:30pm and Saturday from noon to 4:30pm (☎ **212/431-1616**), flies from New York. Now Voyager also offers noncourier discounted fares, so call the company even if you don't want to fly as a courier.

## CyberDeals for Net Surfers

It's possible to get some great deals on airfare, hotels, and car rentals via the Internet. So go grab your mouse and start surfing and you could save a bundle on your trip. The Web sites below are worth checking out, especially since all services are free.

We highly recommend Arthur Frommer's Budget Travel Online (**www.frommers.com**) as an excellent travel-planning resource. Of course, we're a little biased, but you will find indispensable travel tips, reviews, monthly vacation giveaways, and online booking.

Subscribe to Arthur Frommer's Daily Newsletter (**www.frommers.com/newsletters**) to receive the latest travel bargains and insider travel secrets in your mailbox every day. You'll read daily headlines and articles from the dean of travel himself, highlighting last-minute deals on airfares, accommodations, cruises, and package vacations. You'll also find great travel advice by checking our Tip of the Day or Hot Spot of the Month.

Search our Destinations archive (**www.frommers.com/destinations**) of more than 200 domestic and international destinations for great places to stay, tips for traveling there, and what to do while you're there. Once you've researched your trip, you might try our online reservation system (**www.frommers.com/booktravelnow**) to book your dream vacation at affordable prices.

The best part of **Microsoft Expedia's** (**www.expedia.com**) multipurpose travel site is the "Fare Tracker": You fill out a form on the screen indicating that you're interested in cheap flights to southern Africa from your hometown, and, once a week, they'll e-mail you the best airfare deals.

**Preview Travel** (**www.reservations.com** and **www.vacations.com**) is another useful travel site. Reservations.com has a "Best Fare Finder," which will search the Apollo computer reservations system for the three lowest fares for any route on any days of the year. If you find an airfare you like, you can book your ticket right online—you can even reserve hotels and car rentals on this site. If you're in the preplanning stage, head to Preview's Vacations.com site, where you can check out the latest package deals for South Africa and other destinations around the world by clicking on "Hot Deals."

**Travelocity** (**www.travelocity.com**) is one of the best travel sites out there. In addition to its "Personal Fare Watcher," which notifies you via e-mail of the lowest airfares for up to five different destinations, Travelocity will track the three lowest fares for any routes on any dates in minutes. You can book a flight right then and there, and if you need a rental car or hotel, Travelocity will find you the best deal via the SABRE computer reservations system (a huge database used by travel agents worldwide). Click on "Last Minute Deals" for the latest travel bargains.

**Epicurious Travel** (**travel.epicurious.com**), and **Smarter Living** (**www.smarterliving.com**) are other good travel sites that allow you to sign up for weekly mailings of last-minute deals from major airlines.

5. Join a travel club such as **Moment's Notice** (☎ **718/234-6295**) or **Sears Discount Travel Club** (☎ **800/433-9383,** or 800/255-1487 to join), which supply unsold tickets at discounted prices. You pay an annual membership fee to get the

club's hot-line number. Of course, you're limited to what's available, so you have to be flexible.

### In-Flight Comfort & Avoiding Jet Lag

A few basic strategies will go a long way to relieving your discomfort on a long-distance flight. Wear loose clothing and a roomy pair of shoes that are easy to slip into, because your feet will swell en route. Drink plenty of water to avoid dehydration in the air-conditioned cabin, and go easy on the free booze. To while away the hours, bring lots of magazines or a good book. Even if you usually fly coach, you may want to consider a business-class seat for this trip. It won't be cheap, but you will be grateful for the bigger seat, extra legroom, and lower recline on the chair. If you do travel coach, request a bulkhead or exit-door seat as these have more legroom. Some airlines allow you to request seats when you book, but others allocate seats only at check-in—get to the airport early.

Unless you're traveling from Europe, jet lag is a foregone conclusion on the long journey to Africa, so factor this into your itinerary. Don't plan to climb Table Mountain the first morning you arrive, or book a late dinner for your first evening. There is no cure for jet lag, but you will help fight it if you get as much sleep as possible, drink lots of water, and don't overeat. Trying to adapt to your new time zone as quickly as possible, especially at meal and sleep times, is also a good idea. When you're on the plane, move your watch ahead to southern African time (the pilot usually announces the current time at the destination shortly after takeoff) so that you can get out of the habit of thinking about what time it is at home. If it's evening when you arrive, go to bed; if it's day, try to stay awake. If you must nap, keep it short.

If you have time, you can break up your trip with a 1-day stopover in Europe. Book a hotel near the airport and get some much-needed shut-eye.

## BY BOAT

Several cruise companies including **P&O, CTC Cruise Lines, Royal Viking,** and **Starlauro** offer stops in South Africa on their routes. The *RMS St Helena* runs four scheduled services a year on its Cardiff, Wales to Cape Town route. Call ☎ **01326/563-434** in the United Kingdom or ☎ **718/939-2400** in the United States. *Safmarine,* a container-ship operator, offers berths for up to 10 fare-paying passengers on its Tilbury, United Kingdom to Cape Town, Port Elizabeth, and Durban routes. Book through ☎ **01703/33-4415** or fax 01703/33-4416 in the United Kingdom, or ☎ **27/21/408 6911,** fax 27/21/408-6370 in South Africa.

## PACKAGE & ESCORTED TOURS

Before you start your search for the lowest airfare, you may want to consider booking your flight as part of a travel package such as an escorted tour or a package tour. What you lose in adventure, you'll gain in time and money saved when you book accommodations, and maybe even food and entertainment, along with your flight.

### Escorted Tours

Some people love escorted tours. They let you relax and take in the sights while a bus driver fights traffic for you; they spell out your costs up front; and they take you to the maximum number of sights in the minimum amount of time with the least amount of hassle. If you do choose an escorted tour, you should ask a few simple questions before you buy:

1. What is the **cancellation policy?** Do they require a deposit? Can they cancel the trip if they don't get enough people? Do you get a refund if they cancel? If you cancel? How late can you cancel if you are unable to go? When do you pay in full?
2. How busy is the **schedule?** How much sightseeing do they plan each day? Do they allow ample time for relaxing by the pool, shopping, or wandering?
3. What is the **size** of the group? The smaller the group, the more flexible the itinerary, and the less time you'll spend waiting for people to get on and off the bus. Tour operators may be evasive about this, because they may not know the exact size of the group until everybody has made their reservations; but they should be able to give you a rough estimate. Some tours have a minimum group size and may cancel the tour if they don't book enough people.
4. What is included in the **price?** Don't assume anything. You may have to pay for transportation to and from the airport. A box lunch may be included in an excursion, but drinks might cost extra. Beer might be included, but wine might not. Can you opt out of certain activities, or does the bus leave once a day, with no exceptions? Are all your meals planned in advance? Can you choose your main course at dinner, or does everybody get the same chicken cutlet?

*Note:* If you choose an escorted tour, think strongly about purchasing travel insurance from an independent agency, especially if the tour operator asks you to pay up front. See the section on travel insurance earlier in this chapter. One final caveat: Since escorted tour prices are based on double occupancy, the single traveler is usually penalized.

## Package Tours

Package tours are not the same thing as escorted tours. They are simply a way to buy airfare and accommodations, or book a safari, at the same time. For far-off destinations like South Africa, they can be a smart way to go; by using a reputable operator, you put your trip in the hands of someone who knows the area well enough to help you plan the best vacation for your interests. Note that you will pay for the operator's expertise, however, and this book is designed to help you create a great itinerary.

Packages vary widely. Each destination usually has one or two packagers that are usually cheaper than the rest because they buy in even greater bulk. If you spend the time to shop around, you will save in the long run. Also keep in mind that though we recommend companies based in Africa, it is usually easiest to book their services through a representative in your home country. Most of the U.S.- and U.K.-based operators listed below and elsewhere in the book represent several reputable African-based companies. For more safari and tour operators, also see individual chapters. For safaris in Zimbabwe and Botswana, see chapters 9 and 10, respectively.

Highly recommended **Premier Tours** (☎ **800/545-1910** or 215/893-9966; e-mail: info@premiertours.com; www.premiertours.com/) a specialist in southern and eastern Africa, offers wildlife safaris, adventure tours, overland camping safaris, fly-in safaris, special interest tours, and general sightseeing. They also act as an air consolidator and have some of the lowest airfares to Africa. Their safaris range from the do-it-yourself, eco-conscious, participation type to high-end luxury. They are also a great source of advice, with knowledgeable operators—born and raised in South Africa—who can put together an entire itinerary for first-time travelers to Africa, or tailor land- or air-only arrangements to your specifications.

Other recommended operators include: **Abercrombie & Kent Safaris,** 1520 Kensington Rd., Oak Brook, IL 60523-2141 (☎ **800/ 323-7308**) specialists in upmarket safaris in southern Africa. **Ker & Downey** (☎ **713/917-0048**) has a 16-day southern African safari that takes in Cape Town, a Sabi Sand game reserve, the Okavango Delta, and Victoria Falls. Contact them at 2835 Wilcrest Dr., Suite 600, Houston, TX 77042. Less luxurious, **African Travel**, 1100 E. Broadway, Glendale, CA 91205 (☎ **800/421-8907**; fax 818/507-5802); **Born Free Safaris,** 12504 Riverside Dr., North Hollywood, CA 91607 (☎ **800/372-3274**; fax 818/753-1460; e-mail bornfreesafaris@att.net); and **Wildlife Safari,** 346 Rheem Blvd., Moraga, CA 94556 (☎ **800/221-8118;** fax 510/376-5059) also offer game viewing packages for individuals and groups.

Local outfitter **Wilderness Safaris,** P.O. Box 78573, Sandton 2146, in Johannesburg (☎ **27/11/883-0747**) puts together excellent itineraries that cover visits to a variety of Botswana camps and/or Zimbabwe and/or great beach and birding destinations in KwaZulu-Natal. They are recommended for the quality of their guides, and with a maximum of 8 guests on any safari, the quality of the experience, particularly in Botswana, where they operate a relatively large number of camps.

**Conservation Corporation,** Private Bag X27, Benmore 2010, in Johannesburg (☎ **305/221-2906** in the United States, or 27/11/784-7077), concentrates on offering the most luxurious accommodation in reserves throughout southern Africa. If you'd like to include cultural and historical sights in your tour, contact **Springbok Atlas,** P.O. Box 819, Cape Town 8000 (☎ **27/21/448-6545**), one of the oldest South African operators; or **Rennies Travel,** P.O. Box 4569, Johannesburg 2000 (☎ **27/11/407-3211**), one of the largest. For a more intimate experience, look into a minibus tour with **Welcome Tours and Safaris,** P.O. Box 632, Howard Place 7450, in Cape Town (☎ **27/21/510-6001**), or P.O. Box 2191, Parklands 2121, in Johannesburg (☎ **27/11/328-8050**). These operate throughout South Africa and combine natural, cultural, and historical aspects.

## 10 Getting Around

With a well-maintained and organized road system, a good range of car-rental companies, and the best internal flight network in Africa, a combination of flight and road travel is recommended in South Africa—that is, overland to a certain point, and then fly out. With a budget to adhere to, you could choose to travel by bus: The major intercity bus companies are reliable for long-distance hauls, and some are fairly flexible. Then again, if you have time on your hands, nothing beats the romance of rail—if you can afford it, steam into Victoria Falls from Pretoria on the Blue Train.

Note that it takes 2 days to drive to Maun, Botswana, and should you have an emergency on the road, help can take a long time coming. To travel around this country, you'd be best off flying in and booking an organized tour. For more information on overland travel in Zimbabwe and Botswana, see chapters 9 and 10, respectively.

### BY CAR

Given enough time, this is by far the best way to enjoy South Africa, as you wind along relatively empty roads through some of the most spectacular scenery in the world. Certainly in urban centers you'll need a car to get around, as public transport is often unreliable and can be unsafe. All the major car-rental companies have agencies here; as well, there are a host of local companies. All offer much the same deals, though cars are in big demand and short supply during the busiest period, November to April, so be sure to book well in advance. **Britz Africa** (☎ **0800/11-7460)** rents camper vans and 4×4 rentals, and will pick you up in your vehicle from the airport.

**CAR RENTALS** You'll need a driver's license to rent a car and most companies stipulate that drivers should be a minimum of 21 years. Armed with a letter of authority from the rental agency, vehicles rented in South Africa may be taken into Botswana and Zimbabwe, though the latter will require 72 hours notice and additional insurance charges are applicable (for information, call ☎ **27/11/974-2571** ext. **2408**). You can leave the vehicle in these countries for a fee; in South Africa, you can hire a one-way rental car to any of the major cities. It's best to prebook your vehicle. The following major companies have branches in South Africa.

**Avis** (☎ **800/331-1212** in the United States; ☎ **800/TRY-AVIS** in Canada; ☎ **0990/900-500** in the United Kingdom; ☎ **1800/22-5533** in Australia; ☎ **09/526-2847** in New Zealand; ☎ **0800/021-111** toll-free in South Africa; (☎ **263/13/4532** in Zimbabwe; and ☎ **267/66-0039** in Botswana); www.avis.com.

**Budget** (☎ **800/527-0700** in the United States; ☎ **0800/181-181** in the United Kingdom; ☎ **1300/36-2848** in Australia; ☎ **09/375-2222** in New Zealand; ☎ **0800/01-6622** toll-free in South Africa); www.budgetrentacar.com.

**Hertz** (☎ **800/654-3131** in the United States; ☎ **0990/996-699** in the United Kingdom; ☎ **13-30-39** in Australia; ☎ **09/309-0989** in New Zealand; ☎ **27/21/386-1560** in South Africa; and ☎ **263/13/4772** in Zimbabwe); www.hertz.com.

### Demystifying Car-Rental Insurance

Before you drive off in a rental car, be sure you're insured. Hasty assumptions about your personal auto insurance or a rental agency's additional coverage could end up costing you tens of thousands of dollars—even if you are involved in an accident that was clearly the fault of another driver.

Even if you already hold a **private auto insurance** policy, coverage probably doesn't extend outside the United States. Be sure to find out whether you are covered in the area you are visiting, whether your policy extends to all persons who will be driving the rental car, how much liability is covered in case an outside party is injured in an accident, and whether the type of vehicle you are renting is included under your contract. (Rental trucks, sports utility vehicles, and luxury vehicles such as the Jaguar may not be covered.)

Most **major credit cards** provide some degree of coverage as well—provided they were used to pay for the rental. Terms vary widely, however, so be sure to call your credit-card company directly before you rent.

If you are **uninsured or driving abroad,** your credit-card provides primary coverage as long as you decline the rental agency's insurance. This means that the credit card will cover damage or theft of a rental car for the full cost of the vehicle. If you already have insurance, your credit card will provide secondary coverage—which basically covers your deductible.

Credit cards **will not cover liability,** or the cost of injury to an outside party and/or damage to an outside party's vehicle. Since you will be driving outside the United States, you may seriously want to consider purchasing additional liability insurance from your rental company. Be sure to check the terms, however: Some rental agencies only cover liability if the renter is not at fault; even then, the rental company's obligation varies.

The basic insurance coverage offered by most car-rental companies, known as the **Loss/Damage Waiver (LDW)** or **Collision Damage Waiver (CDW),** can cost as much as $20/day. It usually covers the full value of the vehicle with no deductible if an outside party causes an accident or other damage to the rental car. Liability coverage varies according to the company policy. If you are at fault in an accident, however, you will be covered for the full replacement value of the car, but not for liability. Most rental companies will require a police report in order to process any claims you file, but your private insurer will not be notified of the accident.

**Arranging Car Rentals on the Web** Internet resources can make comparison shopping easier. **Microsoft Expedia** (www.expedia.com) and **Travelocity** (www.travelocity.com) help you compare prices and locate car-rental bargains from various companies nationwide. They will even make your reservation for you once you've found the best deal.

### On the Road in Southern Africa

**GASOLINE** Fuel is referred to as "petrol" and is available 24 hours a day in major centers. It costs approximately R2.50 (42¢) per liter (R10/$1.65 for 4 liters, or approximately 1 gallon); credit cards are not accepted as payment. Gas stations are full serve, and you are expected to tip the attendant R2–5 (35¢–85¢).

**ROAD CONDITIONS AND RULES** In South Africa, you'll find an excellent network of tarred roads, with emergency services available along the major highways; you cannot rely on this sort of backup on road conditions in Zimbabwe or Botswana. Driving in all three countries is on the left side of the road—repeat the mantra "drive left, look right," and wear your seatbelt at all times; it's mandatory and in any case, driving skills on the road vary considerably. A broken line means you may pass/overtake; a solid line means you may not. The speed limit on national highways is 120 kilometers/hour (75mph), 100 kilometers/hour (62mph) on secondary rural roads, and 60 kilometers/hour (37mph) in urban areas—stick to them.

**BREAKDOWNS** The **Automobile Association of South Africa (AA)** extends privileges to members of **AAA** in the United States and the Automobile Association in Britain. The toll-free number in South Africa is ☎ **0800/001-0101;** the emergency toll-free number is **0800/03-3007.** Headquarters is AA House, 479 De Korte St., Braamfontein, Johannesburg 2017.

## By Plane

If you have limited time to cover Africa's large distances, flying is your best bet, though internal flights are expensive. Choices in South Africa are limited to **SAA** (☎ **0800/11-4799,** toll free in South Africa or see regional numbers in "Getting There," above), **British Airways/Comair** (☎ **27/11/921-0222**), and **Sun Air** (☎ **27/11/397-2244**). SAA offers the most extensive network, but has slightly more expensive fares. Contact **Nyala Air** at ☎ **27/41/514-117** for charter-flight inquiries.

## By Train

**Spoornet** (☎ **27/11/773-3994,** in Johannesburg; ☎ **27/21/449-5437,** in Cape Town) runs most of the intercity rail services; ticket prices for first class are comparable to a bus ticket to the same destination. Second class costs considerably less, but you'll share your compartment with more people (four in first class, six in second). Coupes in first class take only two people, making them ideal for couples. Note the journey from Johannesburg to Cape Town takes 27 hours—longer than the bus.

If the journey is as important as the destination, splurge on one of South Africa's luxury trains: The famous **Blue Train** (☎ **27/11/773-7631**), a 5-star hotel on wheels, which runs between Pretoria and Cape Town, Pretoria, and Victoria Falls, and along the Garden Route, offers beautiful scenery, great food, plush surroundings (marble en-suite bathrooms, television, fabric-lined wardrobes, a personal butler to take care of your every need), and a formal atmosphere (guests are expected to dress for dinner). Prices include meals and drinks. Another luxury option is **Rovos Rail** (☎ **27/12/323-6052**). Rovos covers similar routes as well as Pretoria to Maputo (via southern Kruger National Park), Cape Town to Knysna, and Pretoria to Swakopmund, a coastal town in Namibia.

### BY BUS

The three established intercity bus companies are **Greyhound, Intercape,** and **Translux.** There's not much to choose between them, though Greyhound offers a pass to frequent users. Johannesburg to Cape Town takes approximately 19 hours. An alternative to these is the **Baz Bus,** which offers a great hop-on-hop-off scheme—a good way to explore the Garden Route if you don't want to rent a car. **Route 49** (☎ **27/21/788-7904**) offers a 24-hour direct bus service from Cape Town to Victoria Falls; at R549 ($91.50) one-way, it's the cheapest way to get there. Phone numbers for the major bus companies are as follows:

- **Baz Bus National** In Cape Town, ☎ **27/21/439-2323;** in Durban, ☎ **27/31/23 6585.**
- **Greyhound** In Johannesburg, ☎ **27/11/830-1301;** in Pretoria, ☎ **27/12/323-1154;** in Cape Town, ☎ **27/21/418-4310;** in Durban, ☎ **27/13/309-7830.**
- **Intercape** In Pretoria, ☎ **27/12/654-4114;** in Cape Town, ☎ **27/21/386-4400.**
- **Translux** In Johannesburg, ☎ **27/11/774-3333;** in Pretoria, ☎ **27/12/315-2333;** in Cape Town, ☎ **27/21/449-3333;** in Durban, ☎ **27/31/361-8333.**

## 11 Tips on Accommodations

For information on accommodations in Zimbabwe and Botswana, see chapters 9 and 10, respectively.

To help you select a place to stay, **Portfolio** (☎ **27/21/686-5400;** www.portfoliocollection.com) brings out an attractive range of booklets profiling the full spectrum of options (from B&Bs to luxurious retreats) across the country. You can utilize their reservation service by calling ☎ **27/11/880-3414** or e-mailing collection@iafrica. com. **Hotelogue** (☎ **27/21/462-5010,** or e-mail info@hotelogue.co.za) offers a similar selection, but concentrates on the upmarket options. Both cover a small selection in Zimbabwe and Botswana. **Conservation Corporation** runs a number of upmarket lodges in southern Africa (☎ **305/221-2906** in the United States or ☎ **27/11/784-7077** in Johannesburg).

A good alternative to hotels, and growing in popularity, are upmarket **guest houses,** which function much like small hotels, with managers rather than owners dealing with the day-to-day running.

Renting someone else's apartment or home is a good option for a longer stay, particularly along the Atlantic seaboard; contact **Cape Holiday Homes** (☎ **27/21/419-0430,** www.capeholiday.com). **Self-catering options** that include a kitchen are good for families, and thanks to **Mr Delivery,** a restaurant delivery service, you won't even have to cook. (See individual chapters for details.)

Should you choose to stay in a **private game lodge** during your safari, you will find a wide range of options and prices. Most basic are the tented camps, which offer a real sense of being in the wild. Luxury options come with all the amenities, and are virtually indistinguishable—except for the odd buffalo wandering the lawn—from luxury hotels. Regardless of the lodge you choose, you can be sure of receiving excellent service and eating well. All meals are included in the rate, and any dietary restrictions can be accommodated with prior notice.

Note that accommodation **prices** differ substantially depending on when you're visiting. Check when booking, but you'll usually find higher prices during the peak seasons of summer and autumn (November to April); and a drop in prices during the low (or "green") seasons of May to October.

## 12 Suggested Itineraries

The 1-week tours below hit the highlights of the various parts of the country for first-time visitors. If you plan to stay longer than 1 week, combine or extend any of the below itineraries to match your schedule.

**THE BEST OF THE CAPE COAST** Spend 2 nights in the Winelands (all within 45 minutes from the Cape Town airport), and spend your days exploring this lush, peaceful region and sampling the terrific wines. On the third day, drive via the N1 to Prince Albert in the Great Karoo and spend the night in this tiny hamlet. Cross the Swartberg pass to Oudtshoorn, visit an ostrich farm and/or the Cango Caves, and then continue on to Wilderness or Knysna. Spend 2 nights here, taking in the indigenous forests and superb Plettenberg Bay beaches (don't forget to visit Storms River Mouth). Drive to George (90 minutes from "Plet") and catch a flight back to Cape Town; spend 2 nights here, and then depart home. Alternatively, drive to Port Elizabeth and spend 2 nights at Shamwari Game Reserve, or book into the luxurious Hacklewood Hill and do a day trip to Addo Elephant Park. (Note that you may want to delete the Winelands from this trip during the winter months May to August, when the region experiences its highest rainfall, and extend your time elsewhere.)

**EXPLORING THE GAME RESERVES AND VICTORIA FALLS** Spend the night in Johannesburg or Pretoria, then set off for Kruger National Park or a private game reserve, overnighting along the way. Spend 3 nights in the Kruger and/or adjacent private game reserve, then fly back to Johannesburg and catch a connecting flight to Victoria Falls. Stay in Vic Falls 2 nights, then return to Johannesburg and fly home.

**THE BEST OF SOUTHERN AFRICAN WILDLIFE AND THE NORTH COAST** Fly to Maun and spend 4 days in the Okavango Delta on safari. From here, fly to Richard's Bay in KwaZulu-Natal, and transfer to Rocktail Bay for a couple days of beach walks and snorkeling. (If you're a keen bird watcher, transfer to Ndumo private game reserve instead.) Extend your stay in this region to 3 days if you're in need of a longer break from civilization, or transfer to Durban for a day and discover South Africa's most multicultural city. Overnight in Durban, and fly out the next day.

## Fast Facts: South Africa

For "Fast Facts" for Zimbabwe and Botswana, see chapters 9 and 10 respectively.

**American Express** **In South Africa** Report card loss to the Johannesburg branch at ☎ **27/11/359-0200.** Other branches are in Cape Town, Durban, Port Elizabeth, Pretoria, and Richard's Bay.

**Banks and ATM Networks** See "Money," earlier in this chapter.

**Business Hours** **Shops** are generally open Monday to Friday, 8:30 or 9am to 4:30 or 5pm, and Saturday 8:30am to 1pm. In smaller towns, they often close between 1 and 2pm. Some of the larger shopping malls (like the V&A Waterfront) are open from 9am to 9pm, daily. South African **"cafes"** (local mini-marts) are often open 7am to 8pm, daily. **Public offices** open at 8am and close 3.30pm, Monday to Friday. **Bank hours** are usually Monday to Friday 9am to 3:30pm, and Saturday 8:30am to 11am. Banks often close from 12:45 to 2pm in rural areas.

**Car Rentals** See "Getting Around," earlier in this chapter.

**Climate** See "When to Go," earlier in this chapter.

**Currency** See "Money," earlier in this chapter.

**Customs** See "Visitor Information & Entry Requirements," earlier in this chapter.

**Documents** See "Visitor Information & Entry Requirements," earlier in this chapter.

**Driving** See "Getting Around," earlier in this chapter.

**Drugstores** Drugstores are called "chemists" or pharmacies; ask the local tourism bureau for directions, see city listings, or look under "pharmacies" in the Yellow Pages.

**Electricity** Electricity in southern Africa runs on 220/230V,50Hz AC and sockets take round- or flat-pinned plugs. Most hotel rooms have sockets for 110V electric razors. Bring an adapter/converter combination, but also be aware that many bush camps do not have electricity at all.

**Embassies and Consulates** The U.S. embassy in Pretoria is at 877 Pretorius St., Arcadia, Pretoria, ☎ **27/12/342-1048.** Other offices are in Johannesburg, ☎ **27/11/331-1681;** Cape Town, ☎ **27/21/21-4280;** and Durban, ☎ **27/31/304-4737.**

**Emergencies** **Ambulance** ☎ **10177** or **999. Police:** ☎ **10111. Fire:** Consult the front pages of the local telephone directory for brigade numbers.

**Holidays** See "When to Go," earlier in this chapter.

**Information** See "Visitor Information," earlier in this chapter.

**Language** There are 11 official languages in South Africa, but English dominates as the lingua franca here, as well as in Botswana and Zimbabwe. It's often a second language though, so be patient, speak slowly, and keep a sense of humor.

**Liquor Laws** Most liquor stores (called "bottle stores" in South Africa) are closed on Saturday afternoons.

**Maps** See "Getting Around," earlier in this chapter.

**Newspapers/Magazines** The best national paper is the weekly *Mail & Guardian,* which comes out every Friday and has a comprehensive What's On section. Local papers are also useful for listings: Purchase the *Star* or the *Sowetan* in Johannesburg, the *Cape Argus* in Cape Town, the *Natal Mercury* in Durban, and the *Eastern Province Herald* in Port Elizabeth. *Business Day* is South Africa's version of the *Wall Street Journal* or *Financial Times.* The *Sunday Times* is the tacky Sunday tabloid, while *The Independent* caters for the more intellectual market. *Eat Out* is an annual magazine that covers top restaurants throughout South Africa. *Getaway* is an excellent monthly magazine that covers destinations throughout Africa and is well worth purchasing for cheap accommodation listings and up-to-date information, while *Out There* is the adventure alternative. The CNA chain sells international press and magazines.

**Police** Call ☎ **10111.**

**Taxes** A value-added tax (VAT) of 14% is levied on most goods and services; check that it's included in any quoted price. Foreign visitors can claim VAT back on goods over R250 ($41.65) by presenting the tax invoice together with their passport at the airport before departing.

**Telephone and Fax** **To call southern Africa from another country:** Dial international access code (United States or Canada 011, United Kingdom or New Zealand 00, Australia 0011), plus country code (**27** for **South Africa, 263** for **Zimbabwe, 267** for **Botswana,** and **260** for **Zambia**), plus local number minus the 0.

**To make an international call:** Dial **09,** then the country code (United States or Canada 1, United Kingdom 44, Australia 61, New Zealand 64), the area code, and the local number.

**To charge international calls:** Dial AT&T Direct, ☎ 0-800-99-0123; Sprint, ☎ 0800-99-0001; or MCI, ☎ 0800-99-0011.

To make a **local call within the same area code,** simply pick up the phone and dial the direct number without the area code. If you are calling within the country to a different area code include the initial zero (0) before the area code and number. When calling a mobile phone number, always include the 082 or 083 area code.

If you have problems getting through to anyone, or need a new number, use the **directory assistance** service by dialing ☎ **1023** for numbers in South Africa, and **0903** for international numbers. Be patient, speak slowly, and check spellings with your operator.

Pay phones require a minimum of 40¢ for a local call; as hotels often charge a massive mark-up, it's worth purchasing a telephone card (used in specific pay phones) for international calls—these card pay phones are also often the only ones working. Cards are available from post offices and most newsagents, and come in units of R10 ($1.65), R20 ($3.30), R50 ($8.35), R100 ($16.65), and R200 ($33.35).

**Vodacom** has 24-hour desks at all major international airports offering mobile phones for rent.

**Time Zone** South Africa is 2 hours ahead of GMT (that is, 7 hours ahead of Eastern Standard Time).

**Tipping** Add 10–20% to your restaurant bill, 10% to your taxi. Porters get around R3 (50¢) per bag. There are no self-serve garages; when filling up with fuel, tip the person around R2 to R5 (35¢–85¢). It's not unusual to leave some money for the person cleaning your hotel room. Be generous if you feel the service warrants it.

**Useful Telephone Numbers** **Computicket** (☎ **27/21/430-8080**) is a national booking service that covers cinema and concert seats, Intercity bus tickets, and national parks. In South Africa, call directory assistance at ☎ **1023** for numbers in South Africa, and ☎ **0903** for international numbers.

**Water** Tap water is safe to drink in all tourist areas. Always check in game reserves.

**Weather** Call ☎ **27/21/40-881** in Cape Town; ☎ **27/12/321-9621** in Pretoria; ☎ **27/31/307-4121** in Durban; and ☎ **27/41/582-4242** in Port Elizabeth.

3

# Cape Town & the Winelands

The oldest port in southern Africa, Cape Town is regularly heralded as one of the most beautiful cities on earth. The massive sandstone bulk of Table Mountain, often draped in a "tablecloth" of clouds, forms an imposing backdrop to the city and the pristine, uncrowded beaches that line the magnificent cliff-hugging coast. Mountainous slopes sustaining the world's most varied botanic kingdom (some 9,000 species strong) overlook fertile valleys carpeted with vines, and from the city's highways you can spot zebra and wildebeest grazing unperturbed.

Cape Town feels very different from the rest of Africa. Situated in the far southwestern corner, it is physically separated from the rest of the continent by a barrier of mountains. The hot, dry summers and cool, wet winters are Mediterranean, while the Atlantic Ocean is as frigid here as it is off the coast of Maine.

Unique, too, is the Cape's architectural heritage—Cape Dutch homesteads, Neo-Gothic churches, Muslim minarets, and English-inspired Georgian and Victorian buildings speak of the multifaceted influences of a colonial past.

Inevitably, colonialism has left its mark on the residents of Cape Town as well; the majority of the population is made up of the mixed blood descendants of European settlers, slaves, and indigenous people. This Afrikaans-speaking group is referred to as the "coloureds," a divisive designation conferred in the apartheid era.

During apartheid they were relocated behind Table Mountain into the grim eastern interior plain, known as the Cape Flats. With the influx of people from impoverished rural regions, this area has grown, and today these squatter towns form a seamless ribbon of cardboard and corrugated iron housing that most visitors glimpse only on their way to the airport.

Since the scrapping of influx control in 1986, the city's population has swelled. Most come from the poverty-struck Eastern Cape, others from as far afield as Somalia, Angola, and Mozambique, making Cape Town one of South Africa's fastest growing cities—and unfortunately, the gangster-ridden Cape Flats have made it the most violent. While the high crime statistics are mostly contained in these areas, visitors are urged to take the precautions they would in any large city.

Should you prefer a quieter setting, just whip straight out to the Winelands, where you can stay amidst some of the best-preserved examples of Cape Dutch architecture and sample award-winning wines. This is a great area to base yourself if you're looking for a relaxing, rural escape, with the bright lights of the city a mere 60-minute drive away, and the coastal towns, lagoons, and forests of the Garden Route within easy striking distance.

## 1 Orientation

### ARRIVING

**BY PLANE** Fourteen international airlines fly directly to **Cape Town International Airport** (☎ **021/934-0407**), a 22-kilometer drive from the center of town. It should take no longer than 20 to 30 minutes to get into the city and surrounds (set aside twice that during the evening rush hours of 4 to 6pm). The **Intercape shuttle bus** (☎ **021/386-4414**) operates half-hourly trips between the airport and the Cape Town train station for R30 ($5). You'll find taxis directly outside the terminals, but the same trip will cost you in the region of R110 ($18.35). Car rental firms have their desks inside the arrival terminals, and a bureau de change stays open for the arrival of international flights.

**BY CAR** If you're traveling direct from Johannesburg, you would drive in on the N1, traveling past the Winelands area of Paarl. From Port Elizabeth, the Garden Route, or the airport, you'll approach the city center on the N2, passing Stellenbosch in the Winelands. The N2 splits into the M3 (the highway that connects the southern suburbs to the City Bowl suburbs), and the Eastern Boulevard, which joins the N1 as it enters the perimeter of town. The entrance to the Waterfront is clearly signposted off here.

**BY BUS** The main intercity buses, Greyhound, Intercape, and Translux, all terminate in the centrally located railway station, at the junction of Strand and Adderley streets. The Baz Bus—the budget travelers' bus, offering hop-on and hop-off options throughout the country—stops off at most youth hostels. (See chapter 2, for regional numbers.)

**BY TRAIN** For information on long-distance trains, call **Spoornet** (☎ **021/449-3871**), though it's worth noting that the bus is quicker. The luxurious **Blue Train** (☎ **021/405-2672**) and **Rovos Rail** Pride of Africa (☎ **421-4020**) arrive here from Johannesburg and Pretoria; both do trips along the Garden Route.

### VISITOR INFORMATION

There is a Western Cape tourism desk at the airport (☎ **021/937-1234**) open from 7am to 5pm daily, but the best place to gather information is at **Cape Town Tourism** (☎ **021/418-5202**) in the Pinnacle Building, at the corner of Burg and Castle streets, 1 block up from the Cape Sun Hotel. Hours are Monday to Friday from 9am to 6pm, Saturday 8:30am to 1pm, and Sunday 9am to 1pm; hours are extended during December and January. **Western Cape Tourism** (☎ **021/426-5647**), which is open Monday to Thursday 8am to 4:30pm, and Friday 8am to 4pm, also has an office here. Other useful city addresses are the **National Parks Board** (☎ **021/422-2810/6**) at 44 Long St. and **Cape Nature Conservation** (☎ **021/483-4051** at 1 Dorp St.).

### CITY LAYOUT

Cape Town is on a narrow peninsula which curls southward into the Atlantic Ocean. Its western and eastern shores are divided by a spinal ridge of mountains, of which Table Mountain is the most dramatic landmark. The city center, located on the western shore and facing north, is known as the **City Bowl,** the "bowl" created by the table-topped massif as backdrop, flanked by toothy Devil's Peak to the east, and the embracing arm of Signal Hill to the west. Suburbs on the slopes overlook the city center and harbor, where you'll find the **Victoria & Alfred Waterfront,** situated at the icy waters of Table Bay. Within easy striking distance from both the City Bowl and the Waterfront are the dense built-up suburbs of **Green Point** and **Sea Point.** Moving farther south, the western slopes of the Cape Peninsula mountain range slide almost directly into the sea, and it is here, along the dramatic coastline referred to as the **Atlantic seaboard,** that you can watch the sun sinking from Africa's most expensive real estate.

This is also the most scenic route to Cape Point, while the quickest way is to travel south via the M3, past the **southern suburbs** of Woodstock, Observatory, Rondebosch, Claremont, Wynberg, Kenilworth, Bishopscourt, and Constantia, and then snake along the **False Bay seaboard** to the Point. These eastern slopes, which overlook False Bay (so called by early sailors who mistook it for Table Bay), are the first to see the sun rise, and have price tags still affordable for locals.

East of the peninsula are the **Cape Flats** and the **"black suburbs"** of Guguletu, Nyanga, and Khayalitsha, reached via the N2. The N2 also provides access to the **Winelands,** which lie north of it. **Stellenbosch** is just over an hour's drive from the center of town, and from here **Franschhoek,** some 85 kilometers (53 miles) northeast of Cape Town, is reached via the scenic Helshoogte Pass. A quicker route to Franschhoek is via the northern-bound N1, the highway which connects Cape Town to **Paarl,** a 40-minute drive from the center of town.

SATOUR's free city map is fine for a shorter trip. If you're planning to spend more than a few days in Cape Town, however, you should consider investing in a detailed street atlas like **Mapstudio's A–Z Streetmap,** sold at most newsagents.

Finally, if you get lost, don't despair—with the various aspects of Table Mountain as a visual guide, it is difficult to stay lost for long.

## Neighborhoods in Brief

Within striking distance of the Waterfront, beaches, and Winelands, and in easy reach of most of the city's best restaurants, the **City Bowl** is the most convenient place to stay. The upmarket suburbs of Oranjezicht, Higgovale, and Tamboerskloof, where a number of elegant guest houses on the mountain's slopes have excellent views of the city and harbor, are particularly attractive for travelers. However, the city center is not safe after dark, so use valet parking if you stay here.

**Victoria & Alfred Waterfront** Most often referred to as the Waterfront, this is considered one of the most successful in the world. Hotels feature magnificent sea and mountain views, and there are numerous shopping, restaurant, and entertainment options right on your doorstep; but you'll pay for the privilege of staying here (the cheaper options just aren't worth it), and it's a little out of touch with the rest of the city, and relatively far from the beach.

**Mouille Point** and **Green Point** These border the Waterfront, with the adjacent **Sea Point** also conveniently close. The beachfront has been largely ruined by the construction of dense high-rise apartments, and pockets along the Main Road are hangouts for hookers and drug dealers. Before the development of the Waterfront, this area used to be the heart of Cape Town's nightlife. There are still a number of excellent restaurants on Main Road, but visitors should exercise caution after dark.

If you're looking for a beach holiday, book a place on the sunny **Atlantic seaboard,** where Table Mountain drops steeply into the ocean, creating a magnificent backdrop to the seaside "villages" of Clifton, Camps Bay, and Llandudno. Besides offering the most beautiful beaches, you'll find the city's most beautiful people strutting their stuff on these pristine, fine white sands.

**Hout Bay** Surrounded by mountains, it has its own harbor, and marks the start of the breathtaking Chapman's Peak Drive, which takes you past Noordhoek, Kommetjie, and Scarborough, before you reach the Cape Point Nature Reserve. These are beautiful areas, but beyond Hout Bay you are a little far from attractions like the Waterfront and Winelands; certainly the city restaurants are out of reach for dinner. Staying here is more likely to appeal on a second trip, or to a family.

**False Bay** Distance from city attractions and the Winelands is also the drawback of these suburbs, which are (driving south to north) Simon's Town, Fish Hoek, Kalk Bay, St James, and Muizenberg. The sea is slightly warmer on this side of the mountain, however, and the dawns can be breathtaking, though you'll miss the sunsets.

**Southern suburbs** Two worth highlighting are Observatory and Constantia. Observatory (less than 10 minutes from town), offers a number of good restaurants and is an interesting bohemian area with many Victorian buildings—its proximity to both the University of Cape Town and Groote Schuur hospital makes for a particularly eclectic mix of people. Considered less brash than the Atlantic seaboard, Constantia is arguably the city's most exclusive address, with the lush surrounds of the Cape's oldest wine-producing area attracting the rich and famous.

**Cape Flats** This is where the majority of coloured people live, many forcibly relocated from District Six (a now-razed suburb once adjacent to the city) by apartheid policies. The residents of the Cape Flats suffer from high unemployment and a lack of cultural identity and hope, and have become a fertile breeding ground for gangster-run urban terrorism. Even farther east are the "black suburbs" of Guguletu and Nyanga and the vast shantytowns of Khayalitsha (visible from the N2 as you drive into town from the airport). None of these areas is recommended for travelers on their own; see "Getting Around" later in this chapter for township tours.

**Winelands** No trip to Cape Town would be complete without at least a day spent here; indeed many prefer to stay here for the duration of their visit—Cape Town lies no more than an hour or so away, the airport 45 minutes. **Paarl** has some of the best accommodation options, on gracious wine farms and old estates, but can be sweltering in summer; make sure your hotel has a pool. The university town of **Stellenbosch** is the cultural center of the Winelands, and its oak-lined streetscape offers the greatest sense of history; this is one place where it's worth staying in town. **Franschhoek**—reached via either Stellenbosch or Paarl—is located in the prettiest of the wineland valleys, and is considered the Winelands' cuisine capital. Deciding where you stay here is ultimately a matter of availability; places situated on wine estates with views of the vineyards and mountains are most desirable.

**Northern suburbs** With their kitsch postmodern palaces and endless "first-home" developments, these suburbs don't really warrant much attention. However, if you're heading north to see the West Coast you could consider stopping at Blouberg Beach for the postcard-perfect view of Table Mountain across the bay. To reach Blouberg Beach, take the R27 Marine Drive, off the N1.

## 2 Getting Around

Contained by the mountain, the city center is small enough to explore on foot. Public transport in Cape Town is marginally better than other South African cities—trains will take you to the southern suburbs and False Bay beaches, and buses to the Waterfront,

Sea Point, Camps Bay, and Hout Bay. To explore the Atlantic seaboard, Cape Point, or the Winelands, you're better off renting a car.

## BY PUBLIC TRANSPORTATION

**BY TRAIN** If you're heading for the southern suburbs, Paarl, or Stellenbosch, the **Cape Town train service** (call ☎ **0800/656-463** toll-free for information) is a relatively reliable mode of transport, though not advisable at night. Shell out the extra rands for first class, though, and avoid overcrowded third-class cars. A recommended trip is the spectacular cliff-hugging route along the False Bay seaboard to Simon's Town aboard **Biggsy's Restaurant Carriage & Wine Bar** (☎ **021/449-3870**) with breakfast, lunch, or snacks on route; the return journey from the city station takes approximately 2 hours (you can hop on at any stop); tickets cost R19 ($3.15), excluding drinks and meals.

**BY BUS** Buses depart from the center of town (principal terminals are around the Golden Acre shopping center on Adderley Street) to Sea Point (R2.40/40¢), Table Mountain cable way (R2.70/45¢), Camps Bay (R4.20/70¢), Kirstenbosch (R3.30/$5.50), and Hout Bay (R6.50/$1.10). Contact **Golden Arrow** (toll free ☎ **0801/212-111** or **021/934-0540**) for times and fares. A bus leaves from Adderley St (in front of the station) to the Waterfront every 15 minutes from 6am to 11pm daily; the trip costs R1.50 (25¢) (call ☎ **021/418-2369**).

## BY CAR

Cape Town is a relatively car-friendly city with a minimum of traffic jams and enough car parks to warrant driving into town—try the **Golden Acre Parking Garage** on Adderley Street or the **Pay & Display** on the Grand Parade or the lot opposite Heritage Square. On the street, self-appointed "parking attendants" will offer to watch your car. It is customary to tip them on your return; R2–R5 (34¢–85¢) is adequate.

There are numerous car rental companies in Cape Town. For a cheaper deal, try **Golden Oldies** (☎ **021/424-3951**) at 150 Buitengracht St. in the city center. For a one-way rental, you'll have to use a company with nationwide offices, such as **Avis** (☎ **021/424-1177**) 123 Strand St. in the city (☎ 021/934-0330 at the airport); **Budget** (☎ **021/418-5232**) 120 Strand St. (☎ 021/934-0216 at the airport); **Hertz** (☎ **021/422-1515**) 139 Buitengracht St. in the city (☎ 021/934-3913 at the airport); or **Imperial** (☎ **021/421-5190**), at the corner of Strand and Loop streets (☎ 021/934-0213 at the airport). For more interesting vehicles (like a Chrysler V6 jeep) contact **Rent 'n Ride** (☎ **021/434-1122**) at 1 Park Rd., Mouille Point.

## BY TAXI

Much cheaper than a metered taxi are **Rikkis,** which keep prices down to R5–R15 (85¢–$2.50) by continuously picking up and dropping off passengers en route. These open-sided, three-wheeled vehicles are restricted to the City Bowl, the Waterfront, and Camps Bay; hail one or call ☎ **021/423-4888** for a pick up from 7am to 6pm.

**Metered taxis** don't cruise the streets looking for fares; you'll have to phone. While expensive, this is the best and safest form of transport after dark. Contact **Sea Point Taxis** (**021/434-4444**) or **Marine Taxis** (**021/434-0434**). Minibus taxis are the main form of transport for most South Africans, but are not recommended for visitors—drivers wait until the vehicle is uncomfortably full before tearing off on their set routes, driving skills are negligible, and innocents are regularly caught in the crossfire of feuding taxi groups.

# Cape Town & the Peninsula Orientation

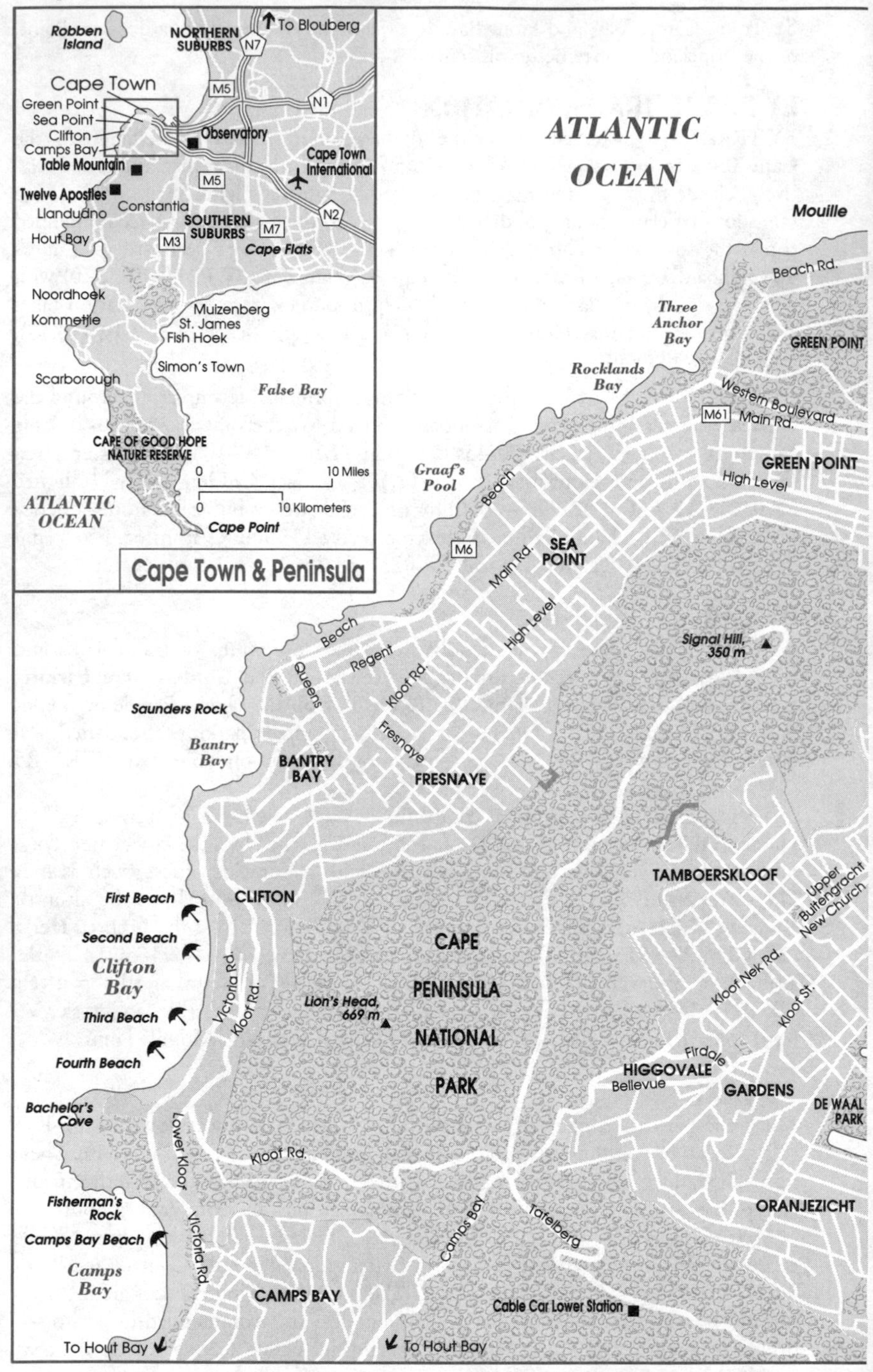

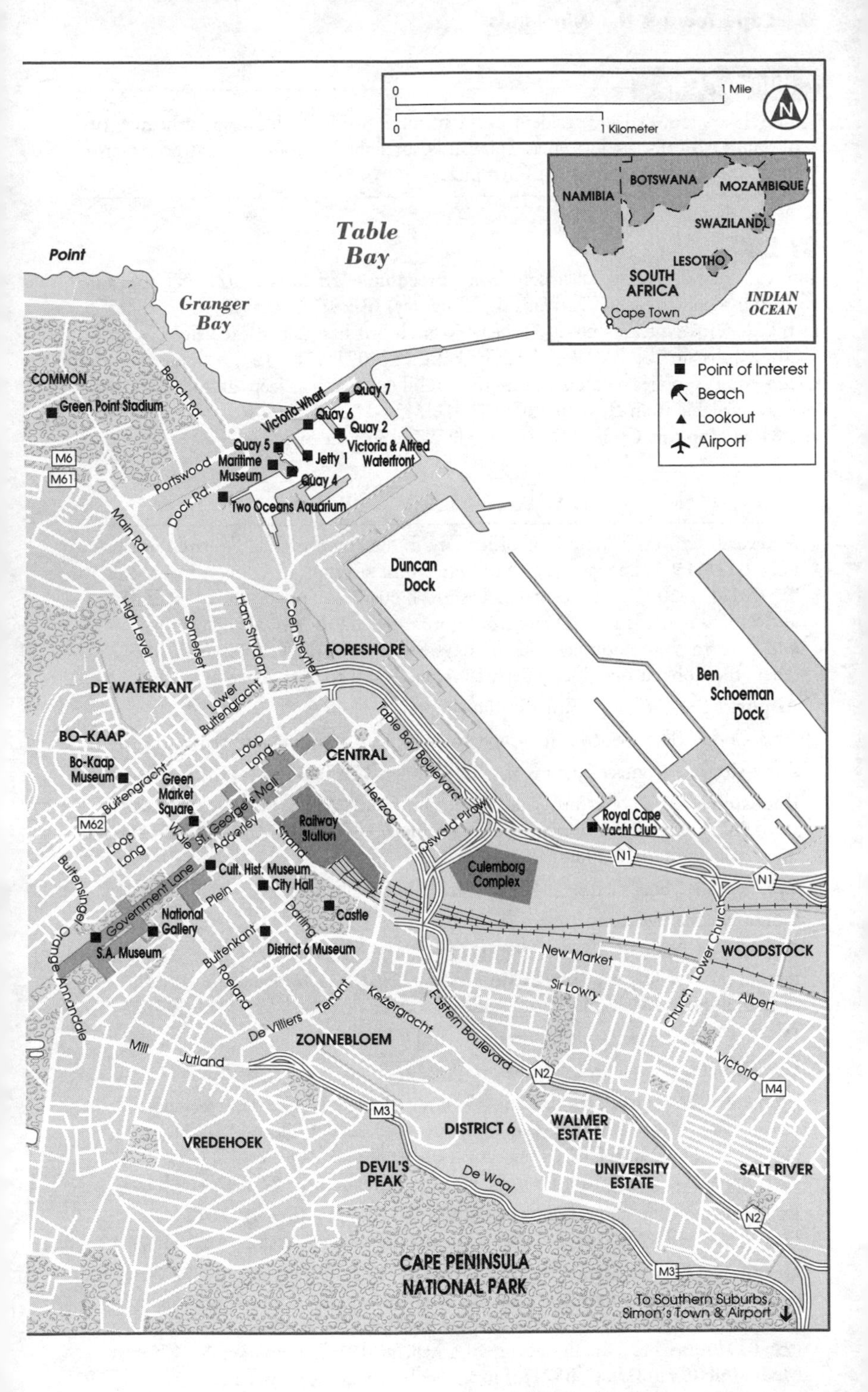
0
1 Mile
0
1 Kilometer
N
NAMIBIA
BOTSWANA
MOZAMBIQUE
SWAZILAND
LESOTHO
SOUTH AFRICA
INDIAN OCEAN
Cape Town
Point of Interest
Beach
Lookout
Airport
Table Bay
Point
Granger Bay
COMMON
Green Point Stadium
Beach Rd.
Victoria Wharf
Quay 7
Quay 6
Quay 2
Quay 5
Victoria & Alfred Waterfront
Jetty 1
Maritime Museum
Quay 4
Portswood
Dock Rd.
Two Oceans Aquarium
M6
M61
Main Rd.
Duncan Dock
High Level
Somerset
Hans Strydom
Coen Steytler
FORESHORE
DE WATERKANT
Lower Buitengracht
Ben Schoeman Dock
Table Bay Boulevard
BO-KAAP
Loop
Long
CENTRAL
Bo-Kaap Museum
Green Market Square
Buitengracht
Hertzog
St. George's Mall
M62
Wale
Adderley
Railway Station
Oswald Pirow
Royal Cape Yacht Club
Strand
N1
Loop
Long
Culemborg Complex
Buitensingel
Government Lane
Cult. Hist. Museum
City Hall
Plein
Castle
National Gallery
Darling
Orange
S.A. Museum
Buitenkant
District 6 Museum
New Market
Lower Church
WOODSTOCK
Annandale
Roeland
Sir Lowry
Albert
Church
De Villiers
Tennant
Keizergracht
Eastern Boulevard
Mill
ZONNEBLOEM
Victoria
Jutland
N2
M4
M3
DISTRICT 6
WALMER ESTATE
VREDEHOEK
UNIVERSITY ESTATE
SALT RIVER
DEVIL'S PEAK
De Waal
N2
CAPE PENINSULA NATIONAL PARK
M3
To Southern Suburbs, Simon's Town & Airport

**Bumper Cars**

The always-crowded and accident-prone minibus taxis, which transport the majority of South Africans, are known as Zola Buds, after the barefoot runner who careened into Mary Decker in the 1984 Olympics.

### BY BIKE

You can hire a Harley-Davidson from **Freedom Africa** (☎ 021/685-7082 or africatour@icon.co.za; 97 Durban Rd., Mowbray). **Bike2Oceans** (☎ 021/423-5555 or bike2oceans@intekom.co.za, 74 New Church St.) has guided excursions as far as Victoria Falls on the BMW F650. **Fly Bike** (☎ 021/421-1328, 5 Somerset Rd., Green Point) supplies scooters and mountain bikes, as well as jeeps and jet-skis. Bicycles are available from **Rent 'n Ride** (☎ 021/434-1122, 1 Park Rd., Mouille Point) and **Mike Hopkins Cycles** (☎ 021/423-2527, 135 Bree St.).

## Fast Facts: Cape Town

**American Express** Main local offices are in the city center at Thibault Square (☎ **021/419-3085**) and at the Waterfront (Shop 11A in Alfred Mall ☎ **021/421-6021**). City center hours are 8:30am to 5pm Monday to Friday, and 9am to noon Saturday. Waterfront hours are 9am to 7pm Monday to Friday, and 9am to 5pm Saturday and Sunday. Seeker's World (☎ 021/419-2861), where the Robben Island ferry departs, is open 8am to 8pm daily.

**Airport** See "Arriving" earlier in the chapter.

**Area Code** The area code for Cape Town and surrounding Winelands is **021.**

**Baby-sitters** Contact Glynnis at Childminders (☎ **083440-4453**).

**Bookstores** For books on Cape Town and South Africa, head for **Exclusive Books** (☎ **021/419-0905**) in Victoria Wharf, Victoria & Alfred Waterfront, open daily 9am to 10:30pm.

**Car Rentals** See "Getting Around" earlier in the chapter.

**Climate** See "When to Go" in chapter 2.

**Doctors & Dentists** Dial ☎ **021/61-3634** or 021/61-2924 for a 24-hour referral service. The **BA Travel Clinic** (☎ **021/419-3171**) is on the 10th floor of the Fountains Medical Centre, Adderley Street.

**Driving Rules** See "Getting Around" earlier in this chapter.

**Drugstores** See "Pharmacies" below.

**Embassies & Consulates** **U.S.:** 4th floor, Broadway Centre, Heerengracht Street (☎ **021/421-4280**); **Canada:** Reserve Bank Building, 30 Hout St. (☎ **021/423-5240**); **U.K.:** Southern Life Centre, 8 Riebeeck St. (☎ **021/425-3670**); **Australia:** 14th floor, BP Centre, Thibault Sq. (☎ **021/419-5425**).

**Emergencies** For an **ambulance,** call ☎ **10177;** for **police** ☎ **10111;** in the case of **fire,** call ☎ **021/535-1100;** for a **sea rescue,** call ☎ **021/449-3500.**

**Hospitals** **Groote Schuur** (☎ **021/404-9111**) in Observatory is the Cape's largest hospital; **Somerset Hospital** (☎ **021/402-6911**) at the Waterfront may be more conveniently located. The closest private hospital is **City Park** (☎ **021/480-6111**), in the center of town, at 181 Longmarket St. Contact **Mediclinic** (☎ **021/883-8571**) if in Stellenbosch in the Winelands.

**Hot Lines** **Police Tourist Assistance Unit** (☎ **021/418-2853**); **Rape Crisis** (**021/447-9762** or **083444-1394** after hours); **Automobile Association** (for vehicle breakdown, ☎ **0800/01-0101**).

**Internet Access** Cape Town Tourism is planning to install computers for visitor use at their offices (see above). You can also pick up your mail at The Virtual Turtle (☎ **021/424-1037**) on the first floor, corner Long and Shortmarket streets, off Greenmarket Square (virtual@turtle.co.za) or at Adventure Village (☎ **021/424-1590**) in Long Street. Visit Cyberspace (☎ **021/887-4022**) in Stellenbosch.

**Maps** See "City Layout" earlier in this chapter.

**Mobile-Phone Rental** You can hire a phone in the International Arrivals terminal at the airport from **MTN Rentals** (☎ **021/934-3261**) or from **Cellucity,** Kiosk 5, Victoria Wharf Centre, Waterfront (☎ **021/418-1306**) for about R40 ($6.65) a day.

**Newspapers & Magazines** The morning paper, *Cape Times,* and the more sensationalist afternoon and evening paper, *Argus,* are sold at most street corners. You'll find international titles at the CNA, at the Waterfront and in St George's Mall.

**Pharmacy** **Lite-Kem,** (☎ **021/461-8040**) at 24 Darling St., opposite the city post office, is open Monday to Saturday from 7:30am to 11pm and Sunday 8:30am to 11pm. **Sunset Pharmacy** (☎ **021/434-3333**) in Sea Point Medical Centre, Kloof Road is open daily 8:30 to 9pm.

**Police** In an emergency, call ☎ **10111.**

**Post Office** The main branch is on the corner of Parliament and Darling streets (☎ **021/464-1700**). Hours are Monday to Friday 8am to 4:30pm (Wednesdays from 8:30am), and Saturday 8am to 12pm.

**Rest Rooms** The city's large population of homeless means the hygiene of public rest rooms is of varying and dubious quality. You're best off going to a coffee shop or restaurant, or visiting a fuel station.

**Safety** The effects of "Business Against Crime," an organization which has installed closed-circuit cameras in town, put more police on the streets, and created 24-hour care centers for Cape Town's street children, are slowly making themselves felt. As in other African cities, however, unemployment and homelessness have resulted in an increase in crime. Muggings can be avoided by staying away from certain areas, particularly at night, and taking the sort of precautions you would in any large city. For detailed advice, pick up a brochure on safety from any tourism office. Be aware of the street children, many of whom beg at large intersections. Visitors are requested to give them food, or to make a donation to one of the childcare centers rather than provide them with cash, which is invariably used to purchase drugs.

**Taxis** See "Getting Around" earlier in this chapter.

**Weather** Call ☎ **40-881.**

## 3 Where to Stay

Renting someone else's apartment or home is a good option for a longer stay, particularly along the Atlantic seaboard; contact **Cape Holiday Homes** (☎ **021/419-0430,** www.capeholiday.com). **Self-catering options:** A fair number of self-catering options,

# Cape Town Accommodations

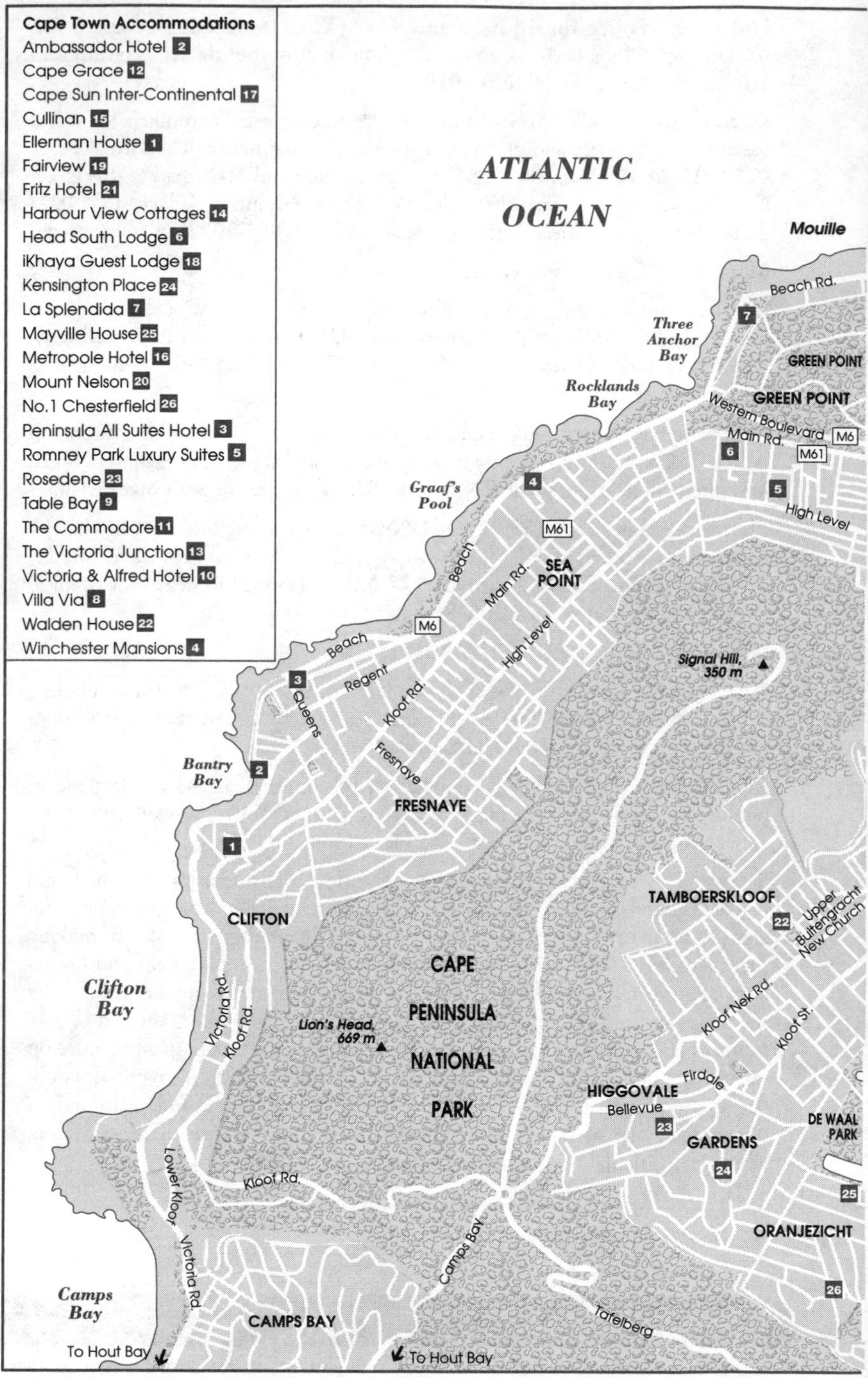

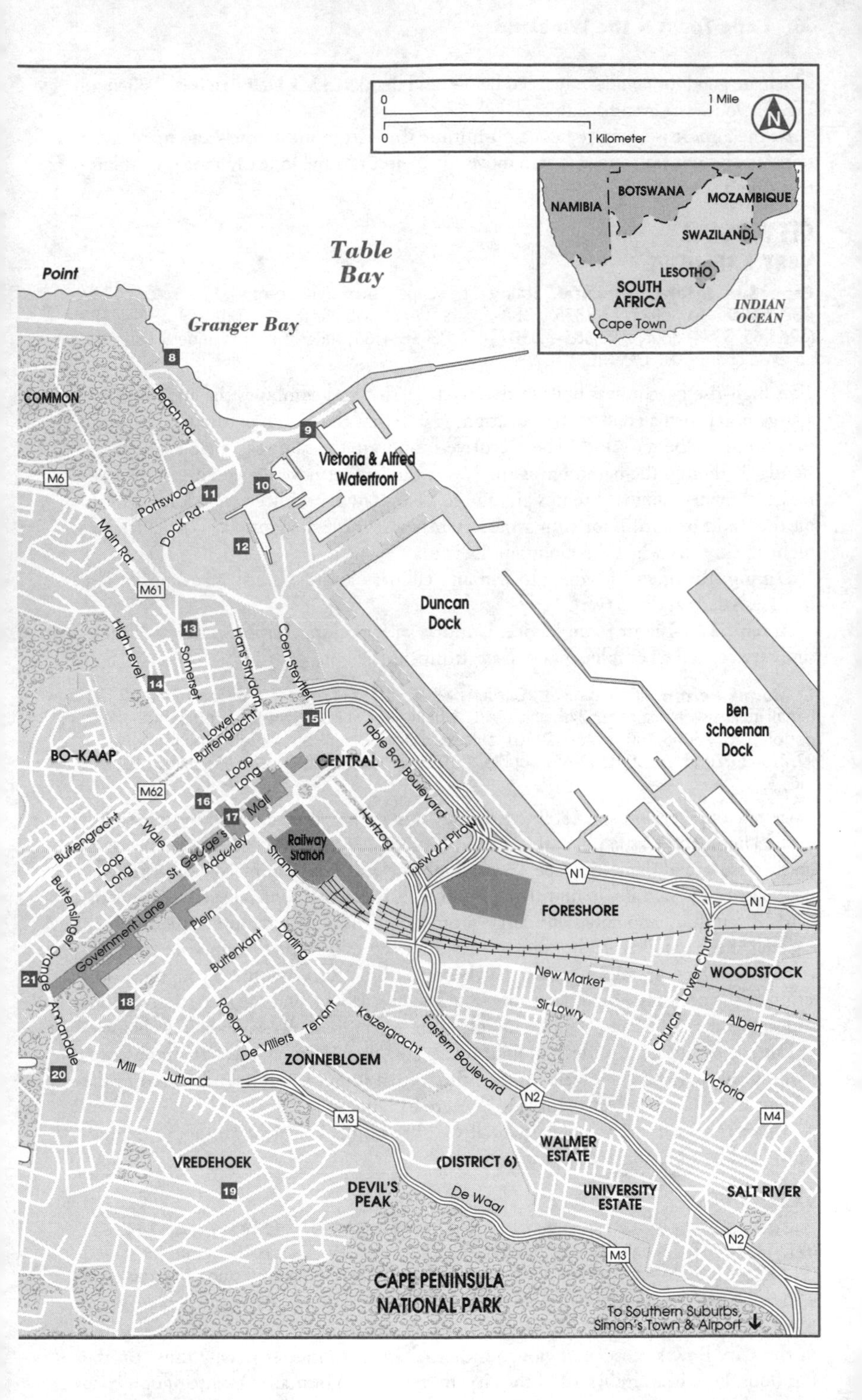

0
1 Mile
0
1 Kilometer
N
NAMIBIA
BOTSWANA
MOZAMBIQUE
SWAZILAND
LESOTHO
SOUTH AFRICA
INDIAN OCEAN
Cape Town
Table Bay
Point
Granger Bay
COMMON
Beach Rd.
Victoria & Alfred Waterfront
M6
Portswood
Dock Rd.
Main Rd.
M61
High Level
Somerset
Hans Strydom
Coen Steytler
Duncan Dock
Ben Schoeman Dock
Lower Buitengracht
BO–KAAP
CENTRAL
Table Bay Boulevard
Loop
Long
M62
Mall
Wale
Buitengracht
St. George's
Adderley
Railway Station
Heritzog
Strand
Oswald Pirow
N1
FORESHORE
Loop
Long
Buitensingel
Government Lane
Plein
Buitenkant
Darling
Orange
Lower Church
WOODSTOCK
New Market
Sir Lowry
Albert
Church
Annandale
Roeland
De Villiers
Tenant
Keizergracht
Eastern Boulevard
ZONNEBLOEM
Mill
Jutland
Victoria
N2
M3
M4
WALMER ESTATE
VREDEHOEK
(DISTRICT 6)
DEVIL'S PEAK
De Waal
UNIVERSITY ESTATE
SALT RIVER
CAPE PENINSULA NATIONAL PARK
To Southern Suburbs, Simon's Town & Airport
8
9
10
11
12
13
14
15
16
17
18
19
20
21

which are good for families, are listed below, and thanks to **Mr Delivery** (see "Where to Dine"), you won't even have to cook.

As the airport is no more than a 30-minute drive from most hotels and many offer transfers, it's not really necessary to move to an airport hotel for early-morning or late-night flights.

## CITY BOWL

### VERY EXPENSIVE

**Cape Sun Inter-Continental.** Strand St., Cape Town (city center) 8001. ☎ **021/488-5100.** Fax 021/23-8875. 388 units. A/C MINIBAR TV TEL. R1,580–1,870 ($263.65–$374) double; R2,585–3,850 ($430.85–$641.65) suites. Children under 18 share at no extra charge. AE, DC, MC, V.

This high-rise beacon was built in the brash 1970s, and combines the anonymity of a large hotel with a good central location. (Note that the Cullinan, though not quite so central, is a better value). The executive rooms are the same reasonable size as the standard (though the bathroom is tiny), but the former have benefited greatly from refurbishment—standard rooms are due to be updated, and need it. Ask for a room on the 32nd or 33rd floor with a mountain view; these are glorious, particularly at night in summer when the mountain is lit up.

**Dining:** Riempies isn't going to win any culinary awards, the standard buffet fare includes salads and a carvery.

**Amenities:** 24-hour room service, laundry, valet parking, airport transfers, limousine service, and a complimentary Waterfront shuttle.

✪ **Mount Nelson.** 76 Orange St., Gardens 8001. ☎ **021/423-1000.** Fax 021/24-7472. E-mail nellress@iafrica.com. 226 units. A/C MINIBAR TV TEL. R2,400–2,760 ($400–$460) double; R2,760–5,700 ($460–$950) suites. Dec 18–Jan 5, 7-night minimum stay, R2,715–3,070 ($452.50–$511.65) double; R3,120–6,520 ($520–$1,086.65) suites. AE, DC, MC, V.

Since opening her doors in 1899 to provide luxury accommodation for the passengers of the Union and Castle Lines, the "Nellie" as she's affectionately known, has been the undisputed grand dame of Cape Town's high society. The Mount Nelson's enduring popularity and inclusion in numerous top hotel lists is due to unparalleled service standards, beautifully appointed and large rooms, and the 9-acre mature gardens which have all the tranquility of the country, despite lying only a 20-minute walk from the city center. Over the years her image had become a little fusty, but today with the acquisition of surrounding properties, some tasteful refurbishing, and the relaxation of dress codes, the likes of U2 and Gaultier mingle with the traditionally white-haired clientele.

**Dining:** A breakfast buffet and light meals are served in the Oasis restaurant, overlooking the large pool and gardens. A more formal lunch and dinner is served in the elegant Cape Colony Restaurant (see "Where to Dine").

**Amenities:** Swimming pools, two all-weather tennis courts, an in-house gymnasium, and hairdressing and beauty salons.

### EXPENSIVE

**Kensington Place.** 38 Kensington Crescent, Higgovale 8001. ☎ **021/424-4744.** Fax 021/ 424-1810. E-mail: kplace@mweb.co.za. 7 units. TV TEL. High-season R800–980 ($133.35–$163.35). Low-season R500–650 ($83.35–$108.35). Rates include breakfast and airport transfers. AE, DC, MC, V. Children 16 and over only.

No expense has been spared in the creation of this modern boutique hotel situated in the City Bowl's most prestigious residential area. Rooms, especially those on the top floor, have beautiful views of the city, harbor, and mountain. A sense of opulence

## Family-Friendly Hotels

Very few places cater specifically for children—babysitters and a pool are usually the sum total of relief therapy for harangued parents. An exception to this is the **Cape Grace** (☎ **021/410-7100**), which is also ideally located in the child-friendly Waterfront area. Corner rooms at the centrally located **Victoria & Alfred Hotel** (☎ **021/419-6677**) can also be combined for families, though they have no pool. **Fairview**'s self-catering apartments (☎ **021/461-3502**), in a quiet suburb on the outskirts of town, offer value for money, and you can call Childminders (see "Fast Facts: Cape Town" in this chapter) for babysitting support. The **Peninsula All Suites** (☎ **021/439-8886**) in Sea Point has a games room set aside for kids, a shuttle service to the beach, a tidal pool within walking distance, and will organize a personal babysitter and itinerary on request. If the general idea is to get the kids away from the city, **Monkey Valley Beach Nature Resort** (☎ **021/789-1391**) is tops, with quaint thatched self-catering cottages ideal for family bonding, a good restaurant with idyllic view, and horseback riding, swimming, volleyball, and long beach walks available. **HoutkappersPoort** (☎ **021/794-5216**) and **Silvermist** (☎ **021/794-7601**) on Constantia Nek are the mountainside versions. Closer to town, the **Vineyard Hotel** (☎ **021/683-3044**) has access to a McDonalds and Cavendish Square's numerous shops and cinemas—a good option for teenage mall rats.

In the Winelands, try Franschhoek's self-catering options or **Mountain Manor** (☎ **021/876-2071**), which offers incredible value.

pervades; the bedrooms are the size of minisuites, and each has a balcony overlooking the city. Dark mahogany pieces are finished with luxurious fabrics, beds are dressed in pale cotton linen, and bathrooms have underfloor heated marble and custom-made bathtubs. The plunge pool on a timber deck is a calm oasis from bustling Kloof Street, a short stroll away. Guests usually choose to dine somewhere in Kloof Street, but dinners can be provided. Despite its size, service is intimate and there's always someone on hand to pour your drink and pass a plate of canapés.

**Mayville House.** 21 Belvedere Ave. Oranjezicht 8001. ☎ **021/461-9400.** Fax 021/461-9419. E-mail: mayville@iafrica.com. www.mayville.co.za. 6 units. A/C MINIBAR TV TEL. High-season R920 ($153.35) double. Low-season R740 ($123.35) double. Rates include breakfast. AE, DC, MC, V. Children 10 and older only.

Situated directly opposite the Molteno Reservoir, this beautiful double-story Edwardian mansion enjoys uninterrupted views of the city, and has been skillfully refurbished. Rooms are spacious; the four upstairs, which open onto the front balcony, have the best views. Numbers 2 and 5 have the biggest bathrooms. Tea and coffee-making facilities, hair dryers, and heated towel rails are standard features. The landscaped gardens are large and feature a private pool; adjacent is the privately accessed honeymoon suite, ideal if you want seclusion, though you'll have to give up the views. There is a small staff, so don't expect 24-hour service—dinners are provided by prior arrangement, but there are no restaurants within walking distance. Secure off-street parking is provided, and business services can be arranged.

**No. 1 Chesterfield.** 1 Chesterfield Rd., Ornajezicht 8001. ☎ **021/461-7383.** Fax 021/461-4688. E-mail: number1@pixie.co.za. 8 units. TV TEL. High-season R880 ($146.65). Low-season R600 ($100). Rates include breakfast and non-alcoholic beverages. AE, DC, MC, V. Children 14 and over only.

Of all the guest houses situated on the slopes of Table Mountain, this provides both the best views of Table Bay and the most beautiful setting—the large, mature garden with oak trees and pool is so inviting you'll find it easy to spend the day here rather than rush off to see the city sights. Hosts Andrew and Charles retain the warmth of a home, and provide intelligent, unobtrusive, and charming service. Furnishings are a little old fashioned (if you prefer designer chic, try Kensington Place), but rooms are comfortable; ask for one with your own balcony. Dinners are provided on request and airport transfers can be arranged.

## MODERATE

**Cullinan.** 1 Lower Buitengragt, Cape Town 8000. ☎ **021/418-6920.** Fax 021/418-3559. 416 units. A/C TV TEL. R530–630 ($88.35–$105). AE, DC, MC, V.

Located at the entrance to the Waterfront and on the outskirts of town, this is the best of Cape Town's new large hotels. The postmodern building, which features a viewing platform inside a clock tower, has been compared to a wedding cake; but if you like kitsch, it's a great choice. Standard rooms are a tad small; executive suites are worth the extra R100 ($16.65), though all rooms have the unfortunately low ceilings of mass, modern construction. Ask for a mountain-view room on the 10th floor or higher. Rooms come with hair dryers and tea- and coffee-making facilities. Dinner, lunch, and room-service meals are supplied by O'Hagan's, which serves standard pub fare. Colcaccio is a short stroll away (see "Where to Dine"). Amenities include an outdoor pool and indoor gym, valet parking, 24-hour reception, room service, same-day laundry service, and an airport shuttle.

**iKhaya Guest Lodge.** Wandel St., Gardens 8010. ☎ **021/461-8880.** Fax 021/461-8889. E-mail: ikhaya@iafrica.com. 16 units. TV TEL. R440–570 ($73.35–$95) double; R480–R650 ($80–$108.35) apartments; R780 ($130) loft. Rates include breakfast. AE, DC, MC, V. Children 12 and over only.

As the name suggests, a strong African theme pervades. Stone-clad pillars, hand-hewn doors, reed ceilings, ceremonial masks, and rough timber chairs create a look that's third-world chic. Accommodation choices include self-catering apartments and a luxury loft; but unless you need the space, the standard and executive rooms offer real value for money. Finished in earthy tones of brown and cream, the hand-carved beds are made up with quality linen; bathrooms have blue-gum floors and brass taps. Each room has its own enclosed patio with chairs; most have a view of Table Mountain and overlook Dunkley Square's bars and restaurants, and there's no shortage of these in the area (a mere 5-minute walk from the center of town). Noise from late-night revelers is occasionally a problem. iKhaya means "the home" in Xhosa, and this is exactly how the laid-back atmosphere feels. Facilities include 24-hour reception, room service, laundry service, fax and e-mail service, and secure parking.

**Walden House.** 5 Burnside Rd., Tamboerskloof 8001. ☎ **021/424-4256.** Fax 021/424-0547. E-mail: walden@grm.co.za. 6 units. TV TEL. R540–600 ($90–$100) double; R600–720 ($100–$120) suite. Rates include breakfast. AE, DC, MC, V. Children 12 and over only.

This quiet, turn-of-the-century guest house offers stylish rooms in one of the city's oldest residential areas. Furnished in pale hues in the Afro-colonial style, rooms are comfortable, with a choice of twin rooms, queen-size beds, or suites. The large suite upstairs, with a door opening onto the first-floor verandah (which features a good view of Table Mountain) is the best in the house. Heated towel rails and brass fixtures are standard in all bathrooms. Breakfasts are sumptuous, with added luxuries like smoked salmon; Kloof Street, with its large selection of restaurants, is a short drive away. Secure parking is adjacent to a lovely small garden, but there's no pool.

**Rosedene.** 28 Upper Kloof St., Higgovale 8001. ☎ **021/424-3290.** Fax 021/424-3481. E-mail: deborah@rosedene.co.za. www.rosedene.co.za. 11 units. TV TEL. R580–720 ($96.65–$120) double. Rates include breakfast. AE, DC, MC, V. Children 12 and over only.

Perched high above Table Bay, where Table Mountain meets the slopes of Lion's Head, this well-appointed guest house offers good views of the city, harbor, and mountain. There's also quick access to Camps Bay and Clifton beaches, and to the cableway; and the restaurants at the top end of Kloof Street are just a stroll away. Ask for rooms 8 through 11—situated on the top floor of this two-story building; they have the best views, but are correspondingly pricier. The small patio features a Jacuzzi and beautifully handcrafted Balinese steamer chairs from where you can watch the cloud "cloth" tumbling down Table Mountain. The Balinese theme is carried throughout. Rosedene also trades in Bali furniture and artifacts—you may even choose to ship home half your room! Amenities include secure parking, 24-hour room service, and same-day laundry. Staff will happily arrange secretarial services and airport transfers.

## INEXPENSIVE

**Fairview.** Ludlow St., Gardens 8001. ☎ **021/461-3502.** Fax 021/461-5555. TV TEL. R295–375 ($49.15–$62.50) studio; R599–685 ($100–$114.15) 2 bedrooms; R865–995 ($144.15–$165.85) 3 bedrooms. AE, DC, MC, V.

This is a good place for families or older travelers who are looking to stay in an apartment, but are worried about staying too close to town. Fairview offers fully equipped studios and two- and three-bedroom flats in a quiet residential area with full security and views of the city. The development is architecturally uninspiring, but the decor is tastefully understated and apartments are serviced daily. Continental breakfasts can be delivered on request. There is a small supermarket a couple of blocks away and a large shopping complex a few minutes drive down the hill. The townhouses are set in lovely gardens, and there is also a smallish pool. If you don't wish to tackle stairs, ask for an apartment on the ground floor; these have good views of the city. Secure parking outside your door.

**Fritz Hotel.** 1 Faure St., Gardens 8001. ☎ **021/480-9000.** Fax 021/480-9090. E-mail: reception@fritzhotel.co.za. www.fritzhotel.co.za. MINIBAR TV TEL. R300–450 ($50–$75) double, including breakfast. AE, DC, MC, V.

Situated on the outskirts of town (a 7-minute walk to the center), the Fritz Hotel is a real bargain. Rooms are furnished in an eclectic fashion, with art deco the main theme, and most are pretty spacious. Ask for rooms 6 and 14; they are by far the biggest, and together with rooms 12 and 7 open onto the first floor verandah. The patio suites on the ground floor are also large, each with its own small garden area. Room 11 has a great view of Table Mountain from the bed and is a steal at only R350 ($58.35). The only meal served is breakfast, but as it's located within walking distance of trendy Kloof Street, you'll be spoilt for choice at mealtime. Unlike most, Fritz Hotel does not supply hair dryers; cupboards are also tiny and there's no pool.

**Harbour View Cottages.** 1 Loader St., De Waterkant 8001. ☎ **021/418-6081.** Fax 021/418-6082. E-mail: elizes@harbourviewcottages.co.za. 30 units. TV TEL. R380 ($63.35) 1 bedroom; R490 ($81.65) 2 bedrooms; R780 ($130) luxury cottages (1, 2, and 3 bedrooms). Rates quoted for two persons sharing; additional person R75 ($12.50). AE, DC, MC, V.

Situated in the oldest residential area of Cape Town, amongst partly cobbled streets and quaint Cape Malay architecture, these self-catering cottages are all distinctly different. It's hard to choose, so specify when booking if you want a plunge pool and/or a really good view, or whether you prefer modern furnishings or Cape cottage (be warned, most cottages have pretty bland furnishings). If you like the latest in fittings and finishes, ask for Harbour Cottage, or the recently completed Harbour Terrace development, which offers an additional 25 loft apartments. This close to town, petty crime can be a problem, but all cottages are burglar-barred to the hilt and some have off-street parking. There is a deli nearby and a number of good restaurants in the vicinity. (The area borders Green Point.) Your fully equipped kitchen can be stocked with groceries before your arrival, and airport transfers can be arranged.

**Metropole Hotel.** 38 Long St., Cape Town (city center) 8001. ☎ **021/423-6363.** Fax 021/423-6370. 33 units. A/C TV TEL. R250–300 ($41.65–$50). AE, DC, MC, V.

The century-old Metropole's claim to fame is its elevator—the second oldest in town, and lined with teak. The only reason to stay here is price; standard rooms are seriously cheap—and they feel that way. Bedrooms are clean and relatively spacious, but mattresses tend to be saggy. This, combined with the street noise, makes for a hotel you don't want to linger in. You are, however, slap bang in the middle of town, perfectly positioned to explore the city sights and within walking distance of the train station, and numerous bars and restaurants. (Take care when venturing out at night.) The restaurant serves so-called French-Continental cuisine, but you'd be better off sampling one of Long and Kloof street's many good restaurants. Valet parking is available.

## WATERFRONT

### VERY EXPENSIVE

**Cape Grace.** West Quay, V&A Waterfront 8002. ☎ **021/410-7100.** Fax 021/419-7622. E-mail: cghres@iafrica.com. www.grace.co.za. 102 units. A/C MINIBAR TV TEL. R1,990–2,180 ($331.65–$363.35) double; R3,030 ($505) 1 bedroom; R4,230 ($705) 2 bedrooms; R5,280 ($880) 3 bedrooms. All rates include breakfast. Children under 12 sharing stay free. AE, DC, MC, V.

Situated on its own promontory and surrounded by water on all three sides, the family-owned Cape Grace is classier than the Table Bay, and is the hotel of choice when the Clintons are in town. Local travel agents voted this South Africa's Top Individual Hotel in 1998.

The standard rooms are luxurious, both in size and furnishings, with French doors opening onto mountain or harbor views; superior rooms are slightly larger, with walkout balconies. All bathrooms are large and come with hairdryers and robes. (At press time, mountain-facing rooms were somewhat marred by the noise of builders on adjacent sites; ask when making your reservation.) The two- and three-bedroom suites have fully equipped kitchens and are ideal for families. The Cape Grace is in fact the most family-orientated 5-star hotel in the country: Children are welcomed with their own cards and gift hampers, the restaurant serves children's portions, and you can hire anything from a car seat to a pram. Like its sister hotels in Johannesburg, the Cape Grace has been furnished much like an English gentlemen's club, with great attention to detail: There is an excellent selection of handpicked books in the library, where complimentary tea, coffee, and sherry are available to guests at any time.

**Dining:** The restaurant, Quay West, is renowned for its simple yet elegant and tasteful menu—it was recently voted top restaurant in the Waterfront.

**Amenities:** Babysitting, pool, laundry and dry cleaning, travel and information desk, modified rooms for travelers with disabilities, 24-hour room service.

**Table Bay.** Quay 6, V&A Waterfront 8002. ☎ **021/406-5000.** Fax 021/406-5767. 356 units. A/C MINIBAR TV TEL. R2,005–2,505 ($334.15–$417.50) rooms; R3,510–14,850 ($585–$2,475) suites. Low-season R1,505–1,880 ($250.85–$313.35) double; R3,710–11,070 ($618.35–$1,845) suites. AE, DC, MC, V.

Competing with the Mount Nelson and Cape Grace as the preferred location for the rich and famous, this glitzy hotel is located in a prime position on the Prince Alfred Breakwater—views are standard features here. It doesn't have the privacy of the Nellie or Cape Grace (Michael Jackson is reputed to have stayed here because he *wanted* to hear his fans chanting in the parking lot), but the service standards are high, with numerous staff on hand to ensure that you don't lift a finger. The public spaces (designed by the Lost City team) are superb: The cavernous lobby, renowned for its large floral displays, is finished in marble and teak, and the comfortable lounge area frames Table Mountain with large triple-volume windows. Standard rooms are comparatively small and dull; opt for a luxury room or suite, or consider the Cape Grace. You're in luck if you're a shopaholic; the hotel is directly connected to the shopping center.

**Dining:** An a la carte menu is available in the Conservatory, which is where breakfasts are served. Lunch and dinner are served at the Atlantic Grill Room (see "Where to Dine").

**Amenities:** Pool deck, beauty parlor, and health and hydro-spa complex.

## EXPENSIVE

**The Commodore.** Portswood Rd., V&A Waterfront 8002. ☎ **021/415-1000.** Fax 021/415-1100. 236 units. A/C TV TEL. High-season R1,015–1,070 ($169.15–$178.35) double; R1,300–2,400 ($216.65–$400) suites. Low-season R600–850 ($100–$141.65) double; R1,040–1,230 ($173.35–$205) suites.

Located 300 meters (984 feet) from the Portswood entrance to the V&A Waterfront, the Commodore offers comfortable rooms at reasonable rates (unbeatable from April to August). The public spaces are large, elegantly furnished, and a tranquil courtyard features a decent-size pool. Rooms, which feature a vague nautical theme, are less memorable, but comfortable. Business-class rooms cost on average R200 ($33.35) more than standard rooms, but they feature extras like minibars, are more spacious, and, as they occupy the top floor, offer the best views. Alternatively, request a room on the 4th or 5th floor.

**Dining:** The Clipper Restaurant continues the nautical theme in decor and offers buffet-type meals, but foodies should head for the Waterfront. Light meals are also available on the terrace adjoining the pool.

**Amenities:** Pool, fully equipped gym, transit lounge, tea- and coffee-making machines in rooms, parking, same-day laundry, 24-hour room service, business service, and a car-rental and tours desk.

**Victoria & Alfred Hotel.** Pierhead, Waterfront 8002. ☎ **021/419-6677.** Fax 021/419-8955. E-mail: vanda@ambassador.co.za. www.ambassador.co.za. 68 units. A/C MINIBAR TV TEL. R1,030–1,200 ($171.65–$200). Children 2–12 years sharing R80 ($13.35). AE, DC, MC, V.

Situated alongside the Alfred Basin's working dock, in the historic 1904 North Quay warehouse now called Alfred Mall, this hotel is the most centrally located Waterfront choice. (Note that while Villa Via is not as conveniently located, it offers better views, a pool, and marginally better rates.) Bedrooms, dressed in wrought-iron and veneer, are, however, disappointingly bland, and go some way to explaining the favorable rate. They are spacious though, each featuring a king-size bed, hair dryer, and trouser press. Rooms on the second floor, particularly 225 through 234, have the best views—be they of Table Mountain and the harbor, or the Waterfront and Table Bay.

**Dining/Diversions:** The Waterfront Café has a reasonably good reputation; you can dine alfresco on smoked crocodile or springbok loin while enjoying the excellent view of Table Mountain. The Green Dolphin, one of Cape Town's premier jazz venues, is in the same building.

**Amenities:** Parking is provided and a regular shuttle bus takes guests to the center of the city.

**Villa Via.** Beach Rd., Granger Bay 8002. ☎ **021/418-5729.** Fax 021/418-5717. E-mail: vvgb@iafrica.com. www.concorde-hotels.com. 201 units. A/C MINIBAR TV TEL. R990–1,770 ($165–$295). Children sharing stay free. AE, DC, MC, V.

Villa Via is located on the outskirts of the Waterfront (500 meters from the entrance), which may account for the relatively low rate. All in all, this 5-star hotel represents very good value for money; but for 5-star service, head for the Table Bay or the Mount Nelson. That said, you can't get closer to the sea than this. The pool (though a little small) is right on the water's edge, and three Villa Via catamarans, moored in the hotel's private marina, are available for guests' use. Almost every room in the hotel has an excellent sea view; all are furnished in dark blues and gold, with a nautical theme. Rooms feature coffee- and tea-making facilities, and hair dryers are provided on request.

**Dining:** It's worth dining at Tobago's, the hotel's restaurant, even if you aren't staying here (see "Where to Dine").

**Amenities:** Travel and information desk, 24-hour room service, laundry service, undercover parking, business and secretarial services, complimentary access to a nearby health club, day membership to the adjacent golf club, and an in-house beauty salon and spa.

## GREEN POINT & SEA POINT

### VERY EXPENSIVE

**Peninsula All Suites Hotel.** 313 Beach Rd., Sea Point 8060. ☎ **021/439-8886.** Fax 021/439-8888. 110 units. TV TEL. High-season R965 ($160.85) studio; from R1,060 ($176.65) suite. Low-season R705 studio ($117.50); from R785 ($130.85) suite. AE, DC, MC, V.

All suites in this time-share hotel face the sea and have large glass doors sliding open onto a private balcony, a great place to watch the spectacular Atlantic seaboard sunsets. Choose between an open-plan studio with private bathroom, a minisuite (specify if you want a private bedroom), or a two- or three-bedroom suite. Sleeper couches are standard, as are hair dryers, ceiling fans, and wall heaters. A portable air-conditioning unit is available upon request. All kitchenettes are fully equipped and suites serviced daily. Reserve early if you intend traveling here during the peak season, December through January.

**Dining:** The terrace-style restaurant, Café Bijou, is open from 7am to 10pm; a full room-service menu is also available.

**Amenities:** Two swimming pools (one heated), gym and games room, complimentary shuttle service, travel desk.

### EXPENSIVE

**Winchester Mansions.** 221 Beach Rd., Sea Point 8001. ☎ **021/434-2351.** Fax 021/434-0215. E-mail: winman@mweb.co.za. 53 units. MINIBAR TV TEL. High-season R765 ($127.50) double; R955–1,600 ($159.15–$266.65) suites. Low-season R630 ($105) double; R790–1,280 ($131.65–$213.35) suites. AE, DC, MC, V.

Built in the 1920s in the Cape Dutch style, this old-fashioned three-story hotel also faces the sea, though it's not as close as The Peninsula or La Splendida—if you leave the windows open, the busy road below blocks out the sound of the ocean. Rooms have recently been refurbished and feature tea- and coffee-making facilities, under-carpet heating, hair dryers, ceiling fans, and are relatively spacious. The Winchester is a popular hangout for locals, particularly on Sundays, when breakfast (often accompanied by live jazz) is served in the beautiful colonnaded central courtyard, built around a fountain and encircled with trees. All meals are served here and in the adjacent restaurant. Weather permitting, the courtyard is another very romantic dinner venue. There is also a small pool.

## Moderate

✪ **La Splendida.** 121 Beach Rd., Mouille Point 8001. ☎ **021/439-5119.** E-mail: lasplendida@hotelogue.co.za. Fax 021/439-5112. 22 units. A/C MINIBAR TV TEL. R420–540 ($70–$90) double; R765 ($127.50) suite; R875 ($145.85) penthouse. Children by arrangement.

If you can't afford the Waterfront or Atlantic seaboard, but want to be close to the ocean, this is a great option. Just minutes from the Waterfront and the city center, this small hotel is separated from the sea only by a road, for the best value-for-money views in town. The art deco exterior wouldn't look out of place in Miami, but the modern interiors are very chic and comfortable. There are a choice of mountain- and sea-view rooms—a sea-view room (reserve early), particularly the penthouse which sleeps four, is worth the extra R120 ($20). Pack your in-line skates, as the promenade stretches all the way past Sea Point. Meals are served at the ground-floor Café Splendide, a stylish venue which serves a mix of Italian and Californian dishes, and opens onto a terrace which features a tiny plunge pool. A potential drawback in winter (June–August) is the noise from the foghorn—this is the closest that boats leaving the harbor come to shore before turning out to sea, and the foghorn makes sure it stays that way.

**The Victoria Junction.** Corner Somerset and Ebenezer rds., Cape Town 8001. ☎ **021/418-1234.** Fax 021/418-5678. E-mail: vicjunt@icon.co.za. 172 units. A/C MINIBAR TV TEL. R755–865 ($125.85–$144.15) double; R1,005 ($167.50) loft apartments (ask for low-season discounts; children's rates negotiable). AE, DC, MC, V.

Situated a few minutes from the city and the Waterfront, with a number of excellent restaurants and nightlife options in the immediate vicinity (including the best gay club in town), this hotel offers the feeling of being at the heart of Cape Town without being in the city center. Featuring exposed brick walls, industrial steel decor, stylized furniture, and some large original artworks, (rather like a South African version of New York loft apartments), the Junction is popular with the film industry types who flock to Cape Town in the summer months. Choose between a standard room (ask for a harbor or mountain view on the 4th floor) or one of the lofts on the 5th floor. Facilities include 24-hour room service, laundry service, a hairdressing and beauty salon, privileges at the nearby Health & Racquet Club gymnasium, and a dedicated shuttle service. The hotel has a lap pool; the Green Point golf course is a few minutes away. The Set is the hotel's theme restaurant, where Mediterranean, Asian, and South African fusion is served under suspended steel frames, booms and mounted cameras. The restaurant also has a full cocktail bar and coffee bar.

## Inexpensive

**Head South Lodge.** 215 Main Rd., Green Point 8001. ☎ **021/434-8777.** Fax 021/434-8778. www.headsouth.co.za E-mail: hedsouth@kingsley.co.za. 15 units. TV TEL MINIBAR. R385–550 ($64.15–$91.65), includes breakfast. Children 17 and over only.

This guest house, a few minutes from town and the Waterfront, and within walking distance of Sea Point's myriad restaurants, is another that offers excellent value for money. Rooms feature stylish art deco–inspired furniture, with walls adorned with Tretchikoff prints. Each room features tea- and coffee-making facilities, hair dryers, underfloor heating and heated towel rails, and daily newspapers are provided free of charge. Owner/manager Jeff Levy has a very hands-on approach, and will gladly assist with restaurant and tour bookings, cycle and in-line skates rental, as well as secretarial, copying, and courier services, e-mail retrieval, and in-room fax. Temporary membership at the local Health & Racquet Club can be organized. Other facilities include laundry services, lock-up parking, and a small pool—dinners are also provided on request. Hookers parade Main Road, but the area is not dangerous; for further peace of mind, there's a 24-hour security guard. Note, however, that for a little more (or, if you're paying the top rates here, less!) you could be staying in a sea-facing room at La Splendida.

## ATLANTIC SEABOARD

### VERY EXPENSIVE

**The Bay Hotel.** Victoria Rd., Camps Bay 8005. ☎ **021/438-4444.** Fax 021/438-4455. E-mail: res@thebay.co.za. 77 units. High-season R1,190–2,480 ($198.35–$413.35) double; R3,400 ($566.65) suites; R5,400 ($900) penthouse. Low-season R680–1,160 ($113.35–$193.35) double; R1,900 ($316.65) suites; R2,860 ($476.65) penthouse. AE, DC, MC, V. Children 12 and older only.

The Bay Hotel's hard-edged architecture and pastel interiors are a bad reminder of the 1980s, but a location directly opposite Camps Bay's palm-lined beachfront provides excellent access to one of the Cape's most beautiful beaches. All rooms are spacious, featuring a small lobby (for unobtrusive room service) and a split-level bed and seating area. Rooms facing the sea are pricey (R1,920/$320 double), but as this is the hotel's raison d'être, you should probably shell out. However, if you've blown your budget, consider booking a cheaper, mountain-facing room and spending your days at the beach and pool (which overlooks the beach), or in one of Camps Bay's excellent sea-facing bars (of which two are in the hotel). Service is good, as the hotel is, after all, a member of Small Luxury Hotels of the World. The hotel provides airport transfers. (Town is a 10-minute drive from here; the airport 30 minutes.)

**Dining:** In-house Tides also has a great view, though the food isn't that good. There's a more happening vibe at Blues, which is adjacent—you can eat here or have a drink at the adjoining Baraza and charge it to your room.

✪ **Ellerman House.** 180 Kloof Rd., Bantry Bay 8001. ☎ **021/439-9182.** Fax 021/434-7257. E-mail: ellerman@pixie.co.za. www.ellerman.co.za/index.htm. 11 units. A/C TV TEL. R2,000–3,200 ($333.35–$533.35); R4,500 ($750) suite. Rates include airport transfer, breakfast, light lunches, laundry, drinks (except wine and champagne), and ad hoc secretarial services. AE, DC, MC, V.

Situated on a spectacularly elevated site overlooking the Atlantic Ocean and premier suburb of Bantry Bay, this Relais & Chateaux member is in a class of its own, and with only 11 rooms is arguably the most exclusive address in Cape Town. Most rooms feature magnificent views from every window (of which there are many) and balcony, but these come at a premium. If you're staying in Room 6 (no view) or Room 3 (view, but no balcony), you can spend your days on the broad patio (where drinks and meals are served) or in the terraced garden with a large pool, from where you can see forever. For a view from your bathtub, book Room 1.

Once the stately residence of Sir John and Lady Ellerman, the house has been meticulously restored to its original early-20th-century splendor, with renovations and additions blending seamlessly. Furnishings are high quality, albeit slightly old fashioned, and numerous original works of art by some of South Africa's most talented artists adorn the walls. Extremely skillful service strikes that delicate balance between intrusive and solicitous, fulfilling your needs before you're aware of them, yet granting every sense of privacy. Amenities include a library, a good wine cellar, a bar with fireplace, and a fully equipped gym, a large pool, and a steambath. The chefs create the menus daily, depending on fresh produce, and special guest requests are welcomed.

## Expensive

**Bali Bay.** 113 Victoria Rd., Camps Bay 8005. ☎/Fax **021/790-6967.** 3 units. TV TEL. R500–1,000 ($83.35–$166.65) studio; R1,600–3,000 ($266.65–$500) apartment; R2,000–5,000 ($333.35–$833.35) penthouse. AE, DC, MC, V.

These modern apartments offer the most tasteful accommodation in Camps Bay, and are a great place to reserve as a group. The studio has a good ocean view and shares a plunge pool with the above apartment, but is a little too close to the road. The apartment and penthouse both have three bedrooms and two bathrooms, an open-plan kitchen, living and dining room, and wraparound balcony. The highly recommended penthouse has a small private garden, and on the top floor, a private plunge pool and patio. Each apartment has a music system, fax machine, monitored burglar alarm, and access to lock-up garages. Camps Bay's restaurants and shops are within walking distance and directly opposite is beautiful Bali Bay, which has a tiny secluded beach.

**Sea Castle.** 15 Victoria Rd., Camps Bay 8005. ☎ **021/438-4010.** Fax 021/438-4015. E-mail: seacastl@iafrica.com. 11 units. TV TEL. High-season R600–1,080 ($100–$180) studios; R675–1,185 ($112.50–$197.50) 1 bedroom; R1,200–2,375 ($200–$395.85) 2 bedrooms. Low-season R450–525 ($75–$87.50) studios; R525 ($87.50) 1 bedroom; R700–800 ($116.65–$133.35) 2 bedrooms. AE, DC, MC, V.

Situated directly across from Camps Bay Beach, this is the self-catering, child-friendly, value-for-money alternative to the Bay Hotel. All apartments have sea views. The living areas, decorated in bright Caribbean-inspired colors, feature ceiling fans, underfloor heating, sleeper couches, and modern, fully equipped kitchens. Some have private Jacuzzis. The sidewalk cafes, restaurants, bars, Theatre on the Bay and Camps Bay supermarket are all within strolling distance.

**Amenities:** 24-hour security, a communal swimming pool, laundry service, e-mail and fax facilities, 24-hour reception, secretarial service, taxi bookings, and airport transfers (by prior arrangement).

## Moderate

**Ambassador Hotel.** 34 Victoria Rd., Bantry Bay 8001. ☎ **021/439-6170.** Fax 021/439-6336. E-mail: reservations@ambassador.co.za. www.ambassador.co.za. 69 units. TV TEL. High-season R850 ($141.65) double; low-season R575 ($95.85) double. AE, DC, MC, V. Extra bed R100/night ($16.65).

Like most of Bantry Bay, this hotel has been built into the cliff-face overlooking the rocks and ocean. The best rooms overlook nothing but the pool deck and the wide, blue horizon. The hotel is in desperate need of refurbishment, however, with stained corridor carpets and some walls showing signs of damp. Do not book a bed here if you cannot get a sea-facing room in the original hotel. (The "executive suites" across the road are too far from the sea). Rooms come equipped with tea- and coffee-making facilities and hair dryers. The Clifton beaches are a pleasant 20-minute stroll or 5-minute drive from here.

**Dining/Diversions:** Both the bar and restaurant (Waves specializes in seafood and is a respected restaurant in its own right) feature the same extraordinary view as the rooms.

**Amenities:** Parking, 18-hour laundry, secretarial services and airport transfers by prior arrangement.

✪ **Monkey Valley Beach Nature Resort.** Chapman's Peak, Mountain Rd., Noordhoek 7985. ☎ **021/789-1391.** Fax 021/789-1143. E-mail: monkey@iafrica.com. 33 units. TV TEL. High-season R700–1,200 ($116.65–$200) double, including breakfast; R1,300–2,200 ($216.65–$366.65) 2-bedroom cottage; R1,500–2,500 ($250–$416.65) 3-bedroom cottage.

(Dec 22–Jan 5, minimum 7-night stay). Low-season R450–700 ($75–$116.65), including breakfast; R1,080 ($180) 2-bedroom cottage; R1,250 ($208.35) 3-bedroom cottage. Cottage rates do not include breakfast. AE, DC, MC, V.

This resort's spectacular location and charming rooms make the 30-minute trip to town worthwhile. In fact, you may never want to leave. The thatched Monkey Valley cottages are situated in the indigenous milkwood forest; most have excellent views of Noordhoek's 8-kilometer-long pristine beach. The alternative mountain view is also beautiful, but not as breathtaking. All the Cape country-style cottages have a deck or lawn terrace with sea views, outside shower, private braai, fireplace, sleeper couch, and are serviced daily. B&B rooms are either in the "Village Inn" (thatched timber cottages, with Victorian fireplaces and Victorian claw-foot bathtubs), or in the more modern Lodge. As the latter are only incrementally cheaper, it's worth specifying a room in the cuter Inn, most of which have sea views. Thorfynn's Restaurant serves healthy farmhouse cuisine, and both the restaurant and bar overlook the sea. Recreation options include the beach, nature walks, nearby tennis and golf, horseback riding, volleyball, a swimming pool, sauna, and natural health program. Airport transfers can be arranged.

## SOUTHERN SUBURBS

### VERY EXPENSIVE

**Cellars-Hohenhort Hotel.** PO Box 270, Constantia 7848. ☎ **021/794-2137.** Fax 021/794-2149. E-mail: cellars@ct.lia.net. 53 units. TV TEL. R1,200–2,150 ($200–$358.35) doubles; R2,300–2,600 ($383.35–$433.35) suites. Children 14 and over only.

With expansive views of the densely forested eastern slopes of Table Mountain behind, and the valley and mountains towering above False Bay in front, the Cellars-Hohenhort is a genteel hotel that would suit the older traveler looking for an out-of-town alternative to the Mount Nelson (though the Mount Nelson is still a better bet). Antique furnishings and original works of art adorn the original Hohenhort manor house; this is also where the best rooms are. All rooms are comfortably furnished with floral fabrics adorning the king-size or twin beds. The hotel is a Relais & Chateaux member, and well deserving of this distinction.

**Dining:** Cellars, where Prince Philip hosted his World Fellowship dinner, is one of the best restaurants in Cape Town (see "Where to Dine"). A second restaurant, the Cape Malay Kitchen, is open for dinner and provides an excellent introduction to regional cuisine.

**Amenities:** A 9-acre garden, two swimming pools, a tennis court, a croquet lawn, and a full-scale golf green designed by Gary Player.

### EXPENSIVE

**Alphen.** Alphen Dr., Constantia 7848. ☎ **021/794-5011.** Fax 021/794-5710. E-mail: reservations@alphen.co.za. 34 units. TV TEL. R795–1,245 ($132.50–$275) double; R1,530 ($255) suite. Rates include breakfast; ask about low-season rates. AE, DC, MC, V.

When the Alphen was built in 1752, the Cloetes had already been farming the Constantia vineyards for a century. Oil paintings of the family forefathers and heirlooms are found throughout the former manor house—look out for the kist that brought their belongings over when the Cloetes sailed over with Jan van Riebeeck in 1657. In stark contrast to the historic estate, the standard rooms are small and uninviting. However, the new luxury rooms are huge, with high ceilings and large bathrooms. They cost the same as the Cellars' most basic unit, but are twice the size. The major drawback here is the proximity to the highway; you hear the low drone as soon as you step out of your room.

**Dining/Diversions:** The restaurant in the manor house enjoys an excellent reputation for both cosmopolitan and traditional cuisine, and the Boer and Brit serves good pub lunches.

**Constantia Uitsig.** Spaansgemacht Rd., PO Box 32, Constantia 7848. ☎ **021/794-6500.** Fax 021/794-7605. 16 garden suites. A/C MINIBAR TV TEL. High-season R998–1,188 ($166.35–$198) double. Low-season R778–880 ($129.65–$146.65) double.

Part of the Constantia Wine Route, the aptly named Constantia Uitsig (*Uitsig* means "view"), has commanding vistas of the surrounding vineyards and mountains. There's a calming sense of rural peace throughout, yet the city center is a mere 15 kilometers (9 miles) away. The 16 well-appointed suites lie in bird-filled gardens; their Cape Dutch architecture echoing that of the 17th century manor house, home to the award-winning Uitsig Restaurant (see "Where to Dine"). La Colombe, the hotel's second award-winning restaurant, features excellent traditional French cuisine (best avoided if you're counting calories). You can sample the local wines at the hotel's tasting center, or order them at dinner. Uitsig's lawns also extend onto a cricket oval—with its unhindered view of the mountains and distant sea, and attractive Victorian pavilion, it is a popular destination for players and enthusiasts from around the world. Other activities include horseback riding, cycling, and golfing. (The Tokai Golf Course is 10 minutes away.)

## MODERATE

**Vineyard Hotel.** Colinton Rd. (off Protea Rd.), Newlands 7700. ☎ **021/683-3044.** Fax 021/683-3365. E-mail: hotel@vineyard.co.za. www.vineyard.co.za. 160 units. A/C MINIBAR (stocked on request) TV TEL. R630–730 ($105–$121.65) courtyard facing; R840–1,050 ($140–$175) mountain facing; R1,198–1,865 ($199.65–$310.85) suites. AE, DC, MC, V.

If you don't mind being 20 minutes from the nearest beach and in suburbia, this hotel's standard mountain-facing rooms—and make sure you stay in one—offer both excellent value for money and spectacular views of the forested mountain slopes. Despite being a short stroll from the large Cavendish shopping center and the Newlands sports arenas, you'll feel as if you're in the middle of the country. Rooms are relatively spacious (no need for the deluxe or suite unless you're staying for a while, or are more than two) and feature basics like tea- and coffee-making facilities, a trouser press, and hairdryers. Facilities include a heated Olympic-size pool set in the 6-acre garden, and a gym. Tours throughout the peninsula, including guided walks up Table Mountain, can be arranged. Breakfasts are served in the Courtyard Restaurant, which is also open for dinner. Au Jardin is one of the Cape's best French restaurants (see "Where to Dine").

## INEXPENSIVE

**Houtkapperspoort.** Hout Bay Rd., Constantia Nek 7800. ☎ **021/794-5216.** Fax 021/794-2907. E-mail: houtkap@iafrica.com. www.houtkapperspoort.co.za. 25 units. TV TEL. R370–520 ($61.65–$86.65) 1 bedroom; R540–770 ($90–$128.35) 2 bedrooms; R620–940 ($103.35–$156.65) 3 bedrooms; R1,590–1,690 ($265–$281.65) 4 bedrooms. Low-season R260–340 ($43.35–$56.65) 1 bedroom; R380–490 ($63.35–$81.65) 2 bedrooms; R390–690 ($65–$115) 3 bedrooms; R1,200 ($200) 4 bedrooms. AE, DC, MC, V.

These stone and timber self-catering cottages are set in spacious landscaped grounds that blend into the forested mountainside. All cottages are well equipped and serviced, and feature private braai areas, while some include fireplaces and underfloor heating. As many are double-storied, specify if you don't want to climb stairs. Amenities include a pool, tennis court, a laundry service, and various walks in the Cecilia State

Forest and Table Mountain Reserve, which the property borders. Breakfast baskets can be delivered to your door. Hout Bay is a 5-minute drive down oak-lined roads, while the center of town lies some 20 minutes away.

An alternative to Houtkapperspoort, which is often full, is **Silvermist** (☎ **021/794-7601;** info@silvermist.co.za), situated directly opposite. These self-catering cottages are more elevated than Houtkapperspoort, affording excellent views of the forested slopes of the mountain; the pool has one of the most breathtaking views in the Cape. The only drawback is the slight rumbling that rises from trucks gearing up and down the Nek—request a cottage as high up as possible. Rates vary from R600–1,800 ($100–$300) in high-season and R470–870 ($78.35–$145) in low-season.

**Rooms.** 113 Lower Main Rd., Observatory (next to Obz Café). ☎ **021/448-9990.** E-mail: barend123@mweb.co.za. 5 units; 3 bathrooms, none en suite. R150 ($25) double.

This small, cheap hotel is situated on Observatory's bohemian high street, with a communal lounge opening onto a balcony that provides a great vantage of the passing parade, and trendy Obz Café below. Proprietor Barend de Wet is one of South Africa's most controversial artists, and his latest "artwork" proves no exception. According to the artist-as-proprietor, your room—dressed and prepared by him—is a work of art. Rooms are spare and clean, though the couches in the lounge need cleaning. Asked if guests, too, are art, Barend is less than forthcoming—seems every artwork needs an audience.

## FALSE BAY

### MODERATE

**Simon's Town Quayside Lodge.** Off Jubilee Sq., St Georges St. ☎ **021/786-3838.** Fax 021/786-2241. E-mail: info@quayside.co.za. 28 units. MINIBAR TV TEL. R500–650 ($83.35–$108.35) double. AE, DC, MC, V.

This new hotel is part of the Simon's Town Harbour development, with a number of shops and the water right on the doorstep, and Boulders Beach a 10-minute walk away. Most of the rooms, in a pleasant nautical theme, have French doors opening onto balconies with beautiful views of the False Bay coast and Simon's Town yacht basin—these are marginally more (R50/$8.35) expensive and definitely worth requesting. Dining is at Bertha's Restaurant. Airport transfers (some 45km/28 miles) can be arranged.

### INEXPENSIVE

**British Hotel Apartments.** 90 St Georges St., Simon's Town 7975. ☎ **021/790-4930.** Fax 021/786-2214. 8 units. TV. R350 ($58.35) double. Children less 50%. AE, DC, MC, V.

Originally built in 1897, the British Hotel has been skillfully converted into four self-catering apartments and four courtyard suites. The spacious three-bedroom, two-bathroom apartments have the better views, with open-plan kitchens, dining and living rooms, and large balconies overlooking the Simon's Town Harbour and Bay. You are 10 minutes from Cape Point, but approximately a 40-minute drive from Cape Town, which makes city dining impractical; but there are a number of good restaurants in the nearby suburb of Kalk Bay, and an excellent bakery and coffee shop adjacent.

## 4 Where to Dine

For centuries Cape Town has set the table for a varied and increasingly discerning audience, with world-class fare augmented by historical venues and great views. For harbor settings and mountain views, head for the Waterfront; for uninterrupted ocean views and great sunsets, go to the Atlantic seaboard. Lunch is best in the southern suburb of Constantia or the Winelands, where you can drink in views of the vineyards and mountains along with a selection of fine Cape wines. For people-watching, take a seat at a pavement café on Greenmarket Square in the center of town.

If you prefer to stroll the streets, taking a more detailed look at menus and venues, head for the restaurant strips of Main Road in Sea Point, or to more charming Kloof Street, which runs down the slope of Table Mountain into town. In the seaside suburb of Camps Bay you'll find another, smaller restaurant strip along the beachfront, a great place to dine in summer, when the sun sets around 8pm.

If you're setting off for Cape Point, a journey that will take you the better part of the day, try and time lunch at one of the recommended restaurants in the Constantia area, or overlooking the False Bay coast. Cape Town's best fish-and-chips takeaway, **Fish Hoek Fisheries** (☎ **021/782-2314** at 43 Main Rd.), is in the appropriately named suburb of Fish Hoek.

If you're staying in a B&B or a self-catering hotel, contact **Mr Delivery** (☎ **021/423-4177** in town; 021/439-9916 in Sea Point; or 021/761-0040 in Constantia) and ask them to drop off a menu. Mr Delivery delivers meals from over 20 restaurants and takeaway joints (some of which are described below), directly to your door.

Finally, make sure to sample at least one dish inspired by the unique hybrid of Cape cultures. This still-evolving "modern Cape" cuisine combines elements of the Portuguese, Dutch, French, German, English, Indian, and Malaysian influences that have made up the city's multicultural past.

## CITY BOWL & SURROUNDS

### EXPENSIVE

**Bonthuys.** 121 Castle St., Cape Town. ☎ **021/426-2368.** Main courses R54–76 ($9–$12.65). Tues–Sat 7–9pm. AE, DC, MC, V. FRENCH.

Entering what appears to be a run-down 19th century warehouse and walking down the narrow peeling corridor does not prepare you for the transformation Ettiene Bonthuys has wrought in the interior, where cobalt-blue walls set off mismatched but beautiful fittings. Chandeliers, tables, chairs, cutlery, and china are as eclectic and artful as the excellent food, which purists consider a bit over the top. Unusual combinations include mussels with banana and apple in an orange sauce, salmon tartare with raw beef fillet and oysters, and poached sole with grilled prawns. If this sounds too mutant, there are less inventive options like saddle of lamb and fillet. No salt and pepper is on the table, the idea being that dishes are perfectly seasoned, but you may request a pepper grinder. The parking lot opposite the restaurant is unguarded.

**The Cape Colony.** Mount Nelson Hotel, Gardens (entrance off Kloof St.). ☎ **021/423-1000.** Two-course lunch special R65 ($10.85). Main course R48–185 ($8–$30.85) dinner. Daily 11:30am–3:30pm and 7–10pm. AE, DC, MC, V. INTERNATIONAL/MODERN CAPE.

This is by far the grandest and most old fashioned of the restaurant options on the Kloof Street strip. Service is discreet and decor is plush, with individual table lamps creating soft pools of light on impeccable table appointments. Food is faultlessly presented with a truly international flavor; in particular look out for Cape Malay kingklip; Australian king prawns; pan-seared Norwegian salmon; tandoori-spiced beef salad; and crispy basil polenta, though the menu changes regularly.

**D'Vijff Vlieghen.** 16 Keerom St., Cape Town. ☎ **021/424-4442.** Main courses R55–63 ($9.15–$10.50). Mon–Fri 12–3pm and 7–11pm; Sat 7–11pm. AE, DC, MC, V. NEW CAPE DUTCH.

# Cape Town Dining

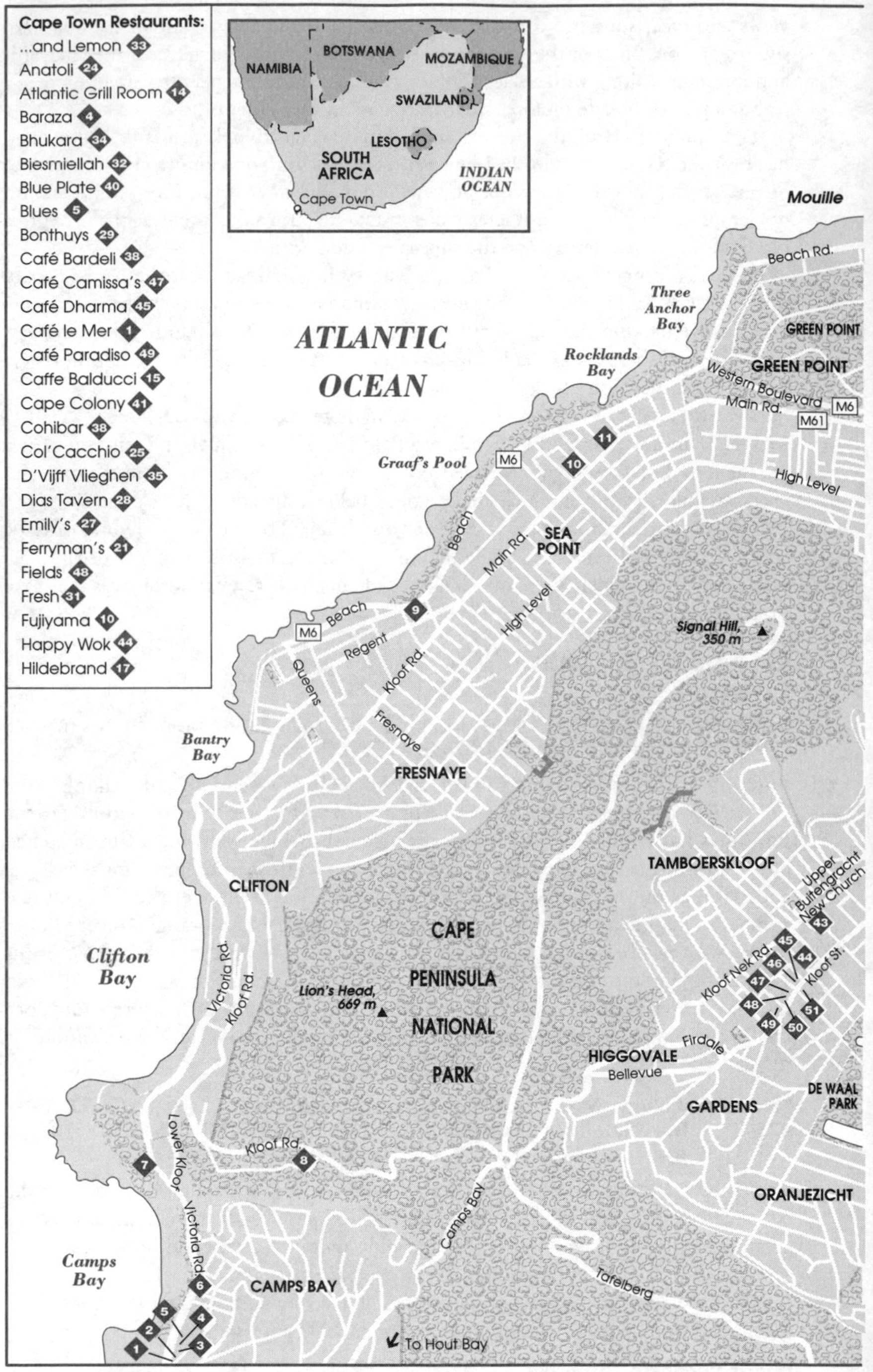

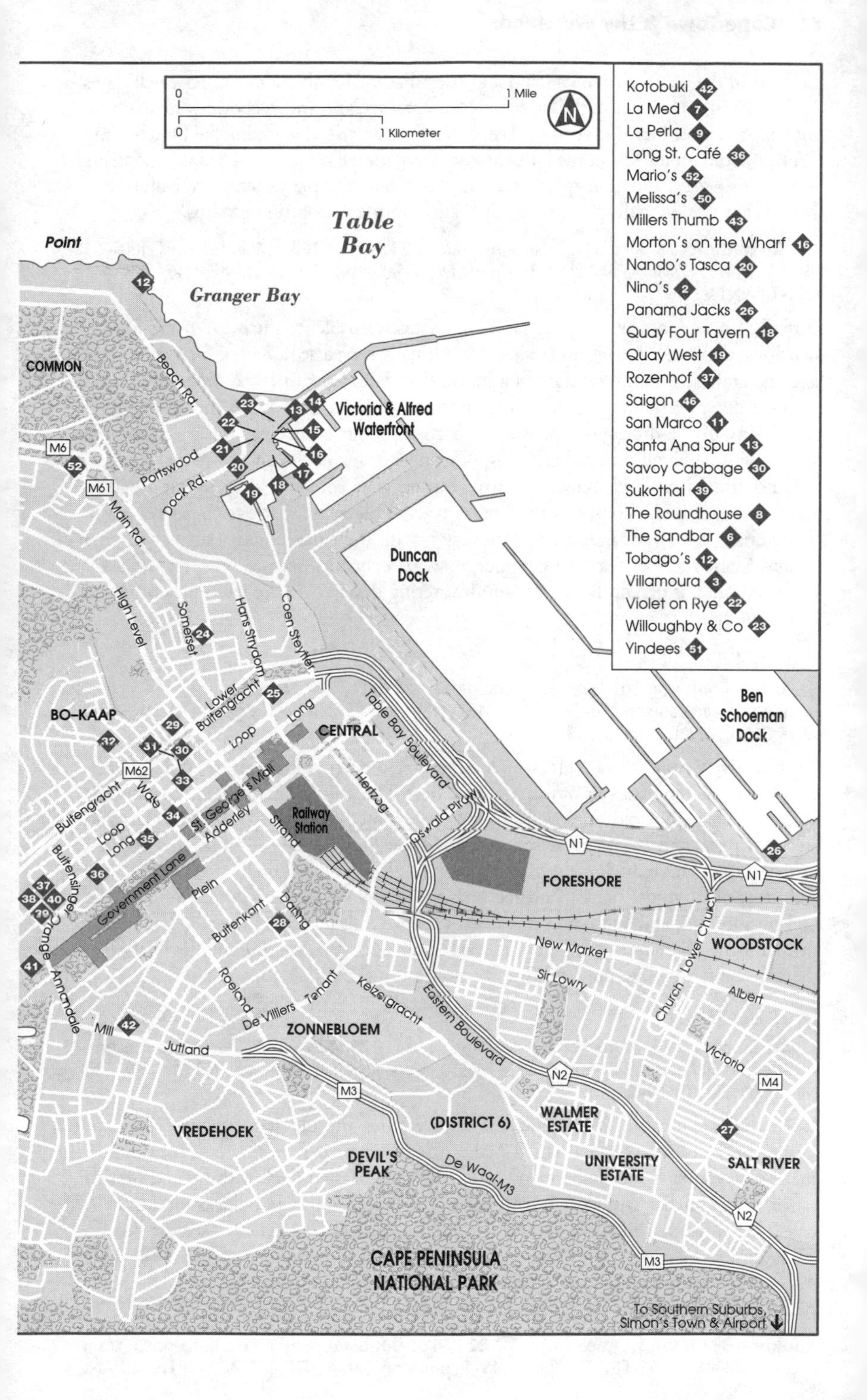
Kotobuki 42
La Med 7
La Perla 9
Long St. Café 36
Mario's 52
Melissa's 50
Millers Thumb 43
Morton's on the Wharf 16
Nando's Tasca 20
Nino's 2
Panama Jacks 26
Quay Four Tavern 18
Quay West 19
Rozenhof 37
Saigon 46
San Marco 11
Santa Ana Spur 13
Savoy Cabbage 30
Sukothai 39
The Roundhouse 8
The Sandbar 6
Tobago's 12
Villamoura 3
Violet on Rye 22
Willoughby & Co 23
Yindees 51
0
1 Mile
0
1 Kilometer
N
Table Bay
Point
Granger Bay
COMMON
Beach Rd.
Victoria & Alfred Waterfront
Portswood
Dock Rd.
Main Rd.
Duncan Dock
High Level
Somerset
Hans Strydom
Coen Steytler
Lower Buitengracht
Long
Loop
BO-KAAP
CENTRAL
Table Bay Boulevard
Ben Schoeman Dock
Buitengracht
Wale
St. George's Mall
Adderley
Strand
Railway Station
Hertzog
Oswald Pirow
Loop
Long
Buitensingel
Government Lane
Plein
Buitenkant
Darling
FORESHORE
WOODSTOCK
Lower Church
New Market
Sir Lowry
Albert
Church
Orange
Annandale
Roeland
De Villiers
Tennant
Keizersgracht
Eastern Boulevard
Mill
Jutland
ZONNEBLOEM
Victoria
VREDEHOEK
(DISTRICT 6)
WALMER ESTATE
UNIVERSITY ESTATE
SALT RIVER
DEVIL'S PEAK
De Waal-M3
CAPE PENINSULA NATIONAL PARK
To Southern Suburbs, Simon's Town & Airport

Located in the old Netherlands Club and the adjacent Rembrandt House (which dates back to 1754), this is one of the classiest venues in the Cape, with a choice of nine dining rooms, each more beautiful than the last. Dishes are described as traditional Dutch using South African products, but the influence of international cooking styles and ingredients is obvious: papaya and bean-sprout salad is combined with prawn tempura; ballotine of Norwegian salmon with spinach, yoghurt, and mint; and poppadom crisps.

✪ **Rozenhof.** 18 Kloof St., Gardens. ☎ **021/424-1968.** Main courses R46–68 ($7.65–$11.35). Mon–Fri 12:30–3:30pm; Mon–Sat 7pm–10:15pm. AE, DC, MC, V. CONTINENTAL.

Rozenhof has been delivering the same understated excellence since 1984; the food is delicious, the service intelligent (waiters have usually served at Rozenhof for some time), and the ambience warm. Located in a house that dates back to 1852, diners are seated in three different rooms, ensuring an intimate experience even when the restaurant is full. Many of the dishes have remained unchanged since opening; the cheese soufflé starter with herb-and-mustard cream is a must, as is one of the linefish preparations—almond crusted on leeks braised in citrus butter, with coriander dressing on a bed of roasted peppers and onions; or served on root-vegetable mash, with a fresh papaya relish. Their crispy roast duck is also a favorite; try it with the citrus brandy sauce or smyrna fig and Marsala sauce. Warm ginger pudding with a chocolate center, served with ginger creme anglaise, is one of the many mouthwatering desserts. Secure parking is provided across the street.

## EXPENSIVE

✪ **Savoy Cabbage.** 101 Hout St., Heritage Sq. ☎ **021/424-2626.** Reservations recommended. Main courses R36–58 ($6–$9.65). Mon–Fri 12–2:30pm; Mon–Sat 7–10:30pm. AE, DC, MC, V. INTERNATIONAL.

This relatively young restaurant, which celebrates the new European trend in "sophisticated peasant" food, is one of the country's best. The venue is stylish (a narrow double volume L-shape; the old brick walls have been exposed and juxtaposed with glass and steel fittings), and the food is interesting. Appetizers include hot-buttered lettuce, anchovy toast and red-wine vinegar sauce; and red pear and plum, pepper cheese, and walnut salad. Two deliciously flavored entrees are the sweetbreads with lemon, chives and mushrooms, and lamb- and rice-filled cabbage rolls poached in broth. The menu, printed daily on a simple sheet of bond paper, changes daily and exemplifies chef Janet Telian's ability to reinterpret and find inspiration in the simplest ingredients.

## MODERATE

**...and Lemon.** 98 Shortmarket St., Heritage Sq. ☎ **021/423-4873.** Reservations recommended. Main courses R35–85 ($5.85–$14.15). Mon–Sat 10am–5pm and 7–11pm. AE, DC, MC, V. INTERNATIONAL.

It's the cool courtyard (which incidentally features the oldest living vine in Cape Town) in the center of town which makes the dining experience here so pleasurable; make sure you have a table here and order the slow-roasted duck with fig and brandy sauce, or the linefish with coriander. Green curries are another popular choice, but the true Thai enthusiast should hold out for a more authentic experience (see the box on Thai dining below). If you can't get a table in the courtyard, **Fresh** (☎ **021/423-4889**), specializing in breakfast and light lunches, shares the venue. There's plenty of parking in Riebeeck Square opposite.

**Bhukara.** 33 Church St., Cape Town. ☎ **021/424-0000.** Reservations recommended. Main courses R28–48 ($4.65–$8). 12–3pm, 6.45–11pm Mon–Sat. AE, DC, MC, V. NORTH INDIAN.

Sabi Sabharwal met his Afrikaans wife in Italy and followed her home, an act of love for which Capetonians are truly grateful. Bhukara—a classy venue that wouldn't look out of place in style-conscious London—specializes in Mugal food and tandoori barbecues. Meats are tender and the flavors full and vibrant: Make sure you try the butter chicken, or hotly spiced tandoori lamb chops. Chefs Sharma and Singh leave no fat on meat and use only the freshest ingredients, including the spices. Their motto "Only the best will do, whatever the cost," must be what kept Shakira and Michael Caine coming back for more. When crowded, acoustics can be a problem.

✪ **Kotobuki.** Avalon House, Mill St., Gardens. ☎ **021/462-3675.** Reservations essential. Rolls (6) R12–22 ($2–$3.65). Two sushi pieces R12–26 ($2–$4.35). Main courses R32–52 ($5.35–$8.65). Tues–Fri 12–2pm and 7–10pm; Sat–Sun 7–10pm. AE, DC, MC, V. JAPANESE.

Kotobuki is the best of Cape Town's surprisingly few sushi restaurants. The fish is so fresh it's almost moving, and despite a venue that resembles an old school hall and harsh lighting, it's virtually impossible to get a table here without booking two days in advance. It's also often closed—if the chef doesn't like the look of the fish that day, he simply won't prepare it. If you can't get a table here but still have a craving for sushi, try **Fujiyama** (☎ **021/434-6885**) in Sea Point.

### MODERATE

**Millers Thumb.** 10b Kloof Nek Rd., Tamboerskloof. ☎ **021/424-3838.** Main courses R32–47 ($5.35–$7.85). Mon–Sat 12:30–2:30pm and 6:30–10:30pm. SEAFOOD.

At this very welcome addition to the Kloof Street strip, you'll find the best fish in the City Bowl. Try the Cajun butterfish (it really is like butter), the yakki soba (chicken, shrimp, vegetable, and cashew-nut stir-fry), or the rigatoni luca (avocado, sundried tomatoes, and olives tossed with rigatoni in a pesto, tomato, cream and white-wine sauce). This former home is unpretentious and casual; try to book a table close to the log fire in winter.

### INEXPENSIVE

**Biesmiellah.** 2 Upper Wale St., Cape Town. ☎ **021/423-0850.** Main courses R25–46 ($4.15–$7.65). Mon–Sat 12–10pm. AE, DC, MC, V. CAPE MALAY.

There are a number of places offering Cape Malay fare, but none is as authentic as Biesmiellah. Run by two generations of the Osman family in the historic Malay quarter of Bo-Kaap, Biesmiellah has been serving the local Cape Muslim community, and increasingly, tourists, for two decades. The *denningvleis,* a sweet-sour lamb cutlet stew, served with saffron rice, almonds, raisins, and mashed potatoes, is recommended, as is the *pienang curry,* a beef cutlet stew prepared with bay leaves. In keeping with Muslim tradition, no alcohol is allowed on the premises. Biesmiellah also offers takeaways—try a roti (flatbread) stuffed with cubed mutton.

**Col'Cacchio.** Seeff House, 42 Hans Stridom Ave. ☎ **021/419-4848.** Main courses R19–49 ($3.15–$8.15). Daily 12–2:30 and 6:30–11pm. AE, DC, MC, V. PIZZA.

If you like your pizza base thin and crispy and your toppings innovative, Col'Cacchio is the best in town. Recommended choices include the Tre Colori (smoked salmon, sour cream, and caviar), and the Prostituto (avocado, bacon, feta, and spinach). Salads are large and fresh (try the smoked chicken and pepperdew), and service is reasonably fast. It's a good venue (large and laid back); but as Col'Cacchio is served by Mr. Delivery, you don't even have to leave home, though the pizzas are definitely best fresh from the wood-burning oven. If you find yourself in the Claremont area, sister restaurant **Morituri** (☎ **021/683-6671,** 214 Main Rd.) serves exactly the same menu.

### Family-Friendly Restaurants

The most family-friendly restaurants are in the Waterfront; **Santa Ana Spur** (☎ **021/418-3620**) tops the list, particularly over weekends and evenings when Chico the Clown entertains with magic tricks. (The Spur chain is designed around the needs of kids, so keep an eye out for any of their branches situated throughout the city). On the other extreme **Quay West** (☎ **021/410-7100**) in the Cape Grace is an elegant but relaxed 5-star experience, with high chairs and children's portions available on request. If pizzas are what's wanted, check out **Col'Cacchio** (☎ **021/419-4848**), though they don't have a separate menu or high chairs. The **Wharfside Grill** (☎ **021/790-2130**) in Hout Bay has a kiddies menu, but no high chairs.

Choices in the Winelands include **Lady Phillips** (☎ **021/847-1346**), **The Green Door** (☎ **021/885-1756**), and **Spier** (☎ **021/881-3096**) in the Stellenbosch area; **Laborie** (☎ **021/807-3095**) in Paarl, and **Chamonix** (☎ **021/876-2494**) in Franschhoek. Le Pique Nique (☎ **021/874-1152**) at **Boschendal,** Franschhoek, supplies special hampers with animal-shaped breads and other child-inspired foods.

**Dias Tavern.** 27 Caledon St., Cape Town. ☎ **021/45-7547.** Main courses R16–80 ($2.65–$13.35). Mon–Sat 12pm–late. AE, DC, MC, V. PORTUGUESE.

This is a bit of a dive, red plastic chairs alternate with booth seats, but Dias is famous for its delicious steak dishes. Try their *Espetada* (chunks of marinated sirloin, skewered and carried, flaming-hot, to the table). Not the venue for vegetarians, Dias does not bother with vegetables; meals are served with a choice of bread or potatoes. Unless you enjoy eating to the live accompaniment of a wannabe Julio Iglesias, don't dine here on Wednesday, Friday, or Saturday evenings.

## THE BEST KLOOF STREET CAFES

If you're looking for something light, stroll down Kloof Street, the road that runs parallel to Kloof Nek, which takes you up the saddle of the mountain and over into Camps Bay, and you'll be spoiled for choice. First off is **Café Paradiso** (☎ **021/423-8653,** 110 Kloof St.), a sprawling terra-cotta villa with Italian-style decor and Mediterranean-style food, near the top end of the Kloof Street strip. Head straight for the mezze buffet where your plate is weighed and you're charged accordingly, or try the chicken-breast salad (with cashew nuts, dried peaches, and a lightly curried mango dressing). A little farther south is ✪ **Melissa's** (☎ **021/424-5540,** 94 Kloof St.), serving the most irresistible cakes and fruit-filled tarts in town. Lunches, which usually consist of a choice of mouth-watering quiches, pasta, and salad, are also popular, so get here by noon if you want a table. With a large selection of magazines, this a perfect place to unwind if you're on your own. You won't be alone for long if you hang out at **Café Camissa's** (☎ **021/424 2289,** 80 Kloof St.), where cool bohemians play backgammon, eat hearty soups, and watch the Kloof Street traffic—this is one of the few places in town that's busy on Sunday nights, when live acts entertain. Adjacent is **Fields** (☎ **021/423-9587,** 84 Kloof St.), a health- and alternative-therapy shop which serves excellent vegetarian and vegan meals and freshly squeezed juices; unfortunately, like Melissa's it closes in the evenings between 7 and 8. Next up is ✪ **Café Dharma** (☎ **021/423-4233**), a great indoor-outdoor venue, dressed in heavy Balinese furniture, and highly recommended for dinner if you want to meet Cape Town's most happening, young (mid-20s and up) crowd. Farther down, close to where Kloof Street becomes Long Street, is ✪ **Café Bardeli** (☎ **021/423-444** in Darters Rd., just off Kloof St.). Situated in the building which houses the Longkloof studios in a large double-volume space, this trendy hangout attracts media types and models; but despite this, the atmosphere is relaxed, the food is good, and prices are low. Behind is **Cohibar** (☎ **021/424-1122**), a London-style cigar bar with leather horseshoe booths and a specialized air-conditioning system; get here early on weekends as members enjoy preferential entry when it's full. The ✪ **Long Street Café** (☎ **021/424-2464,** 259 Long St.) is within walking distance from here (Kloof merges with Long), and is in the heart of backpacker territory—at night, incidentally, this is where you'll find the most laid-back clubs in town.

## WATERFRONT

You'll find the best Waterfront restaurants (for a map, ask at one of the information desks in Victoria Wharf) in the 5-star hotels. **The Atlantic Grill Room** (☎ **021/406-5000,** Table Bay) is expensive, but executive chef Ian Mancais' international cuisine (he has worked in Asia, Polynesia, Indonesia, and France) is excellent, and there are some good modern Cape dishes as well. Try the wood-grilled Natal beef tenderloin with shallot and mustard cream; crayfish baked with salted capers, thyme, and truffle; or smoked barbecued duck with coriander, wrapped in rice paper, pan-fried and served with plum sauce and paw-paw confit. If the food doesn't win you over, there's always the enormous wine cellar and the spectacular view of Table Mountain.

Not to be outdone, **Quay West** (☎ **021/410-7100**) in the Cape Grace is almost totally surrounded by water, and offers tranquil views across the marina. The food is less fussy than the Atlantic Grill Room and the environment a lot more laid back—even children are made to feel welcome. Heart symbols alongside certain dishes indicate healthy choices; of these the smoked chicken, orange and ginger salad, and crisp linefish with sweet-and-sour citrus sauce are recommended.

**Tobago's** (☎ **021/418-5729,** Villa Via) in Granger Bay (adjacent to the Waterfront) has outdoor seating right on the water's edge. This spectacular luncheon setting nicely complements the Caribbean style fusion cuisine; recommended dishes include the crispy roast duck with dates and cherries, the sweet-potato lasagna with spinach and caramelized pumpkin, and the salmon caviar remoulade. **Hildebrand** (☎ **021/425-3385,** Pierhead), an elegant Italian restaurant, is also situated right on the water.

### The Thai Wars

A decade ago, most Capetonians believed that Eastern cuisine started with Chinese and ended with Indian, but all that changed when Larry Chung opened Sukothai, closely followed by Chaiporn Lekcharoensuk's Thaifoon. Competition has been fierce, and now a string of restaurants cater to the growing market. Both offer authentic, delicious Thai cuisine, so base your decision on location: **Sukothai** (☎ **021/423-4725,** 50 Orange St.) is in the Gardens, on the outskirts of town; **Thaifoon** (☎ **021/794-0022** at Groot Constantia Estate entrance) is in Constantia; **Yindee's** (☎ **021/422-1012**) is on the corner of Camp and Kloof streets, and the **Blue Plate** (☎ **021/424-1515**) is at 35 Kloof Street.

For a choice of Japanese, Vietnamese, Indonesian, Chinese, or Thai takeaway, try **The Happy Wok** (☎ **021/424-2423,** 62A Kloof St.). Chaiporn's latest venture, **Saigon** (☎ **021/424-2862**), at the corner of Nickle and Kloof streets, is strictly Vietnamese, and, with elevated views of the city and mountain, offers a romantic dining experience—don't miss the prawn mousse wrapped around sugarcane.

**Panama Jacks** (☎ **021/447-3992,** Quay 500) in the working harbor section—head for the Royal Cape Yacht Club and take the second road left—has no view or elegance, but serves superb, simple seafood dishes steamed, grilled, or flambéed; crayfish (lobster) is their specialty. The best seafood restaurant in the Victoria Wharf shopping center is **Willoughby & Co** (☎ **021/418-6116,** Lower Level, Victoria Wharf); but if you prefer your fish with seagulls wheeling overhead, stop at **Quay Four Tavern** (☎ **021/419-2008,** Quay Four, Pierhead), for their standard pub fare. Right on the water, this is one of the most popular watering holes in town and can become uncomfortably full. **Ferryman's** on East Pier Road (☎ **021/419-7748**) is less boisterous, and the perfect place to sample a fresh draught of Mitchells beer (the brewery is adjacent). **Morton's on the Wharf** (☎ **021/418-3633,** Upper Level, Victoria Wharf), an imitation French Quarter restaurant specializing in Cajun and Creole cooking, is another popular restaurant with good views of the harbor.

If you're simply looking for a break from shopping, you'll find it at **Caffe Balducci** (☎ **021/421 6002,** Quay 6, Victoria Wharf). With the exception of the carpaccio, the Italian/Californian–inspired food isn't that great, but the cappucinos, cakes, and atmosphere make up for it—this is the most elegant café in Cape Town, and the deep leather sofas provide the best people watching.

Vegetarians should head for **Violet on Rye** (☎ **021/21-5443,** Lower Level, Victoria Wharf), a casual cafe and health-food shop; try their butternut and lentil bobotie accompanied by a cool aloe shake. Families with young kids should look no further than the **Santa Ana Spur** (☎ **021/418-3620,** Upper Level, Victoria Wharf), which has a special kiddies' menu, balloons, and activity sheets, not to mention a variety of adult-size burgers, steaks, and ribs. Alternatively, a large and succulent flame-grilled peri-peri or lemon-and-herb chicken breast with chips will run you a mere R20 ($3.35) at **Nando's Tasca** (☎ **021/419-3009,** Piazza Level, Victoria Wharf), which also has excellent views of the harbor and mountain.

## SEA POINT & GREEN POINT

### EXPENSIVE

**San Marco.** 92 Main Rd., Sea Point. ☎ **021/439-2758.** Reservations essential. Main courses R40–110 ($6.65–$18.35). Wed–Mon dinner 7pm–10pm; Sun lunch 12–2:30pm. AE, DC, MC, V. ITALIAN.

Considered by many to be the best Italian restaurant in Cape Town, San Marco has remained unchanged for over 30 years. Dishes are classic Italian: tender calamari seasoned with garlic and chili, escalopes of veal served with capers and lemon, and homemade pastas served *al dente* with freshly herbed sauces. Service is pompous, but super-efficient, and the homemade ice creams and sorbets are out of this world. If San Marco is closed or full, try **La Perla** (☎ **021/434-2471,** Beach Rd.), another excellent Italian restaurant located in Sea Point.

### MODERATE

**Anatoli.** 25 Napier St., Green Point. ☎ **021/419-2501.** *Mezze* (appetizers) R9.65 ($1.60). Main courses R31 ($5). Tues–Sun 7:30–12pm. AE, DC, MC, V. TURKISH.

Housed in an old, gutted warehouse with exposed brickwork and Persian carpets creating a spacious yet warm environment, Anatoli has been serving up Cape Town's best Turkish mezze platter since 1986. With a mezze selection served with loaves of bread so freshly baked they're too hot to touch, most people can't be bothered to order from the main-course menu. Waiters carry the large trays over and describe the dishes, which include hot potato rolls made with cheese, egg, chili, parsley, and baked in phyllo; cold taboulleh made with cracked wheat, mint, tomato, and cucumber; and seriously good *dolmades* (stuffed grape leaves). The dessert tray is no less irresistible. In short, a great, informal atmosphere and relatively inexpensive fare.

### INEXPENSIVE

**Marios.** 89 Main Rd., Green Point. ☎ **021/439-6644.** Main courses R25–55 ($4.15–$9.15). Mon–Sat 12:30–3pm and 7pm–10:30pm. AE, DC, MC, V. ITALIAN.

Don't let the unprepossessing decor fool you; the kitchen serves authentic Italian cuisine, and there is a long list of Capetonian regulars to prove it. Mario passed away back in the early 1980s, but his widow Pina has single-handedly kept the family business growing, now ably assisted by her daughter Marlena. The menu features everything you'd expect from an Italian restaurant (pasta is homemade and delicious), but the specials—almost as numerous as the menu items—are what's really likely to get your mouth watering. Pheasant, guinea fowl, osso bucco—you name it, Pina cooks it.

## ATLANTIC SEABOARD

### MODERATE

✪ **Wharfside Grill.** The Harbour, Hout Bay. ☎ **021/790-2130.** Reservations recommended. Main courses R29–160 (4.85–$26.65). Daily 12–10pm. AE, DC, MC, V. SEAFOOD.

Situated above Mariner's Wharf, with uninterrupted views of the bay, this nautical-theme restaurant is unpretentious and serves seriously good seafood, despite the silly menu descriptions. A recommended starter is the snoek paté, while the linefish is their specialty—served with foamy lemon or garlic butter, it was probably swimming in the harbor a few hours ago. Other favorites include the butter-tender grilled squid steak, the shrimp, and the crayfish, done to a turn. Sirloin and a vegetarian dish are also available; but if seafood isn't your boat, don't drop anchor here.

## SOUTHERN SUBURBS

### VERY EXPENSIVE

✪ **Buitenverwachting.** Klein Constantia Rd., Constantia. ☎ **021/794-3522.** Reservations essential. Main courses R69–112 ($11.50–$18.65). Set-price lunch R105 ($17.50); set-price dinner R194 ($32.35). Tues–Fri 12–1:30pm; Tues–Sat 7–8:30pm. INTERNATIONAL/MODERN CAPE.

Like Uitsig, Buitenverwachting (meaning "above expectation") is situated on one of the historic Constantia wine farms; it is also consistently rated as one of South Africa's top restaurants. Choosing between this and Uitsig is difficult, though the fact that this is a slightly more formal experience may help you make up your mind. Austrian chef Edgar Osojnik experiments with Asian techniques and flavors; one popular starter is prawn wontons with chili-sesame dip. Main courses feature regional specialties like braised springbok or pan-fried rack of lamb. At lunch, choose between a three-course menu (smoked lamb filet on asparagus salad and gazpacho vinaigrette, braised *kalbs tafelspitz* [braised veal] with mushroom-potato puree, and iced chocolate mousse terrine with raspberries, for example) or a shortened version of the dinner a la carte.

**The Cape Malay Restaurant.** Cellars-Hohenhort, 93 Brommersvlei Rd., Constantia. ☎ **021/794-2137.** Set-price menu R105 (17.50) per person. Daily 7–10pm. AE, DC, MC, V. CAPE MALAY.

More of a fine-dining experience than the authentic Biesmiellah, the Cape Malay Restaurant features recipes created by Cas Abrahams, local Cape Malay guru. After snacking on *samoosas* and chili-bites, you are provided with appetizers including *waterblommetjiebredie* (waterlily stew), snoek soup, *smoor snoek* (a tomatoe-onion mixture), and pickled fish. Main courses range from chicken *breyani* (sweet curried rice) to the delicately flavored lamb known as *denningvleis.* Waiters are also on hand with explanations. Leave space for dessert; *boeber* (a spicy milk pudding with flaked almonds and sultanas) and *kolwadjib* (unbaked rice cakes) are recommended.

## EXPENSIVE

**Africa Café.** 213 Main Rd., Observatory. ☎ **021/447-9553.** Reservations essential in season (Dec–Feb). Set-price menu R70 ($11.65) per person. Mon–Sat 6:30–11pm. AE, DC, MC, V. AFRICAN.

Portia and Jason de Smidt serve traditional dishes from all over Africa—you're unlikely to find a better selection on the continent. Meals are brought to your table in bowls, all shared in the African tradition, and you can eat as much as you want. Popular dishes include the Malawi *mbatata* balls (sweet potato and cheese rolled in sesame seeds), Kenyan *irio* patties (potatoes, spinach, and peas), Ethiopian *zambossa* (spicy curried minced meat in pastry), Moroccan chicken-almond pies in phyllo pastry, and Senegaleze papaya (stuffed with sweet potato and potato wedges). Closer to home are the warm Xhosa potbread, made with corn, and the Botswana *seswaa* masala of lean lamb. Desserts are less traditional, but delicious; leave space for the Coupe Mount Kenya (sliced pineapple spiced with cinnamon and nutmeg and served with coconut ice cream), or the Coffee Bay mud pie, a moist chocolate pudding made with nuts.

**Au Jardin.** Vineyard Hotel, Newlands. ☎ **021/683-1520.** Main courses R50–68 ($8.35–$10.15). Tues–Fri, 12:15–2:30pm; Mon–Sat 7:15–9:30pm. AE, DC, MC, V. FRENCH.

In the "global village" syndrome that has resulted in many jacks-of-all-tastes and very few masters, chef/patron Christophe Dehosse's mastery of the cooking principles of one country is refreshing. The floor-to-ceiling view of the gardens and mountains and the good service are appealing, but it's dishes like deboned guineau fowl braised with lemon and thyme, slow-braised lamb shin with cracked peppers and capers, and cold smoked Norwegian salmon on hot potato with cream and chive sauce that have made regulars of local food editors and critics.

✪ **Constantia Uitsig.** Spaanschemat River Rd. ☎ **021/794-4480.** Reservations essential. Main courses R50–73 ($8.35–$12.10). Daily 7:30–9pm and Tues–Sun 12:30–2pm. ITALIAN/PROVENÇAL.

Constantia Uitsig, situated on the wine route of the same name, is regularly rated as one of South Africa's top-10 restaurants. It's hard not to gush over this combination of inspired cuisine and perfect mountain and vineyard views. Chef Frank Swainston changes his menu regularly, but with any luck you'll still find the fish carpaccio and avocado; the *bouchee de moules* (mussels in puff pastry in a spinach and saffron veloute); jointed wild duck with porcini mushrooms served with red wine and mashed potatoes; the slow-roasted rack of lamb; and the *trippa alla Florentina* (thinly sliced grilled venison with pesto, mushrooms, and parmesan). Swainston's *Marquise au Chocolat* is the most sinful dessert ever made.

✪ **Emily's.** 77 Roodebloem Rd., Woodstock. ☎ **021/448-2366.** Reservations recommended. Main courses R45–75 ($7.50–$12.50). Tues–Fri 12–3pm; Mon–Sat 7–11pm. AE, DC, MC, V. AFRO-EURO/MODERN CAPE.

Housed in an unassuming building in an unfashionable suburb, Peter Veldsman and Johan Odendaal refer to their food as "boere-nouvelle" and Emily's as "Cape Town's first Afro Euro Trash restaurant," which gives some idea of the humor prevalent in the decor (which is rather tacky), but not of the excellence of the food, which received a glowing report in the *New York Times* and is regularly sited in the top-10 restaurants by South African food critics. The menu changes constantly, but is always based on quality ingredients—fresh oysters flown in from Namibia, beef specially bred and matured in Kimberley, Northern Cape. Renowned for its baked mussels and oysters, fine pates, and terrines, Emily's is also one of the few places that serves marron (freshwater crayfish). There is a strong emphasis on African spices, with at least one traditional Malay-inspired spiced meat dish on the menu; as well as more European-inspired dishes such as boned chicken stuffed with boned quail and fine mousseline. Ask for a table upstairs with a view of the mountain.

**Novelli at The Cellars.** Cellars-Hohenhort Hotel, 93 Brommersvlei Rd., Constantia. ☎ **021/794-2137.** Main courses R50–64 ($8.35–$10.65) Noon–2pm and 7–9:30pm daily. AE, DC, MC, V. INTERNATIONAL/MODERN CAPE.

When Michelin-rated chef Jean-Christophe Novelli visited the first Cape Gourmet Festival, Liz McGrath persuaded him to take on her Cellars Restaurant, which he has done with great aplomb, installing his protégé, George Jardine, to take care of the day-to-day running. With the formal dining room spilling out onto the verandah and garden and great views of the densely wooded Constantiaberg, this is a great place to lunch. The small menu focuses on light dishes; and the prices, considering the venue, are reasonable. This changes in the evening, when the menu increases tenfold, and the costs seem more justified. Try home-smoked salmon with cardamom-infused orange dressing and herb salad; springbok and pan-roasted fillet of beef served with marrow bone and red-wine jus; or the offal platter, so well presented and flavored that even the uninitiated will forget what they're eating. The 46-page wine list devotes over a page to wines by the glass.

**Parks.** 114 Constantia Rd., Constantia. ☎ **021/797-8202.** Main courses R50–65 ($8.35–$10.85). Mon–Sat 7:30–9pm. AE, DC, MC, V. INTERNATIONAL.

Yet another fine-dining option in Constantia that regularly makes it onto the top-10 list of South African food critics. Hosts and owners Michael and Madeleine Olivier define their food as "classically based comfort food." Doing justice to this description are combinations like crayfish cakes in tempura batter with Thai dipping sauce, the signature duck confit with calvados and green peppercorn sauce, and tender springbok slices with red cabbage, beetroot, and polenta cake. No views, and a bit off the beaten track if you're staying in town, but well worth the effort.

## FALSE BAY

### EXPENSIVE

**Black Marlin.** Main Rd., Millers Point. ☎ **021/786-1621.** Main courses R37–120 ($6.15–$20). Daily 12–3:30pm, Fri–Sat 7–10pm. Closed for dinner in winter. AE, DC, MC, V. SEAFOOD.

Situated on the cliffs overlooking False Bay in what used to be a whaling station (the building dates back to 1814), this restaurant has one of the best sea views in the Cape. Its lies on the undeveloped coastal road that runs between Simon's Town and Cape Point, making it a very popular tourist stop—you won't get a lunch table during the summer season unless you've booked at least 4 days in advance. The coconut prawn tempura is often recommended, but it's dry and the delicate flavor of the prawn is overwhelmed by the coconut and beer batter. Recommended main courses include the kingklip on a spit (wrapped in bacon, the fish is grilled on a skewer and served with rice), the linefish with shrimp sauce, and the grilled sole, served with herb butter.

### MODERATE

**Brass Bell.** Railway station, Kalk Bay. ☎ **021/788-5455.** Main courses R37–105 ($6.15–$17.50). Daily 12–3pm; Mon–Sat 6–10:30pm. AE, DC, MC, V. SEAFOOD.

## The Best Sundown Bars & Restaurants

When the sun starts its slow descent into the ocean, you simply have to be on the Atlantic seaboard soaking up the last of its pink rays. Head over to Kloof Nek, and then turn right down Kloof Road for a meal at **The Roundhouse (☎ 021/438-2320)**, where the predominantly French cuisine (served by a bona fide French eccentric complete with poodles) is not as good as the view (exquisite) or the venue (a former hunting lodge). For a more informal experience, continue down Kloof Road, turn left onto Lower Kloof, and then turn right into Victoria for **La Med (☎ 021/438-5600,** The Glen Country Club, Victoria Rd., Clifton), a rather tacky indoor/outdoor cocktail bar with lawns that run into the rocks and ocean. Burgers, steaks, and seafood are available, as is live music on Wednesday, Friday, and Sunday. Moving south along Victoria Road into Camps Bay you'll find **The Sandbar (☎ 021/438-8336)**, a popular sidewalk bistro directly opposite the beach that serves a mean strawberry daquiri. For an even better view, keep going, passing the Bay Hotel. Adjacent is the Promenade Centre where the ever-popular Blues, Baraza, and Villamoura have the choicest positions on the Atlantic seaboard. The food at **Blues (☎ 021/438-2040)** is of intermittent quality, yet you need to book a dinner table days in advance during the summer months—proof that with a sublime location (not to mention waiters with good teeth) you can get away with anything. ✪ **Baraza (☎ 021/438-1758,** Victoria Road), finished in muted earth tones and furnished with comfortable sofas with a counter that runs the length of the window, is the most stylish bar on the sunset strip. Adjoining Baraza is **Villamoura (☎ 021/438-1850)**, which serves mainly Portuguese fare, though the baroque interior with Miro-style murals is anything but. Their seafood is recommended, but don't come here if you're watching your budget. A block farther on Victoria Road, at Brighton Court, is an Italian cafe/bar/restaurant that offers really good value for money. The place currently has no name (due to a legal wrangle), but everyone knows it as **Nino's (☎ 021/438-2923)**, owned by the same Nino from Greenmarket Square. A burger will set you back R20 ($3.35) and the highly recommended primavera pasta (spinach fried in parmesan and tossed with chopped fresh tomato and garlic), R27 ($4.50). The pizzas are also excellent. If Nino's is full, take a sidewalk table at laid-back **Café Le Mer (☎ 021/438-0156,** shop 3c, the Promenade, Victoria Rd.), which serves light meals all day, and well into the night.

Even Capetonians regularly travel from the city to sit and watch the waves crashing below while enjoying the relaxed atmosphere and classic seafood. Sipho's Pot (linefish, prawns, crayfish, calamari, and mussels served on linguine with a creamy tomato sauce), the homemade crayfish ravioli, and the mixed seafood platter are all good choices. There is live entertainment by local bands in the bar downstairs when fish braais are held over the weekend—and with the railway station directly behind, there's no need to drive here.

### THE BEST BREAKFAST SPOTS

If you're in town, browse through the market stalls at Greenmarket Square, heart of Cape Town since 1710, and then take a table overlooking the square at **Le Petit Paris (☎ 021/237-648)**, on the west corner of Burg Street, or a window seat at adjacent **Nino's (☎ 021/424-7466)**. For those who like their breakfast wrapped in a fresh flatbread, there's **Naked on the Square (☎ 021/424-2953)**.

Alternatively, head for the pedestrianized antique market in Church Street where **Café Mozart** (☎ **021/424-3774,** 37 Church St.) has been serving breakfasts to the strains of Mozart for a quarter of a century. When in the Waterfront, head for the terrace of the **Victoria & Alfred Hotel** (☎ **021/419-6677**) for a glorious view of Table Mountain. At the **New York Bagel** in Sea Point (☎ **021/439-7523,** 51 Regent Rd.), you can watch the chefs prepare your breakfast in front of you (try the crispy rosti topped with salmon and cream cheese). Take the scenic train journey between Cape Town and Simon's Town in **Biggsy's Restaurant Carriage** (☎ **021/449-3870**), and enjoy the passing views of the coast over a cooked breakfast. Biggsy's operates five return trips daily; the trip takes approximately 2½ hours (see "Getting Around").

It means an early wake-up call, but breakfast at the **Two Oceans Restaurant** (☎ **021/780-9200**) in Cape Point and you'll be rewarded with sparkling air and a most magnificent view—the breathtaking sweep of False Bay embraced by mountains. Closer to home (a 5-minute drive from town) is the **Rhodes Memorial Tea Garden** (☎ **021/689-9151,** see below), situated on the slopes of Table Mountain, with views that stretch all the way to the Hottentots' Holland Mountains; this is a great place to orient yourself.

### PICNIC FARE

Table Mountain is one big garden, and its "tabletop" makes a great picnic venue, as does Kirstenbosch, particularly during the summer when sunset concerts are held every Sunday from December to March. **Melissa's** (☎ **021/424-5540;** 94 Kloof St.) has a good deli, as does **Carlucci** (☎ **021/450-795,** 22 Upper Orange) in Oranjezicht; but if you want the best range of delicacies in the Cape, it's worth detouring to Green Point to visit **Giovanni's** (☎ **021/434-6893,** 103 Main Rd.), home of the best cappuccino in town. A close contender, and ideal if you're in the Constantia area is the **Old Cape Farm Store** (☎ **021/794-7062,** Groot Constantia Rd., at the turnoff to Groot Constantia Estate).

Great Winelands options include **Spier** (☎ **021/881-3096**), on the way to Stellenbosch (see "Winelands") where you can either purchase a prepacked hamper or assemble your picnic from the resident deli, and then choose your spot beside the dam and feed the ducks. Le Pique Nique (☎ **021/870-4274**), at **Boschendal** (see below) between Stellenbosch and Franschhoek, will supply you with a hamper filled with local delicacies and set up tables and chairs on their shaded lawns.

## 5 Exploring Cape Town

## Suggested Itineraries

### If You Have 1 Day

Take a leisurely drive to Kirstenbosch Gardens (consider having breakfast at Rhodes Memorial Tea Garden) and spend an hour strolling through the unique flora of the region. Book lunch at one of the recommended restaurants in the Constantia area, the closest wine-producing area to town. Spend the afternoon driving the False Bay Coast, bypassing the turnoff to the Cape of Good Hope Nature Reserve (if you wish to enter here, leave Kirstenbosch off your itinerary) and heading back to town along the spectacular Chapman's Peak Drive during the evening. Time allowing, drive along Signal Hill for an elevated view of the twinkling city before or after dining somewhere in Kloof Street.

# Cape Town Attractions

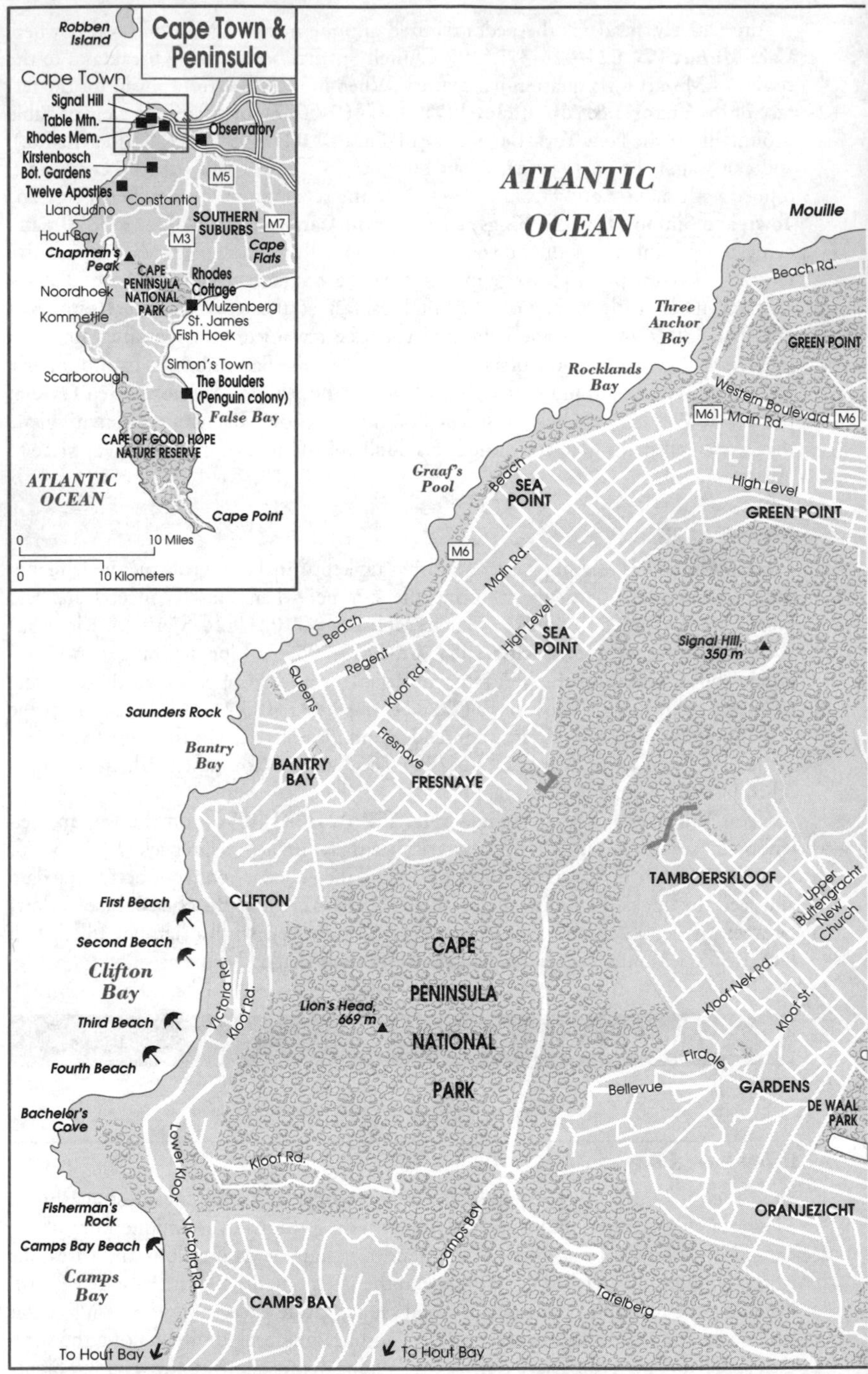

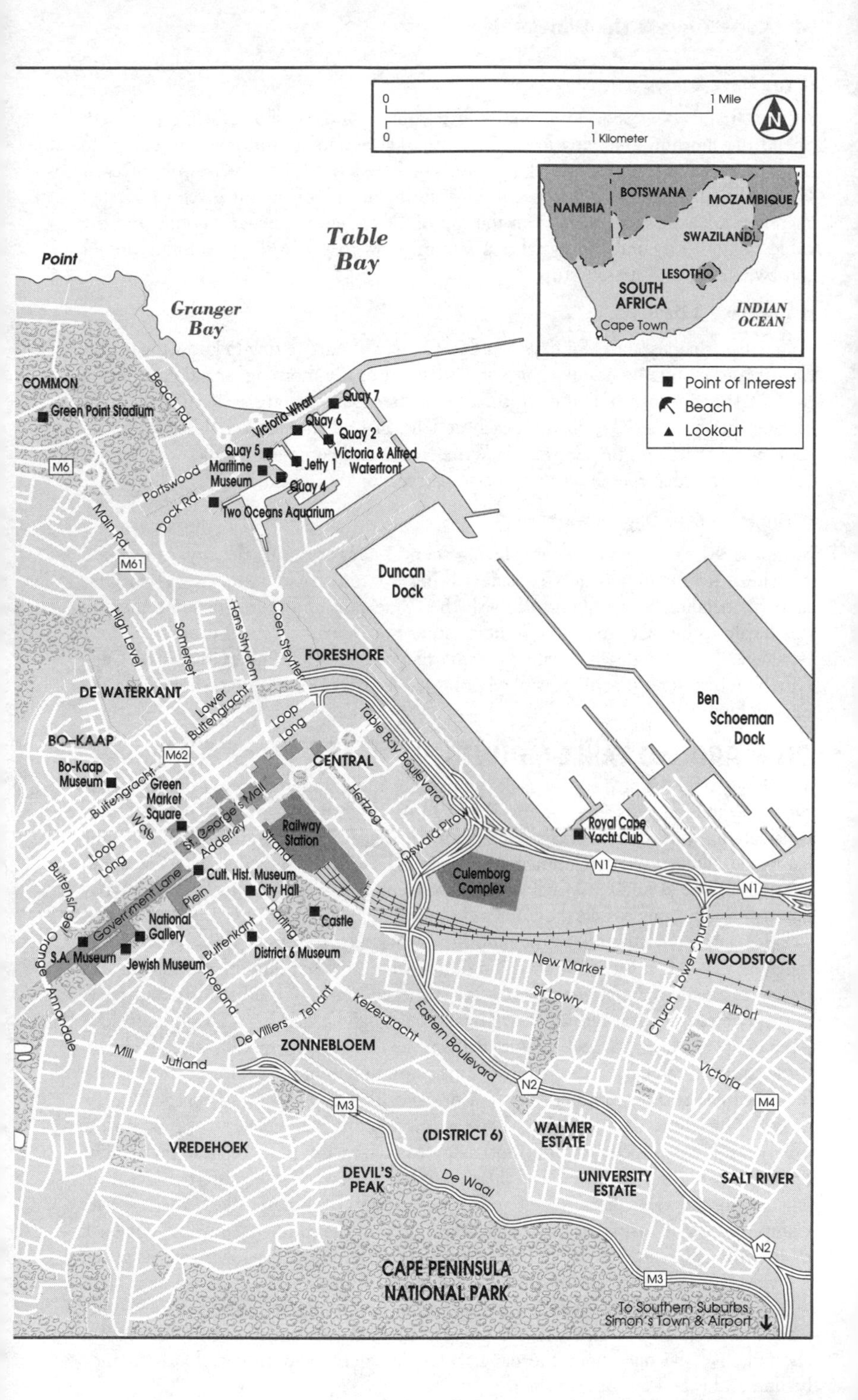

0
1 Mile
0
1 Kilometer
N
NAMIBIA
BOTSWANA
MOZAMBIQUE
SWAZILAND
LESOTHO
SOUTH AFRICA
Cape Town
INDIAN OCEAN
Point of Interest
Beach
Lookout
Table Bay
Point
Granger Bay
COMMON
Green Point Stadium
Beach Rd.
Victoria Wharf
Quay 7
Quay 6
Quay 2
Quay 5
Victoria & Alfred Waterfront
Maritime Museum
Jetty 1
Quay 4
Portswood
Dock Rd.
Two Oceans Aquarium
M6
Main Rd.
M61
Duncan Dock
High Level
Somerset
Hans Strydom
Coen Steytler
FORESHORE
DE WATERKANT
Lower Buitengracht
Loop
Long
Table Bay Boulevard
Ben Schoeman Dock
BO-KAAP
M62
CENTRAL
Bo-Kaap Museum
Green Market Square
Buitengracht
Wale
St. George's Mall
Adderley
Railway Station
Strand
Hertzog
Oswald Pirow
Royal Cape Yacht Club
N1
Loop
Long
Buitensingel
Cult. Hist. Museum
City Hall
Culemborg Complex
Government Lane
Plein
Darling
Castle
National Gallery
Buitenkant
Lower Church
S.A. Museum
Jewish Museum
District 6 Museum
WOODSTOCK
Orange
Roeland
New Market
Annandale
Sir Lowry
Albert
Tenant
Keizergracht
Church
De Villiers
Eastern Boulevard
ZONNEBLOEM
Mill
Jutland
Victoria
N2
M3
M4
(DISTRICT 6)
WALMER ESTATE
VREDEHOEK
DEVIL'S PEAK
De Waal
UNIVERSITY ESTATE
SALT RIVER
CAPE PENINSULA NATIONAL PARK
To Southern Suburbs, Simon's Town & Airport

### If You Have 2 Days

As your first day (see above) was pretty busy, your second day should be more relaxed: Spend the morning shopping in the Greenmarket Square area in town, or complete sections of the suggested city walking tour. Purchase a bottle of wine from Enoteca at Heritage Square (where you may consider dining at one of the three venues located there) to toast the sunset seen from the top of Table Mountain—afternoons find the cable car less busy and it only takes a few minutes to get to the top. Enjoy dinner somewhere on the "sunset" strip.

### If You Have 3 Days

Follow the itinerary above for days 1 and 2. On day 3, start getting to know the Cape's history and culture by heading for Robben Island in the morning, and then taking a tour of the Bo-Kaap and townships in the afternoon. Alternatively, if the sun is blazing, get acquainted with the beach at Clifton or Llandudno. If it's raining, do some wine tasting on the Constantia Wine Route and complete the day with a meal at a restaurant that specializes in modern or traditional Cape cuisine.

### If You Have Four Days or More

Spend days 1 through 3 as above. Having spent 3 days exploring the city, you should now head for the hinterland—consider taking the four passes route (see "Two Dramatic Winelands Drives," below) to visit the Winelands and overnight somewhere in this fertile region. Create a wine route to suit your interests, but make sure you visit Boschendal or Vergelegen Estate to acquaint yourself with fine examples of Cape Dutch architecture. If at all possible, book a table at La Petite Ferme overlooking the Franschhoek Valley.

## ON & AROUND TABLE MOUNTAIN

This huge, time-sculpted slab of shale, sandstone, and granite that rose from the ocean some 250 million years ago, is Cape Town's most instantly recognizable feature. Under consideration for World Heritage Site status, the flat-topped mountain dominates the landscape, climate, and development of the city at its feet, and provides Cape Town with a 6,000-hectare (15,000-acre) wilderness at its center. The best view is from Table Bay (another good reason to take the Robben Island tour, see below) from where you can get some idea of the relative size of the mountain—it can be seen from 150 kilometers (93 miles) at sea. But other views of the mountain are no less beautiful, particularly the wooded **Constantiaberg,** which greets the sun every morning, and the bare buttresses of the **Twelve Apostles,** who are kissed by its last rays. The fact that the mountain alone has more plant varieties than the entire British Isles (some 1,470 species) is flaunted with pride, and it is thought to be the most climbed mountain in the world.

You can ascend the mountain on foot or via cable car, and once there, spend a few hours or an entire day exploring. The narrow table is 3 kilometers long (almost 2 miles), and 1,086-meter (3,562-foot) **Maclear's Beacon** is its highest point. The upper cable station and the Dizzy Dassie restaurant are on the western edge, from which you can view the series of peaks named the Twelve Apostles towering over Camps Bay. Walk eastward, and you'll have a view of the southern suburbs. The back table, with its forests, fynbos, and the reservoirs that supply Cape Town with its water, is a wonderful place to hike, but much of it is off limits.

You will not see many black people ascending the mountain; besides being somewhat inaccessible to residents of the poverty-stricken townships, legends and myths abound, like the one about the dangerous lake snake who creates clouds to hide behind and is best left undisturbed.

## Ascending the Mountain

### ✪ By Cable Car

One of the best ways to experience the mountain is the ascent by cable car. Cars depart every 15 minutes from the lower station (☎ **021/424-5148,** Tafelberg Rd.) daily (weather permitting) from May to November 8:30am to 6pm; and December to April 8am to 10pm. The cost is R60 ($10) return; R32 ($5.35) children 4 to 16. Operating since 1929 but upgraded in 1997, the cable car has a floor that rotates 360 degrees, giving everyone a chance to gape at the breath-taking views during the 4-minute journey up. The upgrade has meant that queues are now much shorter. Even during the busiest months of November to April, the longest you'll wait is 30 minutes. Afternoons are generally less crowded.

### On Foot

The most commonly used route to the top is via **Platteklip Gorge**—the gap is visible from the front, or northface of the mountain. The route starts just east of the lower cable station (see below) and will take 2 to 3 strenuous hours. Make sure to bring water. A more scenic route starts at the Kirstenbosch Botanical Gardens and climbs up the back via **Skeleton Gorge.** It's steep, requiring reasonable fitness, but should take approximately 2 hours to the summit. Rather than walk another hour to the upper cable station, most return by walking down via **Nursery Ravine.** With a choice of over 300 footpaths, the serious hiker might consider consulting one of the many books on the subject: *A Walking Guide for Table Mountain* by Shirley Brossy is recommended. Be aware that the mountain's mercurial weather can surprise even seasoned Capetonians—don't climb alone, stick to the paths, and take water and warm clothes. For guided hikes, contact **Table Mountain Walks** (☎ **021/715-6136**).

### Quick Fix: Driving Up Signal Hill

If you don't have the time or inclination to ascend Table Mountain, drive to the roundabout (traffic circle) at the top of Kloof Nek and take the road right, which climbs the slopes of Lion's Head and Signal Hill. You'll pass one of the domed *kramats* (tomb) of the Muslim holy men which encircle the city and are believed to have protective powers. From the **Signal Hill** parking lot, you can see the sun set over the Atlantic, and when you drive back at night you'll have a magnificent view of Cape Town glittering like a jeweled necklace around Table Mountain. (Please note that you should be careful when visiting Signal Hill after dark. Recently an increase in crime has been reported here.) Drive back to the Kloof Nek roundabout to the start of

### A Devil of a Wind

Legend has it that the "tablecloth," the white cloud that tumbles over Table Mountain, is the work of retired pirate Van Hunks, who liked nothing more than to climb Devil's Peak and smoke his pipe while overlooking Cape Town. One day the devil, not happy that someone was puffing on his patch, challenged him to a smoking contest. Needless to say the competition continues to rage unabated, particularly in the summer months. The downside of this magnificent spectacle is that hurricane-force winds will simultaneously whip around Devil's Peak and rip into the city at speeds of up to 150 kilometers (93 miles) an hour. The "Cape Doctor," as the southeaster is often called, is said to clear the city of pollution, germs, and litter; but most just wish Van Hunks would give it up and stop infuriating the devil. For sanity's sake, head for the Atlantic seaboard, where the most protected beach is Clifton. Alternatively, escape to the Winelands, or visit in March and April, when the wind dies away completely.

**Beware the Giant Hamsters**

On a visit to Table Mountain, you will certainly encounter the **dassie,** or rock hyrax, on the summit. These large, furry, rodent-like animals are (despite appearances) related to elephants; and while they are relatively tame, they do bite.

**Tafelberg Road,** which traverses the length of Table Mountain, for more beautiful views of the twinkling city.

### On the Mountain Slopes

✪ **Kirstenbosch Botanical Gardens.** Rhodes Ave. (off the M5), Newlands. ☎ **021/ 762-9120,** or 021/761-4916 on weekends. www.nbi.ac.za. Daily Sep–Mar 8am–7pm; Apr–Aug 8am–6pm. Conservatory daily 11am–4pm. R10 ($1.65) adults; R5 (85¢) children 6–18. Concerts R30 ($5); R10 ($1.65) children. **Tours:** Guided garden walks are offered every Tues and Sat at 11. More specialized tours can be arranged by appointment for a minimum of four people at R20 ($3.35) per person. Golf cart tours (R12/$2) for the elderly or handicapped are often booked well in advance. To check availability of all tours, call ☎ **021/761-4916.**

Situated on the eastern slopes of Table Mountain, Kirstenbosch is called one of the most beautiful gardens in the world, and is the third-most visited attraction in Cape Town; its shaded lawns and gurgling springs, the perfect antidote to the searing summer heat. With the cultivated sections seamlessly blending into the adjoining nature reserve, some 8,000 of South Africa's 22,000 plant species (including a giant baobab) grow here. There are a number of themed walks and areas; as an introduction to the indigenous flora, the fynbos walk is recommended. The interactive Braille-labeled route, which features plants with fragrance and texture, is also worth experiencing. Of historic interest are the remains of the wild almond hedge that Jan Van Riebeeck planted in 1660 to demarcate the colony from the Khoi. Large sandstone carvings from Zimbabwe are often exhibited in the gardens, and **concerts** are held December to March (for details call ☎ **021/ 761-4916**). The **restaurant** (☎ **021/ 797-7614**) at the gardens is open for breakfast, teas, and lunches; the food isn't bad, and it's a good value, but for great views, stop at the Rhodes Memorial Tea Garden, closer to town.

**Rhodes Memorial.** Off the M5 (De Waal Dr.), Groote Schuur Estate (sign-posted turnoff just after the University of Cape Town). No phone or admission charge. Open 24 hours.

Rhodes Memorial was erected in honor of Cecil Rhodes, the man who, incidentally, donated the land for Kirstenbosch Gardens in 1902. Rhodes made his fortune in the Kimberley diamond mines and became prime minister of the Cape in 1890. A true British imperialist, he "owned" Zimbabwe (previously known as Rhodesia) and it was his life-long dream to see a Cape-to-Cairo railway line built so that the "sun would never set on the British Empire." The memorial (which you can reach by heading back to town on the M3 and taking the Rhodes Memorial turnoff) is an imposing granite staircase flanked by lions and overlooking the Cape Flats and Table Bay. In one of the Cape's most bizarre juxtapositions, herds of wildebeest and zebra graze on the slopes around the memorial, oblivious to rubberneckers driving the M3 below.

The **Rhodes Memorial Tea Garden** (☎ **021/689-9151**), located behind the Rhodes Memorial, is one of the best places to breakfast in the Cape: The food is good, and the views are unbeatable.

## ATTRACTIONS IN THE CITY BOWL

A combination of Cape Dutch, Georgian, Victorian, and 20th century architecture, this is South Africa's oldest and most pleasant city center. The major axis is **Adderley**

**Street,** which runs past the railway station, cutting the city in half. East of Adderley is the **Castle of Good Hope, Grand Parade,** and **City Hall;** west are the more charming shopping areas of which **Long Street** and **St George's Mall** (a pedestrian street), both of which run parallel to Adderley, are the best. **Greenmarket Square** lies between these two streets and Long- and Shortmarket streets. South of Adderley Street (where it takes a right turn and melds with Wale St.) lie the **Company Gardens,** where most of the museums are situated. As the city is small, the best way to get to know is it is on foot (see the "Walking Tour" later in the chapter.)

**Castle of Good Hope.** Corner of Buitenkant and Strand sts. ☎ **021/469-1249.** Mon–Sat 9am–4pm. William Fehr: Mon–Sat 9:30am–4pm. R12 ($2) adults; R5 (85¢) children and seniors.

Built between 1666 and 1679 on the site of Van Riebeeck's original fort, the castle—really a pentagonal fortress typical of the Dutch defense system adopted in the early 17th century—marks the original shoreline which ran the length of Strand Street (*strand* means beach). The long-serving Castle still serves as the regional headquarters of the South African Defence Force, though the most invasive force it's ever dealt with are the tourists ambling through its ramparts and dungeons. There are 30-minute tours departing at 11am, noon, and 2pm, but you're welcome to purchase a map and explore on your own.

Get here at 10am sharp if you want to view the official opening of the castle, called the Key Ceremony, or at 12pm for the Changing of the Guard (Monday through Friday only). You can give the **Military Museum** a miss, but do visit the **William Fehr Collection,** housed in the old governor's residence. An arch-conservationist, Dr. Fehr (1892–1968) collected paintings and graphics which provide some insight into the early colonists and how they were to change the face of the Cape completely. Thomas Baine's painting, *The Greatest Hunt in Africa,* depicts the slaughter of 30,000 animals in honor of the visiting Prince Alfred. (If the collection intrigues you, you can view the bulk of it at **Rust-en-Vreugd,** a pretty, pink 18th-century town house at 78 Buitenkant St.) Contemporary exhibitions are also occasionally held; check the newspaper for details.

An alternative way to experience the Castle is at night: "Ghosts of the Castle" combines a three-course dinner and cabaret-style show celebrating South Africa's cultural past. For those interested, a tour is included in the price. For tickets (R125/$20.85 per person), call ☎ **021/421-1878.**

**South African Cultural History Museum.** 49 Adderley St. ☎ **021/461-8280.** Mon–Sat 9:30am–4:30pm. R5 (85¢); R1 (15¢) children 7–16.

The museum concentrates on the lives of the early Cape colonists, using various artifacts from the 17th, 18th, and 19th centuries, and various drawings and photographs that give visitors an idea of what Cape Town looked like before the land reclamation project and development of the mountain's slopes. One of the most interesting collections is the inscribed "post office stones" under which passing ships would leave their mail. Many of the rooms also house uninspiring and seemingly irrelevant collections of Roman, Egyptian, Greek, and Asian artifacts.

## The Name Game

**Adderley Street** was the name given to the Cape's principal trading street by the grateful Cape colonists after Charles Adderley, a member of the British House of Commons, helped dissuade the British government from dumping their convicts in the Cape. (You will not, of course, find an Adderley Street in Australia.)

**South African National Gallery.** Government Ave. ☎ **021/465-1628.** Tues–Sun 10am–5pm. Free admission.

This small gallery, started with an initial donation by Victorian randlord Sir Abe Bailey, has room to exhibit only 5 to 8% of its collection of over 8,000 artworks. Despite this, and despite a lack of funding, it is considered by many to be the country's premier art museum. Under the expert guidance of Marilyn Martin, the gallery has collected certain works neglected by other South African galleries, including rare examples of what used to be considered handicrafts rather than art, such as beadwork and *knopkierries* (fighting sticks). The gallery also often hosts excellent traveling exhibitions featuring internationally renowned names.

**South African Museum and Planetarium.** Between Government Ave. and Queen Victoria St. ☎ **021/424-3330.** Mon–Sat 10am–5pm. R5 (85¢) adults; children free. Planetarium show daily 1pm. R7 ($1.15) adults (R10/$1.65 combined with museum); ages 3–16 R5 (85¢). Children's show Sat–Sun 12pm.

Founded in 1825, South Africa's oldest museum has some rather old-fashioned views: The display of life-size indigenous people in a natural history museum is an embarrassing faux pas, suggesting as it does that they are part of the animal world. That said, the ethnographic displays are excellent, with displays on traditional medicine, the use of wood (used to tell the time), and African mathematics and alphabetic symbols. The fossil gallery provides valuable insights if you intend moving on to the Karoo, and the Lydenburg heads, which date back to circa A.D.500, are some of the earliest examples of African art. The four-story whale well, hung with two whale skeletons, is another highlight, while the stuffed *quagga* (see below) foal is simply macabre. If possible, plan your visit to coincide with a show next door at the Planetarium; shows change regularly, but with any luck the popular "Astronomy of the Great Pyramids" will be on. "The Sky Tonight," held over weekends, introduces and updates the current constellation in the southern skies.

## VISITING CAPE MUSLIM SIGHTS

On the slopes of Signal Hill—the arm that stretches out of Table Mountain to overlook the city and harbor—is the suburb of **Bo-Kaap.** Home to a section of the Cape's Muslim community (often referred to as Cape Malays despite the fact that only 1% of their forefathers, skilled slaves imported by the Dutch, were born in Malaysia), this is one of the city's oldest and most interesting areas. Narrow, cobbled streets lead past colorful 19th century Dutch and Georgian terraces and quaint mosques; try to visit at sunrise and sunset when the air is filled with the song of the imams in their minarets, calling the community to prayer.

Start at the **Bo-Kaap Museum,** at 71 Wale St. (☎ **021/424-3846**), open Monday to Saturday 9:30am to 4:30pm; R3 (50¢) adults; R1 (15¢) children. The museum gives some idea of the furnishings of a relatively wealthy 19th century Cape Muslim family. The museum also houses exhibits relating to the local brand of Islam. One block south at Dorp Street is **Auwal,** South Africa's oldest mosque, dating back to 1795, and said to be where Afrikaans was first taught.

The protected **historic core** of the Bo-Kaap ranges from Dorp to Strand Street, and between Buitengracht and Pentz streets. You can drive these streets, but they are narrow and full of people—the best way to experience them is on foot, with a local guide. Try **Tana-Baru Tours** (☎ **021/424-0719**), a 2-hour tour which ends with tea and traditional Malay cake at a private home (R50/$8.35 per person).

Alternatively, head up steep Longmarket for tea and traditional *melktert* (milktart) at the **Noon Gun Tea Room and Restaurant** (☎ **021/424-0529,** 273 Longmarket St., Bo-Kaap). The name "Noon Gun" derives from the Signal Hill cannon fired by the South African Navy daily at noon—a tradition that has informed Capetonians of their imminent lunch break since 1806. The tea room features magnificent views of the city and mountain, and serves authentic Cape Malay fare.

The charm of the Bo-Kaap provides some measure of what was lost when **District Six** was razed; opposite the Bo-Kaap, and clearly visible from any raised point, this vacant land is located on the city's southern border. When bulldozers moved in to flatten the suburb in 1966, an estimated 60,000 Cape Muslims (then referred to as coloured) were living in what was condemned a ghetto by the apartheid hardliners. Much like Sophiatown in Johannesburg, District Six housed people from every walk of life—musicians, traders, teachers, craftsmen, *skollies* (petty criminals), hookers, and pimps—and was one of South Africa's most inspired and creative communities, producing potent poets, jazz musicians, and writers. The community was relocated piecemeal to the Cape Flats—a name that accurately describes both the geography and psychology of the area.

Renamed Zonnebloem (sunflower), the District Six area has remained vacant, as even hardened capitalists have spurned development in protest. Many believe that Cape Town's current gangster problems, spawned in the fragmented, angered, and powerless Cape Flats communities, are the price the city has had to pay. Most hope that by returning the land to the original families, the damage done to the national psyche can be reversed. Until then, the scar on the cityscape is a constant reminder.

To better understand this loss, it's worth visiting the **District Six Museum** at 25a Buitenkant St., open Monday to Saturday from 10am to 4:30pm (by donation). In addition to the photographs that go some way toward capturing the energy of its streetlife, the entire suburb has been mapped on the floor, which ex-residents have poignantly re-inhabited by scrawling both names and memories.

For tours that cover both these areas, as well as the Cape Flats and townships, contact **Grassroots** (☎ **021/424-8480**) or **Legend Tours** (☎ **021/697-4056**).

## ATTRACTIONS AT THE V&A WATERFRONT

Redevelopment of this historic core started in the early 1990s, and within a few years the Waterfront had become Cape Town's most fashionable place to eat, drink, and shop. Views of Table Mountain and the working harbor, as well as numerous restored national monuments and a wide array of entertainment options, attract an estimated 20 million visitors a year. It has been cited as the best of its kind, successfully integrating a top tourist attraction with southern Africa's principal passenger and freight harbor. The smells of diesel and fish mingle with the aromas wafting from pavement bistros, tugboats mingle with catamarans, and tourists mingle with, well, tourists. (If you're seeking tattooed sailors and ladies of dubious repute, you'd be better off taking a drive down to Duncan Dock, where the large working ships dock.)

A rather sanitized place (the enclosed shopping center could be in any large city), the Waterfront's **240 stores** are open until 9pm daily, and there is a choice of over **60 restaurants,** as well as **17 movie screens** (☎ **021/418-2369;** for **IMAX,** which shows predominantly wildlife movies, call ☎ **021/430-8025**). Other attractions include the **Scratch Patch,** a toddler's paradise filled with semi-precious stones (☎ **021/419-9429**); the **Telkom Exploratorium** (☎ **021/419-5957**), which makes the science of telecommunications fun; **Cyberworld 3D Simulated Tours,** ideal for cyberspace cadettes; and **The Maritime Museum** (☎ **021/419-2505**), a rather dry exhibition consisting mostly of model ships. For a small additional fee, you can board its floating exhibit: the **S.A.S. Somerset,** the only surviving boom-defense vessel in the world.

There are often live performances at the **Amphitheatre** and the Waterfront's walkways are abuzz with special events during school holidays when children's entertainment steps up—to find out what's on and pick up a map, visit the **Visitor's Centre** (☎ **021/418-2369**), on Dock Road, or one of the information kiosks in the Victoria Wharf shopping center. Both are open from 9am to 6pm. For recommended restaurants and cafes, see "Where to Dine" above.

If you do only two things in the Waterfront, book a **boat trip,** preferably to Robben Island, and visit the **Two Oceans Aquarium.** Most boats and cruises (see "Organized Cruises and Tours" below) take off from Quay 4 and 5, and you can catch the Penny Ferry rowing boat or a Waterfront taxi from the Pierhead Jetty (close to the Alfred Mall and Hildebrand Restaurant) to the aquarium and Robben Island departure point.

✪ **Robben Island Museum.** Tickets and departure from the Clocktower Terminal, adjoining Bertie's Landing. ☎ **021/419-2875** or 021/419-1300. Tours at 10am, 12pm, 2pm, daily. Sat and Sun 4pm. R100 ($16.65) adults; children 4–14 R50 ($8.35).

Only tour groups organized by the Department of Arts, which manages the Robben Island Museum (encompassing the entire island), are allowed to land on the island. Access to the island is limited, and visitors are transported via the *Makana* or the *Autshumato,* luxury high-speed catamarans that take approximately 25 minutes. (Note that the views of Table Mountain and Cape Town as you pull out of the harbor are fantastic—don't forget your camera.) The tour's highlight is the prison where you can view the tiny cell in which Mandela spent most of his 27 years of imprisonment. To make the experience even more poignant, an ex-political prisoner conducts the tour, giving a first-hand account of what it was like to live here. Bus tours of the island provide passing glimpses of the lepers' church and graveyard, PAC-leader Robert Sobukwe's house, and the wardens' village; visitors are then allowed to explore the lime quarry on foot (take sunglasses—the brightness ruined many inmates' and wardens' eyes). Final stops take in Robben Island's wildlife and World War II artillery sites. Tours take 2½ hours and can feel very restricted—during the peak summer season, it's definitely worth looking into one of the museum's special-interest tours, which include seeing the island on mountain bike, birdwatching and the historic village tours. The latter is highly recommended: A fascinating counterpoint to the more publicized prison, the village seems stuck in time, its deserted streets and low fences conjuring up the nostalgic 1950s. To get a real feel for the village (not to mention the most spectacular sunset view of Table Mountain), it's worth spending the night in one of the old wardens' cottages. Contact **Ester Henderson** at ☎ **021/411-1006** or send a fax (021/411-1283) with your expected date and number of people and whether you'll need catering; don't expect any luxuries and take your own picnic hamper with bottled water.

✪ **Two Oceans Aquarium.** Between New Basin and Dock Rd. ☎ **021/418-3823.** Daily 9:30am–6pm. R30 ($5) adults; R16 ($2.65) ages 4–17.

This is by far the most exciting attraction at the Waterfront itself. From the brightly hued fish found on coral reefs to exhilarating encounters with the great white sharks, over 3,000 live specimens are literally millimeters from your nose. Besides the Indian and Atlantic underwater tanks displaying the bizarre and beautiful, there are a number of well-simulated environments including tidal pools, a river ecosystem, and the magnificent Kelp Forest tank. The walk through the aquarium (30 to 90 minutes, depending on how long you linger) ends with an awesome display on deep-sea predators. The aquarium is particularly delightful for children, with child-height window benches throughout and a "touch pool" where they can touch kelp, shells, and anemones under the guidance of trained staff. Special activities for qualified divers include diving with the sharks (10am, 12pm, and 2pm daily) and feeding the Kelp Forest fish by hand.

## Island of Tears

The remarkably varied history of Robben Island goes back some 400 years. It has served variously as a post office, a fishing base, a whaling station, a hospital, a mental asylum, a military base, and—most infamously—as a penal colony, for which it was dubbed "South Africa's Alcatraz." The banished have included Angolan and West African slaves, princes from the East, South African chiefs, lepers, the mentally insane, and most recently, opponents of the apartheid regime. But all that changed on September 24, 1997, when the Robben Island Museum was officially opened by its most famous political prisoner.

In Mandela's words, "Few occasions could illuminate so sharply the changes of recent years; fewer still could bring to sharp focus the challenges ahead." Rising to this challenge is an eclectic complement of staff—artists, historians, environmentalists, ex-political prisoners, and ex-wardens. It's hard to imagine how a group of people with such diverse backgrounds and ideologies could work together, but it seems anything is possible once you've established common ground; in this case, the 586 hectares (1,465 acres) of Robben Island.

Patrick Matanjana, one of the prison tour guides, spent 20 years behind bars on the island. In recent months, he's spent time at Robben Island's bar, fraternizing with the very people who upheld the system he was trying to sabotage. "They know me; they respect me," he says when asked what it's like to sit and drink with former enemies. "We are trying to correct a great wrong. They also buy the drinks," he grins. The island's ironies don't end here. Even the bar, the Alpha 1 Officer's Club, has historic significance: This is where Patrick's latrine bucket would have been emptied in the 1960s and 1970s, before the prisoners had access to toilets (not to mention beds, hot water, or adequate nutrition).

Despite the radical changes, the remaining ex-wardens, now mostly in charge of island security, do not want to leave. "You cry twice on Robben Island," explains skipper Jan Moolman, who first stepped onto the island in 1963 as one of PAC-leader Robert Subukwe's personal wardens. "The day you arrive, and the day you have to leave."

For the many daytrippers, all it takes is the sight of Mandela's cell.

# Walking Tour—City Bowl Highlights

**Start:** Castle of Good Hope

**Finish:** Mount Nelson

**Time:** If you include visits to the major sights, this walking tour will take up most of the day, with no stops it should take about 3 hours. Tailor it to suit your interests and/or time constraints, or follow the shortened version suggested below.

**Best Times:** During the day, Mondays to Fridays, when there are plenty of people around and the museums and shops are open.

**Worst Times:** After 5pm on weekdays, Saturday afternoons, and Sundays, when much of town is deserted.

Kick off by visiting the oldest surviving building in South Africa, the:

1. **Castle of Good Hope.** You can park your car directly opposite, in the **Grand Parade,** where the residents of District Six used to trade. This is where Nelson Mandela greeted a crowd 100,000 strong with the words, "Amandla! Iafrika!

# Walking Tour—City Bowl Highlights

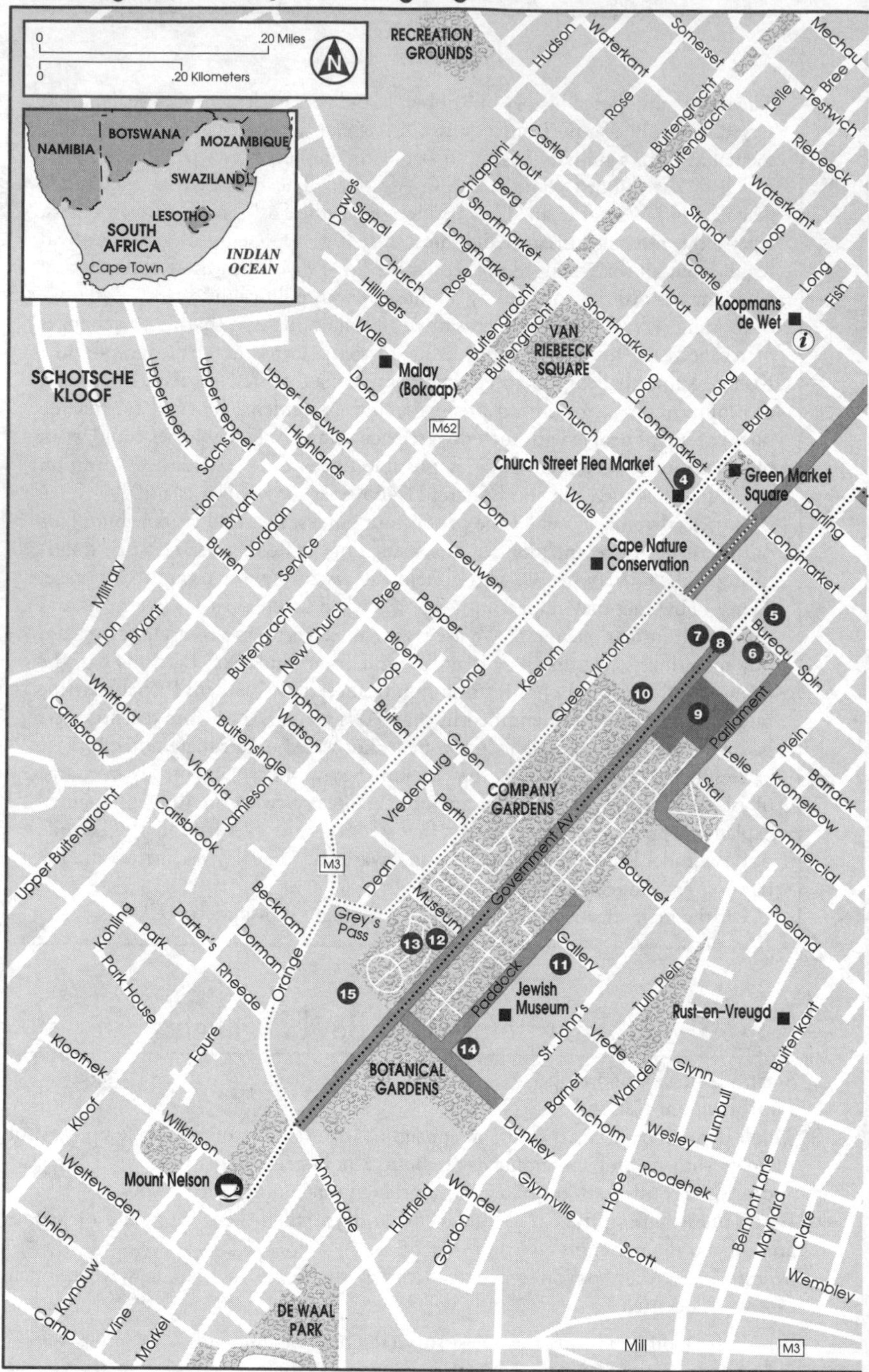

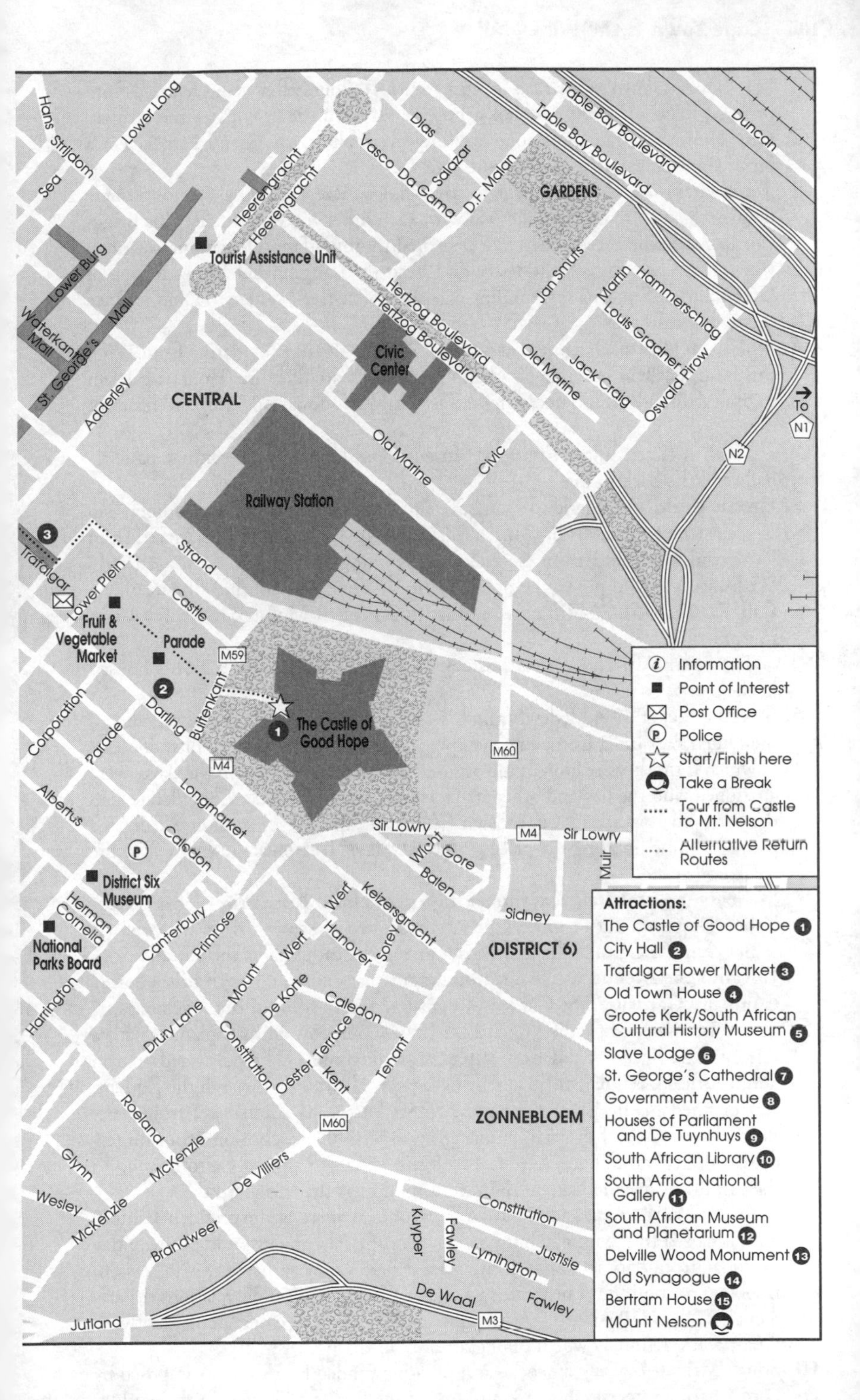
Information
Point of Interest
Post Office
Police
Start/Finish here
Take a Break
Tour from Castle to Mt. Nelson
Alternative Return Routes
Attractions:
The Castle of Good Hope 1
City Hall 2
Trafalgar Flower Market 3
Old Town House 4
Groote Kerk/South African Cultural History Museum 5
Slave Lodge 6
St. George's Cathedral 7
Government Avenue 8
Houses of Parliament and De Tuynhuys 9
South African Library 10
South Africa National Gallery 11
South African Museum and Planetarium 12
Delville Wood Monument 13
Old Synagogue 14
Bertram House 15
Mount Nelson
CENTRAL
GARDENS
(DISTRICT 6)
ZONNEBLOEM
Railway Station
Civic Center
The Castle of Good Hope
Tourist Assistance Unit
Fruit & Vegetable Market
Parade
District Six Museum
National Parks Board
To N1
N2
M59
M4
M60
M3

Mayibuye!" ("Power to Africa! It must return!"), hours after being released from prison on Feb 11, 1990. He spoke these words from the balcony of the former:

2. **City Hall,** the ornate sandstone building overlooking the Grand Parade. For a bit of Cape culture, take a stroll through the:
3. **Trafalgar Flower Market** (next to the Golden Acre Shopping Centre), where flower sellers clutching bunches vie with each other for your trade. This brings you to **Adderley Street,** the city's principal thoroughfare. Depending on time, you might want to cross Adderley and head up **Longmarket Street** to one of **Greenmarket Square's** surrounding cafes for coffee (see "Where to Dine"). Once there, pop into the:
4. **Old Town House,** Greenmarket Square (☎ **021/424-6367**), dating from 1755, this is an excellent example of urban Cape Dutch architecture. Hours are 10am to 5pm daily, admission free. Alternatively, turn left down Adderley and head for the:

   South African Cultural History Museum, passing the 19th-century banking halls and the back of the:
5. **Groote Kerk,** 43 Adderley. If you have time, take a look inside the somber "big church" (the entrance is in Church Sq.). Built in 1841, the pulpit, carved from local stinkwood and Burmese teak, is the work of sculptor Anton Anreith. With nearly 6,000 pipes, the organ is the largest in the southern hemisphere. Call ☎ **021/461-7044** for free guided tours; open Monday to Friday 10am to 2pm.

   The South African Cultural History Museum (☎ **021/461-8280**) is housed in the old:
6. **Slave Lodge,** at 49 Adderley St. Built in 1679 for the gardeners and servants of the Dutch East India Company, the lodge has a few interesting exhibits, not least of which is the cross-section of the original slave tree, under which the slaves were auctioned, and the flag and other artifacts from the Alabama, a Confederate ship that used to re-stock in Cape Town. (Opposite the lodge, in Skin Street, is a plaque commemorating the place where the **Slave Tree** once grew.) Next to the Slave Lodge is:
7. **St George's Cathedral.** This former diocese of Nobel Peace Prize–winner Archbishop Desmond Tutu contains the largest stained-glass window in the country.

   Between the Cultural History Museum and the cathedral is the entrance to:
8. **Government Avenue,** a tree-lined boulevard that runs the length of the lovely **Company Gardens.** The Gardens are a surviving portion of the vegetable gardens commissioned by the Dutch East India Company, and are planted with a variety of indigenous and exotic trees including the oldest cultivated tree in South Africa. Cecil Rhodes is said to have enjoyed strolling through the gardens, and planned his invasion of Rhodesia (now known as Zimbabwe) from here. Beyond is a statue of the man pointing north with the inscription "Your hinterland is there," an oblique reference to his imperialist Cape-to-Cairo dream. To the east of the avenue, take in the various buildings that make up the:
9. **Houses of Parliament** and **De Tuynhuys** (official office of the president). Tuynhuys is closed to the public, but you can tour the Parliament buildings Monday to Friday from 9am to 12pm or attend a debate when parliament is in session. Bookings for both must be made in advance through the public relations department (☎ **021/403-2460**)—with talk of Parliament moving permanently to Pretoria, it's definitely worth calling ahead. On the right is the:
10. **South African Library,** a neoclassical building funded by a wine tax imposed by Lord Charles Somerset in 1818, and one of the first free libraries in the world.

Farther down you'll find the:

11. **South Africa National Gallery** on your left, with the:
12. **South African Museum and Planetarium** on your right. The temple in front of the Museum is the:
13. **Delville Wood Monument,** which honors the thousands of South Africans who died during the Somme offensive in World War I. Opposite the National Gallery is the:
14. **Old Synagogue,** South Africa's first, and home to the **Jewish Museum** (☎ **021/465-1546**). The entrance is in Hatfield Street, and its hours are Tuesday to Thursday 1:30 to 5pm and Sunday 10:30am to noon.

    Keep strolling down Government Avenue, passing the University of Cape Town's art and drama department on your right, until it intersects with Orange Street. On the corner is:
15. **Bertram House** (☎ **021/424-9381**), Cape Town's only remaining red-brick Georgian town house, with furniture and objets d'art dating back to the 19th century. Hours are Tuesday to Saturday, 9:30am to 4:30pm. Admission is R3 (50¢) adults; R1 (15¢) children.

**TAKE A BREAK** Opposite Government Avenue is the grand entrance to the **Mount Nelson,** whose archway was erected in 1924 to welcome the Prince of Wales. Head up the palm-lined driveway for an exceptional high tea. Replenished, you could either stroll back down **Queen Victoria Street,** lined with some of the city's most stately buildings, or return via **Long Street,** an interesting shopping street. If it's too late, take a taxi.

### QUICK FIX

Pressed for time? A much shortened alternative to the above tour is to enter the top end of the **Company Gardens** (that is, opposite the Mount Nelson), stroll down **Goverment Avenue** and visit the **South Africa Museum** and **National Gallery,** including the **Cultural Museum** if you have time.

## 6 Farther Afield: Discovering the Peninsula

✪ **Cape of Good Hope Nature Reserve.** Entrance off M4 and M65. ☎ **021/780-9204.** Sept–May daily 7am–6pm; June–Aug daily 7am–5pm. R10 ($1.65) adults; R5 (85¢) ages 7–17.

Part of the Cape Peninsula National Park (which also encompasses the Silvermine Nature Reserve and Table Mountain), the Cape of Good Hope is most famous for Cape Point, the farthest tip of the Cape Peninsula. There are a number of drives and picnic sites in the reserve, which is home to baboons, eland, ostrich, and bontebok. (Be aware that the baboons, which have become habituated to humans, can be dangerous; keep your car windows closed and never feed them.) The usually wind-swept reserve is pretty bleak, but the coastal views are arresting. The walk along Platboom Beach on the west coast (also popular with windsurfers) is recommended, or follow the turnoff to Buffelsbaai Beach on the east coast, where you can swim or even *braai* (barbecue). The Cape of Good Hope is a rocky beach that marks Africa's most southwestern point. Most head straight for Cape Point, taking the funicular (R20/$3.35 round-trip; R8/$1.35 children) to the viewing platform and lighthouse—the view is spectacular.

### THE CONSTANTIA WINE ROUTE

Groot Constantia is a good place to start your exploration of the Cape's oldest Winelands, an area that comprises **Klein Constantia, Buitenverwachting, Uitsig,**

### House Hunting

If you're interested in house museums, the **Koopmans-De Wet House** (☎ **021/424-2473**), is an 18th-century house with an excellent collection of furniture. You'll find it at 35 Strand St.; it has the same hours and entry fee as the **Bertram House,** which is listed in the Walking Tour. The best is, however, in Stellenbosch. See "Winelands."

and **Steenberg.** All feature Cape Dutch homesteads, oaks, and acres of vineyards, and are some 20 minutes from town. Spending some time here is definitely recommended if you aren't venturing into the surrounding Winelands. If you're looking for an ideal luncheon venue, look no further than Buitenverwachting or Uitsig—these renowned restaurants on the eastern slopes of the Constantiaberg, with views of vineyards and the distant sea, should be high on your priority list.

**Groot Constantia.** ☎ **021/794-5067.** Daily 10–5. R5 museum (85¢), R9 ($1.50) cellar tour, R10 ($1.65) wine tasting. Take the Constantia turnoff the M3; follow the Groot Constantia signs.

Groot Constantia was established in 1685 by Simon van der Stel, the then governor of the Cape, who named it after his daughter Constancia, and planted the Cape's first vines. A century later, the Cloete family put Constantia on the international map with a dessert wine that became the favored tipple of Napolean, Bismarck, and King Louis Philippe of France—even Jane Austen wrote of its "healing powers on a disappointed heart." The outbreak of phylloxera in the 1860s was to bankrupt the family, and the land lay fallow until 1975, when substantial replanting began. Today Groot Constantia is known for its reds, particularly the **Gouverneurs Reserve.** In addition to tasting the wines in the modern cellars here, you can also visit a small museum showing the history of the manor, as well as Cape Dutch house itself, originally designed by French architect Louis Thibault, and furnished in beautiful late-18th-century Cape Dutch furniture. Behind the house are the old cellars, featuring the celebrated pediment sculpted by Anton Anreith in 1791 and now containing an interesting museum of wine.

## A Peninsula Driving Tour

Note that not all the sites are must sees; personal interest should shape your itinerary. As this is a circular route, it can also be done in reverse, but the idea is to find yourself on the Atlantic seaboard at sunset.

**Start:** Take the M3 out of town; this follows the line of the mountain, providing access to the southern suburbs.

**Finish:** Kloof Nek roundabout in town.

**Time:** The full tour will take at least one full day, with a recommended shortened version below for those with less time.

As you start to drive out of town, keep an eye out for the wildebeest and mountain zebra on the slopes of the mountain after you pass the huge **Groote Schuur Hospital** on your left, scene of the world's first heart transplant in 1967. Art lovers should consider taking the:

1. **Mowbray** turnoff and dropping in on the **Irma Stern Museum** (☎ **021/685-5686,** Cecil Rd.; open Tuesday to Saturday 10am to 5pm). A follower of the German expressionist movement, and acknowledged as one of South Africa's

# Peninsula Driving Tour

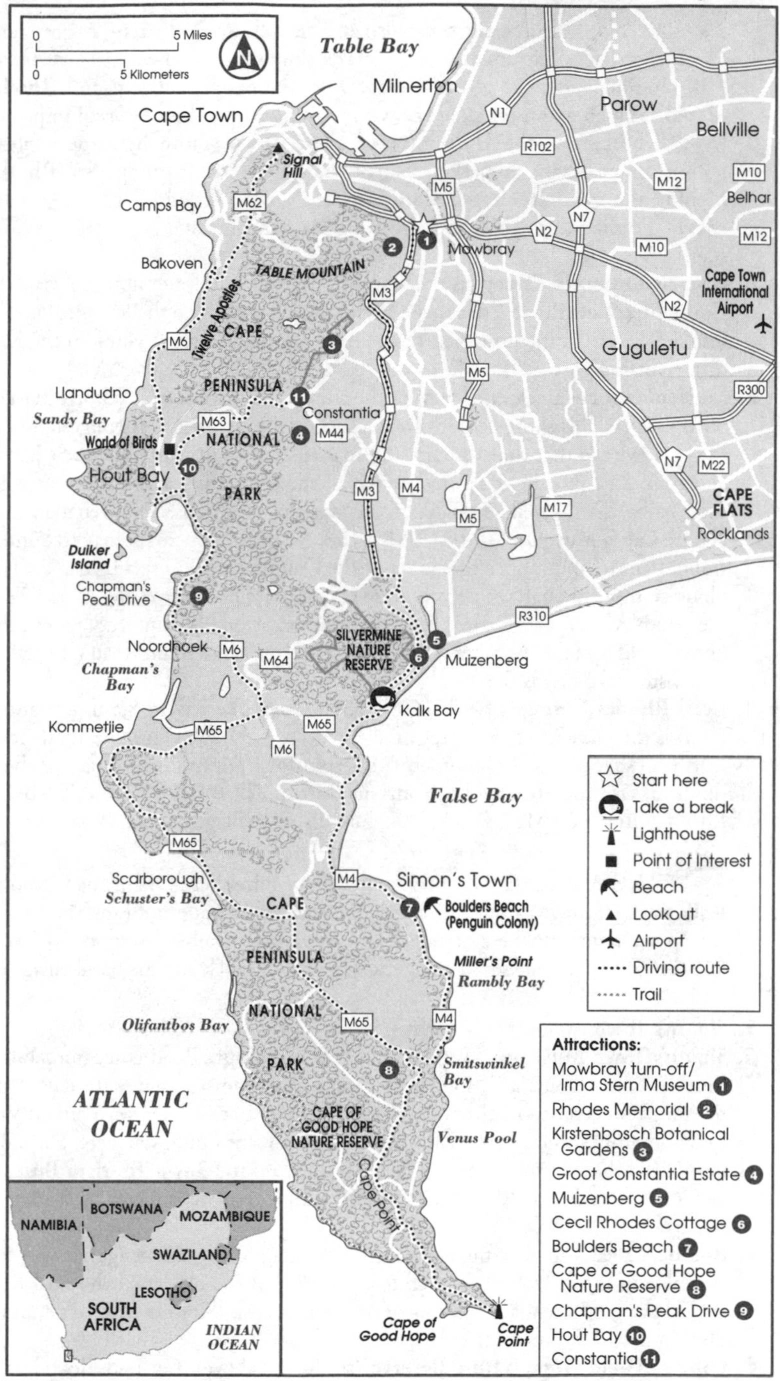

best 20th century artists, Stern was also an avid collector of Iberian, African, and Oriental artifacts. Back on the M3, still traveling south, you will pass **Mostert's Mill,** another reminder of the Cape's Dutch past, on your left, and **Rhodes Memorial** high up on the slopes on your right, followed by a series of imposing ivy-clad buildings—the **University of Cape Town.** From here the suburbs become increasingly upmarket, as you pass both the turnings for **Rhodes Memorial** and **Kirstenbosch Gardens** (see "On & Around Table Mountain" above), heading through the suburbs of Bishops Court and Wynberg for Constantia. Visit the:

2. **Groot Constantia Estate** on the way or set aside a full afternoon to visit the Constantia Wine Route (see above). Keep traveling south on the M3 until it runs into a T-junction, then turn left to the next T-junction where you join the M4; turn right for:
3. **Muizenberg.** For an elevated view of the coast, take **Boyes Drive** (clearly marked off the M4). This short detour of the coastal route is often less congested than the narrow road that runs through the coastal suburbs of Muizenberg, St James, and Kalk Bay, though you'll miss much of the interesting architecture of what used to be the favored seaboard of the wealthy randlords. The Venetian-style **Natale Labia Museum** (☎ **021/788-4106,** Main Rd., open Tuesday to Sunday from 10am to 5pm), once the home of the Count and Countess Labia, is a fabulous example, though the actual house contents are not as riveting. A satellite of the South African National Gallery, there are occasionally some very good exhibitions held upstairs. Another attraction on Muizenberg's Main Road (also called the Historical Mile) is the:
4. **Cecil Rhodes Cottage** (☎ **021/788-1816,** open Tuesday to Sunday 10am to 5pm) is the place where he purportedly died—a remarkably humble abode for a man who shaped much of southern Africa's history. For more information about this area, visit the **Muizenberg Tourism Bureau** (☎ **021/788-1898,** 52 Beach Rd.). Continue on Main Road to the busy fishing village of Kalk Bay.

**TAKE A BREAK** If you've opted for Muizenberg's main road, stop in **Kalk Bay** to browse through a variety of charming antique and junk shops. You can lunch here (try the seafood at the **Brass Bell,** railway station, ☎ **021/788-5455**) or continue south along the M4 to Fish Hoek and the naval village of:

5. **Simon's Town,** where a visit to the:
6. **Simon's Town Museum** (☎ **021/786-3046**) in Court Road is recommended, time allowing. Hours are Monday to Friday from 9am to 4pm, Saturday 10am to 1pm. This is the most charming of the False Bay towns, lined with quaint Victorian buildings, and many regular visitors to the Cape opt to stay here. For more details on what the town has to offer, visit the **Simon's Town Tourism Bureau,** also on Court Road (☎ **021/786-3046**). Top of their list will be a stop at nearby:
7. **Boulders Beach** to view the large breeding colony of jackass penguins who settled here in the early 1980s, much to the horror of the residents who now have to deal with the attendant coachloads of tourists. From Simon's Town it's another 20 minutes to the entrance to the:
8. **Cape of Good Hope Nature Reserve** (see listing above). Once inside, take the Circular Drive to spot game, or the Buffelsbaai turnoff for a beach walk; alternatively head straight for **Cape Point.** From the nature reserve, it's a relatively

straightforward—and spectacular—drive back to town. Take the M65 left out of the reserve (past the **Cape Point Ostrich Farm** (☎ **021/780-9294**), and travel through the coastal towns of **Scarborough** and **Kommetjie** (you can opt to bypass Kommetjie) to **Noordhoek.** Once there, follow the signs for the M6 to Hout Bay, bypassing Noordhoek village and ascending the exhilarating:

9. **Chapman's Peak Drive** (make sure you look back to admire the pristine stretch of Noordhoek's Long Beach). Built between 1915 and 1922, this winding 10-kilometer drive must rate as one of the top in the world, with cliffs plunging straight into the ocean, dwarfing the vehicles snaking along its side. Not surprisingly, hundreds of international car commercials have been shot here. From Chapman's Peak you descend into:
10. **Hout Bay,** where you could head for the harbor and book a cruise to view the seal colony and seabird sanctuary on **Duiker Island** (see "Organized Cruises & Tours") or visit the **World of Birds Sanctuary** in Valley Road (☎ **021/790-2730**). Open 9am to 5pm daily, it is home to over 450 species. From Hout Bay you can now head for leafy:
11. **Constantia** by taking the M63. Alternatively take the coast-hugging M6 to town—with any luck this will coincide with sunset. Follow the M6 (Victoria Rd.) out of Camps Bay and turn right at the sign "Kloof Nek Round House" to snake up the mountain to the Kloof Nek roundabout—if you haven't yet seen the **city lights** from Signal Hill or Tafelberg Road, do so now.

### QUICK FIX

In a rush? The following covers the most spectacular parts of the drive, but cuts out Cape Point. Head out of town by traveling up Kloof Nek Road and descending into Camps Bay's **Victoria Road** (running parallel to the beach), or travel to Camps Bay along the coastal road that starts in Sea Point and winds its way past Clifton. Continue following the coast, past Llandudno into **Hout Bay** and up the spectacular **Chapman's Peak Drive.** Descend into **Noordhoek,** keeping an eye out for the M64 turnoff (also called "Ou Kaapse Weg"), which takes you through the beautiful **Silvermine Nature Reserve.** Once at the bottom of the Silvermine Mountain, follow the signs to the M3, which heads back into town; time allowing, pop into **Groot Constantia** for a wine tasting, or combine this route with a visit to **Kirstenbosch.** With no stops, this drive should take approximately 2 hours.

## 7 Surf & Sand

You'll find Cape Town's most beautiful beaches along the Atlantic seaboard; Clifton, Camps Bay, and Llandudno are the most popular. With four beaches created by large granite boulders, **Clifton** is often the only place where the wind isn't blowing and is good for swimming, but it's a long walk back through the cliff-hugging village to your car. **Camps Bay** is the most popular volleyball beach, and has a number of bars and cafes within strolling distance. Laid-back **Llanduno** is one of the prettiest, though parking can be a real problem during high-season. **Sandy Bay,** adjacent to Llandudno, is the Cape's only (unofficial) nudist beach. Reached via a narrow footpath, it's secluded and popular with gay men and wankers—this is not a great spot for women, unless you're in a group. The pristine, empty 8-kilometer stretch of **Long Beach,** featured in a thousand television commercials, is best traversed on horseback. On the False Bay side, where the water is a little warmer, you could try for the safe waters of **Fish Hoek,** or swim with the penguins at **Boulders.**

For a real taste of the beach—literally!—take up sandboarding (see "Staying Active" below). Practiced mostly by Namibians who've never seen an inch of snow, this is recommended only for the thick-skinned and foolhardy.

## 8 Especially for Kids

Many of the Waterfront activities have been designed with children in mind, making it Cape Town's foremost family destination. The top attractions here are the five-story **IMAX** cinema, which shows predominantly wildlife shows, and the **Two Oceans Aquarium.** The latter often arranges fun sleepovers and excursions to interesting and educational locations for ages 8 to 12. Call ☎ **021/418-2369** to find out what special kids' entertainment will be available when you're in town.

In town, take a look at the whale skeletons in the **South African Museum** (☎ **021/424-3330**), then catch the 12pm **Planetarium** (same phone) show every Saturday and Sunday, where they attempt to answer simple astronomy questions, like "Why is the sky blue?" and "Is the sun round?" To get there, take a stroll through **Government Avenue** (enter from Orange St., opposite Mount Nelson) armed with a bag of nuts to feed the almost-tame squirrels. Afterward, ascend Table Mountain in the rotating **cable car.** For an even bigger thrill, see the mountain upturned by riding the stomach-churning "Cobra" at **Ratanga Junction** (☎ **086/120-0300**), open daily from 10am to 10pm Cape Town's biggest amusement park, 8 kilometers (almost 5 miles) from town off the N1. The Nico Malan and Baxter theatres always stage at least one **children's play;** call Computicket (☎ **021/421-4715**) to find out what's on.

For more active options, chill out with a ball and picnic at **Kirstenbosch,** or head for **Le Pique Nique** at Boschendal, near Franschhoek. Walk through the **World of Birds Sanctuary** (Valley Rd., ☎ **021/790-2730**), in Hout Bay, and then take one of the cruises to **Seal Island,** departing from Hout Bay Harbour. Older kids (there is a height restriction) may enjoy the **Grand Prix Go-Karting** (☎ **021/419-5465**) at an indoor track near the entrance to the Waterfront.

And when all else fails? There's always the beach. Try **Boulders,** where the temperature is slightly warmer, tidal pools are safe, and the penguins add unique entertainment value—visit the **Warrior Toy Museum** (☎ **021/78-1395**) in George's Street, Simon's Town on your way.

## 9 Organized Cruises & Tours

**BY BOAT** One of the best vantages of Cape Town is undoubtedly from the sea. With tours costing R35–80 ($6.85–$13.35) depending on the duration and destination, a sunset cruise from the harbor to Clifton is highly recommended. **Waterfront Adventures** (☎ **021/418-5806**) has a variety of boats. Or you can set sail on **Le Tigre** (☎ **021/419-7746**), a luxury catamaran. To sail to Cape Point, then overnight on the West Coast on the **Maharani,** a beautiful 66-foot naval ketch, call ☎ **082/412-2222. Wildest Water Sports** (☎ **021/438-8270**) specializes in powerboat cruises—ask about their Clifton crayfish braai and jet bikes. (Note that while many offer "Robben Island trips," only boats run by the Department of Arts can actually land on the island; see "Exploring the Waterfront" above.) **Drum Beat Charters** (☎ **021/438-9208**) and **Circe** (☎ **021/790-1040**) both offer 1-hour trips from Hout Bay Harbour to see the Cape fur seals on Duiker Island.

**BY BUS** A large number of operators offer driving tours of the city and its surrounds—recommended companies include **Legend Tours** (☎ **021/697-4056**),

**African Eagle** (☎ **021/794-0378**) and **Welcome Tours & Safaris** (☎ **021/510-6001**). For a personal one-on-one guide, contact **Led Tours** (☎ **021/406-5995**). **Topless Tours** (☎ **021/418-5888**) offers tours aboard an open double-decker bus—this is a great way to orient yourself; you can hop on and off at any of the designated points along the 2-hour city tour. Alternatively opt for their full 7-hour Cape Peninsula or Winelands tours (don't forget the sunblock).

**BY AIR** For an aerial tour of the city or peninsula contact **Court Helicopters** (☎ **021/425-2966**) or **Civair Helicopters** (☎ **021/419-5182**).

**Flamingo Flights** (☎ **021/790-1010**) operates sightseeing tours from a De Havilland Beaver seaplane.

**SPECIALIST TOURS** For a more holistic view of the Cape Town community, contact **Grassroute Tours** (☎ **021/424-8480**). Their 4-hour "Behind the Rainbow Curtain" tour takes in the Cape Muslim culture of the Bo-Kaap, the history of the forced removals from District Six, and introduces you to the predominantly black communities of Langa and Khayalitsha; this can be combined with an afternoon trip to Robben Island. It'll actually work out cheaper, however, if you visit Robben Island on your own steam. Their "Culture of the Cape Fishermen" and "Culture of the Winelands" tours give visitors a greater insight into the lifestyle of the people who man the Cape's oldest industries.

Another highly recommended tour company, **One City Tours** (☎ **021/387-5351**), concentrates on the black Cape Town community: "Xhosas in the Mother City" introduces you to some of the rites and rituals that still exist despite urbanization; "Ekhaya" concentrates on history from a black perspective; "The Gospel Truth" takes you to different church services in the townships; and the "Shebeen Crawl and All That Jazz" is a nocturnal pub crawl through the townships. Note that many of these tours can also be organized through **Adventure Village** (see below).

## 10 Staying Active

For one-stop adrenaline shopping, head straight for **Adventure Village** (☎ **021/424-1580,** 229 Long St.), where the staff will organize bookings for almost every adventure activity under the sun (for numbers not available below, contact them directly). This is also where bookings for the Route 49 bus to Victoria Falls are made, as well as many specialized overland and safari trips throughout southern Africa.

**ABSEILING** **Abseil Africa** will throw you 100 meters (328 feet) off Table Mountain—attached to a rope, of course—making this the world's highest commercial abseil. Chapman's Peak offers an easier descent. Best of all, combine your abseil with a day's kloofing in a nature reserve, ending with Kamikaze Kanyon, a 65-meter (213-foot) waterfall abseil. Contact Adventure Village.

**BALLOONING** Board a balloon in the early morning and glide over the Paarl Winelands—the 1-hour flight takes off every morning from November to April, and includes a champagne breakfast at Grande Roche. Contact **Wineland Ballooning** (☎ **021/863-3192**).

**BIRD WATCHING** The peninsula attracts nearly 400 species of birds; Kirstenbosch, Cape Point, and Rondevlei Nature Reserve are some of the best areas for sightings. For guided tours, contact **Birdwatch Cape** (☎ **021/762-5059**) or **Peregrine** (☎ **021/706-2960**).

**BOARDSAILING** Big Bay at **Blouberg** (take R27 Marine Dr. off the N1) provides consistent wind, good waves, and a classic picture-postcard view of Table Mountain.

Another popular place is Platboom, off the Cape of Good Hope Nature Reserve. Alternatively, head north for Langebaan Lagoon (see "Western Cape," chapter 4).

**CANOEING** **Felix Unite** (☎ **021/683-6433**) offers relaxing river trips on the Breede River. **Real Cape Adventures** (☎ **082556-2520**) has various sea-kayaking routes for novices—request a trip to the rugged coastline of Cape Point.

**DIVING** Wreck diving is popular here, and the coral-covered wrecks at Smitswinkel Bay are particularly worth exploring. Contact **Dive Action** (☎ **021/557-0819**), or **Two Oceans Diving Academy** (☎ **021/419-0521**). (For shark-cage diving, see "Western Cape," chapter 4).

**FISHING** **Wild Thing** (☎ **021/438-8270**), based at the Waterfront, offers 4- or 8-hour big-game fishing trips off Cape Point. **Lloyd** (☎ **021/64-2203**) operates out of Simon's Town on a 12-meter (40-foot) catamaran and also offers bottom/reef fishing. Trout fishing is popular in the crystal-clear streams found in the Du Toit's Kloof Mountains near Paarl (☎ **023/349-1092**) and in Franschhoek (☎ **021/876-2510**), where salmon trout is a specialty on every menu. Guidance for beginners can be arranged by calling **James Warne** (☎ **021/794-5713**).

**GOLFING** Top Cape courses are **Royal Cape** (☎ **021/761-6551**), which has hosted the South African Open many times, **Rondebosch** (☎ **021/689-4176**), and **Mowbray** (☎ **021/685-3018**)—both located off the N2—have lovely views of Devil's Peak (the latter course is the more demanding). **Clovelly** (☎ **021/782-6410**) in Fish Hoek is a tight course requiring some precision. Steenberg (☎ **021/713-2233**) is the course to play in Constantia. **Milnerton Golf Club** (☎ **021/434-7808**) is the only links course in the Cape, with magnificent views of Table Mountain, but is best avoided when the wind is blowing.

In the Winelands, the Gary Player–designed **Erinvale** (☎ **021/847-1144,** Lourensford Rd.) in Somerset West is considered the best, but **Stellenbosch** (☎ **021/880-0103**), on Strand Road, which recently hosted the South African Open, is another worthwhile course, with a particularly challenging tree-lined fairway. **Paarl** also has an attractive option on Wemmershoek Road, call ☎ **021/863-1140.**

**HIKING** Most hikers start by climbing Table Mountain, of which there are a number of options (see "Table Mountain" above). For hikes farther afield, contact **Footprints Adventures** (☎ **021/461-1999**) or Ross at **High Adventure** (☎ **021/ 447-8036**)—as a trained climbing instructor, Ross can spice up your walk with some exhilarating ascents. If you're staying in Stellenbosch, the trails (5.3 to 18km/3 to 11 miles) in the mountainous Jonkershoek Nature Reserve are recommended; call (☎ **021/889-1668**) for bookings. Recommended reading for hikers: *Day Walks in and Around Cape Town* by Tim Anderson (Struik) and Mike Lundy's *Best Walks in the Peninsula* (Struik).

**HORSEBACK RIDING** Take a sunset, champagne, or moonlight ride on the spectacular Long Beach, Noordhoek by contacting **Sleepy Hollow** (☎ **021/789-2341**). Closer to town is **The Riding Centre** (☎ **021/790-5286**), in Hout Bay. To ride through the Franschhoek vines on horseback or in a carriage, stopping for wine tastings, contact the **Mont Rochelle Equestrian Centre** (☎ **021/876-3592**); to do so on pure-bred Arab horses, contact **Paradise Stables** (☎ **021/876-2160**). The **Wine Valley Riding Club** (☎ **082981-6331**) offers a similar service in Stellenbosch.

**IN-LINE SKATING** Rent your wheels from **Rent 'n Ride** (☎ **021/434-1122**) and skate the beautiful beachfront promenade from Sea Point to the Waterfront.

**MOUNTAIN BIKING** There are a number of trails on Table Mountain, Cape Point, and the Winelands, but the Tokai Forest network and Constantiaberg trails are the best; contact **Hopkins Cycle Inn** (☎ **021/423-2527**) or **Rent 'n Ride** (☎ **021/**

**434-1122**) for bike rentals and advice, or **Day Trippers** (☎ **021/531-3274**) for guided rides.

**PARAGLIDING** Soar off Lion's Head and Signal Hill for a jaw-dropping view of mountains and sea, and land at Camps Bay Beach or La Med bar for cocktails at sunset. This is one of the most exhilarating trips in Cape Town, and no prior experience is necessary. Contact Adventure Village directly.

**SANDBOARDING** South Africa's answer to snowboarding takes place on the tallest dunes all around the Cape; contact **Downhill Adventures** for trips and tuition (☎ **082/549-2422**).

**SKYDIVING** Freefall for up to 30 seconds, attached to an experienced instructor. Tandem dives are offered off the West Coast (contact **Adventure Village,** above) or over the Stellenbosch Winelands (contact **Cape Parachute Club,** ☎ **021/58-8514**).

**SURFING** The beaches off Kalk Bay reef and Noordhoek are considered hot spots. Muizenberg and Big Bay at Blouberg (take R27 Marine Dr. off the N1) are good for beginners. Call ☎ **021/788-1350** for the daily surf report and **Downhill Adventures** (☎ **082/549-2422**) for equipment, tuition, and advice.

**WHALE WATCHING** For the best whale watching on the peninsula, drive along the False Bay coast. Fish Hoek is a favorite whale stop. Hermanus—just over an hour's drive on the N2—is considered one of the world's best land-based spots (See chapter 4, "Western Cape").

## 11 Spectator Sports

Every February fashion-victims, designers, and revelers join forces to place their bets at the **J&B Met,** the Cape's premier horse-racing event (☎ **021/762-7777**). The 105-kilometer (66-mile) **Argus Cycle Tour** (☎ **021/683-0913**), which covers some of the most scenic parts of the peninsula, is the largest individually timed bike race in the world, and attracts over 25,000 participants every March, including an increasing number of foreign visitors. The 56-kilometer (35-mile) **Two Oceans Marathon** takes place every April (☎ **021/61-9407**). Both the **Western Province Cricket Union** (☎ **021/64-4146**) and **Western Province Football Union** (☎ **021/689-4921**) call the huge sports complex on Campground Road in Newlands home. (Newlands Stadium is incidentally where the South African rugby team trounced the favored Australians before going on to win the 1995 Rugby World Cup, sparking a euphoria that matched that of election day.) Watch the newspapers for details on upcoming cricket and rugby matches. For major international sporting events, head for the big screens and convivial vibe of the **Sports Bar** in the Waterfront (☎ **021/419-5558**).

## 12 Shopping

You'll find a large selection of shops and hundreds of street hawkers catering to the African art and crafts market, though as none of it is produced locally, you will pay a slight premium—and of course, the better the gallery, the larger the premium. Ask for the Arts & Crafts Map from any Tourism Bureau or follow the guidelines below.

### GREAT SHOPPING AREAS

#### IN TOWN

In the heart of the city center, the cobbled **Greenmarket Square** is brimful of traders selling clothing, crafts, and souvenir or gift items. Weather permitting, it's worth browsing here just for the atmosphere, not to mention the selection of great coffee shops surrounding the square (see "Where to Dine"). It's also ideally situated to explore town's major shopping areas.

**Long Street,** a one-way street running toward the mountain, is 1 block from here: Walk straight up Shortmarket Street and take your first left onto Long for the ✪ **Pan African Market,** (76 Long St., ☎ **021/242-957**), where you'll find an overwhelming choice of African art and crafts. Follow the flow of the traffic to **Church Street,** a section of which is for pedestrians only, 2 short blocks away. Street traders deal in antiques here, and there are a number of interesting shops. On the corner of Long and Church streets is **Peter Visser Antiques** (☎ **021/422-2660**), which specializes in fine art, particularly ceramics, and antiques; the centrally located **Gilles de Moyencourt** (☎ **021/424-0344**), 54 Church St., deals in over-priced but interesting Africana and other quirky antiques; **The Collector** (☎ **021/423-1483**) at 48 Church St., trades in the expensive end of what they term ""tribal" artifacts. On the corner of Church and Burg streets is **African Image** (see "Best Buys," below).

Keep walking down Church Street or Greenmarket Square to **St George's Mall**—a pedestrian street that runs the length of town. There are always buskers and street dancers performing here, and a small selection of street hawkers peddling masks and sculptures. For a larger selection, head 1 block down to Adderley Street, cross via the Golden Acre, and browse the **station surrounds,** where the streets are paved with wood and soapstone carvings. It's also paved with pickpockets, so don't carry valuables here. If you've had your fill of African crafts, head back up to **Long Street** and walk toward the mountain. This is the city's most interesting shopping street—lined with Victorian buildings. Long Street houses numerous antique shops, galleries, porn outlets, hostels, and cafes/bars, as well as a mosque and Turkish baths. If you've got time, check out the funky hairdresser (**Peter the Haircutter,** ☎ **021/424-6768,** 232 Long St.), or purchase your first piece of *droë wors* (like biltong, but sausage) at **Morris the Butcher** at 265 Long St. (☎ **021/423-1766**). There are plenty of places to stop for food, but it's worth highlighting the **Yellow Pepper** at 138 Long Street (☎ **021/424-9250**), for an inexpensive, down-home hot lunch, and **169 On Long** (☎ **021/426-1107**), for its Victorian balcony overlooking the street.

### On the Waterfront

Shopping here is a far less satisfying experience than in the bustling streets of town; Victoria Wharf is at the end of the day simply a glam shopping center with a nice location. However, there are a few gems. Head straight for the **Everard Read Gallery** (☎ **021/418-4527**) to view a small selection of the best contemporary art in South Africa—be warned though, you won't find a bargain here. Adjacent is the Waterfront branch of **African Image** (☎ **021/419-0382**). For more African collectibles and jewelry, take a look at **African Heritage** (☎ **021/421-6610**) and **Out of this World** (☎ **021/419-3246**). If you're going on a camping safari, **Cape Union Mart** (☎ **021/419-0019**) has the best gear in South Africa. For elegant yet casual men's and ladies' wear, visit **Joseph Cotton and Oaktree** (☎ **021/419-7068**). The **Red Shed Craft Workshop** (☎ **021/418-2369**) and **Waterfront Craft Market** (☎ **021/418-2850**) are both predominantly supplied by the local (white) hippie market and are not recommended if you're looking for uniquely African work.

## BEST BUYS

**AFRICAN SOUVENIRS** You can purchase vibrant traditional African fabrics and clothing, like the shirts made popular by Mandela, at **Vlisco** (☎ **021/423-2461,** 45 Castle St., in town), or **Mnandi** (☎ **021/447-7937,** 90 Station St., Observatory). For inexpensive, carved African crafts, your best bet is to browse through the myriad street hawkers' wares, or visit the **Pan African Market** at 76 Long St. (☎ **021/242-957**). For a slightly more expensive but well-chosen selection of indigenous crafts, visit **African Image** (in town, ☎ **021/423-8385;** or the Waterfront, ☎ **021/419-0382**). African Image offers one of the best selections of reasonably priced selections of African art and crafts in the country—look out for their barber signs which hail from Ghana and the Ivory Coast. For a well-picked (but expensive) selection of **South African art** (rather than craft), visit the **Everard Read Gallery** (☎ **021/418-4527**) in the Waterfront.

**FOOD** To sample the best biltong, head for **Joubert & Monty** (☎ **021/425-2961**) in the Waterfront—ask for it slightly moist, and sliced. If you're planning to have a barbecue, purchase some *boerewors* (literally "farmers sausage") from any branch of **Woolworths** (Waterfront location, ☎ **021/419-8250**)—try the Grabouw seasoning. Re-create the mild, slightly sweet curry flavors of Cape Malay dishes back home by purchasing a bag of mixed **spices** from the Ahmed family, proprietors of **Atlas Trading Co,** 94 Wale St., off Adderley (☎ **021/423-4361**).

**GIFTS and SOUVENIRS** For ceramics, check out the paper-thin bowls created by the masterful Anthony Shapiro, available from homeware outfits like **Nocturnal Affair** in the Waterfront (☎ **021/419-2291**); for brightly-hued African-motif tableware, created by popular ceramist Clementina van der Walt, visit the **A.R.T. Gallery** in Paarl (☎ **021/872-3420**)—pick up a brochure from the Paarl Tourism Bureau. For Carol Boyes' sublime pewterware (her cutlery is exported all over the world), visit **Peter Visser Interiors** at 63 Loop St. (☎ **021/422-2660**) or the **Yellow Door** in the Gardens Centre (☎ **021/465-4702,** off Mill and Buitenkant sts.).

**JEWELRY** Local jewelers are well represented at **101 Jewellery Emporium** (☎ **021/423-1211**), at 101 Kloof St.

**WINE** For expert advice on the best wines and export assistance, visit **Vaughan Johnson's Wine Shop** (☎ **021/419-2121**) in the Waterfront, or **Enoteca** in Heritage Square in town (☎ **021/424-9167**), or in Newlands (☎ **021/683-7516**). (Note that exporting wine to the United States and Canada is not easy and may be prohibitively expensive.)

## 13 Cape Town After Dark

Pick up a copy of *What's On in the Cape*, or—even better—purchase a copy of the monthly *SA Citylife* magazine. Alternatively, the weekly *Mail & Guardian* covers major events, as does the local daily *The Argus*—look in the "Tonight" section. You can book tickets to most venues by calling **Computicket** (☎ **021/421-4715**) and giving your credit-card number.

### THE PERFORMING ARTS

Standards are often shaky, but there are notable exceptions—critics here, as elsewhere, pull no punches, so watch the press. Note that if anything directed by Martinus Basson is showing, it's more than likely worth seeing. Drama, ballet, and opera are held at the **Nico Malan Theatre** (☎ **021/421-7839,** DF Malan St., Foreshore); while the **Baxter Theatre** (☎ **021/685-7880,** Main Rd., Rondebosch) features predominantly drama and comedy. The **Theatre on the Bay** (Camps Bay) hosts mostly comedies and farces.

During summer, there are a variety of outdoor venues. **Maynardville Open Air Theatre** (☎ **021/77-8591,** Church and Wolf sts., Wynber) hosts an annual Shakespeare play, which is a great picnic venue. The **Oude Libertas Amphitheatre**

## The Great Gay esCape

Cape Town is fast becoming one of the great international gay destinations—like sister cities San Francisco, Sydney, and Miami, this is a sexy seaside city, with a fantastic mix of indoor and outdoor activities. It's also very gay friendly, and openly promoted as "Africa's Queer Capital." This is hardly surprising, considering that South Africa's constitution is the only one in the world to expressly protect the rights of homosexuals, and Mandela was the first head of state in history to stand up and mention freedom of sexual orientation.

Most gay-friendly venues are situated in and around the City Bowl. The "Gay Quarter"—west of the city in Green Point, centered around Somerset Road and running up the slopes of Signal Hill to Loader Street—is where you'll find the best selection of clubs, bars, bath houses, cafes, and guest houses. Check the local press (*Exit, Outright,* or *Gay Pages*) or Web sites (www.q.co.za or www.queer.co.za) for more information.

**A GAY NIGHT OUT** You'll find that the gay white male subculture is much like that of any western city, and Americans in particular may be amused by the predominance of U.S.-inspired names. Traveling from town to Green Point, the first stop worth considering is **De Waterkant** (☎ **021/425-2478,** 72 Waterkant), a good restaurant with a nice quiet bar. Adjacent is the more buzzy **Manhattans** (☎ **021/421-6666,** 74 Waterkant, corner Dixon), a friendly low-volume chatty bar with a good-value restaurant, which gets busy after 9pm nightly. (Women-only nights are held on the last Thursday of every month.) Down Dixon is **On Broadway** (☎ **021/418-8338,** Corner Somerset and Dixon), a great cabaret and theatre restaurant, with excellent shows (book early for "Mince," featuring South Africa's best female impersonators). Next door is the **Blah Bar** (☎ **021/419-5599,** 21a Somerset), a trendy cocktail and lounge bar that flows out onto the pavement at about midnight. Keep heading down Somerset and look out for **Bronx, Angels,** and **Detour** (same phone for all, ☎ **021/419-8547,** at 27 Somerset Rd., corner of Napier). The three separate venues all connect onto an outdoor alfresco courtyard, but each has its own atmosphere. **Bronx** is a very popular late-night bar with excellent dance tracks by Mitzy the DJ; open from 9pm to 5am nightly, with different events (like lesbian karaoke on Mondays). **Angels** is a club with a large dance floor playing disco and soul; it also has bars, pool tables, and the occasional drag show. Upstairs you'll find **Detour,** a hard-core house and techno nightclub experience, with laser dance floor, bars, backroom, and open-air balcony. It's best Fridays and Saturdays after midnight, and every day in season (December and January). **Bar Code,** (no phone, Hudson St., off Somerset), is a men's-only leather cruise bar—look out for their underwear parties and leather nights. Still in the same area, but getting steamier, the **Hot House** (☎ **021/418-3888,** 18 Jarvis St.) is a European-style men's-only leisure club, with sauna, steamroom, and outdoor sundeck with spectacular view over the city and the harbor.

Moving farther south, into Sea Point, there is **Dominoes** (☎ **021/434-7147,** 100 Main Rd.), a bistro-type bar and restaurant. **Café Erte** (☎ **021/434-6624,**

(☎ **021/808-7911,** Adam Tas Rd., Stellenbosch) hosts dance, opera, and music. Best of the bunch, the ✪ **Spier Summer Festival,** at the open-air amphitheatre at Spier Wine Estate, serves up a varied program featuring a mix of South Africa's best, as well

265a Main Rd.) is a trance cafe with a neo-eastern trippy vibe at night. It's got a very relaxed atmosphere, a friendly staff, and good food for those out very late.

Back in town you'll find **The Brunswick** at 17 Bree St. (☎ **021/421-2779**): Cape Town's oldest gay bar has hysterically funny drag, cabaret, and theater shows, as well as fabulous cocktails and dinners—reservations are crucial. Farther uptown, on Long Street, there are several gay-friendly restaurants. **Lola's** (☎ **021/423-0885,** 228 Long St.) is a fabulous daytime coffee shop, filled with kitsch and collectibles, and frequented by Cape Town's cultural activists. In the evenings it turns into a funky street bar with a cozy dance floor. The **Long Street Café** (☎ **021/424-2464,** 259 Long St.) treats a trendy crowd to a healthy menu and to beautiful bar staff. A little farther up is **Café Bardeli,** (☎ **021/423-4444,** Longkloof Studios, Darters Rd., off Kloof), a cafe, bar, and deli all in one, in a historic tobacco factory. Models and film and TV industry types pack this place in search of the healthy salads and pastas. **Café Camissa,** (☎ **021/424-2289,** 80 Kloof St. ) serves an off-beat gay-friendly crowd home-cooked food, and there are jazz evenings on Sunday from 8pm.

If you venture to Observatory, don't miss **A Touch of Madness** at Café Carte Blanche (☎ **021/448-2266,** 42a Trill Rd., opposite the post office), a cozy restaurant/bar decked out in rich brocades and gilt-framed mirrors, and the adjacent **Fiddlewoods** (☎ **021/448-6687,** 40 Trill Rd.), a lesbian cigar bar that admits only women on Wednesdays.

**GAY EVENTS** Cape Town's biggest gay event and Africa's biggest queer celebration, the annual **Mother City Queer Project,** is held on the first Saturday of December. A massive costume party attended by over 10,000 queers of all ages, with 10 dance floors playing a rich variety of music, each year sees a new theme explored with partygoers dressed in teams with matching costumes. For information, visit www.mcqp.co.za or call ☎ **083309-1553.**

**RECOMMENDED GUEST HOUSES** **Harbour View Lodge and Cottages** (See "Where to Stay") is situated in the heart of the Gay Quarter, within easy walking distance of clubs and bars. **Parkers Cottage** (☎ **021/424-6445,** 3 Carstens, Tamboerskloof), is a graciously decorated Victorian home with four large en-suite bedrooms; this clean, neat home away from home will run you about R300 ($50) per person. **iKhaya Guest Lodge** features funky African decor, stunning views of Table Mountain—all rooms en-suite, private apartments and luxury lofts (see "Where to Stay"). **Clarens Manor** (☎ **021/434-6801,** 35 Clarens Rd., Fresnaye), charging from R250 to R750 ($41.65 to $125) per person, is a gracious home built in 1908 and furnished with antiques—a place to pull out the caftan. Francois, the proprietor, was once the chef for F. W. De Klerk, the last National Party president who contentiously shared the Nobel Peace Prize with Mandela.

—By Andre Vorster, Cape Town's most celeb queen
and "mother" of MCQP (Mother City Queer Projects)

as international talents like Pavarotti and pianist David Helfgott. You can catch a steam train to Spier from the V&A Waterfront, and eat at one of the restaurants or picnic on the Estate lawns. For more information, call ☎ **021/809-1100.**

Check the press to see what's on at **On Broadway** (☎ **021/418-8338,** 21 Somerset Rd., Green Point), Cape Town's most popular cabaret venue—advance reservations for "Mince," a drag show held every Sunday, is essential. (Note that "Mince" also makes the occasional guest appearance at the **Dorpstraat Teater Café** (☎ **021/886-6107,** in Stellenbosch).

Alternatively, check out what's on upstairs at the **Coffee Lounge,** which features fringe theater (☎ **021/424-6784,** Church St.).

## LIVE MUSIC

### JAZZ

For live jazz in town, head for **Kennedy's Cigar Bar** (☎ **021/424-1212**) on Mondays, and **169 On Long** on Thursdays and Fridays (☎ **021/426-1107**)—the latter is a great venue in summer, with a balcony overlooking the street. The **Green Dolphin Restaurant** (☎ **021/421-4771**), in the Waterfront, showcases some of South Africa's best jazz performers daily, but the food is no great shakes. For a more relaxed environment, head for **Dizzy's Jazz Café** (☎ **021/438-2686** in Camps Bay), which also offers live jazz nightly.

For authentic township jazz, you'll have to head into Rylands, to **Blue Note** (☎ **021/637-9133,** open Friday to Monday), or to Guguletu, to **The Kraal Jazz Den** (☎ **021/34-7131**). (To find these venues, it's probably worth going with a guide; call ☎ **021/387-5351.**)

### AFRICAN DRUMS

Every night the sounds of African drums resound down Long Street when the marimba bands play at **Mama Africa** (☎ **021/424-8364**); you're invited to join in at **The Drum Café** (☎ **021/461-1305**) on Glynn Street, Gardens. The best nights are Wednesdays (Mondays feature the women-only circle), and you can hire a drum for R10 ($1.65). Fridays is when live bands perform—don't miss an evening featuring Amapondo or Bayete.

### ROCK

For a more rock/indie sound, head for the **Purple Turtle** (☎ **021/423-6194**), on Shortmarket Street.

### OUTDOOR CONCERTS

Long evenings and late sunsets during summer make outdoor venues a great experience. **Kirstenbosch Summer Concerts** take place every Sunday evening, and may feature anything from the Cape Town Philarmonic to the Cape Minstrels; for program details, call ☎ **021/762-1162.** You can also order picnic meals to pick up when you arrive.

Call ☎ **021/418-2369** to hear what's on at the **Agfa Amphitheatre** at the Waterfront. (See above for Oude Libertas and Spier, amphitheatres located in the Winelands.) For over 150 years, the local minstrel troupes have taken to the city streets at New Year in the annual **"Coon Carnival."** Sporting painted faces, umbrellas, and boaters, they sashay from District Six to Green Point, where they dance and compete at the stadium. For more information, call Cape Town **Tourism** (☎ **021/418-5214**).

## CLUBS & BARS

There are two hot areas in town. Sandwiched between Long and Bree streets, this section of Waterkant Street pumps with a large selection of bars and clubs, but it can be testosterone heavy—the bottom end of Long Street (toward the mountain, near the

Turkish baths) is where you'll find the more laid-back groovers. I've listed some of the best below (but note that clubs come and go in this fickle town).

**The Fez** (☎ **021/423-1456,** 38 Hout St., close to Greenmarket Square) is the latest trendy hangout—Bedouin drapes hang from the ceilings, beautiful girls lounge in comfortable banquettes, and everything's softened with lighting and cocktails. **Rhythm Devine** (☎ **021/423-0333**) at the bottom end of Long Street is a young and friendly club. **Mama Africa** (no phone), **The Lounge** (☎ **021/424-7636**), and **Jo'burg** (no phone) are three venues that are within easy walking distance and in the backpacker precinct. **All Bar None** (☎ **021/425-3961,** 5 Bree St.) is one of the friendliest, vibiest bars in town—definitely call to find out what special events they're planning. Finally, head for **Angels** (☎ **021/419-8547,** Somerset Rd., Green Point); when drag queens are dancing away the night with go-go boys, you know this has got to be the most happening place in town.

### Cigar Bars

The lounge at **La Perla** (☎ **021/434-2471**, Beach Rd., Sea Point) is a classy and highly recommended place to puff away. **Cohibar** (☎ **021/424-1122**) and **Kennedy's** (☎ **021/424-1212**) are good town venues; while traditional cigar evenings are held at **Grande Roche** (☎ **021/863-2727**) in Paarl, and lesbian evenings at **Fiddlewoods** (☎ **021/448-6687,** Trill Rd., Observatory).

## 14 Drinking in the Winelands

South Africa has 13 designated wine routes, of which the area called the Winelands—comprising Somerset West, Stellenbosch, Paarl, and Franschhoek—is by far the most popular. While the towns are all within easy driving distance from each other, there are well over 100 estates to choose from, and first-time visitors are advised to concentrate on those that offer a combination of historic architecture and/or views of the vineyard-clad mountains. True oenophiles should refer to the box "Collecting Cape Wines," below. You can treat the Winelands as an excursion from Cape Town, or alternatively, you can base yourself here. No more than 45 to 75 minutes from the bright lights of the city, this is a great place to visit if you're looking to immerse yourself in rural peace and fine wines.

### QUICK FIX: TWO DRAMATIC WINELANDS DRIVES

Traversing four mountain ranges and encompassing both Franschhoek and Stellenbosch, the **Four Passes Route** will take a full day including a few stops for wine tastings and lunch. Head out of the city center on the N2, bypassing the turnoff for Stellenbosch (R310) and Somerset West (R44) and ascend the Hottentots' Holland Mountains via **Sir Lowry's Pass** with breathtaking views of the entire False Bay. Take the Franschhoek and Villiersdorp turnoff, traveling through the town of Grabouw, and traverse the Groenland Mountains via **Viljoen's Pass.** This takes you through fruit-producing valleys (exquisite in spring when bare brown branches are covered in pink and white blossoms) and past the Theewaterskloof Dam. Look out for a right turn (marked Franschhoek) and ascend the Franschhoek Mountains via the **Franschhoek Pass,** stopping at La Petite Ferme (see below) for tea. Having explored Franschhoek, drive to Stellenbosch via the equally scenic **Helshoogte Pass.** Take the R310 back to the N2 or overnight in Stellenbosch.

The second drive takes in the less well-known Breede River valley and the historic town of Tulbagh. Take the N1 out of town, past Paarl, then tackle the majestic **Du Toit's Kloof Pass** (if you've made a late start, take the tunnel; but it's long and murky—hold your breath). Once through the Du Toit's Kloof Mountains, you enter the Breede River valley, less publicized, but no less attractive than the more famous Winelands areas. Keep an eye out for the turnoff marked Rawsonville, then follow the signs north to Goudini Spa and **Slanghoek.** This scenic backroad meets the R43 in a T-junction—turn left and travel straight through the small town of Wolseley before taking the R46 to **Tulbagh.** Once there, stroll down Church Street to admire the Cape Dutch and Victorian buildings, perfectly restored after an earthquake destroyed them in 1969, and lunch at **Paddagang** (☎ **0236/300-242**): Their *waterblommetjiebredie* (waterlily stew) is arguably the best in the Cape. Then head back to Wolseley where you take the R303 to Wellington via **Bain's Kloof Pass,** another spectacular pass created by the same celebrated master engineer responsible for the Swartberg Pass outside Oudtshoorn. From **Wellington** follow the signs to Paarl where you could overnight, or head for the N1 and back to Cape Town.

## STELLENBOSCH

46km (28 miles) east of Cape Town

The charming town of Stellenbosch was founded in 1679 by Governor Simon van der Stel, who, amongst other achievements, built Groot Constantia and planted hundreds of oak trees throughout the Cape. Today Stellenbosch is, in fact, known informally as *Eikestad,* or "city of oaks." Its beautifully restored streetscape (it has the largest number of Cape Dutch houses in the region) makes Stellenbosch the loveliest of the Winelands' towns. If you have time to explore only a little of the town, start with the oak-lined streets of **Dorp, Church,** and **Drosdty.** The town is also known as the cultural center of the Cape, and has a number of theater options, though the best work is often in Afrikaans. Keep an eye out for listings in the local press or contact the Tourism Bureau to find out what's on at the **Oude Libertas** and **Spier amphitheatres** (see "Cape Town After Dark," above).

### ESSENTIALS

**VISITOR INFORMATION** Stellenbosch **Tourism Bureau** is by far the most helpful in the Winelands, and you'd be well advised to head for their office at 36 Market St. as soon as you arrive—besides giving expert advice on where to stay and what to do, staff distributes the excellent *Discover Stellenbosch on Foot* leaflet, which indicates over 60 historical sites with accompanying text. Call ☎ **021/883-3584** or e-mail them at eikestad@iafrica.com. Their hours are Monday to Friday 8am to 6pm, Saturday 9am to 5pm, Sunday 9:30am to 4:30pm; June to August they're open Monday to Friday 9am to 5pm, Saturday 9:30am to 4:30pm, and Sunday 10am to 4pm.

**GETTING AROUND** **Guided tours** leave the Tourist Bureau every day at 10am and 3pm. If you're overnighting, consider hiring the services of a **specialist guide.** Contact **Dries Smit** (☎ **021/887-2056**) or arrange a twilight walk by calling **Sandra** (☎ **021/887-9150**). The town center is small enough to explore **on foot,** but a **bicycle** (☎ **021/883-9103**) or **scooter** (☎ **021/887-9965**) is a good alternative.

### EN ROUTE TO STELLENBOSCH

**Vergelegen** (☎ **021/847-1334,** open daily 9:30 to 4pm), is the only must-see estate on the Somerset West or "Helderberg" Wine Route, which lies a few kilometers from Stellenbosch. Vergelegen (or, "far location") was built by reprobate Willem Adriaan van der Stel, who took over from his father as governor of the Cape in 1699, only to abuse his power by building Vergelegen on land that did not actually belong to him and by using the Dutch East India Company slaves and resources to compete with local farmers. He was sacked in 1707 and the farm demolished and divided. Today this

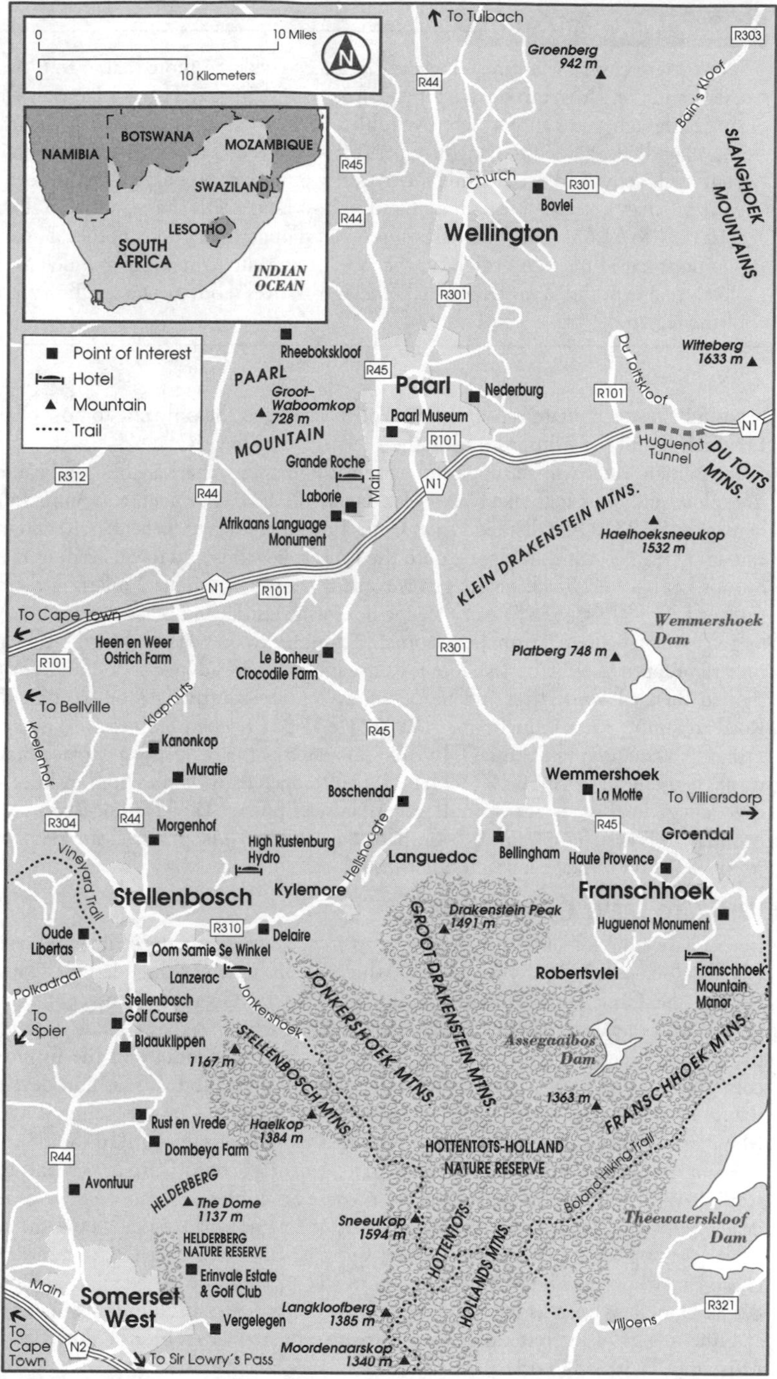
To Tulbach
R303
Groenberg
942 m
R44
Bain's Kloof
SLANGHOEK MOUNTAINS
0
10 Miles
0
10 Kilometers
N
NAMIBIA
BOTSWANA
MOZAMBIQUE
SWAZILAND
LESOTHO
SOUTH AFRICA
INDIAN OCEAN
R45
Church
R301
Bovlei
R44
Wellington
R301
Point of Interest
Hotel
Mountain
Trail
Rheebokskloof
R45
PAARL MOUNTAIN
Groot-Waboomkop
728 m
Paarl
Nederburg
Paarl Museum
Du Toitskloof
R101
Witteberg
1633 m
N1
Huguenot Tunnel
DU TOITS MTNS.
R101
Grande Roche
R312
R44
Main
Laborie
Afrikaans Language Monument
N1
KLEIN DRAKENSTEIN MTNS.
Haelhoeksneeukop
1532 m
N1
R101
To Cape Town
Heen en Weer Ostrich Farm
Wemmershoek Dam
R101
Le Bonheur Crocodile Farm
R301
Platberg 748 m
To Bellville
Klapmuts
Koelenhof
Kanonkop
Muratie
R45
Wemmershoek
La Motte
To Villiersdorp
Boschendal
R304
R44
Morgenhof
Hellshoogte
R45
Groendal
High Rustenburg Hydro
Bellingham
Languedoc
Haute Provence
Vineyard Trail
Stellenbosch
Kylemore
Franschhoek
Drakenstein Peak
1491 m
Oude Libertas
R310
Delaire
Huguenot Monument
Oom Samie Se Winkel
Lanzerac
Robertsvlei
Franschhoek Mountain Manor
Polkadraai
Jonkershoek
JONKERSHOEK MTNS.
GROOT DRAKENSTEIN MTNS.
Stellenbosch Golf Course
To Spier
Blaauklippen
STELLENBOSCH MTNS.
1167 m
Assegaaibos Dam
FRANSCHHOEK MTNS.
1363 m
Rust en Vrede
Haelkop
1384 m
Dombeya Farm
R44
HOTTENTOTS-HOLLAND NATURE RESERVE
Boland Hiking Trail
Avontuur
HELDERBERG
The Dome
1137 m
Sneeukop
1594 m
HOTTENTOTS-HOLLANDS MTNS.
Theewaterskloof Dam
HELDERBERG NATURE RESERVE
Erinvale Estate & Golf Club
Main
Somerset West
Langkloofberg
1385 m
R321
Viljoens
Vergelegen
To Cape Town
N2
To Sir Lowry's Pass
Moordenaarskop
1340 m

### Some Wine Route Tips

Don't try to cover the entire Winelands in a day; tackle no more than 4 to 6 estates a day; and don't forget to book a luncheon table with a view. This is a large and hilly area; although you can get here by public transportation (see "Getting Around," above) and take guided tours, you're best off seeing it by car, so that you can choose your own estates and pace. While the majority of wine estates accept credit cards for wine purchases, keep some cash on hand—most estates will charge between R5 and R10 (85¢ to $1.65) for a wine-tasting session, though many don't bother. Finally, if you don't have time to overnight in the Winelands, but want to see as much as possible, try one of the "Two Dramatic Winelands Drives" above, for a terrific overview of the region.

---

beautifully restored estate is Mandela's favorite, as well as the only one to host Queen Elizabeth II and the Clintons during their respective state visits.

In addition to the wine-tasting center and the homestead, there are beautiful gardens to explore, and tours that take place every day at 10:30am, 11:30am, and 3pm. To get here, pass the R310 (the first road from Cape Town that leads to Stellenbosch) and take exit 43 off the N2, which takes you onto the R44. Follow this into town, keeping an eye out for Lourensford Road. Vergelegen is some 3 kilometers (about 2 miles) farther on this road. The R7.50 ($1.25) entry fee includes wine tasting and cellar tours.

To get to Stellenbosch from here (some 20 minutes away) head back to the R44 and turn right (at the Lord Charles Hotel). Red-wine lovers are advised to look out for the sign to **Rust en Vrede** (rest and peace) along the way—turn right onto Annandale Road to sample these raunchy reds (☎ **021/881-3881,** open 8:30 to 5 Monday to Friday, 9:30am to 1pm Saturday). Families in search of the perfect picnic place should turn left and head for **Spier** (☎ **021/809-1100**), open daily 9am to 5pm. A little farther along the R44 is the turnoff for **Blaauwklippen** (☎ **021/880-0133,** open Monday to Friday from 9am to 5pm, Saturday 9am to 1pm), where from October 1 to April 30 you can take a coach ride through the vineyards.

## What to See & Do in Town

If you have time for only one historic stop in town, make it the **Village Museum** (☎ **021/887-2902;** 18 Ryneveld St.), which comprises the Schreuderhuis Cottage (1709), the Cape Dutch Blettermanhuis (1789), the Georgian Grosvenor House (1803), and the Victorian Murray House (1850). Each house has a guide dressed in the appropriate period costume, and the artful styling and beauty of the furniture, combined with the accessible explanations of the architectural and fashion developments of these eras, make these the best house museums in the country. Open Monday to Saturday 9:30am to 5pm, Sunday 2 to 5pm; admission R10 ($1.65).

From here head south along Drosdty Street, turn right onto Dorp Street, and then stroll down the oak-dappled street to **Oom Samie Se Winkel,** a Victorian-style general dealer bursting at the seams with knickknacks, and a great place to pick up some souvenirs. Pick up some step-by-step bobotie spice packs, a dried-fruit roll, or a few dirt-cheap enamel plates. The charming tea room (☎ **021/887-2612**) behind the shop at 82–84 Dorp St. is open Monday to Friday from 9am to 6pm and Saturday 9am to 5pm.

Other places of interest along Dorp Street include the **Rembrandt van Rijn Art Museum** (☎ **021/886-4340,** on the corner of Dorp and Aan-de-Wagen Weg; open Monday to Friday 9am to 12:45pm, and 2 to 5pm, Saturday 10am to 1pm and 2 to 5pm), housed in a Cape Dutch manor called "Libertas Parva," which displays work by some of South Africa's best artists, and the adjacent **Stellenryck Wine Museum** (☎ **021/887-3480;** same times).

## The Stellenbosch Wine Route

This is the oldest in the country, with 29 estates and farms to choose from, all located on the three major roads radiating from the town center. If you head southwest on the R306, you should consider driving up the pine avenue to the 300-year-old **Neethlingshof** (☎ **021/883-8988,** open Monday to Friday 9am to 5pm, and Saturday and Sunday 10am to 4pm). Then retrace your steps and take the R44 north to visit the beautiful **Morgenhof** (☎ **021/889-5510,** open Monday to Friday 9am to 5pm, Saturday and Sunday 10am to 3pm; from September to May, Saturday and Sunday hours extend to 5pm). A little farther north is the turnoff for **Muratie** (☎ **021/882-2330,** open Monday to Thursday from 9am to 5pm, Friday 9am to 4pm, and Saturday 9am to 3pm), a must for port lovers. **L'Avenir** (☎ **021/ 889-5001**), **Kanonkop** (☎ **021/ 884-4656**), and **Lievland** (☎ **021/875-5226**) are other good estates off the R44. If you're tired of wine, take the 10-kilometer (6-mile) circular drive through the mountainous **Jonkershoek Nature Reserve**—ask for a map from the Tourism Bureau.

## Where to Stay

**Bonne Esperance.** 17 Van Riebeeck St., Stellenbosch 7600. ☎ **021/887-0225.** Fax 021/887-8328. 15 units. MINIBAR TEL. R390–420 ($65–$70) double. AE, DC, MC, V. Children 10 and over only.

In a Victorian villa 2 minutes from Stellenbosch's historical heart, this is one of the best value-for-money guest houses in town. The rooms are on the small side, and some bathrooms are no bigger than a large cupboard, but the decor is charming, the rooms clean, and the management professional. While there are obviously no hotel facilities (staff will only prepare breakfast, but are happy to make restaurant recommendations and bookings), the size of the guest house makes for a great vibe, with the guest-list inevitably cosmopolitan, and the breakfast room and pool area provide ample opportunity to swap wine-tasting tips. There are two lounge-type rooms with TVs, one for smokers, who are requested to refrain elsewhere.

**D'Ouwe Werf.** 30 Church St., Stellenbosch 7600. ☎ **021/887-1608.** Fax 021/887-4626. 25 units. A/C MINIBAR TV TEL (stocked on request). R660–760 ($110–$126.65). Rates include breakfast. Ask for reduced rates May–Aug. AE, DC, MC, V.

Dating back to 1802 and conveniently located in the heart of historical Stellenbosch, D'Ouwe Werf is the oldest existing country inn in South Africa, and retains an old-fashioned country atmosphere. The hotel has been renovated, but there remain a few glimpses into its past, like the elegantly dressed foyer and the name of a visitor from a previous century inscribed in the yellowwood door to one of the rooms. Bedrooms are also extensively furnished with antiques—luxury rooms have real ones, classic rooms have reproductions. The classic rooms are located in the new section and have slightly larger bathrooms; all are equipped with hair dryers and tea- and coffee-making facilities. Staff are friendly and efficient and will make various travel arrangements, including airport transfers. The a la carte restaurant serves filling if rather uninspired meals, and the pool is a pond.

✪ **Lanzerac Manor & Winery.** Lanzerac Rd., Stellenbosch 7599. ☎ **021/887-1132.** Fax 021/887-2310. E-mail: info@lanzerac.co.za. 40 units. A/C MINIBAR TV TEL. Nov to mid-Apr R1,460–2,140 ($243.35–$356.65); Jun–Aug R920–1,300 ($153.35–$216.65); all other times R1,110–1,630 ($183.35–$271.65). Suites R2,860–4,980 ($476.65–$830), depending on size and season. Rates include breakfast. Children's rates on request. AE, DC, MC, V.

## Collecting Cape Wines

The flavor treasures of the Cape are sprinkled across the fan-shaped Cape vineyard region. They are usually found in one of many tiny cellar sales rooms at the end of a farm drive in the foothills of a granite- and sandstone-peaked mountain range. Using Cape Town and its Table Mountain as the handle of the fan, one can collect most of these gems on a circular sweep through the Cape Peninsula and Stellenbosch and Paarl Valleys.

Looking for crisp, firm white wines and succulent sweeties, you should begin in Constantia, just a few minutes from the city center. **Buitenverwachting** ("beyond expectation") regularly delivers the boldest and most spicy Sauvignons, rich honey-like Chardonnay, and a boldly structured, blended red called "Christine." Nearby, **Klein Constantia** competes with an equally dramatically fruited Sauvignon Blanc and one of the sweet wonders of the world, Vin de Constance. To find more of the Cape's great white wines, you should sweep southward around the scenic shores of False Bay to Somerset West and the Helderberg wineries.

**Vergelegen,** spectacularly mounted on the crest of an eroded mountain, produces a steely, racy Sauvignon Blanc, a multitextured Chardonnay, and a lime-flavored Semillon Noble Late Harvest—a sweet wine with a good 20 years of pleasure in the bottle.

On the other side of the Helderberg mountain range, close to Stellenbosch, we meet some great reds: Crescendo from **Cordoba** with its earth and pepper richness and **Grangehurst's** twin red blockbusters, Cabernet Sauvignon-Merlot and Pinotage. Even closer to Stellenbosch, you'll find another example of ripe-fruited Pinotage at **Vriesenhof.**

The Stellenbosch valley floor is bordered to the north by the Bottelary Hills, home to many of the area's best vineyards. The southern slopes, called "Polkadraai," shelter the luscious, sweet Noble Late Harvest wines of **Neethlingshof,** oozing with litchi, kiwi, and apricot fruit; the dense and creamy Pinotage reds from **Uiterwyk;** and two oak-aged white charmers from **Jordan** at the end of the cul-de-sac, where Chardonnay and Sauvignon Blanc develop enhanced fruit flavors. Just over the hill (or by road around the R306), you'll encounter the vine-clad slopes of **Saxenburg,** facing the waves of False Bay, where the Private Collection labels of Shiraz, Cabernet Sauvignon, and Pinotage require reservation and patience to acquire.

The Lanzerac, the Cape's only 5-star hotel to be affiliated to a working wine estate, sits sublimely amidst rolling vineyards in the beautiful Jonkershoek Valley, with spectacular views of the Helderberg mountain range from every angle. Rooms, furnished in expensive furniture and fabrics (though the toiletries are cheap), are what you'd expect from a member of Small Luxury Hotels of the World; luxury rooms are situated in separate chalets for additional privacy. The most expensive option, the Royal Pool Suite, features a private pool; but with three more to choose from, this really is an indulgence. The Lanzerac's position as the Winelands' most upmarket hotel is challenged only by Grande Roche; and while it is not as slick as its Paarl competitor, some would find the Lanzerac more user friendly.

**Dining:** The Governors Hall (see "Where to Dine") represents Stellenbosch's top fine-dining experience; while the Lanzerac Terrace offers an informal alternative.

On the other side of Stellenbosch, in the valley called Jonkershoek, Etienne le Riche crafts a densely hued, chunky Cabernet Sauvignon on a tiny farm called **Leef op Hoop** (Live on Hope) and, near the end of the road, **Neil Ellis** practices his skills with one of the Cape's most respected Cabernet Sauvignons, a rich, complex Chardonnay, and two cool-climate-origin Sauvignon Blancs, from the West Coast (Groenekloof) and South Coast (Elgin).

Nearby, high on the mountain slopes, the tiny **Thelema Vineyards** offer four Cape classic wines: opulent, creamy Chardonnay; gooseberry-flavoured Sauvignon Blanc; a minty Merlot; and probably most revered of all Cape Cabernets, Thelema Auction Reserve Cabernet Sauvignon. Downhill to the west, you'll find **Rustenberg,** home of many of the Cape's great reds over the last 40 years, and where you should search out the labels of Rustenberg and Peter Barlow. Next door, the terraced vineyards of **Morgenhof** produce a notable Merlot with a dark chocolate and coffee character and a firm-fleshed Chardonnay with maturation potential.

Two great Pinotages beckon the traveler toward Paarl, where you'll find Marc Wiehe's **L'Avenir** Pinotage with its fragrant red-currant flavor, which contrasts dramatically with the massive structure and cherry-rich style of the landed Pinotage from neighbouring **Kanonkop.**

Crossing an invisible boundary line into Paarl, first stop should be with **Villiera's** prized champagne-styled bubbly, Tradition, followed by the farm's intensely spicy Bush Vine Sauvignon Blanc. Just for fun, compare this with the nearby **Mulderbosch** Sauvignon.

**Fairview,** with its goat-encrusted tower, produces some of the Cape's most finely modeled wines, with the powerful, peppery Shiraz and plum-like Pinotage providing two standouts.

Two of Paarl's top vineyards specialise in Cabernet Sauvignon and Merlot: The **Veenwouden** Merlot is dense and complex with gentle flavours; while **Plaisir de Merle** has a deliciously soft and round Cabernet Sauvignon. A finely structured Shiraz from **La Motte** completes the lineup from the Paarl and Franschhoek Valley.

—by Graham Knox, wine connoisseur and author of *Cape Wines: Body & Soul*

**River Manor.** No. 6 The Avenue, Stellenbosch 7600. ☎ **021/887-9944.** Fax 021/887-9940. E-mail: rivermanor@adept.co.za. 8 units. TV TEL. R450–550 ($75–$71.65) double; R650 ($108.35) suite. Rates include breakfast. AE, DC, MC, V. Children 12 and over only.

River Manor is a two-story guest house on an oak-lined road which follows the course of the Eerste River, and is a few minutes stroll from the historic attractions of Stellenbosch. If you're staying more than one night, ask for a luxury room (R100/$16.65 more); if you're staying more than two nights, book the suite—a large airy room, and the only one with a small private balcony overlooking the leafy avenue. River Manor will provide picnic baskets and dinner on request, though there are restaurants within walking distance. Rooms come equipped with hair dryers. This is not as well situated as D'Ouwe Werf, and does not offer hotel facilities, but like Bonne Esperance is ideal for the younger traveler looking for value for money.

## Where to Dine

In addition to the restaurants discussed below, keep these other good options in mind. **96 Winery Road** (☎ **021/842-2020,** on the road between Stellenbosch and Somerset West) is often quoted as one of the country's top-10 restaurants, and has a wonderful selection of wines. Nearby **L'Auberge du Paysan** (☎ **021/842-2008,** on Raithby Rd., Firgrove) serves classic French cuisine in a fine-dining atmosphere. To sample traditional food, head for **Pride of the Plate** (☎ **021/887-9991**), on Andringa St., where meals are weighed, or to **De Volkskombuis** (☎ **021/887-2121,** on Aan-de-Wagenweg, off Dorp St.). Both are in town. Other good town venues are **Wijnhuis** (☎ **021/887-5844**) in the Dorpsmeent Complex on Andringa Street, where you can combine good fare with wine tastings of the region's best till 10pm, and **Decameron** (☎ **021/883-3331,** at 50 Plein St.), the best Italian restaurant in town.

**Governers' Hall.** Lanzerac Hotel Lanzerac Rd. ☎ **021/887-1132.** Main courses R45–98 ($7.50–$16.35) Set-price menu R145 ($24.15). 7–10:30am, 12–2:30pm, 7–10:30pm, daily. AE, DC, MC, V. INTERNATIONAL/MODERN CAPE.

Traditional buffet luncheons in this sumptuously decorated dining room lined with gilt-framed oils of past Cape governors combine fine dining with traditional South African fare. Chef Jens Popp even roasts his own Cape Malay spices. Dinner is a choice between a set and a la carte menu, both as influenced by French preparation as by available local ingredients. Main courses include a perfectly prepared fresh linefish, baked in a Parmesan crust on braised fennel roots. West Coast sole was, however, bland and dull. If you'd prefer a less formal experience, the terrace menu provides breakfasts for under R30 ($5) and light meals for under R50 ($8.35). The prawn and chicken curry is a winner.

**The Green Door.** Delaire Wine Farm, Helshoogte Pass, off the R310. ☎ **021/885-1756.** Main courses R28–60 ($4.65–$10). Tues–Sun 12–3pm. AE, DC, MC, V. INTERNATIONAL.

Most come here for the view, which is almost as good as that from La Petite Ferme—the restaurant's verandah overlooks the mountainous Helshoogte Valley, only slightly marred by the R310 twisting below. But people also come in droves for the food, which ranges from Mediterranean-inspired (roasted peppers filled with grilled vegetables) to regional (Franschhoek salmon trout baked with butter, lemon, and herbs) and eastern (an absolutely delicious Thai seafood salad). This is one of the best value-for-money restaurants in the Winelands.

**Lady Phillips.** Vergelegen Farm, Lourensford Rd., Somerset West. ☎ **021/847-1346.** Reservations recommended. Main courses R25–46 ($4.15–$7.65). Tea daily 9:30–11:30am and 3–4:30pm. Lunch daily 12:30–2:30pm. AE, DC, MC, V. COUNTRY FARE.

Lady Phillips describes itself as a tea garden, but make no mistake—this will still give many a Wineland restaurant a run for its money. The small menu changes seasonally, but you can expect simple, flavorful dishes like the specialty pies, filled with guinea fowl, duck with orange, game and apricot, or lamb and rosemary. Vegetarians are well catered for with salads, (grown and picked on the farm), tarts, and the vegetable curry, flavored with traditional Cape Malay spices (cassia, cumin, ginger, and coriander). Book a table under an umbrella in the delightful garden in summer, and in winter make sure you're seated close to the log fire. Note that there's a R7.50 ($1.30) entrance fee to the estate.

# FRANSCHHOEK

33km (20 miles) from Stellenbosch; 79km (49 miles) from Cape Town via Stellenbosch; 85km (53 miles) from Cape Town via Paarl

If you only have time for one Winelands town, head for Franschhoek (French corner), the land Simon van der Stel gave the French Huguenots fleeing religious persecution in 1688. This small valley surrounded by mountains is so lush a local once compared it to "living in a lettuce."

### ESSENTIALS

**VISITOR INFORMATION** **Franschhoek Tourism Bureau** (☎ **021/876-3603**) on the main road going into town, at 85 Huguenot Road, is open Monday to Friday 9am to 5pm, Saturday 9:30am to 1:30pm, and Sunday 10am to 1:30pm. Hours are extended from October to April. Make sure to pick up one of their helpful maps.

**GETTING AROUND** See "Outdoor Activities" earlier in this chapter for information on wine tasting by carriage or on horseback.

### EN ROUTE TO FRANSCHHOEK

You can take the R310 over scenic **Helshoogte Pass** to Franschhoek and Paarl, both of which lie some 30 minutes from Stellenbosch. After 2 kilometers (just more than 1 mile) on the R310, turn left into Idas Valley and head for **Rustenberg** (☎ **021/887-3153**), open Monday to Friday 8:30am to 4:30pm, Saturday 9am to 12:30pm. There is no restaurant on this estate, renowned for its peaceful and beautiful setting, but visitors are welcome to picnic under the oaks. Alternatively, stop for lunch or tea at **Delaire** on the Helshoogte Pass, which has one of the best mountain views in the Winelands (see "The Green Door," above). **Thelema** (☎ **021/885-1924**) is adjacent, and (unlike Delaire) has an outstanding reputation for its wines; though disappointingly, they are often sold out.

Having traversed the pass, you will come to a T-junction where the R310 intersects with the R45—turn left for Paarl; right for Franschhoek.

Be sure to take the turnoff to **Boschendal** (☎ **021/870-4000,** Monday to Saturday 8:30am to 4:30pm; May to October Saturday 8:30am to 12:30pm; December to January Sundays 8:30am to 12:30pm), clearly signposted off the R45. Together with Vergelegen, this is one of the Winelands' most attractive estates, combining an excellent manor house museum with beautiful grounds, and is definitely worth visiting despite being somewhat touristy. Boschendal offers a number of dining options (see below).

### WHAT TO SEE & DO

The following estates, all clearly signposted off Main Road and its extension, Huguenot Road, are recommended. **Bellingham** (☎ **021/874-1011,** open Monday to Friday 9am to 5pm, and Saturday 10am to 1pm) has been producing wine for three centuries. **La Motte** (☎ **021/876-3119,** open Monday to Friday 9am 4:30pm, and Saturday 9am to 12pm) is worth seeing for its modern designer tasting room, not to mention its good wines. Time allowing, visit **Haute Provence** (☎ **021/876-3195,** open daily 9am to 4pm) for its lovely Angels Tears wine, and **Mont Rochelle** (☎ **021/876-3000,** open Monday to Saturday 11am to 4pm, and in September to April, Sunday 11am to 1pm) for its glorious setting—you can also purchase a picnic basket here.

A visit to the **Cabriere Estate** (☎ **021/876-2630,** open Monday to Friday 11am to 3pm) is also recommended—and not just for their excellent bubbly (of which they have five varieties)—with any luck you'll witness a demonstration by winemaker Achim von Arnim who "uncorks" his bottles by slicing the neck off with a sabre.

Huguenot Road finally intersects with Lambrecht Road at a T-junction at the base of the Franschhoek Mountains. Opposite is the **French Huguenot Monument** erected in honour of the French Protestant refugees who settled in the valley between 1688 and 1700. Its three arches symbolize the Holy Trinity. Turn left to drive up the Franschhoek Pass for tea or lunch at **La Petite Ferme** (a must, if you can get a table—see below), passing the **Franschhoek Museum** (☎ **021/876-2532**) on your right.

The museum is open Monday to Friday 9am to 4pm; Saturday 9am to 1pm and 2 to 5pm, and Sunday 2 to 5pm; admission is R4/65¢), but is only worth visiting if you have a real interest in the origins and history of the valley.

Alternatively, turn right and eat at **La Couronne** (see "Where to Stay") or explore the winding roads that take you farther into the Franschhoek Mountains.

## WHERE TO STAY

As this is the prettiest of the valleys, it's worth noting that there are a number of lovely self-catering cottages situated in the vineyards, some with swimming pools and/or fireplaces, most with mountain views. Prices range from R85 ($14.15) to R150 ($25) per person; contact **Klein Dassenberg Cottages** (☎ **021/876-2107**), **Vineyard Cottages** (☎ **021/876-3194**), or **Bird Cottage** (☎ **021/876-2136**). For a cute cottage in town, call **Lavender Cottage** (☎ **021/876-2666**).

### Expensive

**La Couronne.** Robertsvlei Rd. (turn right at the monument), Franschhoek 7690. ☎ **021/876-2770.** Fax 021/876-3788. 10 units. MINIBAR TV TEL. R700–900 ($116.65–$150) double. AE, DC, MC, V.

La Couronne (the crown) is on a hill overlooking the Franschhoek Valley and Mountains; its views are challenged only by those at La Petite Ferme (see below). Until recently the property of the president of the Ivory Coast, the new owners have spent R15 ($2.5) million on refurbishing the home and have turned it into a well-appointed guest house. Every window has a view, and the rooms are spacious, with king-size beds, underfloor heating, and down pillows. Decor is predominantly gold and yellow, with a distinct English-manor influence (ask for number 3, the unofficial honeymoon suite). There are no tea- or coffee-making facilities—a pity as room service is not 24-hour. The spacious bathrooms are cheapened by a bad choice of fittings. The large pool and comfortable and elegant public spaces (once again, all with beautiful views) mean you could easily spend the entire day at the hotel. Meals are excellent, and the young London chef specializes in perfectly prepared steak. Trout fishing is available.

**L'Auberge du Quartier Francais.** 16 Huguenot Rd., Franschhoek 7690. ☎ **021/876-2151.** Fax 021/876-3105. E-mail: res@lqf.co.za. www.lqf.co.za. 17 units. TV TEL. R890 ($148.35) double; R2,400 ($400) suite. AE, DC, MC, V.

Until La Couronne opened, this was the undisputed choice of discerning travelers to the Franschhoek Valley, a cluster of rooms and a library built around a large oval pool, with comfortable and spacious bedrooms. Wood-burning fireplaces ward off winter chills, while ceiling fans dispel some of the heat. The best rooms are 16 and 12; each has a leafy private seating area within the garden. The pool suite, comparable to the Grande Roche and Lanzerac in price, features a private pool in a lovely walled garden. The staff is efficient and the overall service standards are high, but the fact that it is "in" rather than overlooking the valley is a drawback.

### Moderate

**Auberge Clermont.** Robertsvlei Rd., Franschhoek 7690. ☎ **021/876-3700.** Fax 021/876-3701. E-mail: clermont@mweb.co.za. 6 units. TV TEL. R680 ($115) double; R960 ($160) suite. Rates include breakfast. AE, DC, MC, V.

In a working wine farm in the old wine cellar, this auberge is inspired by the tastes and colors of Provençe. Even the gardens, redolent with the scents of lavender and roses, are reminiscent of the South of France. Rooms are large and beautifully decorated; bathrooms are equally spacious with double basins, separate showers, and heated towel racks. Breakfast is served in your room or under the 400-year-old oak trees. For families, there is a spacious three-bedroom, two-bathroom self-catering villa in a formal French garden. Note that the suite is the same price as a room at the superbly situated La Couronne and the pool is on the small side.

**La Petite Ferme.** Franschhoek Pass Rd., Franschhoek 7690. ☎ **021/876-3016.** Fax 021/876-3624. 3 units. MINIBAR (stocked on request) TEL TV. R550 ($91.65) double, includes breakfast. AE, DC, MC, V. No children under 16.

Together with La Couronne, these three B&B cottages offer the very best views of the valley, and from a comfort and location point of view, this is also the best value for money in the valley. Each unit has its own fireplace and private plunge pool, and suites are equipped with every convenience. Every morning a continental breakfast is served on your verandah from where you can appreciate a sweeping view of the valley; luncheons and dinners can be enjoyed at the adjacent restaurant or at Haute Cabriere across the road—as these are currently the best dining options around, you may find it difficult to descend into the valley at all.

### Inexpensive

**Mountain Manor.** Robertsvlei Rd., Franschhoek 7690. ☎ **021/876-2071.** Fax 021/876-2177. 14 units. TV TEL. R360 ($60) double, includes breakfast. Children under 12 stay free, excluding breakfast. AE, DC, MC, V.

This dilapidated hotel is in an exquisite location. Surrounded by trees and mountain views, it seems to be totally in the country yet is only a few minutes from town. The decor is unexceptional and at times downright dubious, but the rooms, while small, are comfortable—and for this price, no one can complain. The Goats Bar and Mountain View restaurant cater for in-house dining, but the beautiful views are somewhat marred by overcooked buffets (the same every night). Foodies are better off heading into town or booking one of their one-bedroom chalets, which have kitchens and braai facilities and cost the same as a standard hotel room. Sporting facilities include squash and tennis courts, a bowling green, horse riding, and a gymnasium, as well as the best located swimming pool in the valley.

## WHERE TO DINE

Franschhoek calls itself "the wine and food capital of the Cape," and while most Capetonians would disagree, it certainly can claim that title in Winelands. In addition to those listed below, two other excellent options are **Monneaux** (☎ **021/876-3386**), located in Franschhoek Country House on the Main Road into Franschhoek and **Topsi & Company** (☎ **021/876-2319**), also on the main road as you're driving into Fran. Monneaux is renowned for its innovative modern French cuisine. Topsi (considered the doyenne of Cape chefs—she was featured in Robert Carrier's *Great Dishes of the World,* Smithmark Publishing) and her vegetarian daughter prepare everything from offal to butterfish. Ideal for parents, **Chamonix** (☎ **021/876-2494**) serves simple, good food and has a grassy area great for kids, as well as a kid's menu. Reservations are essential.

**Boschendal.** Pniel Rd., off R310 between Franschhoek and Paarl, Groot Drakenstein. ☎ **021/874-1152.** Buffet daily 12:15–5pm (arrivals no later than 1:30pm; reservations essential) R107.50 ($17.90) per person. Le Café 10am–5pm daily; R20–45 ($3.35–$7.50). Le Pique Nique, R55 ($9.15) per person, lunch only. AE, DC, MC, V. TRADITIONAL/COUNTRY.

This historic estate offers three different dining experiences. A buffet is served in the original wine cellar, which groans under a variety of traditional Cape Malay dishes like malva pudding (arguably the best in South Africa), Franschhoek specialties like smoked salmon trout, and delicacies like springbok carpaccio with raspberry compote.

This is a great place to break a fast. If you're not that hungry, you can sit at one of the wrought-iron tables under the oaks at Le Café and order one of their delicious quiches (the smoked salmon trout is recommended) or a half baguette with a choice of fillings. You can also purchase a picnic to enjoy on the shady lawns (see below).

✪ **Haute Cabriere Cellar Restaurant.** Pass Rd. ☎ **021/876-3688.** Main courses R26–62 ($4.35–$10.35). Daily 12–3pm; Wed–Mon 7–9pm. AE, DC, MC, V. INTERNATIONAL/SOUTH AFRICAN/MODERN CAPE.

As this restaurant is on the wrong side of the pass for valley views, the designers did the sensible thing and looked inward, over the submerged wine cellar. The rose-covered bunker is almost hidden from the road, and the vaulted ceiling gives it a modern medieval feel. Only the well-respected wines of this estate—chosen to complement each meal—are served, and there are no appetizers or main courses, just full or half portions or shared platters to mix and match. Try the three-cheese risotto with watercress sauce and the roasted loin of springbok with sweet potato, butternut fritters, baby corn, and Ratafia jus. Haute Cabriere has in recent years overtaken Le Quartier Francaise as Franschoek's best—make this your number one choice for dinner, and visit La Petite Ferme for lunch.

✪ **La Petite Ferme.** Pass Rd. ☎ **021/876-3016.** Reservations essential. R25–48 ($4.15–$8). Daily 12–4:30pm. AE, DC, MC, V. CAPE COUNTRY.

If you are only spending one day in Franschhoek, make sure you lunch here: Book a table on the verandah, order the deboned smoked rainbow trout served with a creamy horseradish sauce, and allow plenty of time to drink in both the view and one of the farm's superb wines. Even the locals can't resist dining here—situated on the Franschhoek Pass with a breathtaking view of the entire valley, this family owned and managed restaurant has arguably the best setting in South Africa (though The Green Door at Delaire is a strong contender) and serves simple wholesome fare. (Though popular table seven is considered the prime position and is booked for months in advance, on a recent visit a manager told me that table 4 has just as good a view). The Portuguese-style calamari, marinated in red wine and grilled, is recommended.

**Le Quartier Francais.** Corner of Berg and Wilhelmina sts. ☎ **021/876-2151.** Main courses R38–52 ($6.35–$8.65). Daily 7:30–10:30am; 12;30–2pm and 7–10pm. PROVENÇAL/ MODERN CAPE.

Once considered the best in Franschhoek (and in this haute cuisine environment that takes some doing), Le Quartier overlooks its own sheltered gardens in the center of town. The chef is renowned for her innovative flavor combinations—while dishes like "double-baked blue cheese soufflé with watercress gnocchi and red pepper compote," and "grilled loin of springbok with spiced oranges, warm lentil dressing and celery" deserve rave reviews, my "poached salmon on a salmon and onion fritter" was almost inedible. When in doubt, stick to classics, like the filet of beef served with a béarnaise sauce (predictable but good). There is also a small terrace menu featuring simpler soups, salads, and pastas.

## PAARL

33km (20 miles) northwest of Franschhoek, 56km (35 miles) from Cape Town

Paarl is named after the great granite rocks that loom above the town—the first European party to visit the area in 1657 watched the dawn sun reflecting off the glistening boulders after a night of rain, and named it Peerlbergh (Pearl Mountain). These 500-million-year-old domes are incidentally one of the world's largest granite outcrops, second only to Ayers Rock in Australia. The town's large size makes it a somewhat less attractive destination than the chichi village of Franschhoek and the oak-lined avenues of Stellenbosch, but there are a number of excellent wine estates to visit, and Main Street, with its 2-kilometer (just more than a mile) stretch of beautifully preserved buildings, is definitely worth taking a leisurely drive along.

### ESSENTIALS

**GETTING THERE** To get to Paarl from Franschhoek (some 30km/19 miles northwest), retrace your footsteps down Huguenot Road and take the R303 to Paarl (off the main road, after the turnoff to La Motte). Once in town look out for the first traffic circle and turn left onto Market; keep going until Market meets Main Street.

**VISITOR INFORMATION** The **Paarl Information Bureau (☎ 021/872-3829,** open Monday to Friday 9am to 5pm, Saturday 9am to 1pm, Sun 10am to 1pm) is at 216 Main St. The bureau has a selection of good maps and will assist with restaurant or accommodation recommendations.

### WHAT TO SEE & DO

If you're interested in the history of the area and won't have a chance to visit the Village Museum in Stellenbosch, consider stopping at the **Paarl Museum (☎ 021/872-2651,** 303 Main St.), open Monday to Friday 10am to 5pm, and Saturday 10am to 12pm. It's housed in one of the most attractive Cape Dutch buildings lining Main Street, the old Dutch Reformed parsonage, dating back to 1787. A few blocks away, on Pastorie Street, is the **Afrikaans Taal** (language) **Museum (☎ 021/872-3441,** open Monday to Friday 9am to 1pm and 2 to 5pm), which chronicles the development of the world's youngest language. Most foreign visitors will find a visit to the **Taal Monument** (the large phallic sculpture clearly visible on the slopes of Paarl Mountain) more satisfying (as it were), since the views of the valley and False Bay from here are excellent. To get here, drive down Main Street passing the KWV headquarters on your left and look out for the signs to your right.

Keen shoppers shouldn't miss Clementina van der Walt's **A.R.T. Gallery (☎ 021/ 872-3420,** off R303 to Wellington; open Monday to Friday 9am to 5pm and Saturday 9:30am to 3:30pm) for brightly colored tableware, cutlery, baskets, and textiles.

If you've timed your Paarl visit to coincide with lunch, the restaurant at **Rhebokskloof (☎ 021/863-8386,** open Monday to Friday 9am to 5pm, Saturday and Sunday 9am to 4pm; see "Where to Dine") has the best location, overlooking a lake with swans and adjoining a nature reserve. Drive out of Paarl (toward the N1) along the main road and look out for the sign at Jan Phillips Drive. Alternatively keep heading along the main road and take the R101 southwest for **Fairview (☎ 021/ 863-2450,** Monday to Friday 8:30am to 5pm, Saturday 8:30am to 1pm). The resident goats (milking is at 4pm) and raucous peacocks make this a good family option as does the deli, where you can choose a selection of cold meats and cheeses produced by the estate, and picnic on the lawns.

### WHERE TO STAY

**Grande Roche.** PO Box 6038, Paarl 7622. **☎ 021/863-2727.** Fax 021/863-2220. E-mail: reserve@granderoche.co.za. www.granderoche.co.za. 35 units. A/C MINIBAR TV TEL. Oct–Apr R1,450 ($241.65) double; suites from R1,700 ($283.35). May–Sept R1,200 ($200) double; suites from R1,450 ($241.45). Dec 12–Jan 10 5-night minimum stay; 2-night minimum remainder of year. Rates include breakfast. AE, DC, MC, V. Children 7 and older only.

The worst thing about staying at the Grande Roche is that eventually you'll have to leave. This is 5-star escapism at its best: a beautifully restored 18th century estate surrounded

## The Last Step to Freedom

Paarl made international headlines when President Mandela, who spent his last years here under house arrest, took his final steps to freedom from the Victor Verster prison on the outskirts of town on February 11, 1990. This was the first time South Africans could see how 27 years of incarceration had changed Mandela—in fact, many had never seen his face; for under the Prisons Act, not even old pictures were allowed to be published.

by lush gardens and with the Drakenstein Mountains as dramatic backdrop. The doubles have integrated lounges/bedrooms, but are still luxurious and roomy. Suites have separate lounge areas, enormous bathrooms, separate shower/tubs, and feel like private apartments—especially when you're sipping a pre-dinner glass of wine overlooking rosebushes and trailing vines. Ignore the schizophrenic decor (orange upholstery, rustic thatched roof, and Japanese watercolors) and head for your private terrace or one of the pools. Touches like the good selection of magazines on your coffee table and the welcoming fruit baskets are thoughtful (but the flower in the toilet is less appealing).

**Dining:** The 5-star **Bosman's Restaurant** is a culinary treat not to be missed. See "Where to Dine," below.

**Amenities:** Fitness center, laundry/dry cleaning, hairdressing, massage therapy, 24-hour room service, and pool.

**Lemoenkloof.** 396A Main St, Paarl 7646. ☎/fax **021/872-3782.** E-mail: lemkloof@adept.co.za. 20 units. A/C MINIBAR TV TEL. R400–440 ($66.65–$73.35). Ask for winter specials. Rates include breakfast. AE, DC, MC, V. Children 8 and over only.

Situated in a National Monument, in the historic center of Paarl, Lemoenkloof offers real value for money. Rooms are artfully decorated, featuring a mix of antiques and period pieces, and are equipped with all creature comforts including tea- and coffee-making facilities. Ask for a honeymoon suite if you're staying longer than one night; these larger rooms are a mere R40 ($6.65) extra. A small pool ensures cool summers, and all rooms are carpeted and heated for winter. Owner Hannelie supplies very personalized service and will make various travel arrangements, including airport transfers.

**Palmiet Valley.** PO Box 9085, Klein Drakenstein 7628. ☎ **021/862-7741.** Fax 021/862-6891. E-mail: palmiet@cis.co.za. palmiet-valley.idtravel.net/. 9 units. TV TEL. R690 ($115); R920 ($153.35) suite. Winter rates negotiable. Rates include breakfast. MC, V.

Situated on a working wine farm in a historic homestead dating back to 1717, Palmiet Valley is at the foot of the Drakenstein Mountains, a few kilometres east of Paarl. With 14 golf courses in a 30-kilometer (19 mile) radius, this is a good choice for golfers. Rooms are spacious and—like the entire guest house—furnished with an exquisite selection of antiques. Once outdoors, you can enjoy beautiful views of the surrounding vineyards and craggy mountains from every angle, including the terrace and decent-size pool (essential in summer). Dinners (R100/$16.65; often Cape Malay–influenced and specializing in fish) are served in the period-styled dining room at one table. If you don't want to be forced into a dinner party with people you've never met, your host will set up a more private option. A chauffeur-driven limousine is available for daily charter or airport transfers.

**Roggeland.** PO Box 7210, Northern Paarl 7623. ☎ **021/868-2501.** Fax 021/868-2113. E-mail: rog@iafrica.com. 11 units. TEL. R940–1,100 ($156.65–183.35). Rates include breakfast and four-course dinner with wine. (May–July less 30%.) AE, DC, MC, V.

The visitor's book at Roggeland—another gracious guest house in the Klein Drakenstein Valley—is a who's who of traveling writers and foodies, all of whom rave about this 300-year-old estate. World-famous chef Robert Carrier called it "an inspiration," *Travel & Leisure* described as "one of the world's 20 best hotels," and the *New York Times* named it the "preferred choice of hotel in the Winelands." Furnishings are not as pretty as Palmiet, but rooms are spacious and comfortable, the location is tranquil, the service discreet and efficient, and the food is some of the best in the Cape (see "Where to Dine"). Airport transfers can be arranged, and there is a medium-size pool.

**Zomerlust Guest House.** 193 Main St, Paarl 7622. ☎ **021/872-2117.** Fax 021/872-8312. E-mail: zomer@iafrica.com. www.kontrei.co.za/zomerlust/. 14 units. A/C TV TEL. R820 ($136.65) double; R955 ($159.15) suite. Low-season May–Aug R632 ($105.35); R742 ($123.65) suite. Rates include breakfast. AE, DC, MC, V.

Zomerlust is conveniently located on Paarl's historic Main Street, with most of the bedrooms situated in the original 1865 manor house. The interior is old-fashioned but stylish, with rich, dark furnishings (many of which are antiques), and heavy brocade-like fabrics. Room sizes vary considerably, but most are pretty small—request a large room or the suite if you're staying more than one night. Behind the manor house is the Kontreihuis restaurant serving mostly traditional South African food, with tables that flow out to the gardens and fountain; it's a peaceful haven that contrasts strongly with the busy street entrance. Four more rooms are situated in the original stables, called "Die Stal." Ask for one of the upstairs rooms in this building; these have instant access to the gardens, and are close to the secluded pool area. Facilities include room service, a library, and lounge with fireplace. All rooms are equipped with hair dryers and tea- and coffee-making facilities.

## WHERE TO DINE

**Bosman's Restaurant.** Plantasie St. (in the Grande Roche Hotel). ☎ **021/863-2727.** Reservations essential. Three-course lunch menu R95 ($15.85). Dinner set menus from R149 ($24.85); appetizers R20–40 ($3.35–$6.65); main courses R87 ($14.50). Open daily 7:00–10:30am; 12:00–2pm; 6:30–9pm. AE, DC, MC, V. CONTINENTAL/MODERN CAPE.

The first and only hotel restaurant in Africa to achieve Relais Gourmand status, Bosman's has been wowing local and international food critics alike for years. Menus change daily, but the set-price "Flavours of the Cape" menu's innovative look at traditional fare is particularly recommended—you won't find prawn samoosas, karoo lamb carpaccio, duck bobotie, and biltong tagliatelle anywhere else in the world. Culling a variety of influences, the chefs produce astonishing flavor combinations that dance on the tongue—a trio of tuna is served with a wasabi mayonaise and a sweet balsamic reduction; an *amuse bouche* of marinated kingklip marries soy sauce, cumin, and slivered vegetables. Even the pedestrian black-bean soup is gussied up with swordfish and brandy. Unfortunately, the cuisine is marred by service that confuses sophistication with cloying formality—the incessant readjusting of one's butter knife is intrusive, and a request for a glass of tap water is likely to be met with an upturned nose, not to mention a lengthy wait. Should Bosman's ever refine its service to the level of its food, this will be a fine-dining experience in all senses of the word.

**Laborie.** Taillefer St. (on the main road into Paarl). ☎ **021/807-3095.** Main courses R28–54 ($4.65–$9). Daily 12:30–2pm; Tues–Sat 7–9pm. AE, DC, MC, V. TRADITIONAL/COUNTRY.

Housed in a beautiful Cape Dutch building, furnished with yellowwood tables and stinkwood chairs, this elegant yet laid-back restaurant offers the best value for money in the Winelands. The small menu features simple dishes like chicken pie, tripe, guinea fowl, rump of lion, pork neck, as well as a seasonal dish of the day.

**Rhebokskloof.** Rhebokskloof Estate, Agter Paarl. ☎ **021/863-8386.** Main courses R49–55 ($8.15–$9.15). Thurs–Tues 12:30–2:30pm; Thurs–Mon 6:30–9pm. AE, DC, MC, V. CONTINENTAL.

Yet another restaurant with a superb setting, this one overlooking the estate's manicured lawns and lake, Rhebokskloof offers alfresco dining in summer, and fire-side warmth in winter. Chef Stefan Achterfeld produces innovative fare such as a catch of the day crusted in sesame and coriander and served with ginger butter sauce, a trio of rosti with individual toppings (mushroom ragout, smoked salmon trout, and tomato and cheese), and the ostrich with mushroom and port jus on mushroom risotto. Rhebokskloof is a good alternative to the ever-popular Roggeland.

**Roggeland.** Roggeland Rd. (in the Roggeland Hotel), Dal Josaphat Valley, Northern Paarl. ☎ **021/868-2501.** Reservations essential. R120 ($20) four-course table d'hôte, includes wine. Daily 6:45–10:30pm. AE, DC, MC, V. INTERNATIONAL/MODERN CAPE.

Vying with Bosman as the favorite of Paarl's foodies, this European/Thai/Cape fusion restaurant sits a maximum of 28 guests. The four-course menu changes daily, depending on what's available in the garden and surrounding farms. In summer you might have basil and lemongrass soup; smoked ostrich and roasted pear salad with a green peppercorn and yogurt dressing; musselcracker with red-pepper sauce and barley risotto; and lemon soufflé tart with raspberry sorbet. Winter menus are suitably heavier. Guests are invited to join in an informal wine tasting on the lawns from 6:45pm. Wines are paired with the food, taking the headache out of choosing. As residents obviously enjoy preferential seating, book in advance if you can't spend a night.

4

# The Western & Northern Cape

The Western Cape, Africa's southwesternmost tip, is the most popular tourist destination in South Africa, and with good reason. Besides the sybaritic pleasures of Cape Town and its wine routes (see previous chapter), there is the vast Southern Right whale nursery that stretches along the Cape's southern coast. Some of the best land-based whale-watching sites in the world are in the Overberg, with the whales migrating to its shallow coastal basin to mate and calve from mid-July to November. Adjacent to this area are the coastal lakes and forests of the Garden Route, fringed by the majestic mountains that separate it from the ostrich farms and vineyards of the Klein Karoo, and the distinctive architecture of the small settlements dotted in the vast arid plains of the Great Karoo. This is a beautiful part of the world to explore by car, while the Garden Route should take pride of place on the itinerary for adrenaline junkies, with activities ranging from paragliding courses to the highest bungee-jump in the world.

Moving north up the West Coast you'll find numerous treasures, among them laid-back beach restaurants famous for serving up more than is possible to eat, the bewitching Cederberg Mountains, and—after the first rains fall, usually in August—the annual miracle of spring, as the seemingly barren plains are carpeted with spectacular flower displays. Time allowing, those with a penchant for solitude should venture even farther, into the vast expanses of the Northern Cape and the Kalahari Gemsbok National Park, one of Africa's most unusual game reserves.

The Western Cape is home to the most diverse of the world's six floral kingdoms, with some 8,600 flowering species. Popular indigenous species that have found their way into gardens across the world include the red-hot poker, arum lily, bird of paradise flower, agapanthus, gladioli, and freesias.

## 1 Staying Active

The Western Cape offers the greatest range of adventure activities in the country, and vies with Victoria Falls as "adventure center" of Africa.

**ABSEILING** You can abseil in the Kaaimans river in Wilderness; after warming up with an 8-meter (26-foot) abseil, you take a 45-meter (148-foot) drop into the river, then canoe out. Call **Eden Adventures** at ☎ **044/877-0179.** Even more exhilarating is canoeing over to Knysna's Western Head in the Featherbed Nature Reserve—not least because the drop here is 120 meters (394 feet). Contact **SEAL Adventures ☎ 044/382-6399.**

**BLACK-WATER TUBING** Not quite as exhilarating as white water rafting, but equally inspiring, is a half day spent floating on a tractor tire inner tube on the Storms River. Once you enter the narrow gorge, you can look up to see nothing but the dramatic cliff face, dripping ferns, and a sliver of sky above. Trips cost R150 ($25) per person, including lunch. **StormsRiver Adventures** offers this and a host of other activities in the Tsitsikamma area, call **☎ 042/541-1836** or e-mail adventure@gardenroute.co.za.

**BOATING** **In Hermanus** **Rudy's Ivanhoe Sea Safaris (☎ 08234/40556)** is one of the few operators permitted to offer boat trips to view the Southern Right Whales (R250/$42 per person) on the Gansbaai side of Walker Bay. **In Knysna** With a bar on board, the double-decker **John Benn Ferry (☎ 044/382-1693)** is the most luxurious way to explore the Knysna Lagoon. Weather permitting, the ferry will venture through the heads, a 90-minute trip that costs R33 ($5.50) for adults; R15 ($2.50) for children. **In Plettenberg Bay** Contact **Ocean Adventures (☎ 044/57-35083** or 044/533-5083) for the Garden Route's best marine tours. These 2- to 3-hour trips, which cost R150 ($25) per person, cover everything from maritime wrecks to bird life, but specialize in marine mammals. The more esoteric of the various topics includes the merits of dolphin therapy.

**BOARDSAILING** Langebaan Lagoon on the West Coast is considered one of the best sites in South Africa, particularly in the early afternoon when the wind picks up. You can hire equipment from **The Cape Windsurf Centre** in Langebaan (**☎ 022/772-1114**).

**BUNGEE/BRIDGE-JUMPING** There are two sites: The original Gourits River bridge-jump, between Albertinia and Mossel Bay on the N2, is a 65-meter (213-foot) drop for R150 ($25) per person; while the Bloukrans River bridge-jump R500 ($83.35) per person, 40 kilometers (25 miles) east of Plettenberg Bay, is the highest bridge jump in the world, a stomach-churning 7 second, 216-meter (708-foot) free fall. Both operate from 9am to 5pm daily. Price includes video. Contact **☎ 042/281-1450.**

**CANOEING** With the Garden Route often described as South Africa's "lakes district," naturally one of the best ways to explore it is via its many waterways. Canoes can be rented throughout the area—contact the local Tourism Bureau wherever you are. Recommended canoe trips are the 3-day trail starting at the Ebb & Flow rest camp at **Wilderness National Park** (**☎ 044/877-0197**) and the 1-day canoe trail up the Keurbooms River at Plettenberg Bay. Contact **Cape Nature Conservation** at **☎ 044/533-2125.** The 3-day Wilderness Canoe Trail costs R150 ($25) per person; accommodations, cutlery, crockery and canoes are provided. You will need to supply food and bedding. Canoe rental for the Keurbooms River costs R20/hour ($3.35) per person; contact **Aventura Eco (☎ 044/535-9309)**. To explore the sea, contact **Dolphin Adventures** (**☎ 044/531-6806**) for kayaking tours along the Plettenberg Bay coast.

**DIVING** There are two snorkeling and diving routes in the Tsitsikamma National Park (see below). Gear can be rented from **Diving International** (**☎ 044/533-0381**) or **Beyond the Beach** (**☎ 044/533-1158**) in Plettenberg Bay (ask about Jacob's Reef, another good spot off the Plet coast). **Waterfront Divers** (**☎ 044/384-0831**) can assist with any diving queries or equipment hire in Knysna, and the **Mossel Bay Diving Academy** (**☎ 044/693-1179**) deals with diving trips farther south.

**GOLFING** While George cannot boast a plethora of attractions, it is home to some of the Garden Route's best golf courses—you have to stay at ✪ **Fancourt** (☎ **044/870-8282**) to play at either of its two Gary Player-designed championship courses; if you're not up to par, sign up with the Fancourt Golf Academy. Non-members can play the attractive **George Golf Club** course (☎ **044/8736116**). **Plettenberg Bay Country Club's** 18-hole course (☎ **044/533-2132**) is a pleasure to play, not least because of the beautiful surrounds, as is the Gary Player–designed and owned **Goose Valley** (☎ **044/533-5082**). The Hermanus Golf Club is the best golf course in the Overberg (☎ **0283/21954**).

**HIKING** Most of the country's top hikes are in the Western Cape—hardly surprising considering the combination of coast, mountains, rivers, and flora. For serious hikers, the following four are worth noting: the 7-day **Outeniqua Trail** (☎ **044/382-5466**), which takes you through plantations and indigenous forests (shorter versions available); the 5-day **Tsitsikamma Trail** (☎ **042/391-0393**), an inland version of the more famous Otter Trail, which includes long stretches of *fynbos* (evergreen vegetation characterized by its ability to thrive in harsh conditions) as well as forests and rivers; the 2-day **Harkerville Trail** (also called the mini–Otter Trail, and a good alternative), which features magnificent coastal scenery (☎ **044/382-5466**); and the 5-day **Otter Trail,** South Africa's most popular trail. The latter is a tough coastal walk, taking you through the Tsitsikamma National Park's rivers and indigenous forests, with magnificent views of the coast; its popularity means it must be booked at least a year in advance, call ☎ **021/22-2810.** For the less committed hiker, the 10-kilometer (6-mile) **Pied Kingfisher Trail** in Wilderness National Park covers a variety of beautiful habitats; the 9½-kilometer (almost 6-mile) **Kranshoek Walk** in the Harkerville Forest is a great forest environment; and the 9-kilometer (5½-mile) **Robberg Trail** in Plettenberg Bay is worth exploring for its wild coastline and whale-watching opportunities. The Garden Route Regional Tourism Organization has a comprehensive brochure covering all hikes in the region. Contact them at ☎ **044/874-4040** for a copy, or pick one up from any of the Tourism Bureaus. Note that the **Cederberg Wilderness Area,** with its strange twisted rock formations and tea-colored streams, is a hiker and climber's paradise, though it's off the beaten track (☎ **027/482-2812**).

**HORSEBACK RIDING** **Cilla's Stables** (☎ **0283/23-679**) conducts rides in the Hermanus area. **Cherie's Riding Centre** (☎ **044/343-1575**) offers rides in the Sedgefield area, which include scenic trails along the Swartvlei Lake and forests, as well as a 6-hour beach ride which includes a light lunch. If you're looking for a mount in the Plettenberg Bay area, contact **Equitrailing** (☎ **044/533-0599**) to explore the area's magnificent fynbos on horseback.

**MOUNTAIN BIKING** The Garden Route has numerous trails ideal for mountain biking and plenty of places that rent bikes and provide guides. To tour the foothills of the Outeniqua Mountains (close to George), contact **Eden** (☎ **044/877-0179**) in Wilderness; their half- or full-day tours often combine other activities. All three of the Diepwalle State Forest trails in Knysna are ideal for mountain biking. You can rent bikes from **U-Ride** (☎ **044/382-7785**) in Knysna; they'll either deliver them to you or take you on a guided ride. The **Harkerville red route,** which includes forest, fynbos, and the craggy coastline, is considered one of the best in South Africa—book early. For more information on trails in the Knysna State Forests, contact Mrs. van Rooyen at ☎ **044/382-5466** or Jacques at **Knysna Cycle Works** (☎ **044/382-5153** or e-mail freejacq@mweb.co.za).

When in Plettenberg Bay, you can rent mountain bikes from **Kenburn Cycle** (☎ **044/533-3932**) and **Outeniqua Biking Trails** (☎ **044/57-7644** or 044/532-7644); the latter also offers guided mountain-biking trails in the area.

Joyrides in Prince Albert (☎ **0443/29-1163**) offers both escorted and unescorted trips over the Swartberg Pass.

**MOTORCYCLING** For Harley-Davidson enthusiasts, **Freedom Africa** (☎ **021/685-7082**) offers 5- and 10-day biking tours of the Western Cape.

**PARAGLIDING** Wilderness is considered South Africa's best site for coastal flying, particularly from August to May. Paragliding courses last 7, 10, and 14 days, or you can take a flight with a qualified instructor. Experienced pilots can rent equipment. Contact Bruce Watney from **Wings Over Wilderness** on his mobile (☎ **083269-3608**) or e-mail BruceW@mb.lia.net.

For a bird's-eye view of Plettenberg Bay, take a two-seater glider flight in an open cockpit, R120 ($20) per person—contact **Stanley's Island** (☎ **044/57-9442** or 044/535-9442).

**SHARK-CAGE DIVING** Boats go out from Gansbaai (a coastal town some 30 kilometers [19 miles] east of Hermanus) to Dyer Island. This, and nearby Geyser Island, are popular with the jackass penguin and seal breeding colonies, whose pups are an all-time favorite Great White shark snack—so much so that they call the channel between the islands "Shark Alley"). The sharks are baited, and you stand a good chance of seeing one of them from the boat, if not from the cage, which fits only two people at a time. There are a number of operators, all offering the same service (some even include a pickup from Cape Town) for more or less the same price: R600 ($100) per person, including a meal. As **Infante** (☎ **082455-2438** or 044/691-3796) is the only operator in Mossel Bay, your experience will be less crowded and frenzied than in Gansbaai.

**SKYDIVING/PARACHUTING** If you think bungee jumping is for wusses, try dropping from a height of 900 meters (3,000 feet) with **Skydive Citrusdal** (☎ **021/462-5666**), based in the citrus-growing area 90 minutes north of Cape Town. With 1-day training for the novice costing R430 ($71.65), including the first jump, and additional jumps costing R100 ($16.65), this is the cheapest drop from a plane in South Africa.

**SURFING** You can hire boards and wetsuits from **U-Ride** (☎ **044/382-7785**) in Knysna. U-Ride will also take you to a surf spot appropriate to your experience. **Albergo** (☎ **044/533-4434**) rents boogie boards to surf the "Plet" (Plettenburg Bay) waves. Top spots in the Western Cape include Inner and Outer Pool and Ding Dangs at Mossel Bay; Vic Bay (a good right-hand point break) and Elands Bay, the best spot on the West Coast. For more information, e-mail Paul at nirvan@ilink.nis.za. For advanced and beginner surf training, contact **Charlie Moir** (☎ **021/701-2727**) in Cape Town. **Replay Sports** (☎ **021/25-1056**) buys and sells secondhand gear.

**WHALE WATCHING** Some of the best land-based whale watching in the world happens on the Overberg coast from June to November (see "The Whale Coast,"

## Jaws

Ironically, despite the Great White shark's ferocious reputation, man poses a much greater threat to them than they do to us. Great Whites are currently endangered, and their baiting for sightseers (see "Shark-Cage Diving" above) is contentious in some conservation circles. Many also believe that the recent increase in shark attacks off the False Bay coast is a direct result of sharks associating humans with food.

below). When traveling the Garden Route, keep an eye out from the Brenton cliffs, the heads in Knysna, and the Robberg Peninsula in Plettenberg Bay—all good whale-watching spots, though whales appear all along the southern Cape coast. There is a **Whale Hotline** number that gives updates on where the whales are and answers any queries you may have, call ☎ **0800/22-8222.**

**WHITE-WATER RAFTING** The best white-water rafting in the Western Cape takes place from mid-July to mid-September on the Doring River. **River Rafters** (☎ **021/712-5094**) organizes trips that include an overnight (under a cave overhang) for R595 ($99.15) per person, food and equipment included. River Rafters will assist where possible, but you may have to arrange your own transportation to the base camp, which is 4 hours from Cape Town, in the Cederberg area. River Rafters also runs trips on the Orange River.

## 2 Exploring the Overberg & Whale Coast

During the 17th century, the Dutch settlers saw the jagged Hottentots-Holland mountain range as the Cape Colony's natural border, beyond which lay what they called Overberg, literally "over the mountain." Today this coastal area—wedged between the Cape Peninsula and the Garden Route, with mountains lining its northern border and the ocean on its south—encompasses a vast patchwork of grain fields, fruit orchards, and fynbos-covered hills. There are two main routes through it: the N2, which traverses its northern half and is the quickest way to reach the Garden Route; and the more-circuitous Coastal Route, which most people prefer to take during the whale-watching months. However, those who travel the N2, or drive only the first section of the coastal route as far as Hermanus, miss some lovely points along the Overberg coast. Known as the "the graveyard of ships," this rugged coastline is pounded by both the Atlantic and Indian oceans, which meet at L'Agulhus, Africa's most southerly point. East of this point is Arniston (Waenhuiskrans to locals), a bleak fishing village overlooking a magnificent turquoise bay; and De Hoop Nature Reserve, which vies with the Garden Route's Tsitsikamma as the most beautiful coastal reserve in South Africa.

Besides a wealth of rare fynbos, the Overberg provides visitors with the opportunity to view South Africa's national bird, the elegant blue crane. Sadly, numbers have declined by as much as 90% in some areas, but half of the remaining population has found a haven in the Overberg. Another sanctuary-seeker is the Southern Right whale; these return in increasing numbers every spring to mate and nurse their young off the "Whale Coast." The towns of Hermanus and Die Kelders, which overlook Walker Bay, and Koppie Alleen in De Hoop Nature Reserve are considered the best locations for viewing these oddly elegant, 60-ton, callus-encrusted cetaceans.

### THE COASTAL ROUTE: GORDON'S BAY TO HERMANUS

The coastal route starts at **Gordon's Bay,** an easy 40-minute drive from Cape Town on the N2. Gordon's Bay has an attractive small-craft harbor, but property development and overcrowding has erased much of its former charm. You're best off heading straight for the R44, the coastal road that snakes along the sheer cliffs of the Hottentots' Holland Mountains as they plunge down to the oceans below. Keep an eye out for **whales** and **dolphins** in **False Bay** as you descend the cliffs and bypass the Steenbras River mouth (where you can abseil Kamikaze Kanyon) and Koëelbaai (pronounced *cool*-buy). Between rocky outcrops along this stretch of coast, you'll find small sandy coves shaded by ancient milkwood trees and grassy sunbathing areas.

Having crossed the Rooiels River (named after the red alder trees that grow in the riverine bush up the gorge) and the Buffels River, you enter the built-up village of

# The Western Cape

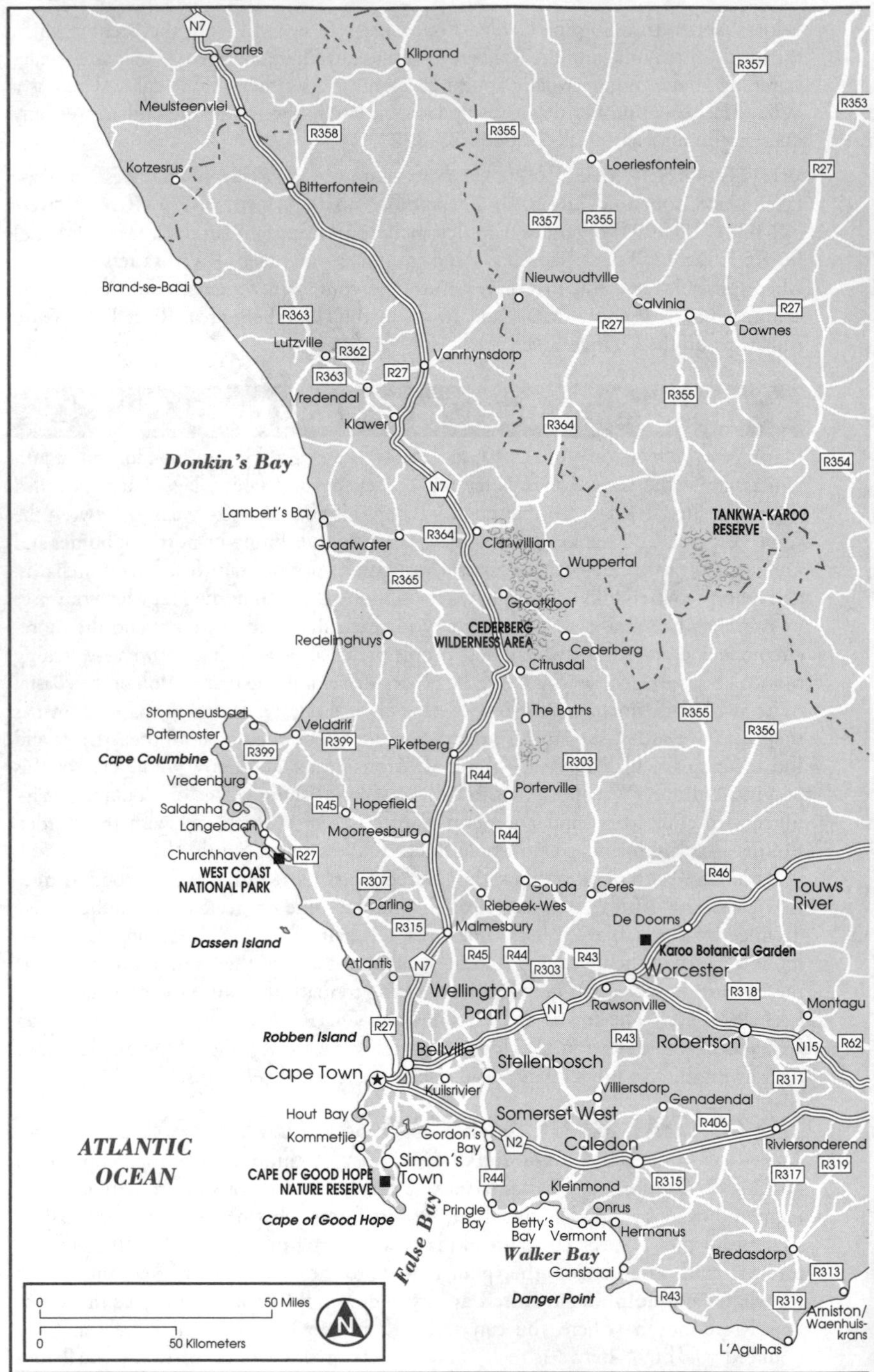

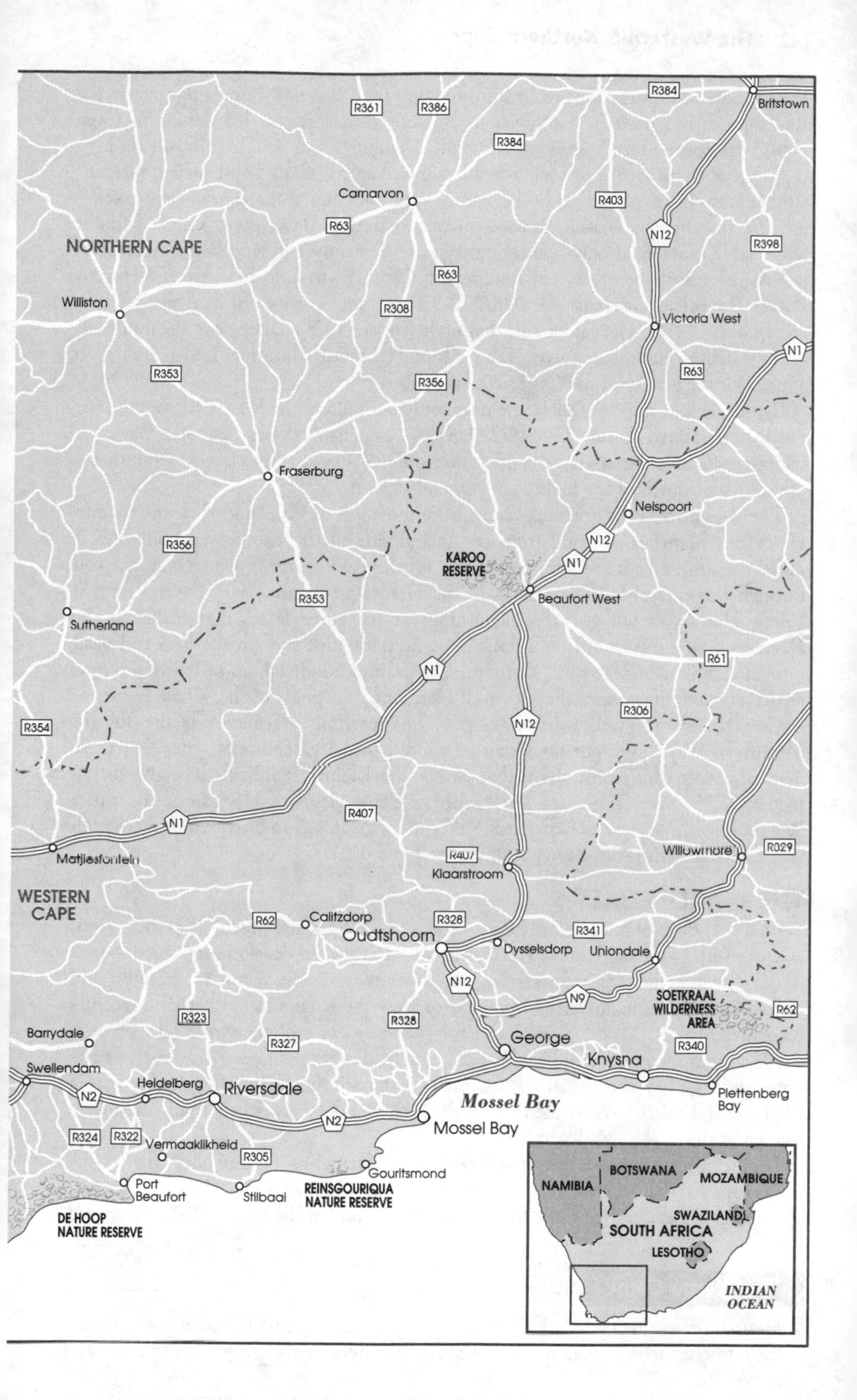
NORTHERN CAPE
WESTERN CAPE
Britstown
Carnarvon
Williston
Victoria West
Fraserburg
Nelspoort
KAROO RESERVE
Beaufort West
Sutherland
Matjiesfontein
Willowmore
Klaarstroom
Calitzdorp
Oudtshoorn
Dysselsdorp
Uniondale
SOETKRAAL WILDERNESS AREA
George
Knysna
Plettenberg Bay
Barrydale
Swellendam
Heidelberg
Riversdale
Mossel Bay
Vermaaklikheid
Gouritsmond
Port Beaufort
Stilbaai
REINSGOURIQUA NATURE RESERVE
DE HOOP NATURE RESERVE
NAMIBIA
BOTSWANA
MOZAMBIQUE
SWAZILAND
SOUTH AFRICA
LESOTHO
INDIAN OCEAN

Pringle Bay, and things don't really improve after that. Just past Pringle Bay, where the R44 cuts inland past the Grootvlei marshlands, is a less traveled detour to **Cape Hangklip** (pronounced *hung*-clip, literally "hanging rock"). This 460-meter-high (1,509-foot-high) wedge of rock was often mistaken for Cape Point, which incidentally is how False Bay came by its name. After skirting three lagoon-type lakes—estuaries blocked by coastal dunes—you reach **Betty's Bay,** where you will find a remarkable number of ugly holiday cottages, one of only two land-based colonies of jackass penguins (the other is at Boulders in Cape Town), and the beautiful **Harold Porter Botanical Gardens** (☎ **028/272-9311**), open daily from 8am to 6pm at a charge of R5 (85¢). The gardens are definitely worth a visit—take one of the four trails leading up the mountain to the **Disa Kloof Waterfall** (duration 1 to 3 hours) to appreciate the beauty of the Cape's coastal fynbos.

If you need to stop for lunch, the next settlement along the R44 is Kleinmond. At the **Beach House Hotel** (☎ **028/271-3130**), which overlooks Sandown Bay's 10-kilometer (6-mile) beach, large panoramic windows provide views of the ocean that is the source of much of the highly recommended food.

The R44 now heads northeastward in the direction of Caledon, while the road to Hermanus branches eastward from the inland side of the Palmiet Lagoon. This is called the R43; take it and keep an eye out for the R320 turnoff, which will take you through the vineyards and orchards of the **Hemel-en-Aarde** ("Heaven and Earth") Valley. Here, you can go on wine tastings at the three farms that make up the **Hermanus Wine Route.** If you don't have time for this, stay on the R43 and head into the hamlets of Hawston, Vermont, Onrus, and Sandbaai, all of which are now virtual suburbs of the sprawling town of Hermanus, "capital" of the Whale Coast.

One last detour well worth taking before reaching Hermanus is the **Rotary Mountain Way.** Look out for a pair of white-painted gateposts on your left; these mark the start of a **scenic drive** that climbs the Kleinriver hills to a height of 900 meters (2,952 feet) above sea level, with excellent views of Hermanus, the entire Walker Bay, and the Hemel-en-Aarde Valley. It's a great way to orient yourself, though you'll have to return the way you came.

## THE WHALE COAST

With a backdrop of mountains, a large lagoon and long white beach, deep rock pools, and a wealth of coastal fynbos, **Hermanus** was destined to develop into one of South Africa's premier holiday resorts. The best times to visit Hermanus are autumn and spring, when aficionados come from afar to view the whales in Walker Bay (recently recognized by the World Wide Fund for Nature as one of the world's 12 premier whale-viewing spots). Humpback, Bryde's, and Minke whales make occasional appearances, but the bay is essentially frequented by the Southern Right whales—due to a high oil and whalebone content, as well as their buoyancy when dead, they were known as the "right" whales to harpoon.

Whales aside, there are the **wine farms** in the Hemel-en-Aarde Valley to visit, the opportunity to have a close encounter with a Great White shark (see "Staying Active," above), long **beaches** to walk, and a number of good **trails** in the Walker Bay and

### The Name Game

Hermanus was named after the Dutch dropout Hermanus Pietersfontein, a part-time teacher who herded a flock of sheep out here in the early 19th century and never left.

Fernkloof Nature Reserves. With Hermanus as your base, the picturesque villages of Arniston, Elim, L'Aghulhus, and Bredasdorp are only a day's excursion away.

## Essentials

**VISITOR INFORMATION** The **Hermanus Tourism Bureau** is on Main Road, next to Volkskas Bank (☎ **0283/22-629,** e-mail: infoburo@ilink.nis/za). Hours are Monday to Saturday 9am to 5pm, and Sunday 9am to 2pm.

**GETTING THERE** **By Car** To rent a car, see "Cape Town Essentials," chapter 3. To reach Hermanus, you can either drive east from Cape Town for about 112 kilometers (69 miles) via the N2, ascending Sir Lowry's Pass with its magnificent views of False Bay (duration approximately 90 minutes, see below) or take the winding coastal route from Gordon's Bay (see above).

**By Bus** Contact **Hylton Ross** (☎**021/511-1784**) for day trips to Hermanus, held on Sundays and Wednesdays. Cost is R180 ($30) per person.

**GUIDED TOURS** **Whale Coast Tours** (☎ **0283/24-063**) offers historic and scenic tours of two reserves, as well as wine-tasting trips. **Foot of Africa Eco Tourism Forum** (☎ **02841/42-584**), based in Bredasdorp, has specialized fynbos tours, as does **Cape Specialist Eco Tours** (☎ **021/689-2978**). The latter is run by a professional botanist and author of a wildflower guidebook to the southern Overberg.

**By Boat** **Hermanus Adventure** (☎ **0283/24-146**) has 2- to 3-hour sundowner cruises on the lagoon and harbor for R50 ($8.35) per person, including a picnic. You can rent anything from motorboats to windsurf boards to explore the lagoon from **The Boathouse** (☎ **0283/77-0925**). **Rudy Hughes** (☎ **02834/40556**) is one of only 20 operators with a permit to offer boat-based whaling expeditions. They cost R250 ($41.65) per person.

**On Foot** **Whale Coast Tours** (☎ **0283/24063**) conducts coastal and mountain guided walks for those wanting a greater insight into the whales, fynbos, or birdlife of the region. Duration of walks varies from 30 minutes to 4 hours.

**On Horseback** **Cilla's Stables** (☎ **0283/23-679**) conducts rides in the mountains and on the beach.

**SPECIAL EVENTS** The annual **MTN Whale Festival,** which features local music, theater, sports, and flower exhibitions, takes place during September, when the local population swells by an estimated 200,000. Contact the Hermanus Tourism Bureau for this year's dates and program.

## What to See & Do

### Surf & Sand

The sweeping curve of **Grotto Beach** can be seen from most vantage points of Walker Bay—this is a great family beach, made for long walks and swimming. Closer to town, **Voëlklip** is where the hip youth hang out; while the closest, **Langbaai** (*lung*-buy), offers the best bodysurfing, though currents can render it hazardous.

### Wine Tasting

The three small wineries that comprise the **Hermanus Wine Route** are all located on the R320 to Caledon, the turnoff to which is 2 kilometers (just over 1 mile) before you get to Hermanus (see "Gordons Bay to Hermanus," above). The first farm you'll come across is **Whale Haven Winery** (☎ **0283/21-585**), established in 1995. Whale Haven is open weekdays from 9am to 5pm and Saturdays from 10:30am to 1pm; there is no charge for tastings. **Hamilton Russell** (☎ **0283/23-595**) has the dubious distinction of producing South Africa's two most expensive wines—a Chardonnay and a Pinot Noir—but here you can sample them for free. Tastings are held weekdays from 9am to 5pm, Saturday 9am to 1pm. Adjacent is **Bouchard Finlayson** (☎ **0283/23-515**), open for tastings weekdays from 9am to 5pm and Saturday from 10:30am to 12:30pm. If you don't feel like visiting the farms, **Hermanus Adventure** (☎ **0283/24-146**) combines wine tastings with a picnic on the slopes of Raed-Na-Gael, overlooking Hermanus and Walker Bay.

### Whale Watching

The once threatened Southern Right whale (a protected species since 1946) is enjoying a major comeback, with the population on the South Africa coastline nearly doubling itself over the past decade. In recent years as many as 2,000 have followed the annual migration from Antarctica, to flirt, mate, and calve in the warmer waters of the southern Cape coast. They appear in Hermanus' Walker Bay during June and, if pregnant, calve during July and August, staying on to nurse their young until November. One can clearly view these playful, gentle giants (sometimes at a distance of only 10m), from the craggy cliffs and rocks that run along the Hermanus shoreline. For the best sightings, take the 12-kilometer (7½-mile) walk along the top of the cliffs from New Harbour east to Grotto Beach and the lagoon. Also recommended are the terraces above the Old Harbour where there's a telescope and a plaque giving basic information about the bay and its whales.

The Old Harbour is a national monument and site of the **Old Harbour Museum** (☎ **0283/21-475**), which is open Monday to Saturday from 9am to 1pm, again from 2 to 5pm, and on Sunday from 12 to 4pm. Restored rowing boats that were used by local fishermen from 1855 to 1961 add a colorful touch, but the interior features a rather uninspiring collection of exhibits like old fishing tackle, shark jaws, and whaling relics. The best reason to visit the museum is to listen to the sounds of the whales in the bay, transmitted through a sonar buoy (though this was not running at press time). Also keep your ears open for the kelp horn—Hermanus is proud of the fact that it is the only town in the world to have a **"whale crier."** During whaling season, Pieter Claasen walks the town streets blowing his kelp horn in a sort of Morse code to alert the town's inhabitants to the presence and whereabouts of whales. If you don't understand the code, never mind; he wears a sandwich board and carries a mobile phone (☎ **083212-1074**). Contact him for reports of whale sightings, or call the toll-free **Whale Hotline** at ☎ **0800/22-8222.**

Note that the limestone cliffs of De Kelders, southeast along the R43, provide another superb view of Walker Bay. If you're looking for more information on the subject, *Whale Watch,* a book by Vic Cockcroft and Peter Joyce, published by Struik and available at most bookshops, offers indispensable insights and tips for whale watchers.

### A Whale of a Time

When it comes to dating, the Southern Right ladies don't have an easy time of it—bulls show no particular preference for their partners and one bull after another will mate with a single female in an effort to be the one to fertilize her. To avoid the onslaughts of these males (who happen to have the largest testes in the mammal kingdom), females often lie on their backs on the ocean floor. However, as they are unable to breathe in this position, they are eventually forced to roll over, exposing themselves to male attentions. After having their way, the males move on, leaving the ladies to fend for themselves (gestation lasts for a year) and to nurse their young.

## WHERE TO STAY

**The 19th Hole Guest House.** 281 Main Rd., Hermanus 7200. ☎ **0283/22-766.** Fax 0283/22-766. 5 units. TV. R300–400 ($50–$66.65) double, includes breakfast. AE, DC, MC, V. Children 10 and over welcome.

The 19th Hole may be on a busy road, but fortunately, all the bedrooms are at the back of the house. Their doors open onto lawns that run into the Hermanus golf course; beyond lie the Raed-Na-Gael Mountains—a truly tranquil sight. Relax in what used to be the clubhouse (hence the name) and watch the golfers trundle along the course, or take a stroll along the cliff paths which lie just across the road. Or, as many guests do, head for the first hole or the swimming pool. Bedrooms are huge and well appointed (hair dryers, tea- and coffee-making facilities, fresh flowers) though the brightly colored decor is not for the fainthearted. Host Brian McFarlane is a keen angler and he occasionally invites guests to enjoy a freshly caught fish for dinner. His boat is also equipped with the necessary equipment to take guests shark-cage diving off Dyer Island.

**Auberge Burgundy.** 16 Harbour Rd., Hermanus 7200. ☎ **0283/70-1201.** Fax 0283/70-1204. 18 units. MINIBAR TV TEL. R580 ($96.65) double, includes breakfast. AE, DC, MC, V. Children by prior arrangement.

An excellent replica of a Provençal or Tuscan villa, the stylish Auberge Burgundy is located opposite the Old Harbour. Rooms are tasteful and spacious, opening onto a balcony with views of either the ocean or the garden, which in spring is redolent with the scent of roses and lavender. Features like underfloor heating, heated towel racks, walk-in dressing rooms, tea- and coffee-making facilities, and hair dryers are standard. The Burgundy (where breakfasts are served) is an excellent restaurant just opposite, but there are a number of other restaurants within easy walking distance. Ask for a room with a view of the ocean, but don't be too disturbed if they're all taken—almost every room has something to recommend it, and the pool deck has an excellent view. The penthouse suite, which sleeps 6, is ideal for families.

✪ **Grootbos Nature Reserve.** ☎ **02834/40-381.** Fax 02834/40-552. 10 units. MINIBAR TV. R1,500 ($250), includes all meals and activities; minimum 2-night stay. Children's rates on request. AE, DC, MC, V. Off the R43, 33km (20 miles) east of Hermanus.

This is the best place in the Western Cape to learn about the eccentricities of the smallest and most diverse floral kingdom in the world. The staff is not only professional, but their enthusiasm and passion for Grootbos is infectious. There's a fynbos drive every morning with one of the resident botanists, and evening walks in Walker Bay with the resident marine biologist. During the day guests are welcome to walk, ride, or bike through the 1,000 hectare reserve, which features amongst other rarities the largest milkwood forest in the world, as well as porcupine, lynx, and bush buck. If the lodge's pool doesn't appeal, Walker Bay Beach is a short drive away. Guests stay in luxurious stone and timber cottages situated throughout the lodge's extensive gardens. Among the many luxury touches is a breakfast served in the privacy of your dining room that awaits your return from the morning drive. Each cottage is a fully equipped open-plan house with large open fireplace, multilevel sun decks, and views of Walker Bay and the surrounding vegetation from every angle. Dinner is a three-course affair that centers on seafood from Walker Bay and homegrown vegetables. There are game dishes in season. Grootbos stipulates a minimum 2-night stay—you'll wish it were three.

✪ **Marine Hotel.** Marine Dr., Hermanus 7200. ☎ **0283/70-1000.** Fax 0283/70-0160. 47 units. TV TEL. R1,000 ($166.65) double; R1,500 ($250) studio; R1,900–2,500 ($316.65–$416.65) suites with ocean view. AE, DC, MC, V. No children under 12.

This grand dame of Hermanus (built in 1890) has had a major facelift, and now offers a truly luxurious option for the moneyed set. Situated on the craggy cliffs close to the town's center and Old Harbour, The Marine has wonderful views of Walker Bay with a large tidal pool for swimming below. Rooms either face the sea, the courtyard (with pool), or have distant views of the mountain; it's worth spending R200 ($33.35) for an ocean view. All rooms are finished in mute modern colors and feature simple luxuries like hair dryers, underfloor heating and heated towel racks; some have air-conditioning and minibars. There are two restaurants: No prizes for guessing what Seafood at the Marine specializes in. The Pavillion has the view, and serves a larger variety of meals.

**Whale Cottage Guest House.** 20 Main Rd., Hermanus 7200. ☎ **0283/70-0929.** Fax 0283/70-0912. 5 units. TV TEL. R300–460 ($50–$76.65) double, including breakfast. Children 2–9 R50 ($8.35), 10–15 half price. AE, DC, MC, V.

Don't let the name mislead you; Whale Cottage is situated on the busy Main Road into Hermanus, and the only whales you'll spot from here are in the photographs that adorn the walls and books. Guests stay in pastel-colored rooms; try booking the Dolphin or Whale rooms as they're slightly larger, and Whale has a working fireplace. Avoid Shell room, which is closest to the road. All rooms have hair dryers, heaters, electric blankets, and radio/alarm clocks; and there is a pool and one mountain bike available for guests' use. Breakfast is served in a large room adjoining the private garden and pool; there is no lounge.

## WHERE TO DINE

✪ **Bientang's Cave.** Off Marine Dr., next to Old Harbour, Hermanus 7200. ☎ **0283/23-454.** Reservations essential. Main courses R14–60 ($2.35–$10). AE, DC, MC, V. Daily 11am–4pm, Sat 6:30–10pm; Sept, Dec, and Easter open daily for dinner; call ahead for exact hours. SEAFOOD.

Few restaurants in the world can best this location—a cave in the rocks just above the sea, with a fabulous view of Walker Bay and the whales at play. Predictably, seafood is Bientang's specialty; the only other meat available is the ham used on their pizzas. One recommended starter is the bouillabaisse, a spicy, tomato-based soup with calamari, prawns, mussels, linefish, and saffron; fresh oysters are also served. One of the two fresh linefish grilled daily is a snoek with the traditional apricot sauce. With the fresh sea breeze to build up an appetite, you might want to try the four-course buffet—salad, bouillaisse, linefish, and dessert—a steal at R85 ($14.15). The pizza oven caters to non-seafood eaters.

**The Burgundy.** Marine Dr. (opposite Old Harbour), Hermanus 7200. ☎ **0283/22-800.** Reservations recommended. Main courses R44–65 ($7.35–10.85). AE, DC, MC, V. Daily (except Sunday dinner) 10–11am tea, 12–2:15pm lunch, 3:15–4:30pm tea, 7–9:15pm dinner. FRENCH/AFRICAN.

Located in the oldest building in Hermanus (the stone and clay cottage was built by a Swedish boat builder in 1875), The Burgundy is regularly voted as Hermanus' best seafood restaurant. The wine list features Hemel-en-Aarde wines and meals are simple, but excellent. Try the Moules Burgundy (plump mussels in a green-peppercorn and mustard cream sauce served on pasta), followed by Poisson Masal (grilled linefish marinated in masala paste and served with a coriander vinaigrette). Vegetarians can enjoy quiche served with couscous or a variety of grilled vegetables. When booking, ask for a table on the veranda or lawn, both overlook Walker Bay, though you're much farther back than at the nearby Bientang's Cave. The Burgundy is also open for tea and scones.

**Cuckoo Tree.** 155 Main Rd., Hermanus 7200. ☎ **0283/23-430.** Dinner reservations essential. Main courses R25–48 ($4.15–$8). AE, DC, MC, V. Mon–Sat 8:30am–5pm. Thurs–Sat 7:30–9:30pm; Dec–Jan open daily 7:30–9:30pm. FRENCH.

Food here, such as crispy duck with orange and *van der hum* (a liqueur) sauce, and pork fillet, stuffed with spinach and feta and done to a turn, offers welcome relief from the plethora of seafood options in Hermanus. If you're looking for comfort food, opt for the delicious fishcakes. The Cuckoo Tree serves teas and sweet treats during the day. Guests can choose to be seated indoors or under a big tree alive with birds (no cuckoos though!).

## MORE WHALE COAST DESTINATIONS

Two coastal destinations east of Hermanus worth visiting are the village of **Arniston** and the ✪ **De Hoop Nature Reserve.** To reach either, head east to Stanford on R43, then turn northeast on R326 for 27 kilometers (16½ miles) before turning right and heading south for Bredasdorp. Once there, you can either immediately go south on R316 toward Arniston, or north on R319 for De Hoop. However, if you want to take a side trip to Africa's southernmost tip, where the Indian and Atlantic oceans meet, turn south on R319 for L'Aghulus. Bar the interesting facts of its location, the place itself has little to recommend a visit, unless you wish to visit the **Lighthouse Museum** (☎ **0281/41-466**), a satellite of the Shipwreck Museum in Bredasdorp (see below). A better reason to take the R319 south is to see the tiny town of **Elim.** Although it's not on the coast, it's interesting from an architectural and cultural point of view. A Moravian mission station originally established in 1824, the entire town remains unchanged and is still inhabited only by Moravian church members who make their living from harvesting fynbos. Reaching it is rather inconvenient though, as it's not on the way to anything (see map), and it's only worth considering if you're overnighting at Arniston or De Hoop. You'll find the **Elim Tourism Bureau** (☎ **028/482-1806,** open Monday to Friday from 9am to 4pm, and Saturday 9am to 12:30pm) in the churchyard.

**Arniston,** a small fishing village and popular getaway, lapped by a startling turquoise sea, lies only 24 kilometers (15 miles) south from Bredasdorp on R316. If you see signs for "Waenhuiskrans," don't panic—Arniston, named after a ship that wrecked here in 1815 (pieces of which are still visible), is also officially called Waenhuiskrans. The name, literally "wagon-house-cliff," comes from a huge cliffside cavern capable of housing several ox-wagons, which can only be visited at low tide.

For over 200 years, local fishermen have been setting out at first light to cast their lines and returning at night to the quaint collection of lime-washed, thatched cottages clustered on the dunes overlooking the sea—these dwellings have collectively been declared a national monument and are picture-postcard pretty, but probably less romantic to live in. You can take a wander through the sandy streets of what is called the **Kassiesbaai Community** on your own, but it's probably more considerate to visit with a local guide. A 90-minute tour costs R25 ($4.15) per person with all proceeds going directly to the community; call ☎ **02847/59-000.** Beyond the cottages lies nothing but 5 kilometers (3 miles) of pristine beach, with no sign of human habitation; it's well worth a walk if the wind isn't blowing. Besides this, there's not much to do but marvel at the unspoiled coastline and swim in the shallow sea, the safest swimming on the Whale Coast.

The ✪ **De Hoop Nature Reserve** (☎ **028/542-1126,** R4/65¢ entry) boasts what many consider to be the best whale-watching spot on the entire coast, Koppie Alleen; but most visitors are here to explore one of the most beautiful coastal reserves in the world—50 kilometers (30 miles) of pristine white beach dunes, limestone cliffs, rock pools, wetlands, coastal fynbos and no one to disturb the peace but antelope and birds.

## A Famous Shipwreck

At the southernmost point of Walker Bay lies Danger Point, an 8-kilometer-long (5-mile-long) peninsula. At low tide you can still see the very rock that struck the *HMS Birkenhead* on February 26, 1852. Within moments it became apparent that the ship was going down fast, and as was the custom, the captain gave the order "Every man for himself." However, the British soldiers on board allegedly lined up on the decks and stood to attention while the women and children were assisted into the lifeboats and lowered into the churning sea. Shortly thereafter the ship sunk, claiming the lives of the 443 courageous men. Shipping history was irrevocably changed with what came to be known as the "Birkenhead drill" or, more commonly, "Women and children first."

More than 20 ships would sink at Danger Point before a lighthouse was commissioned in 1895. To view artifacts recovered from ships that have gone down on this treacherous coast—more than 120 since the earliest recorded in 1673—visit the **Bredasdorp Shipwreck Museum** (☎ **02841/41-240**) on Independent Street, Monday to Friday 9am to 4:45pm; Saturday 9am to 1pm, 2:30 to 3:45pm. In summer, the museum is also open on Sunday from 11am to 12:30pm.

To reach the reserve, retrace your steps from Arniston to Bredasdorp and take the R319 north. After 10 kilometers (6 miles) take the well-maintained dirt road to your right, and simply follow the signs to De Hoop for 60 kilometers (37 miles) before the final turn off. Once in the reserve, there are limited routes (you can drive to the beach or accommodations), and the reserve is best explored on foot or on a mountain bike (though you'll have to bring your own.) Do note that the reserve hours (7am to 4pm) are strictly enforced, and that visitors intending to overnight must report to the reserve office no later than 4pm on the day of arrival.

### WHERE TO STAY & DINE

**The Arniston Hotel.** Beach Rd., Waenhuiskrans. Mailing address: PO Box 126, Bredasdorp 7280. ☎ **02847/59-000.** Fax 02847/59633. E-mail: hotel@arniston.co.za. www.arniston.co.za/ahotel/awelcome.htm. 30 units. A/C (suites only) TV TEL. R570–700 ($95–$116.65) double, including breakfast. AE, DC, MC, V. No children under 12.

If you want to get away from it all, but don't want to stint on luxury, the Arniston Hotel is the perfect solution. Six luxury sea-facing suites are a recent and much-needed addition—the space and furnishings are such a vast improvement on the standard sea-facing rooms as to be almost incomparable—it's definitely worth forking out an extra R200 ($33.35). If you're on a real budget, consider staying in one of the Arniston Seaside Cottages (see below), and having dinner here. There are another 15 rooms facing the pool and courtyard (the advantage are that these are pretty wind-free, but it's a pity to miss out on the view).

**Dining:** The casual Slipway restaurant serves simple meals—the catch of the day (R39/$6.50) grilled and served with vegetables, salad, and fries or rice is an obvious choice. The Dining Room serves a three-course (R79/$13.15) or four-course meal (R89/$14.85), usually with a choice of red meat or fish. Large windows overlook the ocean, but as it's situated on the first floor the views aren't that great.

**Arniston Seaside Cottages.** Huxham St. (follow signs), Waenhuiskrans 7280. ☎ **02847/59-772.** Fax 02847/59-125. 18 units, sleeping 2, 6, or 8. TV. R240 ($40) double. AE, DC, MC, V.

While not on the sea, as the name suggests, all 18 cottages are within walking distance of the beach, and some balconies feature views of the sea and the surrounding dunes. Cottages have all been built in the traditional Arniston style with white walls and thatched roofs, and feature large open log fireplaces, en-suite bedrooms, fully equipped open-plan kitchens, and a wind-sheltered braai area. Cottages are also serviced daily. Furnishings are quite sparse—predominantly pine and cane—but perfectly comfortable. The rooms are generously sized and at a per person price of R120 ($20) regardless of the size of the unit, they're an excellent value. In season, however (December, January, and Easter), you pay for the total number of beds in the unit.

**De Hoop Nature Reserve.** Wydgeleë, Private Bag X16, Bredasdorp 7280. ☎ **028/542-1126/7.** Fax 028/542-1679. 10 units, each with 4 beds. R100–200 ($16.65–$20) per unit. No credit cards. (See above for directions.)

This is one of the most peaceful places on earth, with only a handful of people to explore the 36,000-hectare reserve once the gates close for non-residents at 4pm. The self-catering cottages are basic—two bedrooms, one bathroom and an open-plan kitchen and dining room—and only three are fully equipped. The remaining seven are supplied with a stove, fridge, and electricity; visitors are expected to provide their own bedding, kitchen utensils, and food. Pack an overnight picnic or barbecue; each cottage has its own braai site and wood can be bought at the reserve office. Any other supplies need to be purchased before you enter the reserve. The nearest shop and gas station is at Ouplaas, 15 kilometers (9 miles) from De Hoop, so it's best to stock up at Bredasdorp. Note that you must check in at the office no later than 4pm on the day of arrival. There are also seven campsites. You have to drive a short way to get to the sea.

## 3 Swellendam & the Overberg Interior

Swellendam: 220km (136 miles) east of Cape Town

Most people who choose to drive through the Overberg interior are on their way to the Garden Route, and may rush through without realizing that there are a few excellent pit stops on the way. As you head east from Cape Town on the N2, here are some suggestions of what you can stop and do as you travel.

### EN ROUTE TO SWELLENDAM

After ascending ✪ **Sir Lowry's Pass,** you'll reach the fruit-growing areas of Grabouw and Elgin (the area produces 65% of South Africa's apple export crop) and the first of many farm stalls dotted along the way. **Peregrine** (opposite the Grabouw turnoff) is one of the oldest, and arguably the best—stop here for fresh farm produce and various traditional "road trip" treats (see appendix A, "South Africa in Depth"). This is one of the best places in the Cape to sample biltong and *droë wors.* The bakery is also excellent—the pies, *melktert,* and *koeksisters* are all out of this world. (Note that if you're traveling directly from the Winelands you will join the N2 at Grabouw, via the R45, or a little farther along, via the R43.)

The first detour you might consider is the R406, which loops past the villages of **Genandendal** and **Greyton.** Genandendal is the oldest Moravian mission village in Africa with buildings dating back to 1738. **The Genandendal Mission and Museum Complex,** which is open Monday to Thursday from 8:30am to 1pm and 2 to 5pm; on Friday from 8:30am to 1pm and 2 to 3:30pm; and on Saturday from 9am to 1pm, documents the activities of the missionaries and their flock. The complex includes an old mill, printing works, and a nursery. For **guided tours,** call ☎ **028/251-8582.** Greyton, a few minutes farther east on the R406, was developed much later, and by a more affluent community. Set in the Riviersonderend Mountains, with many beautifully restored buildings, it's a more attractive town than Genandendal, though not as interesting. The main attraction here is the 14-kilometer (8½-mile) **Boesmanskloof Trail,** which traverses the mountains to the town of McGregor. The drawback of this trail is that after overnighting in the mountains, you have to return the way you've come. It's probably better to take the 9-kilometer (5½-mile) walk to Oak Falls—the highlight of the route—instead. For more information, call ☎ **023/625 1621** or 028/254-9620.

Greyton used to be renowned as an artist's haven, but with the influx of tourists and weekenders, most have beaten a hasty retreat deeper into the hinterland. Stop for tea and scones in **The Post House** courtyard, or lunch at **Greyton Lodge** (for both, see "Where to Dine" in Greyton, below). If you've enough time, consider staying overnight at one of the charming accommodation options also recommended below. For **tours** in Greyton, contact Judy Terry (☎ **028/254-9207**); or for more information, call the **Greyton Tourism Bureau** (☎ **028/254-9414**), in the library on Main Street.

To return to the N2 from Greyton, stay on the R406—it becomes a dirt track but is well maintained and rejoins the N2 just before the town of Riviersonderend.

If you skipped the R406 detour to Genandendal and Greyton, you will pass the farming town of **Caledon,** some 110 kilometers (68 miles) east of Cape Town. This is the official capital of the Overberg region, but other than to take a long soak in the Overberger's **hot springs** (☎ **028/214-1271**), there's no reason to stop here. The Overberger is Caledon's 3-star hotel, but the springs, which bubble up into a large Victorian indoor pool, are open to the public Friday to Wednesday from 8am to 7pm, for a fee of R10 ($1.65) per person. To reach them, take the second turnoff into Caledon, opposite the hospital. Swellendam lies some 100 kilometers (62 miles) east.

## SWELLENDAM

Swellendam, a pretty town situated at the foot of the Langeberg Mountains and appropriately billed as "the historic heart of the Overberg," is the perfect half-way stop (for lunch or the night) for visitors driving from Cape Town to the Garden Route.

### ESSENTIALS

**VISITOR INFORMATION** The **Swellendam Tourism Bureau** is in the Oefeninghuis at 36 Voortrek St., ☎ **028/514-2770.**

**GETTING THERE** **By Car** The quickest way to get to Swellendam is via the N2 as described above. Alternatively you can travel the more attractive mountain route, taking the N1 out of Cape Town, turning south on the R60 after Worcester, and then heading south to Swellendam through the vineyards of Robertson.

**By Bus** **Intercape, Translux,** and **Greyhound** pass through daily on their way to the Garden Route. See chapter 2, "Planning Your Trip to Southern Africa," for regional numbers.

**GETTING AROUND** **On Foot** This is the best way to explore the Drosdty Museum complex. Hiking trails in the nearby **Marloth Nature Reserve** lead into the Langeberg Mountains; for maps, contact ☎ **028/514-2648;** to purchase a permit for the popular but tough 5-day **Swellendam Trail,** contact ☎ **028/514-1410.**

**On Wheels** **Bontebok National Park** (☎ **028/514-2735**) lies 7 kilometers (4½ miles) out of town and is accessible by car or mountain bike. You can rent bikes from **Reitzhof** (☎ **028/514-3554**) for R35 ($5.85) per day or from **Swellendam Backpackers Lodge** (☎ **028/514-2648**) for R50 (8.35) per day.

**GUIDED TOURS** Dawie Fourie (☎ **082572/2078**) offers tours of the **Bontebok Park** and mountain surrounds in an open-topped jeep that's ideal for taking photos.

## The Route Less Traveled

To reach Swellendam/the Garden Route from Cape Town, it's worth considering an alternative route, highly recommended for its spectacular mountain scenery and Wineland valleys. With no detours or stops, this **scenic route,** which takes you through the Breede River Valley, will add some 45 minutes to your 2-hour direct journey from Cape Town to Swellendam. Travel north from Cape Town on the N1, through the toll road (R12.80/$2.15 per vehicle) and the Du Toitskloof Tunnel. Time allowing, bypass the tunnel and traverse the **Du Toitskloof Pass,** the soaring mountain and valley views from the 1:9 gradient road are well worth the extra 15 minutes. There's not much to keep you at Worcester, capital of the Breede River region, but the **Karoo National Botanical Gardens** (☎ **023/347-0785**) off Roux Road are open daily 8am to 6pm from August to October, R7 ($1.15) fee. There's no charge November to July. The gardens showcase the weird and wonderful plants from South Africa's semi-arid regions.

From Worcester, head southeast on the R60 to Robertson, keeping an eye out for the ultramodern **Graham Beck cellars** and tasting room (☎ **02351/61-214**), which are worth a stop if you like sparkling wine—his Brut is considered one of the best in the country. Hours are Monday to Friday from 10am to 5pm, Saturday 10am to 3pm, and it's clearly visible from the R60.

From Robertson it's another 20 kilometers (12½ miles) southeast on the R60 to Ashton where you can either choose to traverse the dramatic 10-kilometer (6-mile) **Cogmanskloof Pass** to the pretty town of **Montagu,** where you should then overnight, or keep heading southeast on the R60 to Swellendam. If you choose to stay in Montagu, take an evening stroll to admire the town's Victorian architecture or enjoy a therapeutic dip in the nearby hot springs (though from an aesthetic point of view, these have been ruined by the resort that's sprung up around them). The springs (no phone) are a constant 43°C (109°F), and are open daily from 8am to 11pm, for R20 ($3.35) per person, R12 ($2) per person if you overnight at one of the accommodations below. Recommended places to stay are the intimate **Mimosa Lodge,** an attractive Edwardian two-story house in Church Street (☎ **023/614-2351,** fax 021/614-2418, from R610 ($101.65) double, dinner and breakfast included, ask for winter discounts), and the **Montagu Country Inn,** at 27 Bath St. (☎ **023/614-3125,** fax 023/614-1905, R470/$78.35 double). Both are within easy walking distance of the **Montagu Tourism Bureau,** at 24 Bath St. (the main street) (☎/fax **023/614-2471**), open Monday to Friday from 8:45am to 4:45pm, Saturday 9am to 5pm, and Sunday 10am to 1pm.

Note that you don't necessarily have to retrace your footsteps through the Cogmanskloof Gorge to rejoin the R60 south to Swellendam. If you travel east from Montagu to Barrydale, the N2 and Heidelberg (official start of the Garden Route) can be reached via the pretty **Tradouws Pass.** Alternatively, if you're in the mood for a solitary, dusty drive with wide-open, unpopulated spaces, head northwest (to Calitzdorp) from Barrydale on the R62. Oudsthoorn lies 176 kilometers (109 miles) away.

**OUTDOOR ADVENTURES** Abseiling, kloofing, canoeing, horseriding, and mountain walks and hikes can be organized through **Swellendam Adventures,** ☎ **028/514-2648.**

## HISTORIC SWELLENDAM

Back in the early 1700s, the Dutch East India Company was most perturbed by the number of men deserting the Cape Colony to find freedom and fortune in the hinterland. Swellendam was consequently declared a magisterial district in 1743, making it the third-oldest white settlement in South Africa and bringing its reprobate tax evaders once again under the Company fold. In 1795 the burgers finally revolted against this unwanted interference and declared Swellendam a republic, but the Cape's occupation by British troops later that year made their independence rather short-lived.

Swellendam continued to flourish under British rule, but a devastating fire in 1865 razed much of the town. Almost a century later, transport planners ruined the main road, Voortrek Street, by ripping out the oaks that lined it, ostensibly to widen it. Two important historical sites to have survived on this road are, at number 36, the **Oefeningshuis,** built in 1838, and at number 11, the over-the-top **Baroque Dutch Reformed Church,** built in 1901. The Oefeningshuis houses the Swellendam Tourism Bureau.

The ✪ **Drostdy Museum complex** (☎ **028/514-1138**) comprises the Drostdy, the Old Goal and Ambagswerf (Trades Yard), Mayville House, and Zanddrift, now an excellent day-time restaurant. Start your walking tour before lunch by picking up the excellent free brochure describing the Drostdy complex and exhibits. The Drostdy (which together with the Old Goal is the oldest building in town) was built by the Dutch East India Company in 1747 to serve as residence for the *landdrost* (magistrate) and features many of the building traditions of the time: yellowwood from the once abundant forests, cow-dung and peach-pit floors, elegant fireplaces, and of course the Cape Dutch gables. The Drostdy also houses an excellent collection of late-18th-century and early-19th-century Cape furniture in the baroque, neoclassical, and Regency styles, a small selection of which originally belonged to the Drostdy. Mayville House, reached from the Drostdy via a delightful garden path, is an example of a typical late-19th-century middle-class home. It shows the transitional style of architecture, which combines Cape Dutch and Georgian elements, as well as the introduction of mass-produced goods. Hours are Monday to Friday from 9am to 4:45pm; Saturday and Sunday from 10am to 4pm; admission is R10 ($1.65) adults, R1 (15¢) children.

### WHERE TO STAY & DINE

The best place to eat is ✪ **Zanddrift** (☎ **028/514-1789,** in the museum complex), a country-style restaurant that is open for breakfast, tea, and legendary lunches (book your table well in advance). The soups, salads, and country platters center on what's been picked in the garden, and desserts often feature youngberries. (Swellendam is one of the world's biggest producers of youngberries.)

#### In Greyton

**Greyton Lodge.** 46 Main Rd., Greyton 7233. ☎ **028/254-9876.** Fax 028/254-9672. 18 units. TEL. R450 ($75) double. Rates include breakfast. Children's rates on request. AE, DC, MC, V.

Built as a trading store in 1882, Greyton Lodge is a collection of cottages set around a fragrant garden in close proximity to the mountains. Of these the best are cottages number 4 (a standard room), numbers 8 and 15 (for a slightly higher price), and numbers 7 and 16 (the highest-priced choices with the additional luxury of fireplaces). The rooms are appropriately decorated in an English country style—proprietors Sandra and Philip originally hail from Blighty, and are poncey enough to push the fact that Philip is "Lord of the Manor of Netherdean." Even if you don't overnight here, you should sample their fare; talented chef Antonie was voted the chef of the year in 1998 for the Cape Overberg region, and serves a simple lunch menu which changes seasonally (R18–24/$3–$4) and pricey four-course dinners (R98/$16.35). A starter (usually

### Why Time Stood Still

No one really knows why the Oefeningshuis (built as a place of worship and then used as a school for freed slaves) has clocks carved on each gable end, both forever stopped at 12:15. Underneath one of these is a working clock and it has been suggested that this was used in conjunction with the carved clock to help the illiterate identify the correct time to come for their lessons—when the working clock and carved clock "matched."

---

soup) might be followed by feta cheese soufflé wrapped in eggplant and served on salad leaves and tomato compote, with the main course a choice between fish or beef.

**The Post House.** Main Rd., Greyton 7233. ☎ **028/254-9995.** Fax 028/254-9920. 19 units. TEL. R460–580 ($76.65–$96.65) double. Rates include breakfast. AE, DC, MC, V. No children under 9.

The original post office and the oldest building in Greyton (built in 1860) today forms the reception, English-style pub, and dining room of Greyton's most popular inn. The majority of bedrooms have their own fireplaces, and open onto the central grassy courtyard—choose these rather than rooms in the annex, which is a relatively recent addition. Strangely, considering the moratorium on children, Beatrix Potter characters inspire most of the bedrooms, which have names like Two Bad Mice (the honeymoon suite) and Jemima Puddleduck. Thankfully the furnishings, a comfortable mix of Edwardian antiques and Cape country furniture, are more mature. The public rooms are quaint, with various comfy nooks. The four-course meals are average English fare: Soup may be followed by an avocado crepe, followed by either fresh kabeljou (fish) served with leek sauce, pork filet stuffed with prunes and raisins, or roast leg of lamb. There is a small pool, and riding, fishing, tennis, and croquet can be arranged.

#### In Swellendam

**Adin & Sharon's Hideaway.** 10 Hermanus Steyn St., Swellendam 6740. ☎/Fax **028/514-3316.** 3 units. MINIBAR. R400 ($66.65) double, includes breakfast. MC, V. No children under 14.

Before opening their Hideaway, Adin made a meticulous list of guests' needs, garnered from many interviews. The result is a string of awards, proof of their unstinting hospitality and appreciation for good food. Rooms are spacious, with every comfort, a choice of three coffees and three teas, handcrafted beds with well-sprung mattresses (made by the blind) and a "lest ye forget" box containing everything from headache tablets to condoms. Breakfasts are vast (a rainbow of over 40 jams, all made by Sharon, gives you some idea of what's in store) and what you can't finish you're encouraged to pack as "*padkos*" (literally "food for the road"). In the evenings, guests are asked to join Adin and Sharon for a sundowner and he will recommend a restaurant to suit your tastes—most are a stroll away, as are the Drostdy buildings. Adin also knows the surrounds very well and takes guests for photographic expeditions to the Bontebok National Park (for no extra charge). A very personal experience, this "hideaway" is not for those who enjoy anonymity.

**Herberg Roosje Van De Kaap.** 5 Drostdy St., Swellendam 6740. ☎/Fax **028/514-3001.** E-mail: roosje@dorea.co.za. 7 units. R115–135 ($19.15–$22.50) double, includes breakfast. DC, MC, V. Children by prior arrangement.

You'd be well advised to book this charming country inn in advance. Conveniently located right opposite the Drostdy Museum in a national monument, the rooms are a bit on the small side. However, more than compensating are the tasteful furnishings, the sparkling pool, and the tranquil gardens where guests not keen to wander the museum complex can spend the day. The equally charming restaurant, Roosje Van De Kaap, serves a la carte meals with a strong Italian slant in an informal atmosphere—definitely consider eating here even if you don't stay. Specialties are dishes prepared in the wood-burning oven. Pizzas are popular, and the Roosje Fillet, tender beef medallions prepared in garlic butter and herbs, is an all-time favorite.

**Klippe Rivier Country House.** Box 483, Swellendam 6740. ☎ **028/514-3341.** Fax 028/514-3337. 7 units. TEL. R800 ($133.35) double, includes breakfast. AE, DC, MC, V. From N2 take R60, turn left at four-way stop, follow the signs down the dirt road. No children under 10.

This magnificent Cape Dutch homestead, dating back to the 1820s, is by far the most luxurious address to overnight at in Swellendam. Furnished with beautiful antiques and run like a small luxury hotel, Klippe Rivier is on the outskirts of town, which means you'll have to drive to the Drostdy Museum. Then again, you may be unwilling to leave the peaceful pool or fireside of this gracious estate. Choose between the spacious downstairs suites (each with its own fireplace and walled-in gardens) and the more contemporary upstairs suites (each with a private balcony overlooking the mountains and gardens). For total privacy, request the honeymoon cottage, which is set well away from the main house. Klippe Rivier has its own vegetable gardens and orchards, and fresh milk is collected daily. The three-course dinners featuring country-style cooking (R95/$15.85) start with pre-dinner drinks and can last several hours, concluding in the library or lounge with coffee and truffles. Non-resident guests are welcome, though there are only eight tables; so booking is essential.

## 4 Exploring the Garden Route & Klein Karoo

The Garden Route has become the most popular tourist destination after Cape Town, drawing visitors year-round to its indigenous forests, freshwater lakes, wetlands, hidden coves, and long beaches. In addition to the great variety of outdoor activities that this eco-paradise offers, the mountains that range along the Garden Route's northern border beckon with a series of spectacular passes that cut through to the hinterland of the Klein Karoo. Besides providing a stark contrast to the lush coast, the dusty *dorpies* (little towns) dotted throughout this arid area have developed a distinctive architectural style, the best-preserved examples being found in the tiny hamlet of Prince Alfred. Oudtshoorn is the center of the Klein Karoo, and this is where you'll find the region's most famous attractions: ostrich farm tours, the Cango Caves, and the Swartberg Pass (a dramatic roadtrip connecting Oudtshoorn with Prince Alfred).

The narrow coastal strip that forms the Garden Route stretches from the rural town of Heidelberg in the west, to Storms River Mouth in the east; and from the shore of the Indian Ocean to the peaks of the Outeniqua and Tsitsikamma coastal mountain ranges. This is the official boundary description, but for many Mossel Bay marks the entry point in the west, and Port Elizabeth the eastern point of the route. (See chapter 5, "Eastern Cape," for transport details to Port Elizabeth, as well as for recommended routes between Storms River Mouth and Port Elizabeth.) Of the four major towns, three are coastal—Mossel Bay, Knysna, and Plettenberg Bay—while George, the capital and transport hub of the Garden Route, sits at the foot of the Outeniqua Mountains. Highlights of this region include the Wilderness National Park's "Lake District," where you'll find some of the Garden Route's loveliest coastline; Knysna's lagoon- and forest-based activities; and Plettenberg Bay, which combines some of South Africa's best beaches with beautiful fynbos surrounds. However, the real "garden" of the

Garden Route is the Tsitsikamma National Park, where dense indigenous forests interrupted only by streams and tumbling waterfalls drop off to a beautiful coastline. This is the final stop on the route if you're coming from Cape Town, but it is also the best, particularly for hikers as much of it is only accessible on foot.

There are a number of ways in which you can visit all these areas, and there's certainly enough to keep you occupied for at least 4 days (though many stay as long as 2 weeks). During this time, you may wish to keep moving to fully appreciate what each region has to offer, or, you may decide to take it easy by basing yourself in one or two places. Oudtshoorn and all the coastal towns are within easy driving distance from each other, and the routes you choose will depend on whether you wish to traverse the mountains, explore caves, bike through forests, visit an ostrich farm, paraglide onto the beach, or boat down the many rivers and lakes of South Africa's most famous garden.

## OUDTSHOORN & THE KLEIN KAROO

The Klein ("little") Karoo—a sun-drenched area about 250 kilometers (155 miles) long and 70 kilometers (43½ miles) wide—is wedged between the coastal mountains and the impressive Swartberg mountain range in the north. To reach it from any angle, you have to traverse precipitous mountain passes, the most spectacular of which is the Swartberg Pass, connecting the Klein Karoo with its big brother, the Great Karoo. Unlike this vast dry land that stretches well into the Northern Cape and Free State, the "little" Karoo is watered by a number of streams that flow down from the mountains to join the Oliphants River. Grapes grow here, Calitzdorp producing some of the country's best port, and Lucerne serving as the favored staple of the ostrich diet. (Incidentally, it was the ostrich that put the Klein Karoo on the map: During the late-19th and early-20th century, when the world decided that ostrich feathers were simply the hautest of haute, Oudtshoorn found itself crowned the feather capital of the world.) Today the popularity of the ostrich farms and the Cango Caves—a series of subterranean chambers some 30 kilometers (18½ miles) from Oudtshoorn—mean that no Garden Route itinerary is complete without a sojourn in Oudtshoorn, center of the Klein Karoo.

### ESSENTIALS

**VISITOR INFORMATION** You'll find the Oudtshoorn Tourism Information Bureau (☎ **044/279-2532**) on Baron van Rheede Street, next to the Queens Hotel. Hours are Monday to Friday 8am to 6pm, and Saturday 8:30am to 1pm.

**GETTING THERE** There are no scheduled flights. **By Car** Whichever way you approach it, you have to traverse a pass to get to Oudtshoorn. Via the N1 from Jo'burg or Cape Town, you'll head south on the R407 to Prince Albert before tackling the majestic Swartberg Pass. Alternatively, you approach it from the N2, either branching off via the R62, 14 kilometers (8½ miles) east of Swellendam and then driving via Calitzdorp (where you may be able to fit in a port tasting at Die Krans or Boplaas Estate; see box "The Route Less Traveled," above), or by traveling to Mossel Bay and heading over the Robinson Pass (R328). The latter is preferable if you don't have much time. Oudtshoorn is 88 kilometers (55 miles) from Mossel Bay and 55 kilometers (34 miles) from George.

**By Bus** **Intercape** and **Translux** travel from Johannesburg daily; only Translux travels from Cape Town. See chapter 2, "Planning Your Trip to Southern Africa," for regional phone numbers.

**GETTING AROUND** You can rent a car from **Avis** (☎ **044/272-0711**) on Voortrekker Street. If you need to be picked up and taken somewhere, or want an

# The Klein Karoo & the Garden Route

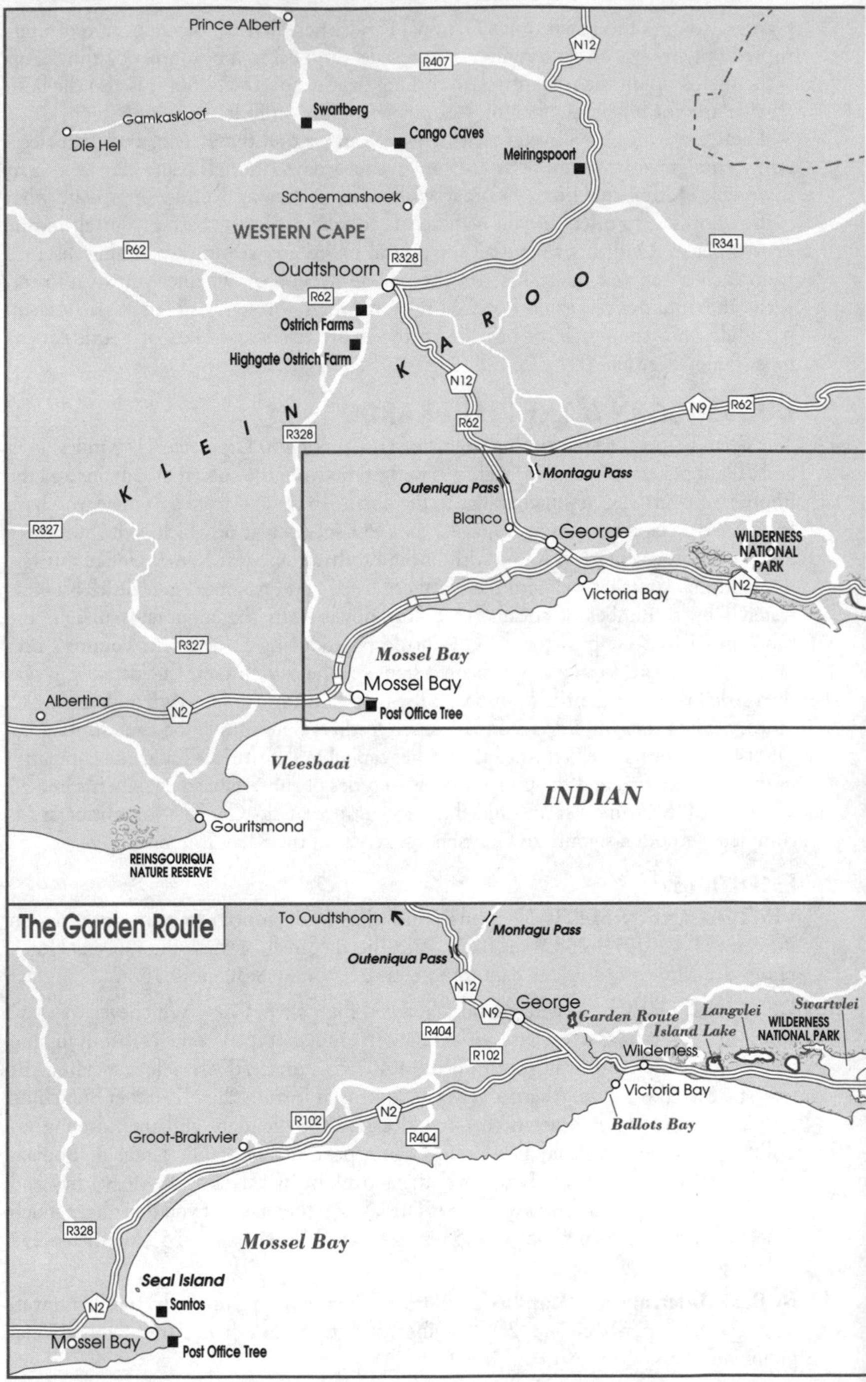

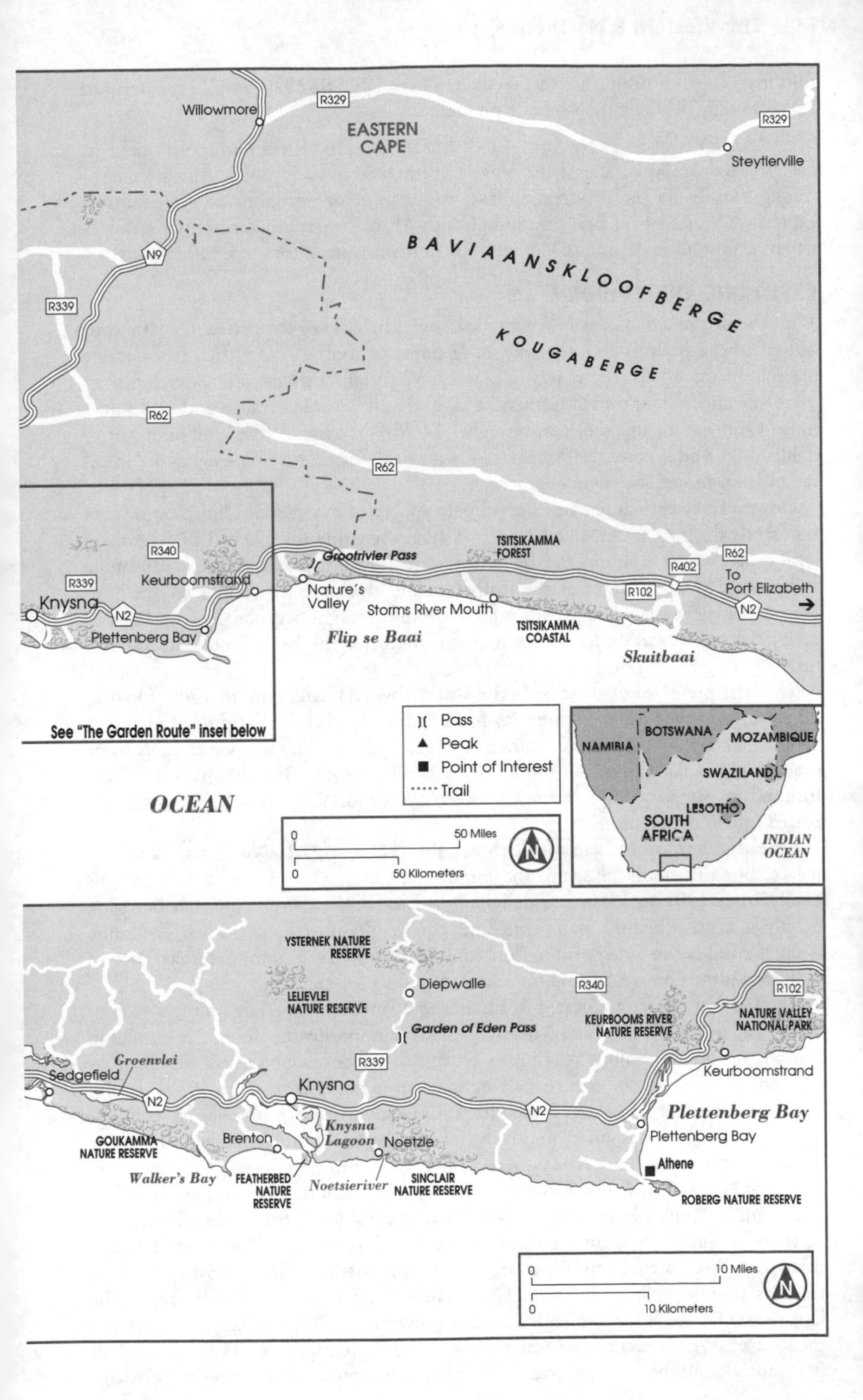

Willowmore
R329
EASTERN CAPE
Steytlerville
N9
R339
BAVIAANSKLOOFBERGE
KOUGABERGE
R62
R62
R340
Grootrivier Pass
TSITSIKAMMA FOREST
R62
R402
R339
Keurboomstrand
Nature's Valley
R102
To Port Elizabeth
Knysna
N2
Storms River Mouth
N2
Plettenberg Bay
Flip se Baai
TSITSIKAMMA COASTAL
Skuitbaai
See "The Garden Route" inset below
Pass
Peak
Point of Interest
Trail
OCEAN
0
50 Miles
0
50 Kilometers
NAMIBIA
BOTSWANA
MOZAMBIQUE
SWAZILAND
LESOTHO
SOUTH AFRICA
INDIAN OCEAN
YSTERNEK NATURE RESERVE
Diepwalle
R340
R102
LELIEVLEI NATURE RESERVE
Garden of Eden Pass
KEURBOOMS RIVER NATURE RESERVE
NATURE VALLEY NATIONAL PARK
Groenvlei
R339
Keurboomstrand
Sedgefield
Knysna
N2
N2
Plettenberg Bay
Knysna Lagoon
Plettenberg Bay
GOUKAMMA NATURE RESERVE
Brenton
Noetzie
Athene
Walker's Bay
FEATHERBED NATURE RESERVE
Noetsieriver
SINCLAIR NATURE RESERVE
ROBERG NATURE RESERVE
0
10 Miles
0
10 Kilometers

informal tour of Oudtshoorn, contact **Nico** (☎ **082979-9003**) or **Bernard** (☎ **083482-3847**) on their mobile phones.

**SPECIAL EVENTS** Every April, Oudtshoorn hosts the Klein Karoo National Arts Festival (**KunsteFees**), one of the biggest cultural festivals in South Africa, concentrating mainly on the preservation and stimulation of Afrikaans as a medium of expression. Some of the best theatre in South Africa is performed here, but unfortunately almost all in Afrikaans. Contact the Tourism Bureau for more information.

## EXPLORING OUDTSHOORN

With the introduction of wire fencing and sweet lucerne to the perfect climatic conditions of the Klein Karoo, the large-scale domestication of the ostrich first became possible in the 1800s. But it was only when Victorian fashion-victims developed an insatiable appetite for ostrich feathers in 1880 that it became a reality, and land values in the Oudtshoorn area shot up overnight. World War I signaled the end of this profitable trade, and it never really recovered, with fickle-dame Fashion seeking her inspiration from more sober sources post war.

However, the ostrich remains the primary source of income for Oudtshoorn, with thousands flocking to see, touch, eat, and (yes) even ride the giant birds. The town itself is also worth exploring for the beauty of its Edwardian and Victorian sandstone architecture. At the height of the feather boom, the so-called feather barons built themselves lavish town houses where they would overnight occasionally (usually after taking communion at the local church), before returning to their marble-floored farmhouses.

The best preserved of these is the **Le Roux Town House,** built in 1909. On 146 High St., it is open Monday to Friday from 8am to 1pm and 2 to 5pm; admission is included in CP Nel Museum's entrance fee (see below). The interior features some original pieces dating back to the Le Roux family's heyday, but the majority of the furnishings—imported from Europe between 1900 and 1920—have been bought and placed in situ by the museum.

**Arbeidsgenot,** on 217 Jan van Riebeeck Rd. (☎ **044/272-2968**), is not a feather palace, but this house museum, the humble abode of C. J. Langenhoven and his family from 1901 to 1950, is a delight, not least because everything has been left exactly as it was when the man penned his noteworthy novels and poems. The house is open Monday to Friday from 9am to 1:30pm and 2 to 5pm; Saturday 9am to 1:30pm. Admission is R5 (85¢) for adults, 50¢ (9¢) for children.

The **CP Nel Museum,** located in a handsome sandstone building on the corner of Baron van Rheede Street and Voortrekker Road opposite the Tourist Information Bureau, has many exhibits relating to Oudtshoorn's boom period, as well as photographs of some of the ostrich palaces that never made it past the 1950s. It also houses a synagogue and exhibits relating to Oudtshoorn's once large Jewish community. (Oudtshoorn was often derisively referred to as "Little Jerusalem" by those envious of the feather merchants' success, most of whom were Jewish.) The museum (☎ **044/272-7306**) is open Monday to Friday from 8am to 5pm, and on Saturdays from 9am to 4pm. Admission is R8 ($1.35) adults, R2 (35¢) for children under 13.

There are many more sandstone buildings, closed to the public but worth taking a drive past. Note particularly **Pinehurst** in Jan van Riebeeck Street, now part of the teacher's training college, and the elegant **Mimosa** on Baron van Reede Street. The latter becomes the R328, which leads out of town to the Ostrich farms (see below), the Rust-en-Vrede waterfall (a 74-meter [243-foot] drop under which you can cool off in summer), and the Cango Caves, Oudtshoorn's biggest attraction after the ostrich.

**South African Anthems**

C. J. Langenhoven was the author of South Africa's national anthem, "Die Stem" ("The Voice"), which is still sung with passionate fervor at international rugby games, though it is less popular with the general population than "Nkosi Sikele'iAfrika" ("God Bless Africa"), South Africa's second anthem inaugurated together with the country's first black president in 1994.

The **Cango Wildlife Ranch,** (☎ **044/272-5593**) off R328, is home to a host of tame farm animals, as well as 500 crocodiles, cheetahs, wild dogs, pumas, jaguars, tigers, and lions. The ranch is to be commended for creating an effective breeding and research center to help deal with endangered species, but if seeing wild animals in captivity depresses you, don't bother stopping here. The ranch is open 8am to 4:15pm daily and admission is R24 ($4), R13 ($2.15) for children aged 4 to 16.

The **Cango Caves** (☎ **044/272-7410**), approximately 30 kilometers (19 miles) from town on the R328, were first explored in 1780 by a local farmer who was lowered into the dark bat-filled chamber now named in his honor. The Van Zyl Hall, 107 meters (351 feet) across and 16 meters (52 feet) high, has some incredible limestone formations. The second chamber was discovered in 1792, and a century later the caves opened as a tourist attraction. Regrettably, they were damaged in the 1960s and 1970s, when the floors were evened out with concrete; ladders, colored lights, and music were installed; and a separate entrance was chipped away for "non-whites" (who had tours at different times). Today the caves enjoy a slightly more respectful treatment, with wardens fighting an ongoing battle to keep the limestone formations from discoloring due to exposure to lights and human breath. There are three tours you can take: the short 30-minute "scenic" tour (R11.50/$1.90), which takes in the first two chambers; the hour-long "standard" tour (R22.50/$3.75), which departs every hour and visits six chambers; or the 90 minute "adventure" tour (R28/$4.65), which covers just more than 1 kilometer (a little more than a half mile), some of which must be crawled—under no circumstances tackle this if you're overweight, claustrophobic, have heart, knee, or breathing problems, or are not wearing sensible shoes and trousers. Certainly the 30-minute tour, which departs hourly on the half hour, is more than adequate—you get to see the most majestic of the million-year-old limestone formations, and the irritating commentary is less likely to infuriate you.

The caves are open from 9am to 4pm daily. Visitor facilities have recently been upgraded and there is a restaurant, a gift shop, and childcare facilities. A new auditorium shows "Cango Two and Three"—areas that have always been out of bounds for visitors.

### VISITING AN OSTRICH FARM

There are four ostrich farms vying for the tourist buck (R20/$3.35) and offering more or less the same 45 to 90-minute tour. These include an explanation of ostrich farming (from incubation to tanning), the opportunity to ride an ostrich, and an ostrich "derby." All offer meals with ostrich on the menu, though you do need to pre-book these. **Highgate** (☎ **044/272-7115**) is the oldest show farm, having opened its doors back in 1937, and the world's largest. Of course big isn't always better, and while the owners are proud of their ability to process thousands of people a day, it can make for a very impersonal experience, particularly if you've been shoved onto the tail end of a large tour group. **Safari** (☎ **044/272-7311**) has the additional benefit of having a feather palace, Welgeluk, on the farm, but you can only look, not enter. Highgate and Safari are on R328 from Mossel Bay to Oudtshoorn, while **Oudtshoorn Ostrich Farm**

(☎ **044/279-1861**) and Cango Ostrich and Butterfly Farm are on the R328 heading out of Oudtshoorn to the caves. Of these, ✪ **Cango Ostrich and Butterfly Farm** (☎ **044/272-4623**) is the best, not least because of its location in the beautiful Schoemanshoek Valley. The owner is adamant that individuals should never be tagged onto large tour groups, and visitors take a brief walk from one process to the next (rather than being driven around the large farm). Finally, while you can sit on an ostrich, they are not raced, saving you the embarrassment of this circus display. You can also end your tour with a wine tasting, thereby sampling the distinctive flavors of the Klein Karoo. Lunch is served in the open air with a great view overlooking the Schoemanshoek Valley. The butterfly component is an additional bonus, particularly for kids.

## A BREATHTAKING DRIVE

For many, the greatest highlight of visiting the Klein Karoo is traversing the Swartberg Mountains to Prince Albert, a charming 18th-century Great Karoo town that lies 100 kilometers (62 miles) north. The circular route described below starts with the Swartberg Pass, but you could choose to begin with Meiringspoort.

To reach the ✪ **Swartberg Pass,** a 27-kilometer (17-mile) gravel road built over 100 years ago by master engineer Thomas Bain, take the R328 (also known as Cango Valley Road) north from Oudtshoorn. About 1 kilometer (a little more than a half mile) before the road terminates at the Cango Caves, you'll find a turnoff to the west, signposted Prince Albert. This marks the start of the pass, which soon begins its steep ascent. By the time you reach the summit, you will have enjoyed stupendous views of the Klein Karoo, which lies some 1,220 meters (4,002 feet) below. Stop to gird your loins, for the journey has only just begun. The northern descent is hair-raising—10 kilometers (6 miles) of zigzags, serpentines, twists, and steep gradients on a narrow dirt road with nothing between you and the abyss but a good grip on the wheel—a truly awesome experience. (You'll note a turnoff to the west that will take you to ✪ **Die Hell,** or Gamkaskloof. This is another magnificent drive, particularly popular with fynbos lovers, but you have to return the way you came and set aside most of the day.) The road continues to twist and turn before finally winding its way out of the Swartberg. At this point, you can either go to Prince Albert or turn back into the mountains and return to Oudtshoorn via Meiringspoort. Opt for ✪ **Prince Albert;** not only is the town an architectural gem, with almost all the buildings preserved and maintained in their original 19th-century form, but there is also an excellent restaurant if you need a break. The **Boere Bistro** in the Swartberg Hotel (see both below) serves delicious traditional Afrikaans food with a menu providing a good glossary of terms. If you're in need of real tranquility, or wish to wander the streets at sunset to view the mix of architectural styles (including Cape Dutch, Cape Cottage, Victorian Cottage, and the classic Karoo flat-roofed house), consider spending the night. Prince Albert's **Tourism Information** (☎ **023/541-1366**), at 42 Church St. is extremely helpful. Their hours are Monday to Friday from 8:30am to 1pm, and 2 to 5pm. (Note that Christiaan de Wit (☎ **023/541-1912**) offers birding trips around Prince Albert, day trips to Die Hell, and will cook for you under the stars with a veld braai.)

To return to Oudtshoorn, take the road back to the Swartberg Pass, keeping an eye out for the R407, which takes you east through Meiringspoort. This is another spectacular drive, though this time the views are up. In prehistoric times, the Great Karoo was a swamp that apparently broke through to the sea at Meiringspoort. The majestic **Meiringspoort Pass,** a natural ravine created by the course of what came to be known as the Groot River, features soaring cliffs and spectacular rock formations. The 25-kilometer (16-mile) tarred road follows and crosses the river several times as it winds through the floor of the gorge. If you have time, be sure to stop at the rest area some 3 kilometers (2 miles) from the northern entrance, and follow the track leading to a pretty waterfall.

## Where to Stay

If you want to stay in Prince Albert, be warned that the only hotel, **The Swartberg** (see below), is extremely popular and often full. However, the extremely helpful local Tourism Information will gladly assist with alternatives. B&B establishments worth noting are **Collins House** (☎ **023/541-1786**), a two-story house in town with a pool, and **Dennehof** (☎ **023/541-1227**), a tranquil oasis on the outskirts.

**De Opstal.** PO Box 1425, Oudtshoorn 6620. Schoemanshoek Valley. ☎ **044/279-2954.** Fax 044/272-0736. 11 units. R370 ($61.65) double, including breakfast. AE, DC, MC, V. Drive 12km (7 miles) north from Oudtshoorn on R328 toward the Cango Caves.

Stopping in Schoemanshoek Valley is an excellent opportunity to get a feel for the rural Klein Karoo. Certainly if you're interested in Afrikaans "boere" culture, De Opstal rates as one of the most authentically Afrikaans guest houses in the country. Matilda de Bod is an eighth-generation Schoeman, still living on the original Schoemanshoek Valley farm, though she and her husband Albertus now share it with guests. The 1830 farmhouse, stables, and milking parlor have all been converted into en-suite bedrooms. The best of these is the huge honeymoon suite, with its large bed and fireplace (essential in winter as windows close with shutters rather than glass). Meals are traditional and hearty, though nothing to write home about, and invariably feature ostrich. Service is friendly, but guests are left pretty much to their own devices. There is a small pool; and children are expressly welcome.

**Queens Hotel.** Baron van Reede St. (next to the Tourism Information Bureau), Oudtshoorn 6620. ☎ **044/272-2101.** Fax 044/272-2104. 40 units. A/C TV TEL. R488 ($81.35) double; R538 ($89.65) family room. Rates include breakfast. AE, DC, MC, V.

This elegantly refurbished hotel is steeped in history. Photographs of the British royal family abound, and there's even an illustration from 1881, with the hotel in the background. Today it makes a most convenient stopover. In addition to the in-house dining room, a number of excellent restaurants are within easy walking distance (we're talking across the road). The CP Nel Museum is adjacent, and the hotel complex boasts the local Tourism Bureau, a hairdressing salon, a beauty salon, a coffee shop, photo-processing center, and the local wine store. The foyer features pale marble, an antique furniture collection, and a large bowl of cut flowers; bedrooms have luxury details like gold-plated door handles and are finished in muted grays, creams, and dark woods. They are a little on the small side, however, and you'd be well advised to book a balcony room facing the beautifully landscaped courtyard and its smallish pool (rooms facing the street are noisy).

✪ **Rosenhof Country House.** 264 Baron van Reede St., Oudtshoorn 6620. ☎ **044/272-2232.** Fax 044/272-2260. 12 units. A/C TV TEL. R590 ($98.35) double, including breakfast. AE, DC, MC, V. No children under 10.

This is the most upscale place to stay in Oudtshoorn: a calm gracious oasis, beautifully furnished, with selected works by famous (white) South African artists and in springtime, a rose-filled garden that assaults the senses. Rooms are built around a courtyard, each with its own entrance. Though each has a different theme, they share the most important characteristics: space, beautiful linens, well-sprung beds, elegant pieces, and tasteful colors. The courtyard contains a large pool, during the searing summer heat this is almost a necessity rather than a luxury. The staff is very eager to please and despite the hotel's small size there are such luxuries as room service. Meals are a five-course affair, served in the original homestead, which dates back to 1852. Ingredients are local with herbs picked fresh from the garden. Appetizers are followed by a choice of three main courses, usually fish, beef, or ostrich, and two desserts.

**Swartberg Hotel.** Church St. (diagonally opposite the Tourism Bureau), Prince Albert 6930. ☎ **023/541-1332.** Fax 023/541-1383. 19 units. TV TEL. Low-season R424 ($70.65), high-season R468 ($78) double; under 12 half price. Rates include breakfast. AE, DC, MC, V.

The Swartberg Hotel has been declared a national historical building, and while the facade is a beautiful example of Victorian-style Karoo architecture, the interior is a little fusty. Rooms feel bare though they're perfectly comfortable. Numbers 2 and 4 are the best choices as they open onto the balcony that runs the length of the facade. The cottage suites, which face the garden and pool area, are ideal for families. In summer traditional luncheons are served under one of the oldest vines in South Africa. For dinner, try the attached Boere Bistro (see below).

### WHERE TO DINE

**Bernhard's Taphuis.** 10 Baron van Reede St. (opposite the Tourism Bureau), Oudtshoorn 6620. ☎ **044/272-3208.** Main courses R29–59 ($4.85–$9.85). MC, V. Open Mon–Sat 11:30am–11pm. TRADIONAL SOUTH AFRICAN/AUSTRIAN.

Austrian Bernhard Esterer received his food training in Austria and Germany, before unexpectedly falling in love with Oudtshoorn and opening his Taphuis four years ago. This has been such a resounding success that he has recently expanded to include the attractive sandstone house next to the original Taphuis. The honest, simple food is typical Karoo, but with an Austrian slant. Ingredients are local—even the olives in the olive bread come from Prince Albert. Ostrich is prepared in six different ways (I recommend the carpaccio), and Karoo lamb is tender and delicious. Another popular dish is *kassler,* smoked pork prepared in muscadel and raisins; this can be combined with the roast pork. Bernhard's new restaurant is modeled very much on a Vienna coffee shop, with 28 specialty coffees and one of the largest cigar selections in South Africa—thankfully there's also a large garden with plenty of outdoor tables.

✪ **Boere Bistro.** Church St. (the main street), Prince Albert 6930. ☎ **023/541-1332.** Main courses R15–33 ($2.50–$5.50). AE, DC, MC, V. Open daily 7:30am–5pm. Formal hotel restaurant open daily 7–11pm. TRADITIONAL AFRIKAANS.

The Boere Bistro is basically the best crash-course in Afrikaans cuisine in the Cape. Try the *boere* burger, a generous homemade hamburger patty served on *roosterkoek* (a Karoo speciality yeast bread) with a *tamatie smoorsous* (relish); or the *vetkoek en mince,* (a deep-fried yeasty dough filled with lightly curried ground beef). There's always a farm-style casserole served with *stampmielies* (a tasty corn dish); and *bobotie* (lightly curried ground beef cooked in a savory egg custard and served with yellow rice) is a perennial favorite. The sweet treats are irresistible—don't leave without trying either *malvapoeding* (a sweet sticky pudding), *souskluitjies* (sweet dumplings served in a cinnamon sauce with cream), or *melktert* (baked milk custard in a light pie crust and dusted with cinnamon).

## MOSSEL BAY—ENTERING THE GARDEN ROUTE

Traveling east on the N2, the first sign of the fast approaching town of Mossel Bay is the sci-fi spectacle of the MossGas oil plant on your left, about 100 kilometers (62 miles) outside the town and some 300 kilometers (186 miles) west of Cape Town. The town does not really improve on closer inspection, but it's a good place to lunch (try the seafood restaurant recommended below) if you haven't stopped elsewhere on the road. Though the historical center (where you will find the Tourism Bureau) has some

**Claim to Fame**

Mossel Bay features in the *Guinness Book of Records* as having one of the mildest all-year climates in the world—it's second only to Hawaii.

charm, and the Bartholomieu Dias Museum Complex is worth visiting if you're interested in the early maritime history of South Africa, this industrialized coastal town has little to recommend it otherwise.

## Essentials

**VISITOR INFORMATION** **The Tourism Bureau** (☎ **044/691-2202**) is in the historical center, at the corner of Church and Market streets.

**GETTING THERE** **By Car** Mossel Bay is approximately 4 hours from Cape Town on the N2. From Oudtshoorn either descend via the Robertson Pass to Mossel Bay, or take the more spectacular Outeniqua Pass to George, some 50 kilometers (31 miles) east of Mossel Bay.

## What to See & Do

Mossel Bay was the site of the first European landing on the South African coast, when Bartholomieu Dias, having battled a fearsome storm, tacked in for water and safety in 1488. The **Bartholomieu Dias Museum Complex** (☎ **044/691-1067**) comprises a collection of historic buildings, of which the **Maritime Museum** is excellent. It relates the early Portuguese, Dutch, and British seafaring history (which is a bit text-heavy), and houses a life-size replica of the caravel in which Diaz set sail in 1487—it's hard to imagine going where no man has gone before in something that looks like a large toy. The ship on display was built in Portugal and sailed from Lisbon to Mossel Bay in 1987 to commemorate the 500th anniversary of Dias' arrival on southern cape soil. The museum, located on Market Street, is open Monday to Friday 9am to 4:45pm, and Saturday and Sunday from 10am to 4pm. There is no admission fee.

Outside the Maritime Museum is the **Post Office Tree,** South Africa's first post office. In 1501 the first of many sailors sent his mail by leaving a letter stuffed in an old boot and tied to the tree. Soon this became an informal postal system, with letters picked up by passing ships and distributed accordingly. Today you can post a letter in a boot-shaped post box and it will be stamped with a special postmark. The only other intriguing museum is the **Shell Museum and Aquarium** (in the museum complex and with the same hours as Maritime), which contains a good selection of shells found off the world's coasts, the emphasis obviously on South African mollusks.

The entire complex overlooks **Santos Beach,** the only north-facing beach in South Africa. You can see Seal Island from here; but in order to view its resident jackass penguin and seal colonies, you'll have to board a yacht. The ***Romanza*** (☎ **044/690-3101**) operates daily, departing every hour from 9am to 5pm. The fare is R30 ($5) per person for one hour. Note that Mossel Bay is also the only place on the Garden Route where you can go shark-cage diving—see "Staying Active" above.

## Where to Stay

**Eight Bells Mountain Inn.** Ruiterbos, Mossel Bay, Western Cape 6500. ☎ **044/631-0000.** Fax 044/631-0004. E-mail: 8bells@mb.lia.net. 24 units. TV TEL. Low-season R360–460 ($60–$76.65); high-season R460–570 ($76.65–$95), double. Rates include breakfast. Children R10 ($1.65) per year of age. AE, DC, MC, V. 35km (22 miles) from Mossel Bay at the foot of the Robinson Pass (R328), 50km (31 miles) from Oudtshoorn.

This inn is run by a family, for families, and has 400 acres of fynbos and forest to explore on foot or horseback; a swimming pool, tennis, and squash courts; billiards, and daily donkey-cart rides visiting a host of farm animals to entertain the kids. There are four accommodation options: The Rose Court rooms are set in the garden, but have no views; the Pool Terrace rooms are close to the pool; Palm Court rooms have their own enclosed patios; and the Swiss Village cabins enjoy the best views and privacy (no children are allowed in this part of the inn). The Swiss Village cabins are the most charming; if you can't book a room here, you might want to settle for a Rose Court room; they are marginally cheaper, yet no worse than the other options. Family rooms share bathrooms. Meals are simple, with dinners a choice between an a la carte menu and a set menu (R65/$10.85 per person). The set menu might include mushroom soup, roast turkey, and spicy banana crepes. There is also a kids' a la carte menu.

**The Old Post Office Tree Manor.** Corner of Church and Market sts., Bartholomieu Dias Museum Complex, Mossel Bay 6500. ☎ **044/691-3738.** Fax 044/691-3104. E-mail: posttree@mb.lia.net. www.isaa.com/posttree. 30 units. TV TEL. R500–600 ($83.35–$100) double, includes breakfast. Children under 12 sharing R65 ($10.85). AE, DC, MC, V.

The best reason to stay at the Old Post Office Tree Manor is its proximity to the museum complex, Tourism Bureau, and the restaurant. "Manor" is a much abused word in South Africa, and this place proves no exception—though rooms are clean and relatively spacious, they are not exactly going to make you feel like the landed gentry. Bright Caribbean-esque colors are apparently chosen to inspire a cheerful mood, but far more uplifting are the views of the ocean (ask for rooms 30, 31, or 20). All rooms have tea- and coffee-making facilities (ask for fresh milk) and hair dryers. If you don't manage to bag a room with a view, repair to the Blue Oyster. This cocktail bar enjoys exceptional views of Munro Bay and its great whale-watching opportunities. Meals (including breakfast) are enjoyed in the Gannet, renowned as one of the Garden Route's great seafood restaurants (see review below).

### WHERE TO DINE

**The Gannet.** Market St., Bartholomieu Dias Museum Complex, Mossel Bay 6500. ☎ **044/691-1885.** Main courses R37–85 ($6.15–$14.15). Mon–Fri 7:00am–10:30pm; Sat–Sun 8:00–10:30pm. AE, DC, MC, V. SEAFOOD.

The Gannet is conveniently located across the road from the museums and a stone's throw away from the Information Bureau. It is considered one of the best seafood restaurants on the Garden Route and, with its range of pizzas, pastas, and meat dishes, even the non-seafood lover won't leave disappointed. The linefish, basted with butter and herbs and grilled or fried to tender perfection, is so fresh it's almost moving. The seafood casserole, baked in a clay pot with a creamy wine sauce, is another house specialty. Beleaguered parents will be pleased to know the restaurant is also child-friendly, with a separate kiddies' menu, though there are no high chairs. Weather permitting, dine alfresco in the garden overlooking the bay, keeping an eye out for whales and dolphins.

## GEORGE & WILDERNESS

Halfway between Cape Town and Port Elizabeth, George may not win any beauty competitions, but it is the commercial heart of the Garden Route, with the most transport connections, a large choice of restaurants, and a comprehensive, helpful tourist bureau. However, it's not worth overnighting in this inland town as its attractions are few and far from scintillating, and the coastal town of Wilderness, which has a number of pleasant accommodation options, is a few minutes drive away.

## Essentials

**VISITOR INFORMATION** The **George Tourism Bureau** (☎ **044/801-9295**) is at 124 York St. E-mail: gardenroute.tourism@pixie.co.za; www.gardenroute.org.za. (Note that if you're traveling from Port Elizabeth, your first comprehensive tourist bureau will be in Knysna [see that section below].)

**GETTING THERE** **By Air** **SAA** (☎ **044/801-8448**) and **Sabena Nationwide** (☎ **044/801-8414**) have regular flights into George Airport (☎ **044/876-9310**) from Cape Town, Johannesburg, and Port Elizabeth. **South Africa Airlink** (☎ **044/533-9041**) flies from Johannesburg to the small Plet airport daily.

**By Train** Comfortable inter-city trains run from Cape Town and Port Elizabeth to George once a week—expect to pay in the region of R115 ($19.15) one-way from Cape Town. Call ☎ **044/801-8202** Monday to Friday, from 10am to 4pm. If you've got money and time to burn, board **Rovos Rail** (☎ **012/323-6052**), which steams into the George and Knysna stations once a month. Tickets are R3,295 ($549.15) per person sharing. The **Blue Train** (☎ **021/405-2672**) also offers Garden Route service. A much better value-for-money option is traveling on the **Union Limited's** steam train, though you'll have to take the full tour (see below).

**By Bus** The intercity buses (**Intercape, Greyhound,** and **Translux**) travel the N2 from Cape Town to Port Elizabeth, but they don't offer a door-to-door service and often don't drive through towns, leaving you stuck at some filling station. See chapter 2, "Planning Your Trip to Southern Africa," for regional numbers.

**GETTING AROUND** **By Car** **Avis** (☎ **044/876-9314**) and **Budget** (**044/876-9999**) both have desks at George Airport. The N2 cuts right through the Garden Route, but make time to explore the roads that venture off it or you are likely to be disappointed. (*Note*: Don't miss the 1-kilometer [just more than half-mile] trail to the Storms River mouth).

**GUIDED TOURS** **By Bus** Outeniqua Coach Tours (☎ **044/874-4940**) and Springbok Atlas (☎ **044/874-1710**) offer various tours of the area in large luxury buses. For a smaller operator, try Eco Bound (☎ **044/873-5881**).

**By Train** Take a luxury steam train tour with **Union Limited,** and travel through the Garden Route and Klein Karoo in elegantly restored en-suite carriages dating back to the 1930s and 1940s. The 6-day Golden Thread Tour sets off from Cape Town to Mossel Bay via the Breede River, then heads for Knysna before steaming back to George and Oudtshoorn, and returns to Cape Town via Paarl. Passengers alight at certain designated stops to explore areas. The 6-day tour costs R3,800 ($633.35) per person, including all side tours, breakfasts, two-course lunches, and four-course dinners. For more information, contact Union Limited, ☎ **021/449-4391,** fax 021/449-4395, e-mail to SteamSA@Transnet.co.za, or visit www.steamsa.co.za.

## What to See & Do

The most interesting exhibits in the **George Museum** on Courtney Street (☎ **044/873-5343**) used to be the P. W. Botha collection, which was personally donated by the hard-line apartheid minister himself. Botha withdrew the collection recently and auctioned them, however, apparently to pay for legal council during his lengthy wrangle with the Truth and Reconciliation Commission. What's left in the museum is a large selection of mechanical musical instruments, a display of the history of the timber industry, and Ruby Reeve's paintings of fairies and pixies. Understandably the museum charges no admission. Hours are Monday to Friday from 9am to 4:30pm and Saturday from 9am to 12:30pm.

**The Name Game**

Legend has it that when a young Capetonian called Bennet asked his wife's hand in marriage she acquiesced only on the condition that he take her to live in the wilderness. The imaginative young man bought a farm, named it Wilderness, and brought his wife home.

---

Really, the best reason to be in George is to board the **Choo-Tjoe steam train** that runs between George and Knysna (though consider starting the journey in Knysna and booking with **Kontours** (☎ **082569/8997**) who will then pick you up at George station). See the Knysna section of this chapter for more information.

You are spoilt for choice when it comes to the number of excellent **drives** that start in George. To do a circular route to Oudtshoorn, take the **Outeniqua Pass** (or R29) to Oudtshoorn, then return via the **Montagu Pass,** a gravel road dating back to 1843. If you're heading farther into the Garden Route, consider taking the **Seven Passes Road** to Wilderness or Knysna. This, the original road linking George and Knysna, doesn't have the great views of the mountain passes, but it takes you through dense indigenous forests, and crosses a number of quaint Edwardian bridges. Alternatively, head down the N2 for the most direct route to the pretty town of **Wilderness**—8 kilometers (5 miles) away via the Kaaiman's River Gorge.

Today **Wilderness** is anything but, with its residential development creeping up the forested hills that overlook the Touw River estuary, and a string of ugly mansions lining the beach; yet it is still the smallest and most tranquil of the coastal towns along the Garden Route. Set around the mouth of the Touw River, it marks the western end of a chain of lakes that stretches some 40 kilometers (25 miles) east, most of which are under the control of the **Wilderness National Park.** While the beaches along this stretch are magnificent, the strong currents regularly claim unsuspecting and inexperienced swimmers. You're better off floating in the tea-colored waters of the **Serpentine,** the waterway that links Island Lake, Langvlei, and Rondevlei to the Wilderness lagoon. Don't be put off by the color, it's caused by plant oxides and perfectly clean. You can explore the area on foot on a number of trails lasting from 1 to 4 hours, or cover some 15 kilometers (9 miles) of inland waterways in a canoe. The **Wilderness National Park reception** (☎ **044/877-1197**) issues trail maps and rents canoes for R14 ($2.35) per hour. Alternatively, ask about the 3-day canoe trail (see "Staying Active" above). Park hours are 8am to 4:30pm from February to November, and until 7pm the remainder of the year. To reach the park, follow signs off the N2, 2 kilometers (just more than 1 mile) east of Wilderness; should you wish to overnight in the park, accommodations options are listed below.

For more information, contact the helpful **Wilderness Tourism Information Bureau** on Leila's Lane (☎ **044/877-0045**). Their hours are Monday to Friday from 8:30am to 5:30pm, Saturday from 8:30am to 1pm, and Sunday from 3 to 5pm.

## A Nearby Cove

Nine kilometers (almost 6 miles) east of George on the way to Wilderness you'll find a turnoff marked **Victoria Bay.** This tiny cove, protected by cliffs, provides wind-free tanning on the tiny sandy beach, a tidal pool, and safe swimming in the surf. "Vic Bay," as locals refer to it, is in fact known as one of South Africa's top surf spots, with a big and long break. Its geography has also kept development to a minimum, with a single row of houses strung along the western cliff. Be warned, however, that the bay becomes a no-go zone during school holidays, particularly Christmas and Easter, as campsites run into the beach and parking becomes a nightmare.

## WHERE TO STAY

### In George

**✪ Fancourt Hotel and Country Club Estate.** Montagu St., Blanco, George 6530. ☎ **044/870-8282.** Fax 044/870-7605. E-mail: hotel@fancourt.co.za. www.fancourt.co.za. 100 units. A/C TV TEL. R1,050–1,600 ($175–$266.65) double; R2,100 ($350) deluxe suites; R2,940 ($490) 2-bedroom suite. AE, DC, MC, V.

There is no doubt that this is the best address in George, with over R300 million ($50 million) invested in the estate's already well-developed facilities and the two Gary Player–designed courses consistently rated among the top four in South Africa. Luckily, you don't have to be a golfer to appreciate the luxurious atmosphere, lovely setting, and helpful staff. Rooms are either in the manor house, or set in the beautifully landscaped gardens. There's not much that differentiates them; though rooms may be slightly smaller in the manor house, they are closer to all amenities. Should you choose to base yourself here for the duration of your stay on the Garden Route, you will not be disappointed.

**Dining/Diversions:** Two bars and four fine-dining options, including George's top Italian restaurant.

**Amenities:** Four tennis courts, two swimming pools, spa, squash, children's entertainment center (baby-sitters on tap), mountain bikes and backpacks for rent.

### In Victoria Bay

**Land's End Guest House.** PO Box 9429, George 6530. ☎ **044/871-3168.** Fax 044/871-0024. www.meditnet.com/~iclub/landsend. 4 units. MINIBAR TV TEL. R300–500 ($50–$83.35). AE, DC, MC, V. At the end of Beach Road, Victoria Bay.

The logo reads: "The Closest B&B to the Sea in Africa," and at 6 meters (19 feet) from the high-water mark, this is no doubt true. Land's End is also the last house on the only residential road in Vic Bay; beyond lie the rocks and the ocean, beside you is the safest swimming bay for miles around. The guest house is run in a very laid-back manner and furnished in a homely fashion. Don't expect luxuries like well-sprung mattresses, but there are lovely touches like complimentary sherry, and standards like tea- and coffee-making facilities and hair dryers. The views from the two self-catering units are fantastic; try to book these rather than the downstairs rooms. If you don't feel like cooking, the local restaurant delivery company will deliver to Vic Bay.

### In Wilderness

**Karos/Möven Pick Wilderness Hotel.** Owen Grant St., Wilderness 6560. ☎ **044/877-1110.** Fax 044/877-0600. 158 units. A/C TV TEL. Low-season R505 ($84.15) double; high-season R720 ($120) double. Children free if sharing with adults. AE, DC, MC, V.

The Wilderness Hotel is apparently built on the site of Wilderness' very first farmhouse, but that's where the romance ends. This huge, impersonal hotel could be anywhere in the world; and very few rooms enjoy any sort of view. You can try to book a lagoon-facing suite on the first floor, but these are limited as many have been sold in timeshare. Rooms all have tea- and coffee-making facilities and hair dryers. Furnishings are old fashioned and tired, though the Swiss-owned group Möven Pick have just purchased the majority of shares in Karos, and a refurbishment program here is apparently a top priority. Breakfast is an additional R50 ($8.35) per person; the buffet dinners, an additional R80 ($13.35).

**Amenities:** Three swimming pools (one heated), tennis, squash, snooker, mini-golf, outdoor chess and bowls, 24-hour room service.

**Moontide Guest Lodge.** Southside Rd. (at the end of the cul de sac), Wilderness 6560. ☎ **044/877-0361.** Fax 044/877-0124. E-mail: moontide@intekom.co.za. www.gardenroute.co.za/wilderness/moontide/. 4 units. MINIBAR (semi-stocked) TV. Low-season R310–440 ($51.65–$73.35); high-season R400–660 ($66.65–$110). AE, MC, V. Children by prior arrangement.

Situated on the banks of the Touw River, in gardens that flow into its tidal waters, this beautiful B&B offers one of the best value-for-money options on the Garden Route. The thatched homestead nestles under milkwood trees, and cottages are set amongst the flowering garden. Guests can choose from the Stone Cottage, Milkwood Suite, the Rondawel, or River Suite. The last is the most luxurious and enjoys the best views; Milkwood, a separate duplex cottage with bedroom upstairs, is ideal for younger couples; Stone Cottage is also separate from the main house and has the largest bathroom (shower only); and Rondawel has both a bathtub and shower in a bathroom that is private, but not en suite. All the rooms are tastefully furnished with handpicked pieces. Guests have exclusive use of the lounge with large log fireplace and sliding doors leading to the terrace overlooking the lagoon. Breakfasts are served here, weather permitting, and the service is friendly. As it's hard to tear yourself away from the tranquility, you may want to dine here. Given notice when booking, your hostess will prepare a simple three-course meal; alternatively take advantage of one of the takeaway joints in Wilderness and ask for a table to be set on the deck.

**Palms.** Owen Grant St. (opposite Wilderness Hotel), Wilderness 6560. ☎ **044/877-1420.** Fax 044/877-1422. E-mail: palms@pixie.co.za. www.palms-wilderness.com. 10 units. TV TEL. Low-season R400 ($66.65) double; high-season R470 ($78.35) double. Rates include continental breakfast. AE, DC, MC, V. Children over 12 only.

Despite being a great deal lower in price, this guest house is a lot classier than the large monolith across the road. Rooms are spacious and are stylishly furnished in crisp whites, deep blues, and black. Green is the other dominant color, supplied by the lush gardens that lead to each room's private entrance, and the red and pink hibiscus flowers make a stark statement against the black marbled pool. Palms is Swiss-owned and managed and things do rather run like clockwork, with four hosts to attend to guests' needs. Note that transfers from and to George's airport (15 minutes away) can be arranged.

**Dining/Diversions:** Palms's restaurant, which serves a set menu for R85 ($14.15), is the best in Wilderness. A typical four-course meal might include the following choices: salmon roses with sweet mustard sauce or Palms vegetable salad with herb dressing; seafood quiche or fettuccine with zucchini sauce; grilled fillet of sole with lemon butter or beef fillet with green-pepper sauce. Finally, there is a choice of desserts. A smaller menu is available on request.

**Wilderness Manor.** 397 Waterside Rd., Wilderness 6560. ☎ **044/877-0264.** Fax 044/877-0163. 5 units. MINIBAR TV TEL. High-season R440–540 ($73.35–$90) double (ask for low-season rates). DC, MC, V.

This well-dressed home, separated from the lagoon by a narrow road and seconds from the boardwalk that snakes along its banks, is constantly being improved upon by owners Marianne and Johan. Guests enjoy exclusive use of the lounge and billiard room, which is skillfully decorated in the Afro-colonial style and offers a wide array of interesting books to page through. Most rooms range along a corridor, which means you don't really enjoy the privacy of Palms or Moontide, nor the anonymity of the Karos; however, this need not be a drawback if you're keen to meet other travelers. The best room by far (and the most private) is the honeymoon suite. Here you can luxuriate in space, and roll around in the beautiful timber four-poster bed. Rooms have tea- and coffee-making facilities and hair dryers. Wilderness Manor does not serve dinner, but there are three restaurants within walking distance.

**Wilderness National Park.** Off N2, 2km (just more than 1 mile) east of Wilderness; follow signs. Book through PO Box 787, Pretoria 0001. ☎ **021/422-2810;** Fax 021/24-6211. E-mail: reservations@parks-sa.co.za. www.parks-sa.co.za. 43 cottages with 4 beds and forest huts and rondawels with 2 beds, not all with bathrooms. R110–154 ($18.35–$25.65) double; R360 ($60) for 4-bedded units. Camping R55 ($9.15) double. AE, DC, MC, V.

Accommodations in the Wilderness National Park (called Ebb & Flow rest camp) offer exceptional value, though some of the rondawels in Ebb & Flow North are very rudimentary and share washing facilities. Your best options are in Ebb & Flow South, the timber "forest huts" numbered 24 to 33. These are slightly raised and built right on the Touw River—you can almost cast for fish from your front door. Bear in mind that only these have en-suite showers and toilets, so remember to specify your requirements. All forest huts have kitchenettes and braai areas. If you're camping, sites 28–40 and 63–65 are also located right on the river. Of the 4-bedded log cabins, which are better equipped if you want to self-cater, units 7–13 enjoy the best location, on the Serpentine River. All units are serviced daily. There is no restaurant or shop, so you'll have to bring your own supplies (there is a small shop in Wilderness) or dine out.

## Where to Dine

The best meals in Wilderness are served at The Palms, see above. At the Fancourt Country Club and Golf Estate (☎ **044/870-8282,** on Montagu Street in Blanco), you'll not only find a fine Italian restaurant (see below), but three more restaurants as well. There's the elegant **Montagu,** for intimate candlelit occasions; the more casual **Grillroom;** and the **Morning Glory,** which specializes in light lunches and health food. Call the above number for all bookings and inquiries. Another restaurant in George worth highlighting is the Reel 'n Rustic, at 79 Davidson St. (☎ **044/884-0707**), where you can enjoy excellent Cajun-style dishes in an atmosphere inspired by the southern United States.

**Copper Pot.** 12 Montagu St., Blanco, George 6530. ☎ **044/870-7378.** Main courses R19–70 ($3.15–$11.65). May–Sept open Mon–Fri 12–2pm, Mon–Sat 6:30–10pm; Oct–Apr daily 6:30–10pm. SOUTH AFRICAN/ECLECTIC.

The Copper Pot has been around for over 20 years, though the new venue—an elegant old house in Blanco—is relatively new. The walls remain the signature deep red though, and owner-chef Anneliese Ocker still provides diners with a range of difficult choices: beef stroganoff prepared with wine, cream, and mushrooms or the ever-popular Beef Wellington? Vegetarian paella, or homemade spinach pasta? Mossel Bay sole, or prawn curry? How about Durban curry? (If you haven't yet sampled traditional South African fare, there's an entire page devoted to it.) Or try the healthy Copper Pot salad with greens and fresh herbs dressed with a light walnut dressing, which just might justify the house specialty, crepes Anneliese (paper-thin, fruit-filled crepes in a liqueur sauce).

**La Cantina.** Fancourt Country Club and Golf Estate, Montagu St., Blanco, George 6530. ☎ **044/870-8282.** R26–98 ($4.35–$16.35). Tues–Sat, 7–10:30pm. ITALIAN.

You'll find George's best Italian restaurant in an estate known for its no-expenses spared attitude. If you're an Italian aficionado, you're unlikely to find any surprises on the menu (note the authentic northern bias), but everything you sample will please. The gnocchi tossed in tomato-and-basil sauce and baked with goat cheese is delicious. Meat lovers face a difficult choice: slices of rare filet, basted with balsamic and rosemary and served on a bed of rocket (arugula), or grilled filet topped with gorgonzola and served on beetroot noodles. End the meal with Genovese pastries filled with wild berries marinated in Kirsch and topped with whipped cream, or take your coffee at one of the estate's bars.

**The King Fisher.** 1 Courtenay St. (opposite the Outeniqua High School's sport fields), George 6530. ☎ **044/873-3127.** Main courses R19–82 ($3.15–$13.65). Open daily 12–3pm and 6–10:30pm. SEAFOOD.

This is not an elegant dining option, but if you enjoy quality seafood, you won't find a better value on the Garden Route. The decor is simple and unpretentious, and the surfer-dude waiters provide friendly service. Main courses are limited to a choice of nine different linefish (all freshly purchased from local fishermen), a range of Mediterranean-style calamari (deliciously tender), and the house specialty: huge, succulent prawns (quite possibly the best on the Garden Route). The King Fisher also serves up pizzas (try the feta-garlic pizza bread as an appetizer) and pastas; but if you're looking for Italian you're better off at La Cantina, on the other side of George.

## SEDGEFIELD & GOUKAMMA RESERVE

The drive from Wilderness to Sedgefield on the N2 is very pleasant, with the Island Lake, Langvlei (long lake), Rondevlei (round lake), and Swartvlei (black lake) on the left and occasional glimpses of the ocean on your right. Sedgefield itself looks very unattractive from the road—a motley collection of shops, estate agents, and service stations—but it's worth turning off and heading for the beach, which is one of the most attractive along this stretch (mostly due to the houses being set back behind the sand dunes). One of the best Garden Route beach walks starts here: During low tide, walk westward to **Gericke's Point,** a low hillock of sandstone where you can pick fresh mussels.

If you're hungry, stop for an Italian meal at **Trattoria Da Vinci** (☎ **044/343-1867**)—the best restaurant in Sedgefield.

Next stop is the **Goukamma Reserve** and **Groenvlei,** or "Lake Pleasant," a freshwater lake within the reserve. There are several day-long **hiking trails** that cover various habitats in the reserve, including a 4-hour beach walk and a short circular walk through a milkwood forest; pick up a Nature Conservation map from the Lake Pleasant Hotel. You can also **rent canoes** from the Lake Pleasant Holiday Resort (☎ 044/343-1985) for R10 ($1.65) per hour. Admission to the Goukamma Nature Reserve is R4 (65¢), and its hours are 8am to 6pm. For more information, contact ☎/fax **044/383-0042.**

### WHERE TO STAY & DINE

**Lake Pleasant Hotel.** PO Box 2, Sedgefield 6573. ☎ **044/343-1313.** Fax 044/343-2040. E-mail: lake.pleasant@pixie.co.za. 33 units. TV TEL. Low-season R530–686 ($88.35–$114.35); high-season R650–840 ($108.35–$140). Rates include breakfast. AE, DC, MC, V. Off N2 in the Goukamma Reserve, 3km (2 miles) east of Sedgefield town, 16km (10 miles) west of Knysna.

Situated on the south bank of Groenvlei, this country-style hotel is one of the few on the Garden Route located in a nature reserve and bird sanctuary. Don't let this mislead you though; the N2 is hardly ever out of earshot. However, the atmosphere is immensely peaceful, and the hotel's popularity proof of its excellent service and value. Guests can choose between classic and luxurious suites—opt for a luxurious suite; a little more money buys more taste, comfort, and privacy, as well as timber sliding doors leading out to the gardens (which overlook the lake), and wrought-iron garden furniture from which to enjoy the view.

**Dining:** Non-residents are welcome to dine here: Simple, reasonably priced pub lunches are served at the Swan, and table d'hôte dinners in the dining room. A typical menu (R80/$13.35 per person) consists of baked brown mushrooms topped with avocado mousse, spring vegetable soup, a choice of fish or meat with seasonal vegetables, two dessert choices, and a cheeseboard. There's also an excellent wine list.

**Amenities:** A bird-hide from which to identify the some 130 species, a number of canoes, maps designating the hiking trails of the Goukamma Reserve, a tennis court, swimming pool, and a beach is also only 2½ kilometers (1½ miles) away.

## KNYSNA

The founder of Knysna (pronounced *nize*-na) was one George Rex; in 1802, at the age of 39, he purchased the farm which included the whole basin containing the Knysna Lagoon. By the time of his death in 1839, he had engaged in a number of enterprises, the most profitable of which was timber, and had persuaded the Cape authorities to develop Knysna as a port. Knysna's development and the decimation of its forests were well underway.

That there are any areas of forests to have escaped the devastation of the 19th century is thanks to far-sighted conservation policies introduced in the 1880s, and today Knysna has the largest areas of indigenous forests left in South Africa. The Knysna elephants have fared less well—attempts to augment their numbers by relocating three young cows from the Kruger failed miserably when it was discovered that the last remaining Knysna elephant was also a female. The surviving cows have subsequently been relocated to Shamwari game reserve in the Eastern Cape. And although the locals are loathe to admit it, the word is finally out: Their pachyderms are extinct, and the only elephants you're likely to see are the ones on road markers warning you of their presence (not to mention the ones that may appear if you over-indulge in the delicious local beer).

Knysna used to be a sleepy village inhabited only by hippies and wealthy retirees, but the last decade has seen a boom in tourism which has changed the town irrevocably—nowhere is this more evident than the congested Main Road that runs through town. Knysna's raison d'être is its large tidal lagoon, around which the town has grown, and the large sandstone cliffs (the heads), which guard the lagoon's narrow access to the sea. The eastern buttress has unfortunately been developed, but this means you can drive to the top of the cliff for good sea views, or to the bottom and walk to the churning mouth. Better still, visit the unspoiled western side—a visit to the Featherbed Nature Reserve should be high on your list of priorities.

### ESSENTIALS

**VISITOR INFORMATION** Head straight for the **Tourism Information Bureau** (☎ **044/382-1610**), on 40 Main St., which is open Monday to Friday 8:30am to 5pm, Saturday 9am to 1pm. From December 16 to January 20, hours change to Monday to Friday 8:30am to 6pm, Saturday 9am to 3pm, and Sunday 10am to 3pm. You can also visit the independent **Info Centre** (☎ **044/382-5878**), open Monday 9am to 5pm, Saturday 9am to 1pm; and from December 16 to January 20, open daily 9am to 6pm. From their kiosk on Main Street, the very helpful Michael du Plessis will not only advise you on what to do, but will also make your Choo-Tjoe steam train, lagoon cruise, and adventure reservations, as well as sort out any last-minute accommodation hassles. He can also be contacted at knyinfo@mweb.co.za.

**GETTING AROUND** For a fun way to get around (not to mention avoid Knysna's traffic congestion), rent a **scooter** or **mountain bike** from **U-Ride** (☎ **044/382-7785**); they also provide canoes and cars (see "Staying Active" for more options). For a **taxi,** call **Benwill Shuttle** at ☎ **083728-5181** or **082962-4498;** they will transport you in and around town at any time.

**GUIDED TOURS** **Forest Explorer** (☎ **044/382-1954**) runs minimum 90-minute orientation tours of Knysna, including the town, the forests, Belvidere, Noezie, the goldfields, and various scenic drives. Personalized tour options are available on request.

**ACTIVITIES** The **Adventure Centre** can organize all your outdoor experiences, from deep-sea fishing and scuba diving to paragliding and abseiling. Contact Stuart on his mobile phone (☎ **083269-8501**).

**SPECIAL EVENTS** Knysna gets rather busy during the Knysna Oyster Festival held every July. For dates and more information, contact the Tourism Bureau.

## What to See & Do in Knysna

The **Choo-Tjoe train,** which runs through the Wilderness National Park along the coast, provides exquisite views of the coastline and of hidden valleys inaccessible by car, and is one of the top attractions on the entire Garden Route. This half-day excursion on South Africa's last scheduled mixed steam train operates on the Outeniqua Preserved Railway, a track that runs between George and Knysna, along valleys and coastal heights inaccessible by car. For more information, see "The Top Attractions" below.

Several companies run **boat trips** on the lagoon, which is home to 200 species of fish, including a rare seahorse (threatened by development), and is a major supplier of oysters—you can expect this delicacy on almost every Knysna menu. Combine a tasting with a trip by boarding **Knysna Ferries** (**044/382-5520**); they run six 90-minute trips a day from Tapas (See "Where to Dine"), or take a lunchtime or sunset trip on the **John Benn Ferry** (☎ **044/382-1693**) through the heads where you can order oysters on board.

Another local product definitely worth trying is the beer. **Mitchell's** (☎ **044/382-4985,** Arend St.) is an independent brewery producing four types of beer, of which the best is the Bosun's Bitter and Foresters Draught. You can either take a 30-minute tour and tasting, or sample them with your meal at any of the Knysna eateries. Ask for directions from the Tourism Bureau.

Alternatively, pack a picnic hamper of oysters and beer and head for the beach. To reach the closest sandy shore, you'll need to head west along the N2, take the Belvidere turnoff and wend your way to **Brenton-on-Sea,** an endless stretch of sand 16 kilometers (10 miles) from Knysna, or head east for **Noetzie Beach,** some 11 kilometers (7 miles) from town. This is a beautiful little beach with the by-now-requisite estuary spilling out into the ocean, but the holiday homes are rather different: five over-the-top crenellated castles overlooking the beach.

## The Top Attractions

✪ **Featherbed Nature Reserve.** Board the Rivercat Ferry at the Municipal Jetty, Remembrance Ave., off Waterfront Dr. ☎ **044/382-1693.** Admission R45 ($7.50); Children 3–12 R25 ($4.15). Lunch extra. Depart daily at 10am (also 9am, 11:15am, and 12:30pm, depending on demand). Duration approximately 4 hours.

If you only have 1 day to spare, make sure you spend it on a tour of the Featherbed Nature Reserve. This privately owned nature reserve on the western head of Knysna is a National Heritage Site and besides being exceptionally beautiful, is home to the endangered blue duiker. Guests are ferried over and then ascend the head in a large open-topped 4×4 vehicle to enjoy the magnificent views of the lagoon, town, and ocean. Qualified guides then lead the visitors down through milkwood forests and coastal flora onto the cliffs and coastal caves on the 2-kilometer (just more than 1-mile) Bushbuck Trail. Meals (an optional extra) are served at the Tavern (main courses range between R15–40 ($2.50–$6.65), and focus on seafood. Guests are then ferried through the narrow entrance to the heads before returning to the mainland.

**Garden of Eden.** Off N2, 16km (10 miles) east of town. Forestry Department, ☎ **044/382-5466.** Admission R3 (50¢). Open daily dawn to dusk.

Despite its romantic name, a visit to this indigenous "garden" is only worth it if you're not intending to visit any other indigenous forests. While the walk does feature some spectacular hardwood specimens, it's too close to the N2 to really enjoy a sense of primal forest, and the signs and cautionary advice regarding the Knysna elephants are a bit of a joke. If you don't mind the rumble of the traffic though, its proximity to the N2 can be an advantage, as you don't need to venture far afield to identify the wide variety of indigenous trees and ferns (all labeled), and the walk shouldn't last longer than 25 minutes. In an improvement on the original, this Eden is wheelchair friendly.

**Holy Trinity Church.** No phone. Take the N2 west, turn off south to Belvidere, and follow signs to church. Open daily 8:30am–5pm.

This diminutive church is one of the most interesting buildings in Knysna. Almost an exact replica of an 11th century Norman church, it was built in 1855 from local stone. The interior features the indigenous timber of the region and pretty stained-glass windows. It's worth visiting the church and then taking a stroll through the streets of Belvidere. Situated across the lagoon from town, this is one of Knysna's most upmarket suburbs; and with strict developmental guidelines keeping it firmly in the past, it is certainly the most attractive. Visitors are no longer allowed to drive around the streets to ogle at the perfect picket-fenced properties, but they are welcome to walk the streets, many of which are still not tarred—no doubt in deference to the sense of 1950s nostalgia that pervades the streets.

✪ **Knysna Forests.** ☎ **044/382-9762.** Admission to forests free or R4 (64¢) during school holidays (see chapter 2, "Planning Your Trip to Southern Africa"). Open daily 6am–6pm. Diepwalle: Take the N2 east, after 7km (4 miles) turn left onto the R339 for 16km (10 miles) before taking turnoff to Diepwalle. Goudveld: Take the N2 west, turn right into Rheenendal Rd.

These, the last pockets of indigenous forest, are located some distance from the town itself: Goudveld State Forest is 30 kilometers (19 miles) northwest of Knysna, while Diepwalle is some 20 kilometers (12 miles) northeast of town. Goudveld is a mixture of plantation and indigenous forest, making Diepwalle, with its ancient yellowwoods, the better option for the purist. Look out for the emerald Knysna Loerie and the brightly hued Narina Trogon in the branches. Diepwalle has three excellent circular trails color-coded with red, black, and white elephant markers. The routes are all 7 to 9 kilometers (4 to 5 miles) long, and the red route is recommended as it features the most water. Unfortunately, it is also the most popular. The elephant trails, as they are known, are also ideal for mountain biking. For more information, see "Staying Active," above.

**Knysna Museum Complex.** Queen St. ☎ **044/382-5066.** Donations welcome. Mon–Fri 9am–4:30pm; Sat 9:30am–12:30pm (Old Goal stays open to 1pm).

The complex consists of the Millwood House and Parkes Shop and Cottage, which covers local history, and the Old Goal. The Old Goal, which is on the corner of Main and Queen streets, is the only museum building that hasn't been relocated to its current position, and was the first government building to be erected in town. Today it houses The Angling Museum, the Knysna Art Gallery, a curio/gift shop, and the Old Goal Café, which serves light meals throughout the day and evening. The most interesting exhibit is found in the Angling Museum: a coelacanth specimen. Before a South

African fisherman landed one in 1938, this living fossil was thought to have been extinct for 65 million years.

**Millwood Gold Fields.** Take the N2 west, turn right into Rheenendal Rd. No phone. Admission free. Open dawn to dusk.

Gold was discovered in the Knysna forests in 1876 and by 1886 there were over 500 diggers panning Jubilee Creek, and a town with six hotels, three newspapers, and a music hall had sprung up. Thankfully they never found much and by the turn of the century Millwood was a ghost town. Millwood Gold Fields is an ongoing project to breathe life back into Jubilee Creek, with abandoned equipment gathered and taken to Bendigo Mine. If you're interested in this kind of thing, or simply feel like taking a drive through the forest (the gold fields are located in the Goudveld State Forest, see above), this is an easy afternoon's outing, albeit a little dull. There is nothing left of the original gold mine village, with all but one of the houses either demolished or dismantled and transported to town after they were abandoned. Ironically two of the best examples now stand in the middle of Knysna where they form part of the Knysna Museum. The only building still standing houses Mother Holly's Tearoom, which dispenses fresh tea, and an adjacent room with photographs that passes as the Materolli Museum.

✪ **Outeniqua Choo-Tjoe.** The Station, Remembrance Ave. ☎ **044/382-1361.** R40 ($6.65) one-way; R50 ($8.35) round-trip; ages 3–16 R30 ($5). Train departs Mon–Sat 9:45am and 2:15pm. Duration 3 hours.

If you didn't have a chance to board South Africa's only scheduled steam train trip in George, be sure to book from Knysna. Most locomotives date back to 1948 (though some are over a century old) with timber-and-leather–fitted carriages dating from 1903 to 1950. Grab a window seat—the views are spectacular—and settle for a truly enjoyable excursion. Light snacks and bar facilities are available on the train. To avoid traveling back the way you came (which will take up the whole day), book through **Kontours** (☎ **082569-8997**). For R80 ($13.35) per person (R50/$8.35 children 3–16), they will provide a map showing the places and points of interest as seen from the train, pick you up at George, and return you to Knysna station. Along the way, a taped commentary will point out additional points of interest from the road. (The reverse trip by arrangement only.)

## WHERE TO STAY

**Belvidere Manor.** Duthie Dr., Belvidere Estate, Knysna 6570. ☎ **044/387-1055.** Fax 044/387-1059. E-mail: blaster@pixie.co.za. 31 units. TV TEL. Low-season R760–980 ($126.65–$163.35) double; high-season R1,320–1,580 ($120–$263.35) double. Rates include breakfast. AE, DC, MC, V.

Belvidere and the St James are the most expensive places to stay in Knysna, but Belvidere's detached cottages, situated on lawns that sweep down to the lagoon, are the most upscale. Its location in the exclusive suburb of Belvidere Estate, with views of town that are a mere smudge on the other side of the tidal waters, validates this reputation (though really, the competition in Knysna is not that stiff). A valid complaint is that Belvidere Manor has been compromised by the addition of a further 16 cottages in their back garden, turning what used to be a very exclusive retreat into a largish hotel. The best units remain the original lagoon cottages, which cost in the region of R200 ($33.35) more. All the cottages are spacious, tastefully decorated, and fully equipped, should you wish to self-cater.

**Dining:** The food served on the verandah of the historic Belvidere House, a proclaimed National Monument, is hard to resist. Succulent butterfish served with sauce béarnaise, rack of karoo lamb with quenelles of couscous, and smoked duck breast are but a few of the mouthwatering dinner dishes, each priced at R46 ($7.65). Lunches are lighter, with salads, burgers, mussels, and baguettes ranging between R12 and R34 ($2–$5.65). Non-residents are welcome.

**Cranmere Stables.** PO Box 144, Knysna 6570. ☎/fax **044/382-1743.** 4 units. TV. Low-season R190–300 ($31.65–$50); high-season R260–430 ($43.35–$71.65). Prices are per unit, which sleep 2, 4, and 5. No credit cards. Off N2, turn off at second jetty after white bridge if traveling east toward town.

Situated well away from the hustle and bustle of Knysna's center, these charming self-catering units offer the best value in town. The best deals are Bridesmaid, the only unit to sleep 2; or, for families, Courtship, which sleeps up to 5. Created by converting the original stables that once housed the Cranmere horses, the units are well equipped, nicely furnished (all with antique brass beds), and still feature the large original yellowood stable doors. Situated on 9 acres of gardens that overlook and run down to the lagoon and private jetty, Cranmere guests enjoy total peace and privacy. The only drawback is that you'll either have to cook for yourself, or venture forth in your car, though Pronto Delivery, a restaurant delivery service, will deliver to your doorstep. See "Where to Dine," below.

**Headlands House.** 50 Coney Glen Dr., The Heads, Knysna 6570. ☎/fax **044/382-7972.** E-mail: headland@knysna.lia.net. 4 units. TV TEL. Low-season: R400–470 ($66.65–$78.35); high-season R550–620 ($91.65–$103.35). Double rates include continental breakfast. AE, DC, MC, V. No children under 16.

While it is unfortunate that the eastern heads have been developed, at least there's a good B&B from where you can enjoy the stunning views of the ocean and lagoon. The house's perch high above the ocean affords great views from all the rooms. If at all possible, book the master suite; with its sliding doors opening onto one of the most dramatic views in the Garden Route, the extra R70 ($11.65) is well spent. Wrought-iron beds were specially built, linens are 100% percale, and duvets are down. With an in-house South AfricaTOUR registered guide, guests are assured of authoritative advice on what to do while in the area. A lounge, bar, and small swimming pool are exclusively for the use of the guests. Headlands doesn't serve meals other than breakfast (continental), but you can order takeaway from Pronto Delivery (see "Where to Dine," below).

**Inyathi Guest Village.** 52 Main St., Knysna 6570. ☎/fax **044/382-7768.** 11 units. A/C TV. R350 ($58.35) double, with continental breakfast; R300 ($50) without. AE, DC, MC, V.

If you want to be in the heart of Knysna, Inyathi offers affordable, tasteful rooms with a great feeling of privacy even though it's just off the busy main road. Innovatively laid out around a green courtyard, many of the double-bedded timber cabins feature beautiful stained-glass windows, and each has a luxurious slipper bathtub. Rooms are small but cute, decorated with an African theme, and come equipped with tea- and coffee-making facilities and hair dryers on request. Continental breakfast baskets are also delivered to your room on request only; alternatively head for Hunters (see below) and blow the money you've saved on accommodation. Tourist information is also within close walking distance. While Inyathi is perfectly comfortable, this is not a luxury destination, and is unlikely to appeal to the older traveler.

**The Knysna Belle.** 75 Bayswater Dr., Leisure Island, Knysna 6570. ☎ **044/384-0511.** Fax 044/382-6971. 6 units. TV. Low-season R240–380 ($40–$63.35); high-season R300–440 ($50–$73.35). All rates are double and include breakfast. MC, V.

The Knysna Belle is architecturally one of the finest waterfront homes on Leisure Isle, and is considered to have the best lagoon swimming in Knysna. Four of the rooms lead out onto the garden and residents' pool—Paquita and Annie Benn have full en-suite bathrooms, while Hettie and Fredheim make up a family suite with shared bathroom. Emu is the lagoon-facing honeymoon suite; besides the unfortunate choice of name (the *Emu* wrecked herself on Knysna's rocks), the furnishings are rather unattractive. If you are on your honeymoon, nothing less than the Captain's Quarters (R800–1,000/$133.35–$166.65) will do. This stunning suite takes up the entire first floor and comprises a queen-size bed, sitting room with fireplace, and a large en-suite bathroom. The large open-plan room is finished in cool whites and grays and features beautiful views of the heads and lagoon. All the Belle's rooms have underfloor heating, coffee- and tea-making facilities, and guests are welcome to use the mountain bikes, tricycles, and the small engine-powered boat.

**Knysna River Club.** PO Box 2986, Knysna 6570. ☎ **044/382-6483.** Fax 044/382-6484. 35 units. A/C MINIBAR TV TEL. Low-season R320–380 ($53.35–$63.35) double; high-season R460–500 ($76.65–$83.35) double. AE, DC, MC, V. Just off Main St. east of town center on N2, take Sun Valley Dr. south; entrance 100m (328 feet).

This award-winning resort built on the northern banks of the Knysna Lagoon is very popular, so book months in advance, particularly if you want to bag a lagoon chalet (which you do!). All the cabins, which are constructed from local timber, are spacious and feature outdoor decks with grills, most with views of the lagoon; and tastefully finished interiors with one-, two-, and three-bedroom configurations, all en-suite. (Note that prices quoted above are for two persons only). The chalets are all well equipped for self-catering and are serviced daily.

**Dining:** If you don't feel like cooking, the resort has an elegant restaurant on the premises, the **River Club Café** (☎ **044/382-1751**), situated in a refurbished Edwardian homestead dating back to 1890. The fresh pasta dishes are highly recommended, as is the linefish. The River Club Café is open for breakfast and dinner daily; for lunch in December.

**Amenities:** Pool, lagoon swimming, canoes, same-day laundry, and baby-sitting.

✪ **Lightley's Holiday Cruisers.** PO Box 863, Knysna 6570. ☎ **044/387-1026.** Fax 044/387-1067. E-mail: sandpoint@pixie.co.za.x. 12 houseboats. Low-season R390/day ($65); mid season R650/day ($108.35); high-season R800/day ($133.35). MC, V. Take Belvidere turnoff from N2; look out for sign.

The best way to escape the congested streets of Knysna is to hire a houseboat and cruise the lagoon. You need no experience to skipper, just switch on and drive (charts, maps, and instructions are supplied by Lightley's). You can fish for dinner from your boat (grunter, kob, shad, steenbras, and leervis are regularly caught) or simply chug along to one of the many restaurants that line the lagoon. Houseboats come equipped with everything: stove, fridge, hot and cold water, chemical toilet, radio/tapedecks, CB radio, electric lights, crockery, and cutlery—just remember to pack towels and detergent, and don't run out of fuel. Lightley's will also rent fishing rods and barbecues, and provide secure parking for your vehicle at their harbor premises. Note that rates quoted above are for Leisure Liners, which sleep 4; Aqua Chalets sleep six, are more luxurious, look better, and cost R180–400 ($30–$66.65) more, depending on the season.

**Old Drift Forest Lodges.** PO Box 461, Knysna 6570. ☎/fax **044/382-1994.** 6 units. TV. Low-season R450–500 ($75–$83.35) double (minimum 2 nights); high-season R900–1,300 ($150–$216.65) (minimum 6 nights). MC, V. 4km (2½ miles) off N2 before Knysna town.

It takes some commitment to stay at Old Drift; not only are you required to spend at least 2 nights (6 in peak-season), but the timber cabins are not that easy to get to—or to tear yourself away from. Set in 120 acres of secluded forest overlooking the Knysna River, the idea is that you unwind and commune with nature, and this does not happen overnight. There are a number of trails through the forest, two-man canoes to explore the river, and excellent bird-watching opportunities from the comfort of your sheltered deck. The cabins are furnished in a homey manner and with a great deal of thought about guests' comfort; cozy ceramic fireplaces and rugs ward off the winter chill, while fans cool off the midday heat. Your hosts will drop off a continental breakfast basket if you choose; otherwise you are unlikely to see them for the duration of your stay. Privacy is key here. The best units by far are ✪ lodges 4 and 7—both for their privacy and views.

✪ **The Phantom Forest Eco-Reserve.** Off Phantom Pass. Mailing address: PO Box 3051, Knysna 6570. ☎ **044/386-0046.** Fax 044/387-1944. E-mail: phantomforest@mweb.co.za. 4 units. MINIBAR TEL. R1,480 ($246.65) double, including dinner and breakfast. AE, DC, MC, V.

This is without a doubt the best accommodation in Knysna, particularly if you're looking for an authentic African decor with strong safari overtones. Located on a 137-hectare nature reserve overlooking the Knysna River, it offers visitors the chance to explore Cape coastal fynbos, estuarine wetland, and indigenous forest. The lodge has been built using only sustainable materials, from the ragged thatch roofs to wood shingle walls, with meandering boardwalks connecting the privately located suites. Each of the suites—which are like luxurious tree houses tucked into the forest canopy—is comprised of a sitting room, bedroom, deck, and large bathroom. Beds are dressed in Swazi cotton sheets, floors are a combination of timber and coir, and every room (including the bathroom) has a magnificent view of the forest and river below. The chemical-free pool also has a magnificent view. Meals are set, with a choice of four appetizers, five main courses, and three desserts. Main courses may include blackened beef filet served with saffron mayonnaise, roasted quail glazed with port, ostrich medallions served with peppered pineapple and red-wine sauce, seared tuna steak, or Plet mountain trout served on rosti—all are well prepared and beautifully presented. Airport transfers from George can be arranged as well as bookings for activities in the Knysna area.

**The St James of Knysna.** The Point, PO Box 1242, Knysna 6570 (phone for directions). ☎ **044/382-6750.** Fax 044/382-6756. E-mail: stjames.knysna@pixie.co.za. 11 units. A/C (master suite) TV TEL. Low-season R460–1,000 ($76.65–$166.65); high-season R800–1,900 ($133.35–316.65). Rates are double, and include breakfast. AE, DC, MC, V.

Situated on the shores of the Knysna Lagoon, with an excellent view of the heads, the St James rather fancies itself as an exclusive club. Certainly its prices warrant a certain amount of exclusivity, as do the limited number of rooms. The three lake-facing suites are obviously the better option, but you pay for the privilege—number 4 has an elevated position, but is a little close to the rumbling N2; number 8 has an outdoor shower; and number 9 has a bathtub that looks directly onto the water. The five garden-facing suites are huge: Despite two double beds, they still feel underfurnished. The garden suites offer the best value and you still get to take advantage of the other perks: lazing on loungers overlooking the lagoon, swimming in one of the two pools, canoeing, setting off on a sundowner cruise, or playing tennis on the floodlit court. The Master Suite enjoys the same views as number 4, but you've got a private sauna and steam room thrown in—for an extra R500 ($83.35), it's a pricey sweat. The staff is very helpful, but there are a few jarring touches: The flowers in the hall are fake; and meals in the hotel restaurant are expensive and don't cater to vegetarians.

## Where to Dine

If your hotel doesn't serve meals and is far from the restaurants mentioned below, try calling **Pronto Delivery** (☎ **044/382-6660**); they'll pick up food from nine different takeaway joints from 10am to 10pm and deliver it to your door.

**Crabs Creek.** On the road to Brenton-on-Sea (6km/about 4 miles from town), Belvidere. ☎ **044/386-0011.** Reservations for 10 or more only. Main courses R17–43 ($2.85–$7.15). DC, MC, V. Open daily 12–3pm and 6–10pm; bar opens 11am. PUB.

People come here in droves, despite the fact that the food isn't that great—beautiful views of the lagoon and a casual holiday atmosphere more than make up for the average fare. During December, when up to 700 people a day descend on the Creek, you'd be well advised to arrive as early as 11am for lunch and 6pm for dinner to choose one of the timber tables ranged along the edge of the lagoon. Start with the mussel soup, and try the "pint of prawns"—these are more like shrimp, but they're very tasty—fried and stuffed into a beer mug. Other popular dishes are the peri-peri calamari heads, liver, and the chicken and chips. During peak-season, service can be slow—order a Mitchell's beer and soak up the sun.

**Cranzgots.** George Rex Dr., The Heads, Knysna 6570. ☎ **044/384-0408.** Reservations essential during high-season. Main courses R22–110 ($3.65–$18.35). AE, DC, MC, V. Open 12–10pm daily; in season till 11pm. SEAFOOD.

If you're driving to the heads, take time out to lunch at this laid-back spot. Superb views of the lagoon and heads mean you hardly have to do the cliff walk. There's nothing fancy about the menu—the seafood lineup includes oysters, fresh linefish, sole, mussels, calamari, calamari steaks, queen prawns, and crayfish (pick one from the tank). If you can't decide, try the seafood combo, a portion of fish, prawns, mussels, and calamari for R60 ($10), or the pricier seafood platter (R200/$33.35), which includes lobster and could satisfy three. Portions are generous, everything is super fresh, including the homemade pasta, and service is fast and friendly. There are pizzas and grill choices for those who prefer looking at the sea to devouring its contents. The biggest drawback is a lack of parking in peak-season.

✪ **Knysna Oyster Company.** Bottom end of Long St., Thesen's Island, Knysna 6570. ☎ **044/382-6941.** Open 9:30am–5pm, extended to 7pm in season (Dec 16–Jan 20) Reservations not accepted. Main courses R17–37 ($2.85–$6.15). AE, DC, MC, V. SEAFOOD.

This no-frills tavern is part of the cultivated oyster farm that Knysna is famous for. You can buy takeaway oysters (a standard dozen, opened, will run you R28/$4.65), or sit down and sample the difference between the cultivated and slightly more expensive Cape coastal oyster. Other light dishes include a plate of garlic mussels (one of the few dishes served hot), a choice of two fish pâtés, and the "cool seafood platter": This includes smoked mussels, fresh oysters, angelfish pâté, peppered mackerel, and salmon. The tavern is right next to the oyster processing facility; for guided tours, contact Toni at the above number in advance.

**La Loerie.** 57 Main St., Knysna 6570. ☎ **044/382-1616.** Reservations essential in high-season. Main courses R37–50 ($6.15–$8.35). AE, DC, MC, V. Mon–Sat 6:30–10pm. INTERNATIONAL.

This is where Knysna's locals head, where husband and wife team Sandy and Abdel have been providing a cozy, intimate venue and quality food for almost a decade. La Loerie is in fact rated as Knysna's best restaurant (though there's stiff competition from Belvidere, see "Where to Stay"). Abdel has no formal training, but the best inspiration: a sincere passion for food. His linefish, fresh from the harbor, and lightly dusted with flour and herbs and pan-fried in butter is excellent, as well as his Shrimp Taj Mahal, cooked with ginger and garlic in a creamy curried sauce. If you've tired of the taste of the sea, try the braised ostrich neck, cooked with red wine, brandy, and mushrooms.

**Pink Umbrella.** 14 Kingsway, Leisure Island, Knysna 6570. ☎ **044/384-0135.** Reservations essential in high-season. Main courses R29–70 ($4.85–$11.65). MC, V. Open daily 9:30am–5pm in season; closed Mondays Easter–Sept. Phone for special dinner and cabaret evenings. SEAFOOD/VEGETARIAN.

Proprietor June Davis has been pulling the crowds into her flower-filled garden for over 17 years now. Her candy-pink cushions and umbrellas may be looking a little worse for wear, but you won't be disappointed with the food. The dahl terrine, made with nuts and lentils and served with an aromatic sauce, is delicious, and her vegetable curry is good enough to turn a hardcore carnivore into a vegan. Other favorites include the tuna and spinach roulade with creamy cheese sauce, and corn and herb pie. The Pink Umbrella is also famous for its wickedly delicious desserts: If "Death by Chocolate" doesn't get you, the "Great American Disaster" surely will. June has a very small wine list, so you're welcome to bring your own. Incidentally, if you can't find the energy to roll home, June has opened a charming guest house above the restaurant; prices range from R260–400 ($43.35–$66.65) double, depending on the season.

✪ **(Jetty) Tapas.** The jetty on Thesen Island (bottom end of Long St.), Knysna 6570. ☎ **044/382-1927.** Reservations not accepted downstairs. AE, DC, MC, V. Main courses R16–21 ($2.65–$3.50). Open 12–10pm daily (bar stays open later). SPANISH/PUB.

Okay, so you've heard about the views from Cranzgots and the laid-back atmosphere of Crabs Creek, but Tapas is the corker. Situated on a jetty built over the lagoon (when the tide's in, you can sit with your feet dangling in the water), this casual tavern is very popular with the young crowd—if you want to escape the masses in December, book a table upstairs in the slightly more formal (and pricey) restaurant. Tapas is based on the Spanish concept of having small portions of food to help line the stomach; just choose a selection of dishes, say two to three per person, share them, then re-order your favorites. Options include garlic mussels, cheese-and-wine mussels, peri-peri chicken livers, chicken wings, marinated calamari, chili calamari with bacon, rosti, rollmops, and a number of cold platters. If you'd prefer a square meal, you can purchase a steak, Portuguese sardines, or fish kebabs (skewered), and then cook them on the grills provided. Tapas is also the best place to sample the local beers; the pub stays open late in season, and if you're looking for some action, this is the place to hang out.

## PLETTENBERG BAY & SURROUNDS

Several kilometers of white sands, backed by the blue-gray outline of the Tsitsikamma Mountains and lapped by an endless succession of gentle waves, curve languidly to create Bahia Formosa—the Beautiful Bay—so dubbed by the Portuguese sailors who first set eyes on it. Over the years its beauty has inevitably drawn an ever-increasing string of admirers, with some 50,000 of Jo'burg's wealthiest individuals descending on the seaside town every December. However, out of season this is a far more laid-back destination than neighboring Knysna; the N2 bypasses the small town center, and the vast majority of holiday homes stand empty.

There's not much to do in Plettenberg Bay itself but head straight for the beach; try **Lookout** on the eastern side or **Robberg** on the west. **Central Beach,** dominated by the time-share hotel Beacon Isle, is where most of the boats launch from. Sadly, money and taste seem to have enjoyed an inverse relationship; huge monstrosities line most of the beachfront, with the exception of the less developed far-western edge of Robberg Beach. **Robberg Reserve,** the rocky peninsula on the western side of the bay, offers fantastic whale-watching opportunities during the course of a 9-kilometer

(5-mile) trail. Be sure to wear sun protection and good shoes as the going gets very rocky. For the less energetic, there are shorter 2½-hour versions; pick up a map from the reserve gate when you pay your R4 (65¢) to get in. The reserve is open February to November from 7am to 5pm daily, and from December through January 7am to 8pm daily.

If the views aren't enough to take your breath away, remember that the **world's highest bungee jump** is only a 15-minute drive east on the N2—for R500 ($83.35), you can have the rare privilege of free-falling for 216 meters (709 feet) off the Bloukrans Bridge, then watch yourself doing it all over again on video (see "Staying Active" above).

Plettenberg Bay (or "Plet" as locals call it) also offers a number of watersports and a good 18-hole golf course. For more information, visit the local **Tourism Bureau** in Victoria Cottage on Kloof Street (☎ **044/533-4065**), its hours are Monday to Friday from 8am to 5pm and Saturday from 8am to 1pm; or contact **Kingfisher Tours** (☎ **044/535-9719**) for guided tours of the area.

If the size of Plet's holiday development depresses you, head 14 kilometers (9 miles) east on the N2, crossing the Keurbooms River, and spend a day on relatively unspoiled **Keurbooms Beach.** This wide beach shares the same bay, and has rock arches and pools to explore, but the swimming is not quite as safe, so take care.

If even this isn't unspoiled enough, travel farther east to Nature's Valley, a tiny hamlet on a wide deserted sweep of beach, or Storms River mouth, both in the **Tsitsikamma National Park. Monkeyland** (☎ **044/534-8906**) just before the Nature's Valley turnoff, is a primate sanctuary where you can meet several species, though the project is still relatively new and finding its feet.

## Exploring the Sea, Air & Water

Don't miss the opportunity to take one of David Rissik's **Ocean Adventures** tours (☎ **044/533-5083**). This personable man's passion and enthusiasm for the ocean is inspiring, and you will be provided with excellent photographic opportunities of the dolphins and whales in this mammal-rich bay, as well as get new insights into the various species' behavior and characteristics. Apart from the resident Bryde whale, Indo-Pacific Humpback, Bottlenose, and Common dolphins who feed in the bay all year-round, Plet also enjoys seasonal visits from the Southern Right, Humpback, and Killer whales during their annual migration. Coastal and pelagic birdlife, and the historical and geological make-up of the bay are also discussed. Tours depart daily at 9am, 12:30pm, and 3pm, weather permitting, and cost R150 ($25) per person. Proceeds benefit whale and dolphin research, conservation, and disadvantaged sectors of the community.

A more removed but no less thrilling way to view Plet's marine mammals is by air—**African Ramble Air Safaris** (☎ **044/384-0080**) offers 30-minute low-level flights over the bay and up the coast, entering the Knysna estuary through the heads, then returning via the forested inland. These require a minimum of two passengers at R200 ($33.35) per person. Mark Andrews also offers personalized "air safaris," taking guests to various destinations including the Shamwari private game reserve (see chapter 5, "Eastern Cape")—a 30-minute flight away.

Plet has two estuaries, and the Keurbooms River in the east is by far the larger. It's definitely worth renting a canoe and paddling upstream to view the lush vegetated banks and birdlife of the Keurbooms Nature Reserve (keep an eye out for Knysna Loeries, Kingfishers, and fish eagles). You can hire your canoe (R20/hour, $3.35) from **Aventura Eco** (☎ **044/535-9309**) (see "Where to Stay," below). Alternatively, for

R35 ($5.85) per person, you can sail up without lifting a finger by boarding the **Keurbooms River Ferries** (☎ **044/532-7876**). Daily scheduled trips, which last approximately 2½ hours, take place at 11am, 2pm, and sundown, and include an optional 30-minute walk. Liquid refreshments are available. Part of the proceeds go to Cape Nature Conservation.

## WHERE TO STAY

If you're looking for a budget self-catering option, you won't do better than **Aventura Eco,** located on the banks of the river in the Keurbooms Nature Reserve and clearly signposted off the N2, 6 kilometers (4 miles) east of Plet. The resort offers four types of self-catering chalets, all fully equipped, serviced, en-suite with TV, and telephones. Call ☎ **044/535-9309,** fax 044/535-9912, or e-mail info@aventura.co.za.

**Hog Hollow Country Lodge.** Askop Rd., The Crags, Plettenberg Bay 6600. ☎/fax **044/534-8879.** E-mail: hoghollow@global.co.za. 12 units. R680–900 ($113.35–$150). AE, DC, MC, V. 16km (10 miles) east of Plet on the N2, follow signs from here. Children by prior arrangement only.

Overlooking the dense indigenous forests that drop away below the lodge and carpet the Tsitsikamma Mountains beyond, Hog Hollow is not where you come for a beach holiday—though the Plet beaches are only a few minutes drive away. Rooms are supremely comfortable (each has a fireplace and hammock) and very private (many are freestanding). Two of the best are also the cheapest: the Formosa and Outeniqua rooms have French doors leading out onto private balconies with hammocks overlooking the verdant gorge. The quaint Tsitsikamma duplexes have similar views, but the bedroom and bathroom are on different levels. Top of the range is the Forest Suites; these are huge, but with no minibar or telephone it's a long walk back to the main house to place your order. For the same money, you're better off staying in the Round House, which is much closer to the main house and has an en-suite master bedroom with a wooden balcony upstairs, and a lounge downstairs.

**Dining:** Hog Hollow is renowned for their food and it truly is exceptional. Dinner is a set affair which will run you R115 ($19.15); ingredients, from the ostrich to the exquisite linefish, are local. Meals are served around the large dining-room table, turning the event into an informal dinner party. The service is excellent.

✪ **Hunters Country House.** PO Box 454, Plettenberg Bay 6600. ☎ **044/532-7818.** Fax 044/532-7878. E-mail: hunters@pixie.co.za. 23 units. A/C (some) MINIBAR TV TEL. R1,460 ($243.35) garden suites; R1,720 ($286.65) premier suites; R2,020 ($336.65) classic suites; R2,780 ($463.35) forest suites. All rates include breakfast. Signpost 24 kilometers (15 miles) east of Knysna, off the N2, 10 kilometers (6 miles) before Plet. Children 12 and over.

This award-winning lodge is the only 5-star hotel on the Garden Route, and it deserves those five stars. Thatched cottages are situated in beautifully manicured gardens and are individually furnished with antiques, each with its own fireplace and private patio. (Note that when it comes to booking your suite, you could request a more masculine room if you find the frills and florals which some of the rooms are decorated in too cloying.) Premier suites are larger, with minibars and underfloor heating, but not necessarily better; it depends very much on how the room has been decorated. Classic suites have private pools and outdoor showers. The Forest Suite features a private lounge, dining room, butler's kitchen, and swimming pool. Meals are enjoyable affairs (see "Where to Dine"), while activities (anything from golf to aromatherapy) can be arranged by the staff. It's the personal, warm service that has earned this luxurious family-run hotel its accolades, including Hotel of the Year in the guest-driven AA awards. Its only drawback is its distance from the beach.

**Mallard River Lodge.** PO Box 532, Plettenberg Bay 6600. ☎ **044/533-2982.** Fax 044/535-9425. E-mail: mallard@pixie.co.za. 4 units. MINIBAR TV TEL. R780 ($180) double, breakfast included. Children 13+ only. Off Rietvlei Rd., signposted 2km (just more than 1 mile) east of Plet.

Mallard River Lodge is perched above the beautiful Bitou River and wetlands, a mere 5 kilometers (3 miles) from Plet's center, yet a million miles from the crowds that descend every December. A truly tranquil retreat, Mallard's luxurious accommodation standards also represent relatively good value for the money. Each huge suite is a free-standing unit with total privacy; the bathroom, bedroom, and private deck all enjoy exceptional views of the wetlands and offer excellent bird-watching opportunities. Fireplaces, double basins, underfloor heating, tea- and coffee-making facilities, and hair dryers are standard in every suite. Proprietor Eve Wilson is responsible for the paintings behind the headboards as well as the food, which is good, though service can be a little shaky—this is not the place to come if you want to be waited on hand and foot.

**Periwinkle Lodge.** 75 Beachy Head Dr. (opposite Robberg Beach), Plettenberg Bay 6600. ☎/fax **044/533-1345.** E-mail: periwinkle.lodge@pixie.co.za. 6 units. TV TEL. May–Aug R400–500 ($66.65–$83.35) double; Sep–Apr R550–750 ($91.65–$125) double. Rates include breakfast. AE, DC, MC, V.

This relatively new guest house has been busy since opening its doors, as it is one of the few that provides guests with excellent access and views of the beach and ocean, which is just across the road. All rooms are spacious and comfortably outfitted with amenities such as tea- and coffee-making facilities, fruit baskets, and heated towel racks, and hair dryers. Rooms 1 and 2 both have balconies and enjoy the best views of the beach and ocean; room 2 has the additional benefit of a fireplace. Even though they're a little cheaper, try to avoid rooms 3 and 4 as they have no ocean views (though the glorious views from all the public spaces almost make up for it). Periwinkle will serve dinners and lunches by prior arrangement, and hosts Colleen and Charlotte are happy to make suggestions and arrangements should you wish to dine out. There's no pool, but with one of South Africa's best swimming beaches so close, who cares?

**The Plettenberg.** 40 Church St., Lookout Rocks. Mailing address: Box 719, Plettenberg Bay 6600. ☎ **044/533-2030.** Fax 044/533-2074. E-mail: plettenberg@pixie.co.za. www.plettenberg.com. 40 units. TV TEL. R1,300 ($216.65) double, no seaview; R1,700 ($283.35) double with seaview; R1,900–3,000 ($316.65–$500) suites with seaview.

Situated on a hill overlooking Lookout Beach, with views all the way to Keurbooms and the blue-gray mountains beyond, the hotel has one of the best vantage points in the country. (Make sure you've booked a room that makes the most of this, as the rooms with views of the parking lot are still pretty pricey.) Full to the rim, the Plettenberg's pool literally seems to drop off into the Indian Ocean. Rooms are individually decorated, and differ somewhat in size; the doubles can be somewhat small. Best (and priciest) are the grand Plettenberg suites, but it's worth noting that a night spent here is worth two or three at the all-inclusive, highly recommended Plettenberg Park. The new Blue Wing has views of the Beacon Isle Beach, but as it's across the road guests occasionally complain of feeling cut off.

**Dining:** The Plettenberg is a Relais & Chateaux hotel, and as such you can expect excellent food in the formal dining room. The emphasis is on seafood, but Karoo lamb is another specialty. Service is attentive, but this is not a place to let your hair down.

✪ **Plettenberg Park.** PO Box 167, Plettenberg Bay 6600. ☎ **044/533-9067.** Fax 044/533-9092. E-mail: plettenbergpark@hotelogue.co.za. 4 units. MINIBAR TV/VCR TEL.

May–Sept R800–1,000 ($133.35–$166.65) double; Oct–Apr R1,200–1,570 ($200–$261.65) double. Rates include all meals, drinks, and laundry. AE, DC, MC, V. Take Robberg Rd. to the Plet Airport for approximately 6km (4 miles); look out for small sign and security gates on your left 10m (33 feet) before the airport. Children 12 and over only.

Situated a few minutes from the town, perched on the cliffs overlooking the Indian Ocean and surrounded by a private nature reserve, this is without a doubt the most exclusive retreat in Plettenberg Bay. Guests are accommodated in the modern Lake House; its northern aspect overlooks a tranquil inland lake, a wild duck sanctuary, while the southern views are of the pounding ocean. Request the view you'd prefer when making reservations. There is a swimming pool as well as a tidal pool and private beach, but it's a long walk back up the cliff-face to the house. Rooms are huge, each with its own fireplace, and well decorated in what has come to be known as the "Afro-colonial" style (natural materials in neutral, earthy tones; crisp whites, and bleached animal skulls). And the small size ensures attentive, personal service; the chef even creates a menu around your needs. If you're looking for a romantic retreat with very little disturbance from the outside world, Plettenberg Park is perfect—the only drawback is that you have to share it at all.

**Southern Cross Guest House.** 2 Capricorn Lane (ask for directions to be faxed), Plettenberg Bay 6600. ☎/fax or **044/533-3868.** E-mail: beach@global.co.za. 5 units. R450 ($75) double, including breakfast. AE, DC, MC, V.

This pale pink and white timber beach house is one of the most beautiful homes in Plettenberg—a sort of plantation-style home that wouldn't look out of place on Long Island. It's also the only B&B in Plet built right on the beach, a boardwalk leads through the vegetated dunes to the western side of Robberg Beach, close to the reserve. This far west, the beach is pretty deserted and provides an excellent sense of getting away from it all. Rooms are tastefully decorated in cool whites (even the rose in each room is white) with an occasional touch of black or natural wood. Bathrooms only have showers, but they're spacious and finishes are expensive. However, the owners (who live upstairs) have definitely bagged the best views—none of the guest rooms enjoy sea views; and unless you close your doors and curtains, they also lack privacy. This is a place to sleep, not unwind. Breakfasts are served in the sunny lounge and dining area or—bliss on a beautiful day—on the patio overlooking the beach and sea.

## WHERE TO DINE

**Blue Bay.** Lookout Centre, Main St., Plettenberg Bay 6600. ☎ **044/533-1390.** Main courses R18–38 ($3–$6.35). AE, DC, MC, V. Mon–Sat 9am–10pm, Sun 6–10pm. LIGHT MEDITERRANEAN.

This is no great location, in a shopping center on the main road, but the food is both good and well priced. Start with thin slices of rare chargrilled ostrich fillet dressed with olive oil and Parmesan, or the freshly baked crisp puff pastry with fresh tomatoes, basil pesto, and sour cream. The spinach salad, made with bacon, Parmesan, avocado, and cashew nuts is refreshing; more filling is the baked potato with tomato salsa, guacamole, and cream cheese. Try the fresh linefish grilled with lemon and fresh herbs and butter if you want something even more substantial. If you've got a sweet tooth, top it all off with the famous Blue Bay phyllo creme brulee—layers of crisp phyllo with creamy custard, pecan nuts, and caramel sauce.

**Brothers.** Shop 4, Melville Corner, Main Rd. (on main circle), Plettenberg Bay 6600. ☎ **044/533-5056.** Reservations essential in high-season. Lunch main courses R12–50 ($2–$8.35); dinner main courses R24–60 ($4–$10). AE, DC, MC, V. Open daily 9am–3pm and 6:30am–10pm; off-season closed Mondays. INTERNATIONAL.

The restaurant was started by—you guessed it—two brothers, one of whom is fortunate enough to be engaged to the excellent chef who helped build both The Plettenberg and Hog Hollow's reputation for fine food. Popular main dinner dishes are rack of lamb, medallions of sweet-and-sour pork served on Chinese noodles, ostrich filet, and grilled linefish. Ask for the specials; oven roasted breast of chicken stuffed with feta, basil, sundried tomato, and wrapped in olive paste and bacon proved so popular it's now part of the permanent lineup. Skewered prawns marinated in fresh coriander, mint, garlic, and olive oil are done to a turn. During the day, a lighter lunch menu of salads, pitas, and bagels is served. Brothers has a view of the distant ocean, particularly from the open-air terrace; try to reserve a table here if the weather's pleasant.

**Hunters Country House.** PO Box 454, Plettenburg Bay 6600. ☎ **044/532-7818.** Reservations recommended for dinner. Lunch main courses R33–70 ($5.50–$11.65); dinner table d'hôte R149 ($24.85). AE, DC, MC, V. Daily 7:30–10am; 12–2:30pm; 7:30–9pm; tea and snack menu available throughout. Watch for the signpost 24km (15 miles) east of Knysna, off the N2, 10km (6 miles) before Plet. CONTINENTAL.

Dining at Hunters is the next best thing to staying here; it's relatively pricey, but worth it. If you're on a budget, breakfast served in the conservatory is an excellent value at R55 ($9.15) per person. If you've opted for lunch, the first difficult choice you face is deciding where to eat. Weather permitting, choose one of the private terraces set amongst the beautiful gardens, as the Tapestry Room, Baronial Hall, and Regency Room really come into their own in the candlelit evenings. The mouthwatering menus have been created by Swiss-born and trained executive chef Walter Butti: Try the creamy butternut soup with king prawns and a light orange foam, followed by rack of lamb basted with pommery mustard and served on Provençale ratatouille with rich port jus for lunch. Dinners are four-course affairs featuring a mix of local ingredients and classic preparations; for those who don't have the stamina, there is also an excellent a la carte menu.

**The Islander.** PO Box 663, Plettenberg 6600. ☎ **044/532-7776.** Reservations essential in high-season. Buffet R98 ($16.35) per person; set menu R50 ($8.35). AE, DC, MC, V. High-season open daily 12–1:30pm and 7–9pm; hours vary off-season; phone ahead. Off N2 between Knysna and Plet (8km/5 miles west of Plet). SEAFOOD.

This family-run restaurant has been going strong for 15 years now, providing diners with an incredible array of seafood dishes. The style is casual, the huge buffets are self-service under simple wood and thatch buildings, but waiters are attentive and always ready to replenish your glass or whip away your plate. Drawing on island cuisine (Indonesia, Polynesia, Seychelles), as well as Portuguese, Creole, and South African traditions, the chefs have done the impossible—create a buffet where almost every dish is exceptional. Vegetarians can enjoy a range of delicious vegetables, and, if given advance warning, the restaurant will prepare something special for them. A few tips: Make sure this is your main meal of the day; don't fill up on the delicious bouillabaisse soup, don't miss the roasted tuna, herbed calamari, sailfish parcels and smoked butterfish, and don't show up without reservations. (During lunch and dinner out of season, a four-course set menu replaces the buffet—this is largely missable.)

**Lookout Deck Restaurant.** Right on Lookout Beach. ☎ **044/533-1379.** Reservations in season essential. Upstairs: main courses R19–45 ($3.15–$7.50). Downstairs: R43–70 ($7.15–$11.65). AE, DC, MC, V. Upstairs: open daily 9:30am–9pm. Downstairs: open Wed–Sun 12:30–3pm and 7–10:30pm. Hours vary off-season; phone ahead. SEAFOOD/AMERICAN.

This is probably the best-placed restaurant on the Garden Route; it's right on the beach, with the water and the Tsitsikamma Mountains stretching beyond. Owner

Chris has developed an upstairs and a downstairs component. On the upstairs deck, simple meals like burgers, mussels, and fish-and-chips ensure a fast turnover of clientele. Downstairs, the slightly more formal menu includes crayfish, calamari, prawns, grilled linefish, and Thai-style stir-fries, the latter prepared in front of you. Both serve the Lookout's famous wild oysters, picked off the Plet coast. The downstairs deck has only recently opened for lunch with the thatched beach bar once again providing unbeatable views. Both sections are glassed in for inclement weather. (Chris claims that some of his most memorable evenings have been in gale-force winter storms.)

## TSITSIKAMMA NATIONAL PARK

Tsitsikamma National Park was created in response to a call for more marine parks made at the 1962 First World Conference on National Parks. Starting from just beyond Keurboomstrand in the west, this narrow coastal belt extends 80 kilometers (50 miles) along one of the most beautiful sections of the southern Cape coastline, and includes a marine reserve that stretches 5½ kilometers (3½ miles) out to sea. The lichen-flecked craggy coastline is cut through with spectacular river gorges, while the cliff surrounds are carpeted in fynbos and dense forest—the fact that the Otter Trail, which takes in the full length of the coastline, is South Africa's most popular trail gives some indication of its beauty (see "Staying Active" for more information).

Tsitsikamma is roughly divided into two sections: De Vasselot (which incorporates Nature's Valley) in the west, and Storms River Mouth in the east. There is no direct road linking them; but it's well worth taking the detour off the N2 and visiting both, though Storms River Mouth is the more awesome sight of the two. To reach Nature's Valley, the only settlement in the park, take the R102 or Groot River Pass, which descends through the dense indigenous forests of the Tsitsikamma. (Note that you do not have to retrace your footsteps; this road loops back to the N2.) One of the best walks to tackle here is the 3-kilometer (2-mile) walk west to the Salt River mouth. (For directions, visit the town's only shop, which doubles up as an informal **Information Bureau.**)

To visit **Storms River Mouth** (and you'd be crazy not to!), take the marked turnoff, some 60 kilometers (37 miles) from Plettenberg Bay, and travel 10 kilometers (6 miles) toward the coast. (Do not confuse Storms River Mouth with Storms River Village, which is just off the N2, and has nothing much to recommend it.) Park hours are from 5:30am to 9:30pm daily, and the entry fee is R16 ($2.65), with ages 2 to 16 half price. You can eat at the rest-camp restaurant, which serves basic meals (steak, fish, crayfish, spareribs, sole, and curries) but has one of the best locations on the entire Garden Route, right on the sea.

### EXPLORING ON FOOT

With no roads connecting sites of interest, this is, for most, the only way to explore the park (there is also a snorkeling and scuba diving trail). The easiest and most popular trail is the 1-kilometer (just more than a half-mile) **boardwalk,** which starts at the Storms River Mouth restaurant and visitors office and winds its way along the mountainside, providing beautiful glimpses of the sea and forest, and finally descending to the narrow mouth where the dark waters of the Storms River surge into the foaming sea. This walk also takes you past the appropriately named **Mooi** (pretty) **Beach,** a tiny cove where the swimming is safe, though the water can be very cold. Once at the mouth, don't miss the excavated cave with its displays relating to the *strandlopers* (beachcombers) who frequented the area over 2,000 years ago. You can cross the suspension bridge that fords the mouth and climb the cliff for excellent ocean views, though it's steep going.

Another rewarding, yet relatively easy walk is the first 3 kilometers (2 miles) of the **Otter Trail,** which takes you to the base of a 50-meter (164-foot) waterfall and beautiful pool close to the shore. Note that unless you have made reservations to walk the trail (it's booked for a year in advance), you are not allowed to continue any farther. To find out more about the various trails, pick up a map from the **visitor's office** at the rest camp. Hours are 7am to 6pm, daily.

### WHERE TO STAY & DINE

**Storms River Mouth Restcamp.** Reserve through the National Parks Board, PO Box 787, Pretoria 0001. ☎ **012/343-1991** or in Cape Town ☎ 021/22-2810. Direct inquiries ☎ 042/541-1607. 46 units consisting of 8-bed, 7-bed, 4-bed, and 2-bed log cabins, 3- and 4-bed oceanettes, and 2-bed forest cabins with no kitchen facilities. Rates start at R120 ($20) for forest cabins (excluding breakfast) and R290 ($48.35) for a 2-bed log cabin (including breakfast). AE, DC, MC, V.

The Parks Board is not about to win any architectural awards, but Storms River is their best attempt by far. Almost all the units enjoy good sea views, particularly the oceanettes. Try to book a ground-floor apartment; in front is a narrow strip of lawn with your own barbecue and beyond lie the rocks and the pounding surf. You can head off into the forest or walk the rocks, at low tide the rock pools reveal a treasure trove of shapes and colors. The only drawback to staying in the oceanettes is that they are farthest from the restaurant, though the drive, which snakes along the coast, is hardly unpleasant. If you're going to have all your meals at the restaurant, consider the forest huts, particularly 1 and 2, which overlook a burbling stream, though the cabins are sweltering hot in peak summer. Of the log cabins, 8 and 9 enjoy particularly good views. The rest camp also has a pool situated within feet of the sea, a relatively well-stocked shop, and self-service laundry facilities.

## 5 The West Coast

The appeal of the West Coast of South Africa is not immediately apparent—windswept beaches, great desolate plains, and low-growing hardy coastal scrubs are not what most holiday-makers are after. The main reason to venture up here is to catch the spring flower displays that can occur anytime from July to early September. The West Coast National Park is particularly spectacular; the Postberg exhibits a flowering extravaganza that rivals the more northerly displays of Namaqualand in the Northern Cape. This aside, there are a few more gems to uncover—though they may pale when compared to the lush beauty of the Cape's southern coast, they are unique to the West Coast, and well worth traveling north for, particularly if you've done the Overberg and Garden Route.

### ESSENTIALS

**VISITOR INFORMATION** The very helpful **West Coast Publicity Association** (☎ **02281/42-261**) is in Saldanha, on Van Riebeeck Street. As there is no other reason to visit Saldanha, you may prefer to go to Langebaan, the closest town to the West Coast National Park and therefore the one that provides the most useful information on the area's best attraction. The Tourist Information (☎ **02287/22-115**) is at the corner of Oostewal (the road in from R27) and Bree streets.

For more information regarding the best places to view flowers at any given time, contact the **Flowerline** at ☎ **08000-1704** or 021/418-3705. This service is available Monday to Friday from August to October.

**GETTING THERE** From Cape Town take the N1 to Paarl for 2 kilometers (about a mile and a half), then turn north onto the R27 to Paarden Island and Milnerton.

# West Coast & Sidetrips to Northern Cape

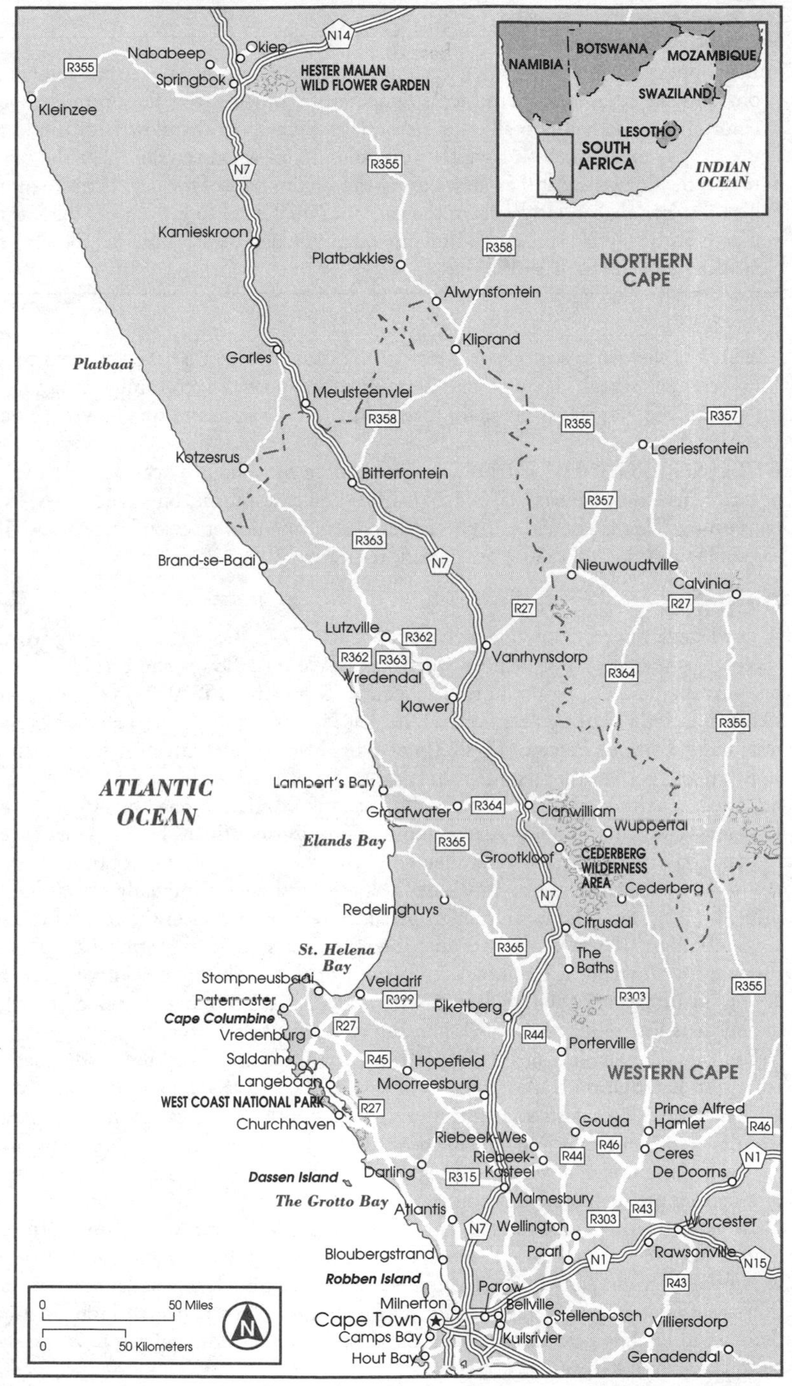

### Flower Viewing Tips

It is impossible to predict when each annual flower season will be, but rainfall is obviously key. Another determiner is temperature, which is why flowers rarely open before 10am and hardly at all on overcast days. Remember that flowers turn toward the sun, so make sure you have the sun behind you when traveling. For the same reason the flowers are at their best during the hottest part of the day, 11am to 4pm. The displays are spectacular from the car, but you'll need to get out of your car to marvel at the myriad species. To find out where the best displays are, call the **Flower Hotline** (☎ **021/418-3705**).

---

The R27 is the main West Coast artery to the coastal towns; it's even referred to as "the West Coast Road." If you intend to travel farther north, say to Lambert's Bay, take the N7 off the N1; this is the main road north to Namaqualand (the flower region) and Namibia.

**GETTING AROUND** The only way to explore the area is by car or with a tour operator. **Welcome Safaris** (☎ **021/510-6001**) takes minibuses on 1- and 4-day 4×4 trips up the West Coast and into the Cederberg during flower season; these are R758 ($126.35) and R5,208 ($868) per person, respectively.

## DARLING

A small town a mere 50-minute drive from Cape Town, Darling is definitely worth visiting, particularly in September when its annual wild flower and orchid show is on—usually held during the third weekend in September (☎ **022/492-3361**)—as well as the **Hello Darling Arts Festival,** held at Pieter Dirk Uys's informal theater and restaurant, **Evita se Perron** (☎ **022/492-3145**) on Arcadia Street. A performance artist famous for creating the marvelous character of Evita—the *tannie* (auntie) who held sway over the imaginary homeland of Bapetikosweti, and now the First Lady of Darling—Uys is one of South Africa's most accomplished satirists. He always manages to make even the most conservative laugh at the country's tragic ironies (not an easy task for a man who dresses up in women's clothing), though admittedly he was hard-pressed during his nationwide tour to persuade people to vote in the run-up to the 1999 elections. If you're not here in September, relax, Evita se Perron has cabaret shows every weekend. Evita presides over most of these, which are held every Friday at 9pm, Saturday at 12 and 9pm, and Sunday at 12 and 3:30pm; but during her September Arts Festival, she steps aside and showcases the best local talents.

You can also sample some of Tannie Evita's traditional fare (try the Madiba lamb curry) at her **Station Café** after the show. Evita se Dagkombuis (literally "day kitchen") serves breakfasts and light meals throughout the day: gay muffins, affirmative tarts, and quite possibly the best toasted sandwiches in the world. To view pure Afrikaans kitsch, take a wander through her **Boerassic Park,** where garden gnomes preside over plastic flowers and political figurines.

To get to Darling, take the R27, or West Coast Road as it's known, and turn off toward Mamre and Atlantis. (There is an old Moravian mission station at Mamre, a worthwhile detour, particularly if you haven't been to the Genandendal mission station mentioned earlier in this chapter in "En Route to Swellendam.") From Mamre the road to Darling cuts through fields of wheat and vineyards, and before you know it, you've arrived in town.

Darling itself is not particularly picturesque. You'll find the most attractive houses lying to the left of the main road. These large Victorian homes have been spruced up by an ever-increasing circle of artists and other city refugees. **The Darling Museum** (☎ **022/492-3361**), on the corner of Pastorie and Hill streets, is open daily from 9am to 4pm. The museum features work by local artists; in particular take a look at the work of the very talented Nicolaas Maritz who recently had a sell-out exhibition in London. The **Tourism Information** office is inside the museum (same number) and will happily dispense various maps, details of nearby flower reserves (don't miss the **Tienie Versveld Wild Flower Reserve**), and any other information needed.

From Darling head back to the R27 to get to the West Coast National Park or Cape Columbine, or take the R307 (a dirt road) to join the N7 toward Lambert's Bay. (Note that if you return via the N7 south, you can visit an **ostrich farm** (☎ **021/975-1905**) just 20 minutes from Cape Town, just off the N7.

## WEST COAST NATIONAL PARK

West Coast National Park encompasses almost 30,000 hectares of wilderness as well as a 16 kilometer–by–4½ kilometer (10-mile–by–3-mile) marine lagoon on which the coastal town of Langebaan is situated. During spring, the park is an almost essential day journey from Cape Town; but the unique coastal fynbos, pristine white beaches, and beautiful lagoon wetlands make a visit advisable at any time. The **Postberg section,** which contains zebra, wildebeest, and gemsbok, is only open during August and September, from 9am to 5pm, when the flowers are usually most spectacular; but the rest of the park is open 24 hours. Look out for the whitewashed settlement at **Church-haven** (marked by the Anglican church of St Peter), which was founded in 1863 by George Lloyd, a deserter from an American merchant vessel. The hamlet enjoys a unique setting on one of the world's greatest wetlands. Overlooking a blindingly white beach and surrounded by salt marshes, the settlement is visited by over 140 bird species (including the greater flamingo), and presides over the calm, almost-warm waters of the lagoon. Be sure to pack a bathing suit.

There are two entrances to the park: one off the R27, some 100 kilometers (62 miles) north of Cape Town, and the other just south of Langebaan. You can see a good deal of it by entering the one and leaving by way of the other, but make sure you visit the **Information Center** at Geelbek, on the southern tip of the lagoon. Light meals are served, and this is the start and end of the **Strandveld Educational Trail.** This is particularly rewarding in summer, when the hides at Geelbek overlooking the lagoon provide views of the thousands of migrant waders and flocks of pelican, flamingo, curlew, and sandpipers. Admission to the park is between R7 and R18 ($1.15–$3) per person, depending on the season. For more information, contact ☎ **02287/22-144**.

### WHERE TO STAY & DINE

**The Farmhouse.** 5 Egret St., Langebaan 7357. ☎ **022/772-2062.** Fax 022/772-1980. E-mail: farmhouse@cis.co.za. 15 units. A/C TEL. R349–449 ($58.15–$74.85) double, includes breakfast. AE, DC, MC, V. Turn left at the "ENGEN" fuel station on to the Langebaan turnoff and follow the signs.

With the West Coast National Park right on your doorstep, and the azure Langebaan Lagoon visible from almost every room, this is the classiest hotel in Langebaan, if not the entire West Coast. The comfortable guest suites, of which 10 have their own fireplace, are very spacious and for an extra R100 ($16.65) it's worth ensuring that you have one with a sweeping view of the lagoon. Numbers 2, 4, 9, 10, and 12 have some of the best views. The latter is a large family room with a king-size bed and two three-quarter beds.

**Dining:** The restaurant, pub, and terrace all enjoy the same beautiful view of the lagoon. A la carte meals include traditional choices like oxtail and chicken pie and, of course, seafood. Their fish barbecue, held on the terrace every Saturday and Sunday, is definitely worth taking a drive out for.

**Amenities:** Pool, and Langebaan's Country Club facilities include golf, tennis, and bowls.

**Kersefontein.** Box 15, Hopefield 7355. ☎/fax **02288/30-850.** 6 units. R470 ($78.35) double, including breakfast. Children welcome. AE, DC, MC, V. Follow signs off route R45 between Velddrif and Hopefield.

Kersefontein, a Cape Dutch farmstead dating back to 1744, is a 90-minute drive from Cape Town; if you can tear yourself away, the West Coast National Park lies under an hour away. This National Monument, masterfully decorated by Graham Viney, is right on the banks of the Berg River and one of the most remote and romantic places to stay on the West Coast. A working wheat and cattle farm in the rugged Sandveld, Kersefontein has been owned by the Melck family since 1770, and the sense of history is almost palpable—you can, for instance, still view the skull of the last Berg River hippo, shot by Martin Melck in 1876 after it bit his servant. The area is ideal for swimming or boating, and there are over 7,000 hectares to explore on foot or by mountain bike. Rooms are in whitewashed and thatched cottages.

**Dining:** You can either request a self-catering room, in which case breakfast will be served at your own dining-room table, or you can join your host Julian in the main house. Given prior notice, dinner can be arranged; the specialty is wild boar, hunted on the farm and served in The Turn and Slip pub, once the old Kersefontein farm bakery.

### COLUMBINE NATURE RESERVE

To reach the nature reserve, stay on the R27 past the West Coast National Park and Langebaan, and then take the R45 west to Vredenburg. Drive through this ugly town and take the 16-kilometer (10-mile) dirt road to Paternoster. To sample a few West Coast delicacies and refreshments, stop at **Die Winkel op Paternoster** (the shop at Paternoster) on the Main Road; alternatively, pass through this tiny village and look out for the sign for the Cape Columbine Nature Reserve.

This 263-hectare reserve is home to a wide variety of flowers; the best time to visit is obviously during spring, but the reserve's superb location is a welcome relief from the coastline's ongoing degradation. The campsites are situated right on the sea, and the hikes are beautiful. Make sure you don't visit during school holidays. (It's even worth avoiding weekends to ensure that you don't have to share this wild beauty with anyone.) For more information, call ☎ **022/752-2718.**

### EXPLORING LAMBERT'S BAY

**Bird Island** is accessed via a stone breakwater in the Lambert's Bay Harbour. This island houses a colony of Cape gannets, jackass penguins, and cormorants—to be amidst the cacophony of a 14,000-strong community all jostling for position on the island is a rare privilege.

Alternatively, book a cruise that takes you out to see the marine life of the bay from the **Lambert's Bay Boat Charter office** (☎ **027/532-1715**). If you wish to stay over in Clanwilliam, at the foot of the Cederberg, it is a mere 65 kilometers (40 miles) away; for dining, try the open-air Muisbosskerm, described above.

## 6 Cederberg

Around 200 kilometers (124 miles) north of Cape Town lies the Cederberg Wilderness Area. This hiker's paradise features majestic jagged sandstone mountains that glow an unearthly deep red when the sun is low; strange-shaped rock formations that dominate the horizon; numerous San (bushman) rock painting sites; burbling rivers to cool off in; a variety of animals such as baboon, small antelope, leopard, lynx; and rare mountain-fynbos such as the delicate snow protea and gnarled Clanwilliam cedar. The only way to explore this area is on foot. In keeping with its "wilderness" designation, there are no laid out trails, though maps indicating how to reach the main rock features, the huge Wolfberg Arch and the 30-meter-high (98-foot-high) Maltese Cross, as well as to the two main Cederberg peaks, are available.

Covering 710 square kilometers (440 square miles), the Cederberg Wilderness Area is reached via a dirt road that lies halfway between the towns of Citrusdal and Clanwilliam. The pretty town of Clanwilliam is the more attractive base, with a few attractions of its own, including the country's main rooibos tea-processing factory, the Ramskop Wildflower Reserve, and a spectacular drive to the nearby Moravian mission station of Wuppertal. Citrusdal's main attraction is The Baths, a mineral spa resort (day visitors R25/$4.15 per person), and the ideal place to soothe aching muscles after a strenuous hike.

You can camp in the Cederberg, or book a self-catering chalet through Cape Nature Conservation; but if you like your luxuries and are particularly interested in rock art, look no further than Bushman's Kloof, northeast of Clanwilliam (see below).

## ESSENTIALS

**VISITOR INFORMATION** The **Clanwilliam Information Centre** (☎ **027/482-2024**) is in the old jail at the far end of the Main Street. Hours are Monday to Saturday from 8:30am to 5pm. To camp or walk in the Cederberg Wilderness Area, you will need a permit from **Cape Nature Conservation** (☎ **027/482-2812** or fax 027/482-2406).

**GETTING THERE** **By Car** Clanwilliam lies just over two hour's drive from Cape Town. Head north up the N7; after approximately 160 kilometers (100 miles), you'll pass the town of Citrusdal to your left. About 28 kilometers (17 miles) farther north on the N7 is the turnoff for Cederberg Wilderness Area; a farther 26 kilometers (16 miles) is the Clanwilliam, also on your left.

**By Bus** **Intercape** (see "Planning Your Trip to Southern Africa" for local numbers) travels the N7 to Namibia. Note, however, that unless you have someone to pick you up, you'll be left stranded on the highway.

## A TEA TOUR

**Taste Rooibos Tea.** 64 Rooibos Ave. ☎ **027/482-2155.** Factory tours Mon–Fri 10am–noon and 2–4pm.

Rooibos (literally "red bush," pronounced *roy*-bos) is a type of fynbos that only occurs in Clanwilliam and the surrounding area. Its leaves have been used for centuries to brew a refreshing, healthy drink, and the tea was first exported during World War II, when the Ceylon variety was scarce. Since then it has become popular in the Japanese, German, and Dutch markets, and research shows some amazing health properties. Rooibos is caffeine-free, and in addition to relieving stomach cramps and infant colic, it is rich in Vitamin C, and contains antioxidants, iron, potassium, copper, fluoride, zinc, magnesium, and alpha-hydroxy acid. It's an acquired taste, but try it with honey and ginger, or lemon, or with milk and sugar.

## WUPPERTAL

It's worth visiting this isolated rural community just to travel the 90-minute dirt road trip from Clanwilliam, with its breathtaking views of the twisted shapes and isolated tranquility of the northern Cedarberg. Once here, you'll feel lost in time: Like many

## Alfresco Dining

One of the great West Coast experiences is sitting on the beach breathing in the aroma of seafood on hot coals and the fresh sea breeze. As you drink in the sun and the sound of seagulls, sink deeper in the sand as course after course keeps flowing, and lick your fingers clean (scrubbed mussel shells are the only cutlery provided), your only worry will be how you're ever going to manage to save enough space for the crayfish still to come.

These eateries are so informal they're hardly restaurants, but if you like casual dining, and don't mind sharing your space with strangers, they are well worth trying out. The food, prepared in the manner of one huge beach braai, is excellent and usually consists of several kinds of fish cooked in various ways (sometimes with jam, a West Coast specialty), *bokkoms* (salted, dried harders, or small fish) with grapes, mussels, calamari, paella, waterblommetjie bredie, and crayfish. There's also piping-hot white bread baked on the beach and served with fresh farm butter and a number of fruit preserves—this is the killer; you'll want to devour an entire loaf, much to the detriment of the remaining courses. The 10-course self-service meal will cost in the region of R90 ($15) per person, with guests supplying their own drinks.

Of the four West Coast alfresco "restaurants," **Die Strandloper** (☎ **083/227-7195**) in Langebaan and Muisbosskerm in Lambert's Bay are the best. Be warned, the Strandloper is a mess, with old fish bones strewn around, dusty bokkoms hanging from bits of netting, and the so-called tables and chairs at inconvenient and awkward heights. The food is, however, excellent, and it's an easy hour's drive from Cape Town.

For hardcore foodies, the classier ✪ **Muisbosskerm** (☎ **027/432-1017**), 5 kilometers (3 miles) south of Lambert's Bay on the Elands Bay Road (3 hours from Cape Town), is worth the effort. It was here that the open-air West Coast restaurant concept was born—for years Edward and Elmien Turner had simply shared their favorite food with friends on the beach, and in 1985 they decided to broaden their guest list. The food is delicious, and you can usually count on yellowtail, steenbras, and kabeljou; fresh green mealies, local potatoes and sweet potatoes, seafood potjies, curried tripe, waterblommetjie bredie, roast lamb, crayfish, mussels, and the legendary West Coast breads and preserves. It's a long drive home after a meal like this, but the Turner family is happy to recommend accommodation options when you phone for reservations.

of the Moravian mission stations in the Cape, ✪ **Wuppertal** looks pretty much the way it did when it was established in the 1830s. In fact, Wuppertal farmers still use sickles to reap, donkeys to thresh, and the wind to sift their grain. You can't miss the **Tourism Bureau** (☎ **027/482-3410**) on the Church Square next to Leipoldt House. This oldest building in the village also houses **The Lekkerbekkie** ("little sweet mouth"), which serves refreshments.

To get to Wuppertal, drive east of Clanwilliam via the Pakhuis Pass on the road to Soetwater. Take the road south some 40 kilometers (25 miles) off the Pakhuis Pass Road at the appropriate sign to the Biedouw Valley. From here you have to travel some 30 kilometers (19 miles) via the Uikyk and Kouberg Passes. To return to Clanwilliam, drive back the way you came, or, if you have a 4×4, continue into the Cedarberg Wilderness Area.

## WHERE TO STAY & DINE

The most luxurious option in Clanwilliam happens to be a B&B. **Saint Du Barrys Country Lodge** has five units, each with a television, telephone, and minibar, and has rates ranging from R290 to R460 ($48.35–$76.65). Call ☎/fax **027/482-1537.**

**The Baths. ☎ 022/921-3609** (for reservations, call from 8am–5pm). Fax 022/921-3609. 18 units consisting of fully equipped flats, duplex flats, and chalets. R160–265 ($26.65–$44.15) double; bedding R10 ($1.65) per bed. AE, DC, MC, V. Turn off to Citrusdal, after 1km (must more than a half mile) turn right, and travel for 16km (10 miles). A shuttle service is provided for those traveling on Intercape.

Established in 1739, this self-catering resort, built around a natural hot spring that bubbles up at 43°C (109°F) is run by the great grandchildren of James McGregor, who bought The Baths in 1903. Unfortunately they've seen no reason to invest much money in the place, and decor is decidedly spartan and old fashioned, though clean. The lovely Victorian sandstone building has six flats accommodating two to four people—if you're fit, request the top floor. The Cape Dutch Dwarsgebou, which dates back to 1738, has duplex flats with views of the back of the mountain where the hot spring bubbles up. However, the cottages, which have their own fireplaces and individual braai areas, are your best bet, though for privacy you should request one as far away from the camping area as possible (Grishold is the farthest). Tours of the working citrus farm and bushman paintings can be arranged. There is a small shop, but you'd be advised to stock up in Cape Town. Understandably, The Baths is very popular during autumn, winter, and spring, so book well in advance.

**Bushman's Kloof.** PO Box 53405, Kenilworth 7945. Lodge **☎ 027/482-2627;** reservations ☎ 021/797-0990. Fax 021/761-5551. E-mail: santrack@ilink.nis.za. www.bushmanskloof.co.za. 14 units. A/C MINIBAR TEL. R1,300–1,590 ($216.65–$265) double, includes all meals and activities. AE, DC, MC, V. Past Clanwilliam turn due east for 34km (21 miles) on Pakhuis Pass; entrance is on right. No children under 12.

This is by far the most luxurious accommodation option in the Cederberg surrounds, with its own private airstrip (it's a 35-minute flight from Cape Town), 7,500 hectares stocked with game and—during spring—filled with flowers, over 125 rock-art sites, and a resident rock-art specialist. Declared a South African Heritage Site, Bushmanskloof is dedicated to preserving the unique biodiversity of the region as well as the history of the San. Early-morning rock-art tours provide visitors with insights into this fascinating community, followed by botanical walks, mountain biking, abseiling, or simply lazing in the river's many rock pools or the swimming pool. Sunset brings game drives in open Land Rovers. Bedrooms overlook the rolling lawns and river and feature modern comforts such as underfloor heating. Ask for rooms in River Reeds or Water's Edge.

**Dining:** Your three-course dinner might start with venison carpaccio or biltong salad, followed by an ostrich, fish, or vegetarian main course and a choice of three desserts.

**Strassberger's Hotel Clanwilliam.** Main Rd., Clanwilliam 8135. **☎ 027/482-1101.** Fax 027/482-2678. 20 units. A/C TV TEL. R290 ($48.35) double, includes breakfast. Children sharing R20–40 ($3.35–$6.65), depending on age. AE, DC, MC, V.

This peaceful country hotel has been run by the same family for over 50 years. Rooms are not particularly tasteful, but they are supremely comfortable and spacious, particularly numbers 2, 8, and 10, which face the street, and numbers 18 and 17.

**Dining:** Meals are served in the main dining room; the classic country inn table d'hôte featuring a soup or fish appetizer followed by a choice of main courses will run you R55 ($9.15). Reinhold's is a restaurant attached to the hotel and is open Monday to Saturday (daily in season). Housed in a restored Victorian house, this is definitely the best place to eat in Clanwilliam, though the menu isn't very imaginative (the steaks are a good bet). Reserve ahead as it's popular with the locals.

**Amenities:** Pool, sauna, and squash court, with golf and tennis nearby.

## 7 Side Trips to the Northern Cape

### A DRIVING TOUR OF NAMAQUALAND

Most of the year, the sandveld region north of the Oliphants River, a vast semi-arid area known as Namaqualand, sees very little visitors. But come the rains in August or September, the seeds that lie dormant under these dusky plains explode into magnificent multicolored carpets, and some 4,000 species burst into vivid bloom. As there are huge distances to cover to get to Namaqualand (Springbok is some 544km [337 miles] from Cape Town), make sure that the season has begun before you set off on a self-drive tour. Getting there is pretty straightforward: The area is reached by the N7 highway, which connects Cape Town with Namibia. If you find the distances daunting, note that **International Airlines** (☎ **021/934-0350**) flies regularly from Cape Town to **Springbok Airport** (☎ **0251/22-380**), where you can rent a car from **Jowell's** (☎ **0251/23-125**).

The seasonal flower displays start quite far south (see "Darling," above), but you enter the more remote and more spectacular flower region soon after the N7 bypasses **Vanrhynsdorp,** 283 kilometers (175 miles) north of Cape Town. This marks the halfway point between Cape Town and Namaqualand's "capital," Springbok. (Note that from Vanrhynsdorp you could head east on the R27 to **Calvinia** as an alternative base from where to explore the surrounding flower routes.) For the best tours in this region, contact **Neil MacGregor** (☎ **02726/81200**), a local farmer who has hosted the likes of David Attenborough while he and his BBC team were filming *The Private World of Plants.*

The first important stop north of Vanrhynsdorp is **Kamieskroon** (174km/108 miles farther on the N7), the last town before Springbok, which lies some 67 kilometers (42 miles) farther north on the N7. Kamieskroon is literally a one-horse town, but it's claim to fame is the nearby **Skilpad** ("tortoise") **Wildflower Reserve** (☎ **027/672-1948**), created by the World Wildlife Fund. The reserve (18km/11 miles west of town on the Wolwepoort Rd.) almost always has rain, and only opens during the flower season from 8am to 5pm. The other reason to stop here is the **Kamieskroon Hotel** (☎ **027/672-1614,** fax 027/672-1675. The hotel charges R461 for a double, including breakfast and dinner, and offers 7-day **photographic workshops** that could transform the way you look at things. Workshops cost R3,700 ($616.65) and are held by local photographers Colla Swart and J. J. van Heerden and internationally renowned Canadian Freeman Patterson.

The best place to stay (and eat) in **Springbok** is the **Springbok Lodge & Restaurant** on the corner of Voortrekker and Keerom roads (☎ **0251/21-321,** fax 0251/22-718), charging R190 ($31.65) for a double. Be aware that while clean, the lodge is far from luxurious. Owner Jurie Kotze is a mine of information, and his restaurant walls are lined with photographs and artifacts relating to the area, including the many gemstones that occur here. Should you need more information, the **Tourism Information Bureau** (☎ **0251/22-011**) is open 7:30am to 4.15pm daily during flower season. It's in a small Anglican church on Namakwa Street. You can also overnight in self-catering chalets at the top attraction, the **Goegap Nature Reserve** (☎ **0251/21-880**). The reserve is open daily 8am to 9pm, and its visitors center is open daily 8am to 4pm. Admission is R5 (85¢) adults, R3 (50¢) children.

**Flower Power**

A square meter (3 square feet) of Namaqualand soil can yield up to 10,600 flower bulbs; this is thought to be the highest density in the world.

Goegap also incorporates the **Hester Malan Wild Flower Garden;** over 100 species of aloes and succulents make this a worthwhile visit at any time of the year. You can traverse the 17-kilometer (11-mile) round-trip in your own car, or go on a 3-hour guided "flower safari." Another option is to rent a bike for R27 ($4.50) a day; a good way to explore one of the 2- to 4-hour hiking trials featuring spectacular flower views.

From Springbok you can head east along the N14 to **Upington,** gateway to the solitary drive north to the Kalahari-Gemsbok National Park.

## KALAHARI-GEMSBOK NATIONAL PARK

This is the highlight of the Northern Cape and a breathtakingly beautiful place. Tucked between Namibia and Botswana, the characteristic rusty-red dunes and wispy blonde grasses contrast starkly with the cobalt-blue skies and support a surprisingly varied and rich amount of game. Species you are likely to site include cheetah, the big-maned "Kalahari" lion, hyena, elephant, jackal, and of course the gemsbok, or oryx.

Proclaimed in 1931, the Gemsbok Park as it's known locally, is the second-largest national park in South Africa: almost 10,000 square kilometers (6,200 square miles) bordered in the west by Namibia, and in the east by the Nossob, a dry riverbed that creates a natural boundary between South Africa and Botswana. There is no fence between the South African park and Botswana's Gemsbok Park (which covers an even larger area), and a joint management committee ensures that the area is run cohesively. Game is free to wander ancient migratory routes in search of water.

For the best game viewing opportunities, make sure you rise early (see "Kruger National Park" in chapter 7 for more game viewing tips), take plenty of extra water, and be prepared to travel long distances—the shortest circular drive is 100 kilometers (62 miles) long.

### ESSENTIALS

**GETTING THERE** **By Car** You can drive here from Cape Town, taking the N7 north to Springbok (see above) or taking the R27 north from Vanrhynsdorp and Calvinia (see above) to Upington. The R360 takes you north to the park. From Jo'burg, it's a 904-kilometer (560-mile) drive: Take the N14 to Kuruman, then the R31 to Hotazel (it really is), across vast empty plains to join the R360 for the final leg to the park.

**By Plane** **SA Airlink** (☎ **054/332-2161**) flies from Johannesburg and Cape Town to **Upington Airport** (☎ **054/337-7900**).

**GETTING AROUND** **Avis** has a desk (☎ **054/332-4746**) in the Upington Airport. They will also drop a car off at the park should you charter a flight directly there. Unless you intend to enter Botswana, you won't need a 4×4 to travel to and around in the park, despite the fact that most of the roads are dirt.

**VISITOR INFORMATION** Direct all booking inquiries to the **National Parks Board,** 643 Leyds St., Muckleneuk, Pretoria (☎ **012/343-1991,** fax 012/343-0905), between 8am and 3:45pm; or 44 Long St., Cape Town (☎ **021/22-2810,** fax 021/24-6211), between 9am and 4:45pm. You can e-mail them at reservations@parks-sa.co.za. The Park is popular, so book well in advance. The **Visitors Centre** (☎ **054/561-0021**) is at Twee Rivieren, at the parks only entrance and major rest

### Lost and Found

The park recently made headlines when the ANC government handed over a large tract of land to the last remaining San still living in the area, thereby bringing to a close centuries of destitution and persecution. The San, not understanding the concept of land ownership, continued to hunt on their ancestral lands after they had been "annexed" by black and white immigrants to southern Africa, and were for many years seen as vermin, and ruthlessly hunted down. The final settlements moved to the inhospitable Kalahari Desert, but even here they were finally ousted. For a greater insight into the fascinating world of these gentle people, read Laurence van der Post's *Lost World of the Kalahari* (Harcourt Brace, 1977).

---

camp. Note that you can enter the Botswana park from Twee Rivieren, but will need to arrange this beforehand through the **Department of Wildlife and National Parks** in Maun, Botswana (☎ **267/66-0376**).

**WHEN TO GO** Rain falls mainly between January and April. The best time to visit is between March and May (autumn), when it's not too hot or dry. In summer, temperatures may exceed 40°C (104°F). In winter, temperatures at night are often below zero. Note that the park's gate hours vary considerably depending on the season and are strictly adhered to—call ahead to find out exactly what they are when you'll be there.

## WHERE TO STAY & DINE

En route from Johannesburg, you'll pass **Tswalu Desert Reserve,** a luxurious private game reserve and the largest privately owned reserve in South Africa. This is where people who find the Parks Board accommodations too primitive come. Call ☎ **0537/819-2111** for more information.

If you get stuck in Upington, book a room at the **Upington Protea** (☎ **054/332-4414,** fax 054/332-1232), and request one that overlooks the river (R295–325/$49.15–$54.15).

There are three rest camps in the Kalahari-Gemsbok National Park, each with chalets and campsites, in the park. **Twee Rivieren** is right at the entrance to the park, and it's a good idea to stay here the first night as you've more than likely covered vast distances to get here. Accommodation is in self-catering two-, three-, four- and six-bed chalets, all en-suite with air-conditioning, fully equipped kitchens, and braai area. These cost respectively R290 ($48.35), R270 ($45), R315 ($52.50), and R330 ($55) a night. There is a restaurant, and though you can buy fuel and basic supplies like milk, bread, wood, frozen meat, eggs, and tinned food, it's best to stock up on a few extras in Upington. There's also a takeaway shop.

Consider spending the next night at **Mata Mata,** 120 kilometers (74 miles) (2½ hours) away and following the course of the dry Auob River, which offers excellent game-viewing opportunities. The camp is a great deal more rustic than Twee Rivieren, and accommodations are limited to six-bed en-suite chalets (R240/$40) and three-bed huts with shared bathrooms and kitchens (R105/$17.50); neither has air-conditioning. There is also no restaurant, though the shop stocks pretty much the same basic supplies.

Alternatively, head for **Nossob,** 160 kilometers (100 miles) (3½ hours) north of Twee Rivieren along the Auob dry riverbed. Nossob is the most remote and considered the best area for lion sightings. Accommodations are in six-bed cottages (R240/$40) and three-bed bungalows, both en-suite, and three-bed huts (R105/$17.50) with communal bathrooms and kitchens. There is no air-conditioning or restaurant, but a shop sells basic supplies. For all park bookings, see "Visitor Information," above.

# Eastern Cape

# 5

Situated between the Western Cape and KwaZulu-Natal, and bordered by the Orange River and Drakensberg Mountains in the north, the Eastern Cape is rarely top of the list of holiday destinations, even for locals. The manufacture of automobiles and farming provide the main sources of income here, but these industries have been unable to generate the sizeable growth needed to absorb the province's large numbers of employed. With the incorporation of two large former homelands, Ciskei and Transkei, in 1994, the Eastern Cape became one of the poorest provinces in South Africa.

That said, the Eastern Cape is, however, an interesting place to visit. Some of the country's most powerful political figures, including Nelson Mandela, were born in the Eastern Cape; and the capital, Port Elizabeth, was a crucial center of the anti-apartheid movement, with a notoriously deadly security police in close attendance. Today a number of good operators offer excellent township tours that provide an insight into Port Elizabeth's role in South African history.

The Eastern Cape is also steeped in English settler history (as opposed to the Dutch influence on the Western Cape), and Grahamstown, 124 kilometers (77 miles) northeast of Port Elizabeth, has particularly fine examples of English settler architecture. Today this university town is an important cultural and educational center and hosts the largest arts festival in the Southern Hemisphere.

Also within easy striking distance of Port Elizabeth is the Addo Elephant Park. If this isn't wild enough, Shamwari private game reserve offers a chance to stay in luxury and tick off the Big Five (though the experience is a poor cousin to the game parks of northern South Africa and Botswana).

Moving north of Port Elizabeth, into the thirstlands of the Karoo, you will find vast uninhabited plains with atmospheric names such as the Valley of Desolation, near Graaff-Reinet, the Eastern Cape's oldest settlement established by the Dutch.

But most visitors head straight for the Eastern Cape coast, where the "perfect wave" breaks in Jeffrey's Bay, and the appropriately named Wild Coast offers a sanctuary for hardcore nature lovers. Here you'll find the country's most inaccessible nature reserves, but with limited accommodation options, bad roads, and circuitous routes, it takes some commitment just to get there.

## 1 Port Elizabeth

763km (473 miles) from Cape Town; 1,050km (651 miles) from Johannesburg

The approach to Port Elizabeth, referred to by locals as "P.E." and by a slightly desperate marketing team as "The Friendly City," is somewhat depressing. Factories alternate with brown brick houses on the freeway in, the ocean breeze is colored by the stench of smokestacks, and a network of elevated highways has effectively cut the center of the city off from the sea. No doubt the English settlers who arrived in 1820 felt even more depressed by the undeveloped shores of Algoa Bay. Today Port Elizabeth is the biggest coastal city between Cape Town and Durban, the industrial hub of the Eastern Cape, with road, rail, and air links to every other major city in South Africa.

There is enough here to keep visitors entertained for a few days, but for most Port Elizabeth is simply an entry or departure point—usually for a trip up or down the Garden Route. If you have a day to kill, and the weather's fine, head for the beachfront. Alternatively take a day trip to the Addo Elephant Park or the multifaceted Shamwari Game Reserve. Or amble along the Donkin Heritage Trail and take in P.E.'s settler history. Whatever you do during the day, try and spend the night at Hacklewood Hill, arguably the finest small luxury hotel in South Africa.

### ESSENTIALS

**VISITOR INFORMATION** The **Port Elizabeth Publicity Association** (☎ **041/55-8884**), open Monday to Friday from 8am 4:30pm, and Saturday and Sunday from 9:30am to 3.30pm, is in the Donkin Lighthouse Building, Donkin Reserve, Central. A recorded touch-tone visitor information service (☎ **041/56-1773**) provides details of transport, tours, what's on, accommodation, and restaurants. The satellite office (☎ **041/55-5427**) is open Monday to Saturday from 9am to 5pm and located on Humewood Road at the Brookes Hill Pavilion.

**GETTING THERE** **By Car** P.E. is on the N2, which runs east from Cape Town to Durban. From Johannesburg you would take the N1 south, then take the N9 south from Colesberg to Middelburg, then head south east on the N10 to join the N2.

**By Air** Port Elizabeth Airport (☎ **041/512984**) is 4 kilometers (about 2½ miles) from the city center. **SAA** (☎ **041/507-1111**) and **British Airways Comair** (☎ **041/51-6055**) have daily flights to P.E. from Johannesburg, Cape Town, and Durban. **Supercab Shuttle** (☎ **041/52-3720**) offers the cheapest transport service from the airport.

**By Bus** Greyhound, Baz Bus, and Translux all travel to P.E. from Johannesburg, Cape Town, and Durban. Intercape runs between P.E., Johannesburg, and Cape Town. (See chapter 2, "Planning Your Trip to South Africa," for numbers.)

**By Train** If you've got the time to spare, this is a great way to get to P.E. from Cape Town. The train leaves at 6:15pm, travel through the Garden Route and Klein Karoo, and arrive the following day at 5:50pm at the centrally located station. For details, call ☎ **041/507-2222** during office hours, or call 041/507-2111 after hours.

**GETTING AROUND** **By Car** To get around P.E. you'll need wheels. **Avis** (☎ **041/51-1306**), **Budget** (☎ **041/51-4242**), **Imperial** (☎ **041/51-4391**), **Tempest** (☎ **041/51-1256**), and **Alisa** (☎ **041/51-6550**), all have desks at the airport.

**By Taxi** **Hurters Taxi Cabs** (☎ **041/55-7344**) offers a 24-hour taxi service.

**By Air** **Nyala Air Charters** (☎ **041/51-4117**) has day trips to Plettenberg Bay and Oudtshoorn, as well as customized charter flights throughout southern Africa. Contact

John Huddlestone (☎ **041/52-2597** or 083/653-4294) for a helicopter trip to Addo Elephant Park or Shamwari, or an aerial tour of P.E.

**GUIDED TOURS OF PORT ELIZABETH & BEYOND** To orient yourself, a 90-minute **Friendly City Tour** (☎ **041/55-1801**), which are held four times daily, is highly recommended. For nature-based tours of the area, contact **Heritage Tours** (☎ **041/52-3216**). These tours concentrate on the fauna and flora of the region. To tour the surrounding townships, visit a shebeen, and share a meal with a Xhosa family, join a **Gqubera Tour** (☎ **041/581-2572** or 082955-1039). **Calabash Tours** (☎ **041/55-6162**) offers a 4–5 hour "Real City Tour" four times a week: This tour takes a look at Port Elizabeth's history and future prospects, and includes a display of traditional dancing and lunch in the townships. Calabash will also take you farther afield. **Fundani Tours** (☎ **041/63-1471**) offers similar tours as well as a 3-day tour that follows the "Footprints of Mandela's Youth." **Pembury Tours** (☎ **(041/51-2581**) has 2-hour city tours, 1-day Addo Elephant Park tours and settler-country excursions, 3-day Karoo tours, and 3-day Garden Route tours. The latter can be combined into a 10-day tour to Cape Town.

### PORT ELIZABETH

**Area Code** Port Elizabeth's area code is **041.**

**Auto Repair** Call **AA Breakdown** (☎ **0800/010101**).

**Emergencies** For an ambulance, call ☎ **041/10177;** National Sea Rescue Institute (NSRI), call ☎ **041/585-6011;** Police Flying Squad, call ☎ **041/10111;** Police, call ☎ **041/34-3434.** If you're in need of a hospital, call Provincial Hospital (☎ **041/392-3911**) or St George's Hospital (☎ **041/33-7921**).

## EXPLORING THE BEACHFRONT

With P.E. enjoying an average of 7½ hours of sunshine a day, the beach is the place to be. The waters of Algoa Bay are safe and warm, and there are more than a dozen beaches in and around P.E. to choose from. The best are some 2 kilometers (just more than a mile) south of the city center. The first crescent is **King's Beach,** ideal for safe swimming, bodysurfing, and walking; it has good family facilities, including a supertube, kiddies' playground, mini-golf course, go-kart race track, and the **McArthur Baths Swimming Pool Complex** (☎ **041/56-3412**), which stretches south to **Humewood Beach,** another good swimming beach. Additional attractions at Humewood include the **Apple Express** (☎ **041/507-2333**), a restored narrow-gauge steam train that runs from Humewood Station in the morning, steams into Thornhill for lunch, and returns in the evening.

The major beachfront attraction is the **Port Elizabeth Museum Complex** (☎ **041/56-1051**), just opposite the beach. The highlight here is the **Oceanarium,** which features dolphin and seal acrobatics (the Oceanarium plays a major role in conservation and its performers were all born in captivity). Its hours are daily 9am to 1pm and 2 to 5pm; with shows at 11am and 3pm. Admission is R15 ($2.50); R7 ($1.15) for children under 14. There is also an aquarium, a snake park, a jungle in the Tropical House, and a museum, which features fossils, historical relics, scale reconstructions of shipwrecks, and an interesting display on the Xhosa. The complex is open from 9am to 4:30pm, daily; entrance fees run from R4 to R15 (65¢–$2.50).

The adjacent Brookes Pavilion has a number of restaurants with views of the beach and ocean (see "Where to Dine"). Humewood Beach is also linked to Happy Valley via a subway; these pond-lined gardens (no phone, open 24 hours) are well worth an amble.

# Eastern Cape

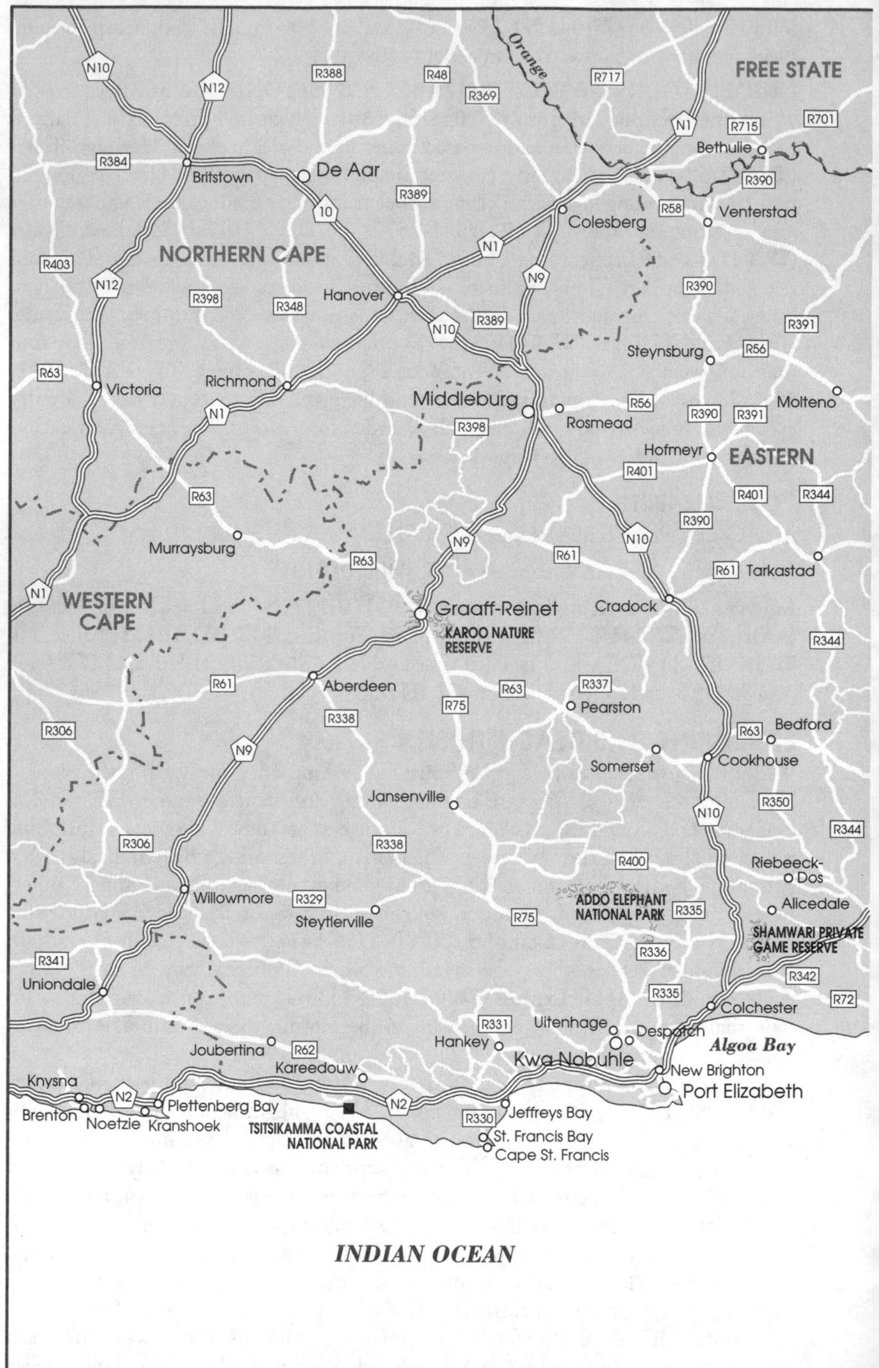

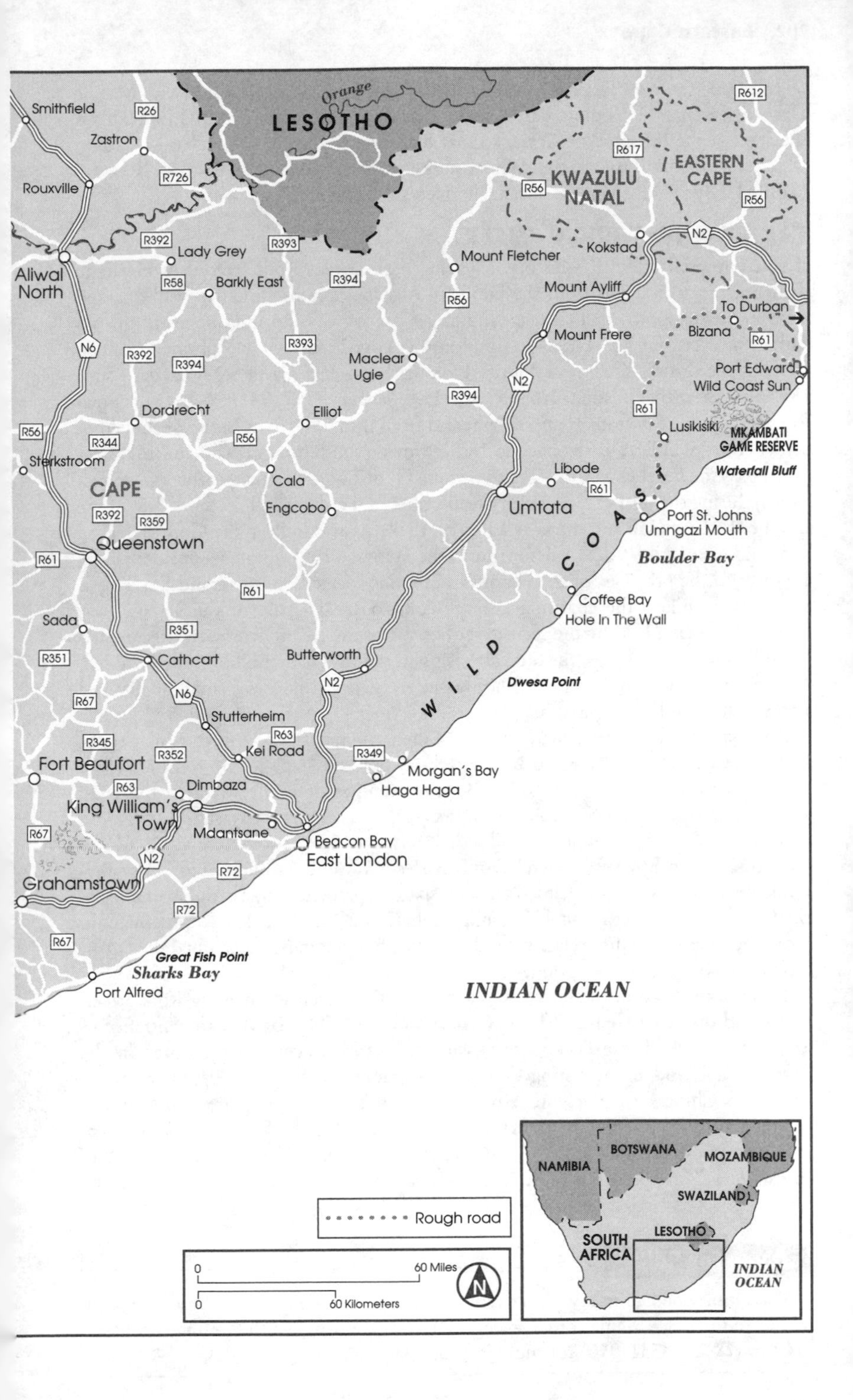
LESOTHO
Orange
Smithfield
Zastron
Rouxville
Aliwal North
Lady Grey
Barkly East
KWAZULU NATAL
EASTERN CAPE
Kokstad
Mount Fletcher
Mount Ayliff
Mount Frere
To Durban
Bizana
Port Edward
Wild Coast Sun
Maclear
Ugie
Dordrecht
Elliot
Sterkstroom
Cala
CAPE
Engcobo
Queenstown
Umtata
Libode
Lusikisiki
MKAMBATI GAME RESERVE
Waterfall Bluff
Port St. Johns
Umngazi Mouth
Boulder Bay
WILD COAST
Coffee Bay
Hole In The Wall
Sada
Cathcart
Butterworth
Dwesa Point
Stutterheim
Kei Road
Fort Beaufort
Morgan's Bay
Haga Haga
Dimbaza
King William's Town
Mdantsane
Beacon Bay
East London
Grahamstown
Great Fish Point
Sharks Bay
Port Alfred
INDIAN OCEAN
N2
N6
R26
R726
R392
R393
R58
R394
R56
R617
R612
R61
R344
R359
R351
R67
R345
R352
R63
R349
R72
Rough road
0
60 Miles
0
60 Kilometers
N
NAMIBIA
BOTSWANA
MOZAMBIQUE
SWAZILAND
LESOTHO
SOUTH AFRICA
INDIAN OCEAN

To escape the crowds, keep traveling the beachfront road until it becomes Marine Drive, then take the Sardinia Bay Road to visit the big dunes of Sardinia Bay. This is the start of the **Sacramento Trail,** a great 8-kilometer (5-mile) coastal walk, a loop which takes you through the **Schoenmakerskop-Sardinia Bay Nature Reserve** (☎ **041/585-9711**). Maps are available from the Publicity Association.

## TAKING A HISTORICAL WALK

If you're interested in P.E.'s history, take the 5-kilometer (3-mile) **Donkin Heritage Trail** (maps are available from the Publicity Association), a self-guided walk marked with a blue staggered line that takes you past 47 places of historical interest in the old Hill area of central P.E. The oldest building is **Fort Frederick** (no phone), built in 1799 by the British. You'll find this overlooking the Baakens River; it's open daily sunrise to sunset; no admission. **No 7 Castle Hill Museum** (☎ **041/52-2515**) is open Tuesday to Saturday from 10am to 1pm and from 2 to 5pm. This is one of the oldest settler cottages in P.E., dating back to 1827. Moving south from here down Bird Street you'll pass the **Feather Market Centre,** where Oudtshoorn's ostrich feathers were auctioned during the turn-of-the-century feather boom. Farther south in the center of the city are the **City Hall** and the **City Library;** the latter was built in the Gothic-Revival style and opened in 1902. (A detour from the Heritage Trail you may consider taking is a visit to the 6th floor of the charmless building located on 44 Strand St.: This is where Steve Biko—the charismatic black-consciousness leader of the 1970s—was killed while being held by the security police. Until the recent Truth and Reconciliation Commission hearings, the official version of events was that Biko slipped and fell. You can visit the room in which Biko was interrogated; it houses a small library and items relating to the man and his past.

Also on Strand Street, at the entrance to the harbor, is the 53½-meter-high (175-ft.-high) **Campanile Tower** (no phone)**;** climb the 204 steps to the top and you'll enjoy an excellent view of the harbor. Built to commemorate the arrival of the 1820 settlers, it has a carillon of 23 bells. Its hours are Tuesday to Saturday 9am to 12:30pm and from 1:30 to 5pm; Sunday to Monday from 2 to 5pm. From here you'll also be able to see the 4-hectare (10-acre) **Donkin Reserve** (no phone), located below Belmont Terrace. This was proclaimed an open space in perpetuity by Sir Rufane Donkin, the Cape's acting governor in 1820, and is where you'll find the large stone pyramid monument he erected to his late wife, Elizabeth, after whom he also named the city—look for the touching inscription.

Moving northeast of the reserve up Havelock street, then south along Rink Street, you'll find the **King George VI Art Gallery** (☎ **041/586-1030**) at the entrance to St George's Park. The gallery features various Victorian artists who painted in the Eastern Cape, and an interesting Oriental collection: The Persian and Indian miniatures and Chinese ceramics are especially worth seeing. Hours are Monday and Wednesday to Friday from 9am to 5pm; Tuesday, Saturday, and Sunday 2–5pm. There is no admission fee. On the first Sunday of every month, St George's Park hosts **"Art in the Park,"** an open-air exhibition of local arts and crafts. East of the Park, on the

### Game For Golf?

The Humewood course, with its sea views and a Victorian-style clubhouse, is considered the best 18-hole course in the Eastern Cape. Contact the **Humewood Golf Club** (☎ **041/531-016**) for more information.

corner of Russel and Cape Road is the **Horse Memorial,** commemorating all those who fell serving their masters in the Anglo-Boer War.

## WHERE TO STAY

**Beach Hotel.** Marine Dr., Humewood 6001. ☎/fax **041/583-2161.** www.pehotels.co.za. 58 units. A/C TV TEL. Non-sea-view doubles R380 ($63.35); with sea view R420 ($70). Children sharing with parents stay free.

This 4-star hotel opposite Hobie Beach (and within walking distance of Humewood Beach's varied attractions) is certainly the best on the beachfront, though it comes nowhere near Hacklewood for luxury and style. You'd be well advised to book a sea-facing room—ask for an executive room with balcony, as they are only marginally more expensive. Rooms have recently been refurbished, but the decor choices are far from memorable. Standard features include hair dryers, private safes, and 24-hour room service.

**Edward Hotel.** Belmont Terrace, Central 6001. ☎ **041/56-2056.** Fax 041/56-4925. 110 units. A/C TV TEL. Standard sea-view double R300 ($50); non-sea-view double R270 ($45). Children R25 ($4.15) extra. AE, DC, MC, V.

Located at the top of the Donkin Reserve in the historical quarter of the city, this two-story Edwardian hotel has a gracious if aged atmosphere. The lift is vintage, corridors are wide, and ceilings pressed and high, but rooms—refurbished over time—are less generous than they were at the turn of the century. Still, they're perfectly comfortable, with the sort of decor you find in chain hotels throughout the world. Once you've drawn the awful net curtains, sea-facing rooms (those on the top floor) provide a sense of space. The major benefit is the hotel's proximity to much of the city's settler heritage and Publicity Association.

**Dining:** The Edwardian Palm Court, a massive conservatory, serves light lunches, while breakfasts and casual dinners (R50/$8.35 per person) are served at Causerie Restaurant. Note that if you're a foodie, you're better off going to a central restaurant (See "Where to Dine").

✪ **Hacklewood Hill Country House.** 152 Prospect Rd., Walmer 6065. ☎ **041/51-1300.** Fax 041/51-4155. 8 units. A/C TV TEL. R1,100 ($183.35) double, including breakfast. AE, DC, MC, V. Children 16 and over.

It's almost worth making a special detour to P.E. to stay at what is rather presumptuously called a "country house" (4 minutes from the airport, Hacklewood is in the heart of Leavy Walmer, and very much in the city). Built in 1898, the Victorian manor house has been artfully converted, with none of the generous spaces of the original home compromised. Certainly if you have a bathroom fetish, these are world-class. Each is bigger than most hotel rooms, and is furnished with the same class and care as the bedrooms. Victorian bathtubs are set in the center of the room, with comfortable seating provided in deep armchairs opposite. The entire house is furnished with beautiful period pieces, with colors and fabrics evincing exquisite taste, and a staff that's eager to please.

**The Heugh Road Guest House.** 55 Huegh Rd., Walmer 6065. ☎ **041/51-1007.** Fax 041/51-4468. 10 units. MINIBAR TV. R250 ($41.65) double, including breakfast. Children under 12 stay free. AE, DC, MC, V.

Your heart might sink as you pull into the parking lot, but the facade facing the busy Heugh Road is where the family stays. Follow the path that runs to the back garden and you enter a courtyard surrounded by spacious suites, each with its own entrance through French doors, some with balconies. The rooms are an excellent value and feature crisp white linens, cool cream walls, and terracotta floors, spacious bathrooms, a

## The 1820 Settlers: Deceit, Despair & Courage

The Industrial Revolution and end of the Napoleonic wars created a massive unemployment problem in Britain. With their underpopulated colony in southern Africa under threat by the indigenous tribes, the British authorities came up with the perfect solution: Lured by the promise of free land and a new life, 4,000 men, women, and children landed at Algoa Bay in 1820, more than doubling the colony's English-speaking population. Many were tradesmen and teachers with no knowledge of farming, and were given no prior warning of their real function: to create a human barrier along the Fish River, marking the eastern border of the Cape Colony. On the other side of this river were the Xhosa. The settlers were provided with tents, packets of seeds, and a few bits of equipment, and given pockets of land too small for livestock and too poor for crops. Pestilence, flash floods, and constant attacks by the Xhosa laid waste their attempts to settle the land, and slowly most of them trickled back into the towns to establish themselves in more secure trades. Here some flourished, most notably those settlers who returned to Algoa Bay or struck out to Grahamstown—interestingly, the latter developed into the Cape's second biggest city, a great trading center dealing with ivory, hides, and wool.

kitchenette (microwave, limited cutlery and crockery, tea- and coffee-making facilities), and comfortable recliners. During the week, your hostess Janet will cook a simple one-course dinner for R30 ($5); alternatively you'll find a number of restaurants within a few minutes walk or drive, though none are P.E.'s best. This guest house is literally 60 seconds from the airport, which means you'll hear the low rumble of planes taking off, but at least you won't miss your flight.

## WHERE TO DINE

**Blackbeard's Lookout & Seafood Tavern.** Brooke's Pavilion, Beachfront. ☎ **041/55-5567.** Reservations recommended. Main courses R30–120 ($5–$20). Mon–Sat 6–11pm. SEAFOOD.

People come here as much for the view as the food—if you haven't caught the dolphin act in the adjacent Oceanarium, you're likely to see one from your table in the Dolphin Room, free of charge. If you can't get a table overlooking the sea, try booking one near the bar; the counter doubles as a top for a large koi fish tank. While there are a few red-meat choices, the emphasis is firmly on seafood: calamari prepared in a number of ways (try the whole tube stuffed with linefish, peppers, mushrooms, onion, and garlic), seafood paella, seafarer's choice (where you create your own platter), linefish, mussels, prawns, crayfish ... the list goes on. The *brodino* dishes—fish cooked with mussels, calamari, tomato, white wine, garlic, and spices in a cast iron pot—are some of the best.

✪ **Le Med.** 66a Parliament St., Central. ☎ **041/585-8711.** Reservations essential. Main courses R24–50 ($4–$8.35). Tues–Sun 12–3pm, 6:30–11pm. MEDITERRANEAN.

The focus here is primarily on countries lapped by the Mediterranean Sea, with decor and food inspired by the owners' experiences of working and traveling in Egypt, Morocco, Nigeria, Israel, Spain, Greece, Turkey, and Italy. Recommended dishes include the trout topped with sour cream and caviar folded over an Israeli potato cake; chorizo sausage flavored with chili, tomato, garlic, and white wine; the Moroccan lamb tajine slow-grilled with prunes, honey, and almonds; and the Grecian filet, which is topped with creamed spinach and feta and flash-baked. Main courses come with couscous, rice, pasta, pasta-rice, or fries on enamel plates or frying pans. Salt- and peppershakers are plain aluminum, and seating is at benches. It's a down-home honesty that works for a large section of the P.E. population; a great place to check out the locals.

## EXCURSIONS FROM PORT ELIZABETH

### PLACE OF THE PACHYDERMS

**Addo National Park.** 72km (45 miles) northeast of Port Elizabeth. ☎ **042/233-0556.** Open daily 7am–6:30pm. Admission R12 ($2). Drive east of P.E. on the N2 for 17km (10½ miles), looking out for the Addo sign/R335; and then travel some 50km (31 miles) north.

Proclaimed in 1931, when only 11 elephants remained in the area, Addo is now home to over 250. With only 14,551 hectares (36,377 acres) for them to roam and accessible waterholes, this easy side trip from P.E. provides an excellent opportunity to view elephants in their natural habitat. Though they are in evidence all year-round, the most attractive time of the year to visit is in spring, when the harsh, prickly Eastern Cape bushveld is softened with flowers, and the gray behemoths can be seen standing in carpets of yellow daisies. Other animals to look out for are black rhino, buffalo, zebra, red hartebeest, eland, kudu, bushbuck, warthog, and a few endemic species such as the unique flightless dung beetle, found almost exclusively in Addo. Despite their size and numbers, it can be surprisingly difficult to spot the elephants in the dense bushveld—always ask at reception where they were last seen, and travel with the map of the park's roads and watering holes that you can pick up at the entrance. Ironically, the best place to view the elephants is usually at the large watering hole situated close to reception and the park restaurant.

To get a good feel for the vegetation of the area, you could tackle the **Spekboom Trail.** Bear in mind you'll see no elephants—this 12-kilometer (7½-mile) walk takes hikers through a fenced-off area that has been untouched by their destructive tusks and trunks for over 40 years.

**Safety tips:** Please note that it is illegal to alight from your vehicle unless at a designated picnic site, and, be aware that no citrus fruit can be taken into the park. This is an elephant delicacy, and can make them quite aggressive when they pick up the scent.

#### Where to Stay & Dine

**Addo Park Rest Camp.** ☎ **042/233-0556.** For reservations, call ☎ **021/22-2810.** Fax 021/24-6211. Reservations@parks-sa.co.za. 42 units, comprising 6-bed cottages, 4-bed cottages, 4-bed forest huts, and 2-bed rondawels. A/C. From R154 ($25.65) double.

With many of the rest camp cottages affording views of the elephants moving through the undergrowth, and the airport an hour's drive away, this is a tranquil alternative to overnighting in P.E. It also allows you can to book a night drive (R60/$10 per person), which is one of the best ways to view the nocturnal activities of carnivores such as the black-backed jackal and bat-eared fox. All units are en-suite, though you need to specify if you want a semi- or fully equipped kitchen, or shared cooking facilities. Units 1 to 6 (2-bed with communal kitchens) have views of the waterhole, as do units 7 and 8 (6-bed with kitchens); units 17 to 24 and 29 to 32 (4-bed) have good views of the park. Residents have access to a tennis court and large swimming pool—essential during the sweltering summer days.

**Dining:** The restaurant serves breakfast from 8:30 to 10am, lunch and teas from 11am to 5pm, and dinners at three sittings: 6, 7, and 8pm. These are basic a la carte meals—chicken, fish, steaks (including kudu and ostrich), and a few traditional dishes like *umcabosi,* a combination of spinach and *pap.*

## SHAMWARI PRIVATE GAME RESERVE

This privately-owned 14,000-hectare (35,000-acre) game reserve prides itself on "conserving a vanishing way of life," and has garnered four international conservation awards. Wildlife had been all but eradicated in the Eastern Cape by the turn of the century, but thanks to the team effort at Shamwari, you can tick off the Big 5, stay in an original 1860 settler cottage, view Xhosa beadwork, and visit **Kaya Lendaba,** a relatively authentic African art and culture village created by controversial *sangoma* (traditional healer) Credo Mutwa. The Kaya gives visitors the opportunity to understand much of Xhosa culture, including initiation ceremonies, dancing, and the tasting of traditional foods—it's well worth visiting for the sculptural quality of the village alone. However, most come for the wildlife, and don't leave disappointed. As is the case with most Mpumalanga reserves, residents go on game drives in the morning and evening in open Land Rovers, with experienced rangers taking you close to rhino, elephant, buffalo, giraffe, hippo, and over 18 antelope species, all successfully reintroduced since 1990. The reserve is also malaria-free, which is a great bonus if you're traveling with kids. The greatest drawback is that Shamwari's lions are kept in large enclosures, though they are scheduled to be released towards the end of 2000. Though for some this adds to the thrill, these lions have come to associate man with food, and traveling through these enclosures is potentially more dangerous than any lion encounter in Mpumalanga or Botswana.

Day-trippers to Shamwari are also welcome. A buffet-style lunch, visit to Kaya Lendaba, and a 3–4 hour game drive will set you back R375 ($62.50). Both day visitors and residents are advised to book in advance; call ☎ **042/203-1111.** Transfers to and from P.E. airport (a 50-minute drive) can be arranged for residents. To reach the reserve by car, follow the N2 on the Grahamstown road for 65 kilometers (40 miles), turn left at the Shamwari sign on to gravel (R342) for 7 kilometers (4½ miles), and turn right at the Shamwari sign. For more information, call ☎ **042/203-1111.**

### Where to Stay & Dine

**Shamwari Lodge.** Bookings: P.O. Box 32017, Summerstrand, Port Elizabeth 6019. ☎ **042/203-1111.** Fax 042/235-1224. www.shamwari.com. 6 units. A/C TV TEL. R4,500 ($750) double, including all meals and activities. AE, DC, MC, V. Children 12 and over.

For the most authentically African experience at Shamwari, choose one of these thatched cottages, furnished in ethnic-chic decor. Traditional African cooking with a European flavor can be enjoyed under the stars around the fireside lapa (boma) or in the dining room. As the lodge is situated far from any of the other accommodation options, and takes no more than 12 guests, guests are assured of the most personal service—then again, service in all the accommodation options is of an exceedingly high standard.

**Long Lee Manor.** For address and telephone, see Shamwari Lodge. 22 units. TV TEL. R3,800 ($633.35) double, includes all meals and activities (winter discounts of up to 40% available). Children under 12 less 50%. AE, DC, MC, V.

Equally luxurious, but more colonial in style, is this pink Edwardian manor, dating back to 1910. Here 42 guests are pampered in four different accommodation options. Book a room in the original manor house as the decor here is truly sumptuous, or choose a garden suite for privacy. The "Sidbury wings" are some way away from public amenities. Lunchtime is usually a buffet, and dinners are superb—formal three-course creations by a cordon bleu chef alternate every other night with a more informal, traditional braai.

## 2 Jeffrey's Bay

75km (46½ miles) west of Port Elizabeth

Situated on the 186-kilometer (115-mile) stretch between Storms River and P.E., this makes an easy detour after or before you've tackled the Garden Route, though the town itself has nothing much to recommend it. However, if you're a surfer, this coastal town will be a top priority on your itinerary. Considered one of the top-three surfing spots in the world, "J-Bay" as it's affectionately known to locals, shot to international fame in the 1960s cult movie *Endless Summer,* which featured the break at Supertubes—the fastest and best-formed break on the South African coast, as well as "Bruce's Beauties," a rare right-point break you'll find a little farther west at Cape St Francis.

### ESSENTIALS

**VISITOR INFORMATION** The J-Bay **Publicity Association (☎ 042/293-2588)** is on the corner of Da Gama and Goedehoop roads and is open Monday to Friday from 8am to 5pm, and Saturday from 9am to 12pm.

**GETTING THERE** Jeffrey's Bay can only be reached by car or bus; take the turnoff south off the N2. The **J-Bay Sunshine Express (☎ 042/293-2221)** is a 15-seater minibus that travels between Jeffrey's Bay and Port Elizabeth and can be booked any time, though it's not ideal if you're only two persons traveling, as you'll pay for the empty seats. The **Baz Bus (021/439-2323)** calls in at the hostels every day on its way to Plettenberg Bay or P.E. The daily **Intercape** (see chapter 3 for phone numbers) travels here from Cape Town, stopping on Da Gama Road, then setting off for P.E..

**GETTING AROUND** Once here, you can get around on foot or by car. **Aloe Africa (☎ 042/296-2974** or 082576-4259) offers tours of the area, including various adventure activities.

### FINDING THE PERFECT WAVE

When it comes to surfing the perfect wave, there's only once place to test your skills: The break at Supertubes, east of the main bathing beach, produces a consistent tube attracting international surf talent all year-round. The other famous break, Bruce's Beauties, lies west at St Francis. This only works in really big swells, and should under no circumstances be attempted by the unskilled. Back in J-Bay, other classic spots worth checking out are Kitchen Windows, Magna Tubes, the Point, and Albatross. To find out what's pumping, pop into **O'Hagans (☎ 042/293-3088,** on Da Gama Road, in front of the Tourism Bureau), where the local surfers hang out. For surf lessons, contact Jason (**☎ 042/933-8015**). A big south swell and light northwest to southwest winds bring about ideal surfing conditions. Note that all these spots can become a little crowded, particularly during the **Billabong Classic Surfing Event** held in July; call the local surf shop **Country Feeling** (**☎ 042/293-1101**). If you prefer body surfing, try Main Beach and Kabeljous-on-Sea; these main swimming beaches are also good for beachcombing for J-Bay's famously beautiful shells.

### WHERE TO STAY

**Diaz 15.** 15 Diaz Rd., Jeffrey's Bay 6330. ☎/fax **042/293-1779.** E-mail: info@diaz15.co.za. www.diaz15.co.za. 8 units. MINIBAR (on request) TV TEL. May–Sept R490 ($81.65) double; Oct–Apr R670 ($111.65) double. AE, DC, MC, V.

Not only is Diaz 15 by far the best guest house in Jeffrey's Bay, it also enjoys one of the best locations on the entire South African coast. A well-cropped lawn abruptly dissolves into Main Beach, and the ocean is literally a stone's throw from your sliding windows. Luxury self-catering apartments cater for the local market—hence their excellent value—and breakfasts are served on request. Given enough notice, proprietor Coenie Nel will stock your fridge for you, and Breakers restaurant (which together with Walskipper is considered J-Bay's best) is a few minutes walk away. Choose between two- and three-bedroom apartments; each bedroom has its own balcony and bathroom (featuring high-pressure showers), kitchens are open-plan and modern, and living rooms are spacious and comfortably furnished with sliding doors opening onto a verandah or balcony. Numbers 3, 5, and 10 enjoy particularly good views of the sea; but if at all possible, book the penthouse for its wrap-around seaviews. Note that P.E. airport is a mere 75 kilometers (46½ miles) away.

## WHERE TO DINE

**Walskipper.** Jeffrey's Bay. ☎ **042/292-0005.** Main courses R30–95 ($5–$15.85). Open daily 12–9:.30pm. Take the road to Aston Bay (next to J-Bay), follow sign to Marina Martinique and Clapton's Beach. TRADITIONAL/SEAFOOD.

If you haven't had a chance to sample the open-air West Coast restaurants, Walskipper offers a fairly similar experience, though the menu here is a la carte. Situated right on the ocean, the restaurant is housed in a simple timber structure. There are no walls, allowing the fresh ocean air to whip up an appetite. Most dishes are cooked over hot coals, and popular choices include the crocodile steak, oxtail in red wine, barbecue chicken, and the Walskipper special—a plate of prawns, calamari, mussels, scallops, and crab sticks. The floor is beach sand, encouraging barefoot informality. Guests are seated on rough benches, wine is served in tin mugs, meals on enamel plates, and chunks of freshly-baked bread and jam accompany every meal. With the sea a mere meter from the restaurant, this is a great venue for families, and kids can take dips between courses.

# 3 Grahamstown

125km (77½ miles) northeast of Port Elizabeth

With a church for every Sunday of the year, Grahamstown is often referred to as the City of Saints, but its history is hardly holy. The town was named after Colonel John Graham who established a garrison here in 1815 with orders to drive the Xhosa eastward over the Fish River—a ruthless expulsion that was to spark off the 100-year Frontier War. Reminders of its English colonial past can be seen everywhere: the streets lined with charming Georgian and Victorian buildings, the only Victorian camera obscura in the Southern Hemisphere, one of South Africa's oldest English-speaking universities, and a number of highly regarded English-style private boarding schools dating back to 1885. But, with the old Fish River frontier a mere 60 kilometers (36 miles) east, signs of the impoverished Xhosa community are equally visible, both on the streets and on the hills surrounding the valley.

As something of a microcosm of South Africa's social and economic problems, Grahamstown is certainly worth visiting, and never more so than in July, when the town hosts its 24-year-old arts festival, said to be the biggest in the Southern Hemisphere, and second in size only to Edinburgh's.

## ESSENTIALS

**VISITOR INFORMATION** The Tourism Bureau (☎ **046/622-3241**) is at 63 High St.; you can also contact them by e-mail: tourgtn@imaginet.co.za or on the Web at www.grahamstown.co.za. Hours are Monday to Thursday 8.30am to 5pm;

Friday 8.30am to 4pm; and Saturday 9 to 11am. (Staff are not that on the ball, but make sure you pick up the Rhodes University's Department of Music & Musicology's concert schedule.)

**GETTING THERE** **By Car** Take the N2 out of Port Elizabeth; some 125 kilometers (77½ miles) northeast is the turnoff for Grahamstown.

**By Bus** Greyhound, Translux and Intercape operate daily between Grahamstown and Port Elizabeth. Grahamstown is roughly 12 hours by bus from Cape Town, Jo'burg, and Durban. All coach queries, call ☎ **046/622-2235.** You can also catch the **Leopard Express minibus** (☎ **046/622-4589**) from P.E. Airport.

**By Train** The Johannesburg–P.E. train pulls into Grahamstown once a day.

**GETTING AROUND** **By Car** You can rent a car from **Avis** (☎ **046/622-8233**) or **Imperial** (☎ **046/622-3841**). Contact **Beeline** (☎ **046/622-5051**) for a taxi.

**GUIDED TOURS** **Lynx thru' Africa** (☎ **082/784-1458**) gives 3-hour city tours for R85 ($14.15) per person; a 5-hour Settler Country tour to Bathurst is R95 ($15.85) per person; and a 4-hour night drive in the nearby Double Drift Game Reserve runs R120 ($20) per person. **Cocks Tours** (☎ **046/636-1287**) has city walking tours for R30 ($5) per person as well as trips to Bathurst and the Sunshine Coast, Addo Elephant Park, and the Frontier Forts and Great Fish River Reserve (prices depend on the number of people in your group).

**SPECIAL EVENTS** Standard Bank National Arts Festival, held every July, is Africa's greatest arts event: Some 600 performances as well as 1,500 musical events are staged over 11 days. To find out what's on, call ☎ **046/622-4341** or visit www.sbfest.co.za. If you decide to attend, remember to pack extra-warm clothes as it's the middle of winter and venues can be draughty.

## ✪ VISITING THE TOWNSHIPS

Despite Grahamstown's patent lack of industry, people continue to pour in from the former bantustan (homeland) of Ciskei. A number of tour guides not only provide insights into the stark contrasts of this growing community, but have come up with some creative solutions to combat its widespread unemployment and feelings of hopelessness. The **Umthati** and **Masithandane** projects help to provide purpose and income to the previously unemployed, and a visit to either is highly recommended. Given prior notice, tours can also include any of the historical and cultural sites of Grahamstown.

An ✪ **Umthati Township tour** (☎ **046/622-5051**) will take you into the heart of the Rini township, where 8 out of every 10 people are unemployed. At Umthati's kitchen gardens and education center you will be served a traditional Xhosa meal, learn something about their culture and customs (including the use of clay for face markings), visit a member's house and local shop, and be introduced to some of the local crafts.

The ✪ **Masithandane Association** owes much of its success to rubbish. Plastic bags—jokingly referred to as the new national flower because of the way they flourish on fences and trees surrounding the townships—are collected by township women, who in return receive a meal. The bags are then skillfully woven by Masithandane members into colorful hats and bags. To visit the Masithandane workshops and enjoy a traditional Xhosa "picnic," contact ☎ **046/622-5944.**

## EXPLORING GRAHAMSTOWN

Start your self-guided tour by driving or walking to the top of Gunfire Hill where the **1820s Settlers National Monument** overlooks Grahamstown, which is situated in a small valley flanked by hills. To your right you will see Makanaskop, where the Xhosa took their last stand against the British. Pop into the monument to view the Cecil Skotnes artworks, then set off for the **Albany Museum** in town (☎ **046/622-2312**) which is open Monday to Friday 9:30am to 1pm, and 2 to 5pm; Saturday and Sunday 2 to 5pm; Admission R4 (65¢), R3 (50¢) seniors and ages 7 to 18. Situated on Somerset Street, the Albany incorporates both the Natural Sciences and the History Museum. The latter has an exhibition on the role of clay in the Xhosa's social life, which is of interest; but for real insight into current issues, you'd be better off taking a tour (see above).

On the corner of Somerset and Prince Alfred streets you'll find the ✪ **International Library for African Music** (☎ **046/603-8557** or e-mail ilcw@giraffe.ru.ac.za, open Monday to Friday 8am to 5pm; donations welcome), which has recordings of traditional African music from southern Africa, as well as from Rwanda, Uganda, Tanzania, and Zaire, and over 200 traditional instruments. The library sells cassettes on request; for an introduction and tour by internationally renowned ethnomusicologist Andrew Tracey (the director), phone ahead and make an appointment.

Nearby is the **JLB Smith Institute of Ichthyology** (☎ **046/603-8425**), open Monday to Friday from 8:30am to 1pm, and 2 to 5pm, where you can view two stuffed specimens of the **coelacanth,** a fish thought to have been extinct for 50 million years until 1939, when J. L. B. Smith identified the specimen caught off the nearby East London coast. Admission free.

No visit to Grahamstown would be complete without a visit to at least one church. At the junction of High and Hill streets, the **Cathedral of St Michael and St George** (☎ **046/622-2445,** free admission) took 128 years to complete. This is the town's most prominent landmark, its spire the tallest in South Africa. Look for the signature mice on some of the wall carvings. The **Methodist Commemoration Church** (☎ **046/622-7210**) is also worth visiting, particularly for its 10 stained glass windows, one of which depicts the arrival of the 1820s settlers. The church, which dates back to 1850, has a Gothic-Revival facade and stands at the top of Bathurst Street. Diagonally opposite is a winged statue of peace, dedicated to the men who died in the Anglo-Boer War. Note the inscription; Rudyard Kipling wrote it especially for the memorial.

Next door to the Methodist Church are the premises of **T. Birch & Co** (☎ **042/622-7010**)—an old-style family store. Purchase something and watch your money fly across the room—they still use the Lamson trolley system, an overhead cash delivery system dating back to the 1950s. (For a stark contrast that is classic Grahamstown, visit **Osher Brothers** on Beaufort Street, who supply the township dwellers.) Alongside Birch's you'll find the **City Hall,** which began its life in 1870 as a memorial tower commemorating the arrival of the 1820 settlers. The city hall was built behind the tower in 1877.

If you do one thing in Grahamstown, visit the ✪ **Observatory Museum** (☎ **046/622-2312**) on Bathurst Street, where you can view a 360-degree view of Grahamstown reflected in the restored Victorian **camera obscura.** The camera is housed in a custom-designed cupola above the home and shop of the eccentric H. C. Galpin, and was constructed by him in the mid-1850s. A watchmaker by trade, Galpin also built a turret housing a clock above his home, the pendulum of which swings in the rooms two stories below. The entire building is today a museum and holds many interesting exhibits relating to Galpin and his hobbies, as well as early-settler artifacts. Hours are Monday to Friday 9:30am to 1pm and 2 to 5pm, and Saturday 9am to 1pm, admission R5 (85¢) adults, R4 (65¢) children. As the cupola holds a maximum of eight people, avoid visiting when there are tour buses parked outside.

## WHERE TO STAY

**The Cock House.** 10 Market St., Grahamstown 6140. ☎ **046/636-1287.** Fax 046/636-1295. E-mail: cockhouse@imaginet.co.za. www.dsa.co.za/cock_house. 7 units. TV TEL. R500 ($83.35) double, including breakfast. R120 ($20) children 4–11 years. AE, DC, MC, V.

Built in 1826, this charming two-story settler house was bought and renovated by owner-managers Belinda and Peter Tudge in 1991. Since then they have hosted a number of illustrious guests (Nelson Mandela, has stayed here twice). Rooms are tasteful and spacious, though the bathrooms above the public spaces are looking a little tired and you may want to opt for a room in the converted stables—of these, the honeymoon suite is the best room in the house. Family rooms sleep four. The Cock House dining room, once a ballroom, is considered Grahamstown's best cordon bleu restaurant and is open for lunch and dinner. Belinda changes her menu every 2 months to ensure that her regular Grahamstown diners are never bored, but typical mains are: deep-fried fillet of kingklip with a parsley, lemon garlic and chili sauce (R44/$7.35); chicken curry flavored with coconut cream (R32/$5.35); roast lamb on the bone with thyme and rosemary gravy (R36/$6); and venison and ostrich pie (R35/$5.85).

✪ **The Hermitage.** 14 Henry St., Grahamstown 6140. ☎/fax **046/636-1503.** 2 units. TV. R220 ($36.65) double, including breakfast. No credit cards.

This is the best B&B in Grahamstown, situated in a beautiful historic home, and decorated with immense flair and impeccable taste by artist Bea Jeffray. There are only two rooms, which is unfortunate, but one is supremely grateful that the Jeffray's are prepared to share their home at all. Of the two, the room overlooking the back garden is far larger, with a small sitting room leading out to the tranquil garden. Every detail is pleasing, and the Jeffrays are charming hosts. The breakfast table is laid with antiques and cut glass. If you don't mind staying at a B&B (and the house and rooms *are* large enough for a sense of total privacy), this is the best place to stay in Grahamstown.

## WHERE TO DINE

✪ **La Galleria.** 13 New St., Grahamstown. ☎ **046/622-2345.** Main courses R26–49 ($4.35–$8.15). Mon–Fri 12.:30–2.:30pm and 7–9.:30 or 10.30pm; Sat 7pm–late. ITALIAN.

When Esme and Gabriele took a 10-month break from this first-rate restaurant they had opened in 1994, Grahamstonians wept. Happily they returned, and are once again providing the best fare in town. Part of La Galleria's charm is the fact that the kitchen is visible from the street—in the afternoon you can look through the window and see the pasta drying for the evening meal. Meals start with the antipasto trolley—a choice of seven—followed by an excellent selection of main courses. Pasta and gnocchi are served with a variety of sauces; try the *barese* (creamed spinach and ricotta with mushrooms and bacon). The pollo cremonese (chicken breasts prepared with herbs and lemon), and the beef filet prepared in red wine and herbs and flambéed are both recommended. Leave space for the dessert trolley; the tiramisu was rated the best in the world by recent Italian guests.

# 4 Graaff-Reinet

254km (157 miles) from Port Elizabeth

Graaff-Reinet, South Africa's fourth-oldest town, is 837 kilometers (519 miles) south of Johannesburg—a good stop-over if you're driving down to the Garden Route. Should you have time to stay awhile, there's plenty to keep you busy, what with 220 national monuments to admire and all its museums within easy walking distance of

**Telephone Tips**

Graaff-Reinet phone numbers are scheduled to change within the lifetime of this edition, probably in 1999. Unfortunately no more exact information was available at press time. The original number is listed first; the new number is listed second.

each other. It is also one of the few towns surrounded by a nature reserve, and there are some worthy side trips to the Valley of Desolation, and to nearby Nieu Bethesda.

## ESSENTIALS

**VISITOR INFORMATION** The helpful Tourist Information Bureau (☎ **0491/24-248** or 049/892-4248) is housed in the Old Library Museum on Church street and is open Monday to Friday 9am to 12:30pm and 2 to 5pm, Saturday 9am to 12pm. Alternatively, visit them at www.graaffreinet.co.za.

**GETTING THERE** **By Car** From Johannesburg you'll travel south on the N1, then take the N9 south at Colesberg to Graaff-Reinet. From P.E. you'll take the R75 north, a 3-hour drive.

**By Bus** **Translux** and **Intercape** buses pull in daily from Cape Town, the Garden Route, and P.E. See chapter 2 for phone numbers.

**GETTING AROUND** The easiest and best way to explore the town is on foot. For a guided tour, contact **William Luckhoff** at ☎ **0491/2-2893** or 049/892-2893. To explore the surrounds, contact **Karoo Connection Adventure Tours** (☎ **0491/23-978** or 049/892-3978 or karoocon@yebo.co.za), who provide the following trips: Valley of Desolation, Owl House, game-viewing drives in the Karoo Nature Reserve, tracking the endangered mountain zebra, horse trails and farm tours, township tours, Anglo-Boer War tours, San/bushman art tours, and a number of walking and hiking tours and light-aircraft trips.

## WHAT TO SEE & DO

Boasting more national monuments than any other South African town, the streets of Graaff-Reinet are a pleasure to simply stroll along, though there are a number of reasonable museums should you wish to scratch beneath the surface of the town. The **Graaff-Reinet Museum** (☎ **0491/23-801** or 049/892-3801) is comprised of four buildings. Hours are Monday to Friday 9am to 12:30pm and 2–5pm; Saturday 9am to 12pm; Sunday 10 to 12pm and 3 to 5pm; admission R8 ($1.35) for three buildings, R10/$1.65 for four buildings. Of these **Reinet House,** a stately Cape Dutch home facing Parsonage Street, is by far the most interesting (admission R5/85¢ for this only). Built in 1812 as the Dutch Reformed Church parsonage, it contains a number of objects used over a century ago, in large airy rooms displaying period furniture, a collection of antique dolls, and various household objects. In the garden you'll find what is claimed to be one of the world's oldest vines—planted in 1870. The stem is now 2.4 meters (almost eight feet) in diameter. Note the hourglass with wings carved on the gable, said to remind us that "time flies"—which is why it's not really worth visiting the **Old Residency** in Parsonage Street, unless you wish to view a large collection of hunting rifles. The **Old Library Museum,** on the corner of Church and Somerset streets, is slightly more interesting, certainly for its collection of fossilized Karoo reptiles that inhabited the area over 200 million years ago. The final building in the museum complex, **Urquhart House** on Market Square, features Victorian furniture, farm implements, and the traditional Cape Dutch peach-pit kitchen floor.

The **Hester Rupert Art Museum** (☎ **0491/22-121** or 049/892-2121), opposite the Drosdty Hotel on Church Street, is open Monday to Friday 10am to 12pm and 3 to 5pm; Saturday and Sunday 10am to 12pm. It houses over 100 contemporary works, but as many are in the same style, and there are no black artists, this is in no way representative of the wealth of South African talent. Admission R1 (15¢).

Other buildings worth noting are the stately **Dutch Reformed Church,** 1 block up from the Old Library Museum, which dates back to 1886, and the delightful **Graaff-Reinet pharmacy,** a typical Victorian chemist that still operates at 24 Caledon St.

## A Couple of Great Side Trips

Graaff-Reinet lies in the center of the 15,000-hectare (37,500-acre) **Karoo Nature Reserve** (daily dawn to dusk, no admission), the highlight of which is the ✪ **Valley of Desolation,** 14 kilometers (8½ miles) from Graaff-Reinet. To view the valley, take the Murraysburg road north, keeping an eye out for the marked turnoff, which is some 5 kilometers (3 miles) from town. The road ascends the Cave Mountains, passing a series of **viewpoints,** before reaching the top. From here, it's a short walk to the canyon lip—the 45-minute looped trail is recommended. Sunset is the best time to visit, when the dolomite towers that soar some 800 meters (2,500 feet) from the valley below turn a deep red, and the pink light softens the Camdeboo plains. On your return, keep an eye out for the endangered mountain zebra—the Karoo Nature Reserve is one of its last remaining habitats.

Another highly recommended excursion is to **Nieu Bethesda;** 50 kilometers (31 miles) northeast of Graaff-Reinet, this typical Karoo *dorp* (small rural town) is in a narrow valley in the foothills of the Sneeuberg Mountains. The village itself is charming; modern-day luxuries like electricity are a relatively recent phenomena, and donkey carts still a main source of transport, but the main attraction is the ✪ **Owl House and Camel Yard** on New Street (☎ **04923/605** or 49/841-1603 (see box "Eyes of Glass & Wings of Cement," below). Another attraction worth visiting is the **Ibis Art Centre Gallery** (☎ **04923/642** or 049/841-1623) on Martin Street, which showcases work by some very talented locals as well as nationally respected artists, and can recommend accommodation options should you wish to prolong your stay.

Tea and light meals are available daily at the **Village Inn** (☎ **04923/667** or 049/841-1635), diagonally opposite the Owl House. There is no Tourism Bureau, but the municipality (☎ **04923/712** or 049/841-1659) will answer any queries (mornings only). To get to Nieu Bethesda, take the N9 northeast to Middelburg for 27 kilometers (17 miles), then take the final turnoff—a well-maintained gravel road—23 kilometers (14 miles) north.

## Where to Stay & Dine

✪ **Andries Stöckenstrom Guest House.** 100 Cradock St., Graaff-Reinet 6280. ☎/fax **0491/24-575** or 049/892-4575. 5 units. A/C. R300–360 ($50–$60) double. Rates include breakfast. AE, DC, MC, V.

Situated in a listed house erected in 1819, the rooms are tastefully decorated. Doors lead from numbers 1, 2, and 3 onto the front verandah and street, and number 5 is the largest and most comfortable. But the main reason to stay here is the food, which is on a par with the very best that Cape Town, South Africa's gourmet capital, has to offer. Beatrice is a self-taught chef, but her passion for the medium has rendered her a true artist. Representative of her creative spirit are an appetizer of smoked loin kudu salad or baked fig with gorgonzola; lightly curried sweet-potato soup with crumbed roasted almonds; and Karoo lamb or deboned quail for a main course. With any luck, dessert will feature the Rolls Royce of bread-and-butter pudding. Beatrice constantly

## Eyes of Glass & Wings of Cement—A Look into the World of Helen Martins

Helen Martins was born in the isolated community of Nieu Bethesda in 1897. After a brief marriage (she terminated two pregnancies, claiming that she was afraid that any children she bore would have horns and cloven hooves; an attitude which repulsed her husband), she returned to the family home to look after her sick, aged parents. In her late 40s after their deaths, she became obsessed with transforming the house into a world of her own making. This project was to absorb her for the next 30 years, totally isolating her from the conservative rural Karoo community, who witnessed in horror the mix of pagan and Biblical images that took over her home and garden.

The interior features large mirrors that maximize the light, and every conceivable surface is covered with finely crushed glass, with colors creating large patterns, including a favored sunbeam motif. No doubt this effectively warded off the long dark lonely nights—in the candlelight, the interior glitters like a jewel. On her porch she perched large cement owls with huge glittering eyes; by the time of her death, there were over 70 of these throughout the house and garden. Helped by her laborer Koos Malgas, and inspired by the words and images of a copy of the *The Rubaiyat of Omar Khayyam,* Helen Martins' inner vision spread into her backyard, eventually surrounding her in a private world of glittering peacocks, camels, mermaids, stars, shepherds, sphinxes, towers, and serpents. But the daily process of grinding glass to decorate her world started to take its toll on her eyesight and, when the thought of perpetual darkness became unbearable, she committed suicide by drinking caustic soda.

Immortalized in the award-winning play and movie *Road to Mecca* (starring Kathy Bates), the Owl House and Camel Yard is today a major source of pride to the Nieu Bethesda community, as one of the world's most inspiring examples of Outsider art. Informative tours are held from 9am to 5pm daily; admission is R7 ($1.15).

darts from the kitchen to ensure that her imaginative meals are to her guests' satisfaction, while Andre describes them seductively and discreetly keeps topping-off wine glasses. A truly marvelous find, and a great shame that there are only five rooms and tables—book early.

**Drosdty Hotel.** 30 Church St., Graaff-Reinet 6280. ☎ **0491/22-161** or 049/892-2161. Fax 0491/24-582 or 049/892-4582. A/C TV TEL. R445–595, ($74.15–$99.15) double. AE, DC, MC, V.

The original home and offices of Graaff-Reinet's first magistrate, this elegant Cape Dutch building is in the heart of the historical center. The gracious public spaces are tastefully furnished with antiques and period artworks, while the bedrooms are all situated in the adjacent Stretch's Court—a row of cottages formerly occupied by freed slaves and dating back to 1855. Most of the standard rooms are cramped and a few have damp walls, making a luxury suite well worth the extra R150 ($30). All the rooms in Ferreira House are charming, particularly F3, which has a fireplace and private garden, and F5, which is furnished in beautiful antiques. Family rooms are available on request. Light meals are served in the garden from 9am to 5pm (the Drosdty's chunky whole-wheat bread is unbeatable) or, in season, there are buffets in De Camdeboo restaurant. Dinner in the old courtroom is a romantic affair with soft light shed by candelabra containing over 144 candles. The seven-course meals feature traditional South African dishes such as *boontjiesop* (bean soup), *kerrievis* (curried fish), and Karoo lamb; R65 ($10.85) per person is very good value.

## 5 The Wild Coast

The northernmost section of the Eastern Cape stretches 280 kilometers (174 miles) from the Kei River in the south to the mouth of the Mtamvuna River, bordering KwaZulu-Natal. The coast is lush and largely uninhabited, with innumerable rivers spilling into large estuaries, waterfalls plunging directly into the ocean, coastal, dune, and mangrove forests, long sandy beaches, rocky coves, and a number of shipwrecks, all of which have earned it the name Wild Coast. This region was part of the former *bantustan* (homeland) Transkei, where any Xhosa that weren't of economic use to the Republic were dumped, and as such it has suffered from overgrazing and underdevelopment, and is one of the poorest areas in South Africa. The coast is difficult to access—dirt roads are pitted with deep potholes, there is virtually no public transport, and limited accommodation options. The only way to reach it is via the N2, which cuts through the middle of the hinterland, passing through valleys dotted with traditional Xhosa huts and the old Transkei capital of Umtata. From Umtata, one of the only two tarred roads leads to the coast, to the town of Port St Johns. The other, a turnoff some 20 kilometers (12 miles) prior to Umtata, leads to Coffee Bay, which is more or less in the center of the Wild Coast, and well set up for backpackers. With the roads to the five beautiful reserves that line the coast in disrepair, the best way to explore more than one area on the Wild Coast is to walk it.

### ESSENTIALS

**VISITOR INFORMATION** There is no central Tourism Bureau. For a Wild Coast Hiking Trail permit, write or fax the **Department of Economic Affairs, Environment and Tourism** (☎ **047/531-2711,** Private Bag X5029, Umtata 5100). Their hours are Monday to Friday 8am to 4:30pm. Make sure they then fax or post you the hiking map for general reference points.

**GETTING THERE** The N2 traverses the length of what used to be called the Transkei, with roads to the coast leading southeast off it. Most roads to the coast are untarred, some are badly marked, and all are time consuming. Beware of livestock on the road and don't travel at night. The best places to stay (see "Where to Stay & Dine") are close to KwaZulu-Natal. You can charter a flight to Umngazi River Bungalows, and the Wild Coast Sun is an easy 2-hour drive south of Durban.

**GETTING AROUND** Unless you're prepared for the unexpected, the best way to explore this coast is with a guide. **Footprints Adventures** (☎ **021/421-1554**) offers an excellent 7-day trail from Port St Johns to Hluleka; hikers are hosted in Xhosa villages along the way. This is one of the most unaffected cultural experiences available to visitors in South Africa. The cost is R1,850 ($308.35), including your transfer to and from Cape Town. Peter Sweeney (☎ **031/86-3292**) provides personalized hikes along the coast, including transfers from Durban. Alternatively, stay in one place—see "Where to Stay & Dine" below for the most comfortable options.

### WALKING THE WILD COAST

The **Wild Coast Hiking Trail** stretches from the Mtamvuna River in the north to the Kei River in the south, but it can be tackled in smaller sections: Umtamvuna to

## Some Wild Coast Hiking Pointers

Besides a tent, sleeping bag, and traveling stove, you should carry water purifiers, a first-aid box, and consider an air mattress, useful for floating your pack across the rivers. A tide table is also vital as you'll need to try to cross the rivers some 30 minutes after low tide—purchase an *Eastern Province Herald* prior to embarking on your journey. Don't swim in river mouths as this is where sharks tend to feed. You may be able to purchase fresh fish and lobster from the locals, but carry your own supplies in case. The trail itself is not well marked, but you won't get lost if you follow the coastline. The trail is not advised for women traveling alone.

Msikaba (3 days); Msikaba to Port St Johns (7 days); Port St Johns to Coffee Bay (6 days); Coffee Bay to Mbashe (5 days); and Mbashe to Kei (6 days). Of these, Port St Johns to Coffee Bay is the most popular walk; it's also worth noting that the walk gets easier the farther south you go. Accommodation is in basic huts (no flushing toilets) spaced some 12 kilometers (7½ miles) apart; but as there is often no communication between Umtata and the "caretakers" of these distant outposts, what you find is very much a matter of luck—be prepared to sleep under the stars.

## WHERE TO STAY & DINE

**The Wild Coast Sun Hotel and Gaming Resort.** P.O. Box 23, Port Edward 4295. ☎ **039/305-2866.** Fax 039/305-1012. 399 units. A/C TV TEL. R713 ($118.85), sea facing; R617 ($102.85), garden facing; children under 18 stay free. AE, DC, MC, V.

As it is situated on the border of KwaZulu-Natal, this is the most accessible hotel on the Wild Coast. Despite its rather tacky South Pacific theme, the resort has a lot going for it, not least its 18-hole championship golf course, designed by Robert Trent-Jones Jr., and rated as one of the best in South Africa. Thankfully day visitors—who arrive in their thousands to try their luck at the tables and slot machines—are kept totally separate from residents, who keep busy water-skiing, windsurfing, jet-skiing, canoeing, parasailing, surfing; playing tennis, volleyball, or squash; horseback riding, and 10-pin bowling. The children's games room is under the supervision of a qualified nursery school teacher. Rooms are relatively spacious and comfortable, if a bit tasteless, and are either sea facing or overlook the golf course. The surrounds are beautiful, and the range of activities make this an ideal family destination, tacked onto a visit to KwaZulu-Natal.

**Dining/Diversions:** There are a selection of bars, movies, and six restaurants to choose from. The Commodore is a plush old-style a la carte restaurant; Chico's serves large buffets including curries, stir fries, pizzas, and salads; the Driftwood Terrace, located on the pool deck, serves light lunches; Castaways serves fast food; and Indigo Café, in the casino, has light meals 24 hours a day.

✪ **Umngazi River Bungalows.** P.O. Box 75, Port St Johns 5120. ☎/fax **0475/64-1115.** 48 units. R400–550 ($66.65–$91.65) double; honeymoon suites R650–750 ($108.35–$125). Rates include all meals. AE, DC, MC, V.

If you want to get away from it all, and sample the subtropical pleasures of the Wild Coast without roughing it too much, this is the coast's finest and best value-for-money resort—you'll want to stay here for the duration of your holiday. Located just south of Port St Johns, Umngazi is situated in its own private nature reserve, overlooking a large estuary and deserted beach, and flanked by dense coastal vegetation. With a safe lagoon, boats and gillies for hire, river trips, skiing, snooker, a salt-water swimming pool, a host of baby-sitters, and a separate toddlers' dining room, it offers the perfect family holiday, yet the honeymoon bungalows are private enough for honeymooners to enjoy. (This is, in fact, where Nelson Mandela chose to spend his first Christmas with Graca). Bungalows are very basic, but feature coffee- and tea-making facilities, en-suite bathtubs, and outdoor showers from which you can watch the dolphins surfing—it's definitely worth requesting a sea-facing bungalow (Brazen Head and units 41 to 43 are choice).

**Dining:** Meals are large buffets featuring fresh salads, choices of fish, meat, and chicken, homemade breads, and cheese, all served in the large thatched dining room. Generally the service is good, though with English very much a second language, patience is, as always, a virtue.

6

# Gauteng & North-West Province

The landlocked provinces of Gauteng and North-West are on the highveld plains of South Africa, and share a common border, but there the similarity ends. While the North-West is characterized by the wide open spaces of great bushveld plains and endless maize fields, Gauteng, the country's smallest and most densely populated province, is typified by an ever-growing concrete sprawl.

Built both literally and figuratively on gold, Gauteng ("place of Gold" in the Sotho language) is the country's most powerful province. It comprises the Pretoria-Witwatersrand-Vaal triangle, a heavily industrialized region upon which three major cities are situated. In the north is Pretoria, currently the administrative capital of the country. Some 50 kilometers (31 miles) south is Johannesburg, the "gold capital of the world" and hub of Witwatersrand (meaning "white-water ridge"), a metropolis that stretches some 120 kilometers (74½ miles) across the province. Southwest is Soweto. Though often described as a township, it is actually a separate city inhabited by an estimated 2 to 4 million souls, almost all of whom are black, and most of whom are poor—an enduring legacy of the country's racist and separatist history.

Most leisure travelers use Gauteng as a gateway to the attractions in neighboring provinces. Of these, the North-West has the most easily accessed game reserves, with the additional benefit of being malaria-free. Pilanesberg Reserve, referred to as the "jewel of the North-West," is the closest. Adjoining is the voluptuous Palace of the Lost City.

## 1 Johannesburg

1,402km (234 miles) from Cape Town, 58km (36 miles) from Pretoria

The bushveld plains that remained unchanged for millions of years were irrevocably transformed when a prospector named George Harrison stumbled onto the richest gold reef in the world in 1886. Within 3 years, a nondescript part of the bleak highveld plains was transformed into the third-biggest city in South Africa, and soon Johannesburg, or "eGoli" as it came to be known, had grown into the largest city south of Cairo. The speed at which it grew was due in part to the power and greed of men such as Cecil Rhodes, whose diamond mines in Kimberley provided him with the capital to exploit the rich gold-bearing reefs of the Witwatersrand, and to the availability of cheap labor. Along with other "randlords," as the most powerful consortium of mining magnates were known, Rhodes founded the Chamber of Mines in 1889 which created common policies regarding recruitment, wages, and working conditions. In 1893 it institutionalized the colour bar, which ensured that black men could aspire to no more than manual labor.

By 1895, the ever-expanding mining settlement far outnumbered the original Boer settlers. Botha, president of the then South African Republic (ZAR), denied these *uitlanders* (foreigners) the vote, and refused to develop an infrastructure to support mining activities. Four years later, the ZAR and Britain went to war, and in 1902 Britain annexed the republic. The British Empire relinquished its hold in 1910 when the Union of South Africa was proclaimed, but for the millions of black migrant laborers who toiled below the earth, working conditions remained relentlessly harsh. By 1946 over 400,000 black people were residing in and around Jo'burg; in August that year, 70,000 African Mineworkers Union members went on strike over their living and working conditions—to no avail, despite the death of 12 men and injuries to over a thousand.

During the 1950's Johannesburg's uniquely black urban culture was given a name. "Kwela" had its own jazzy sounds, heard in the *shebeens* (drinking houses) of Sophiatown, and a slick sophisticated style, as evidenced in the pages of *Drum* magazine. But this was also the decade of forced removals, when thousands were dumped in new suburbs of Soweto, and a consequent growth phase for the African National Congress (ANC), who proclaimed their Freedom Charter—the basis of the current constitution—in 1955 in what is now known as Freedom Square (see "Soweto," below).

But it took another 2 decades before the black majority revolted. On June 16, 1976, police opened fire on a peaceful student demonstration in Soweto and sparked off a nationwide riot—South Africa's black youth had declared war on apartheid. Student activism escalated during the 1980s, and came to a head during the early 1990s, when political parties jostled for power after Mandela's release. Some townships were reduced to utter chaos, with a mysterious "third force" (thought to be state-funded) pouring fuel on the flames. Finally, the 1994 elections brought peace, and Jo'burgers returned to the pursuit of wealth.

However, for many, this has become an increasingly impossible goal. Even the mining industry is in trouble, with long-exploited workers demanding better wages while the gold price drops, and unemployment keeps rising. Crime has bred a culture of fear, and walled neighborhoods, burglar bars, and dogs are common sights. But Jo'burg is the original cultural melting pot, and for every person living in fear, there's another enjoying the New South Africa, finding the city more diverse, vibrant, and exhilarating than ever.

## ESSENTIALS

### ARRIVING

**BY PLANE** Most international flights to South Africa arrive in **Johannesburg International Airport** (☎ **011/975-9963**). **SATOUR** has a branch in the airport's International Arrivals hall (☎ **011/970-1669**), open 7am to 9pm daily; and foreign exchange is available 24 hours.

The airport is 20 kilometers (12 miles) from the city, and a 30–50-minute drive from the northern suburbs. Taxis queue directly outside the terminals—make sure to take a metered taxi. It will cost you about R120–140 ($20–$23.35) to get to Sandton. A cheaper option if you're traveling alone is the **Magic Bus Shuttle** (☎ **011/328-8092,** ticket desk in Terminal 3), which heads for the northern suburbs every 30 minutes, and costs R65 ($10.85) per person. They also offer an exclusive door-to-door transfer/ pick-up; price varies depending on where you're headed, but it's probably only worth it if you're in a group. The **Impala Bus** service (☎ **011/333-3813**), running Monday to Friday and Sunday 5:30am to 10pm, and Saturday 5:30am to 7pm, will drop you off at the Rotunda Building (see "By Train," below) for R40 ($6.65) per person.

**BY TRAIN** Given time there's nothing better than trundling around the country by train, particularly in the legendary **Blue Train** (☎ **011/773-7631**) or the equally luxurious **Rovos Rail** (☎ **012/323-6052** in Cape Town). Both roll in to Johannesburg from Cape Town and Victoria Falls and points adjoining the Kruger; Rovos also operate between Johannesburg and Windhoek (capital of Namibia). However, as all trains arrive at the **Rotunda Terminal** in Braamfontein (☎ **011/725-6431,** at the corner of Rissik and Wolmarans sts.), which is considered a dangerous area, you're better off disembarking in Pretoria. For schedule information on other trains, contact **Main Line Passenger Services** (☎ **011/773-3994**). If you do alight at the Rotunda Terminal, you'll want to get your luggage into a taxi ASAP—Observatory and Melville are relatively close (see "Where to Stay").

**BY CAR** The N1 connects Cape Town with Johannesburg (see box for route tips). Durban is connected to Johannesburg via the N3.

**BY BUS** The intercity buses **Greyhound, Intercape,** and **Translux** (see chapter 2, "Planning Your Trip to Southern Africa" for numbers), all arrive at Park City, next to the Rotunda Terminal. This is an unsavory area, so you may be better off traveling to Pretoria, or hopping in a taxi immediately upon arrival.

### Visitor Information

**Tourism Johannesburg** currently has two offices: one in the center of town, on the 46th floor in the Carlton Towers, Commissioner Street (☎ **011/331-2041**). Hours are Monday to Friday 8:30am to 5pm and Saturday 9am to 12pm. More convenient if you're not venturing into the city is the **satellite office** at Sandton Village Walk, 1st floor (☎ **011/883-4033**). Hours are Monday to Thursday 8:30am to 4:30pm; Friday 8:30am to 4pm; Saturday 9am to 6pm; and Sunday 9am to noon. It's worth picking up a free copy of *Gauteng—The Gateway Province,* which details most of the city's attractions, and has a map of the city and surrounding suburbs—this should suffice if you're only here for a few days.

### Staying Safe

Inevitably, with the promised redistribution of wealth taking a little longer than many expected, the city has become a hothouse for those who have realized that the easiest way to make it is to take it. Carjackings are common; while driving around the city, keep your car doors locked and windows up, regardless of where you are. Though you can be carjacked anywhere, it is more likely to happen in less-populated places, which means locals rather than tourists are targeted. Be aware that should you feel uncomfortable with the situation around you, you are allowed—carefully, of course—to cross against a red light.

Generally speaking, inconspicuous consumption is the order of the day: People who have nothing worth stealing will not be bothered. Make sure you're not carrying anything of obvious value if you're exploring the central business district, Braamfontein, Newtown, Joubert Park, Hillbrow, or Berea (though some say it's worth carrying a small sum of cash to satisfy a demand), and don't look lost. Go into a store if you need to look at a map. If you are ever mugged, don't protest. Just hand over the goods or money and walk away.

**Gone, but Not Forgotten**

Sophiatown, once one of the most vibrant black suburbs (near Melville) was razed to the ground in the 1950s, and ironically renamed *Triomf* (or "triumph"). You can get some sense of what was lost through **Museum Africa's** displays, which include a re-created shebeen (see below).

If this sort of talk makes you nervous, make sure you see the more interesting sites with a guide familiar with the rhythms of the city. Alternatively, book into one of the places recommended below and spend a quiet evening sampling the restaurants in the area.

### City Layout

In the unlikely event that you should want to drive into the city center, get onto the M1, follow the M2 East/City signs, take the Rissik Street turnoff, continue along Rissik, and turn left into Marshall, where you'll see the parking sign for the Carlton Towers. On the northern outskirts of the CBD lie the **inner-city suburbs** of **Joubert Park, Hillbrow,** and **Berea**—do not venture into the latter two areas alone. North of Joubert Park is **Braamfontein,** a business district where the Gertrude Posel Gallery and Rotunda are located. East of town lie the residential suburbs of **Yeoville, Observatory, Bez Valley,** and **Troyville.** Northwest of town lie **Auckland Park,** where the South African Broadcasting Corporation's (SABC) headquarters is situated, and the hilly suburb of **Melville.** Moving in a northerly direction from Braamfontein are the **suburbs** of Parktown, Houghton, Saxonwold, Norwood, Rosebank, Hyde Park, Sandton, Morningside, and Bryanston.

The most important arterial road is the **M1,** which connects the center with the northern suburbs, and eventually meets up with the N3 (from KwaZulu-Natal) and becomes the N1, continuing to Pretoria. Travel south on the M1 past the city and you will reach **Gold Reef City** and **Soweto** (the only reasons to venture south of the city center). If you're traveling between the northern suburbs, you might want to use **Oxford Road,** a major artery that starts in Parktown and goes all the way to Sandton, where it becomes Rivonia Road. Oxford/Rivonia Road lies just west of the M1.

## Neighborhoods in Brief

**City Center** The streets of the town center (which includes **Newtown** on the northwestern outskirts) and the surrounding inner-city suburbs (**Joubert Park, Hillbrow,** and **Berea**) are lined with soaring skyscrapers and crowded with traders. They are a great deal more lively than those elsewhere in the city, but they are also more dangerous. Unless you're accompanied by a guide, you're safer getting a feel for Johannesburg in the slightly less edgy suburb of Yeoville in the eastern suburbs.

If you do head into town, **Diagonal Street,** where you'll find the old beacon marking the southwest corner of the original farm that Johannesburg was built on, is one of the city's most fascinating. Here *sangomas* (traditional healers) selling herbs, bark, and pungent animal bits from the traditional medicine (*muti*) shops, rub shoulders with the suits working on the **Johannesburg Stock Exchange** at 17 Diagonal St. However, the JSE is relocating to the northern suburbs in August 2000, following the trend started by big business in the late 1980s.

The city center's most interesting sights (see "Top Attractions," below) are reasonably safe to visit on your own—the **Johannesburg Art Gallery** has secure parking, and the **Newtown Cultural Precinct,** comprising the Market Theatre, Museum Africa, Kippies jazz club, Gramadoelas African restaurant, the Saturday market, and numerous gallery and performance spaces, has four to five uniformed guards patrolling the area; but be on your guard and don't carry any obviously valuable items with you.

**The Eastern Suburbs** **Yeoville,** east of Berea, has a stronger sense of community than Hillbrow, and is less menacing than the inner-city. With a lower incidence of crime than neighboring Berea and Hillbrow, visitors should feel reasonably safe, provided they don't venture down a side alley for a *tete-a-tete* with one of the many drug dealers pushing their wares. It's possible to explore this area on your own (given the now-repetitive litany, no obvious valuables). Rockey Street, which is lined with bars, clubs, and cafes, has always been one of the city's great places to hang out, but is now becoming seedy. A little farther east is **Observatory,** a quiet area with large houses, some with views (a real luxury in Johannesburg), and a good place to base yourself if you're keen to confront the "real" Johannesburg.

Farther east are **Troyville** and **Bez Valley,** patches of which are slowly being gentrified by the more creative Jo'burgers bored by the soulless northern suburbs and unable to afford Melville.

**The Northern Suburbs** The city center has effectively relocated to the northern suburbs, and you'll find the greatest concentration of hotels, restaurants, and shopping malls here. Locals hang out in the bars and restaurants peppered throughout Parktown, Rosebank, Sandton, and Norwood, and you'll probably find yourself both sleeping and dining in these safer havens as well.

The northern suburb closest to the city is **Parktown,** where the rand lords built their Edwardian mansions. Though this area has largely been destroyed, it is still well worth exploring, particularly for those interested in the architecture of Sir Herbert Baker (see "Guided Tours," below). If you want to drive around on your own, make sure you check out Ridge Road, Jubilee Road, and Rock Ridge Road.

North of Parktown is **Houghton,** a gracious well-established suburb and where Mandela stays when he's in town. Next up is **Saxonwold,** then **Rosebank, Hyde Park,** and **Sandton,** where you'll find the best shopping malls, fortress-like homes and hotels, and a consequently dull street life.

**The Northwestern Suburbs** For a more lively option that's still safer than Rockey Street, head for **Melville,** northwest of Parktown, and no more than a 15 to 20 minute drive south from Sandton.

Adjoining Auckland Park, which is where the SABC (South African Broadcasting Corporation) and RAU (Rand Afrikaans University) are located, Melville has a bohemian mix of residents, including actors, artists, producers, lecturers, architects, and film crew. Considered one of the city's most colorful suburbs, Melville has the added attraction of an adjoining reserve. The **Melville Koppies** (hillocks) **Nature Reserve** (☎ **011/782-7064**) contains remains of both Stone- and Iron Age settlements, which can be seen viewed every third Sunday from September to May, and the **Johannesburg Botanic Gardens** lies in its northeast corner. Come here to drink coffee, play backgammon, dine at one of the many restaurants, or catch the latest jazz act at one of the venues on 7th Street.

## Getting Around

**BY CAR** Like the rest of South Africa, public transport can be unreliable, inflexible, and, after hours, nonexistent. Unless you plan on using a tour operator, Johannesburg

# Greater Johannesburg

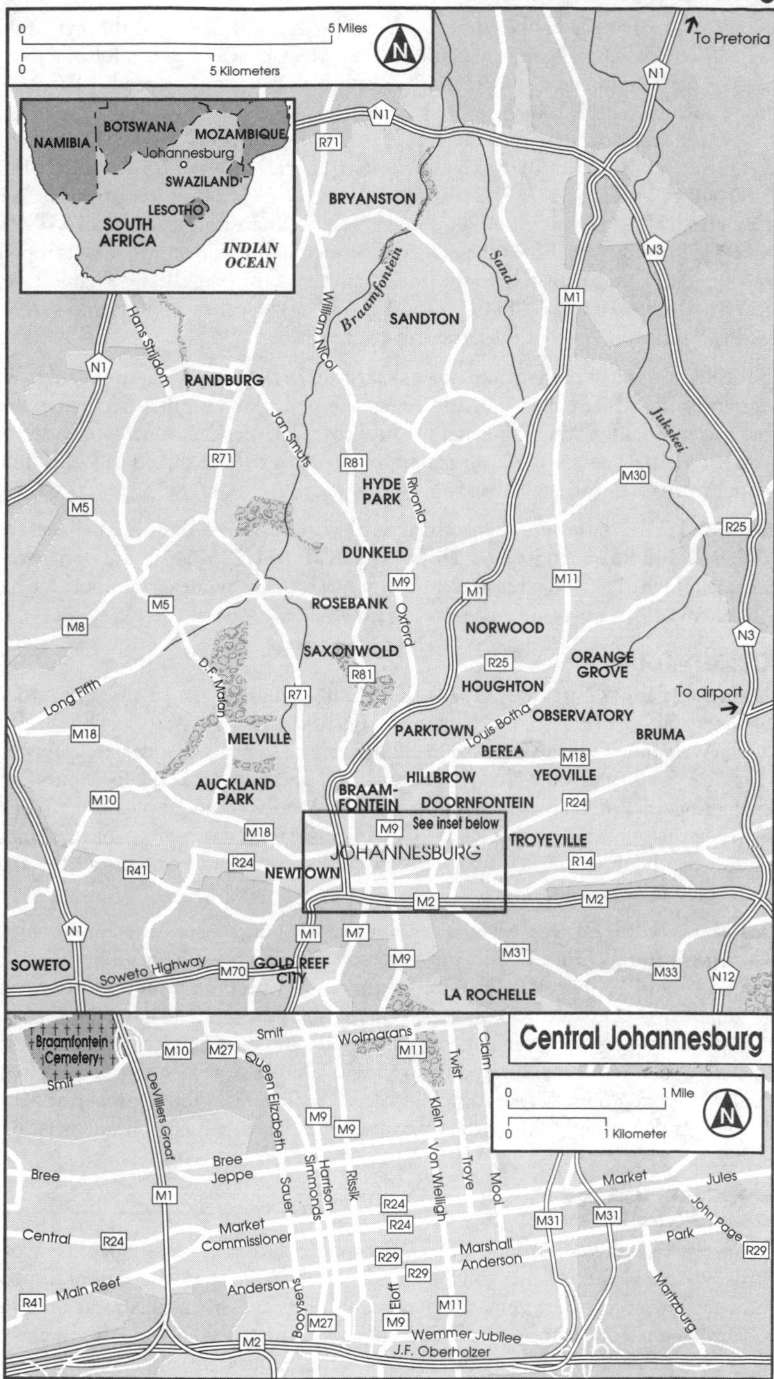

is best explored by car, but be warned: Jo'burg drivers are aggressive, as the myriad skid-marks on the roads will attest, and you will need a map (see "Tourism Johannesburg," above); or if you intend staying for a while, its worth investing in a good *A-Z* (see "Fast Facts: Johannesburg", below).

You can rent a car from **Avis** (☎ **011/974-2571**), **Hertz** (☎ **0800/211-0645** toll-free), **Budget** (☎ **0800/01-6622** toll-free or 011/392-3929) or **Imperial** (☎ **0800/13-1000** toll-free or 011/337-2300), all of which have desks in the airport. **Cheap Car Hire** (☎ **011/648-7300,** 206 Francis St. E, Observatory), and **Apex** (☎ **011/402-5150,** 13 Siemert Rd. at the corner of Siemert and President rds., Doornfontein) offer budget options that have the added advantage of being less desirable to car-jackers. **Britz:Africa** (☎ **0800/11-7660** toll-free) specializes in 4×4s and campers, and will pick you up from the airport in your vehicle.

**Parking** If you're driving into town, **Carlton Towers** has a parking garage with entrances from Marshall, Main, and Kruis streets. Parking on the street is unsafe in town, but shouldn't be a problem in the suburbs recommended below—provided that you *never leave anything in the car in open view;* even a sweater should be locked in the boot. Most hotels offer valet parking.

**BY TAXI** You have to call for a taxi as they don't cruise the streets. **Roses Taxi** (☎ **011/403-9625**) and **Good Hope Taxis** (☎ **011/725-6431**) are both recommended. Don't be tempted to travel by minibus taxi, the mode of transport for most South Africans. At best, it's a hair-raising experience.

### GUIDED TOURS

**Dumela Africa** (☎ **011/837-9928**) runs minibus tours of the city, Gold Reef City, Soweto, and Pretoria (also Sun City, see "Side Trips to North-West Province" below), as do **Welcome Tours** (☎ **011/328-8050**), who also cover Lesedi (see again "Side Trips to North-West Province"). Welcome also goes farther afield to Mpumalanga (including the Panorama Route and Kruger), and to KwaZulu-Natal and the Western Cape destinations. **Springbok Atlas** (☎ **011/396-1053;** www.springbokatlas.co.za/), one of South Africa's biggest and longest-running operators, conducts all the above tours (and more) in large coaches.

**MINE TOURS** If you want to get under Jo'burg's skin—literally—book an ✪ **Operational Mine Visit,** through the Chamber of Mines. Betty Goldie (☎ **011/498-7100**) negotiates a roster of mine visits with the Chamber of Mines every 6 months. As tours are very inconvenient to the mines, try to give Betty at least 1 month's warning. Tours are physically strenuous, and can be psychologically stressful as well; under no circumstances attempt one if you are at all claustrophobic. No one under 16 or over 60 may take part. Tours depart at 7am from the **Chamber of Mines,** located on the corner of Marshall and Sauer streets (or, depending on numbers, Betty

**Survey Says...**

Interestingly, a recent nationwide opinion poll conducted by Independent Newspaper Group and Henry J. Kaiser Family Foundation, USA, with assistance from the *Washington Post,* reports that despite high crime levels, Gauteng residents are the most satisfied citizens in South Africa. This is in stark contrast to the Western Cape, where despite people being by far the best-off in the country (that is, most likely to be employed, educated, fed, have their rubbish removed regularly, and so on), they are the most unhappy with their lot and very dissatisfied with local and national government.

may do a Sandton pick-up). After a brief operational and geological overview of the mine in question, visitors are supplied with full underground gear. Keep in mind that conditions 2 kilometers (just over a mile) below the surface of the earth are humid and hot, and rock temperatures in working mines can reach 55°C (131°F). Even though refrigerated air is pumped through, air temperatures can exceed 32°C (90°F). After a 1–2-hour tour, visitors return to the shaft, shower (towels and toiletries are supplied), watch a gold pour, and, time allowing, visit a miners' hostel. The tour often ends with drinks and lunch, hosted by the mine's management, and costs R250–300 ($41.65–$50) per person.

If all this sounds too daunting, visit the mine at Gold Reef City, or take a **Cullinan Diamond Tour,** which doesn't go underground and is also easier to arrange (see "Pretoria").

**JEWELRY TOURS** Through **Schwartz Jewellers (☎ 011/483-1500)**, you can take a morning or afternoon jeweler's workshop tour (R80/$13.35), and watch over 20 artists creating expensive baubles, or take a full-day tour including a visit to the diamond-cutting workshop where you can witness the transformation from dull pebble to girl's best friend. If it's the latter incarnation that really fascinates you, contact the **Johan Erikson Diamond Centre (☎ 011/970-1369)**, which has a diamond museum.

**ARCHITECTURE TOURS** If your interest is architecture, don't miss a chance to view the Edwardian mansions of Parktown and Westcliff—the very first garden suburbs created by the rand lords at the turn of the century. Contact the **Parktown and Westcliff Heritage Trust (☎ 011/482-3349,** open Monday to Friday 9am to 1pm), to arrange a guided walking or bus tour (R30/$5 per person).

**INNER-CITY TOURS** In the early 1970s, the inner-city suburb of Hillbrow was the cosmopolitan center of South Africa. European immigrants crowded into its high-rise apartment blocks, creating numerous ethnic restaurants, cafes, and shops. The Ponti—the round tower block seen from most areas surrounding the city—had just been completed, and its fur-lined penthouse apartments were the hippest address in the city. Today, despite a murder rate which is the third highest in the country, the hubbub of these lively streets can be a heady experience—particularly when contrasted with the culturally numbing malls of the northern suburbs. To explore you'll need to be accompanied by someone fully familiar with the wild life. Contact Peter Kirchhoff, who owns **Explorers Club (☎ 011/648-7138,** R140/$23.35 double), a guest house in Observatory. Peter offers guided clubbing trips to Hillbrow, his stomping ground, as well as downtown tours.

### Special Events

The city's biggest festival for the performing arts, **Arts Alive (☎ 011/838-6407)**, takes place over 2 weeks in September. The "Jazz on the Lake," which takes place on Zoo Lake (opposite the Zoo), is worth checking out as it often features some of South Africa's best talent. The **Johannesburg Biennale** is an internationally curated exhibition of contemporary arts held at the end of every odd-numbered year (that is, the next one begins October 1999 and ends January 2000). Most of the venues are in the Newtown Cultural Precinct. For more information, call **☎ 011/838-4563.**

## Fast Facts: Johannesburg

**Airport** See "Arriving" earlier in this chapter.

**American Express** There's a branch at Admirals Court, Tyrwhitt Avenue, Rosebank (**☎ 011/880-8382**). Hours are Monday to Friday 8:30am to 4pm, and Saturday 9am to 12pm. For lost or stolen cards, call ☎ **011/359-0111** and ask for the card division.

**Area Code** Johannesburg's area code is **011.**

**Car Rentals** See "Getting Around" earlier in this chapter.

**Climate** See "When to Go" in chapter 2.

**Drugstores** Drugstores are known as chemists or pharmacies in South Africa. Contact **Mediside Dispensary** (☎ **011/883-0322**) from 9am to 9pm daily, or **Daylight Pharmacy** (☎ **011/883-7520**) 8:30am to 8pm daily. (Both are in Sandton). Contact **Morningside Clinic** (☎ **011/783-8901**), off Rivonia Road for 24-hour dispensing emergencies (see below).

**Embassies & Consulates** Note that all embassies are in Pretoria (see below). **Australia,** 292 Orient St., Arcadia (☎ **012/342-3740**); **Canada,** 1103 Arcadia St., Hatfield (☎ **012/342-6923**); **Ireland,** Tulbagh Park 1234 Church St., Colbyn (☎ **012/342-5062**); **United Kingdom,** 255 Hill St., Arcadia (☎ **012/43-3121**); and **United States,** 877 Pretorius St., Arcadia (☎ **012/343-1048**).

**Emergencies** Dial ☎ **10111** for flying-squad police, or ☎ **999** for an ambulance. For car breakdowns, call the **Automobile Association** toll-free at ☎ **0800/01-0101.** In case of fire, call ☎ **011/883-2800** or **011/624-2800.**

**Hospitals** Hospitals with 24-hour emergency rooms include **Johannesburg Hospital** (☎ **011/488-4911**) in Parktown, and **JG Strijdom** (☎ **011/489-1011**) in Auckland Park. The best private option is **Morningside Clinic** (☎ **011/783-8901**), off Rivonia Road.

**Maps** You'll find an array of options at **CNA newsagents.** The *Witwatersrand Street Guide* is the most comprehensive.

**Newspapers/Magazines** Good dailies include *The Star* and *The Sowetan.* The weekly *Mail & Guardian* is published every Friday and offers an excellent overview of national events and listings. *South African City Life* magazine covers events in Johannesburg, Cape Town, and Durban as well as interesting urban issues. You can purchase these at local newsagents. **Exclusive Books** is a good national chain of bookstores; branches can be found in the malls of Hyde Park (☎ **011/788-0998**) and Sandton (☎ **011/883-1010**).

**Post Office** There are additional locations in most suburbs; ask at your hotel. The main Post Office is in an impressive neo-Baroque building dating back to 1897, on the corner of Market and Rissik streets, in the CBD. Hours are Monday to Friday 8am to 4:30pm and Saturday 8am to 12pm.

## WHERE TO STAY

The following options are in areas where you'll be perfectly safe, and relatively close to good restaurants and shops. All can provide shuttle service to and from the airport, which is 25–35 kilometers (15–20 miles) away, or about a 30–40 minute drive. Due to its crime problems, Johannesburg is not a popular leisure destination, and hotels generally cater to businessmen.

### NORTHERN SUBURBS

#### Very Expensive

**The Michaelangelo.** Off Sandton Square, (no street number) West St., Sandton 2146. ☎ **011/282-7000.** Fax 011/282-7171. E-mail: hrmichel@stocks.co.za. www.stockshotel.com. 242 units. A/C MINIBAR TV TEL. R1,280 ($213.35) double; R2,540–4,425 ($423.35–$737.50) suite. One child sharing stays free. AE, DC, MC, V.

A member of The Leading Hotels of the World, the Michaelangelo was voted Best Individual Hotel by the retail trade within weeks of its opening in 1997. As an extension of the Italian-styled Sandton Square (which incidentally means immediate access to restaurants, shops, banks, salons, bookshops, and drugstores), the Michaelangelo is rather like an impenetrable fort. The luxurious rooms are constructed on split levels, affording a generous floor-to-ceiling space. Elegant touches, like the single rose on the sink in the marble bathroom, ensure that the experience is sumptuous. Walls are a tad too thin, so ask for a room far from the elevator bell and one that overlooks Sandton Square's beautifully proportioned piazza.

**Dining/Diversions:** Situated in the Michaelangelo's spectacular atrium, the domed Il Ritrovo Cocktail Bar and Lounge is an elegant place to unwind, and Le Salon De Champagne gives connoisseurs an opportunity to enjoy great champagnes by the glass or bottle. Meals are served at Piccolo Mondo (see "Where to Dine").

**Amenities:** Indoor heated pool with small sun deck, health club with sauna, steam bath, and two personal trainers, laundry, valet parking, car-rental, VIP limousine, and helicopter service, concierge, 24-hour room service, babysitting, in-house nurse. All rooms equipped with safe, hair dryer, and trouser press.

**The Park Hyatt.** 191 Oxford Rd., Rosebank 2196. ☎ **800/233-1234** (in the United States) or 011/280-1234. Fax 011/280-1238. E-mail: parkhyatt@hyatt.ibmmail.com. www.hyatt.com. 244 units. A/C MINIBAR TV TEL. R1,150 ($191.65) double; R1,700–3,800 ($283.35–$633.35) suite. A child sharing stays free. Call reservations to find out about discounts. AE, DC, MC, V.

The Park Hyatt caused quite a stir when it was completed in the early 1990s. Locals considered it a cold, hard-edged, modern monstrosity, but the architects defended the hotel, calling it both a reflection and celebration of Johannesburg. Needless to say, the two opinions are not mutually exclusive. Certainly the Park Hyatt is the ideal businessman's hotel, with many a deal made in its Conservatory and Regency Club Lounge (both serve a mean cappuccino). Rooms are comfortable and spacious, combining ethnic pieces (like bushman-inspired lamp-fittings) with modern finishes. Beds are made up with comforters, which is unusual for a South African hotel. Somehow the attempt to capture the "spirit of modern-day Africa" seems forced, but perhaps this, too, epitomizes the dynamics of business in Johannesburg. Bathrooms are not quite as over-the-top as the Michaelangelo, but gleaming black granite creates a highly polished, slick effect. It's almost worth staying at the Hyatt to order room service; your table is wheeled in, replete with flowers and white linen, and excellent food from No 191 (see below). Ask for a room that faces west so that you can experience a spectacular highveld sunset.

**Dining/Diversions:** You can enjoy a selection of cakes, coffee and canapés in the Conservatory or at the Regency Club Lounge, which offers panoramic views of the city's tree-lined horizon and the best burgers in town. Jabulani is the cocktail and wine bar, and No 191, a large double-volume space well decorated with leather chairs, is renowned for its excellent cuisine.

**Amenities:** Rooftop pool, health club with fully equipped gym, saunas, steambaths, personal trainers, and beauty therapists, laundry, 24-hour room service, baby-sitting, free newspapers. All rooms equipped with safe and hair dryer.

✪ **The Westcliff.** 67 Jan Smuts Ave., Westcliff 2193. ☎ **800/237-1236** (in the United States) or 011/646-2400. Fax 011/646-3500. E-mail: wstcliff@africa.com. www.orient-expresshotels.com. 120 units. A/C MINIBAR TV TEL. R1,250–1,430 ($208.35–$238.35) double; R1,600–3,600 ($266.65–$600) suite. Children 12–18 pay 50%.

Clinging to the steep incline of Westcliff ridge, this exclusive hillside "village" is another of The Leading Hotels of the World. Opened by the Orient-Express group in

March 1998, the hotel is still experiencing some teething problems, but is positioned to be Johannesburg's premier hotel destination for the well-heeled leisure traveler. Accommodation options vary considerably as each room is totally uniquely positioned and sized. All are tastefully furnished, and the bathrooms are the best in the country. If you can't book a room with a view, preferably with a balcony, it's hardly worth staying—looking at a courtyard when you could be gazing out over the green gardens of the Jo'burg Zoo, all the way to the Magaliesberg mountains—will only ruin your stay. Ironically, its biggest drawback arises from its excellent cliffside location; in a rather unwieldy arrangement, cars are left at reception and guests are transported by buggies that ceaselessly traverse the streets. Ask for a unit in Villa 4, appropriately named "Cliffside," which leads into the restaurant (unit 401 leads directly to the pool), or one in 6, 7, and 9, which are close to reception.

**Dining/Diversions:** Breakfast and lunch are served in The Loggia, and dinner in La Belle Terasse. Both offer spectacular views and Northern Mediterranean fare. Afternoon tea and drinks are served in the Polo Lounge Bar and Terrace. Furnished like an gentleman's club, it has a roaring log fire in the winter.

**Amenities:** Two large heated swimming pools, tennis court with resident coach, gym, health and beauty center, golfers enjoy full membership facilities of a nearby club, complimentary shuttle to the shopping districts of Sandton, Hyde Park, and Rosebank; laundry, VIP limousine service, 24-hour room service, newspaper delivery, including *The New York Times* by fax; babysitting. All rooms equipped with VCR, safe, and hair dryer.

### Expensive

✪ **The Grace.** 54 Bath Ave., Rosebank 2196. ☎ **011/280-7200,** or 011/280-7300. Fax 011/280-7474. E-mail: graceres@grace.co.za. www.grace.co.za. 75 units. A/C MINIBAR TV TEL. R990 ($165) double; R1,350–1,950 ($225–$325) suite. No charge for child sharing suite. Call for discounts. AE, DC, MC, V.

Devised as a more intimate alternative to the large city hotel, the family-owned Grace is a gracious residence that feels more like a London gentleman's club than a 75-roomed hotel. In stark contrast to the brutal Hyatt, the Grace is designed to human scale and furnished and finished in the traditional English style. Wood paneling, floral brocades, generous sofas, gold-framed paintings, and well-thumbed books make one feel totally at home in this serene atmosphere. The Grace is also generous, offering everything from complimentary sherry on arrival, to a selection of complimentary teas, coffee, and cakes (a slice of their "melktert," a traditional Afrikaans dessert, is a must) to sample when sinking into a comfortable sofa to read the dailies or books from their ample collection. Fresh milk is supplied with your in-room tea- and coffee-making facilities, and rooms are large and comfortable, with large, luxurious bathrooms. All rooms equipped with safes and hair dryers. The hotel is within walking distance of Rosebank's boutiques, galleries, and art cinemas. The service too is excellent—gracious and personal but unobtrusive, the staff do their utmost to ensure your complete comfort.

**Amenities:** A 25-meter (82-foot) lap pool, croquet lawn, access to Health & Racquet Club, exercise equipment, library, wine cellar, same-day laundry, car rental, VIP limousine, activity desk, 24-hour room service, baby-sitting, newspaper delivery, secure parking facilities.

### Moderate

**10-2nd Avenue.** P.O. Box 2254, Houghton 2041. ☎ **011/483-3037/8/9.** Fax 011/483-3051. E-mail: 10_2nd@global.co.za. 12 units. TV TEL. R760–960 ($126.65–$160), including breakfast. AE, DC, MC, V. Secure parking provided.

At the beginning of each episode of *Egoli,* South Africa's favorite soap opera, the camera sweeps up a driveway to settle on the facade of its most famous house: 10-2nd Avenue, home of the wealthy Vorsters who star in the series. When it's not providing viewers with a glimpse of how the well-to-do live, 10-2nd Avenue serves as an extremely comfortable guest house, located in one of the city's oldest, most gracious suburbs. It's worth asking for one of the luxury double rooms with balcony and view of the well-established garden (though once again, you could be staying at the Grace for this money). Facilities include a tennis court and room service; every room has a hair dryer. A Bentley, Rolls-Royce, and stretch limo are on call for tours and excursions of your choice (10-2nd Ave is 10 minutes from Sandton; golf course, gymnasium, and sports club are within 1 km/just over a half mile). Lunch and dinner are served by prior arrangement.

## Eastern Suburbs (Observatory)

### Inexpensive

✪ **The Cottages.** 30 Gill St., Observatory 2198. ☎ **011/487-2829** or 011/648-4279. Fax 011/487-2404. 13 units. TV TEL. R320–400 ($53.35–$66.65) double, including breakfast. Children R100 ($16.65). AE, DC, MC, V. Secure parking provided.

If The Westcliff is a Mediterranean village, the Cottages are its English counterpart. Set at the end of a gravel drive, in luxuriant well-established gardens that cling to the Observatory ridge, these 13 stone-and-thatch cottages epitomize charm. Each cottage is totally unique, featuring either a fireplace (Hideaway), self-catering facilities (Poolview), great garden views (Fisherman's View), or sweeping views of the suburb (Treetops and Rooftops) or of the ridge (Mountain View). All have private garden areas. Many guests stay for months (Owl View, with a large private garden, is great for this), which gives one some idea of how popular the Cottages are. Breakfast is served in the garden or in the main house, which dates back to the early 19th century. Activities include a rock pool, walking in the 1-hectare (2½-acre) English garden which attracts a wonderful birdlife as well as tackling the adjoining hiking trail to the top of Observatory Ridge. Extra facilities are the complimentary evening newspaper delivery, laundry service, and dinners, served only by prior arrangement (from R50/$8.65). Each room has coffee- and tea-making facilities, and hair dryers are available on request.

## Northwestern Suburbs (Melville)

### Inexpensive

**Melville Manor Guest House.** 80 Second Ave., Melville 2092. ☎/fax **011/726-8765.** 7 units, 2 with no bath. R260 ($43.35) (shared bath); R305 ($50.85). Rates includes breakfast. AE, DC, MC, V. No children under 12.

Melville Manor, an unassuming guest house in all but name, is perfectly positioned for exploring Melville's nightlife on foot. A few blocks away lies 7th Street, renowned for its vibrant street life and excellent bars, galleries, cafes, shops, and restaurants (check out Sam's Café and Bassline, which are written up below). Rooms are simply furnished, carpeted, and comfortable; the best options are numbers 6 and 7, which have their own entrances leading from the pool area. Facilities include a laundry service and telephone and fax access. There is limited off-street parking.

## Near the Airport

### Inexpensive

**Johannesburg International Airport City Lodge.** Sandvale Rd., Edenvale. ☎ **011/392-1750.** Fax 011/392-2644. E-mail: CL_JhbAirport@citylodge.co.za. 160 units. A/C TV TEL. R330 ($55) double; children under 18 stay free. AE, DC, MC, V.

A Select Services hotel, the City Lodge is a functional option if you're concerned about catching an early flight; though bear in mind that Johannesburg's northern suburbs and Pretoria offer much nicer options and are only a 30-minute drive. However, if a half hour extra shut eye means more, or you've spent all your rand, this is your place. It's a mere 4 kilometers (2½ miles) from the airport, with a shuttle every 20 minutes or on request for R12 ($2) per person. Rooms are comfortable and fully carpeted; a sofa-bed is available on request. Amenities include a pool, in-room tea- and coffee-making facilities, 24-hour reception, and same-day laundry.

## WHERE TO DINE

At last count there were over 2,000 restaurants in Gauteng, most of them in Johannesburg. Just about every national cuisine is represented; so if you have a particular craving, simply ask your concierge or host to point you in the right direction. Alternatively, take your pick from the following, located within reasonable distance from the above accommodations, with the exception of the City Lodge. If you like browsing for your dinner, head for Melville's 7th Street, lined with a large choice of restaurants, and take your pick. If nothing appeals, wander down 4th Avenue and 3rd Avenue (perpendicular to 7th Street), which features amongst others the busy **Hard Times Café** (☎ **011/726-2012**) and the recommended **Pomegranate** (☎ **011/482-2366**).

### NORTHERN SUBURBS

#### Expensive

**✪ The Butcher Shop & Grill.** Shop 30, Sandton Square (under the Michaelangelo Hotel). ☎ **011/784-8676.** Reservations required. Main courses R45 ($7.50). AE, DC, MC, V. Mon–Thurs 12–11pm, Fri–Sat 12–11:30pm, Sun 12–10pm. No children under 14. GRILLHOUSE.

According to Alan Pick, who grew up in his parent's Cape Town butcher's shop, "the only vegetarians you'll find in my shop are in the fridge." Alan specializes in—you guessed it—South African meat, generally considered some of the best in the world. Only "super aged" meat is used (that is, carcasses are hung for 3 days, after which time the rump, fillet, and sirloin are "wet aged" for periods varying from 10 days to 2 weeks, and T-bones are "dry aged"). Also available is a daily game dish, which could be ostrich, or an antelope like kudu or springbok. Salads, open sandwiches, and hot dishes are also served.

**Le Canard.** 163 Rivonia Rd., Sandton. ☎ **011/884-4597.** Reservations recommended. Main courses R50–100 ($8.35–$16.65), three-course set-price lunch menu R75 ($12.50). AE, DC, MC, V. Mon–Fri 12:30–2pm, Mon–Sat 7–9:30pm. FRENCH/INTERNATIONAL.

Another consistently good restaurateur is chef-patronne Freda Appelbaum. Her award-winning restaurant, in a Georgian house nestled in a tranquil garden, is reached by driving up a long panhandle that insulates it from Sandton's hubbub. Maitres d'Hotel Chet and Raphael, aided by their experienced team of waiters, ensure excellent service, while Freda produces her classic French sauces—wine, apple, and chestnut for venison, a duet of rosemary and raspberry for flambéed lamb medallions, Pernod for frogs' legs, and fruit and liqueur for the signature duck. The three-course set luncheon menu, which is served on the garden terrace, is highly recommended.

**Leipolds.** Pavilion Shopping Center, Rivonia Rd., Morningside, Sandton. ☎ **011/804-7055.** Reservations recommended. Set-price buffet R59 ($9.85); R72 ($12) with dessert. AE, DC, MC, V. Mon–Fri 12pm until patrons are satisfied. Mon–Sat 7–10:30pm. SOUTH AFRICAN.

If you don't want to venture as far afield as the city center, traditional South African fare is now available in Sandton. Leipolds moved to their new venue 2 years ago and are still serving up a staggering buffet. Their specialty is Cape Malay food like *snoek sambal* (a fish starter), *bobotie* (a mildly spiced curry topped with egg), *waterblommetjie* (water lily) soup, ostrich casserole, and of course the ubiquitous Cape brandy pudding. The buffet allows you to sample a large variety of dishes; try the *mampoer,* a strong white spirit traditionally distilled from peaches, only if you have nothing to do for the rest of the day.

**Linger Longer.** 58 Wierda Rd. W, Wierda Valley, Sandton. ☎ **011/884-0465.** Reservations recommended, especially for dinner. Main courses R60–75 ($10–$12.50). AE, DC, MC, V. Mon–Fri 12–2pm, Mon–Sat 7–10pm. INTERNATIONAL.

In 1976 Walter Ulz opened his restaurant in a Braamfontein pre-war rooming house to much acclaim. Twenty-two years later Linger Longer has followed big business to the safety of Sandton's suburbs, and Ulz is still creating an ambience that patrons find hard to leave. His legendary fare combines classic French principles with eastern flavors—salmon tartare in seaweed with wasabi; trio of venison, lamb, and beef with roasted garlic; and seafood ceviche, marinated with lime juice, honey, chili, and coriander, are favorites. Some combinations, ostrich carpaccio with shucked oysters comes to mind, are a bit over the top.

**Piccolo Mondo.** The Michaelangelo Hotel, Sandton Square. ☎ **011/282-7000.** Reservations recommended. Main courses R65–90 ($10.85–$15). Three-course express luncheon R85 ($14.15). AE, DC, MC, V. Mon–Sun 6:30–10:30am, 12:30–2:30pm, 6:30–10:30pm. AFRO-FUSION/CONTINENTAL.

Executive chef Garth Shnier and his team are part of the new trend combining traditional South African ingredients with international methods. These "Afro-fusion" meals are nothing if not interesting: recommended dishes are baked crayfish on a smoked-tomato risotto served with Cape Malay rice pilaf, and roast rack of Karoo lamb marinated in Bulgarian yogurt. A large antipasto buffet is augmented by the a la carte menu, which is changed daily according to the availability of fresh ingredients. Ask for a table overlooking the square.

## MODERATE

✪ **The Singing Fig.** 44 The Avenue, Norwood. ☎ **011/728-2434.** Reservations essential. Main courses R38–42 ($6.35–$7). AE, DC, MC, V. Tues–Sun 12:30–2:30pm, Tues–Sat 6:30–10:30pm. PROVENÇAL.

A contender for the best duck in town, the Singing Fig is the current hot favorite with Jo'burg's in crowd. The waiters are witty, the wine is well priced, and the people who flock to enjoy it create the ambience. Main courses change regularly, but here's a sample: warm prawn salad with coconut milk and chili-ginger dressing; herb-crusted roast lamb in Port; mussels in orange and fennel sauce; and oxtail simmered in whisky and red wine. The famed duck is served with herbed butternut, potato, and zucchini slices. End the meal with their signature fig ice cream. A truly great food experience.

### Inexpensive

**Iyavaya Mutual Square.** 169 Oxford Square, Oxford Rd., Rosebank. ☎ **011/327-1411.** Reservations recommended. Main course R28–46 ($4.65–$7.65). AE, DC, MC, V. Mon–Sun 12–2:30pm, 6–11pm. AFRICAN.

Colorful Zimbabwean-print tablecloths, Zairian wall-hangings, and Ghanaian masks provide a hint of what's to come: dishes from Kenya, Senegal, Tanzania, Zaire, Ghana, Ivory Coast, and South Africa with Arabian and Indian touches combine for a multicultural dining experience. Mopani worms (worms that feed off the mopani tree) are a popular starter choice as is the Cameroonian banana soup spiced with cardamom.

Favorite main courses include crocodile spare ribs with hot *atchar* (mango pickle with chili), maafe stew from Mali (chicken shreds with okra, moroga, and mushrooms), and the palawa seafood stew, served with traditional *mieliepap* (maize meal). A more conventional choice is Masai filet, beef served with coarsely ground peppercorns and mushrooms. Wash it down with Maroela fruit beer and get your feet tapping to Iyavaya's shebeen sounds.

**Mary-Anne's Restaurant.** The Colony, 345 Jan Smuts Ave., Craighall. ☎ **011/442-3836.** Lunch buffet R35 ($5.85). AE, DC, MC, V. Mon–Fri 12–3pm. VEGETARIAN.

Having opened a successful vegetarian restaurant in a country where people still consider chicken a vegetable, Mary-Anne Shearer has decided to rest on her laurels. New owner Guy Tunmer is now providing Gautengers with all their essential minerals and vitamins, with dishes include chunky soups, vegetable casseroles, fresh salads, pasta, polenta, stir fries, couscous, and quiches. Ingredients are strictly vegetarian, totally organic, preservative-free, and non-irradiated. (Note that drinks are only of the freshly squeezed variety.)

**Renato Trattoria Pizzeria.** 39 Greenhill Rd., Emmarentia. ☎ **011/646-9203.** Reservations essential. Main courses R30 ($5). AE, DC, MC, V. Tues–Fri and Sun 12–1:45pm; Tues–Sun 6–9:45pm. ITALIAN.

Good food and a great atmosphere make this cozy Trattoria, run by charming proprietors Walter and Mario, very popular. Add unbelievably low prices to the formula and you'll understand why it's often a battle to get a table at night. Pizza and pasta dishes are tasty, though not extraordinary; chicken breast with asparagus sauce alternates with trifolato of liver with brandy as house specialties, and the linefish is usually excellent. Strangely, you have to specify olive oil with your salads. A bring-your-own-wine policy at this unlicensed place keeps prices low.

## City Center

### Inexpensive

✪ **Gramadoelas.** Market Theatre Complex, Bree St., Newtown. ☎ **011/838-6960** or 011/838-6729. Reservations recommended. Main courses R30–55 ($5–$9.15). AE, DC, MC, V. Tues–Sat 11:30am–3pm, Mon–Sat 6–11pm. SOUTH AFRICAN.

For 30 years Eduan Naude and Brian Shalkoff have entertained royals, rock stars, presidents, and audiences from all over Africa in this marvelously cluttered restaurant in Newtown's Cultural Precinct. A treasure trove of antiques, African tableware, and artworks from Zulu baskets filled with dried cobs to gourds of spices and grains, Gramadoelas is excellently positioned for those on their way to a little late-night jazz at Kippies or back from a play at the Market Theatre. Some dishes are not for the fainthearted; Hillary Clinton apparently loved the mopani worms, and the *mogodu,* a black tripe and wild African spinach stew, is one of Mandela's favorites. For the more timid, there are prawns, and vegetarian and meat curries.

**Kapitans.** 11A Kort St., Johannesburg. ☎ **011/834-8048.** Reservations essential. Main courses R25–45 ($4.15–$7.50). MC, V. Mon–Sat 12–3pm. INDIAN.

Jo'burg's oldest restaurant (over a century) is still going strong despite its downtown location. Kapitan, who's been cooking curries for 57 years, remembers Mandela sampling his first Campari here. Popular with yuppie stockbrokers from the nearby stock exchange (they love the large selection of Cuban cigars), Kapitans is also a hit with visitors prepared to venture downtown. (Naomi Campbell popped in on one visit.) Beware their Madras curry—it's hot enough to start a fire.

## NORTHWESTERN SUBURBS (MELVILLE)

### Inexpensive

✪ **Sam's Café.** 11 7th St., Melville. ☎ **011/726-8142.** Reservations recommended, essential for window seating. Portions R24 ($4), minimum charge of R40 ($6.65) per person. AE, DC, MC, V. Mon–Fri 12:30–2pm, Mon–Sat 7–10:30pm. MEDITERRANEAN.

Simplicity is the key to this elegantly understated restaurant on Melville's trendiest high street—try and book a table in the room facing it. Big glass windows provide ample opportunity to watch the passing parade while you sample a combination of chef Theresa Beukes smallish portions (try at least two each). Highlights include the warm prawn and zucchini salad, garnished with basil and sun-dried tomato, couscous served with Moroccan-style clams, chourico and bean stew cooked with sage, and chicken breast with watercress and basil. Sticky puddings are legendary, or if you're daring, caramelised camembert with fig preserve; or strawberry, black pepper, and balsamic vinegar ice cream.

## THE TOP ATTRACTIONS

**The Johannesburg Art Gallery.** Joubert Park, parking entrance off Klein St. ☎ **011/725-3130.** Free admission. Tues–Sun 10am–5pm. From the M1 take the Wolmarans turnoff, turn left onto Wolmarans, right onto Wanderers, and second left onto Bok, which runs into Klein.

Predictably, the city's first gallery was financed with the sale of a diamond. In 1904 Lady Phillips, wife of the first chairman of the Rand Mines Company, sold her 21-carat ring to purchase three paintings by Wilson Steer. Over the next 5 years she wrangled money from her wealthy connections to purchase more artworks, and commissioned Sir Edwin Lutyens to design the elegant building that now houses her collection. It is unfortunate that this is in the center of town, as it has arguably the best international collection in South Africa, including works by El Greco, Picasso, Moore, Rodin, and Lichtenstein. Happily, despite ignoring black talent during the apartheid years, they also have a good selection of South Africa's best, including sculptures by Venda artist Jackson Hlungwani and paintings by Helen Sebidi and Alfred Toba. The rather boring Flemish and Dutch collections are more than made up for by the Brenthurst Collection of African Art, comprising curios plundered by European explorers in the 19th century.

**Museum Africa.** 121 Bree St. ☎ **011/833-5624.** Admission R5 (85¢) adults, R2 (35¢)18 and under. Tues–Sun 9am–5pm.

Housed in the old Market Building, and part of the Newtown Cultural Precinct, Museum Africa was opened in 1994 and offers a truly modern take on Johannesburg's history. "Tried for Treason" is an evocative display using video interviews, old radio broadcasts, cartoons, newspaper headlines, and photographs to tell the tale of the 1956–1961 Treason Trial, which put, among others, Nelson Mandela behind bars. "Johannesburg Transformations" includes walkthrough re-creations of shacks, a miners' dorm, and a Sophiatown shebeen (illegal drinking house). Exploring these makeshift rooms, you are accompanied by some well-selected soundtracks from the musical giants Sophiatown and Soweto spawned, like Miriam Makeba and Hugh Masekela. Museum Africa also houses the **Museum of South African Rock Art,** and the less inspiring **Bensusan Museum of Photography and Geological Museum.**

**Gold Reef City.** Off Xavier Rd., (off M1), Ormonde. ☎ **011/496-1600.** Admission R26 ($4.35) weekdays; R30 ($5) weekends; R13 ($2.15) and R15 ($2.50) for seniors; children under 1.2m (4 feet) free. Tues–Sun 9:30am–5pm.

Six kilometers (4 miles) south of the city center, Gold Reef City is built around the old no. 14 shaft of the Crown mines. A supposed re-creation of the Victorian town of the gold-rush era, the "city" houses a variety of gold-related exhibits and museums; avoid those that don't relate to gold, like the Sporting Museum with its collection of rather depressing memorabilia relating to South Africa's sporting heroes. The most interesting activity is the 200-meter (655-foot) descent into the old mineshaft as part of a reconstruction of the mining process (for the real thing, see "Guided Tours," above). After this you can watch gold being poured into bars and minted, and see how newspapers were printed 100 years ago. Dance acts include can-can girls who kick their legs up on the bar counter at Rosie O'Grady's, traditional dance routines, and "mine" dancers who perform gumboot dances. As this is by far the best entertainment here, call ahead for times.

Gold Reef City is billed as a top tourist destination, but it's not all it's cut out to be. During the school holidays its target audience becomes apparent as teenagers jostle for space on the Golden Loop, and toddlers screech on the replica steam train that circles the complex. There is talk of a R650-million ($108,333,336) investment project featuring a casino that would incorporate the existing theme park; but until then, visit a real mine for a more authentic experience. For a more charming one, visit Pilgrim's Rest (see chapter 7).

**Museum of Military History.** 22 Erlswold Way, Saxonwold. ☎ **011/646-5513.** R5 (85¢) adults, R2 (35¢) students, R3 (50¢) seniors. Daily 9am–4:30pm.

Relics of war are not everyone's cup of tea, but this museum is very popular. Besides examples of tanks and aircraft (a Messerschmitt Me-262 jet is one of only two to have survived), a submarine, swords, guns, uniforms, and medals from both World Wars, it houses mementos from every civil war South Africa has fought. The display on Umkhonto we Sizwe, the armed wing of the ANC, highlights the role played by commander Joe Modise, now Minister of Defense.

✪ **Sterkfontein Caves.** ☎ **011/956-6342.** Tues–Sun 9am–4pm. R10 ($1.65) adults, R5 (85¢) ages 6–14. It takes less than an hour from Sandton to the caves; to get here head north up the M1 until it becomes the N1 and keep an eye out for a turnoff signposted 14TH AVENUE; turn right at the stoplight onto Hendrik Potgieter Dr., then travel 900m (2,950 ft.) before turning right onto the M47. Travel for 27km (17 miles), crossing the R28, then turn right onto the R563 (Hekpoort Dr.); stay right, then turn right at the sign that says MAKIETIE. The caves are 1.2km (three-quarters of a mile) farther on the right side.

This treasure trove for paleontologists contains over 600 perfectly preserved hominid fossils, some the oldest surviving in the world, and has provided vital evidence on man's evolution. The caves first leapt to fame in 1947 when Dr Robert Broom discovered "Mrs. Ples," the first known adult cranium of an "ape man," dating back 2.5 million years. They have continued to produce record-breaking finds, most recently in 1998 when a complete skull, dating back 3.5 million years was discovered. There is an excellent guided tour every half hour—it requires some fitness and no history of claustrophobia. Adjacent is the **Robert Broom Museum** of fossils. Currently, this fascinating facility is very underutilized, though this may change should they build a proposed casino complex a few kilometers from the site.

## More Attractions: From African Art to Big Balloons

For art aficionados and anthropologists, the **Gertrude Posel Gallery** on Wits (Witwatersrand University) campus (☎ **011/716-3632,** Senate House, Jorissen St., Braamfontein) has an extensive collection of tribal art and clothing, as well as a fascinating display on South African soccer. It often displays some of the best South African artists, as does the **Standard Bank Art Gallery** (☎ **011/636-4231,** at the corner of Simmonds and Frederick streets), though both are unfortunately located in town.

If the concrete jungle starts to get to you, the **Botanical Garden,** on the banks of the Emmerentia Dam, has the largest rose garden in Africa. The roses are at their best late September and the herb garden is splendid all year-round. Enter off Thomas Bolwer Street. Guided tours are offered on the first Tuesday of every month and begin at 9am; call ☎ **011/782-7064** for more information.

**The Planetarium** (☎ **011/716-3199,** Yale Road, Milner Park) offers an otherworldly escape, and often runs shows on the constellations of the Southern Hemisphere. Show times are Friday 8pm, Saturday 3pm, Sunday 4pm, and cost R16.50 ($2.75) for adults; R9 ($1.50) for children.

If you're not heading for a game reserve, but have always dreamed of having your photo taken with a lion cub, the **Lion Park** (☎ **011/460-1814**) is a 12-kilometer (7-mile) drive northwest of Sandton. Be warned, however, they're not as tame as they look: Stepping out of his minibus for a better photo cost a tourist an arm and a leg—really.

If you have a passion for horses, you can catch a performance by **Lippizaners,** a distinguished breed of all-white horses, every Sunday at 11am. This is the only place outside of Vienna where Lippizaners are trained to "dance" to Verdi, Mozart, and Handel, evidence of both their intellect and total muscular control. The center is in Kyalami (off Dahlia Rd.), halfway between Johannesburg and Pretoria. For more information, call ☎ **011/702-2103.**

If the pace of the city makes you feel like heading for the hills, join Bill Harrop's **Original Balloon Safaris** and discover the most picturesque part of Gauteng, the Magalies River Valley, by air. Flights cost R1,305 ($217.50) per person, last about an hour, and include sparkling wine (served onboard) and a hot breakfast on landing, as well as transfers from the northern suburbs (some 45 minutes away).

## SHOPPING—FLEA MARKETS TO HIGH-END CRAFTS

For crafts and curios, bargained over the ululating of pseudo-tribal dancers, Johannesburg's flea markets are your best bet. Billed as the world's only flea market theme park, **Bruma Lake Market** (☎ **011/786-077/9**), a 10-minute drive from the city center (off Marcia and Allum rds., near Eastgate Shopping Centre), operates daily (300 stalls a week; 600 at weekends), and has plenty of buskers and dancers; but the venue, a man-made lake in Bedfordview, is more than just a little tacky. The **Rosebank Mall Rooftop Market,** which is open every Sunday and public holidays from 9:30am to 5pm, is where the upwardly mobile hunt for anything from olives to antique fetishes. The most authentically African, the **Newtown Market** (☎ **011/832-1641**), opposite the Market Theatre, takes place every Saturday from 7am to 4pm onward. An excellent selection of curios is available, but pickpockets are legendary, so take care.

You can watch all the action from an outside table at **Kofifi** (☎ **011/832-1450**) an informal restaurant that serves traditional African dishes like *pap* and *mogodu* (tripe) as well as curries, steak, and fish, and fries. Less than 1 kilometer (just over a half mile) from here (follow Jeppe St. into Fordsburg) is the **Oriental Plaza shopping center,** specializing in Indian merchandise, particularly fabrics and, of course, spices.

Back in the northern suburbs, **Rural Craft** (☎ **011/788-5821**), in Rosebank's Mutual Gardens, Shop 42E (next to the House of Coffee), markets goods on behalf of the Crafts Association of South Africa, and all profits are returned to the communities. Also in Mutual Gardens is **Afrika Dijalo** (☎ **011/447-9304**), where you can find a good selection of pricey masks and woodcarvings. For a more serious selection of African arts or crafts, visit the **Everard Read Gallery** (☎ **011/788-4805** in Rosebank, 6 Jellicoe

Ave.), considered the best commercial art gallery in the country, or the **Gallery on the Square** (☎ **011/784-2847,** in Sandton City Mall), but make sure your wallet is bulging—a recently advertised Nesta Nala pot would set you back R3,100 ($516.65).

## JOHANNESBURG AFTER DARK

### THE PERFORMING ARTS

Johannesburg vies with Cape Town as the country's center for the performing arts, but most feel that the city of gold wins hands down. There are three main theaters to choose from: **The Market Theatre,** Bree Street, Newtown Cultural Precinct (☎ **011/832-1641**), is famous for having spawned a generation of protest theatre, and is likely to have the best selection of local talent. The **Johannesburg Civic Theatre,** Loveday Street, Braamfontein (☎ **011/403-3408**), is the largest and most technologically advanced theatre in the country; this is where you will find operas, dance troupes, and orchestras performing. The **Alhambra Theatre** (☎ **011/402-6174** for information; 011/402-7726 for tickets, 109 Sivewright Ave., Ellis Park) in Doornfontein is Jo'burg's oldest theatre, and focuses mostly on mainstream drama and comedy. Other options include the **AGFA** theatre (Sandton Square, ☎ **011/883-8606**) and **Windybrow** in Hillbrow (☎ **011/720-7009,** corner Nugget and Pietersen). The latter features all-African casts and crews, and good grass-roots productions; but considering the area, a matinee performance is advisable and even then you may feel nervous. The daily *Tonight* section of *The Star,* the weekly *Mail & Guardian,* and *South African City Life,* supply listings for all these venues. Tickets can also be booked and paid for by phone, call **Computicket** (☎ **011/445-8445** for information, 011/445-8000 for credit-card purchases).

### THE CLUB, PUB, & MUSIC SCENE

Specializing in township jazz, **Kippies** (☎ **011/833-3316**), at the Market Theatre, Newtown (see Museum Africa, above), is a national institution. All of South Africa's best jazz musicians have performed here, and it attracts both established names (watch for Winston Mankunku) as well as new talents. Its only drawbacks are its small size and downtown location (there is secure parking). Attracting a larger, more relaxed crowd these days, and featuring some of South Africa's best talent, is ✪ **Bassline** (☎ **011/482-6915**), a relaxed, informal and intimate jazz club, in Melville (7 7th St.). Dedicated to the blues, with occasional forays into fusion, jazz, and rock 'n' roll, mellow basement supper club **The Blues Room** (Village Walk, Maude St., Sandown, ☎ **011/784-5528**) is becoming increasingly popular, and offers easy access for those living in the northern suburbs. The place to see and be seen is Jabulanis in Park Hyatt (see "Where to Stay").

Back in Melville is **Roxy's Rhythm Bar** (☎ **011/726-6019,** 20 Main Rd.), serving local indie talent to a young crowd (watch for the Springbok Nude Girls). For those following the cigar trend, puff up the hill to **Cigar Exchange** (☎ **011/482-8384**) on the corner of Main and 4th Avenue. **Jargonelle's,** a restaurant in the nearby suburb of Brixton (☎ **011/837-3770,** 110 Caroline St.), is the city's best cabaret venue, offering everything from traditional Venda chants to Afrikaans icons. Reservations essential; call to find out what's on.

Moving east to 206 Louis Botha Ave. in Orange Grove (north of Observatory), ✪ **206 live** (☎ **011/728-5333**) offers a combination of live music and international DJs. Tuesday is drum 'n' bass, Thursday is hip-hop/trance, and Fridays feature live bands. Next door are **208 Lounge Bar** (☎ **011/728-5333**), a cocktail bar, and **Unda Tha Counta** (☎ **011/728-6139**), a drum & bass espresso bar.

Alternatively, warm up at the **Radium Beer Hall** (☎ **011/728-3866** at 282 Louis Botha Ave., Orange Grove). This is one of the oldest bars in Jo'burg (the counter dates back to 1895), and the ambience is warm, the food simple, cheap, and good. When in Yeoville, don't miss **Polli-polli** (☎ **083/770-7913,** 42 Hunter St.) on Fridays and Saturdays.

For a real Jo'burg jive, mingle with the Rainbow Nation to the transfixing sounds of kwaito at **The Palladium** (New Constantia Centre, Cnr. Tyrwhitt and Jan Smuts Ave., Rosebank, ☎ **011/788-5569,** open Wednesday to Saturday).

If hard house and garage are more your scene, get your fix every Friday at **G.A.S.S.** (39a Juta St., Braamfontein, ☎ **011/339-7791**). Anyone wearing full bondage or rubber gets in free (Saturday nights are for gay members only). If your idea of romance is more old-fashioned, an evening of dinner-dancing at the **Silver Rose** (on Saturdays only), in the Rosebank Hotel (see "Where to Stay" for details), is just the ticket.

### FILM

Art-movie aficionados can catch the latest offering at the **Rosebank Mall Art Theatre** (☎ **011/880-2866,** 50 Bath Ave.), South Africa's oldest dedicated art cinema. Or if you like your movies with fantastic city views, head for the **Top Star Drive-In,** situated on top of one of Jo'burg's mine dumps; check local papers for details.

## 2 Pretoria

50km (31 miles) from Johannesburg

An almost uninterrupted ribbon of development connects Johannesburg and Pretoria, yet Pretoria's atmosphere is much more laid back. As the administrative capital of South Africa, it has been home to an increasingly sophisticated population since Nelson Mandela became the first democratically elected president at the Union Buildings, and South Africa reentered the international arena. Despite having been considered an Afrikaner stronghold since 1860, when it was made capital of the ZAR (a Boer republic), and populated with Afrikaans civil servants, a huge majority win for the ANC in the 1995 local elections proved that Pretoria is also, in fact, home to a large black population.

By staying here you'll miss out on Jo'burg's excitement and energy, but Pretoria has enough in the way of cultural and historical sights to fill a day or two before its street life and architecture become monotonous. It is also almost an hour closer to Pilanesberg and the Kruger National Park than Johannesburg. Add to this the fact that Pretoria is far safer and equidistant from Johannesburg International Airport, and staying here starts to make definite sense, particularly in October and November, when its 70,000 jacarandas are in full bloom, and the streets are carpeted with purple blossoms.

### ESSENTIALS

**VISITOR INFORMATION** The **Pretoria Information Bureau** (☎ **012/308-8909**), in the Tourist Rendezvous Travel Center at the corner of Prinsloo and Vermeulen streets is open 8am to 5pm daily. They can supply brochures and maps, as well as their free dining magazine *Be My Guest,* and the *Tourist Quick Reference Guide.* The National Parks Board (where you can make your accommodation bookings), SATOUR, and various other information bureaus are also in the Tourist Rendezvous Travel Center.

**GETTING THERE** **By Plane** Pretoria is some 50 kilometers (31 miles) from Johannesburg International Airport. Most hotels will organize an airport pick-up, as

## Driving from Johannesburg to Cape Town

There are two choices should you decide to drive from Jo'burg to Cape Town. You can drive directly south on the N1 to Cape Town, overnighting at Bloemfontein or at the Karoo National Park (2km/1¼ miles south of Beaufort West); this is marginally quicker (approximately 13 to 14 hours), but the road can get very busy. Another alternative, time allowing, is to travel southwest via the N12, overnighting at Kimberley, where you can take in some diamond history, before heading farther south, where the N12 meets up with the N1 at Three Sisters, some 70 kilometers (43 miles) north of Beaufort West. With no sightseeing, this should take 15 hours.

**VIA KIMBERLEY** Kimberley is approximately 5 hours from Johannesburg, and 10 hours from Cape Town. If you choose to overnight here, book a room at **Edgerton House** (☎ **053/831-1150,** 5 Egerton Rd., Belgravia, 1km/just over a half mile southeast of the center, along Du Toitspan Rd.), where most of Kimberley's wealthiest families lived at the turn of the century. Rates range from R440–950 ($73.35–$158.35). A National Monument, the Edgerton has been elegantly restored and refurbished (this is incidentally where Mandela chooses to stay when in town) and is opposite the **McGregor Museum** (☎ **053/842-0099**), once a sanitarium, and within walking distance of its satellite, the **Duggan-Cronin Gallery,** where you can view numerous photographs taken at the turn of the century. You may choose to end the day with a walking tour of Belgravia; maps are available from the Edgerton or the Kimberley Tourism Office. If you have time to spare, spend another night as there's plenty to do. The excellent **Kimberley Mine Museum** (where you can see the largest man-made excavation in the world is billed as the city's top attraction. Contact **Kimberley Tourism** (☎ **053/832-7298**), in the Civic Complex on Bulfontein Road. Their hours are Monday to Friday 8am to 3pm, and Saturday 8:30am to 11:30pm. (Note that a cheaper accommodation alternative is the old-fashioned **Savoy Hotel,** ☎ **053/832-6211,** at 19 De Beers

will **Kwathlano Tours** (☎ **012/347-1384**), a service that will set you back R55–130 ($9.15–$21.65), depending on how many people are traveling together. A **Pretoria bus shuttle** (☎ **012/323-0904**) connects the airport to the Tourist Rendezvous Travel Center every hour, from 7:15am to 8:15pm, and costs R46 ($7.65) per person. A taxi to the center should cost R180 ($30).

**By Car** From Johannesburg take the M1 north; this becomes the N1 to Pretoria.

**By Train & Bus** **Intercity** trains (and buses) arrive at the train station on Railway Street (☎ **012/315-2757**). Trains, including the Blue Train and Rovos, arrive from Johannesburg, Zimbabwe, Cape Town, Durban, the Kruger, and Namibia. It's better to alight here than in the crime-ridden Jo-burg station.

**GETTING AROUND** Once again, public transport is poor and renting a car or using a tour operator are the only ways to see certain sights, though the center of town is easily walked. The **bus terminal** and information is on Church Square (☎ **012/313-0839**). If you need a **taxi,** call **City Bug** at ☎ **012/663-6316** or **SA Taxi** at ☎ **012/320-2075**—the cars are not always great, but the drivers are. Alternatively head for Tourist Rendezvous, where many of them hang out. For **rental-car** options from the airport, see "Johannesburg: Getting Around." In Pretoria, contact **Avis**

Rd., where rates are from R279 ($46.50) double; but don't expect any luxuries for this price.)

**VIA BLOEMFONTEIN** Bloemfontein is a leisurely 4 hours from Johannesburg, and approximately 8 to 9 hours to Cape Town. There isn't much to see here, but there is an excellent guest house near the city center, regularly voted South Africa's best. **Hobbit House** (☎/fax **051/447-0663**) is at 19 President Steyn Ave., Westdene. Rates are R450 ($75) double, breakfast included, and the three-course meals (served given prior warning) are recommended. Alternatively, avoid town altogether, and head 35 kilometers (21½ miles) south on the N1 until you reach the Riversford exit, off which you'll find **De Oude Kraal** (☎ **051/564-0636;** fax 5640635), a working merino sheep farm. Guests can stay in the restored farmhouse, where there are fireplaces in each room. Rates are R450–630 ($75–$105) double, including a farm-style dinner (expect lamb and large portions) and breakfast.

**KAROO NATIONAL PARK** The park and Beaufort West are approximately 9 hours from Johannesburg and some 4 hours from Cape Town. If you're just too tired to make it to Cape Town, the **Karoo National Park** (☎ **0201/52-828**) is a wonderful place to overnight—you drive only a few kilometers off the N1; but once there, you are in the tranquil nature reserve, surrounded by empty plains and a low ridge of mountains, and a world away from the rumbling highway. Gate hours are 5am to 10pm daily; accommodation is in large self-catering chalets costing R300 ($50) a night, breakfast included. For reservations, which are essential, contact the **Parks Board** in Pretoria (☎ **012/343-1991**) or Cape Town (☎ **021/22-2810**). If the Karoo National Park is full, the **Matoppo Inn** (☎ **0201/51055,** fax 0201/51080, at 7 Bird St.) charges R360 ($60) double. Beaufort West is highly recommended.

(☎ **012/325-1490**), 70 Schoeman St. or **Budget** (☎ **012/323-3658,** 456 Church St. East, Arcadia).

**GUIDED TOURS** **Kwathlano Tours** (☎ **012/347-1384)** conducts excellent tours of the city, and day excursions to Johannesburg, Lesedi, Cullinan, Sterkfontein, the Lion Park, Sun City, and Pilanesberg. **Kevin Kieswetter** (☎ **083/628-1337**) is extremely knowledgeable about the city, and specializes in private tours. **Tebu Travel Tours** (☎ **012/326-2875**) will arrange township tours, including an overnight with a family living there. (For more options, see "Guided Tours" in the Johannesburg section, above).

**CITY LAYOUT** Sights in Pretoria's **city center** can all be explored on foot (see below), including the zoo, which lies just north of the center. Northeast of the center, you will see the Union Buildings, located in **Arcadia,** the suburb in which most of the embassies and consulates are situated. East of the city are the suburbs of **Sunnyside** and **Hatfield,** where most of the city's nightlife options and restaurants are. Southeast of the center lies the upmarket suburb of **Brooklyn.** Together these suburbs form the nucleus of the "Ambassadorial Belt," named for the many embassies and diplomats housed here. South of the city is the Voortrekker Monument, built on a hill, and visible for miles around.

# Pretoria

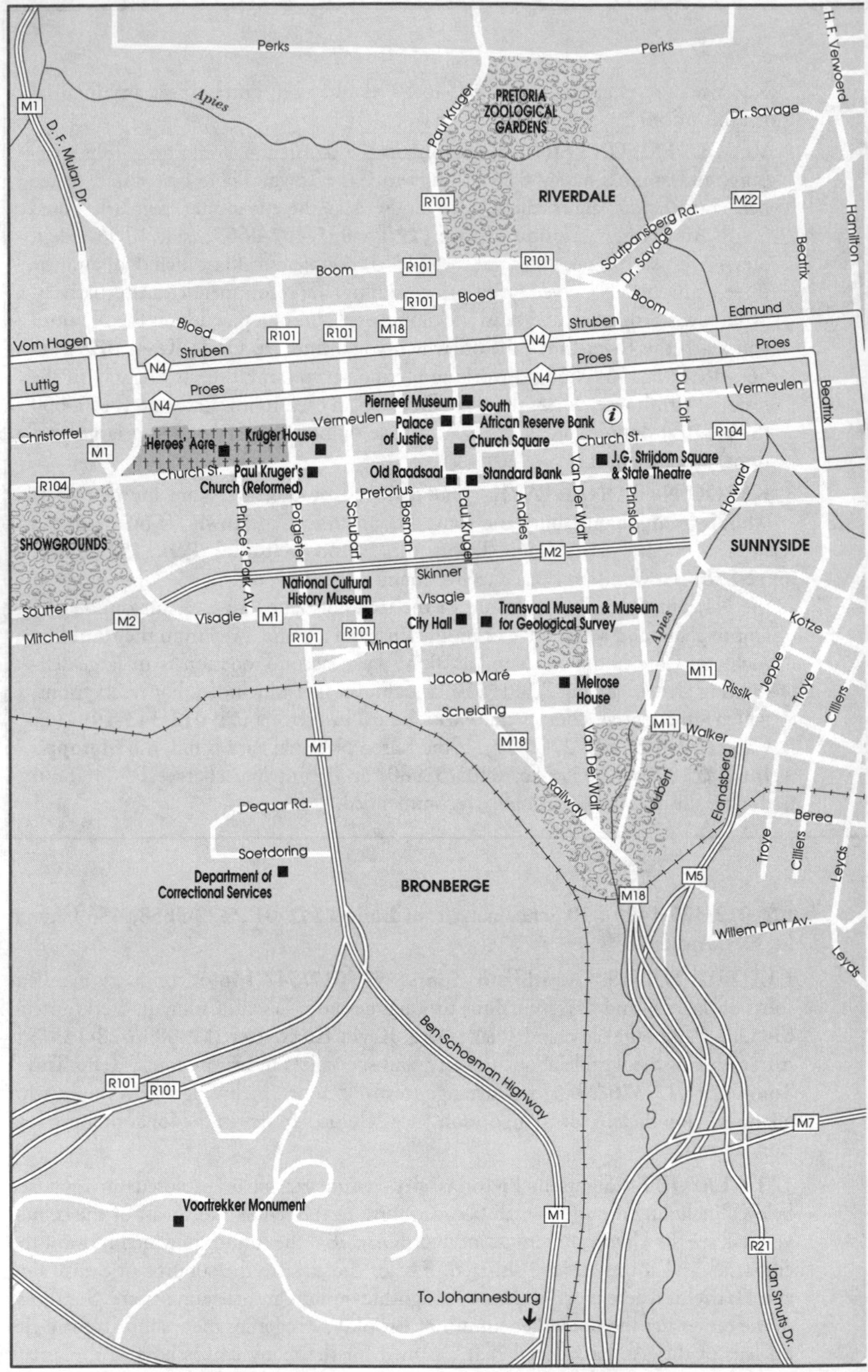

Perks
Perks
Apies
PRETORIA ZOOLOGICAL GARDENS
Paul Kruger
Dr. Savage
H. F. Verwoerd
M1
D. F. Mulan Dr.
RIVERDALE
R101
M22
Soutpansberg Rd.
Dr. Savage
Hamilton
Beatrix
Boom
R101
R101
Bloed
Boom
Edmund
Bloed
R101
R101
M18
Struben
N4
Proes
Vom Hagen
Struben
N4
Proes
N4
Luttig
Proes
N4
Du Toit
Vermeulen
Beatrix
Pierneef Museum
South African Reserve Bank
Palace of Justice
Vermeulen
Christoffel
Kruger House
Church Square
Church St.
R104
M1
'Heroes' Acre
J.G. Strijdom Square & State Theatre
Church St.
Paul Kruger's Church (Reformed)
Old Raadsaal
Standard Bank
R104
Pretorius
Howard
SHOWGROUNDS
Prince's Park Av.
Potgieter
Schubart
Bosman
Paul Kruger
Andries
Van Der Walt
Prinsloo
SUNNYSIDE
M2
Skinner
National Cultural History Museum
Visagie
Soutter
Visagie
M1
Transvaal Museum & Museum for Geological Survey
City Hall
Mitchell
M2
R101
R101
Minaar
Apies
Kotze
Jacob Maré
M11
Melrose House
Rissik
Jeppe
Troye
Cilliers
Scheiding
M11
Walker
M18
M1
Van Der Walt
Railway
Joubert
Elandsberg
Dequar Rd.
Berea
Soetdoring
Troye
Cilliers
Leyds
Department of Correctional Services
M5
BRONBERGE
M18
Willem Punt Av.
Leyds
Ben Schoeman Highway
R101
R101
M7
Voortrekker Monument
M1
R21
Jan Smuts Dr.
To Johannesburg

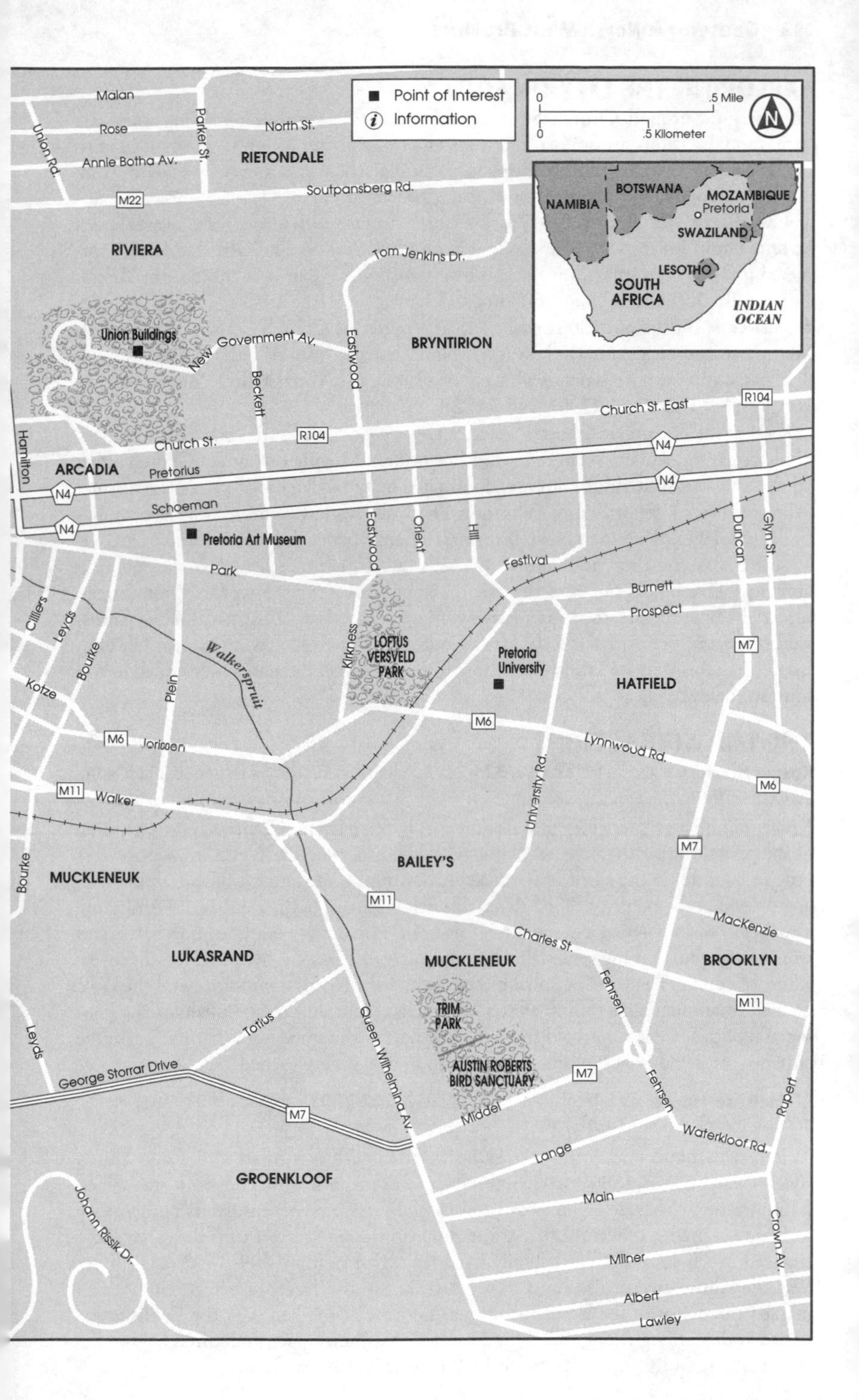
Point of Interest
Information
0
.5 Mile
0
.5 Kilometer
NAMIBIA
BOTSWANA
MOZAMBIQUE
Pretoria
SWAZILAND
LESOTHO
SOUTH AFRICA
INDIAN OCEAN
Malan
Rose
North St.
Union Rd.
Parker St.
Annie Botha Av.
RIETONDALE
Soutpansberg Rd.
M22
RIVIERA
Tom Jenkins Dr.
Union Buildings
New Government Av.
Eastwood
BRYNTIRION
Beckett
Church St. East
R104
Church St.
Hamilton
ARCADIA
Pretorius
N4
Schoeman
Pretoria Art Museum
Orient
Hill
Duncan
Glyn St.
Park
Festival
Burnett
Prospect
Cilliers
Leyds
Bourke
Walkerspruit
Kirkness
LOFTUS VERSVELD PARK
Pretoria University
M7
HATFIELD
Kotze
Plein
M6
Jorissen
Lynnwood Rd.
M11
Walker
University Rd.
BAILEY'S
MUCKLENEUK
MacKenzie
Charles St.
LUKASRAND
BROOKLYN
Fehrsen
TRIM PARK
Totius
Queen Wilhelmina Av.
AUSTIN ROBERTS BIRD SANCTUARY
George Storrar Drive
Middel
Waterkloof Rd.
Rupert
Lange
GROENKLOOF
Johann Rissik Dr.
Main
Crown Av.
Milner
Albert
Lawley

## EXPLORING THE CITY ON FOOT

Pretoria grew around **Church Square,** and it makes sense that a walking tour start here, though visitors are advised that the center of the city is not as safe as it used to be. Don't explore on foot after office hours, particularly not during the weekend. Look out for the following landmarks on Church Square.

**Café Riche** (☎ **012/328-3173,** 2 Church Square), Pretoria's oldest café, and a favorite haunt for the city's workers, is a good place to start. The **Old Raadsaal,** completed in 1891, lies south, on the southwest corner; next to it is the **South African Reserve Bank** (like the Union Buildings, designed by Herbert Baker), and the **Palace of Justice** is on the northwest corner. In the center of Church Square is Anton van Wouw's **statue** of a dour Paul Kruger. (Note that you can visit the house museum of the sculptor, whose work is also on display at the **Voortrekker Monument,** at 26 Clark St., Brooklyn (☎ **012/46-7422**).

West of the Square, on Church Street, is **Heroes Acre,** the burial place for a number of historical figures, and **Kruger House** (see below). Moving east down Church Street you'll come across **Strijdom Square,** dominated by the ugly bust of even uglier former prime minister J. G. Strijdom. (This name has come to have a more sinister connotation since 1993, when namesake Barend Strijdom opened fire on random black targets. Despite showing no remorse, he was subsequently released under political amnesty.) Five blocks north of the square, along Paul Kruger Street, is Boom Street; turn right here for the **zoo.** Alternatively, move south down this road for the **Transvaal Museum,** opposite the **City Hall.** Continue for two blocks, then turn left onto Jacob Mare for **Melrose House.** For more information on the sights mentioned in this tour, see below.

## THE TOP ATTRACTIONS

**Kruger House.** Church St. W. ☎ **012/326-9172.** Admission R5 (85¢). Mon–Sat 8:30am–4pm, Sun 11am–4pm.

Kruger House is on every tour group's itinerary, but as most of the furnishings are simply of the period, rather than the very things Paul and his wife lived with, the house does little to conjure up the spirit of the man. A boy during the arduous Great Trek north, and present at the Battle of Blood River, this first president of the ZAR (Zuid Afrikaanse Republiek) was known as a pious, stern Calvanist. He was also oddly approachable, and would hold court on his verandah, chatting to anyone passing by; provided they were white, of course. There are personal pieces, including his pipes, spittoons, and the knife he used to amputate his thumb after a hunting accident; but the best exhibit is a photograph of the cantankerous old codger sitting next to the stone lions that still guard the entrance to the house. Opposite is the church in which he preached.

✪ **Melrose House.** 275 Jacob Mare St. ☎ **012/322-2805.** Admission R3 (50¢) adults, under 6 free. Tues–Sun 10am–5pm.

This neo-Baroque mansion—a cross between English Victorian and Cape Dutch styles—was built in 1886 for George Heys, who made his fortune from stagecoach transportation. Melrose House has been carefully restored to ensure its authenticity and, unlike many other South African house museums, the furnishings have not changed much since the Heys family lived here. During the 1899–1902 Anglo-Boer War, the House was requisitioned by the British, and the Treaty of Vereeniging, which marked the defeat of the Boers for the second time at the hands of the English, was signed at this dining-room table May 31, 1902. Exhibitions are sometimes held in the conservatory, and you can sip tea in the Prince of Wales Tea Garden.

**Voortrekker Monument and Museum Monument Hill.** 6km (4 miles) south of city. ☎ **012/323-0682.** Monument admission R8 ($1.35) adults, R2.50 (40¢) children. Museum R5 (85¢) adult, R3 (50¢) children. Mon–Sat 9am–4:45pm, Sun 11am–4:45pm.

In 1938 the secret Afrikaner *Broederbond* (brotherhood) organized a symbolic reenactment of the Great Trek, and sent a team of ox-wagons from Cape Town to Pretoria to celebrate its centenary. By the time the wagons reached Pretoria, over 200,000 Afrikaners had joined; all camped at Monument Hill where the foundation stones for the monument were laid. Ten years later, the monument was completed, and the Afrikaner Nationalist Party swept to power. This massive granite structure, sometimes compared irreverently to a large Deco toaster, dominates the skyline at the southern entrance to the city. Commemorating the Great Trek, in particular the Battle of Blood River, the monument remains hallowed ground for Afrikaner nationalists. When *Loslyf,* the first Afrikaans porn magazine, used the monument as the backdrop to their centerfold in its launch issue, nationalists were outraged. Every year on December 16th, exactly at noon, a ray of sunlight lights up a central plaque. (Note that in the marble frieze surrounding the lower hall, you will find no depiction of the many black slaves who aided the Boers in their victory.) The adjacent museum has memorabilia relating to the Great Trek; most interesting is the "female" version of the monument frieze—huge tapestries depicting a romanticized version of the Great Trek's social events. Even more interesting than this sanitized version of the pioneer days are the photographs of the "tannies" (literally "aunties," an Afrikaans term of respect) who created these tapestries. They are the perfect foil to the Afrikaner men; ladies plaiting threads while the men wrest with stone in the main monument.

✪ **The Union Buildings.** Meintjieskop Ridge. ☎ **012/325-2000.** The exterior is accessed 24 hours. Admission free.

On every tour group's agenda, and with the best views of the city, the Union Buildings designed by Sir Herbert Baker are a great place to orient yourself. Probably the best-known creation of this prolific "British Imperial" architect, they are certainly his finest achievement. The administrative headquarters of the South African government and the office of the president since 1913, the office block wings are said to represent the British and Afrikaner people, linked in reconciliation by the curved amphitheater. African natives were, of course, not represented; nor were they allowed to enter the buildings except to clean. In 1994 the buildings and gardens were the scene of huge emotional jubilation as everyone from Castro to Gore witnessed the inauguration of South Africa's first black president and international hero, and African praise-singers in traditional garb exorcised the ghosts of the past. Visitors are allowed to walk around the vicinity and the gardens, but may only enter on official business.

## Other Attractions

**Transvaal Museum.** ☎ **012/322-7632.** Paul Kruger St., S. Mon–Sat 9–5, Sun 11–5. Admission R6 ($1), R3.50 (60¢) children.

The whale skeleton erected outside Pretoria's oldest museum is one of this natural science museum's most impressive exhibits. An uninspiring selection of stuffed animals follows, and many displays resemble high-school projects. However, it's worth seeking out the bits that relate to the development of early man on the second floor, much of which has been based on fossil finds at the Sterkfontein and Kromdraai caves. The **Geoscience Museum** is worth a quick look just to marvel at the earth's myriad colors and textures. **Roberts Bird Hall** is billed as a haven for bird-lovers, but I suspect most birders would find this collection of very dead birds depressing.

✪ **The Pretoria Art Museum. ☎ 012/344-1807.** Arcadia Park, corner Wessels and Schoeman sts. Tues and Thurs–Sat 10am–5pm, Wed 10am–8pm, Sun 12–5pm. Admission R3 (50¢).

The first museum to focus on South African art, this modern building now houses the best collection of work by white South African artists—for instance, it has an even better collection of Pierneefs than the Pierneef Museum in Vermeulen Street. Curators have recently started to purchase work by black artists, including the celebrated Sekoto and Ephraim Ngatane. Currently, the museum has over 3,000 artworks which are regularly circulated by creating themed exhibitions every 2 months, and also features internationally renowned exhibitions, like the recent Leonardo da Vinci Collection.

**The Correctional Services Museum. ☎ 012/314-1766,** at the Prison Reserve in Potgieter St. Tues–Fri 9am–3pm, Sun 10am–3pm. Admission free.

This museum is easily taken in on the way to the Voortrekker Monument. A frightening array of hand-fashioned weapons (even a toilet seat, sharpened, can be life threatening!), as well as artworks made by prisoners are displayed—make sure the resident guide shows you the ingeniously hidden *dagga* (marijuana) pipe in the model train. There is also a replica of Mandela's cell on Robben Island.

**The African Window.** 149 Visagie St. **☎ 012/324-6084.** Open daily 8am–4pm. Admission R5 (85¢).

This new exhibition center of the National Cultural History Museum (and Pretoria's most modern museum) tries hard to celebrate the diverse cultures that make up the South African community. The most successful display is People's Choice, in which selected South African groups (anything from a church to old-age pensioners) are given the opportunity to choose a range of museum-owned objects to display. The objects all have the same function, but different form; themes are simple, such as cooking implements or toys, and provide tactile proof of the underlying heterogeneous nature of the Rainbow Nation.

**Cullinan Diamond Mine Tours.** 95 Oak Ave., Cullinan (40km/25 miles east of Pretoria). **☎ 012/734-0081.** Tours at 10:30am daily, Mon–Fri at 2pm. Ask for Andrew. Admission R25 ($4.15).

Yielding an average 2 million carats a year since 1902, Premier Mines is one of the richest diamond mines in the world. The surface-mine tours include a video of the mining process, a look at the Cullinan Big Hole (40ha/100 acres in area, and 500m/1,640 ft. deep), displays of uncut diamonds as well as of the world's most famous diamonds (the Cullinan, Centenary, and Premier Rose were all unearthed here). The Cullinan, which weighed 3,106 carats, was presented to Edward VII by the Transvaal government. It was divided into 9 jewels, and the 530-carat Great Star of Africa (the largest cut diamond in the world) and the 317-carat Lesser Star of Africa are now on display in the Tower of London, in the Royal Scepter and Imperial State Crown.

## Zoos & Gardens

The 3,500 animals residing in the **Pretoria Zoo** (**☎ 012/328-3265,** off Boom St.) may be living in one of the largest zoos in the world (60ha/150 acres), but a sad air of imprisonment still pervades. They conduct night tours, when you can see the zoo's nocturnal creatures. A good alternative is the **De Wildt Cheetah Research Center** (**☎ 012/504-1921/2,** off Pretoria N. Rd. [R513], Farm #22), internationally renowned for successful breeding and researching endangered species, including cheetah, king cheetah, brown hyena, and the African wild dog, (with only 5,000 left in the world, Africa's most endangered predator). The 3-hour guided tours cost R70

($11.65) per person, take place on Tuesday, Thursday, Saturday, and Sunday at 8:30am and 1:30pm, and are by arrangement only (no children under 6). The tranquil **National Botanical Gardens** (☎ **012/804-3200,** 2 Cuwsonia St., Brummeria; open daily 8am to 6pm; R7/$1.15 adults, R3/50¢ children), which contains every major type of southern African vegetation, is one of Pretoria's top attractions.

## WHERE TO STAY

Accommodations are geared very much toward the diplomatic market, and as yet there is no 5-star hotel. Comfortable apartments with hotel-type facilities or guest houses run like small hotels are the best options; prices are also very reasonable. Most are located in the "Ambassadorial Belt" (Arcadia, Hatfield, Sunnyside, and the upmarket suburb of Brooklyn), which are at most a 10-minute drive away.

Seventeen of Pretoria's best guest houses are represented by the **Harley Group of Gracious Guest Houses** (☎ **012/365-1117;** fax 012/365-1127; e-mail: harleyaccom@intekom.co.za), offering three accommodation categories at three different price ranges. Besides providing a central information and reservation service, the Harley Group will arrange any transfer or rental-car arrangements.

✪ **Rozenhof Guest House.** 525 Alexander St., Brooklyn 0181. ☎ **012/46-8075.** Fax 012/46-8085. E-mail: rozenhof@smartnet.co.za. 6 units. TV TEL. R590 ($98.35) north-facing; R490 ($81.65) south-facing. Rates include breakfast. AE, DC, MC, V. Children 14 and over only.

Built on the former estate of Tielman Roos, one-time deputy minister of the Union of South Africa, Rozenhof has the hushed air that befits a temporary home of important diplomats and well-to-do businessmen. It operates very much as a boutique hotel. In this elegant two-story building with a sweeping staircase leading up to large, spacious bedrooms, the twin-bed north-facing rooms overlook the gardens (numbers 2 and 3, with balconies, are the best), while the south-facing rooms are a little smaller, and are fitted with queen-size beds and en-suite showers only. In winter a fireplace is lit in the comfortable lounge, and you can bone up on South African literature in the Tielman Roos library. There is a 10-meter (33-foot) pool in the garden, adjacent to the verandah where breakfast is served in the summer. Lunch and dinner are available by prior arrangement.

**Sherwood Forest Guest House.** 131 Hugh St., Sunnyside 0002. ☎/fax **012/344-4850.** E-mail: sherwood@qdata.net. 6 units. MINIBAR TV TEL. R350–550 ($58.35–$91.65) double, includes breakfast. AE, DC, MC, V. Children 8 and over only; call for rates.

Situated on the outskirts of the city center, Sherwood Forest (the name was inherited from the previous owner, Mr. John Hood) offers easy access to its sights. Owner Samantha McDonald prides herself on providing all the comforts of a hotel at a fraction of the price. Sherwood is very much a house, however, and some of the rooms are a bit small—not surprisingly "Little John" is one of them. Rooms are painted in rich, warm colors and are comfortably furnished, with the King Edward Suite and Major Oak being the best. Major Oak, a large room with king-size bed (a trifle soft), has its own private entrance and parking space, and has a mezzanine level with an additional single bed. There is no pool, and while a three-course dinner is written up daily, you're better off sampling the fare at one of the nearby restaurants.

**The Victoria Hotel.** Corner Scheiding and Paul Kruger sts., Pretoria 0001. ☎ **012/323-6054.** Fax 012/323-0843. E-mail: reservations@rovos.co.za. 10 units. A/C MINIBAR TV TEL. R750 ($125) double, including breakfast. AE, DC, MC, V.

This is the oldest hotel building in Pretoria, dating back to 1892/6, when it was simply known as the Station Hotel. Located opposite Pretoria's railway station, the Victoria Hotel has been described as the smartest in Pretoria, but this may be because of the associations of luxury that the name Rovos evokes (Rovos, of the luxury steam train trips, owns the Victoria). While rooms have been refurbished in the Victorian style, they lack real style. (Maybe they ran out of money. Or steam.) The most interesting room, Graskop, has two free-standing Victorian baths, but you'll pay an extra R400 ($66.65) for the privilege of having your bath and sharing it, too. The area around the hotel and station is also not very safe, particularly at night. But then again you could just sit on your verandah with a beer (six of the rooms have verandahs for no extra cost), watching the passing parade and waiting for your train to roll in.

✪ **Villa Via.** Corner Orient and Pretorius Sts., Arcadia, 0001. ☎ **012/342-9130.** Fax 012/342-9131. 56 units. A/C TV TEL. R435 ($72.50) studio; R445 ($74.15) 1-bedroom suite; R765 ($127.50) 2-bedroom suite. Rates include breakfast. Check for specials throughout the year. AE, DC, MC, V.

Directly opposite the U.S. Embassy and within walking distance of another 95 embassies, Villa Via is really in the heart of the Ambassadorial Belt. The reception, lounge, bar, and restaurant are housed in a National Monument, but the architecture of the new accommodation block is modern and dull. However, the rooms, all self-catering, are an unbelievably good value. It's worth paying a little more for a one-bedroom suite, which then provides you with a spacious lounge/dining area, TVs in both the bedroom and lounge, a bath with walk-in shower, and a balcony or private garden area with patio furniture—the garden suites are recommended. Safes and hair dryers are standard features. Villa Via's restaurant serves an uncomplicated lunch and dinner menu, which you can have served in your room. Alternatively, the staff will shop for you; simply supply them with a shopping list in the morning, and it will be delivered by 5pm. Other facilities are 24-hour reception/traveler's desk, room service from 6:30am to 10pm, laundry, babysitting, complimentary newspaper, and airport transfers.

## WHERE TO DINE

An increase in petty crime in the center has meant that newcomers tend to frequent the restaurants and bars situated in the "restaurant suburbs" of Sunnyside and Hatfield. When in Hatfield, wander down Burnett and Duncan streets for an overwhelming choice, or head south for Esselen Street in Sunnyside.

If La Madeleine is full and you're craving French fare, head for 525 Duncan St. in Hatfield—the food at **Brasserie de Paris** (☎ **012/362-2247**) is highly recommended.

### EXPENSIVE

**Gerard Moerdyk Park Street.** Arcadia. ☎ **012/344-4856.** Reservations recommended, particularly for dinner. Main courses R50–60 ($8.35–$10). AE, CB, DC, DISC, ER, MC, V. Mon–Fri 12–2:30pm, Mon–Sat 6–9:30pm. SOUTH AFRICAN.

If you haven't yet done the traditional thing, or if you have and love it, Gerard Moerdyk prepares real *boerekos* (literally "farmers food," meaning sweetened vegetables and meat stews). The decor is a little over the top—pink walls, crystal chandeliers, and flounced silk curtains—but you can always avert your eyes to your heaped plate. The Cape Country Sample is an excellent first-time choice: a sample helping of *bobotie,* chicken pie (less than traditional), and *waterblommetjiebredie* (the delicious Cape "waterlily" stew, cooked with lamb). Alternatively, try springbok pie, ostrich egg omelets, or kudu tail in red wine. End the meal with the Moerdyk Cape Brandy Pudding.

✪ **La Madeleine.** 258 Esselen St., Sunnyside. ☎ **012/44-6076.** Reservations essential for dinner. Main courses R49–52 ($8.15–$8.65). AE, DC, MC, V. Tues–Fri 12–2, Tues–Sat 7–until late. FRENCH.

The only real bistro in Pretoria, La Madeleine's credits include a mention in the *Courvoisier Book of the Best* (an international restaurant guide), and is in every local food critic's top picks. When owner-chef Daniel Leusch presents the dishes of the day personally and lovingly, your mouth starts to water. His superb food is a blend of classical methods, creative inspiration, and seasonally fresh products; and as the restaurant holds only 45 people, there is an equally high level of service. Favorites are his legendary rack of Karoo lamb, carpaccio of fresh red tuna, wild pigeon breast with port and pears, and crab served between phyllo rounds on gazpacho sauce. Daniel's wife, pastry chef Karine, is responsible for desserts, including the sinful death by chocolate pudding.

## Moderate

**La Perla.** 211 Skinner St. ☎ **012/322-2759.** Reservations recommended. Main courses R30–55 ($5–$9.15). AE, CB, DC, DISC, ER, MC, V. Mon–Fri 12–2:30pm, Mon–Sat 6–9pm. SWISS-ITALIAN.

Close to the center, and a favorite with the diplomats and businessmen working in the city, La Perla provides welcome relief from the brashness of Hatfield. Expect a dignified atmosphere, classic dishes, cosmopolitan clientele, and staff trained in old-fashioned manners—no waiter would dare to remove a diner's plate before his table had finished. For 16 years brothers Marco and Franco Balmelli have been producing the best beef carpaccio in town, kudu fillet pan-fried in red wine and mushroom sauce, and deboned quails pan-fried with herbs, and poached salmon with sauce hollandaise. Vegetarian dishes are limited.

**Mostapha's.** 478 Duncan St., Hatfield. ☎ **012/342-3855.** Main courses R30–40 ($5–$6.65). AE, DC, MC, V. Mon–Sun 12pm–11pm (or the last customer leaves). MOROCCAN.

At press time, Mostapha's had recently moved from the Yard next door, and the decor looked a little unfinished. A single tented alcove, orange walls, and a few brightly colored cushions seemed a rather half-hearted overture to a Moroccan theme, but thankfully this is not true of the food. Trained in the kitchen of the Royal Palace of Rabat, Mostapha produces truly authentic Moroccan food. The lamb tajine, prepared with onions, saffron, cinnamon, and cardamon, is popular, as is the bastilla, a multilayered chicken phyllo pie cooked with almonds, cinnamon, and ginger. The latter is a little dry for Western tastes; ask if you can have a sauce to accompany it. The wine list is limited, so if possible, bring your own (R8/$1.35 corking fee).

**Mythos.** 1077 Burnett St., Hatfield. ☎ **012/362-6081.** Reservations recommended for dinner. Main courses R24–65 ($4–$10.85). Daily noon–11pm. AE, DC, MC, V. GREEK.

Aspasia and Stratos Malliaros believe that fine cooking first originated in Greece, and that the culmination of the Grecian principles "is a feast fit for the gods at Mythos." It would seem that their customers agree, particularly the large percentage of Greek patrons, always a good sign. *Orektika-Mezethakia* (starters) are the predictable classics—*dolmades* (stuffed grape leaves), taramosalata, fried eggplant slices—while the specialty is, of course, lamb. Try the *Arni sto Harti* (tender lamb roasted in foil). You can either choose to sit on the outside terrace under umbrellas facing Hatfield's "buzziest" street, or indoors on wooden floors under the old pressed-tin ceilings.

## Inexpensive

**Die Jaart Restaurant.** 1204 Duncan St., Hatfield. ☎ **012/342-9950.** Reservations essential on weekends. Main courses R15–39 ($2.50–$6.50). AE, DC, MC, V. Mon–Sat 9:30am until late. Sun 9:30am–6pm. TEA GARDEN/PORTUGUESE.

A favorite hang-out for the arty Afrikaner crowd, this is a delightful setting to enjoy a light lunch or dinner. A courtyard (*jaart*) set among houses that have been converted into decor and craft shops, the atmosphere is alive with gossip-mongers and agony aunts, and the food is simple. Besides the usual sandwiches and salads, there is a strong presence of Portuguese-style meat dishes: kebabs made with beef, game, or chicken, chicken *peri-peri* (a chili sauce), and grilled calamari. Service is unpretentious and courteous, though it may be a bit too laid back for some. Try and book an outside table.

**News Café.** 1 Hatfield Square, Burnett St., Hatfield. ☎ **012/362-7190.** Breakfasts R15–22 ($2.50–$3.65). Main courses R17–35 ($2.85–$5.85). AE, CB, DC, DISC, ER, MC, V. Mon–Thurs 8:30am–11pm, Fri–Sat 8:30am–12am, Sun 9am–11pm; Bar opens 10am–1am; 2am weekends. Evenings, no one under 23 admitted; dress code is smart/casual. GLOBAL/CAFE.

Everything on this menu has been tried and tested, and if dishes aren't ordered daily they're discarded quicker than yesterday's news. The cafe's specialty is the *ziva,* a Yemenite dish of layered dough, folded and toasted with a variety of fillings from all over the world—anything from the Peking Journal (vegetable stir-fry spiked with ginger) to the London Herald (rare roast beef, cheese, gherkin pickles, and olives). A casual venue during the day, with selected newspaper cuttings and TVs for viewing news, the atmosphere changes somewhat in the evening when a casual-smart dress code is enforced and no under-23s are welcome—apparently this protects foreign diplomats and businessmen from Pretoria University's rowdy students.

**The Odd Plate.** 262 Rhino St., Hennops Park Ext. 2, Centurion. ☎ **012/660-3260.** Reservations essential. Lunch main courses R30–32 ($5–$5.35). Dinner R75 ($12.50), four-course table d'hôte. AE, DC, MC, V. Wed–Sat 12pm until late. INTERNATIONAL.

This is a little off the beaten track (15 to 20 minutes south of the center), but if you have your own car, this training restaurant of the Prue Leith College of Food and Wine is worth it. Meals are prepared by students and served on a variety of plates collected by patron Prue and principal Judy Dyason. Plates that haven't made it to the tables decorate the walls of the restaurant, the original Lyttelton Manor House. Classic main courses include roast fillet with borealis sauce, red snapper with grenoblaise, chicken breasts stuffed with mushrooms served with tarragon veloute, or fettuccine with sun-dried tomatoes and olive tapenade. Reservations for an evening in their *boma* (a circular open-air area), sampling bush cooking can also be made.

## 3 Soweto

Dispossessed of their land during the 1800s and further reduced to virtual slavery by taxation, thousands of black men were forced to find work in eGoli. As more and more settled in inner-city slums, the segregationist government's concerns about having blacks nearby grew until, in 1930, a solution was found. A farm, 11 miles to the southwest of Johannesburg, was designated as the new black township. It would now take 3 hours to get to work. There were no roads, no shops, no parks, no electricity, no running water. Public transport and policing were hopelessly inadequate. Not surprisingly, most people refused to move; but in 1933 the government declared the Slums Clearance Act and forcibly evicted blacks from the inner cities. Defeated, these new homeless moved in, and Soweto, acronym for the South Western Township, was born. In 1944, James Mpanza led a mass occupation of open land near Orlando and within 2 years this, the country's first unofficial squatter camp, housed 40,000 people. Rural poverty meant that Soweto remained a magnet for millions searching for a better standard of living, and today Soweto is arguably South Africa's largest city. Population estimates range from 2 to 4 million; with people mistrusting the reasons for compiling a national census, a proper head-count is virtually impossible.

## THE CITY TODAY

Soweto is home to soccer heroes and political MPs, record producers and shebeen queens, multimillionaires and the unemployed, murderers and Nobel Peace Prize winners. Within its boundaries are 48 high schools, the largest hospital in the world, and homes that range from the meanest of shacks in dusty fields to mansions in the area known as "Beverly Hills." Very few white South Africans venture here for pleasure, despite the warm welcome Sowetans are famous for, and the fact that the few *umlungu* ("whitey") inhabitants of Soweto say they feel safer here than in the suburbs. For most, the crime statistics are frightening: Murders are common, and it is estimated that rapes occur every 30 minutes. Undaunted, the Johannesburg City Council has worked out a 4-hour hiking trail through Soweto, but the best and safest way to take in this sprawling city is with a tour operator.

Soweto is massive, consisting of 26 zones, and its sights are not easy to find. Freedom Square, for instance, where the ANC's Freedom Charter was proclaimed to thousands in 1955, is a large dust bowl littered with rubbish, though there are plans to upgrade it. Real insight can only be provided by a knowledgeable guide, preferably one who lives, or has lived, in Soweto. The downside of driving around with a tour group is that it's easy to feel that you are treating people like animals in a reserve. For this reason you are encouraged to get out of the vehicle as often as possible, and talk to the people on the street. It is, after all, a sense of community that distinguishes life in Soweto from that in Johannesburg or Pretoria.

## EXPLORING SOWETO

Soweto, like every other city, breeds entrepreneurs, some a direct result of foreign interest in life on Soweto's streets. In an attempt to differentiate themselves from the market, certain tour operators promise "alternative" experiences (the **Sincere Soweto Company,** since gone belly-up, went as far as including visits to gangsters and carjackers), but the most reliable cover similar ground. This includes exterior views of the homes of the rich and famous, including those of Archbishop Desmond Tutu, Winnie Madikizela-Mandela, and Felicia Mabuza-Suttle, South Africa's very own Oprah; a drive by Freedom Square and the Regina Mundi Church, also referred to as the "Parliament of Soweto"; a visit to the Mandelas' old home; a drive through a squatter camp; and a stop at the Hector Peterson Memorial. Each operator usually includes a pet community project on his 3–5 hour itinerary and ends with a visit to a shebeen. The word shebeen used to denote illegal drinking houses, but today is very much a descriptor of a wide variety of restaurant, club, and pub venues. Note that you are advised to carry extra cash for a meal, donations, and admission fees. Most operators also offer night tours, and can arrange for you to overnight with a Soweto family.

### GUIDED TOURS

**Thaps Executive Tours** (☎/fax **011/985-0689;** 207 Diepkloof Ext.; P.O. Biepkloof; Soweto), runs 2–3 hour tours for R150 ($25). Thabelo Mofokeng, the manager of the company, is a Sowetan native who brings a remarkable depth of knowledge and intelligence to his narratives. He and his operators can also arrange excursions into Johannesburg, Pretoria, Gold Reef City, and the Lost City/Sun City. Tours to Soweto include the standard stops, but longer, more in-depth visits can also be negotiated, depending on your interest.

**Jimmy's Face to Face Tours** (☎ **011/331-6109**) started in 1989, making it the longest-running Sowetan operator. The 3-hour tours (R150/$25) run twice daily, and can feel a little like a production line. In addition, some complain that Jimmy's is showing signs of complacency, and is no longer your best option.

A recommended alternative is **Imbiza Tours** (☎ **011/838-2667;** R165/$27.50), run by hands-on Mandy Mankazana. Specializing in Soweto for the past 6 years, Mandy has five guides working for her (ask for WonderBoy). The half-day route, which may take longer depending on interest, includes a visit to a daycare shack. Imbiza also offers highly recommended night tours, which last from 7:30pm to midnight, and cover a range of venues, including a shebeen and disco.

### THE TOP ATTRACTIONS

The tour operators listed above will make stops at these attractions. As they are rarely visited except by tour groups, phone numbers and operating hours are unavailable.

**Hector Pietersen Memorial.** R5 (85¢) admission.

These makeshift cubicles lined with a series of moving photographs were erected in 1996 in memory of the 1976 student protest, at which police opened fire on hundreds of Sowetan schoolchildren who were peacefully demonstrating against the use of Afrikaans as a medium of instruction in their schools. Included is the infamous shot of Hector Pietersen—one of the young boys who died in a hail of police bullets—being carried by a young man whose face is contorted with disbelief and pain. Hector's sister runs alongside, her mouth a silent wail of grief. The police reported 59 dead; the actual toll was thought to be closer to 500. Children turned on their parents, something hitherto unheard of in traditional society, and destroyed everything they could belonging to municipal authority—schools, post offices, and the ubiquitous beer halls. The police retaliated with arrests, brutal assaults, and killings. These photographs offer a window on the anger, the fear, the aggression, and the grief of these times, after which Soweto and South Africa were never to be the same.

**The Mandelas' Home.** R10 ($1.65) admission.

This simple home (rebuilt after it was razed to the ground during the years of Winnie's persecution by security police) is where the young Mandela couple lived before Nelson's arrest in the 1960s, and where Mrs. Mandela spent many years under house arrest. The four rooms (three before Winnie erected one as a further shield to the bullets that ripped through her house with alarming regularity) are jam-packed with Mandela memorabilia, particularly the hundreds of honorary doctorates awarded Mr. Mandela from universities all over the world. Mr. Mandela did choose to spend his first few weeks of freedom here in an attempt to orient himself, but has subsequently moved to the genteel suburb of Houghton. Very little of the man or his ex-wife clings to the atmosphere, but old bullet holes, a scrawled note from an imprisoned Nelson, and the curator, who is a great fan of Winnie, go some way toward capturing the claustrophobia and isolation Winnie must have felt under almost 20 years of house arrest.

## WHERE TO DINE

**Wandies.** 618 Dube St. ☎ **011/982-2796.** Main courses R26–30 ($4.35–$5). AE, DC, MC, V. TRADITIONAL AFRICAN.

Wandies' walls are papered with business cards from previous visits; from international names like Richard Branson to local celebs like the latest Miss Hillbrow, everyone's been here. The decor is rather unprepossessing—long tables, at lunchtime filled mostly with tourists—but the food is delicious. A selection of chicken, lamb, beef, and sausage stews served with traditional vegetables (mashed carrot and potato, spinach, and potato) and pap (maize meal) are unsophisticated but extremely filling. Rice is optional. The wine list is displayed in a novel way; bottles from various estates and grapes are placed at random on the tables, to pick one take a stroll.

Wandies is a great place, but as you're likely to be surrounded by other tourists, not the most authentic. For that, try an evening tour, and ask for the **Blue Fountain** to be included on the itinerary.

## 4 Side Trips to North-West Province

### LESEDI CULTURAL VILLAGE

The Lesedi Cultural Village is unique in that it comprises four totally separate homesteads, respectively inhabited by a Zulu, Xhosa, Pedi, and Basotho family, all of whom live here permanently looking after the cows, chickens, and tourists that wander through the veld from village to village. Visitors booking **Monati Lunch Experience** (11:30am to 2pm, R165/$27.50 per person, R83/$13.85 children 5 to 12) are taken to only two homesteads. Afterward a traditional singing and dancing session is held in the boma, and a buffet lunch (including pap, spinach, pumpkin, samp, and beans, beef or chicken stew, and beer) is served. To see all four homesteads, which allows for interesting cross-cultural analysis regarding the architectural and social organization and customs of these groups at the turn of the century, you'll have to go on the popular Boma experience (R220/$36.65 per person, R110/$18.35 children 5 to 12). Guests are advised to arrive at 4am, and the evening, which ends with dinner, winds up at about 9:30pm. Dinner (similar to lunch) is shared with members from all four families who will answer any further questions you may have. As the tour does not cover current lifestyles and customs, this is the best time to find out what changes the 20th century has wrought. There are comfortable guest rooms in each of the four village, but these are seldom used.

**GETTING THERE** The cultural village is 45 minutes from Johannesburg. To get here take the M1 north from Johannesburg, then take the N1 West at the interchange (rather than N1 North to Pretoria). Take the Hans Strydom exit off the N1 and proceed along the R512 to Lesedi, on your left-hand side. Lesedi can incidentally be taken in on the way to Sun City. For more information, call ☎ **012/205-1394** or e mail: lesedi@pixie.co.za.

### SUN CITY & THE PALACE OF THE LOST CITY

Set within the southern border of the Pilanesberg National Park, this glitzy Vegas-styled resort is made up of casinos, cinemas, theaters, restaurants, two world-class golf courses, man-made jungles, lakes, and the Palace of the Lost City, arguably the most luxurious 5-star hotel in Africa. Developer Sol Kerzner, the boxer-turned-businessman known locally as the "Sun King" capitalized on apartheid South Africa's stern anti-gambling laws by situating Sun City in the then homeland of Baphutatswana. As an independent state, Baphutatswana was literally a law unto itself, and millions began to swarm to "Sin City," not only to gamble, but to see international acts like Sinatra, George Benson, and Elton John.

#### EXPLORING THE RESORT

The resort is relatively easy to get around, and shuttle buses are constantly moving from one end to the next. A **sky train** takes visitors without cars from the entrance to the entertainment center. Closest to the entrance is the **Kwena Crocodile Sanctuary, Waterworld,** and the **Cabanas,** followed by the **Sun City Hotel, Casino,** and **Gary Player Golf Club.** Adjoining the club to the north is the **Cascades Hotel and Entertainment Centre,** from where you enter the grounds of the Palace of the Lost City, for most, the star attraction.

Built 12 years after Sun City opened, the sheer magnitude of the palace's opulence is proof of how much money has been lost by the those frequenting Sun City's slot machines and tables. Separated from the rest of the resort by "the bridge of time"—a large stone structure that shudders and rumbles at pre-appointed times in a mythical earthquake, and lined with a "guard of honor" of carved elephants—the palace is entered through the massive Mighty Kong Gates. Looking down on the rivers and jungle vegetation, you truly feel as if you are entering another world; it's hard to imagine that a decade ago there was nothing but a dusty, rocky plain here. From the bridge, you can clearly see the "Valley of Waves," where landlocked Gautengers learn to surf on simulated waves, tan on manmade beaches, and hurtle down steep waterslides, reaching speeds of up to 35 kilometers (22 miles) an hour. In the distance, overlooking a lake filled with live flamingoes, is the majestic palace, with what seems like an entire jungle of carved animals in attendance. Surrounding the palace is what must be the most artfully landscaped garden in Africa, featuring five trails through 22 different sections of forest. The theme (that of a lost city, which has been rediscovered and restored) is sometimes carried to a ridiculous extreme, but the craftsmanship is world-class; the fantasy landscape quite overwhelming. But with Michael Jackson a regular visitor and now the majority shareholder, things can only get weirder.

## Sun City Essentials

You can fly to Sun City on **SA Airlink** (☎ **011/394-2430**) or take a bus (book through **Computicket** at ☎ **011/331-9991** or through the Tourism Office in Pretoria at ☎ **012/313-7980**).

Alternatively, it's a 90-minute to 2-hour drive (187km/116 miles) northwest of Jo'burg. You take the N1 to Pretoria, then head west via the N4. Note that nonresidents pay R40 ($6.65) to enter Sun City (of which R30/$5 are "Sunbucks," the "local" currency) and will not be allowed to enter the palace. Overnighters pay no entry anywhere. For more information, call ☎ **014/557-1000** and ask for the Public Relations department.

To organize safari trips into neighboring **Pilanesberg** from Sun City, contact **Gametrackers** (☎ **014/552-1561**).

## Where to Stay & Dine

Most of the restaurants in the Entertainment Complex are grill rooms, pizza dens, and curry taverns. For the best fine-dining experience, book a table at the Palace's **Crystal Court,** where 7-meter-high (23-foot-high) doors open onto rolling views over the Valley of Waves and Californian food is served. Or try the **Villa Del Palazzo,** also at the Palace, which serves regional Italian cuisine.

**The Cabanas.** P.O. Box 3, Sun City 0316. ☎ **014/557-1000.** Fax 014/557-1902 or 014/557-1131. 380 units. A/C MINIBAR (on request) TV TEL R755–870 ($128.85–$145) double. Family rooms R945–1055 ($157.50–$175.85). Children under 18 sharing with parents stay free. AE, DC, MC, V.

Closest to the resort entrance and overlooking "Waterworld" (the resort's largest artificial lake where a variety of watersports are offered), the terraced cabanas are designed to appeal to families. Besides being the most relaxed and casual of the hotels, a fully supervised program of kid's activities and facilities is available at Kwena's Castle, on the Cabana's lawns. Ask for a lake-facing unit. There are three dining options within the hotel. Every night of the week a differently themed buffet is served at the Palm Terrace, or you can enjoy grills at Morula Restaurant or light meals at the Morula Cafe. Guests enjoy access to all the Sun City and Palace facilities, which are immense.

**The Cascades.** P.O. Box 7, Sun City 0316. ☎ **014/557-1000.** Fax 014/557-1902 or 014/557-1131. 243 units. A/C MINIBAR TV TEL. R1,230–1,535 ($205–$255.85) double; R2,750–7,500 ($458.35–$1,250) suite. Children under 18 sharing with parents stay free. AE, DC, MC, V.

A comfortable, and ultimately better value-for-money option than the Sun City Hotel (not to mention more stylish), this is also a very good alternative to the Palace. All rooms are spacious (many with sunken Jacuzzis in the bedroom) and overlook the huge tropical gardens with its waterfalls, weirs, lagoons, and shaded walks. If you ask for a room on one of the top floors, you'll have a view of the Gary Player–designed golf course and beyond, the bushveld plains. The Peninsula Restaurant is set next to a lake, while the Grotto Restaurant and Bar is tucked under a waterfall. Consider dining at the Palace; the walk is short and spectacular.

✪ **Palace of the Lost City.** P.O. Box 308, Sun City 0316. ☎ **014/557-1000.** Fax 014/557-1902 or 014/557-1131. 338 units. A/C MINIBAR TV TEL. R2,085–2,395 ($347.50–$399.15) double; R3,030–21,065 ($505–$3,510.85) suite. Children under 18 sharing with parents stay free. AE, DC, MC, V.

This is one of the most fantastical hotels in the world. From beautiful life-size carvings of animals arching out of fountains and from walls, to tusk-like pens in every room, the decor is totally over the top, and a must for anyone even remotely interested in design. Standard rooms are a little disappointing given the opulence of the public spaces (even the lifts feature exquisite carvings), so make sure you book a lake-facing room, where the view will make up for it. However, if money is no option, there's nothing to beat a suite at the Palace of the Lost City—just ask Michael Jackson.

**The Sun City Hotel.** P.O. Box 2, Sun City 0316. ☎ **014/557-1000.** Fax 014/557-1902 or 014/557-1131. 340 units. A/C MINIBAR TV TEL. R1,135–1,420 ($189.15–$236.65) double; R4,000–5,625 ($666.65–$937.50) suite. Children under 18 sharing with parents stay free. AE, DC, MC, V.

This hotel, situated in the same building as the main casino and nightclub, is the tackiest of the Sun City hotels and best avoided, unless you're solely here to gamble, and want to be as close as possible to the jangling slot machines.

## PILANESBERG NATIONAL PARK

Some 1.4 billion years ago, the Pilanesberg plains were bubbling away in the second largest alkaline volcano in the world. Today the rim of this ancient crater, eroded by time, forms the natural boundary of undulating Pilanesberg National Park. Typified by concentric rings of rocky hills, and centered on a large hippo- and crocodile-filled lake, Pilanesberg is one of Africa's most picturesque parks. It's also definitely the place to view game if you're stuck in Jo'burg with limited time to go elsewhere. In 1979, this once over-grazed farmland was transformed by Operation Genesis, which saw the translocation of over 7,000 animals into the 58,000-hectare (145,000 acre) reserve. These 35 large mammal species include the Big 5, as well as leopard, cheetah, and brown hyena. The park's natural beauty, abundance of wild animals, and lack of malaria have made it one of the area's strongest drawing cards, though most combine a visit with a sojourn at the Palace. However, first-time visitors to the bush should note that this is not the untamed wilderness of, say, Lapalala (see chapter 7, "Northern Province") or Madikwe (see below)—both these malaria-free reserves are some 3 to 4 hours from Gauteng. Pilanesberg's proximity to Sun City and Gauteng means that its well-maintained network of roads can get very busy. On the positive side, this means you're probably more likely to spot your Big 5 (see chapter 7 for game-viewing tips).

### Pilanesberg Park Essentials

The main entrance and reception (☎ **014/555-6135**) are at the Manyane Gate on the eastern side. From Johannesburg take the R24 north to Rustenburg, then follow the R510 to Thabazimbi and turn left near Mogwase. From Sun City, the nearest entrance is Bakubung Gate, west off the resort on the R565. Gates are open April to August, 6am to 6pm, and September to March 5:30am to 7pm. Entry costs R15 ($2.50) per person, and maps are issued as you enter. Guided game drives can be arranged from reception or, if you're staying at Sun City, you can arrange a safari trip in an open-topped Land Rover with **Gametrackers** (☎ **014/552-1561**). Gametrackers also operates hiking trips accompanied by armed rangers (4-person minimum) and hot-air balloon safaris.

### Where to Stay & Dine

If you're looking for a certain level of comfort, but still want to feel as if you're living in the untamed bush, there is only one place worth considering.

**Tshukudu Lodge.** P.O. Box 6805, Rustenburg 0300. Guests are transferred from Bakubung Lodge, located just west of Sun City on the southern edge of the reserve, by vehicle at 2:30pm. ☎ **014/552-1610.** Fax 014/552-1620. 8 units. MINIBAR. Cottages R2,100–2,500 ($350–$416.65); cabins R1,100–1,600 ($183.35–$266.65). Rates include all meals and activities; exclude alcohol. AE, DC, MC, V. Children 12 and over only.

Climbing the 134 steep steps to the lodge (luggage is carried for you), you may be forgiven for cursing Tshukudu, (or "place of the rhino"). Get to the top though, and the panoramic view alone is likely to replenish your reserves. The setting, atop a *koppie* (hill) overlooking a large open plain and waterhole, provides great views of a variety of game from the dining area/bar platform. Run by a mother-and-son team, Alma and Jacques, both sticklers for detail, the luxurious cottages are equipped with everything from binoculars to walking sticks. Designed to make the most of the view, the spacious cottage interior is divided into two distinct areas. The bedroom overlooks a small lounge (with fireplace) that opens onto a private balcony overlooking the plain. The sunken bathtub also has a view of the plain; you won't miss the cheetah kill just because you happen to be taking a bath. Game walks and drives are scheduled daily, and as Tshukudu is located in a private part of Pilanesberg that's inaccessible to the Sun City day-trippers, this is a tranquil experience. Brunch is served after the morning game drive, while high tea (quiche, freshly baked breads, and cakes) is served just before the afternoon game drive. Dinner menus evince a strong traditional Afrikaans influence, with a sit-down starter followed by a potjie (stew) or roast of some sort, accompanied by sweet potatoes and sweetened carrots.

## MADIKWE

In 1991, a 75,000-hectare (187,500-acre) area on the South Africa/Botswana border was proclaimed the Madikwe Game Reserve, thereby transforming a previously overgrazed farming area into South Africa's fourth-largest reserve. Within 6 years, 10,000 animals (28 species, including the Big 5) were once again roaming the Madikwe plains in what was dubbed Operation Phoenix, the largest game translocation exercise in the world. The decision to do this here was based on the area's highly diverse ecozones—bordered by the spectacular Dwarsberg Mountains in the south and the Marico River in the east, the rocky hills, perennial rivers, seasonal wetlands, acacia bushveld, savannah grassland, and Kalahari sandveld allows the reserve to support an unusual range of animal species. Ecologically, Madikwe is better suited to support wildlife than livestock, and today it has the second-largest elephant population in the country, and is one of only three reserves in South Africa that houses a breeding pack of wild dogs. They are Africa's most endangered predator and, as they need a range of some 2000 square meters, are notoriously difficult to fence in. With only two tourist lodges within the entire 75,000-hectare area, it's also large enough to satisfy visitors starved of solitude, something the more popular Mpumulanga reserves can't always deliver.

## Madikwe Essentials

Madikwe is some 280 kilometers (174 miles) northwest of Johannesburg. The River Lodge will arrange air transfers (it's a 45-minute flight). Alternatively, you can travel by car via tarred roads. From Pretoria, this takes about 4½ hours via the N4 through Rustenburg to Zeerust, then heading north R49 to Madikwe's Abjaterskop Gate. The trip via well-maintained dirt roads takes about 3½ hours from Pretoria; ask the lodge to fax you a map. The latter is definitely the recommended route—with no one on the road, and surrounded by bush and classic African skies, the journey itself is a holiday.

## Where to Stay & Dine

✪ **Madikwe River Lodge.** P.O. Box 17, Derdepoort 2876. Reservations ☎ **011/788-1258.** Direct 014/778-0891. Fax 011/788-0739. 16 units. R695–850 ($65.80–$141.60) per person sharing a double. Includes all meals and game activities. AE, DC, MC, V.

A member of the Small Luxury Hotels of the World, Madikwe comprises a compact, central public area—with bird-viewing deck, rock pool with open-plan bar, lounge and dining area—and increasingly private, free-standing thatched chalets, following the curve of the narrow Marico River. Each chalet is attractively furnished with indigenous woods and white linen, and features a split-level bedroom and a lounge, which opens onto a small deck area overlooking the river. Like all lodges, game drives are offered in the morning and evening in open-topped vehicles, with experienced rangers and trackers on hand for identification and explanation. Unlike any other lodge in South Africa, however, Madikwe offers additional "children's game drives," taking into account both their curiosity and limited attention spans. Combined with the fact that this is a malaria-free area, and the variety of game, Madikwe is one of the best young-family destinations in the country. Given prior warning, horse safaris and balloon safaris can also be arranged. Chefs Zebilon and Gaynor specialize in venison dishes for dinners, with continental breakfasts served prior to early-morning game drives, followed by brunch and, in the afternoons, high tea.

# 7

# Mpumalanga & the Northern Province

The Northern Province and its southern neighbor, Mpumalanga, form the northeastern corner of South Africa, and with the neighboring Swaziland, Mozambique, Zimbabwe, and Botswana, make up southern Africa's big-game plateaux. The climate and topography of the region vary from the cool grasslands of the highveld to the subtropical lowveld savannah, and support a number of industries, including agriculture, forestry, mining, manufacture, and tourism.

Most people who come to this region are looking for the romance of precolonial Africa—vast plains of bush savannah teeming with game, rivers swollen with lumbering hippos and lurking crocodiles, dense indigenous jungles alive with twittering birds, horizons shimmering with heat, and nights lit only by stars and crackling campfires. These you will find—and more. Here, too, is the Escarpment, offering some of the country's most breathtaking drives and views; Blyde River Canyon, the third-largest canyon in the world; numerous Stone Age sites; the gardens of the legendary Rain Queen; and a perfectly preserved boomtown that tells of the short but turbulent gold-rush era.

But Kruger National Park is one of Africa's greatest game parks. It is a profound experience coming into contact with Africa's wild animals, and Kruger's first-class facilities make this experience tremendously accessible. Numerous budget accommodation options are scattered throughout the park.

Predictably, even in this scenic environment you cannot escape the contrast that is South Africa; on the park's western flank lie ultra-luxurious private game reserves, with prices that are way beyond even the well-heeled South African. Beyond these are the economically deprived communities of Lebowa, Gazankulu, and Kangwane. Many in these communities resent what they see as a white-man's playground; others are grateful for the employment opportunities which, particularly in the park, have been increasing. But an impoverished and rapidly expanding human population is not the only problem the wildlife sanctuaries face: The vast man-made forests of the Escarpment, claimed to be the largest in the world, are literally sucking the lowveld dry. As the region enters a new century, the challenge will be to find a balance between the needs of industry and those of the communities, pulling them into a general economic interdependence and prosperity for the region, with Kruger National Park at the hub. To a large extent, the growth of tourism is doing just that.

## 1 Staying Active

**BIRD WATCHING** Along with KwaZulu-Natal, Mpumalanga and the Northern Province are the prime bird-watching destinations in South Africa. Many native species inhabit these enormously varying habitats. Over and above either Kruger or the private reserves, **Wakkerstroom,** one of the last remaining grassland regions in southern Africa and a declared endemic bird area by BirdLife International, should be included in the birder's itinerary. Mid-September to the end of March are particularly good months. **Nylsvlei,** a wetland area in the Northern Province, is another good choice. For expert advice and tailor-made tours to these areas, as well as to other top birding destinations in southern Africa, contact **Lawson's Birdwatching Tours** (☎ **013/755-2147**). For tours concentrating on the Escarpment and lowveld, contact ornithologist Dr. Peter Milstein. His services necessitate a stay at his appropriately named **Eyrie Birding Lodge** (☎ **015/795-5775**), 36 kilometers (22 miles) from Hoedspruit on the R531. **Spectra-Ventures** (☎ **013/744-9629**) offers excursions which incorporate aspects such as astronomy, bush cuisine, and cultural storytelling.

**FLY-FISHING** Trout fishing on the highland Escarpment is well established, with an infrastructure of self-catering cottages, guest houses, and lodges situated on well-stocked lakes and streams. **Dullstroom** is the unofficial capital of the trout-fishing areas, and rod rental, fees, and accommodations can be arranged through their helpful Tourist Information Centre, call ☎ **013/254-0254.**

The **Mpumalanga Tourism Authority** also has some helpful information; check their Web site at www.mpumalanga.com/html/wtdfish.htm. **Trout Hideaway's** (☎ **013/768-1347**), self-catering chalets in the Pilgrim's Rest area, are highly recommended, but off the beaten track. For information on trout fishing in the Letaba area, contact **Byadladi Tourist Association,** in Haenertsburg (☎ **015/276-4472**).

**GOLFING** The 9-hole course at **Skukuza** (☎ **013/735-5611**) is quite possibly the most dangerous course in the world—it's unfenced, and wild animals wander the greens at will. Visitors wishing to play here can do so strictly by prior arrangement with chairman Chris van der Linde. More wild golfing experiences await at the exclusive 18-hole course at **Leopard's Creek** (☎ **013/790-3322**—besides the resident leopard, crocs and hippos lurk in the aptly named water hazards. To play here, you'll have to book into the Malelane Sun (see "Where to Stay" in "Lowveld"). Wild animals are also regular visitors to the fairways at the 18-hole **Hans Merensky Country Club** (☎ **015/781-3931**), at Phalaborwa. Book into one of the luxurious Makalali lodges, which lie just under an hour away.

If the thought of meeting a leopard in the rough puts you right off course, choose a scenic option: the 9-hole **Pilgrim's Rest** course (☎ **013/768-1116**) and the more challenging 18-hole championship course at **White River Country Club** (☎ **013/751-3781**) are both popular.

**HORSEBACK RIDING** Many of the Escarpment lodges keep horses, and tourism centers can advise on day rides. A good outfit is **Kaapschehoop Horse Trails** (☎ **013/734-4055**). Situated 36 kilometers (23 miles) southeast of Nelspruit, they offer anything from 2-hour to 2-day trails, accompaniment by experienced guides, a variety of well-schooled horses, and—with traversing rights to 37,000 hectares (92,500 acres) of tranquil forest and open grassland—an environment well worth exploring. Western- and English-style saddles are available. Weekend trails cost R420 ($70) per person; 3-day wilderness trails R650 ($108.35) per person; 5-day pony camps cost R350 ($58.35) per child (8–15 years). Rates include food and lodging.

Highly recommended are the riding safaris that take place in the Northern Province, where you track mammals in the African bush and learn about the local ecology. These are offered by **Equus Horse Safaris** (☎ **011/788-3923**), in the Lapalala Wilderness Area. See "The Waterberg & the Lapalala Wilderness Area," below, for more information.

**HIKING** **SAFCOL** (South African Forestry) has created hiking trails with overnight facilities through some incredibly scenic areas, including the popular 2-, 3-, and 5-day **Magoebaskloof Trails** (R45/$7.50 per person per night), and the 2-, 3-, and 5-day **Fanie Botha Trails** (R35/$5.85 per person per night). Accommodations are bunk beds; showers, flush toilets, wood, and braai facilities are provided.

There are also a number of excellent day trails, most of which are near the Escarpment towns of Sabie and Graskop—the 14-kilometer (9-mile) **Loerie Trail** takes you through some of the region's most attractive surrounds, while the 3-kilometer (2-mile) **Forest Falls Walk** is as pretty as it sounds, and good for those who want to take it easy. If you venture farther north, the 11-kilometer (7-mile) circular **Rooikat Trail,** which follows a stream through the forests of Agatha, is another day trail worth tackling. For excellent advice on all these trails, call Esme (☎ **013/764-1058**), or contact headquarters at ☎ **012/481-3615,** or e-mail ecotour@mail.safcol.co.za.

Another highly recommended hike in the Mpumalanga area is the relatively tough 5-day **Blyde River Canyon Trail,** a 65-kilometer (40-mile) walk that traverses the full length of the Blyde River Canyon Nature Reserve, from the misty heights of God's Window to the tranquil waters of the Blyderivierspoort Dam (tempting in summer, but hikers should be wary of crocodiles and hippos). Hikers' huts are basic: bunk beds, flush toilets, braai sites, pots, and firewood are provided; everything else must be carried in (don't forget toilet paper!). The views and vegetation make this one of the most popular trails in South Africa, so book well in advance (☎ **013/758-1035**).

The **Wolkberg Wilderness** (literally translated, "cloud mountain") area is known for the mists that curl around its rugged peaks, grassland valleys, lush virgin forests, and crystal-clear waterfalls. It's a hardcore hiker's paradise; the basic facilities will run you R3 (50¢) per person per day, and hikers are warned to keep an eye out for snakes. Leopards and the rare brown hyena are also making a comeback since the hunters and marijuana growers who used this area to hide their crops were flushed out in the 1950s. Bring everything, including your own tent and camp stove (no fires are allowed). For information and reservations, contact Cornelius van der Berg at ☎ **015/276-4263** or call the reserve directly at ☎ **015/276-1303.**

For hiking and tracking animals in game reserves, see "Kruger Wilderness Trails," "Lapalala River Trails," and "Where to Stay & Dine in Manyeleti," below.

**HUNTING** Hunting season usually runs from April to September, though some farms enjoy all-year concessions. For more information on procedures and bookings, contact Billy Swanepoel at Mpumalanga Parks Board on ☎ **013/759-5300** or the **Lowveld Hunting Association** at ☎ **013/752-3575.** For softies, there's skeet shooting in the Dullstroom surrounds; note that bookings must be made 3 hours in advance. Call ☎ **013/254-0254.**

**KLOOFING** This is a South African favorite, in which you follow the course of a river by clambering over rocks and boulders and where possible, simply swimming and floating your way downstream. With **Zambezi Spectacular** (☎ **011/794-1707**), you can explore the upper section of the Blyde River, enjoy a light lunch at a breathtaking waterfall, tackle a quick abseil, then pack up and head home. R275 ($45.85) per person; children 12 to 16 R225 ($37.50).

**MOUNTAIN BIKING** Sabie is a bike-friendly area, and **Sondelani Visitor Information** (☎ **013/764-3492**) will assist with finding bikes to rent; expect to pay R60–80 ($10–$13.35) a day, and ask about the Long Tom and Ceylon Trails. Alternatively, you can rent from the **Merry Pebbles Resort** in Sabie (☎ **013/764-2266**); they have their own clearly marked and recommended routes. Another ride worth undertaking if you travel Magoebaskloof/Letaba way is the exhilarating 19-kilometer (12-mile) **Debengeni Downhill,** a forestry road that starts at the top of the Magoebaskloof Pass and plummets down to the Debengeni Falls. To rent a mountain bike in this area, you'll have to stay at one of the hotels listed below.

**RANGER TRAINING** In Sabi Sabi's 3-day ranger training program (☎ **011/ 483-3939**), a maximum of eight trainees stay in a basic tented camp (bush toilet and shower) and are taught such elementary skills as distracting a charging elephant, driving a Land Rover down a perpendicular river bank, shooting a .458 Magnum, reading the stars, and identifying and tracking a variety of game. This is a great way to get to know the bush, R1,200 ($200) per person per night.

**RIVER RAFTING** There are three rivers on which rafting takes place during the summer months (October to May). The tranquil **Sabie River** offers a 3- to 4-hour trip on flat water, covering some 12 kilometers (7 miles). This is ideal for families (6 years and up only). Expect to pay R150–165 ($25–$27.50). Trips down the **Oliphants Gorge** (overall grade II, some IV) are a little more challenging. A 2-day trip, approximately 60 kilometers (37 miles), takes you through spectacular scenery, and the night is spent on a sandy beach flanked by steep mountainside and baobab trees. Expect to pay R650–750 ($108.35–$125) per person. The lower age limit is 12, but minors must be accompanied by parents. The **Blyde River** (a few grade IVs, overall grade III) offers the most exciting rafting in this area. This 8.5-kilometer (5-mile) trip can be completed in one (tiring!) day, but spending a night in the canyon is definitely recommended. The minimum age is 14 or 16, depending on which company you contact; expect to pay R650 ($108.35). For more information on the Oliphants and Blyde rivers, contact **Otter's Den** at ☎ **015/795-5250** or e-mail catfish@mweb.co.za. Other companies that run these rivers are **Hardy Ventures** (☎ **013/751-1693**), **Adventure Seekers** (☎ **021/702-8733**), and **Zambezi Spectacular** (☎ **011/794-1707**).

## 2 Organized Tours

If you don't want to follow the suggestions below for exploring this region in your own car, you may want to consider going with one of these recommended tour operators.

Johan Britz's **EscarpEscapes** (☎ **083/441-7416**) offers 4×4 excursions into the Escarpment forests surrounding Graskop. **Indaba Tours** (☎ **013/737-7115**) has half- and full-day open-vehicle safaris to Kruger—a couple traveling with a registered guide can expect to pay R475 ($79.15) per person for a full day, excluding lunch. They also do the Panorama Route (R525/$87.50) with lunch at Pilgrim's Rest, as well as a highly recommended night safari; these take place in Kapama and include a visit to the Hoedspruit Research & Breeding Centre (R515/$85.85 with supper). Less exclusive (you'll share your vehicle), **Welcome Safaris** (☎ **013/737-7945** or cell 082804-5026) offers all the above, at a lower price—a full-day safari in Kruger will cost only R270 ($45), including lunch. Tours use Skukuza Rest Camp as a departure point. Welcome Safaris also conducts night safaris into the Sabi Sand private game reserve—at R690 ($115) per person, including supper, it's a cost-effective way of seeing the most exclusive game reserve in South Africa.

Pikkie Baker's **Letaba Active Tours** (☎ **015/307-1294**) offers tailor-made tours to suit traveling via the Magoebaskloof region to Kruger.

### Specialist Tours

John Williams at **Monsoon's African Travel and Adventures** (☎ **015/795-5114** or 083/700-8921) will help plan a self-drive itinerary that takes in the less-publicized cultural and archaeological sights in the big-game regions of southern Africa, offering the opportunity to meet the artists and craftspeople whose works stock his gallery. He will also assist visitors in visiting the far reaches of the Northern Province, which is not well geared for tourism. For accompaniment by a specialist guide, be sure to make arrangements well in advance.

## 3 En Route to Big-Game Country

Many travelers going to Kruger or the private lodges nearby fly to Gauteng and then rent a car. The journey, a comfortable 5-hour drive with no major detours, includes some of South Africa's most dramatically beautiful drives, and the surrounds become scenic within 2 hours of leaving Gauteng. The three routes described below take you from the highveld plateau before dropping, usually quite spectacularly, to the lowveld, much of which is taken up by Kruger National Park and the surrounding private game reserves. The best way to savor the journey is to overnight at one of the many places that lie between 2 and 4 hours away from Gauteng and make the most of the Escarpment's dramatic scenery.

The first route takes you via the escarpment towns of **Sabie** and **Graskop** (Pilgrim's Rest is an optional but recommended side trip), before traversing the Escarpment rim along what is called the **Panorama Route**—a spectacular half-day drive. This journey will definitely warrant an overnight stay, preferably two.

The second approach is via **Waterval-Boven** on the N4, the main artery connecting Gauteng with **Nelspruit,** the capital of Mpumalanga—this is ideal if you need to enter one of Kruger's southern gates and don't have time to do much sightseeing on the way.

A lesser-known route to central Kruger, but in parts even more scenic, particularly from June to August, is to follow in the footsteps of the Voortrekkers on the **Great North Road** (N1) as far as **Pietersburg,** then branch off eastward via the **Letaba area,** also known as "land of the silver mist" and also as the "garden of the Rain Queen." This will also necessitate overnighting.

These routes can also be combined or expanded into 3- or 4-day itineraries as there's so much to see, but remember to leave plenty of time to soak up the sights and sounds of the bushveld. If you need to save travel time to do so, your best bet is to fly to Nelspruit airport from where you can drive north and include the Panorama Route or head straight for Kruger.

## 4 Touring the Escarpment

This is the most popular route to big-game country, with roads taking you past endless pine and gum forests, pockets of tangled indigenous jungle, plunging waterfalls, and breathtaking views of the subtropical plains. It is a 4-hour drive from Gauteng, and an easy escape for ever-harassed city dwellers desperate to breathe fresh air and drive around with unlocked doors. Unfortunately the air is not always that fresh; Mpumalanga's industrial activities are responsible for one of the highest acid rainfalls in the world. This is compounded during the dry winter months, when veld fires are rife, coloring the air with a hazy smog that obscures the views. While this is one reason

**Tips for Driving to Kruger**

If you intend to head for Kruger from Johannesburg without stopping over on the way, you should plan your route so that you enter the park via the gate closest to the camp you will be overnighting at. As the park's rules regarding speed limits are strict, driving within the park is slow going. You may arrive at your final resting place within the park later than you had planned, and find yourself unable to check in—camp admission times are also inflexible.

---

to consider traveling via the Letaba area (see below), which is generally greener during this time, there is nothing to match the magnificence of looking down at the lowveld plains from God's Window or watching the Blyde River snake through Blyde River Canyon, thousands of meters below. In addition, the region's popularity makes for a plethora of great accommodation options; it's worth noting that, with the exception of Pilgrim's Rest, overnighting in any of the Escarpment towns would be a mistake, as the surrounding country offers a lot more by way of views and setting.

In short, the route is as follows: After driving to **Dullstroom,** the highest town on the Escarpment, you drop down the eastern slopes via the Long Tom Pass to the forestry towns of **Sabie** and **Graskop.** (**Pilgrim's Rest,** a restored gold-mining village and historical monument, lies another mountain pass away, and warrants a separate visit of a least a half day, excluding travel time.) Graskop is the gateway to the **Panorama Route,** a drive which curls along the rim of the Escarpment, with lookout points peppered along the way that provide relatively easy access to some of the most panoramic views in Africa. Once past the canyon lookouts, the final descent to the lowveld follows the Abel Erasmus Pass to **Hoedpsruit.** You can then either complete the loop and return to Graskop or enter the Kruger via the centrally located Orpen Gate, or the private game reserves of Timbavati, Manyeleti, and Kapama.

## ESSENTIALS

**GETTING THERE** **By Car** To reach the Escarpment from Gauteng, take N12 from Johannesburg, which joins up with N4, the main artery between Gauteng and Mpumalanga. When you reach Belfast, turn north onto the R540 to Dullstroom.

**By Plane** **To Hoedspruit: SA Express** (☎ **015/793-3681**) has daily flights to Eastgate Airport (in Kapama, a private reserve near Kruger) from Johannesburg and from Cape Town three times a week. **To Nelspruit:** Nelspruit Airport is closer to Sabie; see " The Lowveld Route—Gateway to Southern Kruger: Getting There," below, or contact **Airlink** at ☎ **011/394-2430** or 013/741-3536.

**VISITOR INFORMATION** **In Sabie** **Sondelani,** 94 Main St. (☎ **013/764-3492**). Hours are Monday to Friday from 8am to 5pm, Saturday and Sunday 9am to 1pm.

**GETTING AROUND** You can either go with a tour operator (see above) or rent a car and travel at your own pace. **Avis** has a desk at the Hoedspruit Airport (☎ **015/793-2014**).

## DULLSTROOM

At 2,012 meters (6,600 feet) above sea level, Dullstroom (230km/142½ miles northeast of Johannesburg) is the highest town on the Escarpment—expect bitterly cold evenings in the winter, and don't be surprised to find fires lit even in mid-summer. The town dates back to the 1880s, when a committee under the chairmanship of Wolterus

# Mpumalanga & Northern Province

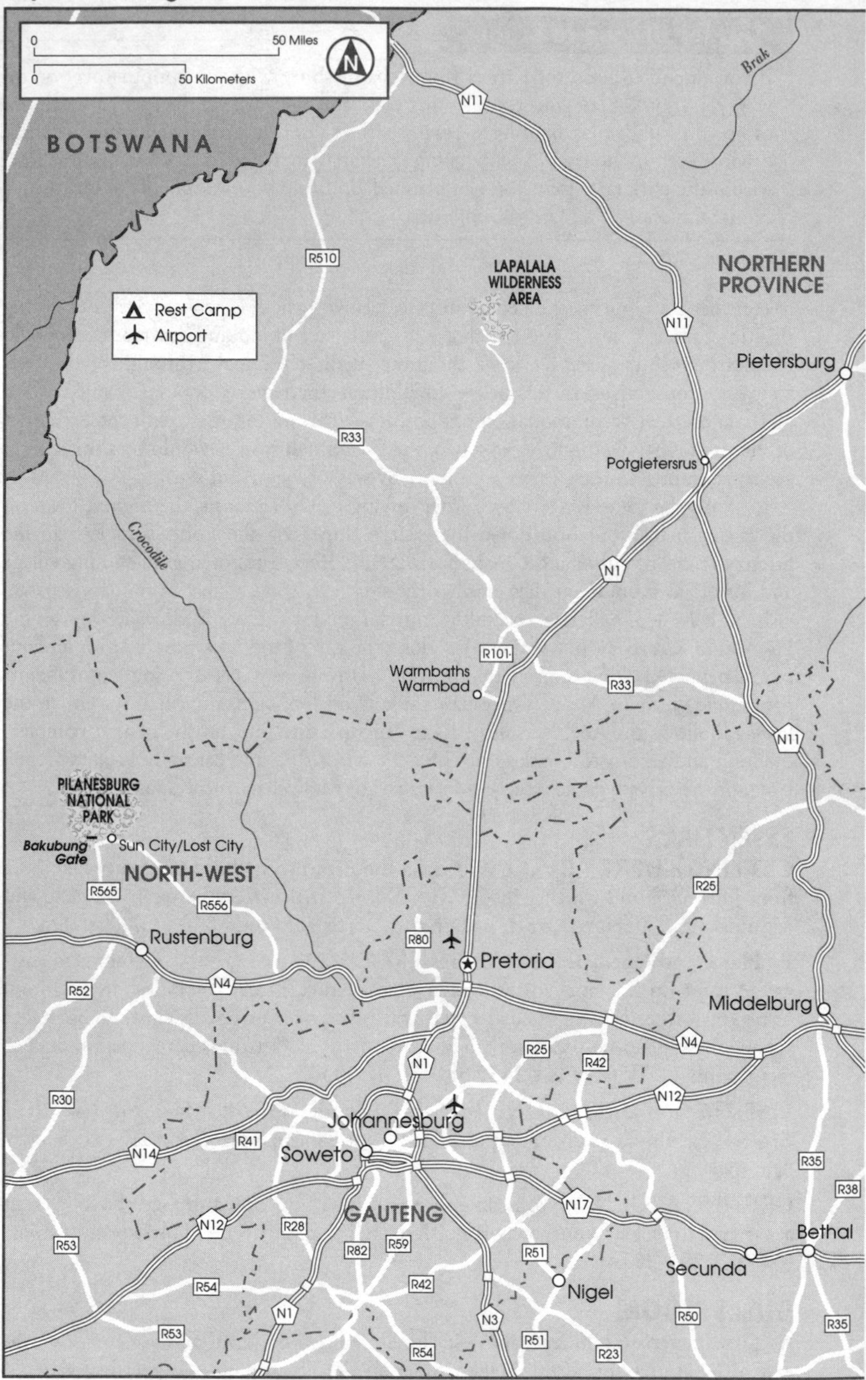

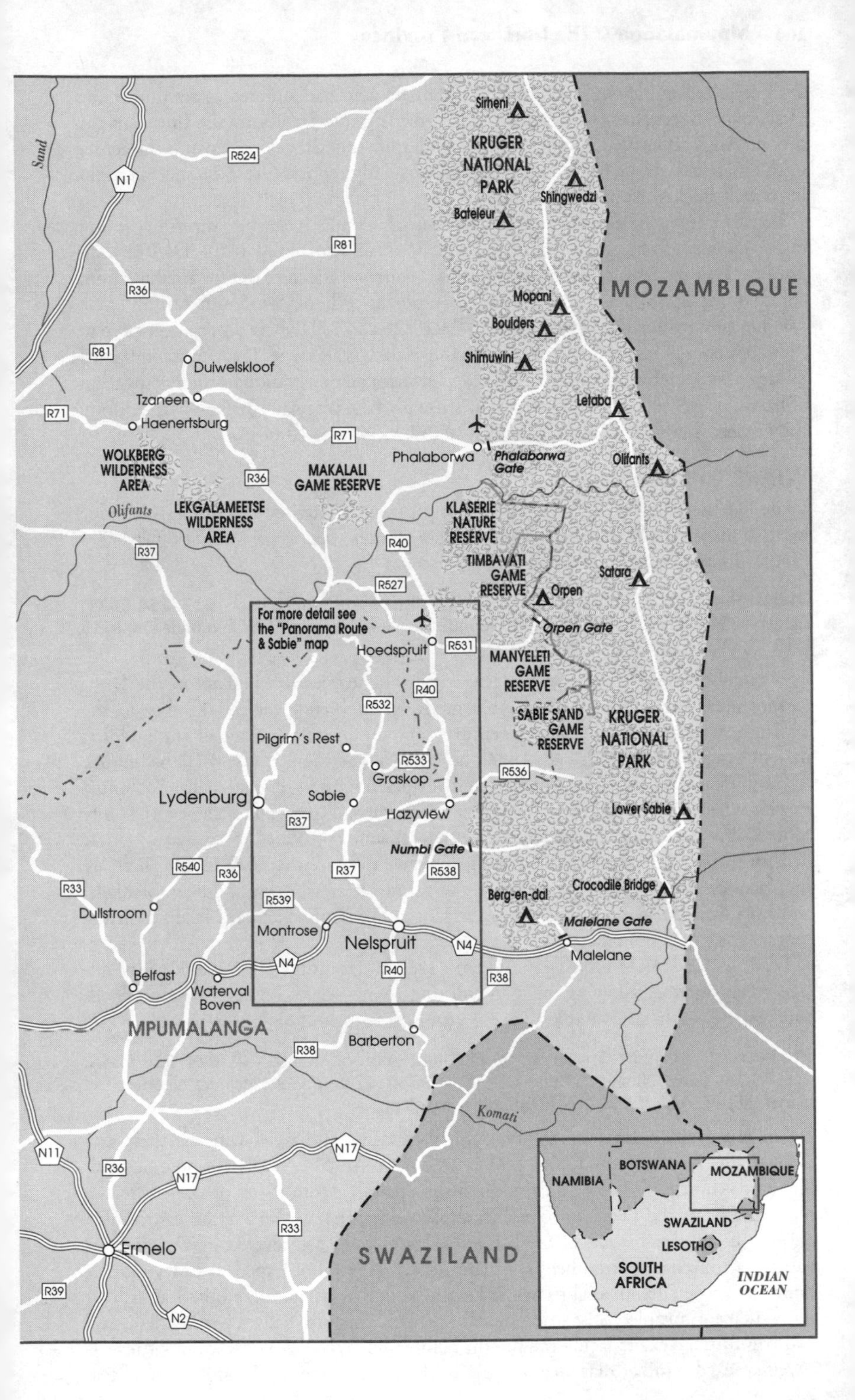

Sirheni
KRUGER NATIONAL PARK
Shingwedzi
Bateleur
MOZAMBIQUE
Mopani
Boulders
Shimuwini
Letaba
Olifants
Phalaborwa
Phalaborwa Gate
Sand
N1
R524
R81
R36
R81
Duiwelskloof
Tzaneen
R71
Haenertsburg
R71
WOLKBERG WILDERNESS AREA
R36
MAKALALI GAME RESERVE
Olifants
LEKGALAMEETSE WILDERNESS AREA
KLASERIE NATURE RESERVE
R37
R40
TIMBAVATI GAME RESERVE
Satara
R527
Orpen
Orpen Gate
For more detail see the "Panorama Route & Sabie" map
Hoedspruit
R531
MANYELETI GAME RESERVE
R40
R532
SABIE SAND GAME RESERVE
KRUGER NATIONAL PARK
Pilgrim's Rest
R533
Graskop
R536
Lydenburg
Sabie
Hazyview
Lower Sabie
R37
Numbi Gate
R540
R36
R37
R538
R33
Crocodile Bridge
Berg-en-dal
R539
Dullstroom
Malelane Gate
Montrose
Nelspruit
N4
Malelane
N4
Belfast
R40
R38
Waterval Boven
MPUMALANGA
Barberton
R38
Komati
N11
N17
R36
N17
R33
SWAZILAND
Ermelo
R39
N2
NAMIBIA
BOTSWANA
MOZAMBIQUE
SWAZILAND
LESOTHO
SOUTH AFRICA
INDIAN OCEAN

Dull collected money in Holland to assist Boers who had suffered losses during the First Anglo-Boer War. The town was razed to the ground again by the British in the Second Anglo-Boer War, but the town grew despite this setback. Today it is the center of the highveld's trout-fishing industry, and regularly reports 6 to 7 pounders caught in its well-stocked dams and streams.

Barring a few good eateries, (see below), there isn't much in town to divert the visitor, but 9 kilometers (5½ miles) north on the R540 to Lydenburg is the **Owl & Oak Trading Post** (no phone), a worthwhile stop if you're on the look-out for anything from embroidered linens to leather fly-fishing equipment or books on South African birds. The Dullstroom **Bird of Prey Centre** (☎ **013/254-0777**), where you can get close to over 20 species of raptors, many of them hand-reared, is also here. If you're accompanied by kids, it's worth timing your visit to coincide with a demonstration by their flying team of hawks, eagles, falcons, and owls. Shows usually take place at 10:30am and 2:30pm, daily except Wednesdays. Admission is R20 ($3.35); under 10 free.

## WHERE TO STAY

If you like the sound of Walkersons, but not the price, **Critchley Hackle,** a sister lodge located in town (☎ **013/254-0145**) offers dinner, bed, and breakfast for R990 ($165) double.

**Dullstroom Inn.** 39 Orange St., opposite the village green. ☎ **013/254-0071.** Fax 013/254-0278. 11 units. R300 ($50) double, includes breakfast. Children under 14, R115 ($19.15). AE, DC, MC, V.

This small-town inn is one of the few family-friendly establishments in the Dullstroom area, and offers an excellent value-for-money stopover on the way to the Escarpment. Established almost a century ago, the original design of the building hasn't changed much, with beds taking up most of the room in the small bedrooms. A busy Laura Ashley decor—florals and stripes abound—doesn't help. You must specify whether you'd prefer a shower or a bathtub and there is a choice of family rooms—ask for Room 1, where you have two separate connected rooms with 3 single beds in the second room; alternatively you'll have to share the same room. There are fireplaces everywhere downstairs, but in the rooms, heaters, carpets, duvets, blankets, and hot-water bottles ward off the Dullstroom chill. Coffee and tea facilities in the room—ask for fresh milk.

**Dining:** Meals (R18–40/$3–$6.65) are served under umbrellas overlooking the village green, weather allowing, or in the dining room—bank on solid comfort food: bangers and mash, steak and kidney pie, oxtail, curries, and of course, trout.

**Walkersons.** 10km (6 miles) north of Dullstroom off R540. ☎ **013/254-0246.** Fax 013/254 0262. 20 units. MINIBAR TV TEL. R1,350 ($225) double, includes breakfast and dinner. AE, DC, MC, V. Children 12 and older welcome.

Set in green, misty surrounds with trout-filled dams and weirs winding their way through the 600-hectare (1,500-acre) estate, Walkersons' grounds are pure Scottish highlands. Inside, the decor only adds to the illusion. From issues of *Majesty* to the photographs of the Duke and Duchess of Windsor, the Walkersons have striven to create a home reminiscent of English aristocracy. Walls are covered in Victorian oil paintings (purchased at Sotheby's, of course), windows are draped in heavy fabrics, floors are carpeted with sisal to which Persian rugs add color, and all the rooms have individual antique pieces. Bedrooms are huge, with king-size beds, a writing desk, and two comfortable chairs facing the fire (lit before you arrive). A cupboard door reveals a well-stocked minibar that includes details like fresh lemon, fresh milk, tea, and real coffee. The lodge also offers a full selection of fly-fishing tackle; and you may encounter up to 12 species of antelope, though the only thing you can point at them is a camera.

**Dining:** Unfortunately, the food doesn't meet the high standards set by the rooms, filet of beef cooked with red-wine sauce was overdone—twice. Quail stuffed with local wild mushrooms was better, and poached trout with white-wine sauce was done to a turn, though a trifle bland.

### Where to Dine

The **Tonteldoos Bistro** (☎ **013/254-0115**) on the main road is the most popular restaurant in town. Try their phyllo parcels of smoked trout with hollandaise, beef filet topped with camembert, or pork chops flamed with *mampoer,* a locally distilled liquor. Or settle for a sandwich made with home-baked bread. Tonteldoos is open for breakfast and lunch daily and for dinner on Fridays and Saturdays. Also on the main road is legendary **Harrie's Pancakes** (closed Wednesdays), ☎ **013/254-0801.** (See "Where to Dine" in "Sabie & Surrounds" for a write-up on the original Harrie's, located in Graskop.) If you're craving a pub lunch, the **Dullstroom Inn** (see above) is recommended. Note that you're unlikely to get a table anywhere on Sundays, when Jo'burg's desperadoes make the 2-hour drive to soak up Dullstroom's country living over lunch before setting off for the traffic jam back home.

## LYDENBURG & LONG TOM PASS

**Lydenburg,** or "place of suffering," was founded by a party of depressed Voortrekkers who, having lost a number of loved ones to a malaria epidemic in nearby Ohrigstad, retreated to its mosquito-free heights in 1849. Happily Lydenburg proved to be a misnomer, and today the town has a substantial center, though there's little to see beyond some interesting examples of pioneer architecture. Among these is the **oldest school building** in the old Transvaal, which dates back to 1851 and is on Church Street. The town is also known for a famed archaeological find: the **Lydenburg Heads,** seven ceramic masks that date back to the fifth century and were discovered in the late 1950s. You can see replicas of the heads (the originals now reside in Cape Town's South African Museum) at the **Lydenburg Museum** (☎ **013/235-2121** ext. **260**), situated in the Gustav Klingbiel Nature Reserve, 3 kilometers (2 miles) out of town on the R37. The museum also has displays dating from the Stone Age to present day, and is one of the better provincial museums in the country. For guided tours (by appointment only), call ahead. There's no admission and hours are Monday to Friday 8am to 1pm, and 2 to 4pm; Saturday and Sunday 8am to 5pm.

Continue on the R37 to **Long Tom Pass,** a place that combines history and fantastic scenery. At 2,150 meters (7,054 ft.), this is the second-highest mountain pass in South Africa. It was named after the Creusot siege guns that the Boers lugged up the pass to try and repulse the British forces during the Second Anglo-Boer War (1899–1902). These guns, or cannons, were known as Long Toms because of their extended necks, which could spit a shell 9½ kilometers (6 miles). Near the summit of the pass, at **The Devil's Knuckles,** a Long Tom replica commemorates the 4-day battle, fought on this mountainside in 1900—the original cannons were destroyed to prevent them falling into British hands. You can still see the holes blasted by the cannons as the Boers retreated down the **Staircase,** a series of hairpin bends that zig-zag down the pass.

Continuing east along the R37, passing the turnoff for Hendriksdal (see "Where to Dine," below), you will come to **Sabie.**

## SABIE & SURROUNDS

The origins of the small forestry town of Sabie (pronounced *sah*-bee) date back to 1871 when a few friends, picnicking at the Lower Sabie Falls, were showing off their marksmanship skills. Bullets chipped the rocks behind the mock targets, revealing a glint of gold, and prospectors followed promptly. The initial boom was short-lived, though the mining industry was still to transform Sabie. The first commercial trees, intended for mine props, were planted in 1876 and today form the heart of what are claimed to be the **largest man-made forests** in the world. To date, over a million acres have been planted with pine and eucalyptus, and many of these are destined to prop up shafts in the mines that run deep below Gauteng's surface. You can find out more at the **Forestry Museum,** which takes up an entire block on 10th Avenue (☎ **013/764-1058**).

The only other sight worth visiting before heading out of town for Graskop (north on the R532) or Hazyview (east on the R536) is **St Peter's Anglican Church,** on Market Square, (though if you are traveling elsewhere in the country, you will soon have your fill of buildings designed by Sir Herbert Baker, South Africa's most famous and prolific architect).

To view some of the area's many waterfalls (see below), head north on the R532. This meets up with the R533 junction, where you will be faced with the choice of turning northwest for Pilgrim's Rest, or heading due east for **Graskop.** Smaller than Sabie, Graskop has the same dual function of servicing its agro-forestry surrounds, and catering to the tourists who flock to see the views that start just north of town. There is nothing to see in Graskop itself, though there's a great place to eat (see **Harrie's** in "Where to Dine," below) and shop (next to Harrie's is **Delagoa** (☎ **013/767-1081**), which has a good selection of well-priced African crafts.)

### VISITING THE WATERFALLS

The area surrounding Sabie and Graskop is renowned for its **waterfalls.** If you only have time to see one, make it **Lone Creek Falls,** reached by traveling 10 kilometers (6 miles) on the Old Lydenburg Road northwest from Sabie. You will pass turnoffs for both the **Bridal Veil** and **Horseshoe Falls** before reaching Lone Creek; entrance is R3 (50¢) per vehicle. Besides being a short walk from the car, this pretty waterfall is also one of the few lookouts in the area that is wheelchair friendly. The single cascade plunges 68 meters (223 ft.) into an attractive pool, and is framed by the lush green vines and ferns of the small damp rainforest. More famous, yet not as spectacular, the **Mac Mac Falls** (on the R532 to Graskop) drop 85 meters (279 ft.) into a steep ravine. This time the view is from above, and is ruined by the construction of wire cages through which you are forced to peer. This was presumably done for one's safety, though the suicidally inclined need only drive a little farther to find an unfenced precipice. Downstream from the falls are the **Mac Mac Pools,** where you can swim (be aware that the turnoff for the pools comes before that of the falls).

A little farther along the R532, you will see the sign for the **Forest Falls,** an easy 3-kilometer (2-mile) trail well worth tackling, time allowing. For more waterfalls, take the Panorama Route following the rim of the Escarpment.

### WHERE TO STAY

✪ **Blue Mountain Lodge.** P.O. Box 101, Kiepersol 1241. ☎ **013/737-8446.** Fax 013/737-8446. E-mail: bluemtnlodge@icon.co.za. 13 units; 2 manor houses. MINIBAR. TEL. R1,200–1,720 ($200–$286.65) double, includes dinner and breakfast. AE, DC, MC, V. Take the Kiepersol turnoff, 28km (17 miles) east of Sabie on the R536, follow for 4km (2½ miles) before turnoff. Children 12 and over welcome, except in Manor House One.

**MacFalls**

Mac Mac Falls derives its name from the nearby mining camp that was established in the 1870s and refers to the great number of Scottish prospectors who came looking for gold.

---

It is impossible to describe the Blue Mountain Lodge without using superlatives—at least when it comes to the Victorian suites and manor houses. While the quadrant rooms are not as pricey, they're also average when compared with the sumptuousness you'll find in the eight separate cottages set below the ponds, palms, pool and dining terrace, and grand staircase that sweep down to more immaculately manicured lawns. From the dark woods and deep-blue walls of the Bismarck Room to the floral and leopard-print Fassler, the suites have only one thing in common: a Versace-like opulence. Do not come here if your taste runs to elegant, spartan minimalism. Bathrooms are equally beautiful and feature ball-and-claw slipper bathtubs and separate showers and toilets. The two huge private manor houses (of which, option one is a slightly better bet) each features two en-suite bedrooms, and one of the lodge's seven excellent chefs are on call to take care of personal dietary needs.

**Dining:** The worst thing about this gourmet haven is trying to choose between the table d'hôte or a la carte selections, both of which change regularly. (Non-residents pay R120/$20 per person for the set menu). Dishes include seared scallops with fresh asparagus in soya, lemon butter, and tomato sauce garnished with slices of lemon grass; seared Mozambican prawns served with a spicy, chunky, Blue Mountain avocado tower; and spicy waterblommetjie and pumpkin soup topped with fresh cream and mint. And that's just for starters. Main courses may include venison served with ginger pumpkin puree and horseradish aioli with spinach, or steamed salmon steaks with tamarind-ginger sauce.

**Casa do Sol.** P.O. Box 57, Hazyview 1242, off the R536, 39km (24 miles) east of Sabie and 5km (3 miles) west of Hazyview. ☎ **013/737-8111.** Fax 013/737-8166. E-mail: casa_do@soft.co.za. 54 units. A/C MINIBAR TV TEL. R880–1,276 ($146.65–$212.65) double, includes breakfast and dinner. Winter rates are lower. Children under 12 R138 ($23); 12 and over, R253 ($42.15). AE, DC, MC, V.

Casa do Sol is a little Mediterranean village, complete with cobbled streets, white stucco walls, and terracotta roof tiles, set in award-winning tropical gardens behind which stretch 500 hectares (1,250 acres) of indigenous bush. The hotel was established in 1968, and still retains a vaguely 1970s feel, despite regular decor updates. There are a number of accommodation options: The A Casa is too small for comfort and has no minibar; while the B Villa, a spacious minisuite with its own private garden area, offers the best value for money. With separate sitting- and cloakrooms, the C and D suites are ideal for families; while the D suites, which are upstairs and feature views of the valley and estate from the private patio, are slightly better if you're prepared to climb a few stairs. Dinners are renowned and offer a choice of three starters and three main courses; vegetarians are well catered for. Casa do Sol also offers minibus tours of the Escarpment, day safaris into the Kruger, and night drives in one of the nearby Sabie Sand private game reserves. This is an all-round excellent hotel, though it doesn't offer the well-bred intimacy of the lodges that lie south in the Kiepersol area.

**Amenities:** Horseback riding, an all-weather tennis court, large swimming pool, bass fishing, boating, and a number of trails are all available at no extra charge. Casa do Sol also offers minibus tours of the Escarpment, day safaris into the Kruger, and night drives in one of the nearby Sabi Sand private game reserves.

**Cybele Forest Lodge.** P.O. Box 346, White River 1240. ☎ **013/764-1823.** Fax 013/764-1810. E-mail: cybele@iafrica.com. 13 units. R990–3,500 ($165–$583.35) double, includes breakfast and dinner. AE, DC, MC, V. Take the Kiepersol turnoff, 28km (17 miles) east of Sabie on the R536; follow for 10km (6 miles) before taking a dirt road to the left marked WHITEWATERS. Look out for the Cybele signs some 12km (7 miles) later. Alternatively, follow signs off the R40 between Hazyview and White River. No children under 10.

Long before crime encouraged Jo'burgers to take regular long weekend getaways, the rooms at Cybele were booked months in advance, and the way you pronounced the name said a lot about how happening you were (it's pronounced "sigh-*bee*-lee"). Even Capetonians traveled north to sample the legendary cuisine and to relax in the subtropical surrounds. Over the years, owners Rupert and Barbara Jeffries have renovated and added a number of cottages, and a pool has replaced the farm dam, but the standard of the food and the beauty of the 120-hectare (300-acre) grounds remain unchanged. However, for these prices rooms are perhaps a little old-fashioned, though the Paddock Suites add total privacy, views of the forest, and the comfort of living in a well-dressed home to the mix. It's worth noting that for this money you could be staying in a private game reserve.

**Dining:** The five-course dinners are the real reason to stay at this Relais & Chateau lodge (though non-residents are also welcome—dinner will run you R120/$20 per person). The original farmhouse, where the lounge and dining room are situated, is wonderful: Rooms are painted in rich, warm colors and are cluttered with an eclectic mix of antiques, English country-style fabrics, kelim rugs, and a few African crafts. Luncheons are usually light (salads, omelets, and terrines), and dinners are either a la carte or set. Appetizers include crumbed mushrooms or Mexican corn soup followed by a choice between artichoke risotto or smoked trout wrapped in spinach. Main courses could be beef filet with red-wine gravy or roast duck with marmalade sauce.

**Amenities:** Horseback riding (the surrounds are truly beautiful), swimming, and trout fishing (tackle is provided).

## Where to Dine

Sabie is the Escarpment town with the most restaurants, but even so the selection is small; **Zeederberg** (see below) is your best option in town itself, and the **Artist Café** is worth a detour. If you want to dine on classic roasts in a first-class coach, replete with starched napkins and fine china, head for the (stationary) **Shunters Express** (☎ **013/764-1777,** off R537, 23km/14 miles from Sabie), where the old White Train is stationed next to a lake. Note also that many of the places listed in "Where to Stay" are renowned for their fine cuisine, particularly **Cybele** and **Highgrove.** If you're staying in the area for more than 1 night, consider visiting one of them just to sample their food. Make sure you book ahead, as seating and portions are often limited.

✪ **Artists Café.** Hendriksdal siding, Hendriksdal, off the R37, 17km (10½ miles) south of Sabie. ☎ **013/764-2309.** Daily 8am–11pm (but call ahead). Reservations recommended. R30–42 ($5–$7). AE, DC, MC, V. ITALIAN.

Surprisingly, this delightful family-run trattoria in the middle of nowhere serves some of the best Tuscan-type fare in the country. In keeping with the simple food, the atmosphere in the restaurant is casual. Menus, which change every few days to make the most of what's available in the vegetable garden, are handwritten, chairs are mismatched, tables are worn wood, and simple dishcloths serve as napkins. Walls are covered with local artworks as well as crafts from across Africa, most of which are for sale.

The wine list features an excellent selection of South African wines and the food is well-priced and delicious—try the slow-roasted free-range duck served with a piquant orange sauce. Seating in the restaurant is limited, so make sure you book ahead during the summer season. (Note that you needn't tear yourself away from the laid-back luxuries of sampling their fine selection of South African dessert wines and port; there are four en-suite bedrooms, available for R370/$61.65 double, including breakfast.)

✪ **Harrie's Pancakes.** Corner Kerk and Louis Trichardt sts., Graskop (23km/14 miles north of Sabie). ☎ **031/767-1273.** 8am–5pm daily. R12.50–22.50 ($2.10–$3.75). MC, V. DUTCH.

You will come across a number of pancake restaurants in the Escarpment towns, all spawned by the success of the legendary Harrie's. Harrie Sietsema, of Dutch descent, opened his doors 14 years ago, and today you can find his restaurant by simply looking for the congregation of tour buses. Tasting one of his thick crepes should definitely be high on your priority list—some of the most popular savory fillings include trout mousse and horseradish, and chicken livers with peppered cream sauce. If you're in time for tea, the black cherries with liqueur sauce is a knockout.

**Zeederberg Coach House.** 10th Ave. (opposite Forestry Museum). ☎ **013/764-2630.** Daily except Tuesday 10am–3pm; daily except Tuesday and Sunday 5:30–11pm. School holidays and long weekends 8pm–late, daily. Main courses R18–65 ($3–$10.85). AE, DC, MC, V. TRADITIONAL/EUROPEAN.

Situated in a charming Victorian house, the very place that Zeederberg's horse-drawn coaches stopped for refreshments over a century ago, this restaurant-cum-bar-cum-coffee shop is owned by local artists Charl and Andrea. Charl is responsible for décor, while Andrea practices her arts in the kitchen—in the past 4 years, Zeederberg's reputation has grown continuously, and is now considered the best in Sabie. Meals are down-to-earth and tasty; specialties include ostrich fillet prepared in a green-peppercorn sauce and served on a bed of homemade pasta; and locally caught trout, smoked, stuffed, pan-fried, or grilled.

## PILGRIM'S REST

The village of Pilgrim's Rest was established in 1873 after "Wheelbarrow" Patterson discovered gold in the stream that flows past what was to become the first gold-rush town in South Africa. Having struck out on his own to escape the crush at Mac Mac, he must have been horrified when he was joined by 1,500 diggers within the year, all frantically panning to make their fortunes. A fair number did, and the largest nugget weighed in at 24 pounds; but by 1881 the best of the pickings had been found, and the diggings were bought by the **Transvaal Gold Mining Estates (TGME).** A century later, the village still looked much the same, and the entire settlement was declared a national monument; the Works Department and Museum Services were put in charge of restoring and preserving this living museum.

If you're looking for historical accuracy, then you'll find Pilgrim's Rest over-commercialized; the town's streets are probably a great deal prettier than they were at the turn of the century, and the overall effect is a sanitized, glamorized picture of life in a gold-rush town. As theme parks go, however, Pilgrim's Rest is a pleasant experience. Most of the buildings line a single main street, and the architecture is of the quaint Victorian variety prevalent in so many of colonial Africa's rural towns—walls are corrugated iron with deep sash windows, and corrugated-iron roofs extend over large shaded *stoeps* (verandahs).

Consider spending the night here, but if you're on a tight schedule, make sure you arrive with plenty of time to explore in the afternoon, or you'll be forced to wait until

9 o'clock the next morning, when the Tourist Information Centre and the museums open up.

## Essentials

**GETTING THERE** Travel north from Sabie on R532. The R532 meets with the R533 in a T-junction; head northwest on R533 for 15 kilometers (just over 9 miles). Pilgrim's Rest is 35 kilometers (22 miles) north of Sabie and about 360 kilometers (223 miles) northeast of Johannesburg.

**VISITOR INFORMATION** Contact the **Information Centre (☎ 013/768-1060)** and ask for John Pringle. The center is clearly marked on the main street. Their hours are daily 9am to 12:45pm; and 1:15 to 4:30pm; they will supply free town maps as well as tickets to the museums, and can book tours for you.

**GETTING AROUND** Pilgrim's Rest has no street numbers; it's literally a one-horse town, with buildings stretched along a main road. Uptown, or Top Town, is literally the higher (and older) part of the main road, while Downtown stretches below the turnoff into town. Most of the tourist sights are situated in Uptown, as is the Tourist Information Office.

## What to See & Do

The three museums in town, the **Dredzen Shop and House Museum,** the **News Printing Museum,** and the **House Museum,** can all be visited with the R5 ticket sold at the Tourist Information Center. They open and close for the day at the same time as the Tourist Information Office, and close for a half an hour at 1pm (as Pilgrim's Rest is effectively owned by the government, it is plagued with a civil-service mentality). Neither of the house museums feels particularly authentic; furnishings and objects are often propped haphazardly and look much the worse for wear.

The **Alanglade Museum** (no phone), which used to house the TGME's mine manager and his family, is more interesting. While the furnishings, which date from 1900 to 1930, are not original, they have been selected and are maintained with more care than those in the house museums. It is set in a forested grove 1½ kilometers (about a mile) north of town. Tours, which cost R20 ($3.35) and include panning for gold nuggets, are offered at 11am and 2pm, Monday to Saturday, and must be booked half an hour in advance from the Pilgrim's Rest Information Centre, where they will supply you with a map of how to get there.

In stark contrast to these museums depicting life at the genteel top, is the **Diggings Museum** (no phone), situated in the creek where the alluvial gold was originally panned. On display is some of the equipment used, as well as a few tents and some wattle-and-daub huts, the very first Pilgrim's Rest buildings. Unfortunately none of the 11 canteens that sprang up during the rush has survived. Demonstrations of alluvial gold panning and guided tours are held at 10 and 11am, and at noon, 2 and 3pm. Admission is R5 (85¢). At the **Reduction Works,** which was undergoing renovations at press time, you can see how gold is processed.

**St Mary's Anglican Church,** seen overlooking the main street as you enter town, is where sinners' souls were salvaged. Higher up the hill, the evocative **Pilgrim's Rest Cemetery** is definitely worth a visit. Besides the tombstone simply inscribed "Robber's Grave"—easily identified because it is the only grave that lies in a north-south direction—the many children's graves are a moving testimony to how hard times really were, while the many nationalities reflect the cosmopolitan character of the original gold-rush village.

### Robber's Grave

Legend has it that the man buried here broke the most serious taboo of the time by stealing gold from a neighboring tent. He was chased out of town, and upon his return promptly shot and buried where he fell. Unlike the good Christians of the time who were buried facing east-west, his grave was dug facing north-west, thereby forever branding him as a sinner.

## Where to Stay

**District Six Miners' Cottages.** Public Works Private X516, Pilgrim's Rest 1290. ☎ **013/768-1211.** Fax 013/768-1113. 6 units. R180 ($30) for 4-bed and R200 ($33.35) for 6-bed cottage. No credit cards.

The District Six cottages date back to the early 1920s. Like the Royal below, each is furnished with a selection of period pieces, though as they fall under the jurisdiction of the Public Works department they are a lot more spartan. Set high up on the hill overlooking the town, accommodations have lovely views from their verandahs, and are serviced daily. Each consists of two bedrooms, a living room, bathroom, and a fully equipped kitchen (though Pilgrim's restaurants are an easy walk down the hill, take the car for the more arduous return journey). Not surprisingly, these cheap, charming cottages are popular—make sure you book ahead. Keys are collected at the Royal Hotel.

**The Royal Hotel.** Main Rd., Uptown, Pilgrim's Rest 1290. ☎ **013/768-1100.** Fax 013/768-1188. E-mail: royal2@global.co.za. 50 units. R510–660 ($85–$110) double, includes breakfast. AE, DC, EC, MC, V.

The Royal first opened its doors in 1873, and over a century later it's still going strong—this is one of the most charming places to overnight on the Escarpment. Besides the 11 original hotel rooms, which are arranged around a small courtyard behind the reception area, the hotel has grown to include 39 rooms located in buildings adjacent to the hotel, all dating back to the turn of the century and impeccably restored and furnished in the Victorian style. The bedrooms, which are relatively small, feature brass beds, many of them four-poster, wooden ceiling fans, and marble-and-oak washstands; only two rooms have showers; the rest are furnished with ball-and-claw bathtubs. This is not a luxurious experience, however—the mattresses are a little monastic and corrugated-iron houses can become bitterly cold in winter. The honeymoon suite, situated in the Bank House, is the only room with a fireplace, and during June and July, when temperatures drop close to freezing, it's worth booking well in advance. The hotel can arrange horseback riding, trout fishing, tennis, bowls, and golf.

**Dining/Diversions:** The buffet breakfasts are lavish, and served in the classy Peach Tree Creek. The Digger's Den (see below), which also has a period feel, is where lunch and dinner is served. Guests can peruse the historic journals and books in the comfortable lounge, opposite which is the Church Bar, one of Pilgrim's Rest's top attractions, though you may prefer to order a pub lunch on the Digger's Den terrace and watch the passing parade.

## Where to Dine

There are a number of places to eat and drink, all ranged along the main road. Besides the reputable **Vine** (☎ **013/768-1080,** see below), you can do a wine tasting at **Edwin Wood's Wine Cellar** (☎ **013/768-1025**), or order pub fare at the bar in the **Royal Hotel.**

## Driving the Panorama Route

This easy, half-day drive takes you past some spectacular views including, from south to north, the Pinnacle, God's Window, Wonder View, the Berlin Falls, the Lisbon Falls, Bourke's Luck Potholes, the Three Rondawels and the Abel Erasmus Pass. The best views are of Blyde River Canyon, the third largest canyon in the world, which marks the sheer 1,600 meter drop from the Escarpment to the warm Lowveld plains shimmering below. Hot air rising over this 'wall' generates the heavy mists and high rainfall which in turn create the unique montane grasslands and riverine forests of the **Blyde River Canyon Nature Reserve** which start just north of Graskop before broadening out to include the Blydepoort Dam, 60km (97 miles) north. To complete the Panorama route as a circular trip (approximately 160km/100 miles) returning to either Sabie or Graskop, set aside a day.

As you follow the tour below, refer to the "Panorama Route & Sabie" map in this chapter for more information.

To drive this route, take R532 north out of Graskop, before turning right on R534. The first stop is the **Pinnacle**—a thin, 100ft-tall quartzite rock topped with trees that juts below the viewpoint—but **God's Window,** 4km (2 ½ miles) further, which offers the first view of the open Lowveld plains, is more impressive. (**WonderView** is a variation of this, and can be skipped if you're pressed for time). The looping R534 now rejoins R532. Turn left and look out for the sign if you want to visit **Lisbon Falls,** which drop 120ft. To continue on to Blyde River Canyon, turn right into the R532, taking in the 159ft **Berlin Falls** on the way. Neither of these signs are essential viewing, but if you're ready for some refreshments, the **Berlin Peacock Tavern** (☎ **013/767-1085**) lies on the way to the Berlin Falls—besides some spectacularly over-the-top baroque decor, the food is delicious, and according to the visitors' book, even rival lodge-owners come here regularly.

Back on the R532, head north for **Bourke's Luck Potholes**—possibly the most overrated sight on the route. Here gold digger Bourke predicted he would strike it lucky, but he found nothing in these large scooped formations, carved by the movement of pebbles and water in the swirling whirlpools created by the confluence of the Blyde and Treur Rivers. Bourke was not the last person to be disappointed by the Potholes—it's a long walk to look at them, and they still reveal very little. Nor does the visitor centre which, in addition to some dry displays regarding the geology of the area, features a few dusty stuffed animals which look

**Digger's Den.** In the Royal Hotel, Main Rd., Uptown. ☎ **013/768-1100.** 12pm–late, daily. R20–38 ($3.35–$6.35). DC, MC, V. TRADITIONAL.

Charmingly restored, with flowers in coffeepots and red-and-white check serviettes evoking a laid-back rustic atmosphere. Specialties include trout roulade, freshly smoked trout, cream cheese and fennel, served with locally grown tomatoes and lettuce; lamb curry, cooked with over 20 herbs and spices, served with *pappadums* (spicy Indian crisp bread); and *bobotie,* a traditional South African dish of ground beef prepared with mild Cape spices before being topped with egg and baked. Terrace specials like *peri-peri* (chili) chicken livers, fish and chips, and venison pie make good luncheon options.

**The Vine.** Main Rd., Downtown. ☎ **013/768-1080.** Reservations recommended over weekends. Open 8am–late, daily. R25–35 ($4.15–$5.85). DC, MC, V. REGIONAL.

close to decomposing. The lichen trail is very easy, and good for children. Gates are open from 7am to 5pm.

Some 20 kilometers north are the **Three Rondawels,** by far the most impressive stop of the entire trip. The name refers to the three circular hut-shaped outcrops which are more or less opposite the lookout, and does nothing to describe the humbling size of what beckons. A sheer drop threatens to pull you off the precipice; below, the Blyde River snakes its way through the Canyon to the tranquil Blyde dam, embraced by green mountains, and beyond, the great Lowveld plains.

If you're feeling thirsty, drop into the **Aventura Blydepoort Resort** (**☎ 013/769-8005**) (the turn-off is a couple of miles north after the Three Rondawels, and clearly signposted), which offers another angle on the Three Rondawels from the restaurant terrace; however, much beyond a toasted sandwich is not recommended.

From here you will descend the **Abel Erasmus Pass,** before passing through the JG Strijdom tunnel—approximately 20 kilometers (12 miles) from here is the turn-off for the **Monsoon Gallery** (**☎ 015/795-5114**), off the R527. Billed as 'rural art and fine craft specialists', the Monsoon has an excellent selection of African crafts and prices are not prohibitive. You can enjoy a light meal at the adjacent **Mad Dogz Café** (**☎ 015/795-5425**) (try the Thai beef salad with fresh coriander and lemon dressing) or visit the **tourism information centre** (part of the Monsoon Gallery), where you can find out more about archaeological and eco-tours.

At this point, you can stay on the R527, heading east for Hoedspruit, where you could visit the **Research and Breeding Centre for Endangered Species** (**☎ 015/793-1633**; see Kapama Lodge, under "Private Game Reserves," below), also known as the Cheetah Project. This is also the way to the **Timbavati** and **Kapama private game reserves.** Alternatively, take the R531 southeast to Klaserie—look for the turn off to **Aventura Swadini** (**☎ 015/795-5141**). From here you can take a 90-minute boat trip on the Blyde Dam to see the mouth of the Canyon and look up at the Escarpment towering above.

Continue on the R531 to enter the Kruger via **Orpen gate** (the closest to the Satara rest camp), or to travel to the **Manyeleti** or northern **Sabi Sand** reserves. To return to Graskop take the R40 south from Klaserie, then follow the R533 from Bosbokrand, climbing Kowyns Pass to Graskop.

In one of the town's turn-of-the-century buildings, and peppered with historical references like the old explosive boxes used as stools, owner-chef Johnny has run The Vine for 30 years and is known as one of the characters of the village. This intimate restaurant-cum-bar is in fact where the Pilgrim's Rest locals tend to hang out after 5, when most of the tourists disappear. Specialties include locally caught trout, prepared with almond stuffing, and traditional oxtail and samp, with beans, onions, and potatoes, and served on crushed corn cooked in milk.

## A Nearby Island Oasis

✪ **Otters Den.** Off R531. P.O. Box 408, Hoedspruit 1380. **☎ 015/795-5250.** Fax 015/795-5250. E-mail: catfish@mweb.co.za. 4 units. R760 ($126.65) per person double, includes dinner, breakfast, and on-island activities. Children under 12 half price; under 6 free. AE, DC, MC, V.

**Cry Me A River**

The Treur (grief) River was named by a group of Voortrekker women who were left behind on its banks by their menfolk for long enough to believe them dead. When the men finally did return, the women had set up camp beside another river, which they named Blyde (or joy) in celebration.

Situated on a densely vegetated island in the Blyde River, this rustic camp is reached by crossing a narrow suspension bridge, symbolizing your escape into the wilderness. The island consists of 50 hectares (125 acres) of forest, veld, and wetland and has 2 kilometers (just over 1 mile) of riverfront on the main channel of the Blyde. The four tented chalets, built on stilts overlooking the river, are a combination of stone, thatch, canvas, and timber, and are simply but comfortably furnished. The central lodge area has a fully equipped kitchen (should you wish to self-cater, though a cook can be arranged), dining room, bar, braai, and sun deck, built around a giant jackalberry tree, and overlooking a natural swimming hole. A qualified botanist and conservationist is on stand-by to take you hiking through the indigenous forest, field, and stream—the island itself has more than 100 indigenous tree species and 200 bird species have been recorded. There are also several dams on the river, offering year-round angling for a variety of fish species. Nearby trails in the Blydepoort Nature Reserve lead you to secluded waterfalls and swimming spots. Day trips to the Kruger and surrounds are available, as well as boat trips to the Blydepoort Dam to see the mouth of the canyon. Otters Den is also one of a small consortium of operators awarded the exclusive traversing rights through the white- and flatwaters that run through the Blyde Canyon (see "River Rafting" in "Staying Active," above). It's a great place to base a river-rafting trip, and special rates are available.

## 5 The Lowveld Route—Gateway to Southern Kruger

Nelspruit is 355km (220 miles) northeast of Johannesburg

Traveling via the N4 to Nelspruit is the most direct way to get to the gates of southern Kruger. A number of lodges adjoining Kruger are also within striking distance, as are the southern Sabi Sand private game reserves. It is not as scenic as the route via the Escarpment; the N4 which connects Johannesburg with Maputo, capital of neighboring Mozambique, takes a lot of heavy traffic and is in the process of being widened and upgraded. From Belfast the views improve somewhat. However, two alternative loop roads that bypass the N4 for part of the way are more attractive and less crowded. As you cannot travel both loops, choose between veering northward to Schoemanskloof from Waterval-Boven, or take the second bypass, which veers southward from Ngodwana—this is the way to reach Kaapschehoop (see "Horseback Riding," above).

### ESSENTIALS

**GETTING THERE** **By Car** Nelspruit is 322 kilometers (200 miles) east of Pretoria on the N4. For the Schoemanskloof Valley 60-kilometer (37-mile) bypass, take the R36 from Waterval-Boven (don't take the turnoff to Lydenburg); and the R36 then becomes the R539 and loops back to the N4. To take the second bypass, look out for the turnoff east to Kaapschehoop, just after the Ngodwana turnoff (some 75 km/46½ miles east of Waterval-Boven).

**By Plane** **Nelspruit International Airport** (don't let the "International" mislead you, this refers only to a few flights from neighboring countries that fly here) is 56

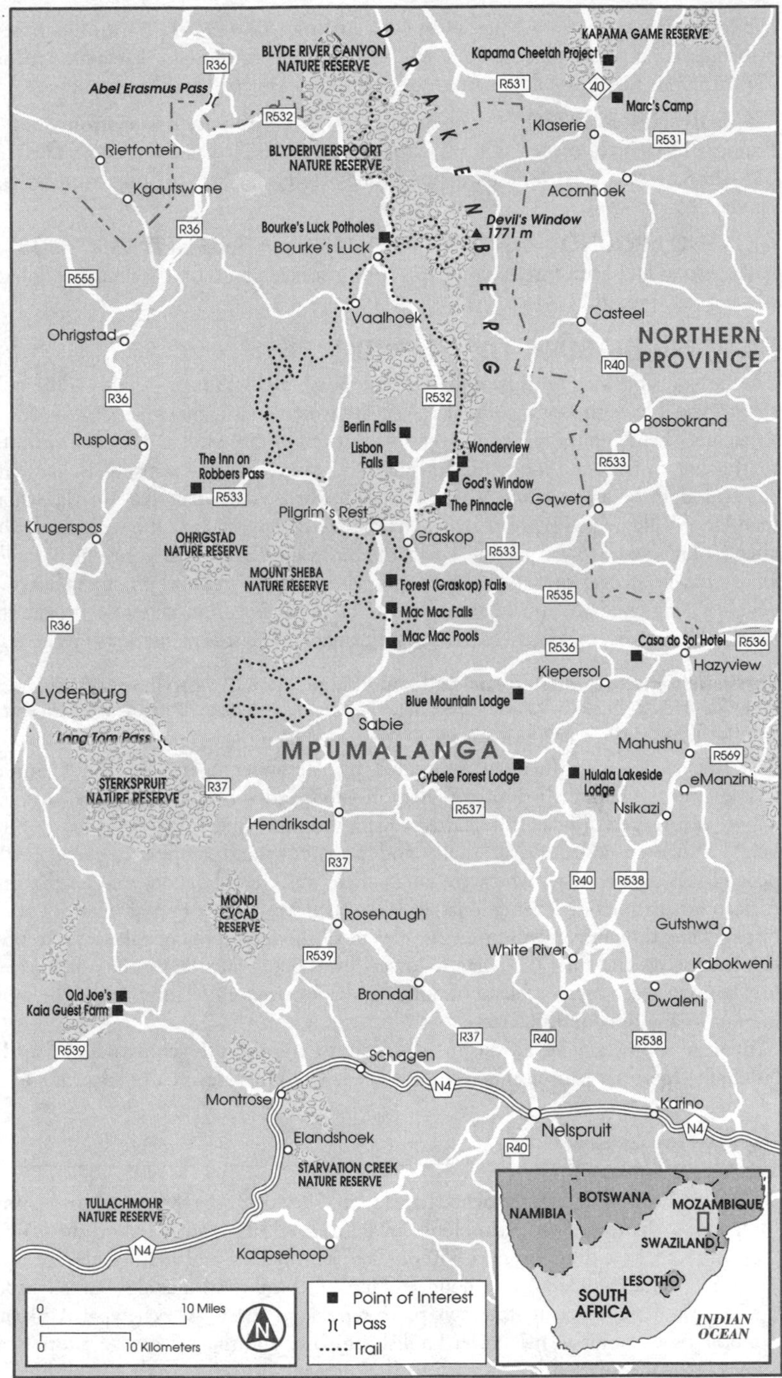

KAPAMA GAME RESERVE
Kapama Cheetah Project
Marc's Camp
Klaserie
R531
40
BLYDE RIVER CANYON NATURE RESERVE
R36
Abel Erasmus Pass
R532
DRAKENSBERG
Rietfontein
BLYDERIVIERSPOORT NATURE RESERVE
Kgautswane
Acornhoek
R36
Bourke's Luck Potholes
Bourke's Luck
Devil's Window 1771 m
R555
Vaalhoek
Casteel
Ohrigstad
NORTHERN PROVINCE
R40
R36
R532
Bosbokrand
Berlin Falls
Rusplaas
Lisbon Falls
Wonderview
The Inn on Robbers Pass
R533
God's Window
R533
The Pinnacle
Gqweta
Pilgrim's Rest
Krugerspos
Graskop
R533
OHRIGSTAD NATURE RESERVE
MOUNT SHEBA NATURE RESERVE
Forest (Graskop) Falls
R535
R36
Mac Mac Falls
Mac Mac Pools
R536
Casa do Sol Hotel
R536
Hazyview
Kiepersol
Lydenburg
Blue Mountain Lodge
Sabie
Long Tom Pass
MPUMALANGA
Mahushu
R569
STERKSPRUIT NATURE RESERVE
R37
Cybele Forest Lodge
Hulala Lakeside Lodge
eManzini
R537
Nsikazi
Hendriksdal
R37
R40
R538
MONDI CYCAD RESERVE
Rosehaugh
Gutshwa
R539
White River
Kabokweni
Old Joe's
Kaia Guest Farm
Brondal
Dwaleni
R539
R37
R40
R538
Schagen
N4
Montrose
Karino
Nelspruit
N4
Elandshoek
R40
STARVATION CREEK NATURE RESERVE
TULLACHMOHR NATURE RESERVE
N4
Kaapsehoop
0
10 Miles
0
10 Kilometers
N
Point of Interest
Pass
Trail
NAMIBIA
BOTSWANA
MOZAMBIQUE
SWAZILAND
LESOTHO
SOUTH AFRICA
INDIAN OCEAN

kilometers (35 miles) from Numbi Gate. **SA Airlink** (☎ **013/741-3536**) flies in several times a day from Johannesburg and once a day from Durban. **Metavia Airlines** (☎ **013/741-3142**) has flights from Johannesburg, Durban, and Mozambique.

**VISITOR INFORMATION** Contact the Nelspruit **Publicity Association,** Shop 5, Promenade Centre, corner of Paul Kruger and Louis Trichardt streets (☎ **013/755-1988** or 013/755-1988). Hours are Monday to Friday 8am to 5pm; Saturday and Sunday 9am to 4pm.

**GETTING AROUND** **Avis** (☎ **013/741-1087**) and **Budget** (☎ **013/741-3871**) have desks at Nelspruit International Airport; or see chapter 6 for car rentals in Johannesburg and Pretoria.

## FROM MIDDELBURG TO NELSPRUIT

The first possible stop on this route is at the **Botshabelo Village**—if this is the only chance you'll have to visit a cultural village, it's worth a visit, though best avoided on weekends when both the village and the adjacent campsite are full and noisy. Returning to the N4 from here, you'll pass through the trout-fishing towns of Belfast and Machadodorp before reaching Waterval-Boven, where you bypass the N4 via Schoemanskloof Valley. The R359 briefly rejoins the N4 before veering off northward again: after 10 kilometers (6 miles), you'll find the **Sudwala Caves,** a labyrinthine complex which has been over-commercialized with false lighting and tacky names, but will delight young children. You'll have to backtrack to the N4 from here to complete the last few kilometers to **Nelspruit,** passing subtropical and citrus plantations on the way.

**Botshabelo Historic Mission and Cultural Village.** 11km (7 miles) from Middelburg on N11. ☎ **013/243-5020.** Mission open daily 5am–6pm. Ndebele Village daily 10am–4pm. R15 ($2.50) per vehicle and R1 (15¢) per person.

The Botshabelo (or refuge) was founded by Alexander Merensky and Heinrich Grutzner of the Berlin Missionary Society in 1865, and within 8 years the village was almost entirely self sufficient. It boasted a print shop (the first Sotho Bible was printed here), a bakery, a brickyard, mills, and a school—and employed some 3,000 people. Among the many who were taught here was Gerard Sekoto, one of the first African artists to enjoy international acclaim. (Unfortunately none of his work is on display here, though you will find examples in all the metropolitan galleries.) To protect themselves and their Christian followers from potential attacks, the missionaries first constructed a **fort**—a blend of Sotho and Western architecture; this is the most interesting building on the reserve.

Besides taking a look at the fort, a visit to the recently constructed **South-Ndebele Open Air Museum** is recommended. The Ndebele are a breakaway group

### Trekker Treat

One good reason to take the Schoemanskloof Valley detour is that you'll pass **Ouma Hannie se Jampot,** Schoemanskloof (☎ **013/733-3301,** signposted off the R539), on the way. In addition to over 350 types of jams, jellies, and marmalades, "Ouma Hannie" (Grannie Hannie, pronounced "honey") produces fruit rolls—an old road-trip treat dating back to the days of the Trekkers—and, as archetypal Afrikaans mother, she is a joy to meet. Her English isn't bad, and she welcomes visitors—call ahead to make sure she'll be around, as she's often out delivering to the establishments that stock what many consider to be the best homemade jams in Africa.

of Zulus who fled from Shaka's tyranny and settled mostly within the borders of latter-day Northern Province and Mpumalanga. Together with the Xhosa and Zulu, they are descended from the Nguni, a cultural group dating back to the 17th century, and the three nations, which make up the majority of the South African population, speak similar languages. The Ndebele are today renowned for their beadwork, the strong geometric designs on the walls of their homes and blankets, and their colorful traditional dress, typified by large metal rings and beaded hoops worn on their ankles, wrists, and necks. Buildings depict materials used from the early–18th century to the present day, and traditionally dressed Ndebele women give explanations regarding their beadwork, clothing, and vibrant artwork. The bold graphics and colors unique to the Ndebele have in recent years literally taken off: Twins Emmly and Martha Masanabo, who live northwest of here, were commissioned by British Airways to paint one of their 747 jets, and BMW has added a Ndebele-painted car to their collection.

**Sudwala Caves.** 33 kilometers (20 miles) from Nelspruit, off R539. ☎ **013/733-4152.** 9am–4:30pm daily. Caves R24 ($4). Dinosaur Park (☎ **013/733-4156**). 8am–6pm daily. R10 ($1.65). Sudwalaskraal Cultural Village (☎ **013/733-3073**). 8:30am–5pm daily. R10 ($1.65) (R15/$2.50, includes dancing). Children half price on all the above.

The caves are thought to extend into the dolomite rock for 32 kilometers (20 miles), of which a mere 600 meters (1,968 feet) is open to the public. Besides their sheer size, these interlinked chambers are worth visiting to view their ancient stalactites and stalagmites—the result of rainwater percolating into the dolomite cracks, dissolving the limestone which drips from the cave ceiling. The caves have a natural ventilation system throughout (they are a constant 18°C/64°F) and have been used by humans for eons, most recently during the 19th century when a Swazi prince took refuge here. These domed chambers, one of which is the largest dolomite hall in the Southern Hemisphere, must have been awe inspiring when lit only with flickering flame; it's a great pity that the current custodians have trivialized the spaces by filling the cave with colored lights and naming these ancient shapes "Weeping Madonna" and "Biltong Forest," to mention but a few of the tacky descriptors. Tours last approximately an hour; as there are no set times, you may have to wait for as long as 35 minutes.

It's no Jurassic, but you (or the kids) may want to take a look at the adjacent **Dinosaur Park**—as much for the life-size models as the indigenous vegetation. Alternatively, visit the **Sudwalaskraal Cultural Village.** Swazi, Zulu, Xhosa, and Ndebele villages have been re-created, but only the Swazi culture is well represented. Tours last about 1 hour.

## Attractions in & Around Nelspruit

Nelspruit, the capital of Mpumalanga, is one of South Africa's fastest growing cities. There is, however, no real reason to stop here unless you want to visit the Lowveld National Botanical Gardens, or are in need of a meal, in which case the prawns at the family-run **Costa do Sol** restaurant (☎ **013/752-6382,** Nel City Shopping Centre on Paul Kruger St.) have been pulling locals in for almost 2 decades.

From Nelspruit, you can head northward on the R40 for the lowveld towns of White River and Hazyview, stopping along the way at the **Kraal Kraft Curios** (☎ **013/758-1229**), which has a good selection of crafts from throughout the continent. If you happen to be in White River over lunchtime, head for **Bagdad Café** (☎ **013/751-1777**, 2km/just over a mile north of White River on the R40 to Hazyview), touted as the trendiest spot in the whole of Mpumalanga by the

30-something local crowd. The food is good, too; try the smoked trout. Call ahead if you'd like to pick up a picnic basket stuffed with homemade bread, cold meats, cheese, pickles, salads, and fruit—perfect if you're about to head into Kruger. **Numbi Gate** is 10 minutes from Hazyview. (Note that you will find the best-priced wood-carved crafts at the curio shop at **Kruger's Numbi Gate** [no telephone], where artists from the region are represented.) **Paul Kruger Gate** is approximately 40 kilometers (25 miles) due east of Hazyview.

Alternatively, if you're headed for **Kruger's southern gates** or one of the hotels or lodges on the Crocodile River, remain on the N4. Bear in mind that if you're pressed for time and due to overnight at Lower Sabie, it's best to travel beyond the Malelane Gate and enter at Crocodile Bridge Gate.

**Lowveld National Botanical Gardens.** Off R40 on the outskirts of Nelspruit. ☎ **013/752-5531.** Open daily Oct–Apr 8am–5:45pm; May–Sept 8am–5:15pm. R5 (85¢) adults; R2 (35¢) students and seniors.

Situated on 159 hectares (398 acres) which include the banks of the Crocodile River, the garden's varied topography has given rise to habitats ranging from riverine forest and marshes to dry woodland and scrub. Approximately 600 plant and 245 bird species occur naturally in the grounds; to these more than 2,000 plant species have been added. In addition to claiming the largest collection of cycads in the world, the garden also contains the largest assortment of indigenous trees in the country. If you have no more than an hour, make sure to explore the South African Forest, which has native trees from the Cape coast to the extreme north; and the African Rain Forest, a re-creation of the ecosystems of the rapidly shrinking forests of Central and West Africa. There are a number of walks, the most satisfying being the 2- to 3-hour trail which winds along the banks of the Crocodile River and takes in all three of the garden's waterfalls. Guided tours can be arranged in advance; alternatively a range of brochures and informative notes are available from the entrance kiosk.

## A Nearby Gold-Rush Village

The discovery of gold in Barberton in 1883 attracted thousands of fortune seekers, among them Graham Barber and his cousins, who found and worked the Barber Reef. In its heyday, during the 1880s, Barberton was a large and lively settlement populated by some colorful characters—one of the most celebrated was Cockney Liz who would regularly auction herself to the highest bidder in the **Phoenix** (☎ **013/712-4211,** 20 Pilgrim St.), where you can still enjoy a drink today. Barberton lies 50 kilometers (31 miles) south of Nelspruit on the R40. With neither the charm nor the accommodations options of Pilgrim's Rest, a trip here makes most sense if you're on your way to KwaZulu-Natal via the small kingdom of Swaziland.

The **Barberton Museum,** 36 Pilgrims St., left off President Street, Barberton (☎ **013/712-4208** or 013/712-2121), has photographs of Cockney Liz and her customers, as well as good displays on the gold-rush era, and will provide you with a map of the Victorian houses that fall under its jurisdiction. These include **Fernlea, Stopford,** and **Belhaven** (built for a wealthy middle-class family in 1904). Museum hours are daily from 9am to 4pm; and admission is free. Tours of Belhaven and Stopford take place at 10 and 11am, noon, and 2 and 3pm.

Barberton is also the only place where you can try your hand at gold panning—tours last about 4 hours and bookings must be made a day in advance: contact the **Valley of Gold Tours** (☎ **013/719-9681**). If you travel here between November and January, you will see colorful displays of the famous **Barberton daisy** (better known as the Gerbera), which was first exported to Kew Gardens in 1884.

## WHERE TO STAY & DINE

### IN SCHOEMANSKLOOF

**Old Joe's Kaia.** Box 108, Schagen 1207. Schoemanskloof, on the R539, 23km (14 miles) from Montrose Falls. ☎ **013/733-3045.** Fax 013/733-3777. www.oldjoes.co.za. 14 units. R780 ($130) double, includes dinner and breakfast. AE, DC, MC, V. Children 12 and over welcome.

Situated on a steep hill overlooking the Schoemanskloof Valley, this is an ideal stopover from Gauteng—a 3-hour drive away—particularly if you've set off late and intend to fit in a full day's sightseeing the following day.

Of the accommodation choices, the generously sized log cabins, which are raised on stilts with views, are the best option—if you can book ahead, ask for number 5. Beds are queen-size, most rooms are carpeted, and there are oil heaters for extra warmth.

**Dining:** Furnishings in the butterfly-themed lounge are tasteful; and the meals, made from fresh, local ingredients, are simple—sandwiches, soups, and salads predominate. Try the trout and garlic pie. Luncheon visitors who are passing through are welcome; a light meal will set you back R10–36 ($1.65–$6).

**Amenities:** Besides relaxing, swimming, bird watching (170 species have been recorded), and walking, croquet and boulle are available.

### IN HAZYVIEW

✪ **Highgrove House.** Off R40, 17km (10½ miles) south of Hazyview. P.O. Box 46, Kiepersol 1241. ☎ **013/764-1844.** Fax 013/764-1855. E-mail: highgrove@ns.lia.net. www.highgrove.co.za. 8 units. TEL. R1,260 ($210) double, includes dinner and breakfast. AE, DC, MC, V. Children 14 and over welcome.

Highgrove's grand tree-lined driveway provides some clue to what lies at the end of the cul de sac—a truly elegant country retreat, where guests are treated like royalty. It's no wonder Highgrove House has won the category for Best Retreat/Small Luxury Hotel in the customer-determined AA Awards for 3 years running.

English country style is a constant theme in South African decor, but here it is particularly well done; the eight garden suites are decorated in pale colors and subtle florals, and feature separate sitting rooms with log fireplaces and double doors that lead onto verandahs with marvelous views over the forest or valley. Fruit and fresh flowers are supplied in every room, and limited room-service is available. The two Orchard Suites, which cost an additional R400 ($66.65), feature private pools, saunas, and minibars. Of these, number one has a beautiful four-poster bed.

**Dining:** Dinners are beautifully presented, though the atmosphere may be a bit formal for someone on vacation—no jeans or sneakers are allowed. Smokers are also not welcome. The six-course table d'ôte dinners (R105/$17.50 per person) change regularly, but a recent meal included mushrooms vol au vents and pimento crostini, butternut soup, and asparagus topped with capers and tomato wontons with lemon-chive butter. Main courses were seared kingklip filets topped with caviar and drizzled with saffron cream, and rump roast encrusted with green peppercorns and served with port-wine jus.

**Rissington Inn.** P.O. Box 650, Hazyview 1242. Off R40, 1km (just over a half mile) south of Hazyview's 4-way stop. ☎ **013/737-7700.** Fax 013/737-7112. 5 units. R180–220 ($30–$36.65) double, includes breakfast. Children half price. AE, DC, MC, V.

What Rissington lacks in style (the honeymoon suite has a false thatch roof jutting over the bed), it makes up for in charm, comfort, and the best food this side of the Escarpment. "I don't know how to cook, but I know how to eat" is how proprietor Christopher Harvie humbly explains his talent. He also promotes a totally relaxing atmosphere—there are no rules, children are expressly welcome, and his reasonable prices extend to the bar, which together with his excellent restaurant is supported by local clientele, many of whom are prepared to travel to enjoy both his food and company. Of the five rooms, Euphorbia is the best option: It faces the sunset, has its own sitting room, and has a king-size bed. Camelfoot, which has two double beds, is a good choice for a small family, though the room is over-furnished. Rissington offers unbeatable value, and with the Numbi Gate 10 minutes away, it makes an extremely comfortable base from which to explore Kruger and the Escarpment surrounds. There is also a large pool.

**Dining:** Chris' menu is strictly a la carte, and as most main dinner dishes cost about R30 ($5), they are an excellent value. The beef Stroganoff is recommended, and if you like your filet medium-rare you'll find a perfect one here.

## Near Paul Kruger Gate

**Karos Lodge.** P.O. Box 888, Hazyview 1242. Off the R536 (Paul Kruger Rd.). ☎ **013/735-5671.** Fax 013/735-5676. E-mail: lodge@karos-hotels.co.za. 96 units. A/C MINIBAR TV TEL. R905 ($150.85) double, includes breakfast and dinner. Children sharing with adults pay for meals only. AE, DC, MC, V.

Situated on 100 hectares (250 acres) on the banks of the Sabie River, Karos is a mere 100 meters (328 ft.) from the Paul Kruger Gate, and yet a million miles from a bush experience. The best reason to stay here is the level of entertainment available for urban kids who might find the Kruger a little too boring. (For more outdoor pursuits, consider staying at Casa do Sol, which is 15 minute away; see "Where to Stay" in "Sabie & Surrounds," above.) Elephants and crocodiles are seen regularly from the raised viewing deck overlooking the river, though with no furniture nor any services you're unlikely to wait around for any length of time. Rooms are tiled, which makes them a little cold, but they're large. An exciting alternative to the rooms in the main two-story building—which despite a few nods to Africa in the foyer, could be anywhere in the world—is to spend a night on the lodge's treehouse platform, accompanied by a ranger. Amenities include swimming pool, tennis court, mini-golf, and games room.

**Dining:** Dinners consist of massive buffets, served in the *boma* (a circular open-air enclosure), with chefs preparing many of the meals in front of you. The results aren't that good, but at least they're varied: grilled calamari, beef steak, stir-fried fish and vegetables, various *potjies* (stews), and a large selection of salads.

## Near Malelane Gate

**Buhala Country House.** P.O. Box 165, Malelane 1320. ☎ **013/790-4372.** Fax 013/790-4306. E-mail: buhala@lbm.co.za. 8 units. TEL. R770 ($128.35) double, breakfast included. AE, DC, MC, V. Off the N4, 12km (7½ miles) beyond Malelane turnoff toward Komatipoort. No children under 10.

With excellent views overlooking the banks of the Crocodile River—opposite of which lies the Kruger—Buhala feels almost as if it's in the park. The indigenous gardens do nothing to detract from this illusion (nor do the browsing hippos), but the accommodations are a lot more comfortable. Rooms are elegant and cool (iron beds, white linen, thatched ceilings), and, for an additional R80 ($13.35), dinner is definitely worth ordering. Sugar Rhodes's cooking is classic: rack of lamb or duckling prepared with glazed oranges, or stuffed veal in phyllo pastry. Her Buhala sauce, a piquant herb-flavored sauce served with filet, is just one reason the lodge keeps placing in the national Country House of the Year awards. If you don't have the patience to watch the game coming to drink while you relax on the large verandah, or add to the list of over 200 species of birds already recorded, the Malelane Gate to the Kruger is a mere

10 minutes away. Buhala will organize tours of the Escarpment as well as safaris into the park—given 2 days notice, even night drives in open-air vehicles can be arranged. With only eight bedrooms, and no children under 10, this is a truly tranquil option; though if you're watching your budget, you're better off booking into the Malelane Sun.

**Malelane Sun Intercontinental.** P.O. Box 392, Malelane 1320. ☎ **013/790-3304.** Fax 013/790-3303. 102 units. A/C MINIBAR TV TEL. R518 ($86.35) double; R1,300 ($216.65) suite, includes breakfast. 2-night minimum. AE, DC, MC, V.

Even closer to the gate than Buhala Country House, the Malelane Sun offers all the comforts and anonymity of a hotel, at a very reasonable price. It's a great way to see the Kruger in style, and although it costs less than the Karos, it's a more luxurious experience. Rooms are all in a single-story building and, while the standard doubles are a tad small, they are elegantly furnished, comfortably carpeted and lead out onto the indigenous gardens—no views though. Suites, of which there are unfortunately only two, feature king-size beds, fireplaces, marble-lined bathrooms, private swimming pools, Jacuzzis, and, weirdly enough, a barbecue. Residents in double rooms share a large attractive pool. The biggest draw is the excellent wooden viewing platform; from this large, comfortably furnished deck within a stone's throw of the Crocodile River, you can sample complimentary cakes and coffee while watching animals on the opposite bank. Another reason you may want to book into the Malelane Sun is the adjacent **Leopard's Creek Golf Course:** Only guests of Malelane are offered the privilege of paying R400 ($66.65) a day to play what has become the most exclusive course in South Africa.

The food, however, is rather disappointing. Large buffets feature overcooked vegetables, stews, casseroles, and roasts, and predictably, venison is a major component.

## 6 The Letaba Area Route

Pietersburg is 330km (205 miles) north of Johannesburg

This lesser-known route to central Kruger is in parts even more scenic than the others, and is particularly attractive during the winter months, when much of the highveld and the Panorama Route are dry and burnt brown. It is also ideal if you are entering the Kruger via the Phalaborwa Gate, or the lodges in the Makalali, Timbavati, and Manyeleti private game reserves. (*Note:* If you're heading for the Kruger's northernmost reaches, stay on the N1, taking the R524 turnoff at Louis Trichardt to the Punda Maria Gate.)

### ESSENTIALS

**GETTING THERE** **By Car** Head north on the N1 Toll Road (make sure you have R50/$8.35 cash on hand) from Gauteng and don't stop until you get to Pietersburg, a 330-kilometer (205-mile) drive, which should take approximately 3 hours. From Pietersburg, head due east on the R71.

**By Plane** Three times daily, **SA Airlink** (☎ **015/781-5823**) flies into Hendrick van Eck, which borders the centrally located Kruger Gate, Phalaborwa.

**VISITOR INFORMATION** You can get information from **Letaba Tourism** (phone only)(☎ **015/276-4307**), or visit the **Byadladi Tourist Association,** Rissik Street, next to Greenwoods, in Haenertsburg (☎ **015/276-4472**); or if you're traveling the other way (that is, from Kruger to Johannesburg via Letaba), visit the **Tourist Information Centre in Tzaneen,** at 23 Danie Joubert St. (☎ **015/307-5979**).

**GETTING AROUND** **By Car** **Avis** (☎ **015/781-3169**) and **Budget** (☎ **015/781-5404**) both have desks at the Phalaborwa Airport.

**By Guided Tour** For organized tailor-made tours of the region, contact **Letaba Active Tours** (☎ **015/307-1294**).

## EXPLORING THE AREA BY CAR

The only sight worth taking in before turning onto the R71 is the **Bakone Malope Open-Air Museum,** a North Sotho cultural village, which is a few minutes drive from Pietersburg (see below). Some 30 kilometers (19 miles) from Pietersburg on R71 you will see a huge Star of David etched onto the hill overlooking a small settlement. This is the **Zion City Moria,** headquarters of the African Zionist Church, the biggest Christian congregation in South Africa. An estimated 3 million members make the annual pilgrimage to Moria every Easter—with minibus taxis stuffed to the brim and their drivers on a mission from God to get there by Good Friday, this is definitely not the time to troll around the area. However, if you do get stuck here, you'll at least come across some interesting photo opportunities.

About 10 kilometers (6 miles) farther on the R71 is the turnoff for the **Wolkberg Wilderness Area,** a 22,000-hectare (55,000-acre) nature reserve which has some excellent hiking trails (see "Hiking" in "Staying Active," above).

Continuing on R71, you will reach the old gold-rush village of **Haenertsburg,** where the dense forestation that typifies the Letaba region begins. There is no real reason to stop in here unless you want to break for refreshments at the **Greenwood's Trading Post** (☎ **015/276-4204**), visit the Tourist Information Centre, or browse for crafts at **The Elms** (☎ **015/276-4405**)—this is not a great selection of African curios; crafts are more of the pottery and homemade jam variety. You can, however, make trout-fishing inquiries, as well as purchase tackle and licenses from The Elms. All the above are situated on Rissik Street, the town's only main road.

One of the area's main attractions is the **Cheerio Gardens** (☎ **015/276-4424**), on a cherry and azalea farm on the outskirts of town, signposted off the R71; but unless the trees are in full bloom (usually during October), or you're desperate for a cup of tea, the drive that awaits is a lot more spectacular. On the same turnoff as Cheerio Gardens is the **Wegraakbos Dairy** (☎ **015/276-1811**), where cheese is still made in the traditional way.

After Haenertsburg you can choose between following the R71 to **Magoebaskloof,** or taking the **Georges Valley Road** (R528), which follows the slopes of the Wolkberg mountain range. Both routes are rewarding, following winding mountain passes offering dramatic views of dense forests and large still lakes before reaching Tzaneen; though the steeper gradients of the R71, and the fact that it has two of the top attractions, swing the balance somewhat in its favor.

If you do travel the Georges Valley Road, 5 kilometers (3 miles) along it you'll find the turnoff to writer John Buchan's memorial. His 1910 book *Prester John* immortalized the area. There's a good view of the **Ebenezer Dam** from here (which is a lot more attractive than its name). To get closer, travel a little farther on the R528 and take the Ebenezer Dam turnoff—incidentally, this road joins up with the R71. Farther on the Georges Valley Road lies **Tenby Gardens** (☎ **015/307-2507**), a tea room and gift shop with the best selection of crafts in the area (the competition is not very stiff, so don't hold your breath). This is an informal tourist information center, with leaflets on display and a helpful staff.

If you have decided on the R71 route through the Magoebaskloof, you will drop 56 kilometers (183 ft.) in under 6½ kilometers (4 miles) as you wind down the

Drakensberg Escarpment to the subtropical lowveld. On the way you'll enjoy beautiful views of the valleys and ravines named after Makgoba, chief of the Tlou tribe, who hid out here after refusing to pay taxes to Paul Kruger's government. Needless to say, he was finally tracked down and beheaded for his recalcitrance. It is said that his spirit still lives here, though thankfully there is little evidence to support this. Look out for the turnoff marked HOUTBOSDORP, which takes you on a 12-kilometer (7½-mile) route into the **Woodbush State Forest.** Here you'll find the largest area of indigenous forest in the Northern Transvaal, and excellent views of the lowveld to the east. The picturesque **Debengeni Falls** lie just east of here, and are reached by following the road that finally returns to the R71 via the De Hoek State Forest. This is also where the 3-day **Magoebaskloof Trails** start (see "Hiking" in "Staying Active," above).

After the turnoff to Debengeni and De Hoek, the woodlands change into subtropical plantations of avocado, banana, mango, pawpaw, nuts, kiwi, and lichi; and rolling hills of soft, green tea bushes. A visit to **Pekoe View,** the Sapekoe Estate's tea garden is highly recommen3ded, even if only to take in the spectacular view (see below).

If you turn south at the T-junction with the R36, you will get to **Tzaneen** in approximately 5 minutes; but if you turn north to **Duiwelskloof,** you can have a drink in a baobab tree and visit the home of the Rain Queen on the way there (see the box below). This circular route will add approximately 100 kilometers (60 miles) to your journey.

Having finally descended to the rather uninteresting town of Tzaneen, which marks the transition from Escarpment to the lowveld, a visit to the impressive **Tzaneen Museum** is recommended.

To overnight, or lunch while taking in more spectacular views, head for the lofty heights of **Agatha,** an area located 15 kilometers (9 miles) south of Tzaneen, where you'll find the most beautiful gardens and the best accommodation option, The Coach House, in the area. There are also some excellent walks, like the **Rooikat Trail** (pronounced *roy*-cut; see "Hiking" in "Staying Active"), which takes you through the New Agatha State Forests.

From Tzaneen you are poised to enter big-game country: Travel for another hour east on the R71 and you'll reach **Phalaborwa,** one of the Kruger's central gates—ideal if you're on your way to Letaba or Olifants Rest Camp. This is also where you will find the **Hans Merensky Country Club** (see "Golfing" in "Staying Active," above). Just inside the Kruger's Phalaborwa Gate is the **Masorini Open Air Village,** a reconstruction of an Iron Age village based on findings in the area that date back to A.D. 800. It has no explanatory boards, so without a guide it's not very enthralling.

If you're booked into the lodges in the **Makalali, Timbavati,** or **Manyeleti private reserves,** or need to enter Kruger at the **Orpen Gate,** you will travel down the R36 southeast from Tzaneen. The R36 joins the R527 a few kilometers after the Strijdom Tunnel. (See "The Panorama Route," above, for traveling details and sights from here.)

## THE TOP ATTRACTIONS

**Bakone Malapa Museum.** 9km (6 miles) southeast of Pietersburg on R37. ☎ **015/ 295-2867.** Mon 8:30am–12.30pm; Tues–Fri 8.30am–12.30pm and 1.30–3.30pm. Admission R3 (50¢); kids under 18, R1.50 (30¢).

While this cultural village is not in the Letaba area, it is easy to take in on the way to or from Letaba. Bear in mind that this really is home to the people who live here, and the villagers prefer prior notification of an upcoming visit. Another reason to call ahead is to ensure that Bernard, the extremely knowledgeable tour guide, is on duty.

The village displays the traditional living arrangements and ways of life of the ancestors of the North Sotho, with special reference to the Bakone, an ethnic grouping within the North Sotho people. Like the excellent Simunye in KwaZulu-Natal, the museum does not ignore the fact that once this culture came into contact with the colonialists it changed irrevocably, and there is a modern section of the village included in the tour. Not surprisingly, this is where the villagers choose to live. The tour takes approximately 30 to 40 minutes and displays authentic utensils and dress. Male and female societal roles are displayed and described in both traditional and modern society. Included in the negligible admission price are San rock paintings dating back to A.D. 1000, as well as the remains of a Ndebele iron and copper smelting works.

**Debengeni Falls.** Off the R71 (turnoff north, at Bruphy Sawmills). ☎ **013/764-1058.** 7:30am–5pm. Admission R5 (85¢) per person; R10 ($1.65) per picnic site.

Translated, Debengeni means "place of the big pot"—a reference to the huge potholes created by the scouring of the pebbles and boulders that cascade down the rockface above. If you're traveling through the Magoebaskloof in the summer, these "pots" are the best natural swimming pools in the area, though care must be taken if you explore in the river—the wet rocks are extremely slippery. There is a circular walk that takes approximately 15 minutes to complete, and picnic and braai facilities under the trees which line the falls; but it's been a long time since anyone did any on-site maintenance or picked up cigarette butts, and one can't help wondering what the admission fee is used for.

**Kings Walden Gardens.** Agatha Rd., 12km (7½ miles) from Tzaneen. ☎ **015/307-3265.** Open daily, weather permitting, from sunrise to sunset. R5 (85¢) admission.

A number of farm gardens in the area are open to the public—so many, in fact, that the tourism office offers a Letaba Garden Route—but if you see only one, it should be Kings Walden. With broad swathes of color and artful landscaping, this is the sort of grand country garden you'd expect to find in England or France—though in bloom the purple-blue Jacaranda blossoms are a dead giveaway, as is the setting. Floating 1,050 meters (3,444 ft.) above sea level, the gardens have been laid out so as to suggest a ship setting sail into the skies, with the grounds falling away on three sides and the grand "decks" providing dramatic views of the undulating lowveld as it meets the foothills of the Drakensberg. Trees, walls, and statuary are covered in moss and lichen, testimony to the damp conditions that often prevail as mists and clouds descend on the gardens. This serves only to heighten their ethereal, romantic beauty, as do well-positioned ponds and mirrors. The gardens were started in 1934 by Elsie Tooley, and are now in the care of her daughter, Tana Hilton-Barber. Day visitors are provided with tea and scones, though there's sometimes a wait for them.

✪ **Pekoe View.** Sapekoe Dr., the turnoff lies south off the Magoebaskloof Rd., or R71. ☎ **015/305-3241 ext. 213** or 083627-1494. Open daily 10am–5pm. Factory tours Tues–Sat 11am. R10 ($1.65), includes a cup of tea.

Undoubtedly the top attraction in the area if you enjoy tea, and worth a visit even if you don't, the Pekoe View Tea Gardens are reached through an evergreen sea of tea

### A Sacrificial Slide

Apparently the Tlou people used to make sacrifices to the spirits at Debengeni Falls; as nothing has been offered to appease them since Makgoba, chief of the Tlou tribe had his head chopped off for evading taxes, this may explain how the falls have managed to claim so many human lives, despite signs posted of the danger of using the wet rockface as a natural slide into the potholes.

bushes and have breathtaking vistas of the estate's plantations. From these 3,300 hectares (8,250 acres), the Sapekoe pickers produce approximately 10,000 tons of tea a day in summer—over two-thirds of South Africa's production. Tours of the tea estate's factory, adjacent to the gardens, take between 40 and 60 minutes. During this time you will walk through the entire factory (noisy during summer, when it runs 24 hours a day), and learn the delicate art of making tea. In this region, the teamaker is as respected as a vintner, and the taster's palate is as discriminating as a wine taster's. At the end of the tour, visitors participate in a tea tasting—it's surprisingly easy to tell the difference between an A-grade and the lower-grade teas. The gift shop sells dried tea, as well as locally grown macadamia nuts, jars of pepperdews (small, sweet peppers), and Avodeau skincare products, a good local range made from avocado (almost half of South Africa's total crop is produced in this area).

✪ **Tzaneen Museum.** On the grounds of the Tzaneen Library, Agatha St. ☎ **015/ 307-2425.** Mon–Fri 9am–5pm; Sat 9am–1pm. Donations welcome.

If you're interested in African art and history, this is undoubtedly one of the top provincial museums in the country. The museum, containing the private collection of dedicated curator Juergen Witt, consists of four small rooms filled with over a thousand well-traveled exhibits relating to the traditions and history of the North Sotho, Tsonga, and Venda. In addition to documenting the development of sculptural art over the past century, Mr. Witt actively encourages it: Outside the museum, you will meet mythical creatures from Tsonga tales. These carvings were commissioned by Mr. Witt in order to keep oral traditions alive and to offer a focal point for children who visit the museum, many of whom are brought by parents wanting to encourage an interest in their own culture. Ethnological artifacts include weapons, pottery (covering a period of nearly 2,000 years), basketry, beadwork, initiation figures, pole-carvings (the world's largest collection), as well as old books and documents relating to the area. One of the most exotic exhibits is the royal drum used in the service of the great grandmother of the present Rain Queen Modjadji, which dates back to 1850. Like the excellent Vukani Museum in KwaZulu-Natal, funding is an ongoing problem, and exhibits are neither labeled nor professionally displayed. However, this is more than compensated for by the enthusiastic staff, who happily guide visitors through the rooms; visits of up to 3 hours are not uncommon. Mr. Witt is usually at the museum, but visitors with specialized interests are advised to contact him well in advance—although the sensitive, Stone Age material is not usually on display, arrangements to view it can be made. As entrance is free, try to help the museum out by donating generously.

## WHERE TO STAY & DINE

✪ **The Coach House.** P.O. Box 544, Tzaneen 0850. ☎ **015/307-3641.** Fax 015/ 307-1466. 45 units. A/C MINIBAR (in premier rooms) TV TEL. R640–800 ($106.65–$133.35) double; R900 ($150) suites. AE, DC, MC, V. Take Agatha Rd., turn left at the top of the hill onto Old Coach Road. Children over 14 only.

The only hotel in the Northern Province to have a 5-star SATOUR grading, The Coach House combines an exceptional location with high service standards and fine cuisine. Situated on a 560-hectare (140-acre) working fruit and nut farm, the well-established gardens are a riot of color, even in winter, and almost every room has a spectacular view and a verandah to enjoy it from (the views from rooms 1 to 6 and 21 to 24 are particularly outstanding). You can choose from a standard double, a premier double, or a suite—the expensive suites add nothing but a wall between the bedroom and lounge—but if you're willing to spend an additional R160 ($26.65), the supremely comfortable premier double is definitely worth it. These give you a choice of large twin beds or a king-size, as well as a fireplace, minibar, writing desk, lounge

## Get Drunk in a Trunk & Visit the Garden of a Queen

To visit the Gardens of the Rain Queen, take R36 north when approaching the T-junction from Magoebaskloof Road (R71). This takes you past the town of **Duiwelskloof.** Approximately 6 kilometers (4 miles) north of Duiwelskloof is a turnoff for Modjadji and Sunland Nursery; turn right here, and after 4 kilometers (2½ miles) turn left onto Leeudraai Road, where you will find the **Big Baobab** (☎ **015/309-9039**). Measuring almost 47 meters (154 ft.) around, its "owners" claim that this is the biggest baobab in the world. The tree has been used as shelter for thousands of years by both humans and animals, but it took a man like Doug van Heerden to transform the 6,000-year old Baobab into its present incarnation. Having cleared the floor and squared the back, Mr. van Heerden has built a bar in the center, complete with seating, lights, draught machine, and sound system. Unfortunately, you have to make a group booking to sample the draught, though if you call well in advance, van Heerden may make an exception. Despite its ignoble new function, the tree continues unperturbed: It drops its leaves in winter, flowers in spring, and provides a good deal more than shade to hot visitors every summer. Admission is R10 ($1.65).

Travel back down Leeudraai Road and turn left to follow the signs to the **Modjadji Cycad Reserve** (☎ **015/23252 ext. 21;** R2/35¢ admission plus R5/85¢ per vehicle), home of the elusive Rain Queen, who lives in protected isolation in the area. Cycads are the most primitive seed-bearing plants, with species dating back between 60 and 300 million years to when dinosaurs roamed the earth. The Modjadji Palm usually grows to 5–8 meters (16–26 feet), but, thanks no doubt to the protection of the Rain Queen, more of these trees grow here than anywhere else in the world, and some have reached heights of 12 meters (39 feet). There are a few short pleasant walks, a picnic site, and a basic information center dedicated to the ancestors of the Rain Queen, a dynasty of females who have ruled over the area since the 16th century. Even the mighty Zulu kings held the Rain Queen in awe, and each seldom-seen matriarch hands over her rain-making secrets to a daughter, after which some say she commits suicide, thereby maintaining the illusion of immortality. Modjadji, the first Rain Queen, is said to have been the inspiration for the immortal queen in Rider Haggard's 1887 classic novel *She.* The monarch does make the occasional appearance, and certainly her powers are in evidence every summer, when the Letaba area is shrouded in mists, and the high rainfall turns the area into a lush, evergreen garden.

area, and a hidden service hatch through which your early-morning tea and coffee is delivered. Bathrooms feature two basins and a bidet.

All rooms include details like a variety of books, fresh fruit, and a tin of homemade biscuits. Even the ubiquitous hotel postcards are thoughtfully accompanied by a few stamps. Furnishings throughout the hotel are very much in the English country style, with floral fabrics, historical illustrations, and a mix of antiques and reproduction furniture.

**Dining:** Even if you're not overnighting, The Coach House is an excellent place to visit for a meal, particularly lunch so that you can enjoy the views. Chef Lucas Ndlovu is internationally renowned; his specialties include avocados (picked on the farm) filled with prawns and topped with a cognac sauce, local Bonsmara beef with béarnaise, deboned Sabie rainbow trout stuffed with spinach, and venison medallions en croute with marula (a local fruit) jelly. A five-course menu will run you R125 ($20.85), while mains alone range between R30 ($5) and R55 ($9.15).

**Amenities:** Solar-heated pool, croquet, mountain biking, billiards, gym, and sauna. The Rooikat Trail through the Agatha Forests starts half a mile away, and four other trails of varying lengths start on the grounds (ask reception for a map). Trout-fishing permits arranged. All rooms have hair dryers.

**Kings Walden.** P.O. Box 31, Tzaneen 0850. 12km (7½ miles) from Tzaneen on the Agatha Rd. ☎ **015/307-3262.** Fax 015/307-1548. 4 units. R320 ($53.35) double, including breakfast. No credit cards.

This is very much a home, and if you prefer anonymity and slick service you'd be better off staying at The Coach House or Magoebaskloof Hotel. It's the gardens of this working farm that make it a worthwhile stopover, and to that end try to book the Oriental Room as it's the only one with a view of the garden and has doors leading to the pool. While there is no doubt that Tana Hilton-Barber, the eccentric and charming hostess, has creative flair (to see the Asian influence in the Oriental Room takes some interpretive powers), her talents are better employed in the garden. However, rooms are comfortable, Tana an excellent cook, and her husband David a keen walker and very knowledgeable about the area. Meals (which must be organized well in advance) often feature avocado (it's a working avocado farm). Avocado and pecans may be followed by soup (carrot and orange is popular), a choice of chicken or beef, and strawberries and lavender ice cream. It's worth noting that The Coach House, which serves the best food in the entire province, is a short drive away.

**Magoebaskloof Hotel.** Off the R71, Magoebaskloof Pass. ☎ **015/276-4276.** Fax 015/276-4280. 60 units. TV TEL. R400 ($66.65) double, including breakfast. (During July and August this rate also includes dinner; minimum 2-night stay.) AE, DC, MC, V.

This is a warm, generous, and friendly hotel—from the zealous porter to the well-priced wine list, there are no hard edges or nasty surprises (except for the shaggy carpets, but I was assured that they are in the process of replacing these). Best of all, "we love children," the room's directory states in no uncertain terms; and in an area not renowned for this sentiment, this open embrace will come as a relief for beleaguered parents. Rooms are all spacious and comfortable. The best are numbers 42 to 47, which are on the third floor and feature beautiful views of the Magoebaskloof Valley and Dam. Every morning, guests are provided with the day's weather forecast, sunrise and sundown time, and current phase of the moon, together with complimentary morning tea and coffee—a nice touch you'll pay a lot more for at The Coach House.

**Dining:** The restaurant has a good reputation (and some beautiful views), though some dishes are to be avoided—the onion soup is a definite no-no. Try the Magoebaskloof Pot, tournedos of beef served on spätzle and topped with mushrooms, crumbed fried fruit and sauce béarnaise.

**Amenities:** Swimming pool, children's playground, squash court, bowling green, and two pubs. Complimentary tea and coffee. Rooms have hair dryers. There are a number of excellent walks and rides in the area—ask at reception.

## 7 Kruger National Park

Southern (Malelane) gate: 428km (265 miles) NE of Johannesburg. Northern (Punda Maria) gate: 581km (360 miles) NE of Johannesburg.

Proclaimed by South African president Paul Kruger in 1898, this jewel in the National Parks Board crown stretches 381 kilometers (236 miles) from the banks of the Crocodile River in the south to the Limpopo River in the north and covers almost 2½ million hectares (6 million acres)—a figure that is constantly being added to by the removal of fences running between the park's western flank and the adjacent private game reserves. Even more impressive than its size, however, is the diversity of life it sustains: 16 ecozones (each with its own geology, rainfall, altitude, and landscape) are home to over 500 bird species and 147 mammal species, including over 2,000 lions, 1,000 leopards, 1,800 rhinos, 8,000 elephants, and 22,000 buffaloes. Cheetahs, wild dogs, hyenas, zebras, giraffes, hippos, crocodiles, warthogs, and a large number of antelope also roam Kruger's open plains and waterways. Plant life is rich and varies from tropical to subtropical; almost 2,000 species have been identified, including some 450 tree and shrub species and 235 grasses. The opportunity to see wildlife is superb—many people report seeing four of the Big 5 (the most elusive being leopard) within 1 day.

Kruger also has a number of archaeological sites, the most interesting being the recently-opened Thulamela, a 12th-century stone-walled village overlooking the Luvuvhu River in the north. Others include the Stone Age village at Masorini and San engravings and paintings. The latter can be visited at Crocodile Bridge hippo pool or on the Bushman and Wolhuter Trails. Historical sites relating to early European explorers and Kruger's beginnings are also dotted throughout the park.

Parks Board officials make no bones about the fact that their main concern is wildlife; *Homo sapiens* are a necessary nuisance. Though an effort is made to service visitors' needs, like offering escorted night and day drives (highly recommended unless you're going on to a private game reserve), rules (like gate opening times) are inflexible, staff can be bureaucratic, and, as services are geared toward the self-catering South African market, you're pretty much expected to toe the line. Here's how.

## ESSENTIALS

### ARRIVING

**BY PLANE** You can fly directly into the park. **SA Express** (☎ **015/793-3681**) flies Johannesburg to **Skukuza** (the biggest rest camp and park headquarters) three times a day (R1,300/$216.65 round-trip). **Nelspruit International Airport** (56km/35 miles from Numbi Gate) is well positioned to enter the southern gates: **SA Airlink** (☎ **013/735-5645**) flies here several times a day from Johannesburg and once a day from Durban; and **Metavia Airlines** (☎ **013/741-3142**) has flights from Johannesburg, Durban, and Mozambique. Phalaborwa's **Hendrick van Eck Airport** borders the central area and is ideal for Letaba and Oliphants camps; **SA Airlink** (☎ **015/781-5823**) flies there three times daily. Hoedpruit's **Eastgate Airport** is good for the central and southern gates; the closest camp is Satara. **SA Express** (☎ **015/793-3681**) has daily flights from Johannesburg, and from Cape Town three times a week.

**BY CAR** There are eight entrance gates, most a comfortable 5- to 6-hour drive from Johannesburg or Pretoria. The closest gate, Malelane, is 428 kilometers (265 miles) from Johannesburg, while Punda Maria (the farthest) lies 581 kilometers (361 miles) northeast. **To the southern gates: Malelane** (take the N4, passing Nelspruit, and look out for the signpost), **Crocodile Bridge** (take the R571 north off the N4), **Numbi** (take the R40 off the N4 north, keep heading north, following signs to the R358, then east on R569), and **Paul Kruger** (take the R536 east from Sabie). **To the central gates: Orpen** (off R40 heading south from Hoedspruit, take the R531 east) and **Phalaborwa** (from Pietersburg, take the R71 east). **To the northern gates: Punda Maria** (from Pietersburg, take the N1 north, then take the R524) and **Parfuri** (from the Punda Maria Gate, take the park roads). Allow sufficient traveling time to the park, as entrance-gate hours (see "Fast Facts," below) are strictly adhered to.

### Visitor Information

All inquiries and applications should be made to the **National Parks Board,** 643 Leyds St., Muckleneuk, Pretoria (☎ **012/343-1991**), fax 012/343 0905, between 8am and 3:45pm); or 44 Long St., Cape Town (☎ **021/22-2810,** fax 021/24-6211, between 9am and 4:45pm). You can also phone the park directly at ☎ **013/735-5159;** e-mail them at reservations@parks-sa.co.za; or visit their Web site at www.parks-sa.co.za or www.ecoafrica.com/krugerpark/. Reservations can also be made through **Computicket** (☎ **011/445-8100**). The park's headquarters are situated at Skukuza Rest Camp, located in the southern section, on the banks of the Sabie River (see below).

### Getting Around

**BY CAR** It's best by far to explore at your own pace in a rental car. **Avis** has a desk at the Hoedspruit Airport (☎ **015/793-2014**); at Nelspruit International Airport (☎ **013/741-1087**); at the Phalaborwa Airport (☎ **015/781-3169**); and at Skukuza Airport (☎ **013/735-5651**). **Budget** operates from Nelspruit Airport (☎ **013/741-3871**) and Phalaborwa Airport (☎ **015/781-5404**). Also see "Guided Game Drives," below—guided drives are an excellent way to get to know the park before setting out on your own.

### When to Go

Each season has definite advantages. Between October and March, when summer rains (often in the form of dramatic thunderstorms) have transformed the dry landscape into a flowering paradise, the park is alive with baby bucks and migratory birds, but temperatures can soar above 40°C (105°F), dropping to 20°C (68°F) in the balmy evenings, the dense jungle-like foliage hides much of the game, and the malaria risk is at its highest. In the winter, when water is scarce and the plant life dies back, animals are easier to spot, especially at waterholes and riverbeds. However, as this is the most popular season, you will have to share your sightings with other motorists. The days are warm, but temperatures can drop close to freezing at night, and units are not heated. Try to avoid going during the school holidays, particularly in winter, when the park is packed to capacity.

## Fast Facts: Kruger National Park

**Admission Hours** **For the Park** Entrance gates open January to February from 5:30am to 6:30pm; March 5:30am to 6pm; April 6:00am to 6pm; May to July 6am to 5:30pm; August to September 6am to 6pm; October 5:30am to 6:00pm; and November to December 5:30am to 6:30pm. **For the rest camps,** the gates follow the same hours except in the summer months (November to January) when they open an hour earlier (that is, 4:30am). Camps are fenced off to protect residents from predators. If you're changing rest camps, try not to travel more than 200 kilometers (124 miles) to ensure you get to your new camp before its gates close. Operating hours for camp receptions are 8am to 5:30pm; for shops 8am to ½ hour after camp gates close; for restaurants 7 to 9am, 12 to 2pm, and 6 to 9pm.

**Bank & ATM Networks** There is a bank and ATM at Skukuza.

**Driving Rules** Unlike private game reserves where rangers are free to drive off road, everyone at Kruger drives on roads; the public on approved roads only. (The speed limit is 50kmph on paved roads; 40kmph on gravel roads; 20kmph in rest camps; 30, 25, and 15 mph, respectively). If photographs of fatally

# Kruger National Park & Private Game Reserves

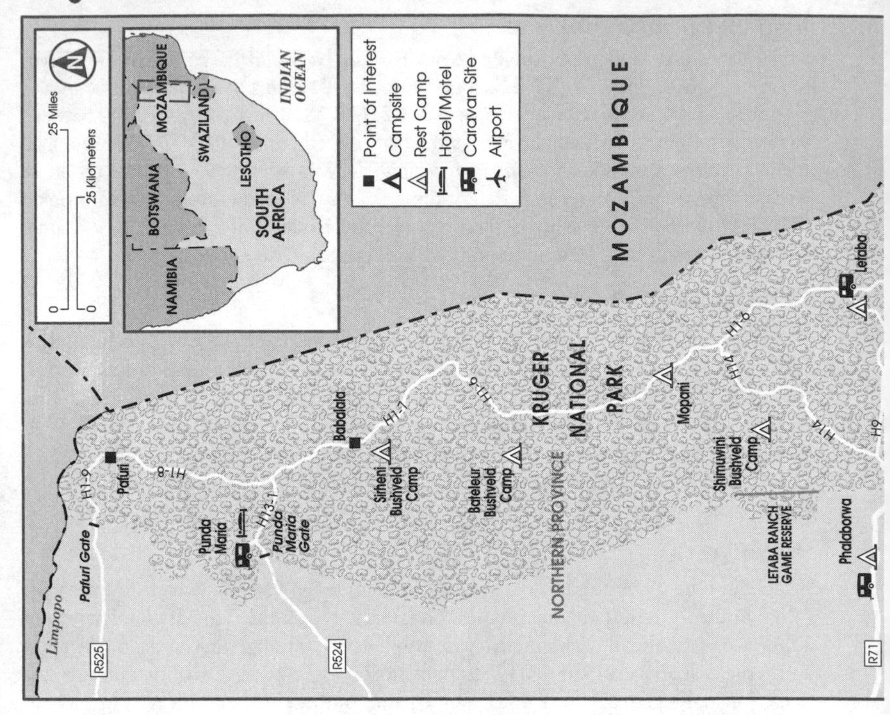


maimed animals don't help ensure that these are adhered to, speed traps do. Stay in your vehicle unless at a designated picnic site.

**Fees** Admission is R30 ($5) per person and R24 ($4) per vehicle; children 2 to 15 R15 ($2.50).

**Fuel** There is a fuel/petrol station in every rest camp and at all the gates except Malelane and Paul Kruger. You must pay in cash.

**Malaria** The highest risk is between October and May, during which time a course of prescription anti-malaria drugs is essential. In most cases, you will have to start a course before you set off for Kruger and continue after your return. However, these drugs are not always totally effective; it's best to avoid being bitten. Repellants containing di-ethyl toluamide are best, but only work for 6 to 8 hours. Apply to exposed skin before sundown, when mosquitoes start to feed, and wear loose clothes that cover arms, legs, and ankles. Clothes can be washed in an insecticide for extra protection, and citronella used as a supplementary deterrent. Remember that perfumed products attract mosquitoes, so this is no time to splash on the Chanel. You'll want to burn coils or use vaporizing mats at nights as camps have no provision for hanging mosquito nets. (Repellants and coils can be purchased from rest camp shops, or are supplied in rooms.) Finally, if you develop symptoms—which are not unlike flu—have a blood test immediately as early diagnosis and treatment can mean a quick recovery. For more information, see chapter 2.

**Medical Emergencies** There is a doctor in Skukuza (☎ **013/735-5638**). If you need help during the night, drive to the your camp gate and beep. The closest hospitals are in Hoedspruit and Nelspruit.

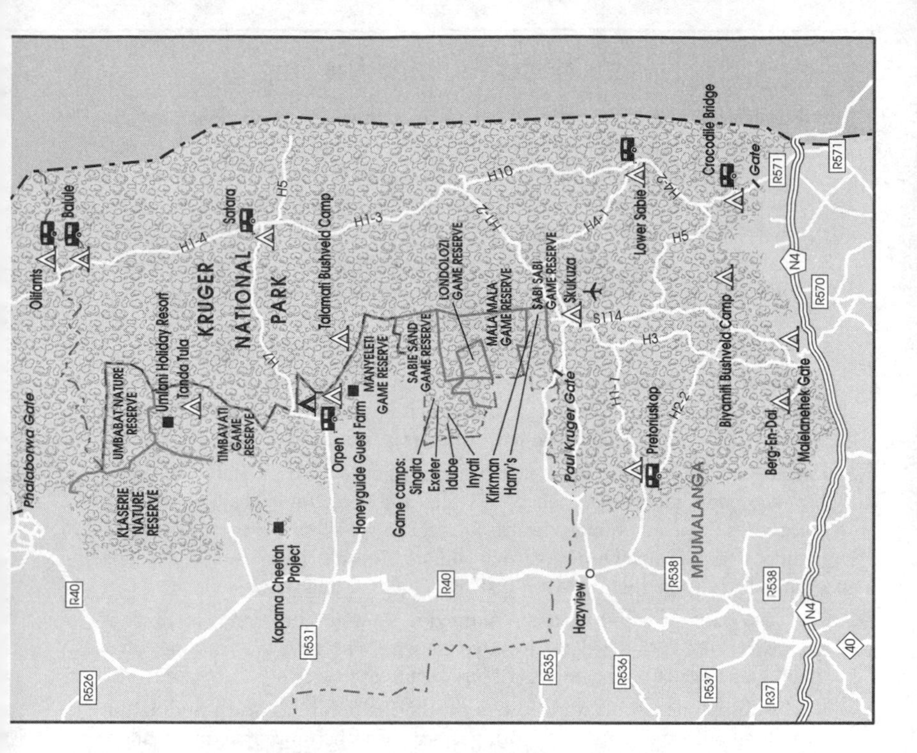


**Money** South African rand, traveler's checks, Visa, MasterCard, Diners Club, and American Express are accepted.

**Reservations** Preference for choice units is given to written applications (this includes fax and e-mail) received 13 months in advance. Pay your deposit as soon as possible to ensure the booking—this can be done over the telephone with a credit card.

**Safety** Don't let the tarred road fool you—once you have left the safety of your fenced-off rest camp, you really are in the wilds. Under no circumstances should you leave your vehicle unless at a designated picnic site; one ranger who left his game drive to take a quick leak didn't survive, and you probably wouldn't, either. When in camp, try not to be frightened by spiders and other small insects you may encounter; unlike mosquitoes they can do you no harm. Snakes are a rare occurrence in camps; if you do spot one, alert reception.

## EXPLORING THE PARK

Despite the many defined ecozones (16 in all), to the untrained eye much of the park looks the same, with a major portion covered with a large shrub-like tree called mopane. You'll find the most variation in the south and far north of the park—old bush hands in fact divide the park into three distinct regions: The south, they call the "circus"; the central area, the "zoo"; and the north, the "wilderness." These are apt descriptions, particularly in the crowded winter months, when the human population soars in the south, while the less-accessible north remains a calm oasis.

**Southern Kruger** supports some of the richest game concentrations in Africa, which in turn attracts the most people. The busiest—and often very rewarding—road

## Tips for Better Wildlife Viewing

1. **Purchase a map** that indicates all rivers, dams, dirt roads, lookout- and picnic points. These are available at all rest camp shops. Though the tone is a little schoolmarmish, the illustrated *Make the Most of the Kruger* will tell you what ecozone you're in, which species you should look out for, and point out the geology and historical sites. The *Find It* booklet is a shorter version.
2. Between picnic spots there are no restrooms, fuel stops, or shops, so **plan your journey** and make sure you have something to drink and eat in the car should you wish to stay with a sighting for some time.
3. The **best time** to view game is in the early morning and late afternoon. Animals don't move much in the heat of the day, so try and set off as soon as the camp gates open (4:30 to 6:30am, depending on the season). Hopefully camp gate hours will be extended in the near future.
4. You're bound to bump into something if you follow a river. Traffic allowing, always **stop on bridges** when crossing and look for crocodiles, herons, leguaans (large amphibious lizards which can grow up to 3 meters/10 feet), hippos, and so on. During winter you are almost always assured of seeing animals at a waterhole or dam; just park your car and wait.
5. A stationary car with binoculars pointed in a certain direction is an obvious clue. It is not considered bad form to ask what they have spotted (but you're unlikely to get a polite answer if you obscure their view).
6. Most first-time visitors want to tick off the Big 5, but it's worth finding out more about other species. Sighting a wild dog becomes that much more exciting when you know there are fewer than 400 left in the park.
7. Bring a good pair of **binoculars** and drum up some enthusiasm for the vegetation—that tree you stop to admire may reveal a leopard.

linking Skukuza to Lower Sabie Rest Camp is often referred to as **Piccadilly Highway** and motorists have been known to jostle each other to get a better view of lions and even to create traffic jams around great sightings. (This is not helped by the recent news that Kruger's lion population is being decimated by a form of TB.)

The **central area** still features a wide variety of species, particularly around Satara Rest Camp. A little more laid back, with fewer camps, but with a reputation for the highest concentration of lions, this area still attracts its fair share of tourists.

Most of the 7,500-odd resident elephants are found north of Olifants Rest Camp, but mile after mile of dense mopane scrubland makes even these huge animals difficult to see. The **northern part** of the park is probably not the best destination for a first-time visitor, unless it's combined with a sojourn in the south; but this so-called wilderness has definite advantages for real bush lovers, not least because there are fewer people. As you travel farther north, the mopane is broken by the lush riverine vegetation of the Shingwedzi, the baobab-dotted sandveld, and finally, the tropical floodplains that lie between the Luvuvhu and Limpopo Rivers. This northernmost part of the park is in fact at the crossroads of nine of Africa's major ecosystems, and the countryside is full of contrasts. This is also where you'll find one of the subcontinent's most important settlements of the stone or Zimbabwe culture (see "Stonewalling" later in this chapter). Take at least 5 days to include the north in your Kruger itinerary.

8. **Drive slowly**—sharing the shadow of the tree you just whizzed past could be a pride of lions. (The recommended speed for viewing is 25kmph/ 15 mph).
9. Dirt roads give a great sense of adventure, but **don't shun the tar roads:** Besides being quieter, less dust makes for tastier grass verges.
10. Every now and then, **stop the car,** switch the car engine off, and open the window. Listen to the sounds of the bush. The loud crack of a breaking branch could be a nearby elephant. Squirrels and birds make raucous alarm calls when there is danger nearby. Kudus (large antelope) bark when frightened.
11. Vultures wheeling above may indicate the presence of predators, as may fixed stares from a herd of zebra or giraffe. A cloud of dust usually hovers over a large herd of moving buffalo.
12. **Consult the animal-sightings book** kept in reception at your rest camp—many animals are territorial and don't cover huge distances. Some experts advise that you concentrate on a smallish area, getting to know the movements of the animals, rather than driving all over the park.
13. **Animals have right of way** on the roads. If a group of elephants is crossing, keep a respectful distance, switch the car off, and wait. If you're lucky enough to spot a black rhino (which has a hooked lip rather than the wide, square lip of the white rhino), be very wary.
14. **Never feed the baboons and monkeys** that hang out at picnic sites; this is tantamount to signing their death warrant as they then become increasingly aggressive and have to be shot.
15. Most importantly, **be patient.** The only way you'll ever witness a kill, or any interesting animal interaction, is by watching a situation unfurl.

## Picking a Picnic Spot

The designated sites dotted throughout the park are the only places visitors are allowed to alight from their vehicles. Maps (see "Tips for Better Wildlife Viewing," below) will indicate where these are located, as well as which facilities each has. (These may include rest rooms, boiling water, barbecues, seating, shade, telephones, educational displays, and shops manned by attendants who sell wood, hot refreshments, and cold drinks.) The two best-equipped and most popular sites are **Nkulu,** on the Sabie River between Skukuza and Lower Sabie (that is, off Piccadilly Highway) and **Tshokwane,** named after an elephant bull that frequents the area. The shop here sells everything from scones to brandy. Less busy, and with good game- or bird-viewing opportunities, are **Orpen Dam,** an elevated picnic spot overlooking the water, east of Tshokwane, and **Parfuri,** considered the best in the park, but located in the far north.

## Guided Game Drives

A **day drive** (R115/$19.15 per person) is a good idea to help you get oriented; they also allow you to travel park roads which are usually inaccessible to tourists and have the animals around you identified without looking at a book. Call your camp's reception office at least one week in advance to arrange one. **Night drives** (R100/$16.65), in which groups of up to 50 are driven around by experienced rangers, give visitors an opportunity to view the nocturnal activities of animals such as bushbabies, porcupines, civets, hyenas, honey badgers, and aardvarks. Despite, or perhaps because of, a ranger recently being attacked by a leopard on one of these drives, they are usually fully booked by the time you arrive; so many now book them upon confirmation of their accommodation booking. Be warned, however, that nocturnal animals are shy, and on a bad night sightings can be frustratingly rare.

For private tour operators offering game drives in the park (the advantage being that these trips cater for far fewer people), see "Organized Tours" at the beginning of this chapter.

### WILDERNESS TRAILS

These 3- or 4-day trails offer the only opportunity to experience the real essence of the African bush in Kruger. While you are unlikely to see as much game on foot, and you won't get as close to most animals as you can in a vehicle (animals don't associate the smell of gasoline with humans), you will be introduced to the trees, insects, and animals that make up the surrounding bush under the protection of an armed and experienced ranger, and stay in base camps that have been selected for their natural beauty. (Note, however, that unlike the Lapalala and Umfolozi Trails, you'll return to the same base camp every night.) Accommodations are in thatched A-framed two-bed huts with reed-walled solar-heated showers and shared flushing toilet. Besides bedding, towels, cutlery, and food, the park supplies rucksacks and water bottles. Drinks (which you must supply) are kept cold in gas fridges. Age limits are 12 to 60 years, and a reasonable degree of fitness is required as you will be covering 8–15 kilometers (5–9 miles) a day.

A maximum of eight people can be accommodated. There are a choice of seven trails: The **Napi, Bushman,** and **Wolhuter** are all situated in the southwestern section, known for white rhino, granite hills, and San rock paintings. The **Metsi-Metsi,** which overlooks a small waterhole, and the **Sweni,** which overlooks the marula and knobthorn savannah, are in the central area, known for its lions; while the **Nyalaland,** situated in the pristine northern wilderness, is situated in the sandveld's fever tree and baobab forests. The vegetation, views, and birdlife more than make up for its lack of game. **Olifants Trail,** which overlooks the perennial Olifants River, west of its confluence with the Letaba, is particularly scenic and one of the most popular.

Trails cost R1,075 ($179.15) per person. Reservations need to be made at least a year in advance, though cancellations do occur. For more information, check the park's Web site (www.ecoafrica.com/krugerpark/bushcamp.htm#trails) or request a brochure. See "Essentials," above, for telephone numbers and addresses.

## WHERE TO STAY & DINE

If you are looking for luxury (we're talking double beds, TV, radio, room service), you'll want to stay in one of the hotels or guest houses situated on Kruger's periphery (for these, see "Where to Stay & Dine" in the "Lowveld" section, above). The Parks Board runs their camps like large hostels; and while for South Africans there is a certain nostalgic charm in coming back year after year to find the same impala-lily and bird fabric on every curtain, cushion and bed, *Custos Naturae* stamped on every sheet, and the kudu crest embossed on every bright-green soap, it's not everyone's idea of a holiday. However, if you are prepared to rough it a little, these accommodations situated throughout the park are scrupulously clean, relatively comfortable, and unbelievably cheap.

*Note:* If you're traveling during the summer with kids, book into camps with swimming pools: Berg-en-Dal, Pretoriuskop, Mopani, and Shingwedzi. There are facilities for travelers with disabilities at Crocodile Bridge, Berg-en-Dal, Lower Sabie, Skukuza,

### Stonewalling

As the major focus of the park authorities is wildlife, not archeology, the discovery of **Thulamela** was kept under wraps for some 10 years before it was examined and finally opened to the public. Excavations show this settlement was first occupied around the 12th century, and that during the 16th century when the inhabitants would have enjoyed increasing wealth and access to sophisticated trade routes, the dry-stone walls (walls made without any form of mortar) were built. These stone walls link the site to the great stone cities found in Zimbabwe. Thulamela was abandoned in the mid-17th century, at more or less the same time the Europeans started to colonize southern Africa under the leadership of Jan van Riebeeck.

---

Satara, Olifants, Letaba, Mopani, Shingwedzi, Jakkalsbessie, Nwanetsi, Pretoriuskop, and Tamboti.

## Rest Camps

The most popular accommodations are the main **rest camps,** which offer a variety of cottages, bungalows, huts, and safari tents. All units are furnished, albeit sparely, and semi-serviced (that is, beds are made and floors are swept, but you'll have to do your own washing up). Water is scarce, so en-suite usually means flushing toilet, sink (often in the bedroom), and shower. The bigger camps are like small suburbs and are designed to encourage interaction between guests (units are close together and often emulate the old *Voortrekker laager,* a circle, facing inward), so there is very little privacy, and—unless you're here to photograph another kind of wildlife, the South African *braaier*—not the best of views. Always check to see whether you can book a perimeter unit, as these face into the bush, albeit through a fence.

The three- to four-bedroom **guest cottages** represent the top accommodation option in each rest camp. It's well worth investigating these if you are traveling with friends, as they offer the most privacy and small luxuries (like a bathtub).

With the exception of Balule, Orpen, and Crocodile Bridge, you can also expect a restaurant and/or cafeteria, first-aid center, shop, communal and/or private cooking facilities (each unit has a built-in *braai,* or barbecue), coin-operated laundry, public phones, and a petrol (fuel) station in every rest camp.

The restaurant food (usually a three-course set menu, with minimum choice) varies between edible and filling. Meals consist of a soup starter followed by a main course (goulash, baked fish, chicken casserole, roast beef, and the like), and desserts of the "ice cream with chocolate sauce" ilk. Lunch will run you R44 ($7.35), dinner R55 ($9.15). The service can be slow and indifferent, and the atmosphere nonexistent—far better to barbecue, which is what most visitors do. Most basics like milk, bread, butter, wood, dishwashing liquid, tea, tinned products, cereal, cold drinks, firelighters, and wood can be purchased from the camp shop, but don't expect anything fresh, nor delicacies like olive oil, balsamic vinegar, or fresh fruit. Meat is frozen, and potatoes, tomatoes, and onions are usually the only vegetables available. Vegetarians and epicurians are advised to shop at a supermarket in one of the Escarpment towns before entering Kruger. The wine selection in the camp shops is surprisingly good—if you don't know what you're looking at, choose Nederburg, an old standby.

### The Top Rest Camps

**Berg-en-Dal.** Malelane Gate, southern Kruger. ☎ **013/735-6106.** Fax 013/735-6104. 94 units, consisting of 3-bed bungalows, 6-bed family cottages, and guest houses (all en-suite). Rates start at R275 ($45.85) double.

Berg-en-Dal is one of Kruger's newest rest camps, and as such is rather different from its predecessors: Gone are the characteristic round *rondawels*, and walls are finished in ugly brick face. Perhaps this is supposed to evoke the granite surrounds—besides being the ideal habitat for leopard and rhino, Berg-en-Dal's hilly terrain comes as some relief to the reserve's mostly flat bushveld. The two-room, 6-bed family chalets are a great deal more spacious (try and book number 26). Each unit has an enclosed patio and braai area, offering a sense of privacy that is lacking in so many of the other camps. However, in true puritan Parks Board style, any attempt at romance is foiled by the beds, which are not only single, but built-in. Berg-en-Dal is one of only four camps that has a pool—a real bonus in summer. The indigenous gardens are also very attractive—a walk along the well-shaded walkway which faces the Matjulu Dam is tantamount to a quick crash course in "Trees of the Kruger." Where the trail leaves the river and follows a narrow path through dense indigenous bush, Braille signs are set out to guide the visually impaired through the plants and animal skulls that are displayed. The dam itself sees much animal and bird activity, although you may have to sit on one of the benches and wait for it: crocodiles lurk—and hunt—in its waters.

**Lower Sabie.** Crocodile Bridge Gate, southern Kruger. ☎ **013/735-6056** or 013/735-6057. 97 units, consisting of 2-bed en-suite bungalows with and without kitchenettes; 2-, 3-, and 5-bed huts with communal bathrooms; 5-bed family cottages; and a guest house. All but huts en-suite. Rates start at R105 ($17.50) double.

Lower Sabie overlooks the Sabie River and is one of Kruger's most pleasant camps, particularly if you manage to bag one of the units with a waterfront view: 11 to 24 or 73 to 96. (3 to 10 also have river views, but they are a little too close to the camping and caravan area, which can be noisy during school vacations.) Just about every animal has been spotted drinking from the banks of the Sabie Riverbanks; and at night (if you switch your fridge off) you'll fall asleep to the grunting of hippos. Elephants are often found just west of the camp, and with two dams in the immediate vicinity, Lower Sabie provides an excellent base for observing wetland birds. Every unit has a braai, but most have no cutlery or crockery, though the basics can be hired for a small fee (R10/$1.65) from reception. Once again there is no privacy, as most units share walls, but the nine o'clock curfew makes it bearable. Walk along the paved walkway that overlooks the Sabie River at night with a torch: The red eyes you light up probably belong to hyenas, tempted by the smell of braaiing meat.

**Skukuza.** Paul Kruger Gate, southern Kruger. ☎ **013/735-5629** or 013/735-5159. Fax 013/ 735-2305. 197 units, consisting of 2- and 3-bed rondavels with and without kitchenettes; 4-bed cottages; and guest houses. All en-suite. Rates start at R275 ($45.85) double.

Just east of the Paul Kruger Gate, you will find Skukuza, so-called capital of Kruger. Skukuza (or "he who sweeps clean") refers to Kruger's first warden Stevenson-Hamilton, who set up his base camp here (see "Recommended Reading," above). Today Skukuza accommodates some 1,000 people in prime game-viewing turf. This is an ideal spot for first-time visitors, though it would be a pity if this were your only experience of the park, as it really is like a small town. Besides the people and cars, there is the noise of airplanes landing, though this doesn't seem to distract the many visitors strolling along the wide walkway that follows the course of the Sabie River. Accommodation is in a range of thatched en-suite units, the best of which are the family cottages. All rondawels have fridges on their verandas; most also have kitchens. Rondawels 88 to 98 have the best riverfront views. For the budget-conscious, there are furnished East African–style tents; but you have to share bathrooms and kitchen facilities with the hordes of campers and RV-drivers who descend on the camp, particularly in winter.

The Stevenson-Hamilton Information Centre has many old books and interesting exhibits relating to Kruger's past.

**Amenities:** Two restaurants, library, airport, car rental, garage, bank, post office, and doctor.

**Letaba.** Phalaborwa Gate, central Kruger. ☎ **013/735-6636.** Fax 013/735-6662. 112 units, consisting of 2- and 3-bed bungalows with and without kitchenettes; 3-bed huts with communal bathrooms; 6-bed guest cottages and guest houses. All but huts en-suite. Rates start at R120 ($20) double.

This rest camp is set in elephant country, just where the mopane terrain starts to become monotonous. The location, on a large bend of the Letaba River, sees plenty of activity, particularly in the winter. The nearby Engelhardt and Mingerhout Dams are also excellent. Unfortunately very few of the units have views, but the restaurant has one of the best; lunch while watching various plains animals wandering down for a drink. Accommodation is in thatched units set in the gardens that are shaded by well-established apple leaf trees, acacias, mopane, and lala palms—ask for a unit on the perimeter fence as game often venture quite close. Furnished safari tents are a budget alternative, but you'll have to share bathrooms and kitchen facilities. Even if you don't overnight at Letaba, pachyderm-lovers should visit the Information Centre, which has an excellent exhibit on the elephant's social development and physical characteristics.

✪ **Olifants.** Phalaborwa Gate, central Kruger. ☎ **013/735-6606.** Fax 013/735-6609. 114 units, consisting of 2- and 3-bed rondawels; a 4-bed family cottage; 4-bed guest cottage; and guest houses. All en-suite. Rates start at R315 ($52.50) double.

Situated on a hilltop 100 meters (330 ft.) above the banks of the Olifants River, with views of the vast African plains that stretch beyond to the hazy Escarpment, this smallish camp is a favorite, and you'd be well advised to book as soon as you read this. Units 1 to 24, which are situated along the camp's southwest perimeter, not only have the most spectacular views of the river and the animals that are constantly in attendance, but are also the most private—it's almost worth rearranging your trip until one is available! One feels less caged in than at Kruger's other camps; while all camps are surrounded by wire fencing to keep predators out, the sudden drop below Olifants' bungalows means that the expansive views are totally uninterrupted. The verandah, which like many of the Kruger units incorporates both kitchen and dining area, is where you drink it all in. There is also a shaded public lookout platform on the cliff-line, should these highly sought-after units be booked. Throughout the day, animals drink from the pools, watched by basking crocodiles. Birds, in particular eagles, wheel below, searching for prey, and it feels as if you're quite literally on cloud nine. If you bother to venture from your verandah, the nearby Ngotso Dam usually has plenty of game around it.

**Satara.** Orpen Gate, central Kruger. ☎ **013/735-6306.** Fax 013/735-6304. 165 units, consisting of 2- and 3-bed bungalows with and without kitchenettes; 5- and 6-bed cottages; and guest houses. All en-suite. Rates start at R275 ($45.85) double.

The second-biggest, and one of the three most popular camps in the Kruger (the others being Skukuza and Lower Sabie), Satara is located in one of the finest game-viewing areas in the park. The rich basaltic soils support the sweet grasses that attract some of the largest numbers of grazers (such as buffalo, wildebeest, zebra, kudu, impala, and elephant), which in turn accounts for what is considered to be the largest lion population in the park. Just as well, for the setting and housing are rather disappointing: five massive *laagers*, each 25-rondawel strong, with verandas all facing inward. The best options are the units in the semi-circles that face the veld (numbers 161 to 179), though without any animal activity it's rather flat and boring, and you have to look at it through the electrified fence. Best to spend a lot of time in your car exploring. (The road that runs just south of Satara toward Gudzani Dam is famously beautiful, with wonderful views over the river in the summer, and the area around Tshokwane is said to have the highest concentrations of lions in the world.)

✪ **Punda Maria.** Punda Maria Gate, northern Kruger. ☎ **013/735-6873.** Fax 013/735-6873. 24 units, consisting of 2-bed bungalows with and without kitchenettes; and 4-bed cottages. All en-suite. Rates start at R255 ($42.50) double.

Very few people have the time to travel this far north, which is just one of the reasons Punda Maria—which is close to the Zimbabwean border—is the number-one choice for wilderness lovers. Built in the 1930s, this small, thatched, and whitewashed camp retains a real sense of what it must have been like to visit Kruger half a century ago. All units have fridges, but you must specify one with kitchen facilities if you don't want to live on restaurant food. The area does not support large concentrations of game, but it lies in the sandveld where several springs occur, and borders the lush alluvial plains, making it a real must for birders. There is a nature trail that winds through the camp, and the area surrounding the camp is scenically splendid. Head north to the Luvuvhu River, the only real tropical region of the park, to spot a variety of birds including the colorful Narina trogon. Overlooking the river is one of the Kruger's most interesting archeological sites, Thulamela (see "Stonewalling," earlier in the chapter). A little farther east along the river is the most beautiful picnic site in Kruger, Parfuri, which lies under massive thorn, leadwood, and jackalberry trees, with water constantly on the boil for tea.

### Other Camps

**Crocodile Bridge.** Crocodile Bridge Gate, southern Kruger. ☎ **013/735-6012.** Fax 013/735-6012. 20 units, consisting of 2- and 3- bed huts. All en-suite. Rates start at R275 ($45.85) double.

Located right at the Crocodile Bridge Gate, on the southeastern edge of the park, Crocodile Bridge is a little too close to civilization for comfort. On the other side of the river are the farms that neighbor Kruger, and you might just as well be there, ensconced in a comfortable guest house. Facilities reflect the fact that this camp is not particularly popular (for instance there's no restaurant), and it's really only worth staying overnight if you know you're not going to make it to Lower Sabie in time. You're in prime game-viewing territory once you've left the camp behind, and the route to Lower Sabie is famed for its sighting of rhino, buffalo, lion, and cheetah; so drive slowly and keep your eyes peeled.

**Pretoriuskop.** Numbi Gate, southern Kruger. ☎ **013/735-5128.** Fax 013/735-5339. 138 units, consisting of 4-bed huts and family cottages. Rates start at R90 ($15) double.

Named after Willem Pretorius, a Trekker who perished on the 1848 expedition to Delagoa Bay, Pretoriuskop is Kruger's oldest camp, and can house nearly 350 guests. However, most visitors only stop 1 night as it is only 8 kilometers (5 miles) from the Numbi Gate and they prefer to get deeper into the bush—the road to Skukuza is usually very rewarding. The sourveld (coarse sandy soil and clay that appears on top of granite) surrounds are good for spotting giraffe, kudu, and white rhino; but as a rule, the area is not the best for viewing game. If you are overnighting, make sure you're booked into the family cottages, which are more comfortable than the huts. Ask for unit 109, a 2-bedroom family cottage built for Princess Elizabeth's (the present-day queen) anticipated visit in 1947. Just as well she couldn't make it, for while the cottage is spotless, it is not exactly fit for a queen. Pretoriuskop has a granite-lined swimming pool.

**Balule.** Phalaborwa Gate, central Kruger. ☎ **031/735-6843.** Fax 031/735-6843. 6 units, consisting of 3-bed huts with shared bathrooms (no en-suite units). Rates start at R85 ($14.15) double.

Balule is hardly a rest camp; there are no shops, no restaurants, and no electricity—light is supplied by candles and lanterns. The huts have no real windows, let alone fans or air-conditioning, making them very unsuitable for summer no matter how much you want to get back to basics. Bathrooms and cooking facilities are shared; and no night or day drives are offered. Nights are great, with the sound of the bush clearer than any other camp; but if you like your creature comforts, head for Olifants, which is only 11 kilometers (7 miles) away.

**Orpen.** Orpen Gate, central Kruger. ☎ **013/735-6355.** Fax 013/735-6355. 15 units, consisting of 2-, 3-, and 6-bed cottages. All en-suite. Rates start at R140 ($23.35) double.

Orpen, one of the Kruger's smallest camps, is on the periphery of prime game-viewing country, about a third up the park's western boundary. Despite its reputation for fine game viewing, it is literally on the border, and it is therefore unlikely that you'll want to stay here unless you are worried about making it to the next camp before the gates close. Predators, including lions, leopards, cheetahs, hyenas, and wild dogs, are regularly seen in the area. Beyond the east-facing perimeter fence is a small waterhole that often attracts elephants. To explore the most scenic drive in the area, follow the Timbavati River for 32 kilometers (20 miles) to the Timbavati picnic site. If you are on your way to Satara, make sure you take the dirt road detour past Rabelais Dam.

**Mopani.** Phalaborwa Gate, northern Kruger. ☎ **013/735-6536.** Fax 013/735-6547. 102 units, consisting of 6-bed cottages; 4-bed luxury huts; and 4-bed huts. All en-suite. Rates start at R315 ($52.50) double.

Completed in 1990, Mopani overlooks Pioneer Dam and is the most modern camp in Kruger. There are a few public viewpoints, but they are rather small—more than five people and you have to look over someone else's head. You can bypass this problem by booking one of the popular units with a view of the dam (numbers 9–12, 43 and 45, 47–54, and 101–102). Unlike most of the other camps, which are grassed, here an attempt is made to blend in with the environment, and there are a few magnificent baobabs. Mopani is also one of the few camps with a swimming pool. Its biggest drawback is its location—despite intense concentration, all you're likely to see on the 74-kilometer (46-mile) drive north from Phalaborwa is mile after monotonous mile of rolling mopane.

**Shingwedzi.** Punda Maria Gate, northern Kruger. ☎ **013/735-6806.** Fax 013/735-6832. 80 units, consisting of 2- and 3-bed rondavels; 2- and 5-bed original chalets; and the guest houses. All en-suite. Rates start at R115 ($19.15) double.

Named after the Shingwedzi River, this medium-size rest camp is surrounded by flat mopane shrubveld, making for less than ideal game viewing, though this is prime elephant territory. You won't find the impala antelope this far north; but the bright pink and white impala lilies, planted over 60 years ago to break the monotony of the mopane, are one good reason to visit the camp. Two even better reasons are the old-style accommodations and the pool. Make sure you are booked into an A-ring chalet, the original wattle-and-daub buildings date back to 1933 and still retain a frontier-like atmosphere. (Note, however, if this is really what you're looking for, you should keep heading north to the Punda Maria rest camp.) The route following the course of the Shingwedzi River south past the Kanniedood Dam is considered to be one of the best in the Kruger.

### BUSHVELD CAMPS

The six bushveld camps are much smaller than the major rest camps. They have no restaurants or shops, so you must be prepared to do your own cooking, and any last minute shopping will have to be done at the nearest rest camp. However, most units are more spacious than rest camp options, and all are en-suite and feature well-equipped kitchens with braai spots. Only residents are allowed to travel the access road, which makes them an excellent get-away-from-it-all option. Best of all, night drives are in vehicles that accommodate 8 to 10. You pay a little more for the greater seclusion, but it's still a bargain.

The centrally located **Talamati** (☎ **013/735-6343**) (close to the Orpen Gate) and southern **Byamati** (☎ **013/745-6171**) (close to Malelane Gate) are particularly popular, located as they are in Kruger's game-rich areas and with a handful of one-bedroom cottages available. (**Jakkalsbessies,** the small exclusive camp located close to Skukuza, was at publication about to be privatized. For the most recent update on when this highly recommended camp will reopen, contact Skukuza ☎ **013/735-5629.**)

Shimuwini, Bateleur, and Sirheni are all located in the northern section of the park. **Shimuwini** (☎ **013/735-6683**), which is reached via the Phalaborwa Gate, and **Sirheni** (☎ **013/735-6860**), which is half way between Shingwedzi and Punda Maria, both have scenic waterside settings that attract a variety of game and birds. They also have one-bedroom cottages. **Bateleur** (☎ **013/735-6843**) is the oldest bushveld camp and—with only seven thatched units—the most intimate. The closest gate to Bateleur is Phalaborwa. Accompanied walks are offered at Biyamiti, Shimuwini, and Bateleur. These are an excellent alternative to the wilderness trails; book at least a week before. Rates range from R345 ($57.50) double, accommodation only, to R895 ($149.15) for four persons.

### PRIVATE CAMPS

The four private camps, with en-suite units that sleep 12 to 19 people, need to be reserved en bloc and are therefore only suitable for groups. Of these, **Nwanetsi** is reputed to support some of the densest concentrations of game in the park, though the camp itself isn't great—no electricity or pools makes for sweltering summers. **Boulders** is the best-looking camp, but is situated in the boring mopane plains. For more information on these, contact Kruger reservations (see "Visitor Information," above).

### CAMPING

Campsites are available at Balule, Berg-en-Dal, Crocodile Bridge, Letaba, Malelane, Maroela, Lower Sabie, Pretoriuskop, Punda Maria, Satara, Shingwedzi and Skukuza, and range from R40 ($6.5) to R75 ($12.50). Every site has a barbecue and many also have electricity; you will need to bring all your own equipment though, including a tent. Campers enjoy shared bathrooms (shower/toilet blocks) and kitchens, and have access to all rest camp facilities.

## 8 Private Game Reserves

Flanking the western section of Kruger Park and covering over 150,000 hectares (375,000 acres) are South Africa's most famous private game reserves, owned by groups of freehold landowners and concession-holders with traversing rights. With most of the fences that separated the private reserves from Kruger finally down, animals are able to follow natural migratory routes to some extent, and you will find as many species in these reserves as you will in Kruger. However, that is where the similarity ends.

## Dangerous Animals & Defensive Plants

- The term Big 5 originated in the days when Africa's big game was hunted by gun rather than camera, and referred to the five animals that were most dangerous when wounded: lions, leopards, elephants, black rhinos, and buffaloes.
- The docile-looking hippo is responsible for more human deaths than any other mammal in Africa (which kind of blows the theory that vegetarians are less aggressive!).
- The most dangerous animal in Africa is smaller than your pinky nail—check under "Fast Facts: Kruger National Park," above, for tips on protecting yourself from malaria-carrying mosquitoes (who just happen to be female).
- While cheetahs hold the undisputed place as the fastest animals on earth (reaching speeds of up to 120kmph/75 mph), third place is shared by the lion, wildebeest, and—believe it or not—the ostrich (which can reach speeds of up to 80kmph/50 mph). These birds also pack a mean punch.
- When an acacia or mopane tree is heavily browsed upon, its damaged leaves release a chemical into the air, which alerts the remaining leaves to imminent danger. These leaves quickly manufacture a foul-tasting substance to reduce their palatability. Leaves begin to taste so bad that the browser moves away, giving the tree time to recover.

The difference between a visit to Kruger and these reserves is so big as to be almost incomparable. In addition to the excellent service you receive from the moment you sign in, most lodges serve good food (all meals are included in the rate), though you will have to share your table with your game-drive companions. Meals are usually buffets, with breakfasts featuring a selection of cereals and fresh fruit, jams, and freshly baked bread and toast. Hot breakfasts are cooked to order, and usually comprise eggs, sausage, bacon, and tomato, or omelets. A very few lodges offer special treats like eggs benedict or Florentine. Lunch is the lightest meal, with interesting salads, cold meats, and cold pastas available. As breakfasts are served late (after the morning game drive), some lodges prefer to skip lunch altogether and serve a high tea at 3pm, with quiches and cakes. Dinners usually feature grilled or roasted meat, providing visitors with an opportunity to taste at least one species spotted earlier that day—springbok, impala, and warthog are particularly popular. Lodges are willing to cater for special dietary requirements, but require advance warning as new supplies take time to arrive in the bush. If you're a vegetarian or keep kosher, definitely warn the lodges prior to your arrival. Almost every lodge rotates dinners from their dining room to the ever-popular open-air boma (an open-air enclosure), to surprise bush dinners, with tables set up under trees or in riverbeds.

The best reason to visit a private reserve is the proximity you will enjoy to the bush and wildlife. Besides the luxurious accommodation options that make the most of the bushveld surrounds, you will be taken within spitting distance of animals in open Land Rovers by rangers who will give a running commentary on anything from the mating habits of giraffe to the family history of a particular lion. Animals in these reserves, particularly Sabi Sand, are so used to being approached by vehicles that they almost totally ignore them—you can trail a leopard at a few feet without it so much as glancing backward. Two-way radios between rangers ensure good sightings, though these can be marred when three to four vehicles converge on the same spot.

Guests are taken on a 4-hour game drive in the morning and again in the evening, with stops in the bush for a hot drink and muffins in the morning and cocktails in the evening. It can be bitterly cold in the winter, and you may want to opt for an escorted walk after breakfast—another service included in the rate.

The drawback to all this? A hefty price tag. However, if you've come to South Africa to see big game, it's definitely worth delving a little deeper into your savings and spending at least 2 nights in a private game reserve, preferably three. Prices (which are often quoted in U.S. dollars and include everything but your bar, telephone, and souvenirs) do vary considerably, and it is possible to find budget options, the best of which are described below.

*Note:* An admission fee is charged at the gates of these reserves, so make sure you have at least R30 ($5) on hand if you're traveling by road.

## WHERE TO STAY & DINE

There are three major private reserves bordering each other and Kruger, Timbavati, Manyeleti, and Sabie Sand. Each has a number of camps and luxury lodges promising sightings of the Big 5. Lodges and camps need adequate warning to stock up on fresh produce (remember, all meals are included in the rates below), and many are extremely popular, so booking ahead is essential. Winter is their slowest time and it's worth calling to check on any special deals: Most lodges drop their prices from May to August; some by as much as 50%.

At an additional cost, all camps and lodges will organize pick ups from any of the nearby airports (see "Getting There" in "Kruger Essentials," above), as well as arranging transfers to or from competitors, should you be fortunate enough to have the time and money to visit more than one. If you are driving, the camp will fax you directions when you make your reservation.

### IN TIMBAVATI

Timbavati, which is next to Kruger's central section, is famed for its white lions (unfortunately none currently reside here, though you'll see plenty of the tawny types). While it offers a comparable game experience to the much-vaunted Sabi Sand, the vegetation is less arresting, and rhino are scarce. It has far fewer camps, and the rates are generally friendlier, though you'll find the best budget options in its southern neighbor, Manyeleti.

**Umlani Bushcamp.** Mailing address: P.O. Box 26350, Arcadia, Pretoria 0007. ☎ **012/329-3765.** Fax 012/329-6441. E-mail: umlani@cis.co.za. 8 units. R1,940 double ($323.35), includes drinks. Children under 12 R485 ($80.85). AE, DC, MC, V.

Umlani offers an affordable and authentic bush experience—there are no formal gardens, very few staff, the huts are basic, the en-suite showers are outdoors, and at night the camp is lit only by firelight and paraffin lamps. There are also no official camp guards to escort you as you follow the flame-lit sandy walkway to your bed; suddenly the huts, which during the day seem a little too on top of each other, are reassuringly close. During the day as you swing in the hammock waiting for a predator to come padding down the dry Nshlaralumi riverbed, the tranquil camp is far too laid back to promote paranoid feelings. Marco and Marie-Louise Schiess are the 30-something owner-managers who have created this rustic haven, and every effort has been made to retain a sense of what it's like to camp in the middle of the bushveld; there's even a stilted treehouse overlooking a waterhole where you can spend the night with only the sounds of nocturnal animals for company. Food isn't bad (though unlike most other lodges there's no great selection), and drinks are included in the rate, which elsewhere

**No Kidding Around**

Bear in mind that many camps and lodges do not welcome children; over and above a concern for other guests' peace is their belief that the bush itself has too many inherent dangers, not least of which is the ever-present threat of malaria (see "Fast Facts: Kruger," above). Even if they are allowed, young children may not go on game drives and you will have to sign an additional indemnity form. As none of the lodges are fenced off from predators, you are advised to exercise extreme caution—under no circumstances are guests, whatever their age, to walk about unaccompanied after dark.

can add a hefty fee to an already weighty bill. Umlani is small, but with traversing rights on Tanda Tula, it effectively covers 10,000 hectares (25,000 acres), and regularly has good sightings, not to mention good luck: At press time, Umlani had a den of endangered wild dog breeding on their land. A great bush experience, for the young at heart.

✪ **Tanda Tula.** Mailing address: P.O. Box 32, Constantia 7848. ☎ **021/794-6500.** Fax 021/794-7605. E-mail: cuisine@iafrica.com/giraffe@ilink.co.za. www.tandatula.co.za. 12 units. TEL. R3,172 ($528.65) double. Off-season R2,292 ($382). AE, DC, MC, V. Children 12 and over only.

Tanda Tula's accommodations are in tents, but don't let that mislead you. These East African safari-style tents come with en-suite bathrooms (specify shower or bathtub or both) and timber deck floors. Little details like bedside lamps and comfortable wicker chairs help you enjoy the comfort of a well-furnished room, while the tent walls do nothing to filter out the sounds of the surrounding wilds—this is an excellent way of getting really close to the bush without giving up comfort. The eight tents are all privately situated, each with its own furnished *stoep* (verandah). However, as the surrounding bush is quite dense, you're more likely to spend time in the elegant and comfortably furnished open lounge and dining area which provides a waterhole view, and leads out onto the lawns and pool (a resident warthog family keeps these lawns well-clipped). This is where drinks are served, as well as lunch, and at night a huge fire is lit, even if dinner is served in the adjacent boma. Dinners usually include game and with any luck you'll be surprised with a bush barbecue, served in a riverbed. Tanda Tula means "to love the quiet," and the staff do everything possible to ensure that you can do just that. Game drives on the 20,000 hectares (50,000 acres) that the lodge has access to are productive, and the rangers are extremely professional. Generally service is immensely personal and warm.

**Ngala.** Mailing address: Private Bag X27, Benmore 2010. ☎ **011/784-7077.** Fax 011/784-7667. E-mail: reservations@conscorp.co.za. 21 units. A/C TEL. R5,400 ($900) double; low-season R3,516 ($586). Children under 11 R1,350 ($225). AE, DC, MC, V.

Operating within an area which has been donated to the National Parks Trust, Ngala was the first contract reserve established between the Kruger and a private company. Fortunately that company is Conservation Corporation (ConsCorp), South Africa's premier safari operator. Ngala Lodge has all the luxuries one has come to associate with this sophisticated outfit, with one or two drawbacks inherited from the previous camp. Units are not designed with privacy in mind, the lodge accommodates a lot more people than is usual in a private game reserve, and the general feeling is more that of a small hotel than a safari camp. These quibbles aside, Ngala offers excellent service, the best food in the Timbavati (ConsCorp chefs are all carefully handpicked and provide huge buffets to satisfy all tastes), and—with exclusive operating rights within 14,000 hectares (35,000 acres) of land—one of the best game-viewing experiences in the world. It is also a child-friendly lodge, with baby-sitters available, and enough noise from other people's children to enable guilt-ridden parents to relax. Children under 6 are not allowed on game drives. Thatched cottages, all connected with narrow paved walkways leading through lawns, are carpeted and well furnished.

Under the stars in the open-air boma, dinner tables are set with cut-glass crystal, silver, and starched white table cloths. A massive thatched roof covers the central living area where deep armchairs and a large log fireplace beckon, and the pool and sundeck overlook a small waterhole which, despite the noise from generators and the occasional lawnmower, attracts various game. There is a doctor on 24-hour call.

## In Manyeleti

Manyeleti, the region between Timbavati and Sabi Sand, is actually still a public reserve. During the apartheid era, when blacks were not allowed to vacation in Kruger, this was considered "their" reserve—and a visit to the original Manyeleti Rest Camp makes Kruger look like a luxury option. Only three operators have been given concession rights to operate private camps within the reserve, which means that at any given moment there will be a maximum of seven vehicles traversing its 23,000 hectares (57,500 acres)—sightings are sometimes shared, but you have a good chance of not seeing another vehicle for the duration of your drive. This is not a luxury the more expensive lodges in the Sabie Sand reserve can offer (though they may provide every other form of pampering).

**Honeyguide.** Mailing address: P.O. Box 786064, Sandton 2146. ☎ **011/880-3912.** Fax 011/447-4326. E-mail: hguide@global.co.za. 12 units. R1,334–1,460 ($222.35–$243.35) double. AE, DC, MC, V. Children 12 and over only.

A member of the upscale Classic Safari Camps of Africa, Honeyguide is one of the best value-for-money camps in the country. Due to the exclusivity of their concession area, no other game-viewing vehicles are found in their part of the reserve. Guests are encouraged to get out of the vehicle and walk to really experience the bush, and the in-camp experiences can be extraordinary. (During my visit, the camp managers were having a hard time dissuading a herd of persistent elephants from treating the camp's small swimming pool as their personal watering hole.) Like Tanda Tula, Honeyguide accommodates guests in East African–style tents, but at these prices you can't expect the same level of luxury. Without fans, tents can become very hot in summer and, as they are pitched on concrete slabs, cold in winter. Beds have basic foam mattresses, though linens are good. All feature simple luxuries like en-suite showers and flushing toilets. Guests can choose between tents or suites (these are simply larger tents). The most private option is suite number 4, which has a view from the shower. Suites have galvanized tin bathtubs (this is as close to *Out of Africa* as it gets), but they're not very comfortable. Generally the standard tents, which are marginally cheaper, have better views. Their furnished timber decks overlook the dry riverbed and riverine vegetation. You may want to spend some time here as the central thatched living area is sparsely furnished. Dinners are served in the boma, under the stars. Early-morning drums alert you to the dawning game drive, and tea is brought to your tent—a luxury even the most upmarket camps don't offer. Popular foot safaris are run from Honeyguide's more rustic camp, the **Outpost,** at a cost of R400 ($66.65) per person per night.

**Khoka Moya.** Mailing address: P.O. Box 298, Hoedspruit 1380. ☎ **015/793-1729.** Fax 015/793-1729. E-mail: khoka@country-escapes.co.za. 8 units. R1,700 ($283.35) double; low-season R790 ($131.65). AE, DC, MC, V.

This charming little lodge offers the cheapest winter rates around. Accommodations, which are a little more luxurious than Honeyguide's, are in raised thatched-and-timber cabins connected to each other via wooden walkways. Even animals think these blend well with the environment; a wild dog recently chased an impala right past the lounge. All cabins are en-suite with showers only and each comes with a comfortable chair, sisal carpet, attractive duvets, his and hers basins, bedside lamps, tables, and fans. The main lounge, dining room, and bar area is comfortable and homely; there's even a TV, though you're viewing needs will have to be satisfied with wildlife videos. The pool is larger than most, and the camp's many trees attract lots of birdlife—it's not uncommon to spot over a hundred species during a 3-day visit. Game viewing is good, given the varied terrain and the fact that there are so few vehicles to share sightings with. This is a good bet for families or for couples traveling together; ask for the Lion or Rhino cabins, which are slightly separate from the rest. Khoka Moya also operates a rustic trails camp (from R300/$50 per person per night, minimum of four people; maximum of eight), situated on stilts overlooking a dam in an area not traversed by roads.

## In Kapama

Kapama does not actually border the Kruger, but it is large enough (12,000 hectares/30,000 acres) to support the Big 5, and has the convenience of having a commercially serviced airport, Eastgate, on the reserve. Currently, it is also the only private game reserve that provides day and night game-viewing drives for non-residents, call ☎ **015/793-1633.**

**Kapama Lodge.** Mailing address: P.O. Box 1511, Hoedspruit 0127. ☎ **015 793-1038.** Fax 015/793-1039. 20 units. A/C MINIBAR TEL. R4,000 ($666.65) double. Call for winter rates. AE, DC, MC, V. Children over 12 only.

No expense has been spared in developing this relatively new deluxe lodge, and the investment is already paying off. Since opening, the lodge has entertained the likes of Sir Peter Ustinov, Mia Farrow, and the kings of Netherlands and Belgium. The main buildings, which are linked by winding timber walkways, overlook a lake and are decorated with expensive furniture that looks as if it still needs to be worn in a little. The most memorable room is the lounge, which is dominated by a massive elephant head—thankfully, not real. The thatched chalets are comfortably furnished with king-size beds, though the Olde Worlde bush style is a little old-fashioned. Rooms do not have good views, and the windows are small, leaving one feeling a little cut off from the bush. Twelve thousand hectares (30,000 acres) and high animal densities assure guests of good game viewing; though when compared to those lodges adjacent to Kruger, you may feel as though you're driving through a large zoo. The lodge's main advantage is its proximity to Eastgate Airport, which saves on traveling time. It also houses the famous **Hoedspruit Research and Breeding Centre for Endangered Species** (☎ **015/793-1633**), where guests are given the opportunity to view the rare king cheetah as well as lions, buffaloes, rhinos, and wild dogs. Visitors can also witness the feeding sessions of various rare African vultures.

## In Sabi Sand

Sabi Sand, which encompasses the southern lowveld, enjoys a reputation for being the most game-rich area in the country. Hardly surprising then that it houses the largest number of luxury camps, of which established names like MalaMala and Londolozi are bandied about in the most exclusive circles.

**Djuma.** Mailing address: P.O. Box 338, Hluvukani 1363. ☎ **013/735-5118.** Fax 013/735-5070. E-mail: djuma@iafrica.com. www.djuma.co.za. 7 units. A/C. R2,840 ($473.35) double. Low-season R1,900 ($316.65). Children under 12 half price. AE, DC, MC, V.

Djuma, one of the most affordable camps in Sabi Sand, is accessed via Gowrie Gate on one of the worst dirt roads in Mpumalanga. It's best to fly in on the **Djuma Shuttle**, a fly-in package which can be arranged through the lodge. Once there, you will enjoy the splendid isolation as Djuma's access to 9,000 hectares (22,500 acres) makes it one of the largest land users in the Sabi Sand Reserve, yet only puts out three vehicles at any given time. Guests are also not constantly interrupted by the crackling of the radio as rangers tip each other off to sightings—rangers sensibly use headsets, a practice in vogue at MalaMala. Djuma's main bar and lounge area is an unusual double-volume construction featuring immense wooden poles and spacious timber decks. Areas of it look distinctly tired and unused though, which is a pity as it must have been magnificent in its heyday, and there are some good views from the top deck. The three-sided chalets are situated throughout the garden. They are comfortably furnished; though from a style point of view, aspects such as the homemade light fittings leave a lot to be desired. Make sure you're not booked into the honeymoon room during the winter as the summer ventilation holes turn the room into a fridge. Food is average, with quiches, pizzas, pasta, and a choice of salads for lunch, and two meat options such as impala or filet (make sure this isn't overcooked) for dinner. Despite these drawbacks, Djuma's staff is excellent, and the game viewing pure Sabi Sand. Waterbuck and a magnificent kudu browsed meters from us while a giraffe wandered closer for a look—and that before we had even set off for a game drive. Djuma is also the site of the world's first "cyber-game park," with Web cameras situated in the reserve. Check it out at www.africam.co.za.

**Exeter.** Mailing address: P.O. Box 2060, Nelspruit 1200. ☎ **013/741-3180** or 013/741-3181. Fax 013/741-3183. E-mail: exeter@cis.co.za. Exeter Lodge, 10 units. Leadwood Lodge, 5 units. A/C. Exeter Lodge R3,700 ($616.65) double. Leadwood Lodge R900 ($150) double. AE, DC, MC, V. Children 12 and over only.

Stuffed animal heads watch unperturbed as a lion leaps just short of its impala prey—a testament to the taxidermist's skill, and an exercise in bad taste. And that's just for starters: Skins and busy animal prints attest to an ethnic style gone wrong and, while Exeter Lodge's decor might feature in a David Lynch movie, it's not exactly soothing. Tastes differ though, and on other aspects Exeter cannot be faulted, though their traversing rights are relatively limited: 6,000 hectares (15,000 acres).

However, if you're prepared to cook for yourself, Exeter's **Leadwood Lodge** is an unbelievable value-for-money gem, the best in Sabi Sand and a far better alternative to Kruger. In a prime position overlooking the Sand River, the five spacious suites each have private en-suite outdoor showers, sliding timber doors that lead out onto the verandah and barbecue, and fully equipped kitchens with staff on hand to assist with cleaning. Catering aside, you enjoy all the luxuries of the private game reserve: an experienced ranger and tracker to take you on game drives, guided bush trails following the course of the river, a pool, and even a boma, should a group wish to book the lodge. (Exeter also has the Hunter's Lodge for a maximum of eight.) Once again the furnishings aren't great, but this kind of value makes them a lot more palatable.

**Leopard Hills.** Mailing address: P.O. Box 3619, White River 1240. ☎ **013/751-2205/9.** Fax 013/751-2204. E-mail: ecologics@soft.co.za. www.soft.co.za/tourism/leopardhills. 5 units. A/C MINIBAR TEL. R2,595 (432.50) double. Low-season R1,390–1,790 ($231.65–$298.35). AE, DC, MC, V. Children 12 and over only.

You won't find the class of Singita, Londolozi, or even MalaMala here, but you won't find their price tags either. Situated in the western sector of the Sabi Sand, Leopard Hills is a relatively new lodge with good specials worth asking about, particularly during winter. Like so many others, the lodge overlooks a waterhole, but your vantage point is much higher, and the views of the African bush savannah go on forever. These can be enjoyed from the public areas as well as from the huge bedroom, the showers (there's a his and hers), and the Victorian bathtub. The chalets are decorated in an overtly African manner: rough untreated timber, bamboo blinds, leopard-print pillows, concrete and sisal floors, billowing mosquito nets, and muted brown walls. Wraparound glass frontage completes the picture. Leopard Hills offers total privacy, but staff do have limited resources. At press time, there was only one vehicle, a bit of a squeeze if the lodge is full. It is, however, state-of-the-art, with specially designed seats to help ensure absolute comfort while you traverse the 10,000 hectares (25,000 acres) to which Leopard Hills has access. Meals are average; there's usually a buffet with a choice of two main dishes and an assortment of vegetables or salads.

✪ **Londolozi.** Mailing address: Private Bag X27, Benmore 2010. ☎ **011/784-7077.** Fax 011/784-7667. E-mail: reservations@conscorp.co.za. Bush Camp, 8 units. Main Camp, 10 units. Tree Camp, 6 units. A/C MINIBAR TEL. R6,600–7,200 ($1,100–$1,200) double. Children under 11 R1,650–1,800 ($275–$300). AE, DC, MC, V.

On land inherited from their father in 1969, the Varty brothers built four simple huts, which are still standing, and offered basic safaris with the emphasis on conservation. Today Londolozi has three totally separate luxury camps, Bush, Main, and Tree, and offers such a high standard in accommodation, cuisine, and game viewing, that it has become the model upon which all the subsequent Conservation Corporation lodges (see "Package Tours" in chapter 2) are based.

The vegetation surrounding the camps (which are built on the banks of the Sand River and within walking distance, but out of sight of one another) is the closest to jungle you'll find in the predominantly bushveld savannah. Of the three camps, Main is possibly the best option—slightly less expensive, yet with large granite en-suite bathrooms and beautifully appointed bedrooms. You will find everything you need to create a perfect atmosphere of romance—mood lighting is controlled from a bank of switches and dimmers—and both your king-size bed and bath overlook a large private timber deck with plunge pool. Barring the noise from the filter, relaxing in the pool while antelope browse in the jungle below is pure heaven. There are two extra-luxurious suites that form part of Main Camp, called the Granite Suites. If you book number one, you will find yourself swimming in a private pool that drops onto the boulders that form the Sand River's banks; and it's close enough to hear the river running from your bath. The six Tree Camp units have the added luxury of *salas,* private platforms joined by a small boardwalk to your room and used for meditation and relaxation. It's hard to leave these rooms, but with over 15,000 hectares (37,500 acres) to traverse, there are excellent game-viewing opportunities, not least of which is finding the famed Londolozi leopards, aided by some of the best trackers in the business.

Another good reason to venture from your room is the meals. Buffet tables groan under a vast selection of meats and vegetables (this is after all a Relais & Chateau lodge). The fact that Londolozi does not have a low-season rate speaks for itself—book now if you can.

**MalaMala.** Mailing address: P.O. Box 2575, Randburg 2125. ☎ **011/789-2677.** Fax 011/886-4382. E-mail: jhb@malamala.com. www.malamala.com. Main Camp, 25 units. Kirkman's Kamp, 18 units. A/C MINIBAR TEL. Main Camp R5,400–5,800 ($900–$966.65) double; children under 12 half price. Kirkman's Kamp R3,200 ($533.35). AE, DC, MC, V. Children over 12 only.

Unparalleled game viewing has made MalaMala the top private game reserve in Africa, or at least the most recognized. In 1998 it won *Travel & Leisure*'s "Best Hotel in the World" for the second year running, *Condé Nast Traveler's* "Top Hotel in Africa and the Middle East," and the Travel Industry Award's "Top Game Lodge in South Africa."

As the largest of the privately owned reserves in the Sabi Sand, MalaMala shares an unfenced border of 30 kilometers (19 miles) with Kruger and the Sand River flows through most of its length. Not only are you likely to see the Big 5 in 1 day (last year, they recorded Big 5 sightings on 332 days), but you'll get a certificate to prove it, and see a wealth of other species besides, particularly in winter. The excellent rangers, all of whom are graduates in the natural sciences, act as hosts at MalaMala, serving you drinks and taking all their meals with you. Leon, who has worked here for over 6 years, is particularly recommended for his deep knowledge and love of the bush, as well as his ability to attract birds by imitating their calls. On the downside, you are unlikely to ever see a black or female ranger at MalaMala (unlike its neighbor Londolozi), and a sense of the old South Africa still prevails. Accommodations are also disappointing; furnishings are old-fashioned and there's none of the style of more sophisticated neighbor, Londolozi. However, rooms are spacious and comfortable, with his and her bathrooms and aluminum windows and doors sliding open to reveal manicured lawns leading down to the Sand River. Food is nothing to write home about, though the evening atmosphere in the huge boma, lit by flames, is superb.

Situated farther south, ✪ **Kirkman's Kamp** is a great option. It has fewer units, decor that pays homage to hunting days of yore, plenty of wildlife wandering onto its lawns, and prices almost half those of the less-personal Main Camp. It also boasts the only tennis court in the wilds. At press time, **Harry's Camp** (the budget option) was in the process of being relocated; it will no doubt continue to offer a great game-viewing experience for a reasonably affordable rate.

**Notten's Bush Camp.** Mailing address: P.O. Box 622, Hazyview 1242. ☎ **013/735-5105** or 013/735-5750. Fax 013/735-5970. 7 units. R2,300 ($383.35) double. AE, DC, MC, V. Children over 8 only.

Wedged between MalaMala in the east and Sabi Sabi on the west, this small camp—one of the few places where the owners are still very much the managers—is an oasis of calm. Gilly and Bambi Notten have created a home-away-from-home atmosphere (lions are framed next to family photos); and if the number of repeat visits is anything to go by, this is a winning formula. The raised open verandah, where the substantial tea and breakfast are served, provides a wonderful view of the waterhole and surrounding grass plain where just about every mammal under the African sun has been spotted. There has even been a kill right on what could be considered their front lawn. Most of the rooms are tiled with attractive slate and warmed with sisal carpets. If you prefer a cozier look, rooms 3, 6, and 7 are carpeted. Rooms 6, 2, and 4 enjoy the best views. Rooms have no electricity and showers are heated by an old donkey boiler. Notten's employs a Shangaan ranger, Joe, whose bush knowledge makes a refreshing change. Do at least one drive with Grant Notten, who seems set to take on the family business; he is a most attentive host and, having grown up in the area, knows it intimately. The only major drawback here is that due to the camp's size (2,500ha/6,250 acres), you will not spot as much game as on neighboring territories.

The food is excellent. In place of lunch, there's usually a high tea, and dinner features one dish rather than a buffet. While all camps in the private reserves force a dinner-party atmosphere by having you dine with your game-drive companions, here the atmosphere is distinctly better, probably because one has a real host and hostess at the table.

**Sabi Sabi.** Mailing address: P.O. Box 52665, Saxonwold 2132. ☎ **011/483-3939.** Fax 011/483-3799. E-mail: com@sabisabi.com. www.sabisabi.com. Selati Lodge, 8 units. Bush Lodge, 27 units. River Lodge, 23 units. A/C MINIBAR TEL. Selati R5,200–6,200 ($866.65–$1033.35) double. Bush and River, R4,800–5,200 ($800–$866.65) double. AE, DC, MC, V. Children 12 and over only at Selati, and 6 and over only at Bush and River Lodges.

Situated in the southern part of the Sabi Sand, with the Sabie River creating a border with Kruger, Sabi Sabi's Bush and River Lodges have more than satisfactory game viewing, but accommodations are old-fashioned and there are a relatively large number of units. You're much better off booking into their latest, Selati, previously a hunting lodge and family retreat and named after the famed turn-of-the-century railway line that ran through this area and into Kruger Park. The line was famed for its dangers and completed at great human cost; the train was once derailed by a charging elephant and travelers often had to climb trees to escape marauding lions.

Selati's rooms are filled with vintage railway memorabilia, turn-of-the-century antiques, and old sepia photographs depicting these early days. With only eight thatched suites, it's a decidedly more exclusive experience. Like Notten's, there is no electricity, the flicker of oil lamps and lanterns heighten the sense of romance as the evening light fades. Suites are in thatched free-standing chalets and are spacious and well furnished, with dark stinkwood beds offset by embroidered cream linen and swathes of white mosquito netting. (Note that only two of the eight suites have double beds; unfortunately, these happen to be the more expensive options). The en-suite bathrooms also have private outdoor showers. Breakfasts and lunches are served under leadwood and jackalberry trees; dinners are served in the farmhouse kitchen or the boma. For Sabi Sabi's 3-day ranger training program, see "Staying Active," above.

✪ **Singita.** Mailing address: P.O. Box 650881, Benmore 2010. ☎ **011/234-0990.** Fax 011/234 0535. E-mail: reservations@singita.co.za. Ebony Lodge, 9 units. Boulders Lodge, 9 units. A/C MINIBAR TEL. R6,800 ($1,133.35) double. AE, DC, MC, V. Children over 12 only.

If the makers of James Bond films needed a new set for the home of a decadently rich baddy, Singita's Boulders would make the shortlist. This is a truly modern lodge, the most expensive in South Africa, and it doesn't disappoint. Each unit is the size of a house and features a massive Balu teak deck and private pool, sliding glass walls, a stone fireplace, en-suite bathroom with Victorian-style bath, a beautifully furnished lounge, and a king-size bed dressed in embossed linen. Colors and textures are organic and combine stone, polished concrete, timber, granite, and ceramics, all in muted browns, creams, grays, and browns—ochre is as bright as it gets. The lodge buildings are low impact, with suites built into a raised section overlooking the Sand River, which both subtly hides the suites from each other, yet affords excellent views. While you might find it difficult to leave your room at Londolozi, here it is virtually impossible. Why bother when you can enjoy a massage or facial on your private deck, watching the wildlife on the open plains beyond the river? However, with traversing rights to over 18,000 hectares (45,000 acres), you'll want to take at least one game drive. For most customers, the experience is awesome, though some find it a little too cut off from the bush. (Sister outfit **Ebony Lodge** features much the same standard of luxury, but is inspired by the old colonial style, and no match for Boulders.)

Singita is run by professional hoteliers and, like Londolozi, is a Relais & Chateaux lodge, offering a high standard of cuisine and a choice of 12,000 bottles of wine. Wine tastings can be conducted here; a fine way to preempt a visit to the Cape. Breakfast options include perfectly cooked eggs Benedict and the three-course lunches and dinners (mains always feature a choice of at least two meats: lamb or kingklip; ostrich or chicken) are served in the stone-walled dining room, boma, bush, or—real luxury—on your private deck.

## In Makalali

If you're not hung up on ticking off the Big 5, the Makalali conservancy, which lies farther north, extends over 10,000 hectares (25,000 acres) and has lions, leopards, rhinos, and elephants. For some the absence of buffalo (due to foot-and-mouth regulations) is not a great loss; though reputedly extremely dangerous when wounded, they provide as much viewing excitement as a herd of cows. The area is also of geological interest, with quartz rock crystals strewn throughout the conservancy. The long-term plan is to keep increasing the conservancy area, eventually creating a corridor connecting it to the Kruger. In the meantime, it provides visitors with extremely reasonable rates.

**Makalali Private Lodge.** Mailing address: P.O. Box 785156, Sandton 2146. ☎ **011/883-5786.** Fax 011/883-4956. E-mail: makalali@icon.co.za. 6 units in 4 camps. Aug 1–Apr 18 R1,980 ($330) double; Apr 19–July 31 R1,287 ($214.50) double. Children under 12, 50% off. AE, DC, MC, V.

The year Makalali opened, *Tatler* magazine voted it the "Most Innovatively Designed Hotel in the World." Architect Silvio Rech has combined architectural styles from all over Africa—shaggy East African roof thatching adorns mud and stone walls, while rugged North African–inspired turrets create a sense of mythical village palace. There is not a right angle to be seen; hardly surprising since everything is handcrafted, from the tap handles to the built-in chairs and the large metal screens that divide the large rooms into bed- and bathroom. Bleached skulls are displayed like totems, and the sense of macabre is heightened at night, when the dark rooms flicker with shadows and hide the sharp rocks that protrude from the walls. Makalali consists of four camps—each with its own swimming pool, boma, and enclosed lounge and dining area—situated on various points of the Makhutswi River, which flows for approximately 8 months of the year. Rooms are huge and totally private; each features a fireplace as well as a *sala,* joined to your hut via a boardwalk, where the resident masseuse will see to your needs. Try and book a room in camp 4, where the rooms are most dispersed and you reach your public areas via a swingbridge—very romantic. Camp 2 is ideal for birders, while 3 has a lovely pool. Whatever you do, don't get stuck with room 4 in camp 1; it's too close to the kitchen.

Makalali's food regularly features in national food critics' top selections. Young chef Liesl Roos (a graduate of Emily's, see "Cape Dining" in chapter 3) has embraced the idea of pan-African cuisine with more success than most. Dishes like grilled kingklip in chermoula (a spicy Moroccan marinade) ensure that she is regularly included in food critics' listings of the top places to eat in the country.

Additional activities include river rafting, golfing, Escarpment tours, and a visit to a Shangaan cultural village and the Hoedspruit Cheetah Breeding Project.

**Garonga.** Mailing address: P.O. Box 2417, Parklands 2121. ☎ **011/327-0161.** Fax 011/327-0162. E-mail: pulselac@sprintlink.co.za. 6 units. Oct 1–Apr 30 R2,300 ($383.35) double; May 1–Sept 30 R1,980 ($330) double. No single supplement. Children under 12, 50% off. AE, DC, MC, V. Children over 8 only.

Garonga's approach to the bush experience is more "soul safari" than big game. While boundary fences between it and Makalali have been down for some time, providing access to four of the Big 5, the emphasis is on "re-earthing" the senses rather than tracking down large mammals; though they are there: A herd of elephants hanging out on the access road made us very late for lunch. This is the perfect place to end a frenetic vacation, with no scheduled game drives imposed on you (though there is a ranger on standby), an easel, pencils, and small Zen garden in your room, and an aromatherapist/reflexologist to further help de-stress you. The central living areas are tasteful, the accommodations sublime. Situated on raised platforms along the seasonal Dhlulamiti River, the six units have low adobe walls, colored a warm pink by mixing local river sand into cement, which are topped by a vast tent of cream canvas. King-size beds are swaddled in acres of white muslin and a large hammock swings above every deck. Due to water restrictions, the en-suite bathrooms have no bathtubs, though you have a choice of indoor or outdoor shower. For those who love to soak, there is a private bush bath that the staff sets up with candles and bath salts—champagne is an optional extra for the decadent and recently married. Guards (who keep well out of sight) are a whistle away should a breaking twig alert you to approaching game. Manageress Penny and chef Claire are incredibly flexible and imaginative. Guests are pampered with meals served by the fire, next to the pool, beside the wine cellar, or on your deck, in the bush, on a hill, or in the hide. If you tire of your bedroom, you can spend the night alone in the hide; this is definitely recommended in the summer. Both Penny and Claire were at Singita before joining Garonga, which gives some idea of the level of professionalism, though nothing can prepare you for the standard of the cuisine. Suffice to say that you can take a finicky foodie here and watch him relish every mouthful. A honeymoon couple recently spent a week here and promptly booked a 2-week return trip for their anniversary—I can't think of a nicer way to celebrate.

## 9 The Waterberg & the Lapalala Wilderness Area

Approximately 350km (217 miles) north of Johannesburg

Three hours north of Johannesburg is the Waterberg, a 150-kilometer-long (93-mile-long) mountain ridge that rises quite dramatically from the bushveld plains to 2,085 meters (6,939 ft.) above sea level. Besides being a malaria-free area, it is substantially less populated than the big-game country that lies to the east of the Escarpment. With no major roads and only one town (Vaalwater) within a 15,000-square-kilometer (9,300-square-mile) area, the Waterberg is almost totally devoid of humans, and one of the most pristine wilderness areas in the country.

There are three major players in the Waterberg: At the western end of the range is the National Parks Board's **Marakele Park** and the adjacent **Welgevonden Reserve**—both of these feature the Big 5, but most areas are accessible only to four-wheel drive vehicles and are privately owned. Separated from these two reserves by a large area of game and hunting farms is the 35,382-hectare (88,455-acre) **Lapalala Wilderness,** the second-biggest privately-owned game reserve in Africa, and internationally renowned for its black rhino conservation and environmental education efforts—over 45,000 pupils from all over the world have been hosted by the Lapalala Wilderness School.

Bisected by 45 kilometers (28 miles) of the great Lephalala River, the terrain is rocky and wild, with sheer cliffs, clear mountain streams, and grass-covered plains that sustain a large number of mammals, though you won't see elephants or lions. The reserve is managed by the indomitable Clive Walker, Chairman of the Rhino & Elephant Foundation, whose most recent project is the creation of a **Waterberg Centre** to incorporate his Rhino Museum with a new Cultural & Natural History Museum. The centre is easily taken in on the way to Lapalala's reception.

Entrance to the centre, which at press time only included the **Rhino Museum,** is R3 (50¢) and hours are daily from 9am to 5pm. The Rhino Museum has displays featuring the history of the rhino, from its evolution to present-day conservation efforts (it is one of the world's most threatened large mammals). The **Cultural & Natural History Museum,** due to open at the end of 1999, will house various objects found in the area dating human occupation of the area back to one million years. Inquiries regarding the Rhino Museum should be directed to ☎ **014/7552 ext. 4041** or fax 014/765-0116, or e-mail chw@ref.org.za.

## ESSENTIALS

**GETTING THERE** **By Car** Take the N1 north from Johannesburg or Pretoria; take the turnoff for Nylstroom after toll gates, then head 72 kilometers (44½ miles) northwest for Vaalwater. Lapalala lies north of here (the entrance is some 70km/43½ miles from here). A map will be faxed to you when you book.

**VISITOR INFORMATION** The Waterberg Centre is due to open a Tourism Information Office at the end of 1999. All Lapalala queries should be directed to their Johannesburg office (☎ **011/453-7645** or fax 011/453-7649). See "Rhino Camp," below, for address.

**GETTING AROUND** Drivers have limited access within Lapalala—once you have reached your camp, you have to explore the reserve on foot or horseback, though you can make inquiries about game drives at reception. Rhino Camp guests are taken on morning and evening game drives daily.

## EXPLORING THE REGION

### ✪ BY HORSE

The best way to get to know this region is by tracking animals and learning about the local ecology on horseback. **Equus Horse Safaris,** 36 12th Ave., Parktown North, Johannesburg 2193 (☎ **011/788-3923**), has two options. **Bush camp safaris** (R1,080/$180 per person per day) last as long as you wish, and are based in a tented bush camp located beside a shaded stream. There are four tents, each with two single beds and an en-suite bathroom. Dinners are three-course, and there is a natural rock pool to cool aching muscles in. Horses are excellent and guides are experienced—both in the bush and on horseback. Riders are offered a choice of English or trail saddles, and are grouped according to their abilities. The tempo of the ride varies depending on the surrounding terrain and presence of wild animals. **Luxury wilderness safaris** (R1,380/$230 per person per day) operate in much the same way, but you'll move from camp to camp for 8 nights. Take a look at their Web site at www.equus.co.za, or e-mail them at equus@equus.co.za. Note there are no trails in November.

### ON FOOT

The **Lapalala River Trails** are another great way to explore the region. Like the Kruger trails, these take a maximum of six or eight people and are led by an experienced, armed guide. Unlike Kruger, every night is spent in a different camp. Hikers are accommodated in two-bed huts and share a "bush" toilet and wash under hand-filled, bucket showers. **Four-day trails** cost R1,285 ($214.15) per person; **weekend trails,** which cover approximately 25 kilometers (15½ miles), are R800 ($133.35) per person—both follow the course of the river as it tumbles over rapids and through gorges, and visit some archeological sites. Rates are all-inclusive except for alcoholic drinks; specify food or drink preferences when booking. You need bring nothing but your personal belongings, which are then transported for you. Central reservations are in Johannesburg (☎ **011/453-7645** or fax 011/453 7647). See "Rhino Camp," below, for address.

## WHERE TO STAY & DINE

If you're looking for luxury, try the **Mekweti Safari Lodge** (☎ **083/458-6122,** fax 083/459-1153) in the Welgevonden Game Reserve. En-suite chalets house a maximum of 10 guests, and the $250-$400 per night charge includes meals, ranger-led game drives and walks, and transfers between lodge and Welgevonden (pickups and dropoffs are at noon at the main gate). In the US, bookings can be made through **Premier Tours ☎ 800/545-1910.** No children under 12 are allowed.

For solitude at a much lower price, book any one of Lapalala's 10 **Rustic Bush Camps**—self-catering camps located in the bush or next to the river, all with flush toilets—of these the aptly named 'Lookout' enjoys the most spectacular setting. Once settled, you are on your own (not even cleaning staff intrude), and as driving in the reserve is not allowed, you won't come across another human until you leave. Black rhinos are in a separate part of the reserve, and camps are fenced off, leaving guests free to wander at will. Every camp has somewhere to swim, though visitors are warned that as crocodiles and hippos are present, the river should be approached with extreme caution.

The tented **Rhino Camp** is the only way to explore the Lapalala in a vehicle, and it is highly recommended.

**Rhino Camp.** Central reservations: P.O. Box 645, Bedfordview 2008. **☎ 011/453-7645.** Fax 011/453-7649. 4 units. R1,380 ($230) double. Children 8–12 R215 ($35.85). AE, DC, MC, V. Note that reserve gates open at 8am and close at 5:30pm from April to August, and at 6:30pm from September to March. Vehicles are left at Rhino Camp reception and guests transported to the camp. There are two check-in times daily: 10–10:30am and 2–2:30pm.

This tented camp is Lapalala's luxury option. Facilities are pretty much the same as those in the private game reserves adjacent to the Kruger, with meals, game drives, and bush walks included in the rate—an unbelievably good value. The four en-suite tents are set on platforms and are situated so as to offer maximum privacy. The dining room and lounge is an open thatch-and-wood structure adjacent to the boma. Not surprisingly, the emphasis is very much on tracking black rhinos, and guests are given the rare opportunity of getting really close to one—Bwana, a young black rhino orphan found abandoned in the sanctuary and hand-reared by Mrs. Walker. Munyane, a young white rhino also hand raised, and Motlo, a hippo, are other orphans you may encounter, though the Walkers are trying to wean Motlo of humans. Guests can also be taken to view the many rock paintings and Iron Age sites in Lapalala and visit the new Waterberg Centre.

# 8 KwaZulu-Natal

Demarcated in the west by the soaring Drakensberg Mountains, its southern tip and eastern border lapped by the warm Indian Ocean, KwaZulu-Natal is often described as the country's most "African" province. Its subtropical latitude translates into long, hot summers—at times oppressively humid—and balmy winters, while the warm Mozambique current ensures that the ocean is never more than 2 to 3 degrees cooler than the air. These sultry conditions have not gone unnoticed by its landlocked neighbors, however, resulting in an almost unbroken ribbon of development along the coastal belt south of the Tugela River, a region dubbed "the Holiday Coast." In its center is Durban, Africa's busiest port, and the region's industrial and tourism hub.

The region north of the Tugela River is known as Zululand, where the amaZulu rose to power during the early 19th century under the legendary Shaka. Zululand is also home to the KwaZulu-Natal game reserves, some of which are Africa's oldest wildlife sanctuaries. A mere 3 hours drive north of Durban, you can see the Big 5 at Hluhluwe-Umfolozi Game Reserve, and cruise the waterways of the Greater St Lucia Wetland for hippo and croc. North of the wetlands, divers explore the rich coral reefs off Sodwana Bay, with the privileged few heading for 60 kilometers (37 miles) of pristine coastline at Rocktail Bay, and—in the far northern corner of the province—the Kosi Bay Nature Reserve. Inland are Mkuzi and Ndumo, the country's premier bird-watching reserves; while adjoining Zululand to the west are the famous battle sites of the many wars fought among Zulu, British, and Boer during the 19th century.

Pride of place for those in search of real tranquility and breathtaking beauty must however go to the Drakensberg, site of over 22,000 ancient rock paintings, and southern Africa's most majestic mountainscape.

## 1 Staying Active

**BIRD-WATCHING** The two best bird-watching destinations in the country are located here. A 4-hour drive from Durban is **Mkuzi,** run by the KwaZulu-Natal Nature Conservation Services (KN NCS). Facilities aren't great (for example, it has no restaurant), but the park is magnificent. Contact Peter Lawson, **Lawson's Birdwatching Tours** (☎ **013/755-2147**), who operates throughout southern Africa and

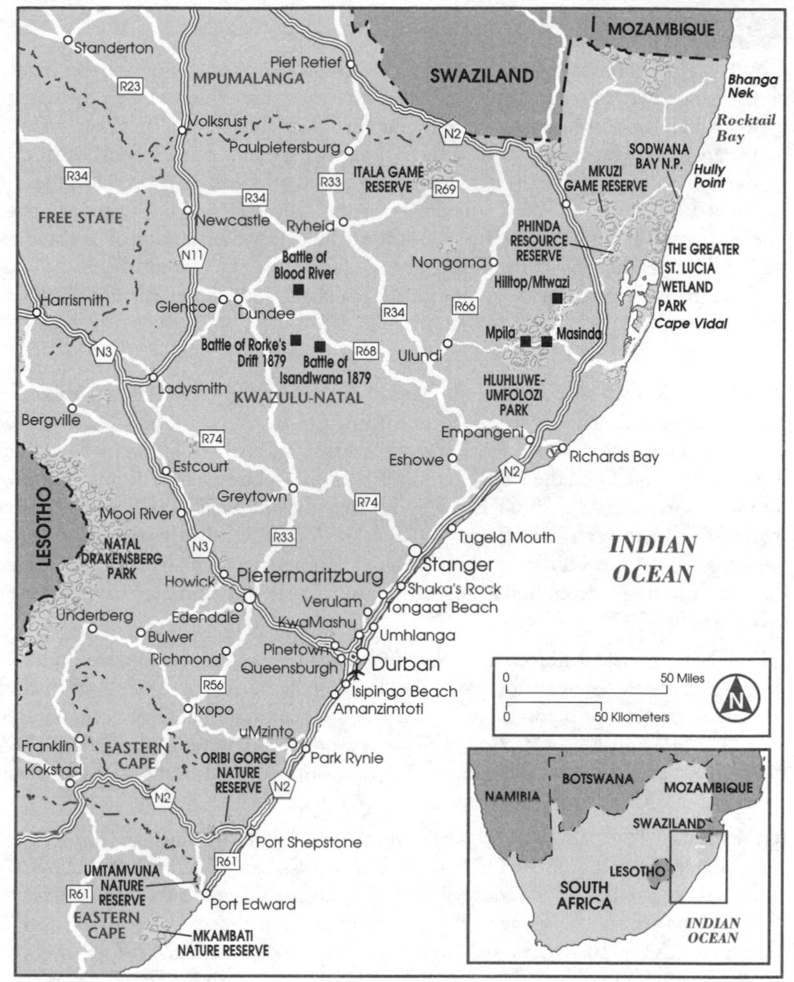


invariably includes Mkuzi in his fully catered bird-watching safaris, or local outfit **Ukubuka Bird Safaris** (☎ **035/573-1080**). Alternatively, head for the laid-on luxuries of ✪ **Ndumo Wilderness Camp,** on the border between KwaZulu-Natal and Mozambique. Located within the exquisite Ndumo Game Reserve, this area is often compared with the Okavango, with pans and jungle simply teeming with over 400 bird species—60% of South Africa's birdlife. The camp offers eight well-appointed tented "rooms," each situated on a raised wooden deck and linked by a boardwalk under a canopy of giant fig trees. For more information, contact **Wilderness Safaris** at ☎ **011/883-0747,** fax 011/883-0911, or e-mail: info@sdn. wilderness.co.za; or one of the general safari tour operators who represents them in your country. (See chapter 2, "Planning Your Trip to Southern Africa", for recommended operators.) For organized bird-watching outings in the Durban area, contact the **Wildlife Society of South Africa,** 100 Brand St., Glenwood (☎ **031/201-3126**).

### The Name Game

When Portuguese navigator Vasco da Gama dropped anchor here off the east coast on Christmas Eve, 1497, he named it "Natal" (nativity), little knowing that the subtropical paradise was already populated by the "people of heaven," or "amaZulu." During the apartheid years, Natal became the holiday playground of white South Africa, but the area north of the Tugela remained KwaZulu, (kwa meaning "place of"), the Zulu "homeland" under apartheid, ruled over by the Zulu king and birthplace to opposition party IFP, led by Mangosuthu Buthelezi. The province was united as KwaZulu-Natal after the 1994 elections, but continues to be administered by both Pietermaritzburg, the "heritage city" of the old Natal, and Ulundi, center of Zululand.

---

**DIVING** Known as "the grand old man of diving" on this coast, **Andy Cobb** offers tuition or guided dives along Aliwal Shoal (off the South Coast, between Scottborough and Umkomaas, a premier spot to see sharks); and trips to Sodwana Bay (Zululand), where you'll find the 2-, 5-, 7-, and 9-mile reefs—considered the four best dives in the country. Contact Andy's **Eco-Diving Expeditions** at **☎ 031/96 4239.** Alternatively, call **Sodwana Dive Retreats** (**☎ 031/307-4902**), they're based at the local resort, and offer good tuition and accommodation packages. Qualified divers looking for self-catering accommodations in Sodwana should contact **Coral Divers** (**☎ 0331/45-3076**).

**FISHING** **Lynski Charters** (**☎ 031/561-2031**) conducts comfortable and challenging deep-sea fishing trips from the Durban harbor; your catch may include marlin, barracuda, or shark, though note that a tag-and-release policy is encouraged. Beginners are also welcome. Trout fishing is a popular pastime in the Drakensberg, particularly at Loteni and Kamberg KN NCS camps situated in the southern Drakensberg. Call **☎ 0331/845-1000.**

**GOLFING** There are over 60 courses to choose from, 11 of which are regularly featured in South Africa's top 50. Of these the **Durban Country Club** (**☎ 031/23-8282**) is considered the best in the country. The majority are found on the South Coast, or "Golf Coast" as it's also known. Here, San Lameer and the Wild Coast are rated in South Africa's top 10, and Southbroom and Selbourne follow hard on their heels. All except Southbroom offer excellent accommodation options on the estates; all are right on the coast and within easy driving distance of each other. The 4-star hotel at **San Lameer** (**☎ 039/313-5141**)—a parkland course that winds its way through a nature conservation area—is geared toward families' needs; while the stately **Selborne** (**☎ 0323/975-3564**) offers silver-service standards; and Pennington is for those who wish to escape the pitter-patter of little feet. **Southbroom** (**☎ 039/31-6051**) is the shortest course, and much easier than San Lameer, but the narrow fairways, plentiful water features, and dense indigenous coastal bush are still challenging; for accommodations, contact **Southbroom Lodge** at **☎ 03931/78-310.**

To really put your game to the test, you'll have to play the **Wild Coast Country Club** (**☎ 039/305-2799**), which is on the border of KwaZulu-Natal and the Eastern Cape. Designed by Robert Trent Jones, this is one of the most attractive courses in southern Africa—there are six par threes, but two of these don't have fairways from tee to green, just lined gorges and, on the 13th, there's a waterfall. For more information about these and other courses on the Golf Coast, contact John Tack at **Hibiscus Publicity Association** (**☎ 03931/22-322**).

**HIKING** Trails worth highlighting in Zululand are the 2-, 3-, and 4-day wilderness trails in **Mkuzi** and **Umfolozi Game Reserves;** those in the latter are considered the best in the country. East of these the **Mziki Trail** (St Lucia Greater Wetland) comprises three 1-day loops of 10–18 kilometers (6–11 miles) that explore the estuary shore, dune forests, and coastline of the park. North lies Kosi Bay's 4-day guided **Amanzamnyama Trail,** which takes in all four lakes, the coral reefs, pristine beaches, and the country's largest mangrove forest. The Drakensberg is, however, the premier hiking spot; contact the **Mountain and Backpackers' Club** (☎ **031/86-3970**). Alternatively, book the **Giant's Cup Hiking Trail** direct through the KN NCS (☎ **0331/845-1000**). This popular 3- to 5-day hike is clearly laid out and ideal for reasonably fit hikers. Accommodation is in huts; all you need to bring is food, camping stove, and sleeping bag. Cost is R30 ($5) per person, per night; organize your return trip through **Giant's Cup Motors** (☎ **033/702-1615**).

**HORSEBACK RIDING** This is a great way to explore the Drakensberg. The 2- and 3-day trails departing from **Hillside Camp** in Giant's Castle are highly recommended. Accommodation for these guided trails (R230/$38.35 per person, excluding food) is in huts and caves in the mountains. Half- and full-day rides are also available. Bookings must be made well in advance through **KN NCS** (☎ **0331/845-1000**).

**PARAGLIDING** **Sky Tribe** (☎ **031/202-6019**) offers motorized and non-motorized tandem flights and courses in the Durban area (launch sites depend on wind direction). Tandem flights cost R150 ($25); courses are R1,350 ($225).

**SURFING** To rent a surf board, contact **Surf Zone** (☎ **031/36-8459**) at 38 West St. in Durban. Good surf spots around the city are North Beach and the adjacent "Bay of Plenty" (both the venue for the Gunston 500). Check out Green Point, Scottburgh, The Spot, Warner Beach, and Cave Rock; the latter has an excellent right reef break. For advanced and beginner surf training, contact **Ocean Sports Centre** (☎ **031/368-5318**) or **Pro Surf Coaching** (☎ **031/368-5488**) in Durban. Also in Durban, **Secondhand Surf Shop** (☎ **031/332-1875**) buys and sells secondhand gear.

**SWIMMING** The entire coast is popular with swimmers, and shark nets protect the main swimming beaches from Port Edward to the Tugela; note, however, that many beaches shelve suddenly into deep surf, with strong undertows—swim only where boards indicate safety, or where there are lifesavers in attendance. (Keep an eye out for portuguese man-of-war.) North Beach is the most popular beach for Durbanites, while Umhlanga, less than 30 minutes from town is more popular with tourists. If you prefer your water without waves, head for the **Rachel Finlayson Baths** (☎ **031/37-2721**), a saltwater pool on Marine Parade.

**WHITE-WATER RAFTING** For 2-day trips on the Buffalo River (grade 2 to 4 rapids), Zululand, call **Isibindi River Explorers** (☎ **0322/947-0538**).

## 2 Durban

1,753km (1,087 miles) from Cape Town, 588km (365 miles) from Johannesburg

The Union Jack was first planted in Durban's fertile soil in 1824, a year after George Farewell fortuitously discovered its harbor. Only after the fledgling settlement was formally annexed in 1844, however, was the dense coastal vegetation gradually consumed by buildings with broad verandahs, and civilized with English traditions such as morning papers, afternoon tea, and weekend horse racing.

Sugar became the region's "white gold," and large fortunes were made by so-called sugar barons. The most famous of these was Sir Marshall Campbell; today his home is one of Durban's main attractions, and one can still travel along the beachfront in the two-wheeled "rickshaws" he introduced to the city in 1893. The world's voracious appetite for sugar was also responsible for the strong Indian influence on Durban's architecture, cuisine, and customs—during the 19th century, thousands of indentured laborers were shipped in from India to work the sugar plantations, and today Durban houses the largest Indian population outside of India.

South Africa's third-largest city, Durban attracts the lion's share of South Africa's domestic tourists. Well over a million locals visit every year, joined by a further 40 to 50,000 international tourists. Most come to what the tourism authorities have dubbed "the Holiday Coast"—a strip that stretches from Port Edward (where it borders with the Eastern Cape in the south) to the Tugela River in the north. However, Durban itself (located in the center of the Holiday Coast) is definitely worth exploring for a day or two before heading west to the Drakensberg or north for the game parks and marine reserves of Zululand. With limited time and a desire to experience the essence of South Africa's most multicultural city, a walking tour of the Indian District, where Indian shops and markets are interspersed with Zulu hawkers touting traditional wares, is a must. For visitors intent on a beach-based holiday, the North Coast is recommended, particularly the less-developed stretch beyond Ballito.

## ESSENTIALS

**VISITOR INFORMATION** You can make all your travel arrangements at the Tourist Junction, where **Tourism Durban** (☎ **031/304-4934;** funinsun@iafrica.com, open Monday to Friday 8am to 4:30pm, Saturday to Sunday 9am to 2pm) is located, as is the **KN NCS** (same phone). The Tourist Junction is in the Old Station Building, 160 Pine St. Tourism Durban also has a satellite beach office (☎ **031/332-2595**) at Ocean Sports Centre, Lower Marine Parade, and an airport office (☎ **031/42-0400**), in the Domestic Arrivals terminal.

**GETTING THERE** **By Plane** **Durban International Airport** is 15 kilometers (9 miles) south of the city center. For arrival and departure information, call ☎ **031/42-6111;** for reservations, call ☎ **031/361-111.** There are always taxis lined up outside, but a far better plan is to use the **airport bus service** (☎ **031/42-6111**) that travels between the Domestic terminal and the SAA building in Aliwal Street every hour from 6am to 9pm. For 24-hour service, call **Super Shuttle** (☎ **0860/333-444**). There is a bank at the International terminal, which opens for arrivals.

**By Train** Durban Station (☎ **031/308-8118**), on NMR Avenue is the central point for KwaZulu-Natal's extensive rail network. Mynah buses leave every 15 minutes for the city center.

**By Bus** Country-wide operators **Greyhound, Intercape,** and **Translux** (see chapter 2, "Planning Your Trip to Southern Africa) all arrive and depart at the station complex.

**By Car** The N2 from Cape Town runs parallel to the coast as far as Zululand; the N3 to Johannesburg meets the N2 at Durban.

**WHEN TO GO** The best time to visit is February to mid-May, when it's not too humid. The temperature ranges between 16°-25°C (61°-73°F) winter and 23°-33°C (73°-91°) summer (September to April).

**GETTING AROUND** **By Car** The city center is relatively small, but to explore farther afield you're best off renting a car. **Avis** toll-free ☎ **0800/02-111, Budget**

toll-free ☎ **0800/01-6622** and **Imperial** toll-free ☎ **0800/13-1000,** all have offices at the airport. For a cheaper deal, call **Windermere Car Hire** (☎ **031/23-0339**). You can pick up free **city maps** from the Tourist Junction, but for longer stays it's worth considering a more detailed **Mapstudio** map, available from any CNA.

**By Bus** The city center, beachfront, and Berea are serviced by **Mynah** (☎ **031/309-4126**) and **Aqualine** (☎ **031/309-5942**) buses. You can catch the **Umhlanga Express** (☎ **031/561-2860**) to Umhlanga Rocks from the Tourist Junction; to travel farther north, catch the **Interport** bus (☎ **0351/91-791**). For coaches to the South Coast, contact **Margate Mini Coach** (☎ **03931/21-406**); to the Wild Coast Sun (just beyond KwaZulu-Natal's southern border; see chapter 5) contact **U Tour** (☎ **031/368-2848**).

**By Taxi** The three-wheeled Asian-style **tuk tuks** queue 24 hours a day on Marine Parade (opposite the aquarium) and will take you anywhere in central Durban, as will "**mozziecabs**" (jeeps), though they must be contacted in advance (☎ **031/368-1114**). Alternatively, call **Aussies** (☎ **031/309-7888**) or **Zippy** (☎ **031/202-7067**), both reputable cab companies. **Super Shuttle** (☎ **0860/333-444**) offers a personalized transfer service to any destination in KwaZulu-Natal, and provides baby seats on request.

**Guided Tours & Cruises** Guided **walking tours** of the city can be arranged through Tourism Durban (see above). They depart at 9:45am, end at 12:30pm, and cost R25 ($4.15) per person. The **Oriental Walkabout** covering the Indian District is particularly recommended. **Hamba Kahle Tours** (☎ **031/707-1509**) has a Shebeen Crawl, a night out in one of the black townships with traditional meal, beer, and live music, for R130 ($21.65) per person. **Welcome Safaris** (☎ **031/561-1095**) conducts a variety of tours including half-day tours of Kwamashu township, and trips to Cape Town. **Zululand Tours** (☎ **031/37-4232**) and **Strelitzia Tours** (☎ **031/86-1904**) all offer scheduled and tailor-made tours of the city center, Valley of a Thousand Hills, Zululand game reserves, and cultural villages, St Lucia Wetlands, battlefield routes, and the Drakensberg. Strelitzia Tours can also arrange special-interest tours for golfers, divers, and deep-sea fishermen.

Board **The African Queen** (☎ **031/561-2887**), a luxury charter yacht, for a champagne breakfast, a high-noon, or sunset cruise. Trips last 2 to 4 hours and cost from R95 ($15.85) per person. Less romantic are the engine-powered **Sarie Marais Pleasure Cruisers** (☎ **031/305-4022**). Choose between deep-sea (departs 3pm) or bay cruises (departs 11am), Monday to Saturday. For further options, contact the **Durban Charter Boat Association** (☎ **031/301-1115**).

**CITY LAYOUT & SIGHTSEEING TIPS** Sightseeing in the city can be divided into roughly three areas: the **city center,** which encompasses the buildings and memorials surrounding Francis Farewell Square, as well as the Indian District; and the tacky **"Golden Mile,"** which runs east of the city, following the beachfront; and—at more or less 90 degrees to the Golden Mile—**Victoria Embankment** (or **Esplanade**), which runs along the harbor's edge, creating the city's southern border. The western outskirts of the city are also important, particularly **Berea,** where you'll find some top attractions and many of the city's best restaurants. Ironically, this upmarket residential suburb borders **Cato Manor,** an African squatter camp with Hindu temples and subtropical vegetation. This is a excellent place to view Durban's unique cultural melting pot. If your time is limited, focus on the city sites and those situated in the Berea area rather than the Golden Mile. The harbor is worth visiting to board a short cruise or visit the BAT Centre.

# Durban

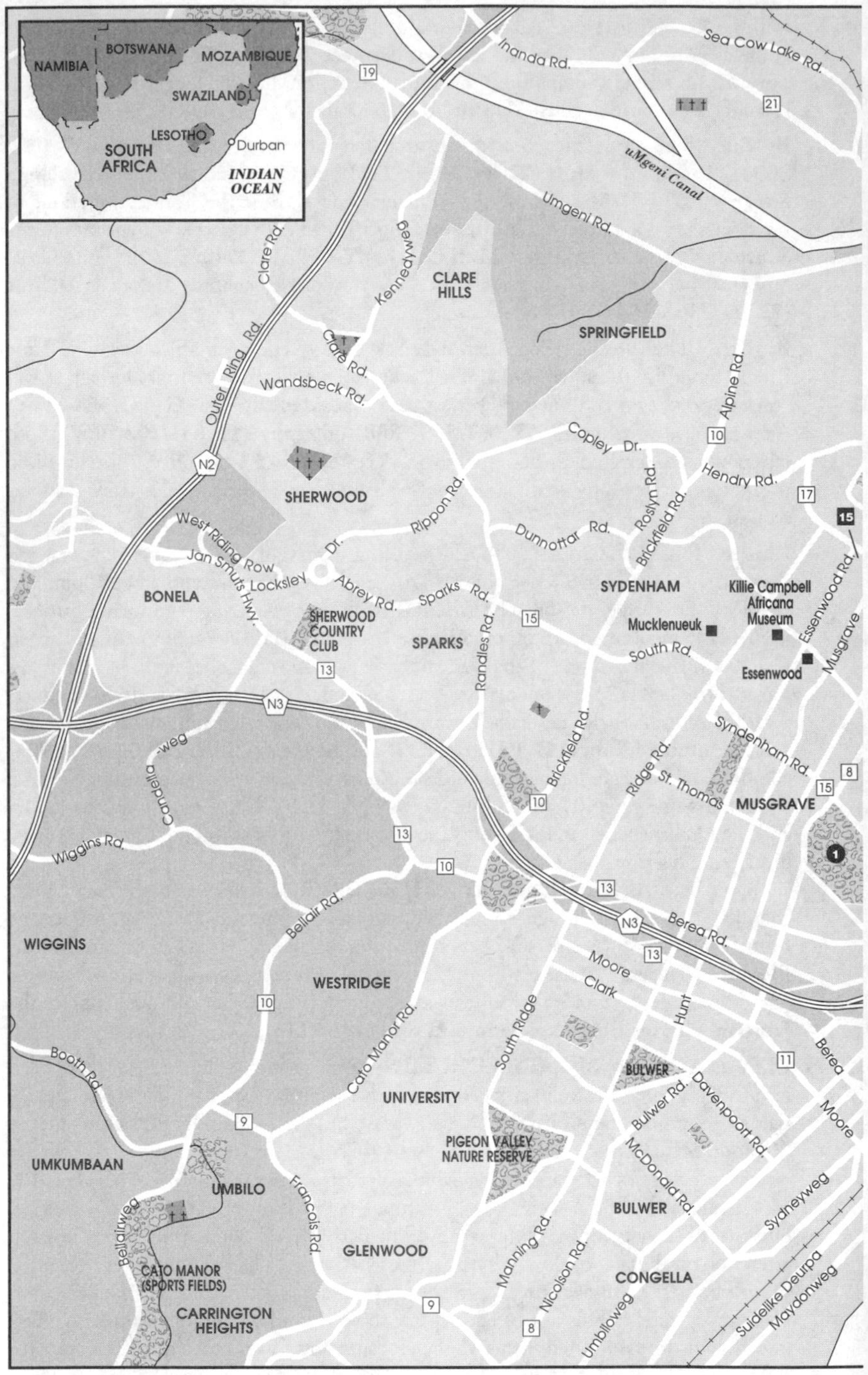

NAMIBIA
BOTSWANA
MOZAMBIQUE
SWAZILAND
LESOTHO
SOUTH AFRICA
Durban
INDIAN OCEAN
Inanda Rd.
Sea Cow Lake Rd.
uMgeni Canal
Umgeni Rd.
Clare Rd.
Kennedyweg
CLARE HILLS
SPRINGFIELD
Outer Ring Rd.
Wandsbeck Rd.
Alpine Rd.
Copley Dr.
Hendry Rd.
SHERWOOD
Rippon Rd.
Roslyn Rd.
Brickfield Rd.
Dunnottar Rd.
West Riding Row
Jan Smuts Hwy.
Locksley Dr.
Abrey Rd.
Sparks Rd.
BONELA
SYDENHAM
Killie Campbell Africana Museum
Mucklenueuk
Essenwood Rd.
Musgrave
SHERWOOD COUNTRY CLUB
SPARKS
Randles Rd.
South Rd.
Essenwood
Candella -weg
Syndenham Rd.
Ridge Rd.
St. Thomas
MUSGRAVE
Wiggins Rd.
Bellair Rd.
Berea Rd.
Moore
Clark
WIGGINS
WESTRIDGE
Cato Manor Rd.
South Ridge
Hunt
Berea
Booth Rd.
BULWER
UNIVERSITY
Bulwer Rd.
Davenport Rd.
Moore
PIGEON VALLEY NATURE RESERVE
UMKUMBAAN
UMBILO
Francois Rd.
McDonald Rd.
Sydneyweg
Bellairweg
BULWER
CATO MANOR (SPORTS FIELDS)
GLENWOOD
Manning Rd.
Nicolson Rd.
CONGELLA
CARRINGTON HEIGHTS
Umbiloweg
Suidelike Deurpad
Maydonweg

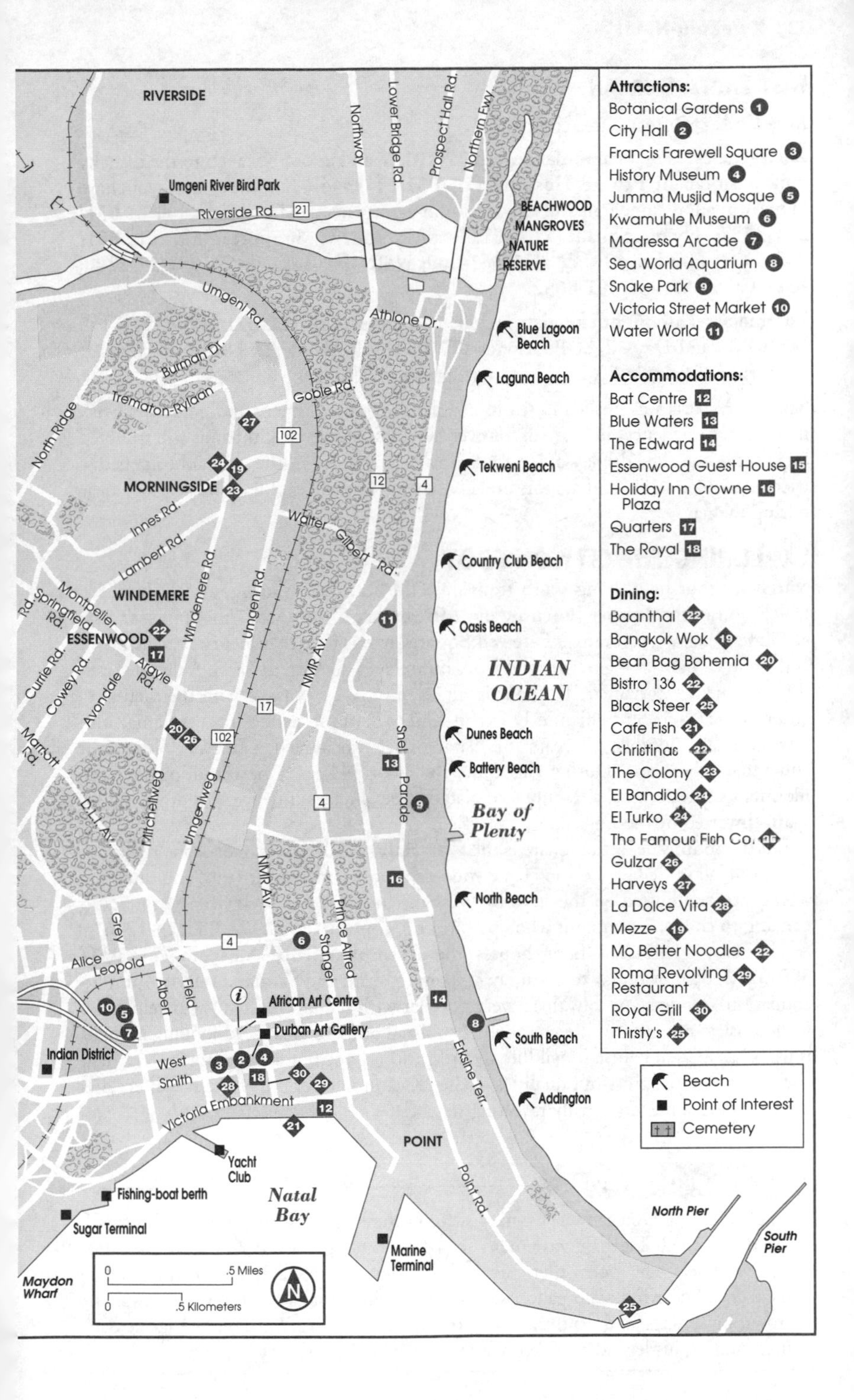
Attractions:
Botanical Gardens 1
City Hall 2
Francis Farewell Square 3
History Museum 4
Jumma Musjid Mosque 5
Kwamuhle Museum 6
Madressa Arcade 7
Sea World Aquarium 8
Snake Park 9
Victoria Street Market 10
Water World 11
Accommodations:
Bat Centre 12
Blue Waters 13
The Edward 14
Essenwood Guest House 15
Holiday Inn Crowne Plaza 16
Quarters 17
The Royal 18
Dining:
Baanthai 22
Bangkok Wok 19
Bean Bag Bohemia 20
Bistro 136 22
Black Steer 25
Cafe Fish 21
Christinas 22
The Colony 23
El Bandido 24
El Turko 24
The Famous Fish Co. 25
Gulzar 26
Harveys 27
La Dolce Vita 28
Mezze 19
Mo Better Noodles 22
Roma Revolving Restaurant 29
Royal Grill 30
Thirsty's 25
Beach
Point of Interest
Cemetery
RIVERSIDE
Umgeni River Bird Park
Riverside Rd.
Northway
Lower Bridge Rd.
Prospect Hall Rd.
Northern Fwy.
BEACHWOOD MANGROVES NATURE RESERVE
Umgeni Rd.
Athlone Dr.
Blue Lagoon Beach
Burman Dr.
Laguna Beach
Trematon-Rylaan
Goble Rd.
North Ridge
MORNINGSIDE
Tekweni Beach
Walter Gilbert Rd.
Innes Rd.
Lambert Rd.
Country Club Beach
Windemere Rd.
Umgeni Rd.
WINDEMERE
Montpelier Rd.
Springfield Rd.
ESSENWOOD
Oasis Beach
NMR Av.
INDIAN OCEAN
Curie Rd.
Cowey Rd.
Avondale
Argyle Rd.
Marriott Rd.
Snel Parade
Dunes Beach
Battery Beach
D.L.I. Av.
Mitchellweg
Umgeniweg
Bay of Plenty
NMR Av.
North Beach
Prince Alfred
Stanger
Grey
Alice
Leopold
Albert
Field
African Art Centre
Durban Art Gallery
Indian District
West
Smith
Erskine Terr.
South Beach
Victoria Embankment
Addington
POINT
Yacht Club
Natal Bay
Fishing-boat berth
Sugar Terminal
Point Rd.
North Pier
South Pier
Marine Terminal
Maydon Wharf
0 .5 Miles
0 .5 Kilometers
N

## Fast Facts: Durban

**Area Code** Durban's area code is **031.**

**Emergencies** For an **ambulance,** call ☎ **10177** and ask to be taken to the casualty unit at **Entabeni Private Hospital** (☎ **031/81-1344**), but make sure you have money for admission. Staff will also treat non-emergencies. **After-hours,** call ☎ **031/301-3737; Flying Squad,** ☎ **10111; SAP Tourist Support Unit,** ☎ **031/332-5923; Fire brigade,** ☎ **031/361-000; NSRI** (sea rescue), ☎ **031/37-2200; Rape Crisis,** ☎ **031/301-8652.**

**Pharmacy** **Late-night chemists** include Medicine Chest (☎ **031/305-6151**), 155 Berea Rd., and **Day-Night Pharmacy** (☎ **031/368-3666**), 9A Nedbank Circle, at the corner of Point and West (the latter offers free delivery).

**Safety** Malaria was pushed north to Zululand by development and pesticides, with no reported incidences in Durban for over 50 years. However, Durban is still troubled by street crime. The display of wealth is unwise anywhere in the central business district or Golden Mile, and visitors are advised to do their explorations of these areas during the day.

## EXPLORING THE CITY ON FOOT

Start your tour by walking south from the **Old Station Building,** at 160 Pine St., which houses the **Tourist Junction** and **African Art Centre** (see "Shopping for Arts & Crafts," below), to **Francis Farewell Square.** It was here that Henry Francis Flynn and some 20 hard-living traders and ivory hunters set up shop in 1823. A decade later, the settlement was named "Durban" in an attempt to curry favor with the then governor of the Cape, Sir Benjamin D'Urban, and to gain protection from the amaZulu. It would take another 20 years for Natal to be proclaimed a British colony and annexed to the Cape. During this time, the Voortrekkers came trundling over the mountains and declared a Republic of Natalia (see "Pietermaritzberg"), but were once again thwarted by the English.

On the south side of the square is the **City Hall** (1910), a stone-for-stone replica of the City Hall in Belfast, Ireland. Time your visit for Wednesday at 1pm, and catch the weekly concert hosted on the steps by Durban Arts; it could be anything from Zulu dancing to choirs. To find out who's performing, contact Patrick (☎ **031/23-1236**).

The City Hall's first floor houses the **Natural Science Museum** (☎ **031/300-6212;** open Monday to Saturday 8:30am to 4pm, and Sunday 11am to 4pm; no admission). Understandably, this is very popular with school children (who help make it the busiest museum in the country). The usual array of very dead-looking animals is useful as a crash course in wildlife identification if you're traveling north. Kids will also appreciate the gross-out qualities of the "Kwanunu" section, where the insect displays include some large, truly revolting roaches.

### A Hero and His Horse

The Zulu king Dingaan was as mistrustful of the English as he was of the Boers. He razed the small Durban settlement in 1838, forcing the English settlers to take refuge at sea. The Boers then moved to annex the town, but were thwarted by teenager Dick King, who galloped some 1,000 kilometers (620 miles) to Grahamstown in 10 days, and drummed up a rescue detachment. You'll see the statue commemorating his legendary ride on Victoria Embankment.

One floor up is the excellent ✪ **Durban Art Gallery** (☎ **031/300-6238**) open Monday to Saturday 8:30am to 4pm, and Sunday 11am to 4pm; no admission). Back in the 1970s, this was the first national gallery to recognize African crafts as art, and today it has arguably the most representative and exciting collection of traditional and contemporary South "Africana" art in the country. Don't miss the temporary **red eye @rt** exhibits, held on the first Friday of every month (see "Durban After Dark").

East of the City Hall, facing Aliwal Road is the **Old Court House.** As the first public building erected in Durban (1866), this is an excellent example of the Natal Verandah style, and today houses the rather dry **Local History Museum** (☎ **031/300-6313;** open Monday to Saturday 8:30am to 5pm, and Sunday 11am to 5pm). Wander past the costumes worn by the disparate groups that made up Durban society over 200 years (look out for the beadwork items), or poke around the reconstruction of Henry Francis Fynn's wattle-and-daub hut, apparently the first in Natal (but otherwise totally unremarkable).

Far more interesting is the **Kwa Muhle Museum** (130 Ordnance Rd.), an annex of the Local History Museum which illuminates how the segregationist policies of the city affected the majority of the city's population. It's a 10-minute walk north up Aliwal Road to where it intersects with Ordnance Road, but as this does not ideally position you to tackle the Indian District, it should possibly be seen as a separate trip.

From the Local History Museum, it's a 15-minute walk east to the **Golden Mile** (you can also take a mynah bus from the depot diagonally opposite the museum, on West Street), and a 15-minute walk west to what is known as Durban's central ✪ **Indian District.** As the latter is by far the more interesting option, head down West Street, then north up Grey. In Durban's most fascinating streetscape, the Indian general dealers trade in everything from spices and *sari* fabrics to fresh fish and meat, while Zulu street hawkers ply passersby with *muti,* or traditional medicine (baboon skulls, bits of bark, bone, and dried herbs), to heal wounds, ward off evil spirits, or to cast a spell. While on Grey Street, look out for **Patel's Vegetarian Restaurant** (for address, see "King of Curry," below) or **Simply Veg** at 326 Grey Street. Both are excellent places to sample Durban's Indian fare. West off Grey Street is the **Madressa Arcade,** a bazaar where you will be exhorted to spend your rand on cheap rubbish, mostly from China. Either walk through to Cathedral Street, or follow Grey for another block and admire the gilt-domed minarets of **Jumma Musjid Mosque** (corner of Queen and Grey), the largest mosque in the Southern Hemisphere. Visitors are welcome to enter provided they remove their shoes; for a guided tour, call the **Islamic Propagation Centre** (☎ **031/306-0026**).

To get into the sway of traditional Indian music, head down Queen Street and take your pick from the selection at **Bombay House** (☎ **031/306-0466;** 36 Lockhart Arcade, on Queen St.). West lie the purple minarets of the bright pink and purple **Victoria "Street" Market** (☎ **031/306-4021,** open Monday to Friday 6am to 6pm, Saturday 6am to 2pm, and Sunday 10am to 2pm), on the corner of Queen and Russell streets. This garish building was built after a fire destroyed much of the original Indian market, and has become increasingly touristy; but you can still purchase fresh meat, sticks of incense, patterned stencils to henna hands and feet, stick on dots for foreheads, and bags of spices whose names (Atomic Bomb and Mother-in-Law Exterminator, for example) provide some guide to chili content. If the meat market doesn't kill your appetite (the offal shops are pretty, well, awful), pick up a couple of *samoosas* (vegetable- or meat-filled pastries) upstairs at the **Market Snack Bar** (☎ **031/304-4934**). If you still have time, take a look at the **Emmanuel Cathedral** built in 1910. Southwest of the market, on Cathedral Street, its Gothic-Christian facade is a stark contrast to the surrounds. Farther south lies the **West Street Cemetery,** where a number of local historical figures lie buried, including Henry Francis Flynn and Durban's first mayor, George Cato.

### QUICK FIX

Park your car in the Nicol Square parkade (R2/35¢ per hour) on the corner of Commercial Road and Grey Street. Cross Commercial and turn left to reach Grey Street. Note **Eve's Elegance** (☎ **031/306-4925**), a 100-year-old bridal boutique, great if you're looking for glam 'n' glitter. Right is the **Ajmeri Arcade** (☎ **031/306-3343**), crammed with shops—walk through to view **Emmanuel Cathedral;** directly opposite is **Madressa Arcade,** which takes you back to Grey Street. Walk up Grey to see the mosque and Victoria "Street" Market (see above).

## OTHER TOP ATTRACTIONS

✪ **Kwa Muhle Museum.** 130 Ordnance Rd. ☎ **031/300-6313.** Daily 8am–4pm. Free Admission.

This stimulating museum's stated aim is to provide an awareness of urban African life, including residential and workplace experiences and struggles, and their role in the making of the city. Certainly anyone interested in South Africa's history of race relations should not miss an opportunity to view the exhibition titled the "Durban System." This provides a graphic explanation of how the System, a municipal race policy which evolved in Durban in the early 1900s, granted itself sole monopoly on the brewing and distribution of beer (provided traditionally by women), which it sold through "African-only" beer halls. Proceeds were in turn used to finance the administration and control of black labor in this very building; these were the offices of the Bantu Administration Board, where the city's black inhabitants were "processed." It is a highly evocative exhibit, and an accompanying audiotape ensures that the information is accessible. The "Pass System" exhibition, located toward the back of the museum, is comparatively text heavy, but provides some insight into the humiliation and hatred evoked by the hated "pass books" that controlled the influx and movement of black people throughout the country from 1948 to 1986.

**Botanic Gardens.** Sydenham Rd., Berea. ☎ **031/201-3022.** Daily 7:30am–5:15pm. Sept 16–Apr 15, 7:30am–5:45pm. Orchid House daily 9:30–5pm. Free. From City Hall head west down Smith, which becomes Berea, and follow the signs down Edith Benson to Sydenham.

This 20-hectare (8-acre) oasis, established in 1849, is famous for its cycad collection, particularly the rare *Encephalartos woodii,* believed to be extinct in the wild. Other highlights are the "Palm Walk," the herb garden, the fragrant frangipani collection, and the orchid house, which has over 3,000 species. A favorite photographic backdrop for Durban's brides, the gardens are a calm counterpoint to the city, and a good place for a picnic, particularly on Sundays, when the Natal Philharmonic Orchestra often performs. Call Tourist Information or the gardens for details.

✪ **Killie Campbell Museum.** Corner Marriott and Essenwood rds. (off Musgrave Rd.). Berea. ☎ **031/207-3432.** Mon–Fri 8:30am–4:30pm, preferably by appointment. R15 ($2.50).

Housed in Muckleneuk, the neo–Cape Dutch home that sugar baron Sir Marshall Campbell built for his family in 1914, this museum is arguably Durban's top attraction. Tours are conducted by the knowledgeable Jenny Harkness, and take in the gracious gardens, the furniture and paintings collected by Cambell's son (whose private hunting farm became what is today the private game reserve Mala Mala), as well as the extensive library and ethnological artifacts collected by his anthropologist daughter, Dr Margaret "Killie" Campbell. The latter, known as the **Mashu Museum of Ethnology,** is considered one of the country's finest collections of African artifacts and is the highlight of the tour. Killie collected tribal utensils, ornaments, art, musical instruments, sticks, beadwork, and various items of clothing—look out for the necklace of redcoat (British) buttons worn by Zulu warriors as a sign of bravery. She commissioned over 250 illustrations from Barbara Tyrrell, who in the early 1940s set off into relatively uncharted areas in a battered old 1934 Chevy to record people in tribal dress. Hairstyles and the colors and patterns of clothing were unspoken indications of, among other things, marital and tribal status. Tyrrell's photos provide invaluable insights into this subtle and largely vanished code of communication.

✪ **Umgeni River Bird Park.** 490 Riverside Rd., Durban North. ☎ **031/579-4600.** Daily 9am–4:30pm. Adults R10 ($1.65), R6 ($1) children under 12. Free flight bird shows held Tues–Sun at 11am and 2pm. (From the M4 take Riverside/Umgeni off-ramp).

The Umgeni Bird Park—rated as one of the top three of its kind in the world—is situated near the banks of the Umgeni River and its natural features include a 30-meter-high (98-foot-high) cliff face and four waterfalls. Over 300 species from around the world are housed in large aviaries, four of which are walk-through, and each is planted with palms, cycads, and other tropical plants. The variety of colors and sounds is astounding, and somehow the lush environment makes up for the fact that most of these hapless creatures are caged. The educational bird show, in which handlers introduce a variety of birds (including a parrot, crane, vulture, pelican, and fish eagle) and demonstrate their flight patterns, is definitely worth catching, particularly if you're accompanied by kids.

### The Top Temples

You can see a variety of Hindu temples by traveling along the **Umgeni Road** (turn right off Ordnance), but visitors interested in monolithic architectural sites should consider taking the short trip south to view the **Temple of Understanding** (☎ **031/403-3328**), the largest Hare Krishna temple in the Southern Hemisphere. The temple is open daily for free guided tours from 10am to 1pm; take the Chatsworth turn off the N2 south, look out for the temple and follow the signs. It's a more interesting drive to the **Shree Ambalavaanar Alayam Hindu Temple** (☎ **031/261-8114**) in Cato Manor. The valley has a history of forced removals, but the vacant land was once again filled in the 1990s and is today a vibrant black township with Hindu temples in the middle of the white townships. Exit town on the M13, take the Brickfield Road exit and turn left onto the M10; this becomes Bellair, the road that winds its way through the Cato Manor Valley. Look out for the facade with brightly painted representations of Ganesha, Shiva, and Vishnu at 890 Bellair (on your right if you're coming from town). This national monument, its doors dating back to 1875, is particularly worth visiting around Easter, when the annual Hindu firewalking festival is held.

Another national monument is the **Shri Jaganath Puri Temple** (no number, corner Catherine and Plane sts.) in Tongaat. Some 40 kilometers (25 miles) north of Durban off the N2, this sugar cane town is home to the oldest Indian community in South Africa. A replica of the larger Jaganath Temple at Puri in India, it was built in the early 1900s by the late Sanskrit scholar Pandit Sirikishan Maharaj.

## ESPECIALLY FOR KIDS

Having visited the Local History Museum (see above), take the kids to the tawdry delights of Durban's **Golden Mile** as the 6-kilometer (4-mile) stretch from Addington Beach (south) to Blue Lagoon Beach (north) is dubiously named. (Do be careful about displaying your valuables and do not leave bags unattended.) The following covers the main highlights of this area.

At the south end, where South Beach Walk becomes Lower Marine Parade, is **Sea World** (☎ **031/337-4079,** open daily 9am to 9pm; R27/$4.50 adults, R17/$2.85 children), which comprises a relatively small aquarium (skip this if you're on your way to Cape Town and visit the Waterfront aquarium instead), as well as dolphin, seal, and penguin shows. Call ahead for times. The reef-tank fish are hand-fed daily at 11am and 3:30pm, while sharks are fed on Tuesday, Thursday, and Sunday at 12:30pm. If you're here on a Saturday or Sunday, walk north to **Funworld** (☎ **031/332-9776**), which offers a variety of rather sedate rides for kids, including a cableway that traverses the length of the amusement park. All rides open at 11am on weekends. Funworld is opposite the Edward Hotel, and there is no admission, but rides cost R4–6 (65¢–$1). Visit **Mini Town** (☎ **031/337-7892,** Marine Parade; R10/$1.65 adults, R5/85¢ children) where comparatively giant kids wander through replicas of Durban's most famous buildings, or the reptilian splendor of adjacent **Fitzsimon's Snake Park** (☎ **031/337-6456,** 240A Lower Marine Parade; open daily 9am to 4:30pm; R10/$1.65 adults, R5/85¢ children). Afterward, catch a **rickshaw ride** along the beachfront (runners operate from Mini Town; rides cost R18/$3 with a photo). **Waterworld** (☎ **031/337-6336**), open 9am to 5pm daily from September 23 to April 30 and June 25 to July 25; May open Saturday and Sunday only; 3 and under free; 3 to 12 R23/$3.85; 12 and up R30/$5) is a few minutes drive farther north, between Battery Beach Road and Snell Parade. This large variety of water-propelled slides and rides will take care of water-babies for the better part of a day; or take a break during the midday sun and visit **Umgeni River Bird Park.**

## SPECTATOR SPORTS

Durban hosts a number of major sporting events, including the grueling 90-kilometer (56-mile) **Comrades Marathon** in June, and the 175-kilometer (110-mile) **Dusi Canoe Marathon** in January, both of which start in Pietermaritzburg and end in Durban. The **Rothman's July Handicap,** South Africa's premier racing event, takes place every year at Greyville Racecourse. This is also the month the **Gunston 500** is held. As the world's longest-running pro surf competition, this is where the world's top surfers and local bathing beauties battle for supremacy. Also in July is the annual **"sardine run":** this is a unique phenomenon, during which sardines/pilchards migrate north in gigantic shoals, closely followed by frenetic game fish and keen anglers. Driven ashore in sheer panic, they beach themselves where locals simply shovel them into buckets.

For details on these and other events, pick up a copy of *What's On in Durban and KwaZulu-Natal,* issued free by Durban Tourism.

## SHOPPING FOR ARTS & CRAFTS

Surprisingly, the Tourist Junction is a great place to start your spending spree. The **Matombo Gallery** (☎ **031/304-9963**), which sells a good selection of Zimbabwean soapstone sculptures, is worth a quick look; but the **African Art Centre** (☎ **031/304-7915;** open Monday to Friday 8:30–5pm, and Saturday 9am–2pm), is one of the best places in the country to examine the woodcarvings, ceramics, beadwork, baskets, tapestries, rugs, fine art, and fabrics created by predominantly Zulu craftsmen and artists. Staff here are extremely knowledgeable and helpful (ask for development director Anthea Martin), and it's worth buying at least one item, as proceeds are reinvested in the development of local talent. However, for real bargains head down Victoria Embankment and enter the harbor for the **BAT shop** (☎ **031/332-9951;** open Tuesday to Sunday 10am to 5pm) in the **BAT Resource Centre** (☎ **031/332-0451,** Craft Harbour, 45 Maritime Place, Victoria Embankment). Established in 1995, this is Durban's largest and most innovative community arts center, with several art studios where you can watch artists at work, a few excellent shops, a restaurant, and an evening music venue. If you plan to shop on a Friday afternoon, hang around until the harbor lights come on, then soak up some good local jazz. Another BAT Centre shop worth seeing is the **Bayside Gallery** (☎ **031/368-5547;** open Tuesday to Sunday 10am to 4pm), which has a very good selection of South African talent—look out for the Carol Boyes pewterware, Barbara Jackson ceramics, and the artful creations from Ardmore Studio in the Drakensberg. Finally, keen shoppers should not miss the **KwaZulu-Natal Society of the Arts (NSA) Gallery,** at 166 Bulwer Rd., Glenwood (☎ **031/202-3686;** open Tuesday to Friday 10am to 5pm, Saturday and Sunday 10am to 4pm), where a large selection of local and imported crafts are on offer; these often include work by master craftspeople such as woodcarver Vuminkosi Zulu and potter Nesta Nala.

For an informal shopping experience, trawl the street hawkers who line the entire **Marine Parade** beachfront, or head for the **Amphitheatre Flea Market** (north of Marine Parade, between Snell Parade and the Bay of Plenty), held every Sunday. The brave should also consider visiting the **Dalton Road Market:** a truly African market not aimed at tourists, this is where craftsmen sell traditional items such as the *amabheshu* (apron), *izimboko* (staff), and shields to Zulu men wishing to participate in ritual dances.

## WHERE TO STAY

Most of Durban's hotels line the beachfront, one seedier than the next—an exception is the Edward. Unlike Cape Town and the Garden Route, most hotels have a year-round rate, with few season-specific bargains. Note that as the center of town is only 17 kilometers (10½ miles) from the airport, it should be unnecessary to book into a nasty airport hotel to catch a late-night or early flight.

### VERY EXPENSIVE

**The Royal.** 267 Smith St., Durban 4000. ☎ **031/304-0331.** Fax 031/304-5055. E-mail: theroyal@iafrica.com. 271 units. A/C MINIBAR TV TEL. R1,250 ($208.35) double. AE, DC, MC, V.

This 5-star hotel is a member of The Leading Hotels of the World and—besides offering terrific views of the busy port and city—its high levels of service are extraordinary, and every staff member is primed to make you feel special. Rooms, finished in indigenous yellowwood and blue fabrics, look a tad dated, bathroom fittings in particular have seen some wear, but they are supremely comfortable. Located opposite the City Hall and near the Palyhouse Theatre complex, you are also perfectly positioned to explore the city center.

**Dining/Diversions:** The Royal offers four dining options. Top of the Royal on the top floor is where you breakfast with spectacular bay views; the Royal Coffee Shop is a great Viennese-style coffee shop on the ground floor; the Ulundi serves authentic Durban curries; and the Royal Grill is renowned for its haute cuisine (see "Where to Dine").

**Amenities:** Facilities include a rooftop pool deck with informal bar, squash courts, and fully equipped health club. Airport transfers can be arranged.

### EXPENSIVE

✪ **The Edward.** 149 Marine Parade, Durban 4000. ☎ **031/337-3681.** Fax 031/332-1692. E-mail: the.edward@movenpick.co.za. 101 units. A/C MINIBAR TV TEL. R855 ($142.50) double; suites R1,000–1,395 ($166.65–$232.50). All rates include breakfast. Children sharing stay free, 5 to 12 get half-price breakfast. AE, DC, MC, V.

The grand dame of Durban since the 1920s, the Edward has played host to princes and presidents, field marshals and millionaires, movie stars and holy men, and is quite simply the best hotel on the beachfront. Its substantial facelift 3 years ago has in fact put it firmly in the running for best hotel in the city, giving the Royal a run for its money, despite the Edward's rates being substantially lower. Its close proximity to both the city sights (it's a 10-minute stroll to the center) and the Golden Mile (just across the road) is ideal. This is also a great family hotel, particularly considering that children sharing the spacious executive double (the cheapest room, but with a bay window overlooking the beachfront, and two double beds) stay free. Even the deluxe double, which has a separate lounge with dining room table, a writing desk in the bay window, and a separate balcony, is a steal at R1,000 ($166.65). Ask for room 211 and you'll have the pleasure of knowing how the Dalai Lama experienced his stay in Durban.

**Dining:** Breakfasts are served in the Brasserie, lunch and dinner at the Smorgasbord (a huge buffet that suffers from the master-of-none syndrome). Alternatively you can dine at the Mandarin, which serves Chinese food.

## MODERATE

**Essenwood Guest House.** 630 Essenwood Rd., Berea 4001. ☎/fax **031/207-4547.** E-mail: paddyc@iafrica.com. 5 units. A/C MINIBAR TV TEL. R450–560 ($75–$93.35) double, includes breakfast. AE, DC, MC, V. Children 12 and over only.

If you don't enjoy the anonymity of a hotel, and would like to experience first-hand what it's like to live in the most sought-after residential area in Durban, than Essenwood House is ideal. A rose-tinted colonial homestead built in 1924 in a large tropical garden with a pool, this was originally the family home of one of Durban's sugar barons. Paddy and John, themselves formerly sugar cane farmers, have restored the house, furnished it with tasteful antiques and artworks, and—thankfully—opened it to guests. There is one smallish room (no view) and four spacious suites (all with views of the city and distant ocean); request one of the two with private, broad verandahs. The city center and Morningside's restaurants are a mere 5-minute drive from here, Umhlanga a farther 30 minutes, but it's hard to tear yourself away from the twinkling lights and total tranquility of this gracious home. Dinners can be arranged given prior warning.

**Holiday Inn Crowne Plaza.** 63 Snell Parade, Durban 4000. ☎ **031/337-1321.** Fax 031/368-5299. Mikej@southernsun.com. 457 units. A/C MINIBAR TV TEL. R550–585 ($91.65–$97.50) double; R660–2,200 ($110–$366.65) suites. AE, DC, MC, V.

Of the four Holiday Inns on the beachfront, this one is by far the best. Walk into the foyer, and the strong smell of incense from Jewel of India, the hotel's upmarket North Indian restaurant, permeates the air. Next to you is a tall Zulu porter decked out in traditional skins and *knobkerrie* (fighting stick). You could only be in Durban. Once in your room, however, you need to look out at the window (all rooms are sea-facing) to remind yourself that you're right on the Durban beachfront, as furnishings are standard Holiday Inn fare—unless of course you're in a Zulu suite, in which case your eyes will be assaulted by geometric and animal patterns gone wild. (Note, however, that while the suites are super-spacious, you could be in the more intimate and classier Edward. Note, too, that although this hotel is also opposite the beachfront, it is not as central as the Edward.) Ask for a deluxe room; for very little extra (R35/$5.85), you gain more space. The family rooms, which features two double beds, are also very good value at R585/$97.50 (kids stay free). Dining options are varied: besides the Indian option, you could dine at Daruma, the city's best sushi restaurant; the Restaurant Continental, which serves a boring but filling buffet; and Derby's Corner for pub lunches. Facilities include two outdoor swimming pools and a fully equipped gym.

**Quarters.** 101 Florida Rd., Durban 4001. ☎ **031/303-5246.** Fax 031/303-5269. 25 units. A/C TV TEL. R660–715 ($110–$119.15) double. AE, DC, MC, V. Children by prior arrangement.

Comprising four Victorian houses set on fashionable Florida Road (see "Where to Dine"), Quarters is a classy, intimate hotel and the best-dressed joint in town. Sensuous textures include suede, velvet, cotton, coir, and grasscloth, all in muted neutrals, with chrome and stainless steel fittings to finish. Walls feature striking black-and-white photographs of South African life by Angela Shaw. All rooms are relatively spacious and feature queen-size sleigh beds, tea- and coffee-making facilities, and are double-glazed to eliminate neighborhood noise—though this is scant protection from the sound of the person above flushing his/her toilet—ask for a room on one of the top floors. Bathrooms are huge and well designed; specify shower or bathtub. Meals are served in the Brasserie, which has a small but good menu (the fish dusted with almonds is highly recommended), which can also be delivered to your room. Alternatively, there are 30 restaurants within a 5-kilometer (3-mile) radius, many within walking distance. The greatest drawback here is the service, which is nowhere near as classy as the decor.

### INEXPENSIVE

**Blue Waters.** 175 Snell Parade, Durban 4000. ☎ **031/332-4272.** Fax 031/337-5817. E-mail: Bwhotel@dorea.co.za. www.bluewatershotel.co.za. 360 units. A/C TV TEL. R320 ($53.35) double; R430 ($71.65) suite. Rates include breakfast. Children 2 to 12, R30 ($5) extra; 12 and over (adult rate of) R160 ($26.65) extra, sharing. AE, DC, MC, V.

You don't book into the Blue Waters for a luxury experience—the price precludes it—but for anyone interested in 20th-century design, and unafraid of kitsch, this hotel is a gem. Commissioned by present owner and architect Robin Jiran after a trip to Miami, the original hotel (now the south wing) was completed in 1957, while the east and north wings were added in the early 1970s. Despite looking a little run down, it has a number of classic features: the glass wall in the indoor pool, which looks into the Cascades function room; the Coimbra bar, which has original Hille bucket chairs and Michael Leu prints; and the Deco-inspired spiral staircase in the lobby, designed by Antonio Avelini. As the hotel sits on the northernmost tip of the Golden Mile beachfront (a 20-minute stroll from the city center), you should request a sea-facing room, available with doubles or twins, or three or four beds. All meals are buffet, and served in the Versailles Restaurant.

## WHERE TO DINE

A combination of creative cooking, gracious venues, and balmy weather makes the Durban restaurant scene the country's most exciting after Cape Town. Windermere and Florida Roads are particularly rich in choice. (Both are situated in Morningside, which lies on the western outskirts of town.) Starting at the town-end of Windermere is **Bean Bag Bohemia** (☎ **031/309-6019,** #18), a laid-back venue serving light meals; pastas are recommended. If downstairs is too rowdy, head upstairs where the vibe is mellower. Keep going to #411, where you'll find **El Bandido** (☎ **031/303-3826**), and the adjacent **El Turko** (☎ **031/237-8983,** #413) serving Mexican- and Middle Eastern–inspired food, respectively. Make sure you book a table at these hip restaurants because both are often packed to capacity, despite tables spilling out onto the street. Diagonally opposite is **Mezze** (☎ **031/23-4127,** #440 at the corner of Windermere and Innes). This modern venue with big glass windows opening onto the street is a great place to enjoy essential Greek fare; the grilled calamari with cayenne pepper, garlic, and lemon; and black mushrooms stuffed with spinach and feta are recommended. Also on this corner is **The Colony** (☎ **031/23-8270**), a more upmarket venue, where owner

Brian Beatt specializes in serving excellent game dishes, curries, grills, and fish in a discreet colonial atmosphere. For Thai food, prepared by imported chefs, keep heading down Windermere for **Bangkok Wok** (☎ **031/23-3211,** #440).

You can also order excellent food prepared by northern-Thai chefs, and sit on a verandah overlooking Morningside's Florida Road, at number #138, **Baanthai** (☎ **031/303-4270**), sandwiched between **Christina's** (☎ **031/303 2111**), where you can enjoy value-for-money four-course menus, and **Bistro 136** (☎ **031/303-3440**), where Swiss-trained chef/patron Willi serves up classic continental fare. Other Florida Road treats are **Quarters Brassiere** (#101, see "Where to Stay") for great sandwiches, and **Mo Better Noodles** (☎ **031/23-4193,** Shop 5, Florida Centre, 275 Florida Rd.) a London-inspired noodle bar populated with trendy patrons.

**Harvey's.** 77 Goble Rd., Morningside. ☎ **031/23-9064.** Reservations recommended. Tues–Fri noon–2pm; Mon–Sat 7–9:30pm. R40–63 ($6.65–$10.50). AE, DC, MC, V. INTERNATIONAL.

Crowned Durban's best in both 1997 and 1998 by the local branch of International Wine and Food Society, this stylish restaurant is known for its innovative flavor combinations, excellent presentation, and efficient service. The menu changes regularly, but main courses may include Australian tiger prawns flamed in brandy and finished with a light Café de Paris butter sauce; linefish meuniere, dusted with roasted hazelnuts in a nut butter with balsamic vinegar; duck confit with a cider, green peppercorn, and calvados creâm with caramelized apples; roulade of fresh pasta, spinach, wild field mushrooms, and ricotta cheese, smothered (literally, unfortunately) in a sage butter sauce. Despite their accolades, visitors may find that the experience is not that memorable; the menu makes no attempt to incorporate local cuisine, and the venue, a converted house styled in a postmodern fashion, could be anywhere.

✪ **La Dolce Vita.** 1st floor, Durban Club, Durban Club Place, off Smith St. (next to Nedbank). ☎ **031/301-8161.** Reservations essential, particularly for dinner. R30–55 ($5–$9.15). Mon–Fri 12–2:30pm, Mon–Sat 6:30–10:30pm. AE, DC, MC, V. ITALIAN.

In the sexiest venue in Durban, the gracious space of the colonial Durban Club is imbued with the sense of a special occasion. And, as La Dolce Vita enjoyed a reputation for fine Italian cuisine for some 25 years before it moved to the club in 1997, the food does not disappoint. Service is slick, the ambience discreet and dignified (but not stuffy), and the food traditional old-style Italian. Steak tartare (mixed at the table), *tagliolini all'Aragost* (pasta with lobster sauce), roast rabbit, tripe and mushrooms, and filet of lamb (the house specialty), are all recommended. Prawns are either grilled or curried, in the only nod to local custom. Ask for a table at one of the windows overlooking the palm-lined Victoria Embankment and yacht basin. Afterward, retire to a sofa in the comfortable anteroom, and indulge in a post-dinner drink or a cigar—a fitting end to a meal in this baronial atmosphere.

**Royal Grill.** Royal Hotel, Smith St., Durban. ☎ **031/304-0331.** Mon–Fri 12:30am–2:30pm, Mon–Sat 6–10pm. Set lunch R88.50 ($14.75); Dinner (a la carte only) R62–165 ($10.35–$27.50). AE, DC, MC, V. CONTINENTAL.

This venue—the 70-year-old flagship of the Royal—rivals La Dolce Vita's. Plush velvet banquette seating, chandeliers, antique dressers, and stained-glass skylights create what many consider to be the most romantic dining room in the country. Service, however, is in a class of its own. The Royal Grill would run the danger of being fusty, were it not for the witty Indian gentlemen who run it like a well-oiled machine. A few have been serving here for 25 years. The set luncheon starts with offerings from the chef's table (a buffet of perfectly prepared, tastefully combined, and beautifully presented dishes), followed by a choice of two soups, a choice of four main courses, and the dessert trolley. This is an excellent value at R88.50 ($14.75) per person. If this sounds too heavy, luncheon guests may also choose from the dinner menu, which is fully a la carte—Supreme of Chicken, filled with lobster and spinach, is recommended; as are the kudu loin steak with sherry sauce and grilled porcini, and the Old Man Steak, beef filet in a mustard cream sauce and brandy, prepared at your table.

### Table with a View, Please

If you've ever thought the world revolved around you, **Roma Revolving Restaurant** (☎ **031/337 6707,** John Ross House, Victoria Embankment) is the place to prove it. Enter John Ross House from a slightly seedy side alley off the Victoria Embankment, whoosh up 32 floors in the small lift, and you'll step directly into a plush 1970s haven. One of only 40 revolving restaurants in the world, the Roma provides great views of the city, harbor, and beachfront from every table, as the restaurant revolves completely every 60 minutes. The service is excellent and, best of all, the classic Italian fare is good (though not exceptional). For a more one-dimensional, but no less spectacular take on Durban, head south down Point Road to **The Famous Fish Co** (☎ **031/368-1060,** Kings Battery North Pier). Seated right at the harbor entrance, diners on the deck are often meters away from the towering tankers, luxury liners, and sailboats that enter and depart Africa's busiest harbor. The theme is nautical, the menu seafood dominated and good (though the calamari errs on the tough side). Directly below Famous Fish and enjoying similar views are the **Black Steer** (☎ **031/368-4030**) a chain-restaurant specializing in ribs and burgers for family clientele and **Thirsty's Tavern** (☎ **031/ 337-9212**) which serves lighter pub-type meals at great value (R15/$2.50 for a plain burger), though it can get very crowded and rowdy. **Café Fish** (☎ **031/301-3102,** Yacht Mole, Victoria Embankment), situated in the middle of the yacht marina, opens at 7:30am for breakfast and serves lunch until 4pm, daily; despite the name, the lamb pot roast is popular. Finally, the best place for breakfast is a table on the **Terrace** at the Edward Hotel, in the heart of the Golden Mile (see "Where to Stay").

## Durban After Dark

For a night out at the theater, head for **The Playhouse** (☎ **031/369-9444,** 29 Acutt St.), a mock-Tudor venue that hosts the best local talent (look out for performances by the Playhouse Dance Company, now called the Fantastic Flying Fish Dance Company) as well as international acts like the Jim Rose Circus and the Russian Ballet. Call ahead or pick up a free copy of *Playhouse News* from the Tourist Junction. Also find out what's happening at the **Elizabeth Sneddon Theatre**'s lunch-time concerts. You can see anything from a traditional Zulu *maskandi* performance to a modern jazz recital here.

These concerts are held every Monday at the University of Natal, South Ridge Road (☎ **031/260-1111**).

**Café Fish** (see above) becomes a watering hole for Durbanites after 5pm—it's considered *the* place for a sundown G&T—and often rocks till 2am. Strictly cash only. On Fridays and Saturdays, head deeper into the harbor to catch the popular jazz sessions at the **BAT Bar** (☎ **031/332-0451**), from 5:30pm onward. Look out for local favorite, Busi Mhlongo. For more of a beach vibe, just cross the road from North Beach and walk upstairs to **Joe Cool's** (☎ **031/332-9697**), where you can watch the beach babes stalking surfers.

On the first Friday of each month, go to the **Durban Art Gallery** (☎ **031/300-6238**), where Durban's hippest kick-start their weekends with the "**red eye @rt**" exhibition, Durban's hottest art happening. Shows have a strong performance element,

## King of Curry

Durban is the next best place to India for sampling Indian food, and the city's Indian District is a great starting point for a cheap lunch. If you're ravenous, try a *bunnychow* takeaway from **Patel's Vegetarian House** (☎ **031/306-1774;** Rama House, Grey St., next to SK Naidoo's Sari Boutique). This scooped out, half-loaf of bread stuffed with curry is unique to Durban. If the heat has you beat, a *Malai Kofta* from **Aangans** (☎ **031/307-1366;** 86 Queen St.) might be more appropriate—these minced cottage cheese and potato dumplings filled with mixed fruit, cream, *kimis* (nuts), and simmered in cashew gravy are a steal at R13 ($2.15). Alternatively, try the creamy butter chicken for only R20 ($3.35). If you don't want to eat in the Indian District, the **Ulundi** (☎ **031/304-0331;** 267 Smith St.) in the Royal Hotel is conveniently situated near Francis Farewell Square, but be warned—it's pricey. If you have time to sample only one Indian restaurant, make it ✪ **Gulzar** (☎ **031/309-6379;** 71 Stamford Hill Rd., Greyville), considered by food critics to be the best Indian restaurant in town. Proud proprietor Rajen Frank specializes in authentic north and south Indian cuisine, and provides excellent guidance to new terms in his menu. Food is cooked to order, thereby enabling diners to control the spiciness of the curry, and the ambience is ideal for a romantic night out. The prize for the best venue must, however, go to **Jaipur Palace** (☎ **031/83-0287;** 3 Riverside Complex, North Way, Durban North), where diners enter large carved entrance doors (imported from Delhi) and cross marble-inlayed floors to be seated under a central chandelier and frieze copied from the Rambach Palace near Jaipur. The food is also highly recommended; executive chef Salil Fadnis, trained in New Delhi, incorporates flavors characteristic of the various regions of India.

and are followed by a range of music from drum & base to *kwaito,* South Africa's homegrown brand of house music. For late-night drinks and coffee, pull into **Beanbag Bohemia** (see "Where to Dine"), an Art Deco cocktail bar with a bohemian vibe, open until 1am. Alternatively try **News Cafe** (☎ **031/201-5241;** at the corner of Essenwood and Silverton), where cocktail orders are delivered to a jungle beat.

If you're in the mood for a club crawl, start with **Colours** (☎ **031/337-4569,** 60 Smith St.), where a combination of kwaito, hip-hop, and R&B should get you moving, then move on to **Crash!** (☎ **031/304-6524,** Main Concourse, Durban Station), touted as Durban's flashiest nightclub. Hedonists should head straight for **330** (☎ **031/337-7172,** Point Rd.); rated by travelers as one of the best clubs in the world, this is where Durban's techno-ravers do their thing (open Saturdays only). End the evening at **Anno Domini** (Hermitage Lane, Small Craft Harbour, off Victoria Embankment, no phone), where chill-out music greets the dawn every night except Saturday; or just head straight up the coast for sunrise over the ocean. If you'd prefer a more cultural spin on the evening, head for **Stringfellas** (☎ **031/332-8951;** Corner Point and West sts.), the most popular Indian club in town, and check out the Eastern rave culture. (Note that you can also catch the latest Bollywood movie at the 400-seat **Isfahan Cinema** (☎ **031/306-2979** in the City Center.) Finally, if you're unfortunate enough to be caught after dark in Pietermaritzburg (see below), head for **Crowded House** (☎ **031/45-5972**) at 93 Commercial Rd. and lose yourself on the large dance floor.

## SIDETRIPS FROM DURBAN

### PIETERMARITZBURG

Pietermaritzburg lies 80 kilometers (49½ miles) northwest of Durban, and visitors with time enough to come here, should make the most of it by taking in the **Valley of a Thousand Hills** along the way. However, neither the "heritage" capital or the evocative-sounding valley (which in reality could be described as Valley of a Thousand Hovel-covered Hills) merit more than a brief detour on your way to the battlefields or Drakensberg. The chief draw of the valley, besides shopping for African curios, is **Phezulu,** one of the most accessible Zulu cultural villages (see "Zululand," below).

To reach the valley, head for Pietermaritzburg northwest from Durban along the M3, following the Pinetown Road signs. Take the Hillcrest/Old Main Road turnoff to the right, and follow the Old Main Road or R103 along the valley, which finally rejoins the M3 to Pietermaritzburg.

Other than its name (the town is named after Trekker leaders Piet Retief and Gerrit Maritz), you'd be hard-pressed to find evidence of Pietermaritzburg's Afrikaner origins; no doubt this is because the British annexed it a mere 4 years after the Boers declared their Republic of Natalia in 1838. "Maritzburg" as it's known to locals, is very proud of its British colonial architecture (the **City Hall,** built in 1901, is reputedly the largest red-brick building in the Southern Hemisphere), but its streetlife is dominated by the largely Zulu and Indian population.

#### What to See & Do

For free maps of the city and more information, visit the helpful **Tourist Information Bureau** at Publicity House, opposite the Tatham Gallery (☎ **0331/45-1348;** 177 Commercial Rd.). Hours are Monday to Friday 8:30am to 4:30pm, Saturday 8:30am to 12:30pm.

Most consider Pietermaritzburg's highlight to be the ✪ **Tatham Art Gallery** (☎ **0331/42-1804;** Commercial St., open Monday to Friday 10am to 5pm; no admission), situated in the old Supreme Court (built in 1871) diagonally opposite the City Hall. The Tatham features a predominantly European collection including minor works by Degas, Renoir, Picasso, Matisse, and Hockney, with a much smaller, but equally interesting collection of South African artworks. Adjacent is the **Old Natal Parliament Building** on the corner of Commercial and Longmarket streets; take a drive down Longmarket to view a fine collection of Martizburg's English-colonial buildings, all dating back to the turn of the century. Parallel to Longmarket is Loop, where you'll find **Natal Museum** (☎ **0331/45-1404,** 237 Loop St., open Monday to Saturday 9am to 4:30pm, and Sunday 2 to 5pm). This is yet another lovely building dating back to the early 1900s, but otherwise filled with stuffed animals and birds, reconstructed street scenes, San caves, and dinosaurs. Highlights are the Traditional Cultures and Crafts display; and the effects relating to the French Prince Imperial, son of Napoleon III, who lived and was buried here after falling in the Anglo-Zulu war in 1879, thereby ending any hope of restoring the Napoleons to power in France. You'll find more exhibits on the Prince at the Cultural Centre in the **Voortrekker Museum** (☎ **0331/94-6834,** corner of Longmarket and Boshoff sts.), which is open Monday to Friday 9am to 4pm, Saturday 8am to 12pm; and charges no admission. Incidentally, it is on the very site of the original Church of the Vow, built by the Trekkers in 1841 to commemorate their victory at the Battle of Blood River.

#### Where to Stay & Dine

**Redlands Hotel & Lodge.** 1 George McFarlane Ln., Wembley, Pietermaritzburg 3201. ☎ **0331-94-3333.** Fax 0331/94-3338. E-mail: redalands@ mweb.co.za. 12 units. A/C TEL

### Pietermaritzburg's Claim to Fame

On June 7, 1893, a young lawyer named Mohandas Ghandi, recently arrived in Durban, found himself stranded at the Pietermaritzburg Station after being ejected from a whites-only first-class carriage. He spent the night mulling the incident over in the waiting room and, according to the great man himself, "[his] active non-violence started from that day." Mohandas (later to become Mahatma) was to spend the next 21 years peacefully fighting the South African laws that discriminated against Indians before leaving to liberate India from English rule. You can visit the platform where Ghandi was unceremoniously dumped (at the seedy end of Church St.), or the **Ghandi statue** (near the City Hall end of Church St.).

TV. R465 ($77.50) double; R525–625 ($87.50–$104.15) suite. Children under 12 stay free. AE, DC, MC, V.

Situated in tranquil park-like surrounds on the northern outskirts of town, this is by far the best place to stay in Pietermaritzburg. Public spaces and rooms are spacious, comfortable, and tastefully decorated in the English-colonial style; facilities include tea- and coffee-making facilities, room service, a large pool, and tennis court. Breakfasts, costing R30–40 ($5–$6.65), are served at tables overlooking the pool or in the elegant dining room. Light meals are available throughout the day, and the a la carte dinner menu includes linefish, steak, trout, duck, and a large selection of salads. Surrounded by trees and lawns, you could be in the country—ideal as the center of town is in reality a mere 6-minute drive away.

## The Holiday Coast

The coast south and north of Durban is a 5-hour drive from dry, dusty Jo'burg, and even less from the Free State. With every middle-class family demanding their place in the sun, this subtropical belt south of the Tugela River has been swallowed up by condominiums, time shares, brick-face homes, and tatty caravan parks, ruining, at least for nature lovers, almost the entire "Holiday Coast." Thankfully, however, there are a few areas where the lush coastal vegetation hides all signs of human habitation—from the beach at least. The fecund vegetation is, in fact, the saving grace of this coastline; wild banana trees and masses of flowering shrubs and trees, often alive with monkeys, do much to soften concrete lines.

## Exploring the South Coast

Unless you're traveling to or from the Eastern Cape, wish to dive the Aliwal Shoal, or are here on a golfing vacation (see "Staying Active," above), the 160-kilometer (99-mile) South Coast stretch, incorporating the "Hibiscus Coast" and "Strelitzia Coast," is best avoided in favor of the less-developed North Coast. There are a few pretty reserves, the most popular being **Oribi Gorge Nature Reserve (☎ 039/679-1644)**, but they are small, and the contrast with their surrounds, such as the sugar mills, only serves as a depressing reminder of how much was lost during the last century's avaricious development. Steam train enthusiasts could, however, consider boarding the **Banana Express (☎ 039/682-4821)** for a 90-minute ride, or for a full day's excursion to Paddock via the Oribi Gorge. KwaZulu-Natal's narrow-gauge steam train rolls out of Port Shepstone, less than an hour's drive south from Durban and a 15-minute drive north from Margate, where you will find the region's **Publicity Association (☎ 031931/22-322;** fax 03931/21886; ybiscus@iafrica.com). Staff here will give you advice on where to stay, should you be forced to overnight in this area, and are well equipped to create golfing itineraries.

## Exploring the North Coast

The most popular seaside suburb on the North Coast (comprising the "Sugar Coast" and "Dolphin Coast") is **Umhlanga Rocks,** a 20-kilometer (12-mile) drive north of Durban (pronounced *um*-shlung-ga), and originally part of Marshall Campbell's sugar estate. Facilities are well developed, with plenty of accommodation options, designated safe bathing areas, and lifeguards. The region's **Sugar Coast Tourism Bureau** (☎ **031/561-4257**), open Monday to Friday 8:30am to 1pm and 2 to 4:30pm, is also situated here, on Chartwell Drive (clearly marked as you enter Umhlanga from the N2). Come here first if you intend venturing inland, to the rolling sugar cane fields.

If you're tired of sunbathing and swimming, the one noteworthy place worth visiting in Umhlanga itself is the offices of the **Natal Sharks Board** (☎ **031/566-1001,** Umhlanga Rocks Dr.). One of the most prestigious centers of shark research in the world, the board offers informative audiovisual presentations about these awesome predators. Presentation hours are Tuesday to Thursday at 9am, with additional showings Monday to Thursday at 12pm, 1pm, 2pm, and 3pm. Get there for the first showing at 9am, or at 2pm, and you can watch a shark being dissected (caught no doubt in the Board's nets). Currently the most viable protection for swimmers, these controversial nets are responsible for the deaths of hundreds of sharks (up to 14 species swim off this coast) as well as numerous rays, dolphins, and endangered turtles. If the thought of these innocent creatures' plight makes you uncomfortable, take a look at the informative display about the history of shark attacks along the coast.

While Umhlanga is conveniently close to Durban, beach-lovers looking for safe, uncrowded beaches are urged to head farther north. In and beyond Ballito, development starts to taper off, and the standard of accommodation increases dramatically. Zimbali Lodge (see below) is the Holiday Coast's premier resort. At Blythedale, roughly 25 kilometers (15½ miles) north of Ballito and 70 kilometers (43 miles) north of Durban, a total ban on high-rise construction has created the best preserved beach on the Holiday Coast, while 13 kilometers (8 miles) farther the tiny hamlet of Zinkwasi is the least developed beach resort on the North Coast, and marks the end of the Holiday Coast. If you intend spending some time in this area, contact the **Dolphin Coast Publicity Association** (☎ **0331/61-997,** fax 0331/62-434) in Ballito.

### The Best of the Tidal Pools

At Shaka's Rock, a seaside suburb 49 kilometers (30 miles) north of Durban, Zulu men apparently leapt into the surf to prove their manhood during the reign of Shaka. For those less challenged by testosterone levels, there are two lovely tidal pools at **Salt Rock,** where the Zulu women used to collect their salt. To find them, drive along the Shaka's Rock beachfront and look for the large Salt Rock Hotel, which overlooks the pools (incidentally built and owned by the Hulett family, a name you'll see on most South African sugar). For keen swimmers, an even better option is the large tidal pool built at **Thompson's Bay,** reputedly Shaka's favorite seaside relaxation spot. To find it, simply walk south from Salt Rock toward Ballito, which lies 6 kilometers (4 miles) south. Once in **Ballito** you have a choice of two more rock pools.

### Where to Stay

**Beverley Hills Hotel.** Lighthouse Rd., Umhlanga Rocks 4320. ☎ **031/561-2211.** Fax 031/561-3711. 88 units. A/C MINIBAR TV TEL. R1,390–1,780 ($231.65–$296.65) double. R2,100–2,420 ($350–$403.35) suites. One child sharing stays free; two by arrangement. AE, DC, MC, V.

This is the most upmarket address in Umhlanga, and an alternative to the Royal in town. Unfortunately, most of the staff (the doorman being a notable exception) seem a tad too snooty for what is, after all, a beach resort. An extensive facelift has rendered the pale-pastel foyer very grand, though the recently tiled rooms could be described as bland, and the spacious suites as bordering on bad taste (salmon-pink damask wallpaper and gray tiles?!). Almost all rooms, however, enjoy excellent views of the beach and ocean as do the large pool and deck. Guests have a choice of two dining rooms: La Provence, an elegant room off the main lounge, where breakfast, lunch, and dinner are served (predominantly French cuisine), or the Cabin. The latter features wooden ceilings and paneling, specializes in seafood, and is a popular venue even amongst Durbanites, particularly on Sundays. Staff are happy to arrange tennis courts, deep-sea fishing, bowling, horseback riding, gyms, golf, and squash for guests, as well as trips to the nearby game reserves and Durban's top attractions. Airport transfers are also happily arranged; at most this is a 40-minute trip. (Note that for the same money you could stay at Zimbali—10 minutes farther north; 100 times classier.)

✪ **The Boat House.** 33 Compensation Beach Rd., Ballito 4420. ☎ **0322/96-0300.** Fax 0322/ 96-0184. E-mail: boathouse@iafrica.com. 8 units. A/C TV TEL. R500–600 ($83.35–$100). AE, DC, MC, V. Children 12 and over.

A real gem, the Boat House offers excellent value and superb service, though the seaside suburb of Ballito is nothing to write home about. Pieter de Kock traveled the country, sampling the best guest houses in every province, before creating his own. Not surprisingly, it's one of the best, with a tastefully executed nautical theme and excellent service via Pieter and his partner Maylene. Ask for one of two front rooms for the best views, but don't despair if these are taken—all rooms are spacious, beautifully appointed, and comfortable. Besides, the house is right on the beach; walk past the pool, open the little garden gate, and your feet sink into the sand. Breakfasts are innovative and beautifully presented, and dinners (on request) delicious, though Pieter is happy to make dinner bookings (as a chow-hound, his advice is honest and critical).

**Cabana Beach.** 10 Lagoon Dr., Umhlanga Rocks 4320. ☎ **031/561-2371.** Fax 031/ 561-3522. faranam@cabanabeach.co.za. 217 units. A/C TV TEL. High-season from R1,320 ($220). Low-season from R880 ($146.65). Rates include breakfast. Children under 18 stay free, and pay R25 ($4.15) for breakfast. AE, DC, M, V.

This time-share resort offers almost the same view as the Beverley Hills Hotel (in fact, it's directly in front of the main swimming beach), but with none of the formality—nor of course, the luxuries. All rooms have balconies overlooking the ocean, but tower rooms command the best views; ask for the highest available. Built in the late 1970s, the hotel is showing its age slightly, particularly in design: rough-textured walls are evocative of a Mediterranean villa, bamboo, and cane furniture is old-fashioned but functional. Units are designed around the needs of families, (units sleep from 2 to 8), with fully equipped kitchens and full servicing. Alternatively, there's always **Razzmatazz** (see below), which is managed separately from the hotel, but is conveniently on the premises. Facilities include two swimming pools (adult and family), squash courts, tennis courts, gymnasium, two more restaurants, children's entertainment program, and babysitting. Airport transfers can be arranged.

✪ **Zimbali Lodge & Country Club.** P.O. Box 404, Umhlali, 4390 (off M4 just before Ballito on the North Coast). ☎ **0322/538-1007.** Fax 0332/538-1019. E-mail: kgarrat@sunint.co.za. 76 units. A/C MINIBAR TV TEL. R1,195 ($199.15) double; R2,080 ($346.65) suite. Rates include breakfast. Children's rates by arrangement. AE, DC, MC, V.

Opened in 1998 to much acclaim, Zimbali (a 42km/26-mile/30-minute drive north of Durban) has brought some much needed class to the Holiday Coast. Totally surrounded by secluded indigenous forest, the lodge is inspired by the architecture of tropical climates, with local influences including the nearby sugar baron estates and Indian temples. The opulent interior (decorated by Wilson & Associates, responsible for Palace of the Lost City) is arguably the country's finest example of the Afro-colonial chic style. From staircases to trusses, beds to deckchairs, each item is beautifully crafted and custom-made—down to the organic ashtrays, made from seedpods. Set on a bluff, the buildings (including bedrooms, which are situated in the gardens surrounding the lodge) overlook a natural lake, surrounded by forested hillsides, and beyond, the ocean. There is a large pool for swimming; alternatively guests can walk or be transported to the private beach, play tennis, bird watch, book a treatment at the resident spa, or play the Tom Weiskopf–designed 18-hole championship golf course. All meals are served in the indoor/outdoor restaurant overlooking the 120-acre (300-hectare) estate. A la carte luncheons are followed by table d'hôte dinners—a typical menu offers a choice of three appetizers (crayfish salad, beef consommé, or asparagus), three main courses (grilled sirloin steak or ostrich filet, grilled linefish, oven-baked chicken breast), and three dessert choices. There are also daily specials, such as chicken curry or a seafood platter.

### Where to Dine

**Razzmatazz.** Umhlanga Rocks. ☎ **031/561-5847.** R35–100 ($5.85–$16.65). Daily 12–3pm and 6:30–10pm. SEAFOOD/GAME.

People come here as much for the view—with most tables situated on a deck overlooking the beach, you can't get closer to the ocean—as for the food. All the house specialties are recommended: calamari is pan-fried with butter, garlic, a touch of chili, and fresh cream; linefish is prepared with cream, wine, mushrooms, and shrimp and served in phyllo baskets; and langoustines are steamed with lemon grass and fresh herbs and served in a Chinese bamboo basket. Game dishes are also excellent: ostrich filet is prepared in a Cape gooseberry sauce, guinea fowl is deboned (heavenly!) and roasted with apple and calvados. Service is super quick, and the ambience laid back, with plenty of bikinis and bare feet as befits a place this close to the sea.

## 3 Zululand

Crossing the Tugela River (88 km/54½ miles north of Durban), traditionally the southern frontier of Zululand, it soon feels as if you've entered an entirely new province. Passing a largely poor, rural population, on increasingly bad roads, you are now traveling the ancestral lands of the Zulu, and the designated Zulu "homeland" prior to 1994.

Most visitors to Zululand spend at least 2 days at Hluhluwe-Umfolozi. This park is home to the Big 5, and has the best wilderness trail in the country. In addition, its proximity to Durban (less than 3 hours north) makes it South Africa's most accessible game reserve, and its varied vegetation and top accommodations give Kruger stiff competition. But if your idea of the "wild life" is pausing your pursuit of lions with a drink poured by your personal ranger, look no farther than Phinda. Northeast of Hluhluwe and bordering Mkuzi, this luxurious private game reserve is close enough to the coast to add diving with dolphins, sharks, and tropical fish to your Big 5 experience.

A number of reserves make up the Greater St Lucia Wetland Park, a top destination for fishermen, divers, and birders. Encompassing as it does the foothills of the Lebombo Mountains, wetlands, forests, lakes, and the coral reefs off the coast, the park is a paradise, though purists will find the shoreline ruined by 4×4 drivers who use the beach as a quick and easy alternative to the potholed highway. To find the highlight of the coast, travel farther north to Rocktail Bay where no more than 22 guests at any given time find themselves alone on a 60-kilometer (37-mile) stretch of pristine beach. For those with more time (and less money), a sojourn in the far northeastern corner, where a chain of lakes empty into the beautiful Kosi Mouth, is definitely recommended, though you will need to rent a 4×4.

## ESSENTIALS

**VISITOR INFORMATION** The **uThungulu Regional Council** (☎ **035/789-1404;** uThungulu House, Kruger Rand St., Richard's Bay, open Monday to Friday from 7:30am to 4pm) is the central bureau for the Zululand area; but as this large industrial port (173 kilometers/107 miles north of Durban) has nothing to recommend it beyond its air links, the best regional office to visit en route is **Eshowe Publicity** (☎ **035/474-1141**) on Hutchinson Street, Eshowe.

**GETTING THERE By Air** The quickest way to get to Zululand is to fly to **Richard's Bay Airport** with **SA Express** (☎ **035/786-0301**) from Durban or Johannesburg and rent a car here.

**By Car** The N2 leading north out of Durban traverses the Zululand hinterland; east lie the coastal reserves, Phinda private game reserve, and the birding reserves (Ndumo and Mkuzi); west lie Hluhluwe and the majority of Zulu museums and cultural villages. From Gauteng take the R29 through Piet Retief to Pongola; this becomes the N2 south.

**By Bus** Contact **Translux, Greyhound** (see chapter 2, "Planning Your Trip to Southern Africa" for regional numbers), or local outfit **Interport** (☎ **0351/91-791**) to travel from Durban or Johannesburg to Richard's Bay.

**SAFETY** October to February, the best time to visit the Maputaland beaches, is also prime time for mosquitoes. Northern Zululand (Ndumo, Kosi Bay, Rocktail Bay) is a high-risk malarial area, while there is a medium risk in the Greater St Lucia Wetland Park, depending on the time of the year. For the most up-to-date advice, contact your doctor or call the CDC (see "Planning Your Trip to Southern Africa", chapter 2).

**GETTING AROUND By Car** Once here you'll have to contact a tour operator or rent a car as there is virtually no public transport in Zululand (Rocktail Bay supplies transfers, however). To explore Kosi Bay on your own, you'll need to hire a 4×4. Car rental, including 4×4s, can be arranged through **Avis** (☎ **035/789-6555**), **Budget** (☎ **035/789-7011**), or **Imperial** (☎ **0800/11-8898** toll-free). All are in the airport.

**Guided Tours Brett Adventure Tours** (☎ **032/456-3513**) specializes in Zululand, from golf and sugar farms to Maputaland and Zulu experiences. **African Tracks** (☎ **0351/97-3156**) tends to concentrate on a more upmarket experience; or you can contact **Dinizulu Safaris** (☎ **035/562-0025**). For tour operators departing direct from Durban, see "Durban Essentials," above. With the exception of Hluhluwe-Umfolozi Reserve, all the major sites are east of the N2.

## DISCOVERING ZULU CULTURE

**Zululand Historical Museum.** Nongqayi Rd. (marked off the R68). ☎ **035/474-2419.** Daily 9am–4pm. R6 ($1) adults, R1 (15¢) children.

Housed in Fort Nongqayi (1883), where the Natal "Native" Police were garrisoned, the Zululand Historical Museum traces the history of the fort and the "enslavement" of the Zulu due to a poll tax. The beadwork collection, dating back to the 1920s, is worth seeking out as is King Mpande's "worldchair" (see "The Rise & Fall of the amaZulu" box, below). There is also a collection of John Dunn's furniture. (The son of settlers, Dunn became King Cetshwayo's political advisor, and was the only white man to become a true Zulu chief. Embracing Zulu polygamy by taking 49 wives, he almost single-handedly spawned Eshowe's coloured community.) The fort is surrounded by

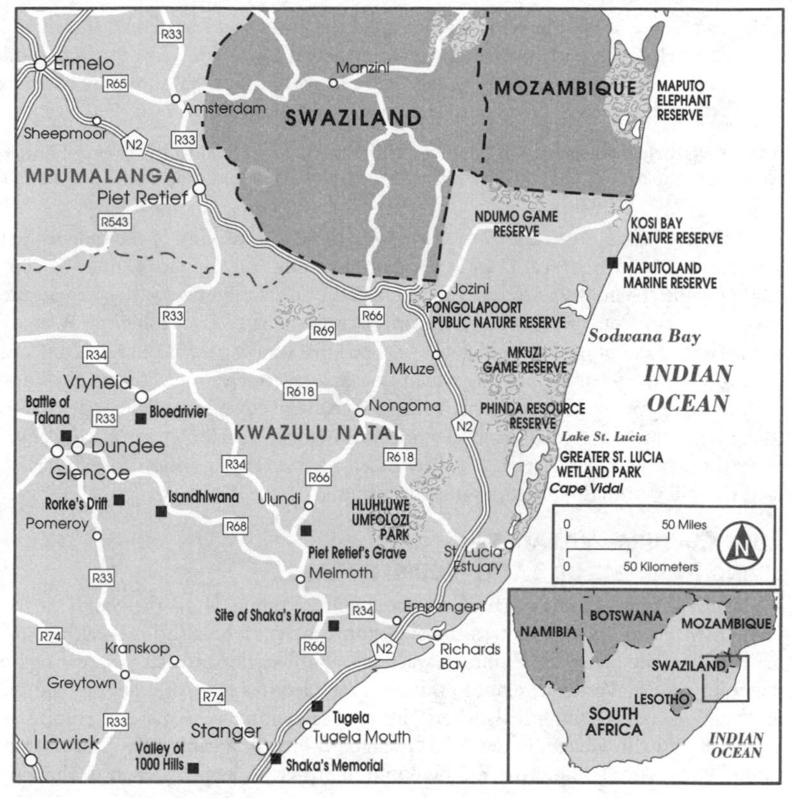


large grounds, and has a 20-minute trail leading to the Mpushini Falls, and a 1-hour self-guided walk through the Dhlinza Forest.

✪ **The Vukani Collection Museum.** Osborne St. ☎ **035/474-1254.** For tours, call ☎ 0354/75-274. Open Tues–Thurs 9am–1pm. Special tours on request. Donations welcome.

While westerners head for cultural villages, many urban Zulu parents bring their children here to gain insights into the rituals, codes, and crafts of the past. This is the finest collection of Zulu traditional arts and crafts in the world, and a visit to the unassuming Vukani Museum is essential for anyone interested in collecting or understanding Zulu art, particularly traditional basketware. Curator Corinne Mahne will, for instance, explain how master weaver Hlabisa Reuben Ndwandwe chooses from a palette of 18 different indigenous dyes to color the ilala palm and local grasses used in weaving, and what the significance of the symbols are, as well as the impact of tourism on the traditional craft.

Another highlight is the collection of pots made by master potter Nesta Nala (her work is also on display at the Durban Art Gallery and is sold in international galleries throughout the world). Nesta walks for miles to find the correct clay before grinding and mixing, then sunbaking her paper-thin shapes and firing them in a hole in the ground. Pots are finally rubbed with fat and ashes, applied with a river stone. Keep an eye out for another award-winner, Allina Ndebele, whose tapestries are inspired by Zulu myths and legends as told to her by her grandmother. Only a third of the collection (some 3,000 pieces) is on display in the small space available, and work is not well labeled; but with the curator on hand to explain every item, this is still one of the best museums in the province. Donate generously. (For real shopping bargains, ask for directions to the Vukani Association shop on Main Rd.)

**Ondini Historical Reserve.** Off Cetshwayo Highway, the dirt road to the Cengeni Gate of Hluhluwe-Umfolozi. ☎ **035/870-2050.** Mon–Fri 8am–4pm, Sat–Sun 9am–4pm. R6 ($1) adults, R3 (50¢) children.

In 1873 Cetshwayo, little knowing that he was to be the last king of the independent Zulu nation, built his royal kraal at Ondini (meaning "the heights"), housing some 5,000 people. There were originally 1,500 huts, but only the *isigodlo* (royal enclosure) has been rebuilt on the original foundations uncovered by archeologists. A model shows the full extent of the original village. The kraal is now part of the KwaZulu Cultural Museum, a separate building which houses a few interesting artifacts, including the original silver beer mug given to King Cetshwayo by Queen Victoria in 1882 (there is a replica in the Zululand Historical Museum)—small compensation considering the destruction that the British wreaked on his empire—should he have ever used the mug, it no doubt left a rather bitter taste.

## Zulu Cultural Villages—Living Museums or Tacky Tourist Traps?

The Zulu is often cited as one of the most culture-proud of all the South African "tribes," many still practicing traditional customs such as lobola (bride-wealth), ritual dancing, and the carrying of "cultural weapons" (knobkerries and assegais) as a sign of masculine pride. Western interest in this group has led to a large number of Zulu cultural villages being established, where turn-of-the century customs and culture are explored. Visits to villages follow a fairly standard format: Visitors may be presented to the "chief," from whom the Zulu cultural interpreter asks permission to show the guests around the *kraal* (a series of thatched beehive-shaped huts encircling a central cattle enclosure), the physical, social, and spiritual center of the homestead.

Zulu "actors," dressed in skins and beads, play out traditional roles, while the guide explains the layout of the kraal and activities. Most visits include lunch and offer overnight accommodation in huts—plumbed and electrified—in the unlikely event that visitors should wish to prolong their stay. Lunch consists of traditional dishes like *phutu pap* (crumbly maize porridge), beans, sweet potatoes, and pumpkin, served with a stew, as well as western-style cold meats and salads.

The greatest drawback is the lack of relevance—with the exception of Simunye, these villages don't adequately deal with the changes that the 20th century has wrought. However, seen as "living museums," they offer an interactive opportunity to understand the customs of the 19th century, particularly if combined with a visit to one or more of the recommended museums (Killie Campbell, Zululand Historical, Vukani Collection, and Ondini). How you finally rate the experience is a matter of personal opinion; at worst these villages serve a much needed employment function. Take your pick from the following.

**Phezulu.** ☎ **031/777-1000.** Off the R103 to Maritzburg, 30 minutes from Durban, in Valley of a Thousand Hills. Shows daily at 10 and 11:30am, 1:30 and 3:30pm. R25 ($4.15) adults, R10 ($1.65) children (excludes lunch).

If you're looking for a quick crash-course within easy reach of Durban, this is the best cultural village on the Holiday Coast. Shows kick off with a sample of Zulu dancing, and the tour of a tiny village lasts no longer than 30 minutes, during which your guide, the charming Washington (off on Tuesdays), provides visitors with an entertaining,

## The Rise & Fall of the amaZulu

The proud amaZulu have fascinated westerners ever since the first party of British settlers gained permission to trade from the great Zulu king Shaka, known as "Africa's Napoleon" for his military genius. As king, he was to unite the amaZulu into the mightiest army in the Southern Hemisphere, and develop better fighting implements and tactics, including the highly successful "horns of the bull" maneuver to outflank the enemy. In 1828, Shaka was murdered by his half-brothers Mhlangana and Dingaan, and Dingaan was crowned king.

Distrustful of the large number of "white wizards" settling in the region, Dingaan ordered the massacre of the Trekker party led by Piet Retief, whom he had invited—unarmed—to a celebratory banquet at his royal kraal **uMgungundlovu.** (A *kraal* is a series of thatched beehive-shaped huts encircling a central, smaller kraal, or cattle enclosure.) Dingaan paid heavily for this treachery at the **Battle of Blood River** (see "A Brief History of the Battlefields," below), where the Zulu nation suffered such heavy casualties that it was to split the state for a generation. In 1840, he was killed by his brother Mpande, who succeeded him as king.

The amaZulu were reunited again under Mpande's eldest, Cetshwayo, who, having in turn murdered a number of his siblings, became king in 1873, and built a new royal kraal at Ulundi. Though by all accounts a reasonable man, Cetshwayo could not negotiate with the uncompromising English, who now wanted total control of southern Africa, with no pesky savages to destroy their imperialist advance on the gold fields. In 1878 the British ordered Cetshwayo to disband his army within 30 days, give up Zululand's independence, and place himself under the supervision of an English commissioner. This totally unreasonable ultimatum, designed to ignite a war, resulted in the **Battle of Islandwana,** and England's most crushing defeat (see the "Battlefields" box, below). Nine months later on July 4, 1879, 5,000 British redcoats under a vengeful Lord Chelmsford advanced on Ulundi and razed it to the ground. A captured King Cetshwayo was exiled to Cape Town and later England; then reinstated as a puppet in 1883.

This was to be the last Anglo-Zulu battle; the might of the Zulu empire had been broken.

Today the core of **uMgungundlovu** (or "secret place of the great elephant") has been rebuilt, and there is a small museum (☎ **035/450-2254**) and a memorial to Piet Retief and his 100-strong delegation. You can also visit a reconstruction of the **royal kraal** at Ondini, near Ulundi. To get here, take the R68 off the N2 to Eshowe, stopping to visit the **Zululand Historical Museum** (clearly marked off the R68) and the **Vukani Collection** in Eshowe first. Note that after Melmoth, the R68 veers off to Babanango; take the R66 to get to Ulundi. To include a detour to uMgungundlovu, take the R34 to Vryheid and look for the turnoff on your left. You will have to retrace your steps back to the R66 and turn left to Ulundi. (Should you want to continue on to **Hluhluwe-Umfolozi,** a 30km/19-mile dirt road connects Ulundi to Cengeni, the western entrance to the game reserve.)

albeit basic introduction to customs and beliefs. Commercial, but bite-sized chunks of information make this very user friendly for short attention spans. Tickets include entrance to the Assagay Safari Park, home to crocodiles, snakes, and a children's animal farm.

**Dumazulu. ☎ 035/562-0144.** Off the N2, 10km (6 miles) south of Hluhluwe Village and 39km (24 miles) north of Mtubatuba Village. Shows daily 8:15am, 11am, and 3:15pm; evening shows at 6pm by request only. R50 ($8.35). Lunch R45 ($7.50).

Situated between Hluhluwe and St Lucia, and close to Mkuze, this is a good option for those who don't have time to venture east of the N2. Dumazulu (thundering Zulu) is a bigger operation than Phezulu and a longer tour; over 50 Zulu residents (overseen by anthropologist Graham Stewart who has studied the Zulu culture since 1967) strive to convey the customs and traditions practiced during the reign of Shaka. Adjacent to the village is a crocodile park and snake pit with over 100 species of indigenous snakes. Take a look at the lodge, the exteriors of the units are inspired by the Swazi, Sotho, Venda, Xhosa, Tsonga, Tswana, Ndebele, and Zulu.

**KwaBhekithunga. ☎ 0354/60-0644.** Stewart's Farm, off the R34 between Empangeni and Melmoth. Tours conducted by prior booking only. R85 ($14.15) without meal; R105 ($17.50) with meal.

Slightly off the beaten track, with no set times, KwaBhekithunga (known to the tongue-tied as "Stewart's Farm") was not built purely as a commercial enterprise, but is the home of Mbhangcuza (Thomas) Fakude and his family. As in other villages, the structure, social order, traditional dress, crops, food storage, hut building, and the role of women and *sangomas* (traditional healers) are explained. Guests also sample traditional beer, prepared by Mazungu, Thomas' wife, and end the experience with a traditional meal.

**Shakaland. ☎ 0354/60-0912.** 14km (9 miles) past Eshowe on the R68. Shows at 11am and 12:30pm, daily. R115 ($19.15) adults, R57.50 ($9.60) children under 12. Fee includes lunch.

The most unashamedly commercial of them all, Shakaland was built as a set for the local TV series *Shaka Zulu,* in 1985, and today this theme park (run by the Protea Hotel group) pulls in the coach parties. The kraal is huge and, with views of the Entembeni hills and Umhlatuze Lake, has one of the most attractive locations. If you do decide to spend the night, ask for huts 21 or 37, which are the most secluded.

Traveling 160 kilometers (99 miles) from Durban to participate in a 3-hour-long tour (called the "Nandi experience" in honor of Shaka's mother) takes some commitment, but this is a slick and informative production, with 70 dancers providing more drama than usual to the dance routine.

**✪ Simunye Pioneer Settlement. ☎ 035/45-3111.** Take the D256, 6km (4 miles) south of Melmoth (look out for wagon wheel), then travel 12km (7½ miles) to the Trading Store. R595 ($99.15) per person, including all meals and cultural program. 18 units.

This is by far the most authentic Zulu cultural village, and the only one to tackle contemporary Zulu culture. If you decide to visit, however, you'll have to set aside 24 hours, as visitors must spend the night. The experience starts upon arrival when guests take the hour-long journey to the settlement via horseback or ox-cart. Simunye (meaning "we are one") celebrates true Zulu hospitality, and visitors can choose to stay in the traditional village or in the stone-and-thatch lodge situated across the Mfule River. These beautifully crafted units were hand built by the community (the hand-filled "hot-rock" baths are particularly attractive, though a little awkward to get in and out of) and are very comfortable, even without modern-day luxuries like electricity. Your hosts, the Biyela clan, are directly linked to the Royal House of Zulu; the patriarch prince's forebear, Mkhosana, led the Zulu regiment that defeated the British at Isandlwana. The sense of pride and history is tangible, the explanations in-depth, and the surroundings of Simunye (a declared National Heritage Site) typical of Zululand.

## HLUHLUWE-UMFOLOZI GAME RESERVE & SURROUNDS

Established in 1895, Hluhluwe-Umfolozi, once separate reserves, is one of the oldest wildlife sanctuaries in Africa. United in 1989, when the land between them was proclaimed the "Corridor Game Reserve," the reserve today covers 96,453 hectares (38,581 acres), and is the province's premier wildlife destination, and the second most popular park after Kruger. Though only a twentieth of the size of its Mpumalanga competitor, the reserve offers a chance to see a large variety of wildlife, with 84 mammal species (including the Big 5, cheetah, hyena, wild dog, wildebeest, giraffe, hippo, and zebra), some 60 reptile species, and over 300 bird species living within its borders. Many visitors actually prefer its varying altitudes and consider this unique combination of forest, woodland, savannah, and grasslands, and its hot, humid, wet summers, the "real" Africa—well worth visiting in addition to Kruger.

The ✪ **wilderness trails** are particularly highly recommended. Conducted by rangers from March to November in the 25,000-hectare (10,000-acre) Umfolozi wilderness, an area where access is permitted only on foot or horseback, they are considered the best way to experience the bush. Unlike Kruger, where walkers return to the same camp every night, provisions and luggage are carried by donkeys to new sites, providing hikers with a sense of heading deeper into the jungle. Trails must be booked through the **KN NCS** (see "Hilltop Camp" details, below) and cost R1,000 ($166.65) per person (4 nights), R900 ($150) per person (3 nights), and R620 ($103.35) per person (2 nights).

Whether on foot or in a car, this is without a doubt the best place to spot rhino, particularly white (or square-lipped) rhino, which the KN NCS single-handedly brought back from the brink of extinction.

The **Hluhluwe-Umfolozi** reserve is open daily April to September, 6am to 6pm; and October to March from 5am to 7pm. Admission is R25 ($4.15) per vehicle and R6 ($1) per person. Guided 2-hour walks (R40/$6.65) take place in the early morning and afternoon, as do the 3-hour game drives, (R75/$12.50 per person, R37.50/$6.25 children). The reserve lies approximately 280 kilometers (173½ miles) north of Durban, with two entrances leading off the N2. Travel 3.4 kilometers (2.1 miles) past the Mtubatuba road junction before taking the R618 left, then turn left again after 21 kilometers (13 miles), and enter via **Mambeni Gate.** Alternatively, stay on the N2 until you see a sign that says Hluhluwe Village. Turn left here (opposite direction) and enter via **Memorial Gate.** (If you're running late, the latter is the quickest way to Hilltop Camp, particularly considering the strict adherence to the 40kmph [25mph] speed limit.) Hilltop is 16 kilometers (10 miles) from Memorial Gate, which should take approximately 40 minutes. The third entrance, **Cengeni Gate,** is approached from the west, 30 kilometers (18½ miles) from Ulundi. To drive the 79 kilometers (49 miles) from Cengeni to Hilltop should take a little more than 3 hours.

### WHERE TO STAY & DINE

There are three public rest camps in Hluhluwe-Umfolozi, two of which (**Masinda** and **Mpila**) are located in Umfolozi, where a camp chef cooks meals with ingredients provided by visitors and guests share communal ablution facilities. While these enjoy good locations, particularly Mpila, and offer the additional thrill of not being fenced off, **Hilltop Camp** in the Hluhluwe section is rated as one of the best in the country, with excellent facilities, views, and comfortable accommodation.

**Hilltop Camp.** KN NCS, P.O. Box 1750, Pietermaritzburg 3200. ☎ **0331/845-1000.** Fax 0331/845-1003. (Direct inquiries, but no bookings, ☎ 035/562-0255.) 70 units, consisting of 2-bed huts (no bath), 2-bed rondawels, 2- and 4-bed chalets, and one 9-bed lodge. From R220 ($36.65) double; R440 ($73.35) for 2-bed fully equipped chalet. AE, DC, M, V.

## The Great White Rhino Recovery

The recovery of the world's white rhino population—from fewer than 100 individuals in the 1920s to over 7,000 worldwide today—is largely due to the efforts of the Natal Parks Board (now the KwaZulu-Natal Nature Conservation Services [KN NCS]). Early conservation efforts ensured a steady increase in numbers at Hluhluwe-Umfolozi, giving rise to Operation Rhino in 1961, whereby surplus numbers of white rhino were relocated to other protected areas and to private land. By 1997 this worldwide distribution had reached a total of 3,912, and white rhino numbers had increased to such an extent that it was the first species to be removed from the World Conservation Union's Endangered List in 1994. There are hopes of the same success with the extremely rare black rhino (incidentally, the same color, but slightly smaller, and with a distinctive hooked lip). There are currently only 2,640 in the world, of which 1,080 are in South Africa; most in KwaZulu-Natal, which has the world's second largest population (after Namibia).

Appropriately named, this relatively luxurious KN NCS camp commands lovely views of the surrounding hills and valleys, and offers a variety of accommodation options. The budget rondawels share ablution and kitchen facilities, while the en-suite 2-bed chalets all feature bar fridges and tea- and coffee-making facilities; some have equipped kitchenettes. The 4-bed chalets all have equipped kitchens. For some of the best locations, request numbers 10 to 14, 28 to 33, or 44 to 49. The shop sells basic provisions (frozen meat, firelighters, liquor, camera film). Units are all serviced daily, but you do have to wash your own dishes, which is just one more reason to book a table in the Mpunyane restaurant (it also happens to offer good value and serves some of the best food in Zululand). If nyala steak is on the menu, order it; this shy, pretty antelope is delicious, though relatively uncommon in the north. There is also a bar/lounge area attached to the reception. Facilities include a large pool, babysitting, fax, limited laundry, and fuel station. Note that Hilltop is an excellent base, not just for the reserve, but also for day forays to MkuzI, Dumazulu, or Lake St Lucia.

**Zululand Tree Lodge.** 12km (7½ miles) from entrance to Memorial entrance gate to Hluhluwe. Private Bag X27, Benmore 2010. ☎ **011/784-7077.** Fax 011/784-7667. E-mail: reservations@conscorp.co.za. 24 units. MINIBAR TEL. High-season R2,640 ($440). Low-season (Apr 19–July 31) R1,740 ($290). Rates include game drives, all meals, and laundry. AE, DC, MC, V.

Located in the 1,500-hectare (6,000 acre) Ubizana Reserve, the Zululand Tree Lodge's thatched bedroom units are freestanding, and built on stilts within a fever tree forest. French doors open from the spacious bedroom onto a balcony, underneath which animals graze on the sweet grasses. Managed by the super-slick Conservation Corporation (who owns the more luxurious Phinda), this is an expensive alternative to Hilltop, but ideal if you want everything done for you. The reserve has a variety of game, including rhino, giraffe, wildebeest, zebra, and warthog, but it's tiny—for an opportunity to see the Big 5, you'll have to visit nearby Hluhluwe. Visitors are taken on morning and evening game drives in the small reserve, and rangers also plan additional expeditions to Dumazulu, MkuzI, Hluhluwe, and Lake St Lucia, all within easy driving distance.

## THE GREATER ST LUCIA WETLAND PARK

From the **Mfolozi swamps** in the south, this park stretches northward to incorporate the **St Lucia Game and Marine Reserves, False Bay Park, Cape Vidal, Sodwana**

**Bay,** and **Mkuzi Game Reserve.** A vast area (260,000ha/104,000 acres) and one of the three most important **wetlands** in Africa, it encompasses five distinct ecosystems, including the Lebombo Mountains, the dry savanah and thornveld of the western shores, the mangrove forests, and vegetated sand dunes of the eastern shores, the Mkuze swamps (home to the rare Pel's fishing owl), and the great estuary and offshore coral reefs. For many the highlight is **Lake St Lucia.** A 38,882-hectare (15,552-acre) expanse of water dotted with islands, it supports an abundance of wildlife, including Nile crocodile, hippo, rhino, elephant, buffalo, giraffe, and various antelope; as well as numerous waterbirds, including pelican, flamingoes, herons, fish eagles, kingfishers, geese, and storks. The lake is flanked on the west by typical bushveld terrain and on the east by the highest forested dunes in the world. These contain large deposits of titanium and zirconium, and conservationists waged a long-running war with mining consortia over their fate, a battle they recently won. (Unfortunately no one is likely to do battle with the hundreds of 4×4 drivers who barrel along the "protected" beaches, not least the KN NCS who earn a great deal of revenue from the permits they sell.)

The easiest way to explore the lake is to catch a ride on the KN NCS's 80-seater **Santa Lucia (☎ 035/590-1340**). Guided tours depart daily at 8:30am, 10:30am, and 2:30pm, and last up to 2 hours. The launch point is clearly marked off the R618 east, which leads to St Lucia Village, located at the mouth of the St Lucia Estuary. There's not much to see in the village, though the **St Lucia Information Centre (☎ 035/ 590-1247**), at the corner of Katonkel and McKenzie streets, is very helpful with regard to advising on accommodation or dining options, none of which are very exciting.

The town's top attraction is the informative **Crocodile Centre (☎ 035/590-1093,** McKenzie St.), open 7am to 5pm daily, feeding time Saturday at 3pm. Part of the KN NCS's conservation campaign (the ugly critters are in fact an essential part of the ecological cycle), the center has interesting displays and ponds with all the African species of crocodile—though you will certainly spot at least one of the estimated 2,000 Nile crocs that lurk in the lake if you take a cruise on the Santa Lucia. Swimming in the lake is obviously strictly prohibited (not to mention a bad idea).

The only other reason to be in St Lucia Village is to visit **Cape Vidal,** located in the St Lucia Wetlands National Park (though with numbers restricted to 100 day-visitor vehicles, and the journey from the village over a rough dirt road taking almost 2 hours, you should consider staying at the camp, see below). A **whale-watching tower** provides an excellent view of passing marine mammals (including 18-m/59-ft-long whale sharks), while the offshore reef makes the sea safe for swimming and ideal for snorkeling. If you think this sounds like an unspoiled paradise, be warned: The beach is part of the 4×4 "highway" stretching from St Lucia to Sodwana Bay. For totally untouched beaches, you have to travel even farther, north of Mabibi.

The **western shore** of Lake St Lucia offers a few rudimentary camps used primarily by local fishermen and bird watchers, but keen birders should head north for **Mkuzi Game Reserve** (open April to September 6am to 6pm, October to March 5am to 7pm; R25/$4.15 per vehicle, R6/$1 per person), which is connected to the coastal plain via the Mkuzi River. Reached via the N2 (take the Mkuze Village turnoff; the Emshopi Gate entrance is 28km/17 miles farther), this reserve has 430 species of bird on record, which is indicative of the varied vegetation and landscape. Maps are issued at the reception office; make sure you don't miss the two bird hides at **Nsumo Pan,** where you can picnic and watch the changing spectacle on the waterway. This is also the start of the 3-kilometer (2-mile) circular **Mkuzi Fig Forest Trail,** one of the area's rarest and most attractive woodlands.

Last, but certainly not least, of the Greater St Lucia Wetland Park attractions is **Sodwana Bay,** South Africa's diving mecca (see "Staying Active," above). Here, the warm Agulhus current is responsible for some 1,200 varieties of fish, second in number only to the Great Barrier Reef. This is the best place in the country to become a qualified diver; but if you just want to snorkel, head for Jesser Point.

During December and January, when the loggerhead and leatherback turtles nest on the beach, the KN NCS conducts guided turtle tours (bookings at the park reception), though visitors should note that this is also the busiest time of the year in terms of human activity, and can be quite unpleasant for anyone seeking solitude.

## WHERE TO STAY & DINE

The only dining options are in St Lucia Village, but don't expect miracles—you're a long way from civilization. **Mujadjis (☎ 035/590-1093,** 9 McKenzie St.) is considered the best restaurant in town, but the predominantly seafood menu is uninspiring. **Quarterdeck (☎ 035/590-1116)**, also on McKenzie Street, is also known for its seafood and popular with a young crowd. If you're cooking, buy fresh fish from the **Fishing Den** next door; they also sell tackle and bait should you opt to catch it yourself.

There are a few B&B and hotel options in St Lucia Village, but the village itself holds few attractions; the self-catering units offered by the Natal Parks Board, while rudimentary, are at least within reserves and parks. Of these, **Cape Vidal** on the coast and **Mantuma Rest Camp** in Mkuzi Game Reserve are the best. Camp Vidal's options consist of a campsite and 29 5- and 8-bedded fully equipped log cabins in the dune forest near the beach. There is a shop, but you're better off stopping for provisions in St Lucia Village. Mantuma is the main public rest camp in Mkuzi, and offers a number of options—ask for the 3-bed, en-suite safari tents. There is a shop at reception, but again, it's best to stock up at Mkuze Village.

Divers wishing to explore the coral reefs in St Lucia Marine Reserve should try the 5-bed log cabins in **Sodwana Bay Park,** which is the closest you can get to the bay itself. Provisions should be bought in town, 8 kilometers (5 miles) west of the camp. Except for campsites, all queries and bookings must be made through **KN NCS** head office: Reservations, P.O. Box 1750, Pietermaritzburg 3200. **☎ 0331/845-1000.** Fax 0331/845-1003. E-mail: smathap@kznncs.org.za. For **camping,** contact **Cape Vidal Officer in Charge,** Private Bag X01, St Lucia Estuary 3936. **☎ 035/590-1404;** or **Mkuzi Camp Superintendent,** P.O. Box X550, Mkuze Village 3965. **☎ 035/673-1001.** However, if you've no budgetary constraints, indulge in the pure luxury of Phinda.

**Phinda Private Game Reserve.** Private Bag X27, Benmore 2010. **☎ 011/784-7077.** Fax 011/784-7667. E-mail: reservations@conscorp.co.za. Rock and Vlei, 6 units each; Forest 16 units; Mountain 20 units. A/C MINIBAR TEL. Rock and Vlei year-round R6,000 ($1,000). Forest and Mountain high-season R2,580 ($430); low-season (Apr 19–July 31) R1,680 ($280). Rates include all meals and activities within the reserve. AE, DC, MC, V.

Adjoining Mkuzi Game Reserve in the south, the 17,000-hectare (6,800-acre) Phinda Resource Reserve covers seven ecosystems, including sand forests, mountains, wetlands, and river valleys, and is home to the Big 5. Wildlife numbers are not as abundant as in Mpumalanga, but visitors are here for the exceptional range of experiences available (referred to as Phinda Adventures) and/or to experience the stylish accommodation options. Each of the four camps, which operate separately, from each other, is a member of Small Luxury Hotels of the World. When Conservation Corporation (CC) launched **Forest Camp** in 1993, the Zen-like glass boxes—each privately located within a torchwood tree forest—were lauded as the most stylish bedrooms in Africa. However, some might find the forest a bit gloomy, and the units are starting to show signs of wear. A better (though more expensive) alternative is **Vlei** (pronounced *flay*), six glass-fronted timber dwellings on stilts located a discreet distance from each other, each with a private plunge pool overlooking marsh- and woodland. Equally exclusive, **Rock Camp** consists of six adobe-like chalets, built into the mountainside, also with private plunge pools, and overlooking a watering hole. **Mountain** is the oldest and least modern of the four camps, but is the most family friendly, and has excellent views of the distant Lebombo Mountains and surrounding plains.

**Dining:** Meals are standard Conservation Corporation fare—large buffets feature a large selection of salads and cold meats, with gestures to pan-African spices, while dinners are usually grilled over an open fire.

**Amenities:** Besides game drives and guided bushwalks, there are diving expeditions to the coral reefs at nearby Mbibi and Sodwana, flights over the surrounding Maputaland wilderness (including to Lake Sibaya, the largest freshwater lake in Africa), deep-sea fishing, black rhino trailing in Mkuzi, and canoeing and cruising the Mzinene River. Airport transfers from Richard's Bay are also offered.

## MAPUTALAND RESERVE & KOSI BAY

Home of the Tonga and Mabudu peoples, the northeastern corner of KwaZulu-Natal is the most remote part of the province, with large tracts accessible only by 4×4. Combined with the total ban on vehicles on the beach and outboard motors at sea, this inaccessibility has protected it from development, and the coastline is absolutely pristine. However, poor infrastructure, uncomfortable distances, and the high malarial risk mean that a minimum stay of 3 days is needed to really validate the effort it takes to get here, though there's plenty to do—sunbathing, snorkeling, fishing, bird watching (there's an excellent chance of spotting the rare palmnut vulture), canoeing the lakes, and sampling the local ilala palm wine.

South Africa's largest freshwater lake, Lake Sibaya lies only 10 kilometers (6 miles) north of Sodwana; but if you're headed for Rocktail or Kosi Bay, this is a major detour by road, and there's nothing much to do here. To get to **Kosi Reserve** (R15/$2.50 vehicle, R7 ($1.15) per person), take the road to Jozini (east of the N2, and possibly the last place to refuel), then head north at the fork signposted KOSI, KWANGWANASE, NDUMO.

The road to Kwanwanase (103km/64 miles) is badly potholed, but can be driven in a 2×4.

Kosi is about 15 kilometers (9 miles) northeast of Kwangwanase via dirt road. You will, however, need a 4×4 (and guide) to get to the mouth (some 5km/3 miles from the camp), where one of the most impressive views in the country overlooks Kosi Bay (in reality an estuary), laced with intricate Tonga fish traps and unchanged for centuries. Turning back you can see each of Kosi's four lakes, linked by narrow channels, extend inland for some 20 kilometers (12 miles). **Lake Amanzamnyama** ("dark waters") is the most southerly lake, fringed by large subtropical swamp and raffia palm forests, and accessible only by canoe or guided hike. (Ask the KN NCS about the 4-day guided **Amanzamnyama Trail,** which takes in all four lakes, coastal dunes, raffia

### Turtle Tracking

The best time to visit the Maputaland beaches is from October to February, when conservation officials take groups on nocturnal wanders along the beach to witness the myopic leatherback and loggerhead turtles struggle ashore to lay their eggs.

Current theory suggests that the female of the species, some of whom have swum as far as 3,500 kilometers (2,170 miles), recognizes the scent of the beach where she was born and heaves herself ashore to produce the next generation—a cycle believed to date back 600 centuries.

forests, coral reefs, and beaches.) There is a KN NCS campsite at Kosi Bay, with three chalets, but as it has no organized cruises or even canoes for hire, and inaccessible roads, you're better off booking into one of the few resorts in the area and using their facilities and guided expeditions.

### WHERE TO STAY & DINE

Note that if you wish to stay at one of the places below, that you will drive to a meeting spot in your 2×4 where a 4×4 vehicle will pick you up. There are no restaurants in this area.

**Kosi Forest Camp.** Reservations through P.O. Box 275, Umhlali 4390. ☎/fax **0322/947-0538.** 8 units. R1,392 ($232), including all meals and excursions. Drops 20–30% in winter, call ahead. AE, DC, M, V. Pick-up point for 2×4 vehicles is 9km (5½ miles) south of Kwangwanase.

This camp is well positioned for forays on the southernmost lake, and activities organized by your hosts, a young couple in their 20s, include guided canoeing, bird watching, fly fishing, forest walks, palm-wine tasting, turtle tracking, and reef snorkeling. Public spaces look unfinished and unlived in (clearly everyone spends their days outside), but safari-style bedrooms—discreetly placed along a sandy walkway that winds away from the main lodge for maximum privacy—are quaint in a rustic sort of way. The outdoor bathrooms with bathtubs sunk into the sand, trees for towel racks, and stars peppering the "ceiling" are fantastic. Meals are casual affairs, shared around a communal table, and may include baked *bringal* (eggplant), feta and tomato as an appetizer, local fish or chicken in phyllo baskets for a main course, followed by brandy snaps with lavender cream. They will cater to any requirements given prior notice.

✪ **Rocktail Bay.** Reservations through Wilderness Safaris, P.O. Box 78573, Sandton 2146. ☎ **011/883-0747.** Fax 011/883-0911. E-mail: info@sdn.wilderness.co.za. 10 units. R1,750 ($291.65), includes all meals and activities. Children under 12 sharing R437 ($72.85). AE, MC, DC, V. Collection point is at the Forest Reserve Gate; you will be given a map.

This is a castaway fantasy come true: 10 thatched en-suite chalets (small but adequate, and simply decorated) raised on stilts into the forest canopy, each with its own wooden deck and within close walking distance of the beach. There are no telephones, TVs, or radios to disturb, and—with the exception of guests—no one to bump into on the 60-kilometer (37-mile) shoreline. There is a charming lounge/pub area (decorated with shells) with small plunge pool, and a dining area where all meals are served around a communal table. Meals are simple, but well cooked. Lunches are light and feature salads and quiches, while dinners are a sit-down three-course affair with limited choice (anything from roast lamb to pan-fried fish). With advance notice, any dietary needs will be taken into consideration. A boardwalk winds from the lodge through the dune forest to the beach and ocean, which appear totally deserted.

Armed with flippers and snorkel (supplied by the lodge), you discover a startling world of color beneath the surface, with numerous tropical fish to identify when back in camp. Nature walks, drives in 4×4 vehicles, and picnics to Black Rock (another excellent snorkeling spot) are arranged, and, in summer, there are sea turtle expeditions. A highly recommended experience for stressed city dwellers.

## 4 The Battlefields

Ladysmith: 251km (155½ miles) northwest of Durban; Dundee: 320km (198 miles) north of Durban

Most of the battles fought on South African soil took place in the northwestern corner of KwaZulu-Natal, where rolling grasslands were regularly soaked with blood as battles for territorial supremacy would in turn pit Zulu against Boer, Brit against Zulu, and Afrikaner against Brit. The official Battlefields Route covers four wars, over 50 battlefields, and 14 towns, and includes numerous museums and memorials to the dead and victorious; but few would argue that the heroic Anglo-Zulu battles that took place on January 22, 1879 at Isandlwana and Rorke's Drift—immortalized in the movie *Zulu,* starring Michael Caine—are the most compelling, and best for those with limited time.

Another site worth investigating is that of the Battle of Blood River, which took place 41 years earlier, this time between the Trekkers and Zulus. This victory was to validate Afrikaner arrogance and religious self-righteousness. Given time, visitors should also visit Ladysmith to immerse themselves in the siege which jump-started the Second Anglo-Boer War—it would take the world's mightiest nation three years and thousands of pounds to defeat one of the world's smallest, and embroil some of the century's giants, like Winston Churchill and Ghandi.

This is one area where a guide is almost essential, and top of the line is David Rattray (see below), with an award-winning performance that regularly reduces onlookers to tears. If, however, you are eager to tackle a self-guided tour, but are unfamiliar with the historical background of the wars, a brief chronological account is supplied below.

## ESSENTIALS

**VISITOR INFORMATION** The central **Battlefields Bureau** (☎ **036/637-2992** or route@battlefields.org.za) is in Ladysmith at 46 Murchiston St. and is open Monday to Friday 8am to 4pm, Saturday 8am to 12pm. If you're not venturing this far south, contact the **Dundee Publicity Association** (☎ **0341/22-121**) on Victoria Street, Dundee (open Monday to Friday 9am to 4:45pm and Saturday 9am to 12pm), for any additional information you may need.

**GETTING THERE** **By Car** Ladysmith is 251 kilometers (155½ miles) northwest of Durban on the N11 (off the N3). Dundee is 320 kilometers (198 miles) north of Durban, and is reached via the R33.

**By Bus** **Greyhound** and **Translux** (see chapter 2, "Planning Your Trip to Southern Africa," for phone numbers) both travel through Ladysmith daily.

**SPECIAL EVENTS** 1999 marked the centenary commemoration of the Second Anglo-Boer war (also called the "South African War"), with various events taking place during the course of the year and continuing into the next century. For details, contact ☎ **036/637-8230.**

## VISITING THE BATTLEFIELDS BY GUIDED TOUR

There is an excellent **Battlefields Guide** which covers all the sites and battles in detail, with an accompanying map, available from the above publicity associations and many of the museums; however, exploring with a guide is definitely recommended. The best, **David Rattray,** is based at his lodge at **Fugitives' Drift** (☎/fax **034/642-1834,** see also "Where to Stay"). A consummate storyteller, his tours may err on the historical side, but his detailed research on the individuals who fought on both sides of the Anglo-Zulu war humanizes the battles, and even those who hate history are enthralled. Space allowing, non-residents may join his tours at a cost of R295 ($49.15)—to avoid disappointment, make sure he's available, and bear in mind that he does have some competent guides working for him. Alternatively, purchase his taped tales; the series *The Day of the Dead Moon* is highly recommended, particularly if combined with site visits. The audiocassettes are available direct from Fugitives' Drift or from the Talana Museum (see below).

## A Brief History of the Battlefields

The first major battle in this area took place some 48 kilometers (30 miles) east of Dundee, at what came to be known as **Blood River.** Following the treacherous murder of Retief and his men (see "The Rise & Fall of the amaZulu," above), and Dingaan's ruthless persecution of white settlers, Trekker leader Andries Pretorius moved a Boer commando of 464 men to a strategic spot on the banks of the ironically named Ncome ("peace") River, where he created an impenetrable *laager* (a circular encampment of wagons, with oxen in the center) with 64 ox-wagons, and prayed for victory. On behalf of the Boer nation, Pretorius made a solemn vow to God that should they survive, Afrikaners would hold the day sacred in perpetuity. On December 16, 1838, the Zulus attacked. Three times they were driven off by fire before Pretorius led a mounted charge. Eventually, the Zulus fled, leaving 3,000 dead, and the river dark with blood. Not one Boer died, giving rise to the nationalistic Afrikaner myth that their Old Testament God had protected them against invincible odds to prove to them that they were His chosen race. Today December 16 remains a national holiday (though renamed Day of Reconciliation), and visitors can view the eerie spectacle of a replica laager, 64 life-size ox-wagons cast in bronze, at the original site of **Blood River Battlefield.** The site is off the R33, and is open daily 8am to 5pm.

Zulu might rose again under Cetshwayo. This did not fit in with British imperialist plans and, having delivered a totally unreasonable ultimatum, three British columns under an over-confident Chelmsford marched into Zululand in January 1879. On January 21, Chelmsford set up temporary camp at **Isandlwana Hill** and, believing that the Zulu army was elsewhere, took a large detachment to support a reconnaissance force, leaving the camp defenseless. Six kilometers (4 miles) away, 24,000 Zulu soldiers sat in silence. At about 11:30am the following day, a British patrol stumbled on them and watched in panic as the Zulu warriors surrounded them, chanting their famed rallying cry, "Usutu" (oo-*soo*-too).

Other guides worth mentioning are "Zulu-phile" **Steven Kotze,** who majored in Zulu War Studies (see Isibindi under "Where to Stay," below); **Pat Rundgren** (☎ **0341/24-560**), an avid researcher and collector based in Dundee; **Maureen Richards** (☎ **036/631-1233**), an expert on the Anglo-Boer War; and **Fred Duke** (☎ **0381/80-7835**), who specializes in the Zulu battlefields in the Vryheid area (this includes the Battle of Blood River). Natural scientist **John Turner** (☎ **0358/35-0062**) combines battlefield tours with trips to Hluhluwe-Umfolozi.

## THE TOP ATTRACTIONS

**Talana Museum.** Off R33, 1½ km (1 mile) from Dundee on the way to Vryheid. ☎ **0341/22-654.** Mon–Fri 8am–4:30pm; Sat 10am–4:30pm; Sun 12–4:30pm. Admission R8 ($1.35), children R1 (15¢).

The various buildings, which comprise this museum are set in a 50-hectare (20-acre) park. The subject matter is extensive, and features the social, economic, agricultural, and industrial history of the area—the latter has some relevance as Dundee was defended by the British mainly because of its industrial wealth—but for most the displays in **Talana House,** which cover the rise of the Zulu, Boer, and Zulu conflicts, as well as the two Boer wars, are the only exhibits worth inspecting. It is a pleasant place

Two hours later, 1,329 of the 1,700 British soldiers were dead. Survivors fled across **Fugitives' Drift,** where more died, but two men made it to the nearby mission station called **Rorke's Drift,** where a contingent of 139 men, of which 35 were seriously ill, were waiting with provisions for Chelmsford's return. With seconds to spare, the men barricaded themselves behind a makeshift wall of army biscuit boxes, tinned meat, and bags of maize meal, and warded off the 4,000-strong Zulu onslaught. The battle raged until dawn, when the Zulus finally withdrew. Only 17 British soldiers died at Rorke's Drift, and 11 Victoria Crosses were awarded—more than at any other battle in British history. Six months later, on July 4, 1879, the Zulus suffered their final defeat at Ondini.

A year later the British would begin a new brawl, this time with the Boers, and though a peace treaty was signed in March 1881, it sowed the seeds for the Second Anglo-Boer War, a 3-year battle that captured the world's attention and introduced guerrilla warfare. On October 20, 1899, the first battle was pitched on **Talana Hill,** when 14,000 Boers attacked 4,000 British troops. The Brits managed to repel the attackers, and on November 2, the little town of **Ladysmith** was besieged by the Boers for 118 days. Thousands died of disease, trapped without access to clean water, while many more fell as the British tried to break through Boer defenses. (Winston Churchill, covering the war for the *London Morning Post,* narrowly escaped death when the train he was traveling on was blown up by Boers some 40km [25 miles] south of Ladysmith.)

The most ignominious battle during this time took place on **Spioenkop** (literally "spy's hill") when Boers and Brits battled for this strategic position until both sides believed they had lost. The British were the first to withdraw, leaving the astonished but triumphant Boer in force on this strategic hill (off the R600). Two years later, after the ruthless scorched-earth policy of the British, the Boers acceded defeat.

to start your battlefield tours, and the Miner's Rest Restaurant, located in one of the small cottages on the grounds, is a good place to stop for tea and lunch.

**Rorke's Drift.** Off the R68, 42km (26 miles) from Dundee on the road to Nqutu. ☎ **0346/42-1687.** 8am–5pm daily. Admission R6 ($1), children R3 (50¢).

Located in the reconstructed hospital (where the 100 men holed up for 12 hours, and successfully warded off 4,000 Zulus led by Cetshwayo's brother, Dabulamanzi), this is the most evocative interpretation center on the route. Realistic scenes are augmented by battle sounds and electronic diagrams depicting the sequence of events. An added bonus is the adjoining **ELC Craft Centre** (☎ **0346/42-1627**), where you can browse for textiles, carpets, tapestries, and pottery. Many of the tapestries on display at the excellent Vukani Collection Museum (see above) originated here.

**Isandlwana Battlefield.** Off the R68 between Nqutu and Babanango. No tel. 8am–5pm daily. Admission R6 ($1), children R3 (50¢).

Not much marks the battle of the Isandlwana, but it's worth trying to imagine 20,000 Zulu men streaming forward to deliver the most crushing defeat the mighty British Empire was to suffer in Africa, all at the hands of "savages armed with sticks." Cairns mark the places where British soldiers fell and were buried. The British were horrified to find their men disemboweled—proof, they thought, of the savagery of the Zulu. In fact, the Zulus were honoring the men by setting their spirits free. There is an interpretation center, manned by curator Kenneth Buthelezi, whose forefathers took part in the battle.

**Ladysmith Siege Museum.** Murchison St. (the main road running through Ladysmith), next to the Town Hall. ☎ **036/637-2231.** Mon–Fri 8am–4pm; Sat 9am–1pm. R2 (35¢)adults, R1 (15¢) children.

If your interest is the battle between the Boers and the British, this is an essential stop. Displays and photographs vividly depict both the wars that so greatly affected 20th-century South Africa, and the appalling conditions at the end of the siege, when 28 to 30 people died daily. Purchase one of the museum's self-guided pamphlets, the *Siege Town Walkabout* or the *Siege Driveabout.*

Diagonally opposite is the **Royal Hotel** (☎ **036/637-2176**). This historic hotel, regularly shelled by the Boers as it harbored the most privileged of the Brits, is a great place to stop for lunch.

## WHERE TO STAY & DINE

There are no real restaurants in the area. Your best option in Dundee is the **Miner's Rest Restaurant** (see Talana Museum, above), which serves light lunches like chicken pie and salads. The **Royal Hotel** (see above), with a choice of three dining rooms serving Italian, continental, or a buffet, is your best bet in Ladysmith. Most guides will include picnic lunches on request. All meals are included in the lodges discussed below.

**Fugitives' Drift Lodge.** (8km/5 miles south of Rorke's Drift, off the D31) P.O. Rorke's Drift 3016, KwaZulu-Natal 3016. ☎/fax **034/642-1843.** R1,750 ($291.65) double, includes tour and meals. DC MC V. Children 7 and above.

Situated within a 1,000-hectare (400-acre) nature reserve with river frontage and a view of the Isandlwana hilltop and the graves of the soldiers that died here, David Rattray's lodge is right in the heart of battlefield history. Certainly this is one reason to find yourself at this Natural Heritage Site, Rattray himself is another. The large lounge/dining area, where the communal dinners are held, is like a small museum, crammed with battlefield memorabilia and books. The extensive, well-manicured lawns overlook the Buffalo River Valley where antelope, giraffe, wildebeest, and zebra can be spotted. Rooms are very spacious, but if you're looking for more stylish accommodation, or if David Rattray is on holiday, you're better off at neighboring Isibindi, which offers a far more reasonable rate.

**Isibindi Lodge.** 9km (5½ miles) south of Rorke's Drift. Reservations through P.O. Box 275, Umhlali 4390. ☎/fax **0322/947-0538.** Direct ☎ 034/642-1620. R1,300 ($216.65) double, includes meals and game drives. R810 ($135) in winter. AE, MC, V.

The rooms at Isibindi take a traditional Zulu beehive hut as their departure point, and must rate as the most successful blend of western and African architecture in Zululand. Each spacious hut, tastefully furnished with all the creature comforts, has French

### Ghandi's War

Ghandi enrolled with the British Army as a stretcher bearer during the second Anglo-Boer War, and encouraged other Indians to do the same. He naively hoped that by serving the British loyally in their time of need, they would in turn grant India's independence.

doors opening onto a small balcony, which is stilted over a precipice, affording wonderful views of the Buffalo River Valley. Guests have a choice of activities: a Zulu cultural experience (R98/$16.35), including a visit to a homestead to watch Zulu dancers and sample a traditional meal; tracking wildlife in an open vehicle; river rafting down the Buffalo River; and battlefield tours, undertaken by Steve Kotze, the resident guide and Zulu War specialist (a full day costs R95/$15.85). Meals are exceptionally good, and may include citrus segments topped with herbs and olive oil, followed by warm apple and phyllo served in custard, roast venison with orange marmalade sauce, and a selection of homemade ice cream.

## 5 The Drakensberg Mountains

The Drakensberg extends from just north of Hoedspruit in Mpumalanga 1,000 kilometers (620 miles) south to the mountain kingdom of Lesotho, where a series of spectacular peaks some 240 kilometers (149 miles) long creates the western border of KwaZulu-Natal—it is this border that most refer to when they speak of the Drakensberg. Known as uKhahlamba (or "barrier of spears," to the Zulus), they were renamed "Dragon Mountains" by the Trekkers seeking to cross them. Both are apt descriptions of South Africa's premier mountain wilderness, the second largest range in Africa. The main range falls within the Natal Drakensberg Park, a semi-circle that forms the western boundary of the province. Of this, the northern and central sections are most spectacular, a hiker's paradise.

Other highlights are the many San rock paintings in what could be described as the largest open-air art gallery in the world; the chance to spot rare raptors; or simply the chance to take a breather in Champagne Valley or Cathedral Peak. As winter snowfalls and summer rainfalls can put a damper on hiking expeditions, the best times to explore the Berg, as locals call it, are spring and autumn.

### ESSENTIALS

**VISITOR INFORMATION** The **Drakensberg Publicity Association** (☎/fax **036/448-1557**) is based on Thatham Road in Bergville. Hours are Monday to Friday 9am to 4pm. If you're not traveling north, pop into the **Ietz Nietz Info and Coffee Shop** (☎ **036/488-1180**) on the Main Road in Winterton. As much of the Berg falls under the protection of the KN NCS, inquiries may also be directed to their head office (for details see Tendele in "Where to Stay," below).

**GETTING THERE** **By Car** Roads to the Berg all branch off west from the N3 between Maritzburg and Ladysmith. Take the N3 north out of Durban, then the R74 west to Winterton (for Cathedral Peak or Giant's Castle), or travel farther to Bergville for the turnoff to Royal Natal National Park, which lies some 45 kilometers (28 miles) away from the town.

**By Bus** Most hotels offer transfers from the **Greyhound** or **Translux** terminals in Estcourt and Ladysmith (see chapter 2, "Planning Your Trip to Southern Africa" for regional phone numbers). There is, however, no transport to any of the Natal Parks Board camps.

**By Plane** **Nac Helicopters** (☎ **031/563-8361**) will fly you direct from Durban at a cost of R8,500 ($1,416.65) for four people.

**GETTING AROUND** There are no connecting road systems, making long circuitous routes necessary to move from one part of the Berg to the next. It's best to base yourself in one area and explore your surrounds on foot.

# Drakensberg

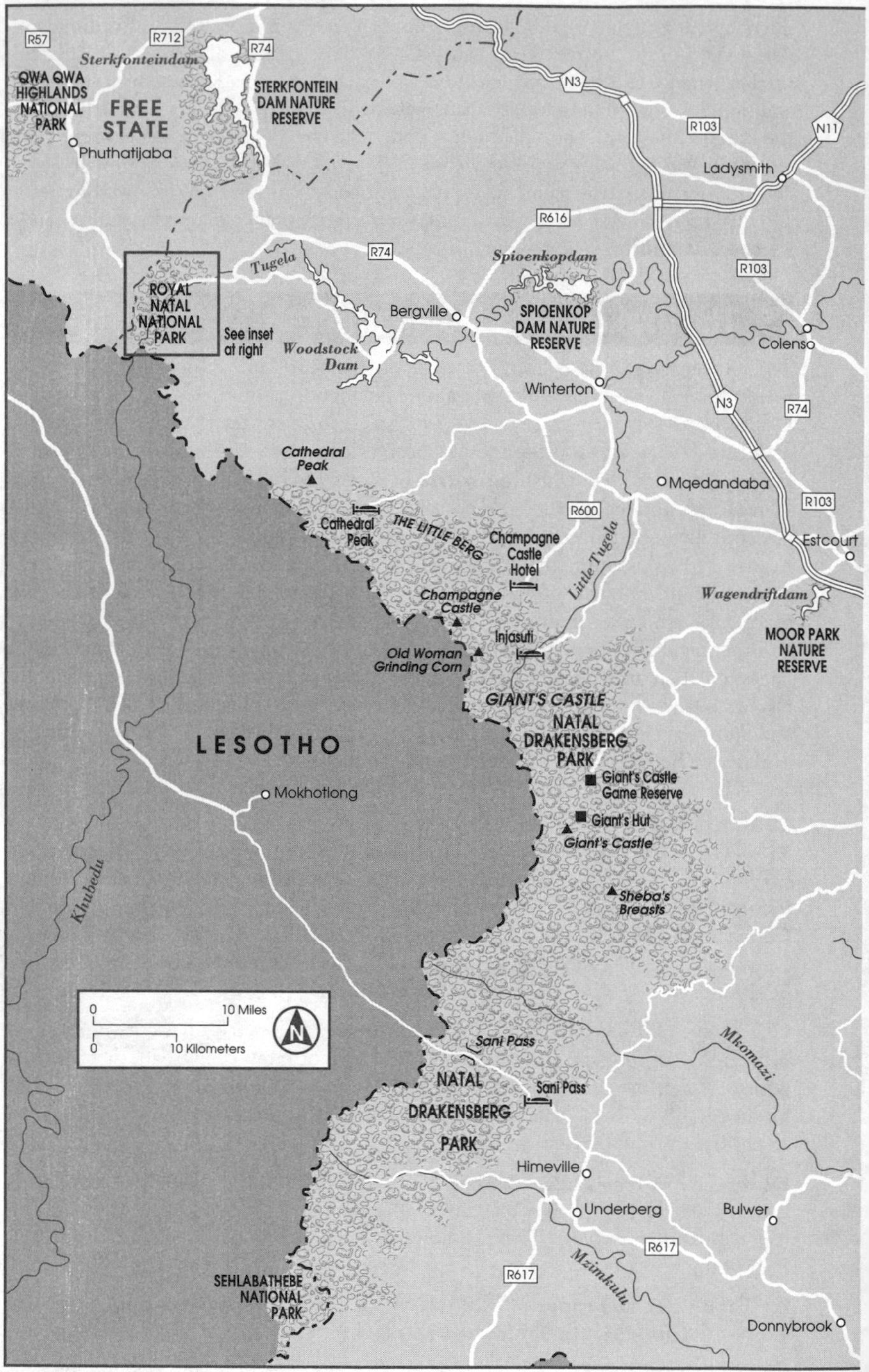

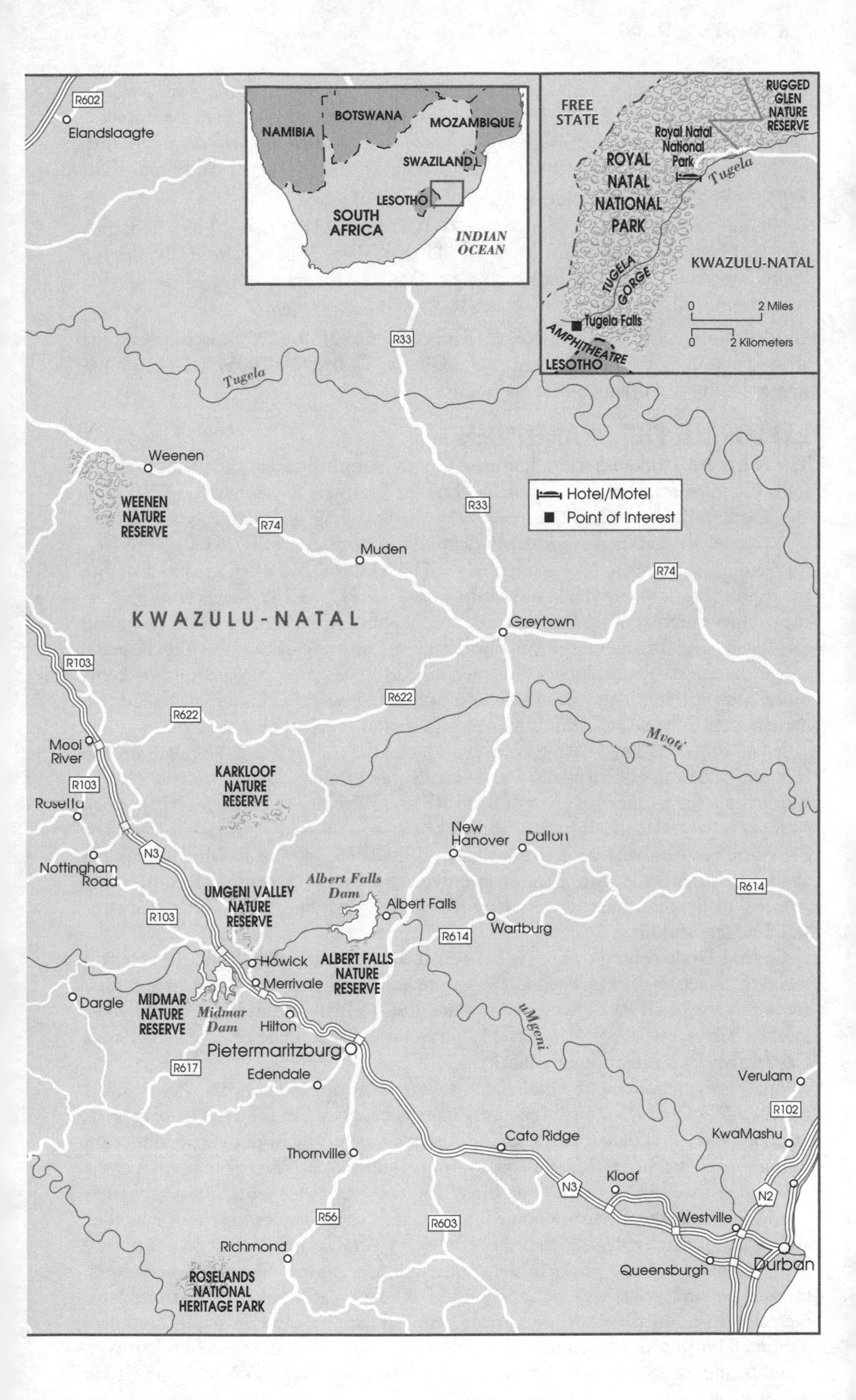

NAMIBIA
BOTSWANA
MOZAMBIQUE
SWAZILAND
LESOTHO
SOUTH AFRICA
INDIAN OCEAN
FREE STATE
RUGGED GLEN NATURE RESERVE
Royal Natal National Park
ROYAL NATAL NATIONAL PARK
Tugela
TUGELA GORGE
KWAZULU-NATAL
Tugela Falls
AMPHITHEATRE
LESOTHO
0 2 Miles
0 2 Kilometers
R602
Elandslaagte
R33
Tugela
Weenen
WEENEN NATURE RESERVE
R74
Hotel/Motel
Point of Interest
Muden
KWAZULU-NATAL
Greytown
R103
R622
Mvoti
Mooi River
KARKLOOF NATURE RESERVE
Rosetta
New Hanover
Dalton
N3
Nottingham Road
Albert Falls Dam
Albert Falls
R614
UMGENI VALLEY NATURE RESERVE
Wartburg
Howick
ALBERT FALLS NATURE RESERVE
Merrivale
Dargle
MIDMAR NATURE RESERVE
Midmar Dam
Hilton
uMgeni
Pietermaritzburg
R617
Edendale
Verulam
R102
Cato Ridge
KwaMashu
Thornville
Kloof
N2
R56
R603
Westville
Richmond
Queensburgh
Durban
ROSELANDS NATIONAL HERITAGE PARK

**On Foot** Walks range from a few hours to several days. Detailed maps are available at Parks Board camps, the departure point for all of the best hikes. The best book is David Bristow's *Drakensberg Walks: 120 Graded Hikes and Trails in the Berg* (Bhb Intl. Inc.), which is light enough to carry, and available from the Parks Board shops. (For more information see "Staying Active, Hiking," above.)

**By Plane** **Mount Aire** in Winterton (☎ **036/468-1141**) offers 20-minute flights over the mountains. **Nac Helicopters** (☎ **036/468-1088**) operates from Champagne Sports Resort, and has champagne sunset cocktails in the mountains. Guests staying at the Cathedral Peak Hotel have access to the hotel's helicopter.

**Guided Tours** **Midlander Trips & Tours** (☎ **0332/30-4293**) specializes in the areas surrounding the Drakensberg, while **Gibela** (☎ **031/29-7005**) has a combination of hiking and driving in the mountains.

## EXPLORING THE DRAKENSBERG

The **Northern Drakensberg** is dominated by the **Amphitheatre,** a dramatic crescent some 8 kilometers (5 miles) long, flanked by the Sentinel (3,165 meters/10,381 feet) and Eastern Buttress (3,047 meters/9,994 feet). Falling within the 8,000-hectare (3,200-acre) **Royal Natal National Park** (open 24 hours, daily; R7/$1.15 entry fee), it's the most awesome rock formation in the Drakensberg, and often used to promote the region. This is where you'll find **Mont-aux-Sources,** at 3,282 meters (10,765 feet) the country's highest peak, and source of five of South Africa's major rivers, including the Tugela. The **Tugela Gorge Walk** will take you past the base of the **Tugela Falls,** where the Tugela River plunges 948 meters (3,109 feet) from the plateau, its combined drop making it the second highest falls in the world. The 6-hour round-trip departs from Tendele and affords marvelous views of the Amphitheatre.

If you don't feel like walking, you can ascend the top by traveling north on the R74 and taking the Oliviershoek Pass, past the Sterkfontein Dam until you get to a T-junction where you turn left onto the R712, following the signs to Witsieshoek Mountain Resort. Just before the resort, take the road marked Sentinal Car Park, the departure point for the steep 2-hour hike to the summit of Mont-aux-Sources via chain ladder. Anyone with a reasonable degree of fitness can complete this, a fact attested to by the quantities of litter along the way. The views, litter notwithstanding, are stunning.

**Central Drakensberg** comprises four distinct areas: **Cathedral Peak** in the north; followed by relatively populated **Champagne Valley,** where most of the Berg resorts are based; the Natal Parks Board–controlled areas of **Injasuti** (an isolated wilderness ideal for hikers, and at 3,459 meters/11,345 feet, the Berg's highest peak); and **Giant's Castle,** famous for its rock paintings.

The easiest mountain to climb (a 9-hour round-trip) is Cathedral Peak (3,004 meters/9,853 feet), which, conveniently, has the best hotel in the Drakensberg at its feet. However, it is **Giant's Castle Game Reserve** (open daily April to September 6am to 6pm, and October to March 5am to 7pm; admission R7/$1.15) that attracts the most committed hikers. Each of the three KN NCS camps (Injasuti, Hillside, Giant's Castle) serves as the departure point for numerous trails, serviced by overnight huts and caves. Initially established to protect the eland, Africa's largest antelope, the reserve is today one of the best places in the country to spot **raptors** like the Cape vulture, black eagle, and jackal buzzard, and one of the few places you'll see the rare lammergeier or "bearded vulture" (occurring only here and in the Himalayan foothills). Visitors keen to spot the lammergeier—thought to be an evolutionary link between vultures and eagle—should visit the ✪ **Lammergeier Hide** (☎ **036/353-3616;**

R75/$12.50 per person; reservations made as much as a year in advance are essential), where carcasses are laid out every Saturday and Sunday from May to September.

Giant's Castle is also where you'll find the most easily accessed **San rock paintings.** There are over 500 in the **Main Caves,** a 2-kilometer (1-mile) walk from the KN NCS rest camp, where a guide controls visitor numbers (entry daily on the hour, from 9am to 3pm; fee R7/$1.15 per person).

The other main cultural attractions of the Berg are found in Champagne Valley, along the 32-kilometer (20-mile) tarred drive (R600) from Winterton. First up is award-winning **Ardmore Studio** (take the D275 off R600; ☎ **036/468-1314;** open daily 9am–4:30pm), where zany ceramic sculptures and crockery are created by a collective of some 40 Zulu and Sotho artists, under the auspices of Fée Berning and Bonnie Ntshlintshali. The studio itself is rather unimpressive, but the work—displayed in galleries around the world—is well worth taking a look at. A little farther along the R600, you'll see a signpost for the **Drakensberg Boys' Choir School** (☎ **036/468-1012**), one of the world's most famous. You can hear their heavenly voices on Wednesdays (and some Saturdays) in the school auditorium, though be warned: The material, which includes some rehashed love ballads and folk songs, is a little kitschy for most. Visit them from 3:30 to 6pm, for a fee of R50 ($8.35) per person.

If you have time to venture into the **Southern Drakensberg,** don't miss the **Sani Pass.** The highest pass in South Africa, this is a hair-raising route leading to the independent state of Lesotho, known as "the roof of Africa," accessible only in a 4×4. **Sani Pass Carriers** (☎ **033/701-1017**) operates bus services from Maritzburg and Durban to hotels in the Sani Pass area, and organize trips up the pass into Lesotho for horse riding and walking trips. (Americans, Canadians, Europeans, Australians, and New Zealanders need only a passport to enter Lesotho.)

## WHERE TO STAY & DINE

Hikers wanting to overnight in the mountains must book their huts and caves through the KN NCS office closest to the trail; below are the best bases for walking—hikes start literally from your front door. Visitors on their way to the Northern Berg can stop for a meal at the **Leaning Tower of Pizza** (☎ **036/438-6480**), which is off the Northern Berg Road (and clearly visible). If you're on your way to the Central Berg, you'll find the best places for lunch off the R600. The **Thokozisa Mountain Café** (13km/8 miles from Winterton; ☎ **036/488-1273**) serves light meals made with organic produce; a little farther is **The Nest** (☎ **036/468-1068**), where filling meals (roasts, cottage pie) are served in a rather fusty atmosphere. Should you wish to overnight in Champagne Valley, the old-fashioned **Champagne Castle Hotel** (☎ **036/468-1063,** fax 036/468-1306; also off the R600) is closest to the mountains and enjoys the best views, though it's nowhere as remote or charming as Cathedral Peak, and has silly rules like shirt and tie for dinner. Note that there is a small entry fee (R7/$1.15) into all the parks.

✪ **Cathedral Peak.** P.O. Winterton KwaZulu-Natal 3340. ☎/fax **036/488-1888.** E-mail: cph@ls.lia.net. www.cathedralpeak.co.za. 90 units. TV TEL. R510–900 ($85–$150), includes dinner and breakfast. Children under 10 sharing R25 ($4.15). AE, DC, MC, V. From Northern Berg travel 44km (27 miles) southwest from Bergville; from Durban travel to Winterton; the hotel lies 40km (25 miles) west of here; all routes clearly signposted Winterton.

This is without a doubt the best option in the Drakensberg. The only hotel situated in its own valley, at the base of the mountains within the Natal Parks' protected area, it offers great views, comfortable rooms, a super-friendly staff, and a relaxed atmosphere. Even getting here is a good experience, with a road that provides charming vignettes of rural bliss. Book a luxury room; they cost very little more, and are the most modern, with French doors opening onto the gardens, and some with excellent views of the mountains. The varied facilities also make this one of the best family resorts in the country—besides hiking, activities include playing the 9-hole golf course, swimming, bowling, playing tennis, squash, or volleyball, horseback riding, and taking helicopter sightseeing trips (offered daily). Trails start from the hotel (which has a model of the area for quick identification), and maps are provided. The 11-kilometer (7-mile) Rainbow Gorge round-trip is recommended. Meals are huge buffets with a large variety of dishes. Some are exceptionally tasty; others suffer from standing around. But there is at least something for everyone, including finicky kids.

**Giant's Castle. ☎ 036/353-3718.** Bookings through KN NCS Reservations (same details as Tendele, below). 20 units, consisting of bungalows, cottages, and huts. From R230–780 ($38.35–$130) double.

This camp is very popular due to its proximity to Main Caves and the Lammergeier Hide. Self-contained bungalows are equipped with cutlery, crockery, and bedding, but no kitchens—once again there is the strange Natal Parks Board phenomenon whereby you hand your provisions over to the camp chef, tell him what you'd like him to do, then wait to sample his cooking prowess. It's a schlep to leave your bungalow to cook in the communal kitchen; try the braai outside your door instead. Giant's Castle also has a shop with basic provisions, but visitors should definitely stock up before arriving. This is also a filling station, the only one in the reserve.

**Injasuti. ☎ 036/488-1050.** Reservations through KN NCS (same details as Tendele, below). 19 units, consisting of 6- and 8-bed units. From R130 ($21.65) double. Campsites R20 ($3.35) per person. 50km (31 miles) from Winterton and Estcourt via the R615.

Situated in the northern part of Giant's Castle, and the only dwellings at the end of a dirt track, this is a true wilderness camp, and, with 10 different day hikes, a hikers' haven. Bungalows are very simply furnished and strung in a straight line, fronted by a stream that's great for paddling, should you consider bringing the family. The most interesting rock paintings are at Battle Cave, where a series of paintings depict what appears to be armed conflict between San groups. Current thinking is that it represents a battle taking place in the spirit world, as the San were not known to be territorial. To view the paintings, you will need to be accompanied by a guide—book for this or one of the overnight caves at reception on your arrival. There is a basic shop at Injasuti, but provisions should be purchased at Winterton or Estcourt. Like most Parks Board camps, cutlery, crockery, cooking utensils, and bedding are supplied.

**✪ Tendele Hutted Camp. ☎ 036/438-6411.** Reservations through KN NCS, P.O. Box 1750, Pietermaritzburg 3200. **☎ 0331/845-1000.** Fax 0331/845-1003. E-mail: smathap@kznncs. org.za. 29 units, consisting of 2- and 4-bed bungalows, 2- and 4-bed chalets, and 6-bed cottages. From R280–780 ($46.65–$130) double (or more). No campsites.

Situated deep within the Royal Natal National Park, with awesome views of the Amphitheatre, this is by far the best KN NCS camp. It is, however, no well-kept secret, so book early. The cheapest units have kettles, toasters, fridges, and cutlery, with chefs on hand to cook ingredients supplied by you in communal kitchens. A shop at the Royal Natal National Park Hotel is stocked with basic provisions (frozen trout, wood, tinned food, milk, and bread), but for fresh supplies stock up in Bergville. The closest restaurant is at the Royal Natal National Park Hotel, which serves old-fashioned food (meat and two veg, all well cooked).

# Victoria Falls & Vicinity

9

*by Tracey Hawthorne*
*with Pippa de Bruyn*

Straddling the western border between Zimbabwe and Zambia, at the point where the Zambezi River drops into the Batoka Gorge, Victoria Falls is justifiably called one of the Wonders of the Natural World. Famously described in 1855 by explorer David Livingstone as being of such magnificence that they must have been "gazed upon by angels in their flight," and named by him for his Queen, Victoria, the falls are the world's largest, spanning almost 2 kilometers (just more than a mile) and dropping some 100 meters (328 ft.) (twice the height of Niagara). The sight of over 500 million liters of water per minute crashing downward at 160 kilometers per hour (99mph) is not one easily forgotten and, on a clear day, the veil of roaring spray can be seen from up to 80 kilometers (50 miles) away. The rain forest, on the cliff opposite the falls, is nourished by this spray that gave the falls their local name: Mosi-Oa-Tunya or "the smoke that thunders." (Actually, it's Leya-Tonga, for "the water that rises in the air," but a little romanticism never hurt anyone.) The forest, which is protected by the Victoria Falls National Park, is one of the few places in this area in which you will find no walls or concrete pathways, no gift stalls or refreshment kiosks, no advertising boards or other commercial distractions.

Vic Falls, as it's most commonly called, is also the overland crossroads of southern Africa. People come not only for the spectacle of the falls and to immerse themselves in the surrounding national parks, but also to partake in some of the many activities available—not for nothing has this area been dubbed the adventure-sport center of southern Africa.

But if you want to slow down and take life easy for a few days, Vic Falls is a great place to do that as well. As you relax on a front verandah or in the gardens of one of the many local hotels, you can watch elephants ambling down to drink at the river, monkeys gamboling across the grass, hippos snorting, and crocodiles patrolling the waterways of the great Zambezi.

## 1 Orientation

### VISITOR INFORMATION

You'll find the **Victoria Falls Publicity Association** at 412 Park Way (☎ **263/13/4202;** Fax 263/13/3362). Their hours are Monday to Friday 8am to 5pm, and Saturday 8am to 1pm. However, they're not really that helpful, and you'll be better off going to the **Backpacker's Bazaar,** across the road at Shop 5, Victoria Falls Centre, ☎/fax **263/13/2189, ZAIBMGLL@ibnmail.com**. This independent service will direct you to the best tours and activities available.

# GETTING THERE

## BY PLANE

See "Getting There" in chapter 2, "Planning Your Trip to Southern Africa," for details on flying to Zimbabwe. **Victoria Falls Airport** (☎ **263/13/4250**) is about 20 kilometers (12 miles) south of the town. Most hotels offer a complimentary shuttle service, but there is also an **Air Zimbabwe bus** that meets incoming SAA and Air Zimbabwe flights and charges about Z$30 (80¢) to take you into town. (A taxi will sting you for Z$120/$3.15 for the same trip.)

The main gateway airport is **Harare International Airport** (☎ **263/14/575-528**) in the capitol, Harare. It's 12 kilometers (7 miles) from the airport to the city; bus service takes approximately 20 minutes, taxi service about 15.

## BY TRAIN

The **Blue Train** (P.O. Box 2671, Joubert Park 2044, South Africa; ☎ **27/11/773-7631;** fax 27/11/773-7643; bluetrain@transnet.co.za. www.bluetrain.co.za) is the last word in getting from A to B in serious style. The "Zimbabwe Spectacular" takes the well-heeled on an unforgettable journey between Pretoria and Zimbabwe, via Johannesburg, Gaborone, Botswana, and Bulawayo, Zimbabwe, ending at the Victoria Falls Station. Your fare covers all meals, beverages, and room-service snacks. From January 1 to April 30 and September 1 to December 31 the one way fare is R10,700 ($1,783) double. The rest of the year the price is R7,490 ($1,248). The train runs once every two months, leaving Pretoria on Thursday at 8:50am and arriving in Victoria Falls on Saturday at 9am. Passengers must hold valid passports and visas; documents are inspected on the train.

**Spoornet (Transnet)** (☎ **27/12/315-2401**) in South Africa charges R250 ($41.65) per person (first class), R175 ($29.15) second class, R105 ($17.50) economy class, one-way, not including meals. Children under four accompanied by an adult travel free; children between five and 11 years old pay half price. Breakfast is R18 ($3) per person, bedding R20 ($3.35) per person. Passengers must hold valid passports and visas; customs and immigration officials inspect travel documents at the border post. Service is overnight weekly between Pretoria/Johannesburg and Bulawayo. From Bulawayo you can catch **Rail Safaris Train de Luxe**'s (☎ **263/19/332-284**) steam train to Vic Falls, stopping at Hwange en route. The cost is about R1,800 ($300), including meals.

**Rovos Rail** (☎ **27/12/323-6052,** fax 27/12/323-0843; rovos.rail@pixie.co.za) in South Africa is a luxury train that gives the Blue Train a run for its money. Rovos runs

**Phone Tips**

This chapter contains phone numbers for three countries. So that you'll know which country each is in, all phone numbers in this chapter start with the country code. Remember to drop these codes and add a zero (0) to the city code before calling locally. Phone numbers starting with **263 are in Zimbabwe;** those beginning with 27 are in South Africa; those starting with 260 are in Zambia. For more information, see "Telephones" under "Fast Facts," below.

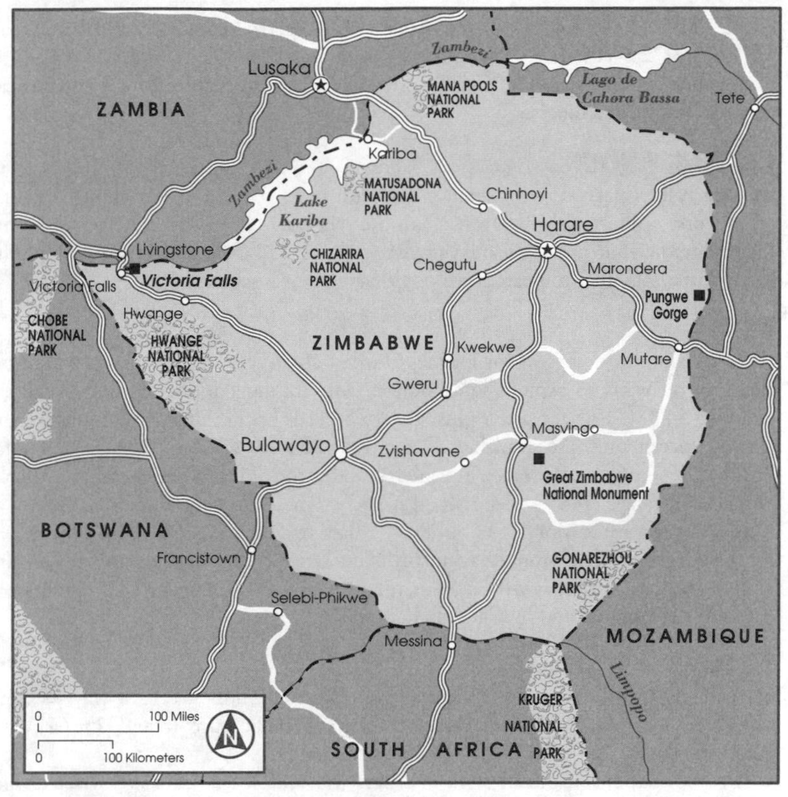


between Pretoria and Victoria Falls, departing on Thursday at 10am and arriving on Saturday at 11am. The train carries a maximum of 72 passengers. Costs are R6,995 ($1,165.85) per person sharing a De Luxe suite and R9,500 ($1,583.35) per person sharing a Royal.

### By Car

If you're driving from South Africa, you'll pass through the border at Beit Bridge (about 5 hours from Jo'burg). From here, follow the A6 to Bulawayo (about 7 hours), then the A8 to Victoria Falls via Hwange (about 4 hours). As the trip is so long, you're best off spending the night in either Bulawayo or northern South Africa. From Harare, take the A5 to Bulawayo, then the A8 to Vic Falls (about 9 hours).

### By Bus

**Route 49** (☎ **27/21/426-5593,** fax 021/423-0411) has weekly trips in a new Mercedes bus from Cape Town (overnighting in Buluwayo) and from Johannesburg, R670

#### Planning Tips

For more essential information on Zimbabwe, including customs, getting there, travel documents, health, and more, see chapter 2, "Planning Your Trip to Southern Africa."

and R300 ($111.65 and $50), respectively; zimcaper@dockside.co.za. **Blue Arrow** (☎ **263/4/729-514** or 263/4/729-518) and **Translux** (☎ **263/4/725-132**) run from Harare to Vic Falls. (See "Getting Around by Bus" in chapter 2 for South African regional Translux numbers.)

## GETTING AROUND

Victoria Falls Village is a very small place, with most attractions in walking distance, or, at worst, a short taxi ride away. Taxis are relatively cheap and easy to hail within the village (or your hotel will call one for you). To go farther afield, for example, to Livingstone, Zambia, you can drive, or ride a bike or a scooter.

### BY CAR

If you're going to rent a car for journeys farther afield, consider getting a 4×4, especially if you want to explore some of the surrounding national parks—you'll pay around Z$400 ($10.50) per day plus about Z$5 (15¢) per kilometer. For longer-term rentals, special rates are available. **Hertz** (☎ **263/13/4772** or 263/13/4297; fax 263/13/2097) offers a full range of vehicles, and is the only car-rental company in the village to arrange cross-border rentals. Contact them at Bata Building, Park Way Drive, Victoria Falls, Monday to Sunday 7:30am to 5pm. **Avis** (☎ **263/13/4532**) is on the corner of Livingstone Way and Mallett Drive. For more information on driving in southern Africa, as well as on insurance and regional numbers for rental agencies, see "Getting Around by Car" in chapter 2.

### BY SCOOTER & BICYCLE

You can rent your two-wheeled transport from **Beano's** (Shop 307, Park Way, ☎ **263/13/3398,** open daily) or from **Bush Trackers Bicycle Hire** (Stand 258A, Adam Standers Dr., ☎ **263/13/2024**).

For information on out-of-town transfers, car and truck rentals, and repair and maintenance service, contact **United Touring Company** (UTC), 1st Floor, Zimbank Building, ☎ **263/13/4267,** fax 263/13/2074; utcvfl@comm.sol.sprint.com. They're open Monday to Sunday 8am to 7pm.

### BY TRAIN

"Steam" safaris, operated by **Victoria Falls Safari Express** (☎ **263/13/4682;** Customs House, Railway Station, Victoria Falls; e-mail: fallsexp@mail.pci.co.zware a fantastic way to cross the mighty Zambezi via the Victoria Falls Bridge. From the comfort of a 1922 Class Ten steam locomotive, you'll pass through tropical forests and see wildlife in its natural habitat.

### BY BOAT

Breakfast, lunch, bird-watching, and sunset **river cruises** are operated by a number of companies. All cruises take place on the calmer, game-rich waters above the falls, and are usually in large, twin-deck boats—a wonderful way to enjoy the water wildlife, including hippos, elephants, and aquatic birds. Companies that operate river cruises are **Mosi-Oa-Tunya Cruise Company** (299 Rumsey Rd., Victoria Falls; ☎ **263/13/4264,** fax 263/13/4780); **River Cruise African Eagle** (African Eagle Tours, Elephant's Walk Shopping Centre, 273 Adam Stander Rd., Victoria Falls; ☎/fax **263/13/4554**); **Kalambeza Safaris** (Park Way, Victoria Falls; ☎ **263/13/4480,** fax 263/13/4644). Other companies include **Dabula Safaris, Shearwater Adventures,** and **Zambezi Wilderness Safaris** (see addresses below); and **United Touring Company** (see above).

# Fast Facts: Zimbabwe

**American Express** The Victoria Falls office is in Manica Travel Services, Phumula Centre (☎ **263/13/113-4402**).

**Airport** See "Getting There," earlier in this chapter.

**Banks** There are a few local banks along Livingstone Way should you need local currency. Try **Zimbank, Barclays,** or **Standard Chartered.** Bank hours are Monday to Tuesday and Thursday to Friday 8am to 3pm, Wednesday 8am to 1pm, and Saturday 8 to 11:30am.

**Business Hours** Banks are open Monday, Tuesday, Thursday, and Friday 8am to 3pm; Wednesday 8am to 1pm; and on Saturday 8 to 11:30am. **Shops** are open from 8am to 5pm, and Saturday afternoons and Sundays. However, some small shops and cafes have longer hours, and there are a few day-night pharmacies in the main centers.

**Car Rentals** See "Getting Around," earlier in this chapter, and also "Getting Around by Car," in chapter 2.

**Climate** See "When to Go," in chapter 2.

**Currency** See "Money," in chapter 2.

**Doctor** **Phumula Centre Surgery.** Suite 10, Second Floor, Phumula Centre (☎ **263/13/4292,** fax 263/13/3294). Hours are Monday to Friday 9am to 5pm, Sun 10am to noon. **Victoria Falls Surgery** (☎ **263/13/3356,** fax 263/13/4646), on West Drive, is open Monday to Friday 9am to 5pm, Saturday 9am to 1pm, and Sunday 10 to 11am.

**Documents** See "Visitor Information & Entry Requirements," in chapter 2.

**Driving Rules** See "Getting Around by Car," in chapter 2.

**Drugstore** Drugstores are called chemists or pharmacies in Botswana. **Victoria Falls Pharmacy** is in Shop 3, Phumula Centre, Park Way (☎ **263/13/4403,** fax 263/13/4639). After hours, call ☎ 263/13/4336 or 3339. Open Monday to Friday 8am to 6pm, Saturday 8:30am to 1pm, and Sunday 9am to noon.

**Electricity** Electricity in southern Africa runs on 220/230V,50Hz AC and sockets take round- or flat-pinned plugs. Bring an adapter/voltage converter, but also be aware that some bush camps do not have electricity.

**Embassies & Consulates** All offices are in Harare. The **U.S. Embassy** (☎ **263/4/794-521**) is at 172 Herbert Chitepo Ave. The **U.K. High Commission** (☎ **263/4/79-3781**) is at Samora Machel Ave.; the **Australian High Commission** (☎ **263/4/75-7774**) is at 53 Samora Machel Ave.; the **Canadian High Commission** (☎ **263/4/73-3881**) is at 45 Baines Ave.; and the **New Zealand High Commission** (☎ **263/4/72-8661**) is at 57 Jason Moyo Ave.

**Emergencies** For **Medical emergencies** contact **Medical Air Rescue Service,** 162 Courtney Selous Crescent (☎ **263/13/4646;** e-mail: marketing@mars.co.zw). For an **ambulance,** call ☎ **994;** for the **police,** call ☎ **995;** to report a **fire,** call ☎ **993.**

**Information** See "Visitor Information," in this chapter and in chapter 2.

**Language** English is the official language, but the most widely spoken languages are Shona and Ndebele.

**Police** For the police, call ☎ **995.**

**Safety** Consult your physician (or a travel-health specialist) before leaving about starting a course of anti-malarial prophylactics, and note that children under the age of 12 are generally not allowed in game lodges unless special arrangements have been made with the management. For more information, see "Health, Safety & Insurance," in chapter 2.

**Taxes** Sales tax is *not due* if payment is made from any foreign source (that is, by bank draft, foreign credit card, traveler's checks) *prior to arrival* in Zimbabwe. Tax *is* due if paid in cash (regardless of currency). Tax is 15%; tourists do not pay this on accommodations. All goods in shops already have tax included in the price.

**Telephone** The Zimbabwean telephone exchange is temperamental (and can be, at worst, hair-tearingly frustrating), and you will find that at certain times of the day it is impossible to get through to any number you dial. The best times are early in the morning and in the evening. Remember, this chapter lists numbers for Zimbabwe, South Africa, and Zambia, indicated by their country codes.

**To call southern Africa from another country:** Dial international access code (United States or Canada 011, United Kingdom or New Zealand 00, Australia 0011), plus country code (**27** for **South Africa, 263** for **Zimbabwe, 267** for **Botswana,** and **260** for **Zambia**), plus local number minus the 0.

**To make an international call:** Dial 00, wait for dial tone, then the country code (United States or Canada 1, UK 44, Australia 61, New Zealand 64), the area code, and the local number.

**To charge international calls:** Dial AT&T Direct at ☎ **110-98990.** At press time, Sprint and MCI did not have international toll-free access numbers from Zimbabwe.

**To make a local call:** Drop the country code and add a zero (0) to the city code. The city code for Victoria Falls is **013.** Do not dial the zero (0) in front of the city code when calling from outside the country.

**Time Zone** Zimbabwe is 5 hours ahead of GMT, or 7 hours ahead of Eastern Standard Time.

**Tipping** For a meal, leave 10%; for small services such as hotel porters carrying your bags, tip Z$76–114 ($2–$3) or the equivalent. Guides should get Z$50 ($1.30).

**Water** You are advised not to use water in the country's dams and rivers for swimming and drinking as it may be infected with bilharzia. Tap water in cities is generally considered safe, but should you venture into rural areas, you'll be better off drinking bottled water.

## 2 Staying Active

Most of the hotels in Victoria Falls have tour desks in-house, and will arrange reservations and give advice on all the activities listed here. Alternatively, visit one-stop adventure shop **Safari Par Excellence** in the Phumula Centre, Parkway, in Victoria Falls Village (☎ **263/13/2051-2054**).

**BUNGEE JUMPING** The checklists of most adventure-sportsmen aren't complete until they've done the heart-stopping 111-meter (364-ft.) bungee off the Vic Falls Bridge. The first jump off the bridge was in 1991; the commercial operation began in

1993, and since then well over 50,000 people have done the jump. The cords stretch to about three times their length, stopping the jumper about 10 meters (33 ft.) from the boiling waters of the Zambezi River in the Batoka Gorge.

Reservations can be made from 9am to 1pm, and from 2 to 5pm daily (except in the event of heavy rains between November and February, and spray between April and June) at the Victoria Falls Border Bridge. Because the bridge lies in a "no-man's land" between the Zimbabwean and Zambian border posts, jumpers and spectators are issued a gate pass when they go out onto the bridge, which must be presented to the immigration officials on their return. Allow about an hour before your jump to get from the village and go through all these formalities. The cost is about Z$3,420 ($90) per person, with a same-day second jump running Z$1,710 ($45); Visa and MasterCard are accepted. Keep in mind that fees are non-refundable, even if you chicken out and don't jump. The minimum age is 14; those under 18 must have a parent or a guardian sign an indemnity form. For more details, contact **African Extreme Bungi** (☎ **260/3/324-231,** fax 260/3/324-238, in Zambia; e-mail: extreme@zamnet.zm; www.zamnet.zm/zamnet/extreme/bungi.htm).

**CANOEING** If you're into a more relaxed pace, try a Zambezi Wine Route, in which you are paddled downstream in a three-seater. Despite its name, there are no estates to stop at en route, but you will be given the opportunity, while on the water, to sample some Zimbabwean wine. South African wines are also included as are a range of other beverages, both alcoholic and non-alcoholic. As there are no rapids on this trip, you won't get your hair wet.

Other similarly sedate canoeing trips are primarily game-viewing expeditions, which may last anywhere from a half day to up to 10 days, with nights spent camping alongside the river. For outfitters, see "Riding the Zambezi River," above.

**FLYING** A flight over the falls can even include some game viewing if you feel like it. Adrenaline junkies opt for **microlights,** choosing between a tricycle-style microlight in which you sit behind the pilot, and an ultralight with a Plexiglas windshield. Rides can be anywhere from 15 minutes to an hour—dangerous, sure, but you can't beat it for excitement. The cost is approximately Z$3,040 ($80) for 15 minutes. Contact **Bush Birds Flying Safaris** in Vic Falls (Shop 307, Park Way, ☎ **263/13/3398;** e-mail: vlazim@samava.co.zw; www.samava.co.za/vlazim) or **Batoka Sky** (☎ **260/3/32-3672,** fax 260/3/32-4289) in Livingstone, Zambia. Batoka, incidentally, has a camera attached to the wheels; your pilot will take a photograph of you at the most appropriate moment—flying past the Falls.

Not sailing as close to nature (or, for that matter, the wind) as in a microlight, but certainly safer, are the helicopter and plane trips offered by **United Air** (☎ **263/13/4530**) and **Southern Cross Aviation** (☎ **263/13/4618**), c/o Elephant Hills Intercontinental. Fax 263/13/4609. Approximately Z$2,470 ($65) for 12 minutes (helicopter), Z$1,520–2,280 ($40–$60) for 15 to 40 minutes (plane).

**GAME VIEWING** There is a huge range of game-viewing options available, including bird-watching trails, walking safaris (usually led by an armed guard), and game drives (both day and night) in the Zambezi National Park. Almost all the safari operators based at Vic Falls offer a range of similar game-viewing activities, with some putting on special trips of their own design. There is a glut of companies offering game-watching options, so don't immediately go for the biggest—the smaller outfits, although not necessarily cheaper, are often able to offer more personalized service. At press time, you could expect to pay Z$1,900–3,420 ($50–$90) for walks (including lunch) and about Z$1,900 ($50) for drives. In addition to those companies listed

## ✪ Riding the Zambezi River

Due to popular demand, a number of companies offer white-water rafting and canoeing, and the competition is stiff. If you're on a budget, call around to find out who's currently offering the best deal. All are located in Victoria Falls.

- **Shearwater Adventures** (☎ **263/13/4471,** fax 263/13/4341), Soper's Arcade, Park Way.
- **Safari Par Excellence** (☎ **263/13/2054**), Pumula Centre, Park Way. There is another office at the corner of Livinstone and Park Way (☎ **263/13/4424** or 2051, fax 263/13/4510; e-mail: spevfa@africaonline.co.za www.itech.co.za/safpar).
- **Frontiers Rafting** (☎ **263/13/5800,** fax 263/13/5801), 3 Park Way.
- **Kandahar Safaris** (☎ **263/13/4502,** fax 263/13/2014), Shop 9, Soper's Arcade, Park Way.
- **Zambezi Canoe Company** (☎ **263/13/2058**), Shop 14, Soper's Arcade, Park Way.
- **Zambezi Jet Boat Journeys** (☎ **263/11/207-518,** fax 263/13/2233), 338 Wood Rd.
- **Zambezi Odyssey** (☎/fax **263/13/4239**), 237 Soper's Crescent.

here, you can contact **Safari Par Excellence, United Touring Company,** and **Shearwater Adventures** (address above). All companies are in Victoria Falls.

- **Dabula Safaris** (☎ **263/13/4453**), 309 Park Way.
- **Touch The Wild** (☎ **263/13/4694**) c/o Victoria Falls Hotel, Mallet Drive.
- **Zambezi Wilderness Safaris** (☎ **263/13/4637,** fax 263/13/4417), c/o Ilala Lodge, Livingstone Way.
- **Charles Brightman/Van Carter Safaris & Bushwalks** (☎ **263/13/5821,** fax 263/13/3305), 487 Marula Crescent.

**GOLFING** While not usually considered an adventure activity, crocodiles in the water hazards, antelope and warthogs in the rough, and the trumpeting of elephants in the background make the Elephant Hills Intercontinental golf course a rather exhilarating experience. Add to this the constant presence of the falls—the 6,205-meter (6,784-yard) course is at times just a stroke from the roaring Zambezi River—and you're looking at a most unusual course, considered one of Africa's finest. For details, contact **Elephant Hills Intercontinental** (☎ **263/13/4793,** fax 263/13/4655), or for reservations in the United States, call ☎ **800/327-0200.**

**HORSEBACK RIDING** Game-viewing on horseback is particularly recommended as it provides visitors with an opportunity to get closer to game than they can on foot or in a car. **Zambezi Horse Trails** (contact them through Safari Par Excellence, see above) is a small privately owned company, which has been operating in Victoria Falls since 1989. Day rides, which range from 2 hours for novices to 7 hours for experienced riders, take place on 30,000 hectares (12,000 acres) of the Matetsi River Ranch, which borders the Zambezi National Park. Keen riders can also sign up for 2- and 3-day rides that range farther afield. Riders are accompanied by an experienced guide with an extensive knowledge of the flora and fauna of the area.

✪ **WHITE-WATER RAFTING** Operators specializing in white-water rafting out of Victoria Falls pride themselves on offering the best commercially run rapids in the world. You need to be reasonably fit (not only to deal with the grade 3–5 rapids, but also for the walks both down into and up out of the gorge). You should also be a competent swimmer, and not mind getting wet. Don't worry if you haven't done anything like it before—organizers offer dry-ground preparation before launching onto the water, and each raft is accompanied by a skilled river guide. The best time for rafting is when the water is low and the rapids impressive, in September and October. (In April and May, when the water is particularly high, some rafting companies close altogether.) You should be aware that there is a certain level of danger, and that the rapids claim a few lives every year, though these are usually kayakers. The approximate cost for a half day is Z$2,850 ($75); for a full day, Z$3,420 ($90). Prices include lunch, drinks, and all equipment. If you have enough time, it's definitely worth spending more time on the river—ask about the 3-, 5-, and 7-day trips offered by most operators. Two of the best known outfitters are **Shearwater Adventures** and **Safari Par Excellence** (see "Riding the Zambezi River," above). The latter have introduced some of the most hair-raising ways to brave the rapids: in a tandem kayak (just you and a guide) or alone, on a boogie board. Boarders don't do as many rapids, but spend some 4 hours catching the waves created by a selection of grade 3–5 rapids.

## 3 Where to Stay

Victoria Falls Village is small and nowhere is too far from the central attraction. All the hotels mentioned below handle reservations for all activities at the falls and can arrange transport. Note that most people opt to stay on the Zimbabwean side of the falls, benefiting from the infrastructure of the commercially oriented village; but if you're here to commune with nature, make sure you stay some way from the village, preferably on the Zambian side, where most lodges are situated on the shores of the Zambezi.

### IN ZIMBABWE

**Elephant Hills Intercontinental.** P.O. Box 300, Victoria Falls. ☎ **263/13/4793** or 263/13/4799. Fax 263/13/4655. Reservations in the United States, call ☎ **800/327-0200.** E-mail: zimsuncro@zimxun.co.zw www.zimbabwesun.com. 276 units. A/C TV TEL. Z$11,932 ($314) double; Z$17,898–23,864 ($471–$628) suite. Rates include breakfast. AE, DC, MC, V.

Four kilometers (2½ miles) from the falls, Elephant Hills is a monstrous structure that continues to spark much derision, notably from those who can't afford to stay here. However, while the spreading building is not particularly environmentally sensitive—its rough, dark-gray exterior is, one presumes, intended to resemble an elephant—it is one of only two hotels in Victoria Falls that offers 5-star accommodations, with excellent service, value-for-money food, and a variety of entertainment options. On the grounds are a casino, shops, an 18-hole golf course (famous as much for its greens as for the wildlife on its fairways), tennis and squash courts, a bowling green, sauna, two swimming pools, and a choice of four bars.

Inside, natural stone, fabrics, wood, and other elemental materials and designs have been used to pleasing effect, and all the bedrooms are off an open-air atrium where an ornamental rain forest, a flowing stream, and fountains have been created. The rooms themselves are decorated in vibrant, ethnic colors and feature comforts like a CD player, VCR, hair dryer, and tea- and coffee-making facilities.

**Dining:** The Samukele restaurant and bar seats 180 people and offers—in addition to spectacular views—buffets, poolside dining, and a nightly show featuring people dressed in animal costumes and masked men on stilts. Breakfast, buffet lunch, and either buffet or a la carte dinner are served. The Kasibi outdoor terrace has tables under a thatched roof and a distinctly ethnic feel.

**Ilala Lodge.** 411 Livingstone Way, Victoria Falls. ☎ **263/13/4737.** Fax 263/13/4417. 16 units. A/C TV TEL. Z$10,868 ($286) double; Z$5,434 ($143) per person. Rates include breakfast. DC, MC, V.

This is a small hotel, but pleasant, offering mid-range motel-type accommodations an easy 10-minute walk from the falls. It's put together very much along an African theme, with thatched roofs, African paintings and fabrics, and cane furniture. Food is reasonably good, and the rooms are modern. The hotel's not fenced in, so don't be surprised if you hear the sounds of elephants feeding outdoors late in the evening.

**Sprayview Hotel.** Reynard Rd., Victoria Falls. ☎ **263/13/4344.** Fax 263/13/4713. E-mail: sprayvw@amcaonline.co.za 58 units (including four family suites). A/C TEL. Z$2,280 ($60) double; Z$874 ($23) per child 3–11 years sharing. Rates include breakfast. AE, DC, MC, V.

Situated about 1 kilometer (just over a half mile) from the town, Sprayview offers motel-style accommodation (with parking outside of each room), and each unit has a private balcony. Well suited to families with smaller children, it has a swimming pool, a children's playground, and a supervised children's TV room. For the adults, there is an a la carte restaurant (Carlos'), a resident's lounge, the Rainforest Cocktail bar (open all day), and a pool bar. There are also gift shops, tour desks, and car-rental desks within the hotel.

**Victoria Falls Hotel.** Mallet Dr., Victoria Falls. ☎ **263/13/4203** or 4751. Fax 263/13/4586. 181 units. A/C TV TEL. Z$14,668–15,732 ($386–$414) double. AE, DC, MC, V.

Built in 1904 for Rhodes's Cape-to-Cairo railway, in the 20th-century imperial manner, the Victoria Falls Hotel was once all columns, arched loggias, and verandahs; its rooms lofty and airy. A total revamp in 1996 with a new decor leaning toward discreetly opulent Edwardian, restored the hotel to its heyday as one of renowned hostelries of the British Dominions. Once again a serene place of understated elegance, the hotel offers everything a discerning guest could possibly expect, including three restaurants, several guest lounges, curio shops, a hair salon, a swimming pool, and tennis courts. From the generous, sweeping terrace (where traditional afternoon high tea may be taken) overlooking the rambling gardens, there is a view directly up the Batoka Gorge to the elegant iron single-span arch bridge. A path through the gardens leads to the falls themselves, and there is a 30-minute trail that descends into the gorge to the river itself.

**Dining:** The Livingstone Room serves breakfast from 7 to 9:30am daily, and dinner daily from 7 to 9:30pm. Dinner requires formal dress, and no children under 12 are allowed. There's a band Tuesday to Sunday evenings. Jungle Junction has superb views of the bridge, and serves an a la carte lunch daily from 12:30 to 2:30pm to the sounds of a marimba band. The buffet dinner served daily 7 to 10pm, is accompanied by Shangaan dancers and a local choir. Children's meals are available.

✪ **Victoria Falls Safari Lodge.** Stand 471, Squire Cummings Rd., Victoria Falls. ☎ **263/13/3201.** Fax 263/13/3205. E-mail: saflodge@vfsl.gaia.co.za. www.vfsl.co.za. 72 units. A/C TEL. Z$13,604 ($358) double; Z$16,340 ($430) suite. Rates include breakfast. AE, DC, MC, V.

Located 3 kilometers (2 miles) from the town center (and the falls themselves), this lodge is set high on a plateau that forms a natural boundary to the Zambezi National Park. Guests must be accompanied by guides when walking outside the perimeters of the resort, a reminder of how close to nature you are. It really is an unfenced wildlife area. A winner of the "Best Zimbabwean Lodge" (voted by tour operators) for three years running, it is constructed on 11 levels, much like an open-plan thatched tree house, overlooking a waterhole. All the rooms have spectacular views of the bushveld. The African decor uses natural fabrics and materials to great effect. All the rooms have glass doors that open onto private balconies, and one of the standard twin rooms has been specially designed for guests with disabilities. The attention to detail here is also worth mentioning—there are mosquito nets and pads, insect repellant, and sunblock in each room, as well as complimentary binoculars, the better to appreciate the wildlife spectacle right on the doorstep. Young children are not encouraged, but cots and babysitters are available. The hotel has a TV lounge with satellite link. For dining, see Boma under "Where to Dine," below.

Another option is **Songwe Point Village,** a village developed and managed by the lodge and about 15 kilometers (9 miles) away, which offers visitors a unique 24-hour opportunity to experience African life and culture. It is situated in Zambia, overlooking the 200-meter (656-ft.) Zambezi Gorge and surrounded by vast areas of protected World Heritage land. Guests can stay overnight in one of eight thatched huts. No children under 12.

## IN ZAMBIA

✪ **Matetsi Game Lodges.** Reservations through Private Bag x27, Benmore 2010, South Africa. ☎ **27/11/784-7077.** Fax 27/11/784-7667. E-mail: reservations@conscorp.co.za. Water Lodge: 3 camps, 6 units each. Safari Camp: 12 units. A/C MINIBAR TEL. Z$26,600 ($700) April to October; Z$22,800 ($600) November to March. Rates includes all meals, game activities, and laundry. AE, MC, V.

The South African–based company Conservation Corporation brought, in the late 1990s, a new type of sophistication to the Zimbabwean hospitality trade. The Matetsi Game Lodges (40km/25 miles) upstream from the falls) are situated on 50,000 hectares (20,000 acres) adjacent to the Zambezi River. Previously a hunting-concession area, Matetsi is now home to herds of buffalo, elephant, and sable, which range freely throughout the vast, unfenced area. The Matetsi Water Lodge buildings use teak, slate, and thatch, and have views of the river sweeping past. Shaded by mangosteen and waterberry trees and set on 15 kilometers (9 miles) of river frontage, the lodge consists of three small, elegant camps of six suites, each with plunge pool, en-suite bathroom, and a private river verandah from which guests have uninterrupted views of hippos and other waterlife. Superlative cuisine prepared by accomplished chefs is served on riverside dining decks under trees. The Matetsi Safari Camp is situated at the edge of an open grassland system where wildlife gathers. It has 24 beds in 12 luxury safari tents with en-suite bathrooms. Swimming pools and tree-shaded decks complete this idyll.

**The River Club.** For reservations, contact Zambezi Wilderness Safaris (see above). P.O. Box 60469, Livingstone, Zambia. ☎ **263/4/73-9977.** Fax 263/4/73-9985. E-mail: Reservations@legends.co.zw. 10 units, sleeping 20 guests. From R2,880 ($480) double; July–Dec R1,650 ($275) double. Rates include all meals and drinks. (Note that although the River Club is in Zambia, its phone number is in Zimbabwe, as above.)

Neighboring Tongabezi (see below), and vying for the position as the most exclusive address in Zambia, is this romantic retreat on the banks of the Zambezi. Owned/managed by ex-British Army officer Peter Jones, The River Club is the most overtly colonial of the Zambian lodges; meals are served under the stars by uniformed waiters wearing fezzes, after which guests can play a game of croquet before they retire to huge four-poster beds swaddled in mosquito nets. A highlight are the baths, which are almost within touching distance of the Zambezi.

**Thorntree Lodge.** Reservations through P.O. Box 1395, Randburg 2194, South Africa. ☎ **27/11/888-3500.** Fax 27/11/888-4942. E-mail: safpar@harare.iafrica.com. www.zambezi.com/safpar/thorn.html. 8 units, consisting of 6 twin-bed en-suite tents and 1 en-suite double lodge with private deck overlooking the Zambezi River. Z$8,360 ($220) per day double. Rates include drinks and meals. DC, MC, V.

Located on the banks of the Zambezi, 15 kilometers (9 miles) upstream from the falls, within the Mosi-Oa-Tunya National Park, Thorntree uses all-natural materials including indigenous woods and thatching to blend into its riverine environment. The lodge offers a very personal experience, and invariably guests enjoying the sunset on the deck of the centrally situated lounge are treated to the sight of elephants following an age-old migration route running directly in front of the lodge. Lodging is in tents built under stone and thatch, and each room has an en-suite bathroom and a private verandah overlooking the river. Comfortable pontoon boats take guests onto the river, while game drives and cultural visits are also available. The lodge is associated with Safari Par Excellence, and can easily arrange all adventure activities.

✪ **Tongabezi.** Private Bag 31, Livingstone, Zambia. ☎ **263/32/3235** or 263/32/3296. Fax 263/32/3224. E-mail: tonga@zamnet.zm. 13 units. From R3,084 ($514) double, including food and drinks. MC, V.

Situated 20 kilometers (12½ miles) upstream from the Falls, and overlooking a broad expanse of the Zambezi, Tongabezi Lodge is set in a grove of African Ebony trees. Guests can choose between tented cottages, each with a private verandah overlooking the river, or the eccentrically decorated houses, of which Tree House and Honeymoon House are particularly popular. For those who don't mind roughing it (i.e. flushing toilets and running cold water, but hot bucket showers and candles only), a stay at their Island Camp, called Sindabezi, is highly recommended. Located on an island 3 kilometers downstream from Tongabezi Lodge (towards Victoria Falls), each of the four thatched chalets has magnificent views of the river, and of the nearby flood plain of the Zambezi National Park. Access is from Tongabezi Lodge only, by motorized banana boat (20 min.) or by canoe (1 hr.). From July to March, Tongabezi also organizes trips to and champagne lunches on Livingstone Island, just feet from the main Falls. They can also arrange overnight trips, but you may find that the roar of the Falls keeps you from sleeping. At certain times of the year (usually September to December) you can swim in the natural pools on the edge of the Falls.

Tongabezi is particularly recommended for birdlovers, not least because ornithologist Bob Stjernstedt, renowned for consistently scoring rare sightings, resides here. Tongabezi is also famed for its food, prepared by a team of Zambian chefs.

## 4 Where to Dine

Victoria Falls is known for its wild water and wildlife, not for its cuisine. Don't expect miracles from the few restaurants in the village (they are mainly steakhouse-type places). If you want an upmarket experience, you'll have to visit one of the hotels listed above, of which Victoria Safari Lodge's Boma (reviewed below) is the best. If you're just looking for a friendly place to fill up before launching into your next adventure, try **The Cattleman** (Phumula Centre, Park Way, Victoria Falls, ☎/fax **263/13/4767**), which styles itself as the "home of the famous Zimbabwe steak," but also offers vegetarian options. They are fully licensed for wine and beer and open daily from 9am to 3pm and 6 to 11pm. Alternatively, the **Croc & Paddle Bar & Restaurant** (Elephant's Walk Shopping Village, Adam Stander Dr., Victoria Falls, ☎/fax **263/13/3365,** zambezi@coldfire.dnet.co.zw), has a view of the falls from a balcony and draws the crowds by offering satellite coverage of news and sports. Hours are daily 11am to 11pm.

**The Boma.** In the Victoria Safari Lodge. ☎ **263/13/4725.** Open daily year-round from 7pm until late. Reservations recommended. AE, DC, MC, V. ZIMBABWEAN.

The Boma, situated in the Gusu Forest and partly open to the night sky, promises a unique cultural experience that involves all the senses. On arrival, guests partake in a hand-washing ceremony before sampling traditional beer and snacks. The four-course meal combines a la carte starters with a barbecue buffet that includes such local delicacies as mopani worms and game stews (although more standard fare and vegetarian dishes are also available). Entertainment is provided by Shangaan dancers and singers and a local witchdoctor, as well as the restaurant's traditional storyteller who tells guests more about the country's folklore, culture, and heritage. Transport is available for a fee, to guests of all hotels situated in and around Victoria Falls.

## 5 What to See & Do

Victoria Falls Village still retains some of its olde-worlde "jungle junction" charm, but as all its available energy is given over to the pursuit of the tourist buck, it's not a town you tarry long in.

Most are here to participate in myriad adventure activities, but when all is said and done, it is the falls themselves that are the star of the show. There are three great vantage points, each offering a different angle, and it's well worth trying to cover all of them: Walking through the rain forest directly opposite the falls in the Vic Falls National Park; seeing them from the Victoria Falls Bridge; and seeing them from the Zambian side, in the Mosi-Oa-Tunya Park.

### SOAKING UP THE FALLS

✪ **The Victoria Falls National Park.** No phone. Adjacent to Victoria Falls Village. Admission Z$190 ($5). Open daily 6am–6pm, later during full-moon nights.

The Victoria Falls National Park, all 2,340 hectares (936 acres) of it, runs in a narrow strip along the southern bank of the Zambezi River and protects the sensitive rain forest around the falls. You will definitely get soaked on a visit to the park, so rent a raincoat or umbrella at the entrance, and remember to put your camera in a waterproof bag. A trail runs through the rain forest, and side trails lead to good viewing points over the falls, the best of which is Danger Point. There is a statue of David Livingstone on a terrace next to one of the ✪ **Devil's Cataract** view points. Try to come when the moon is full—the park stays open later so that visitors can witness the lunar rainbow formed by the spray.

**Victoria Falls Bridge.** No phone. Open 6am–8pm daily.

Built in 1905, this was an integral part of Cecil John Rhodes's dream of "painting Africa [imperial] red from Cape to Cairo," and you can still see steam trains chugging across its span, the backdrop of white rising spray a magnificent counterpoint to the black smoke that billows from their engines. The bridge serves as a rail and road link between Zimbabwe and Zambia and is located within a World Heritage Site. You do have to pass through Zimbabwean immigration and customs control to get onto the bridge which, depending on the crowds, can take up to half an hour. From the bridge, you'll get a great view of the Boiling Pot and a section of the falls themselves. And the sight of people hurling themselves from the center of the bridge into the gorge below,

### Courtin' the Zambezi River God

Every year Nyaminyami, the Zambezi River god, claims one or two of the 40,000 lives that hurtle down his course. It is said that by wearing his serpent-like image around your neck, you will escape harm. Hundreds of hawkers in and around the falls make a living selling Nyaminyami necklaces, which forever brand you as a brave warrior who has ridden the mighty Zambezi River.

---

tied to life by a springy rope, might even convince you to try this adrenaline-raising drop (see "Bungee Jumping," above).

✪ **The Mosi-Oa-Tunya National Park.** No phone. On Livingstone Rd., 10km (6 miles) south of Livingstone. No admission. Open daily year-long 6am–6pm.

Located on the Zambian side, this small park offers a more spectacular vantage point than its Zimbabwean counterpart during high water (April to June), as the view is less obscured by spray. The park is also a sanctuary for white rhino, buffalo, zebra, sable, giraffe, wildebeest, and a wide variety of birds. Note that you will have to cross a border post to get here and purchase a day visa, Z$380 ($10).

## MORE SIGHTS

**Zambezi National Park** in Park Way (adjacent to the village) extends 38 kilometers (23½ miles) westward along the Zambezi River from Victoria Falls and southward for up to 24 kilometers (15 miles). It is a convenient wildlife viewing area for tourists based at the falls, particularly in the dry season (September and October) when it is easiest to see game. Animals in the park include various types of antelope, elephants, zebra, buffalo, giraffe, and warthog. Crocodile, once almost exterminated by indiscriminate hunting, have been successfully reintroduced by the commercial crocodile farms based at Victoria Falls. Entrance is Z$190 ($5) per vehicle; entry into the rain forest is Z$380 ($10). Fishing camps, bush camps, and other rustic accommodations are available. For more information, contact the National Parks Central Booking Office (☎ **263/4/70-6077**), Department of National Parks and Wildlife Management, P.O. Box 8151, Causeway, Harare, Zimbabwe.

There are two main viewing drives in the park. The **Zambezi Drive** is entered via a gate close to Victoria Falls town and runs for 38 kilometers (23½ miles) along the riverbank. Another entrance gate, 6 kilometers (4 miles) south of the town, provides access to the **Chamabonda Drive,** which follows the Masuie River. The main Victoria Falls–Kazungula road also crosses the park.

Speaking of crocodiles, if you have time visit the **Zambezi Nature Sanctuary** (☎ **263/13/4567**) in Park Way, where at around 11am you can see these charming reptiles being fed. It's open daily from 8am to 4:30pm and entrance costs Z$380 ($10).

# 6 Shopping

Street hawkers are a dime a dozen, and can get rather pushy; but they're all prepared to bargain, and picking up small gifts to take home is a cinch. However, if you're into more serious articles (Zimbabwean sculptors are world-renowned for their soapstone creations), consider visiting the following.

**Falls Craft Village.** Stand 206, Soper's Crescent, off Livingstone Way. ☎ **263/13/4309.** Open daily 8:30am–1pm, 2–5pm. Entrance Z$25 (65¢).

Get right into the spirit of the place and visit the Falls Craft Village. Next to the gift shops is a complex consisting of the reconstructed homes of five different Zimbabwean tribes. (If you're thinking of braving the rapids on a boogie board, it might be a good idea to have your fortune told by the local witchdoctor.)

**Soper's Curios.** 1911 Adam Stander Rd., Victoria Falls. ☎ **263/13/4361.** Fax 263/13/4440. Open Mon–Sat 8:30am–5pm, Sun 9am–1pm. AE, DC, MC, V.

This little enterprise has been trading in Zimbabwean artifacts since 1911. Just round the corner from the Craft Village, you can buy wood and soapstone souvenirs here (some of which are carved on site in the Craft Village).

**Elephant Walk Shopping Village.** 273 Adam Stander Rd., Victoria Falls. ☎ **263/13/4608** or 263/13/4404. Fax 263/13/3284. E-mail: elewalk@africaonline.co.zw. AE, DC, MC, V.

If the call of the mall is too loud to resist, this is the place to go. Packed with clothing, gift and furniture shops, cafes, galleries, and a museum, there's something here for everybody. Visit the **Elephant Walk Tribal Art Gallery** for authentic tribal art collected from all over Africa; **African Heritage** for crafts and carvings; **Kwa-Zambezia** for handmade pottery and clothing; the **River Trading Post Art Studio** and **Studio Africana** for original African wildlife art; and the **Trading Company** for Zimbabwe-style housewares. And when you get weary, pop into the **Coffee Shop** for coffee and homemade cakes or a light meal.

## 7 Side Trips from the Falls

### HWANGE NATIONAL PARK

Hwange National Park, 200 kilometers (124 miles) from Victoria Falls, is said to contain the widest variety and greatest density of wildlife in the world. Its 14,651 square kilometers (9,083 square miles) are covered mainly by Kalahari sand, with flat plains and large natural pans, and granite outcrops in the north. The pans fill up in summer and game viewing is more difficult at this time, because of the long grass and the fact that the wildlife no longer needs to converge in one area to find water. Plenty of antelope (16 species), a few black rhino (the white variety has, sadly, been wiped out by poachers), elephants by the thousand, lion, hyena, leopards, crocodiles, and more than 400 bird species may be spotted in this park, and all types of accommodations are available. Contact **The Warden,** Main Camp, Private Bag DT5776, Dete, Zimbabwe. ☎ **263/18/331** or 263/18/332.

Alternatively check out **Hwange Safari Lodge,** situated in a 110,000 hectare (44,000-acre) private game park at the border of Hwane. The lodge has 94 rooms; contact them at ☎ **263/4/737-944;** fax 263/4/734-739; e-mail: randburgof@zimsun.co.za.

### KARIBA

One of the world's largest artificial lakes, the Kariba Dam lies astride the country's northwest border with Zambia. Ringed by blue mountains, the lake, said to be the color of crushed foil, is accessible by visitors to Victoria Falls via daily plane connections. Kariba's sunset cruises and houseboat accommodation are legendary. For more information, contact **Wilderness Safaris** in South Africa (☎ **27/11/883-0747;** fax 27/11/883-0911; or e-mail: info@sdn.wilderness.co.za).

Three resorts run by **Zimbabwe Sun** (☎ **263/4/737-944;** fax 263/4/734-739; e-mail: randburgof@zimsun.co.za www.zimbabwesun.com/) operate out of Kariba. The resorts are Katete Safari Lodge, Bumi Hills Safari Lodge, and Forthergill Island.

# 10

# Botswana

*By Tracey Hawthorne*

The tranquil Okavango Delta, a 15,000-square-kilometer (9,300-square-mile) inland flood plain, fans out in the northwestern corner of Botswana, creating a paradise of palms, papyrus, and crystal-clear channels, and backwaters. Set in a massive sea of desert sand, this fragile wonderland of waterways, islands, and forests is an oasis for birds and animals, drawn to its life-giving waters from the surrounding thirstlands. Here, the evening air is filled with the sounds of birds calling, frogs trilling, and antelope rustling in the reeds; herds of wildebeest, hartebeest, buffalo, and zebra roam the islands, elephants wade across channels guarded by hippos and crocodiles, and predators rule the night.

But it is not only animals and birds that are attracted to this huge, verdant oasis. Because the area is so sensitive, the Botswana government operates a policy of low-volume, high-income tourism, making it a pricey holiday destination—but this doesn't stop thousands of tourists from flocking to one of the world's most game-rich and unspoiled wilderness areas. To service these visitors, scores of safari companies have been established in and around the delta and Moremi Game Reserve, situated in the northeastern sector of the delta. Because it is both expensive and complicated to travel independently in Botswana (huge distances are involved and the road network is poor), and particularly in the delta itself, visitors are advised to contact one of these companies to arrange their trip. Most offer full-package holidays that cover the delta and surrounds, and will organize everything for you, including flights, transfers, accommodation, and game-viewing trips by boat and vehicle.

Once there, travel in this area is very much, as Robert Louis Stevenson once wrote, "travel for travel's sake"—the excitement is not necessarily in the destination, but in the journey itself. A leisurely float in a *mokoro* (wooden dugout canoe) along limpid channels between emerald vegetation and past towering palms and bright green banks of papyrus, interspersed with short game-viewing walks on the islands, is an experience of a lifetime.

Bear in mind that if you do a "whistle-stop" visit, flying in one night and out the next day, you are likely to be disappointed. The delta has its own unique moods and rhythms, and to experience these you'll need at least 2 full days.

There is more to Botswana than the delta, however. To the northeast lies Chobe National Park, a 12,000-square-kilometer (7,440-square-mile) home to some 35,000 elephants; the remote eastern

**Planning Tips**

For more essential information on Botswana, including customs, getting there, travel documents, health, and more, see chapter 2, "Planning Your Trip to Southern Africa."

corner just over the border from South Africa is the Tuli Block; and to the southeast are the spectacular Makgadikgadi and Nxai Pans, where the space is so vast that, it is said, you can hear the stars sing. Most safari companies include the Chobe and its surrounds on their itineraries, and some visit the pans.

Like so many of Africa's wilderness areas, the delta is under threat from human need. A shortage of good grazing in adjacent lands makes the lush grass within the delta a standing temptation to stock farmers, especially in times of drought. The demands of Botswana's diamond-mining industry and the ever-expanding town of Maun (gateway to the delta), both thirsty for water, pose an ongoing threat to the delta's precious liquid reserves. Conservationists have long been lobbying to have the delta proclaimed a World Heritage Site, so far without success. All of which means that—should you wish to experience the untamed Africa of Hemingway, Roosevelt, and Blixen—a trip here should enjoy the highest priority.

# 1 Tips on Traveling in Botswana

## DRIVING

Don't rent a car to drive into the delta unless you're a seasoned rally driver who thinks nothing of water hazards. For the game parks, a 4×4 is advisable; but keep in mind that if you rent a car, particularly a 4×4, you'll have a great deal of freedom, but you won't necessarily save money. Try **Avis** (☎ **267/66-0039**), which has a stand opposite the airport (no street address) in Maun; and in the **Gabarone Airport** (☎ **267/31-3093**). Avis charges P125 ($28.40) per day plus P1.25 (30¢) per kilometer for a small car; P270 ($61.35) per day plus P2.55 (60¢) per kilometer for a 4×4. You can also call **Holiday Car Hire** at Nekdi Road, Broadhurst Industrial Area, Gaborone (☎ **267/3122**). To rent a car, you must be 25 or older. Your home driving license is good for 6 months (as long as it's in English).

Driving is on the left, overtaking on the right. Speed limits vary, and are signposted on the larger roads. Be on the alert in the country districts for game and domestic animals crossing the road. It is the law to wear a seatbelt at all times; but if your car was manufactured without seatbelts, you will not be fined.

For more information on driving in southern Africa, as well as on insurance and regional numbers for rental agencies, see "Getting Around by Car" in chapter 2.

## ACCOMMODATIONS

A holiday spent in Botswana, and particularly in the delta area and its surrounds, is not a "hotel" experience. Most of the lodges and camps are built of and furnished with wood and/or canvas with soft furnishings that range from comfortable rustic to spectacularly colonial in style. In the tented camps, accommodation is in generously sized safari tents (big enough for an adult to comfortably stand up and move around in) and the food is usually prepared in tented "bush kitchens." In those camps that don't have en-suite facilities, chamber pots are provided for use during the night.

Visitors to the delta should bear in mind at all times that they are in a wilderness area: Even those animals that look cute are wild and should not be approached. Most

**Phone Tips**

This chapter contains phone numbers for both Botswana and South Africa. Those in **Botswana** start with the country code **267;** those in **South Africa** have the country code **27.** See "Telephone" under "Fast Facts" for moere information.

of the camps and lodges are unfenced, and animals, including dangerous ones like hippos, lions, and elephants, roam through them. For sensitive and sensible visitors, this provides a unique opportunity to see wild animals in their natural setting; those who do not respect the laws of the wild will ruin the experience for themselves and for others and quite possibly put themselves in danger. Even when you're safe in a safari vehicle on a game drive, your ranger will caution you not to stand up, make sudden or loud noises, or otherwise draw attention to yourself. It is probably not necessary to point out that lions and crocodiles are dangerous; however, you will hear more than once that hippos kill more humans in Africa than any other animal, and you should take this seriously. They may look harmlessly ponderous, but can move amazingly fast and are absolutely lethal when provoked. Even some of the smaller animals should be treated with a great deal of respect: The honey badger, a dear-looking little creature with a pretty "saddle" of coarse, light hair, is the most tenacious of adversaries, and even lions keep their distance. They have a very loose, thick coat that affords them excellent protection, and razor-sharp claws. When cornered, they are fearsome indeed.

There are no telephones in the delta. The camps communicate with Maun and each other via radio, and can transmit emergency messages this way.

The camps and lodges in the delta and Chobe/Savuti areas put a high premium on hospitality. Many of them are run by husband-and-wife teams, and others are managed by small teams of passionate, dedicated people. A typical day in a delta camp will begin very early, just before sunrise, with coffee or tea and biscuits to warm you up before your game drive. (It is often very cold; remember to take a warm jacket.) After breakfast, guests may be taken on a walk, or on a mokoro trip along the channels, with lunch being enjoyed on an island somewhere far from the camp. Guests frequently opt to sleep during the heat of the afternoon, before regrouping for an evening game drive. After dinner, it is not unusual for guests to be entertained by the camp manager or one of the local guides, who will thrill them with stories of life in the delta. Copious amounts of wine are often drunk at these times—don't forget to ask for an escort back to your room or tent after dark.

## DINING

Botswana doesn't have an ethnic cuisine to call its own, and food in the camps and lodges is generally designed to appeal to a wide range of cosmopolitan tastes. Although standards vary, most pride themselves on serving wholesome, home-baked fare, and many cater for vegetarians.

Generally in the lodges and fixed camps, kitchens are surprisingly sophisticated and the dishes that come out of them delicious. Some employ chefs who design menus of international standard. Expect the choice of a full English or continental breakfast, including fresh fruit, imported at great expense. Lunchtimes comprise a cold buffet or, if you're on the water or exploring outside of the camp at midday, a picnic lunch made up of cold cuts, salads, breads, cheeses, and fruits; while dinners are usually three-course meals running the gamut of soup or cold starter, a substantial main course (a roast, a pie, curry, or similar), and a dessert. Many camps bake their own bread, cakes, and muffins. Morning and afternoon tea are institutions at most lodges. Game is served in

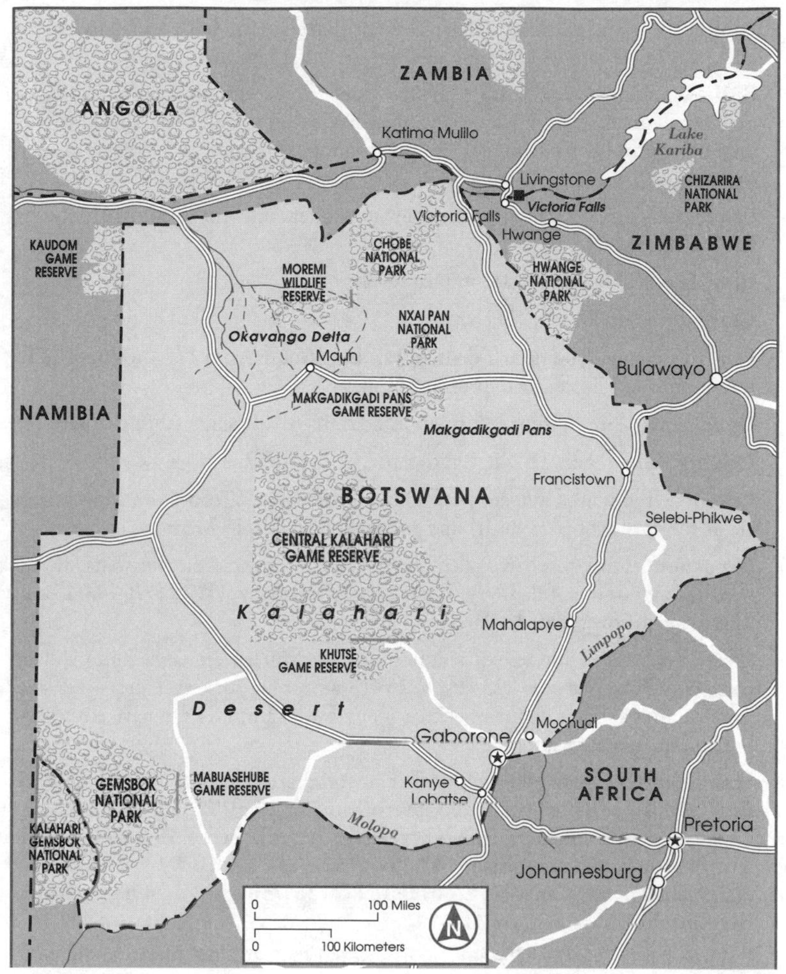


some lodges (although not in those situated within game reserves), so more adventurous diners can experiment with crocodile steaks, gemsbok (oryx) fillets, and the like.

On the traveling safaris, food is simpler but usually perfectly palatable—and designed, as elsewhere, to cater for a wide variety of tastes. If you have any specific dietary requirements, or are a finicky eater, it's best to warn the safari operator or camp well in advance; once there, the chef is restricted to what's been flown in.

South African beers and wines are available in all lodges and camps.

## Fast Facts: Botswana

**American Express** The office is in **Manica Travel Services,** Botslano House, The Mall, Gaborone. ☎ **267/35-2021.**

**Airport** See the "Getting There" sections in this chapter as well as in chapter 2.

**Banks** In Maun **Standard Chartered** and **Barclays** are both open Monday to Friday from 8:15am to 12:45pm, and Saturday 8:15am to 10:45pm.

**Business Hours** **Banks** are generally open from 9am to 2:30pm Monday, Tuesday, Thursday, and Friday, 8:15 to noon Wednesday; and 8 to 10:45am Saturday. **Shop hours** are 8am to 1 or 2pm Monday to Friday, and 8:30am to 1pm Saturday.

**Car Rentals** See "Driving" earlier in this chapter, and also "Getting Around by Car" in chapter 2.

**Climate** See "When to Go" in chapter 2.

**Currency** See "Money" in chapter 2.

**Dentist** Should you need a dentist, call **Dr. Victor Ajayi** (☎ **267/66-1023**), top floor, Roots Tower, Old Mall in Maun.

**Documents** See "Visitor Information & Entry Requirements" in chapter 2.

**Driving Rules** See "Driving" above and in chapter 2.

**Doctor** If you need a doctor, call Dr. Jourdan (☎ **267/66-0482**). His offices are at the corner of Moremi III and Mogalakwe roads, in Maun.

**Drugstore** Drugstores are called chemists or pharmacies in Botswana. If you need a prescription filled, try **Okavango Pharmacy** (☎ **267/66-0043**) in Maun's main street, next to Barclays Bank.

**Electricity** As in the rest of southern Africa, you'll need an adapter/voltage converter. Botswana uses 220–240V 15–13 amp plug sockets. Plugs are 2- and 3-pin, round and flat. Remember that many bush camps do not have electricity, but run on generators.

**Embassies & Consulates** Note that all offices are in Gaborone. The **U.S. Embassy** is on Embassy Drive, Government Enclave (☎ **267/353-982,** fax 267/356-947); after-hours emergency telephone number is ☎ 267/357-111. The **British High Commission** (☎ **267/352-841**) is at 1079 Queen's Rd.**;** fax 267/356-105. The **Canadian Consulate** (☎ **267/304-411**) can be reached at P.O. Box 1009; fax 267/304-411.

**Emergencies** **Medical Rescue International** (☎ **267/30-1601**); ambulance, call ☎ **997;** fire, call ☎ **998;** police, call ☎ **999.**

**Hospitals** **Maun General Hospital** (☎ **267/66-0444**) is 2 kilometers along the main Ghanzi Road in Maun.

**Information** See the "Visitor Information" sections in this chapter and in chapter 2.

**Language** English is widely spoken.

**Police** Call ☎ **999.**

**Safety** Consult your physician (or a travel-health specialist) before leaving about starting a course of anti-malarial prophylactics, and note that children under the age of 12 are generally not allowed in game lodges unless special arrangements have been made with the management. For more information, see "Health, Safety & Insurance" in chapter 2.

**Taxes** Botswanan general sales tax is 10% and is included in all prices quoted in this chapter, unless otherwise indicated.

**Telephone** Phone calls can be made from any post office or business that provides office services. Public call boxes are found in towns. Remember, this chapter lists numbers for Botswana and South Africa, indicated by their country codes.

**To call southern Africa from another country:** Dial international access code (United States or Canada 011, United Kingdom or New Zealand 00, Australia 0011), plus country code (**27** for **South Africa, 263** for **Zimbabwe, 267** for **Botswana,** and **260** for **Zambia**), plus local number minus the 0 at the beginning of the city/area code.

**To make an international call:** Dial 00, wait for dial tone, then dial the country code (United States or Canada 1, United Kingdom 44, Australia 61, New Zealand 64), the area code, and the local number.

**To make calls within Botswana:** Drop the 267 country code; there are no area codes.

**To charge international calls:** The toll-free international access code for **Sprint** is ☎ **0800-180-280.** At press time, there was no international access code for AT&T and MCI.

**Time Zone** Botswana is 2 hours ahead of GMT, or 7 hours ahead of Eastern Standard Time.

**Tipping** Tipping is at guests' discretion, but a good rule of thumb is P22–44 ($5–$10) per person per day, to be shared among the staff. The average for guides is P22–31 ($5–$7) per day.

**Water** Water in all the camps is drinkable, but most camps/lodges do supply mineral water. There is some disagreement about the safety of water in the smaller towns—to be on the safe side, drink bottled water or bring along a purification system.

## 2 Going on Safari

Most people find it simpler and more cost effective to use a tour operator to plan their entire trip. Packages include, among other things, the flight to Botswana, travel to and accommodation in Maun, transport to the lodge or base camp, accommodation, food, soft drinks; game-viewing, fishing, and photographic expeditions; professional guides, boat hire, and *mokoro* trips. There are at least 50 lodges and camps in the delta region, some comprising tents, others reed-and-pole, others brick under thatch.

There is a plethora of safari operators based in and around Maun and the delta. They offer a variety of packages to suit a range of interests and pockets, from fly-in safaris with accommodation in luxurious lodges to "all-hands-on-deck"–type trips with nights under canvas. It's advisable to opt for the latter, as this way you'll experience more than one region. You will need to shop around to find the operator who will offer you the closest to what you want for your budget. Those listed below are among the most reputable, having been around for long enough to have established their credentials. Other trustworthy operators, particularly those that offer specialist safaris, are listed later in the chapter. Also keep in mind that though we recommend companies based in Africa, it is usually easiest to book their services through a representative in your home country. Most of the U.S.- and U.K.-based operators listed in this book represent several reputable African-based companies.

*Note:* Most of the camps and lodges listed in the "Where to Stay & Dine" sections later in this chapter don't have separate rates, as they operate as part-and-parcel of fly-in safari packages, and are usually booked and paid through safari operators, rather than directly. In the safari sections that follow, rates are given for package and per-day trips where possible.

## RECOMMENDED OPERATORS

- **Desert and Delta Safaris/Afroventures** See also specific tour information under "Specialist Safaris," below. In South Africa: P.O. Box 1200, Paulshof 2056 (☎ **27/11/807-3720;** fax 27/11/807-3480).
- **Gametrackers** In South Africa: P.O. Box 782607, Sandton 2146 (☎ **27/11/781-0137;** fax 27/11/781-0733; e-mail: gres@iafrica.com; www.gametrackers.NET). In the United States: Contact **Orient-Express Hotels,** 1155 Avenue of the Americas, New York, NY 10036 (☎ **212/302-5055;** fax 212/398-7746). In the United Kingdom: Contact **Orient-Express Hotels,** Sea Containers House, 20 Upper Ground, London SE1 9PF (☎ **0171/805-5060;** fax 0171/805-5908).
- **Hartley's Safaris** In South Africa: P.O. Box 69859, Bryanston 2021 (☎ **27/11/708-1893;** fax 27/11/708-1569).
- **Ker & Downey** In the United States: 2825 Wilcrest Dr., Suite 600, Houston, TX 77042-6007 (☎ **800/423-4236;** fax 713/937-0123). In Botswana: P.O. Box 27, Maun (☎ **267/66-0375;** fax 267/66-1282, e-mail: debster@kerdowney.bw; www.kerdowney.com). A 14-day "Classic Botswana" tour covering Chobe, Linyanti, the Okavango Delta, and Victoria Falls, with an optional extension to the Makgadikgadi Pans was available at press time for P23,232 ($5,280) per person (including air fare from the United States) sharing in a twin.
- **Moremi Safaris & Tours** In Botswana: Private Bag 26, Maun (☎ **267/66-0351;** fax 267/66-0571). In South Africa: P.O. Box 2757, Cramerview 2060 (☎ **27/11/465-3824;** fax 27/11/465-3779; e-mail: moremi@yebo.co.za; www.moremi.co.za).
- **Okavango Tours and Safaris** In the United Kingdom: Gadd House, Arcadia Avenue, London N3 2TJ (☎ **0181/343-3283;** fax 0181/343-3287; e-mail: info@okavango.com). In Botswana: P.O. Box 39, Maun (☎ **267/66-0220** or 267/66-0339; fax 267/66-0589). A 14-night safari to Botswana's Okavango Delta, Moremi Wildlife Reserve, Linyanti and Kalahari regions, including the flight from London for P28,336 (£4,048) per person sharing. For ground arrangements only, you could deduct about P4,900 (£700).
- **Premier Tours** (☎ **800/545-1910** or 215/893-9966; email: info@premiertours.com; premiertours.com) has some of the best value-for-money, all-inclusive safaris on the North American market. Working in conjunction with South African–based **Drifters Adventours,** they run extremely low-cost participation camping safaris to Botswana and other parts of southern Africa.
- **Wilderness Safaris** **In South Africa:** P.O. Box 5219, Rivonia 2128 (☎ **27/11/807-1800;** fax 27/11/807-2110). In Botswana: Private Bag 14, Maun, Botswana (☎ **267/66-0086;** fax 267/66-0632).

## SPECIALIST OPERATORS

### Mobile Tented Safaris

These range from basic to very luxurious, depending on your budget and what you want to get out of your trip. Participants are transported in a suitably modified vehicle, and camp overnight at predetermined destinations. **Abercrombie & Kent's**

"Botswana Hemingway" is a luxury option, which incorporates the desert (the Kalahari), the delta, and the savannah (the Chobe). It lasts for 11 days and costs P33,200 ($7,550) per person sharing. In the United States, contact them at 1520 Kensington Rd., Oak Brook, IL 60523-214 (☎ **800/323-7308**); in the United Kingdom, Sloane Square House, Holbein Place, London SW1W 8NS (☎ **0171/730-9600**); in South Africa, at 31 Harley St., Ferndale, Randburg, or P.O. Box 782607, Sandton 2146 (☎ **27/11/781-0740,** fax 27/11/781-0733).

**Desert and Delta Safaris/Afroventures** (see above) runs a number of more affordable, "limited-participation" safaris (clients are required to do some of the work themselves, such helping to put up and break camp, and making their own beds). The 10-day "Botswana Explorer," which takes in the Okavango, the Chobe, and the Victoria Falls, costs P7,392 ($1,680) per person, while the 8-day "Specialist Safari," which includes the Kalahari and the Okavango, costs P7,106 ($1,615) per person. Prices are inclusive of everything except airfare.

**Penstone Safaris,** P.O. Box 330, Maun, Botswana. (☎ **267/66-1721;** Fax 267/66-1722) puts together tailor-made safaris for groups of friends or families. You can choose between a fully serviced safari, which costs between P1,320 ($300) and P2,200 ($500) per person per day, depending on the number of people making up the party, and a limited-participation safari costing between P1,100 ($250) and P1,980 ($450) per person per day.

### Mokoro Safaris

These usually start with a flight from Maun to a base camp in the delta in a light plane. Here, you will either venture out daily in a mokoro, returning each evening to the comfort of your tented camp, or spend any number of days out in the channels camping on islands. Walking and driving game-viewing trips are usually included.

In Botswana, contact **Gunn's Camp:** Private Bag 033, Maun (☎ **267/66-0023;** fax 267/66-0040; E-mail: gunnscamp@info.bw). Gunn's Camp charges P436 ($99) per person per day, excluding park fees, camping fees, and flights, but including all camping and cooking equipment, food (on a self-prepare basis), and a mokoro with licensed guide. **Wilderness Safaris** and **Okavango Tours and Safaris** (for both, see address and other details above) also offer mokoro safaris.

### Horseback Safaris

**Okavango Horse Safaris (Pty) Ltd** in Botswana, Private Bag 23, Maun (☎ **267/66-1671;** fax 267/66-1672; e-mail: ohsnx@global.bw; www.okvangohorse.com), run in the western region of the delta, allowing you to get farther into the delta and closer to game than is possible on foot. A maximum of eight riders is taken, and the safaris last between 5 and 10 days. The minimum riding ability required is a mastery of the basic aids, ability to post to the trot for stretches of 10 minutes at a time, to be comfortable at all paces, and to be able to gallop out of trouble. The maximum weight limit is 95 kilograms (210 lbs.). The accommodation provided in the fly camps is camp beds in dome tents. Three meals a day are provided, with the emphasis on fresh foodstuffs (vegetarians are catered for). The cost is P1,298 ($295) per person per night sharing, including accommodation, meals, guiding, riding, game drives, walks, and mokoro rides; air transfers (Maun to the lodge) cost P638 ($145) per person round-trip. Children are accepted (at the same rate as adults), but must be able to prove that they are strong, confident riders. There are no credit-card facilities at the camp.

### Houseboat Safaris

The Kubu Queen riverboat (book through **Wilderness Safaris,** see above) is hired out on a charter basis, at P1,738 ($395) per person per night (a minimum of three people is required), all inclusive. Two tender boats accompany the houseboat, so clients wishing to go on fishing or game-viewing trips, or stop for walks on islands, can do so. Clients are accompanied by a guide and a hostess. The boat accommodates a maximum of four people in two comfortable double cabins on the lower deck, with adjacent hot/cold shower and a separate flush toilet. The upper deck consists of a cane lounge area, cocktail bar, and sun/viewing deck. The Kubu Queen is not a big-game experience, as this region of the delta has water from horizon to horizon; but hippo, crocodile, sitatunga, and lechwe are often sighted. There is also great fishing for tiger fish and bream, and the bird watching is exceptional (keep a sharp eye out for Pel's Fishing Owl, an unusual rust-colored species).

### ✪ Elephant-Back Safaris

The view from atop an elephant, riding high through the bush, is unbeatable. Both photographic and hunting safaris are available at:

**Abu Camp** in Botswana Private Bag 332, Maun (☎ **267/66-1260;** fax 267/66-1005; e-mail: ebs@info.bw). For a 5-night, 6-day, all-inclusive (except for airfare), elephant-themed safari, expect to pay about P26,400 ($6,000) per person. The atmosphere at this camp on the western side of the delta is one of "the ultimate house party," created each week for a maximum of 10 guests. Accommodation is in luxurious, custom-designed tents raised on teak decking and overlooking a lagoon. Each has an en-suite bathroom. A safari chef cooks magnificent meals catering to all tastes and dietary requirements. There is also a lounge tent and a well-stocked library. The chief elephant is Abu, star of motion pictures such as *The Power of One.* He leads a herd of 13 African elephants, comprising five adults and eight youngsters. Guests are transported in comfortable, custom-made saddles on these most effective of 4×4s. Elephants can not only cope in water and sand with equal ease, but can also get very close to other game.

### Fishing Safaris

Situated on a secluded wooded island to the northwest of the Okavango Delta's Panhandle, **Nxamaseri Lodge,** Private Bag 23, Maun (☎ **267/66-1671;** fax 267/66-1672; e-mail: ohsnx@global.bw), offers accommodation for 12 people in six thatched en-suite chalets overlooking the Nxamaseri Channel. The waters surrounding Nxamaseri sport over 80 varieties of fish, including 11 species of bream and the well-known fighting tiger fish. All species are caught on both lure and fly, from specially designed flat-bottomed boats. Tiger fish and bream are caught year-round; African pike and catfish are caught from August to December. The tiger fish record is 6.8 kilograms (15 lbs.); the bream record is 3.2 kilograms (7 lbs.). All equipment is provided, but guests are welcome to bring their own. The all-inclusive rate is P1,210 ($275) per person sharing per night. Children under 2 are welcome at no charge; from ages 2 to 12 at half the adult rate. There are no credit-card facilities at the lodge.

## PLANNING YOUR OWN TRIP

Traveling under your own steam at your own pace could be the adventure of a lifetime, but bear in mind that getting around Botswana can be difficult and frustrating, not to mention dangerous. It's far safer (as well as easier) to go with a safari operator. Distances are huge, and fuel, water, and general supply points are few and far between—it is not unusual to find garages without fuel stocks. You need to plan for every eventuality, and bring everything from extra gas, food and water, to spare car parts, first-aid kits, cooking fuel, tents, and sleeping bags. Should you have an emergency, help could be a long time arriving. To get to any given destination often involves two and sometimes even three modes of transport (car or 4×4, light aircraft, and boat, for instance). Finding your own way through the delta itself and, to a lesser degree, parts of the Chobe area, is especially problematic. Journeys to and through the central and southern Kalahari regions can be downright hazardous. Park fees are steep (P50/$11.35 per day plus P20/$4.55 per person per night camping fee).

A good middle ground for those who want a taste of "do-it-yourself" coupled with the security of experienced backup, is ✪ **Oddball's.** Run by **Okavango Tours & Safaris** (see above), Oddball's, situated close to the Moremi Game Reserve, is a base camp for self-catering mokoro and walking trails, and a good jumping-off point for just about anywhere in the delta. You bring your own tent and sleeping bag (or you can rent a tent). There are communal ablution blocks and a kitchen. You can purchase your food here, which they will cook for you, but you can also stock up with foodstuffs in Maun before traveling into the delta. (Bear in mind that Botswana imports much of its fresh produce, which, having reached Maun after a few days of bouncing along hot, dusty roads, is often in a less-than-appetizing condition.) Prebooking is essential.

However, if you're absolutely determined to go it alone, refer to the "Getting Around" sections below for specific guidelines and information.

## 3 Maun, the Central Okavango Delta & Moremi Game Reserve

The small but sprawling town of Maun is the regional center of Ngamiland (northwestern Botswana) and the gateway to the delta. Not so long ago, progress (in the form of tarred roads and a couple of garish shopping malls) began creeping into this frontier town that once resembled the Wild West. As the starting point for most trips into the delta, Maun has an airport, two open-air shopping malls, three banks, and numerous hotels and lodges, and a plethora of safari tour operators, most of which are based or represented here. Maun makes a good base for exploring, as you can organize a lodge or mobile safari; a game-viewing, birding, hunting, fishing, or photographic expedition; vehicle or boat rentals, and aircraft charter.

### ESSENTIALS

#### VISITOR INFORMATION

See also chapter 2, "Planning Your Trip to Southern Africa," for resources before you go. There is an information center in the airport in Maun, call ☎ **267/650-357.** For information on the parks, contact the **Department of Wildlife and National Parks** (☎ **267/66-0368**) in Maun.

### GETTING THERE

#### BY PLANE

See "Getting There" in chapter 2, "Planning Your Trip to Southern Africa," for details on airlines that fly to Botswana. **Maun's** airport is just south of the delta, or your private camp may arrange for you to fly directly there. This is a very exciting way to travel, and being a passenger in a light plane that has to "buzz" an airstrip, to clear it of herds of grazing zebra before landing, is a great way to start your holiday.

#### BY CAR

From Johannesburg/Pretoria it's about a 5 hour trip via the N1 north to Potgietersrus, and the R35 to Groblersbrug (Martin's Drift on the Botswana side) border post. The border is open 8am to 4pm. Once in Botswana, travel via Palepye and Serule to Francistown (4 to 4 hours), then to Nata. From Nata allow a whole day (say 8am to mid afternoon) for the long, very hot drive across part of the Kalahari to Maun.

## GETTING AROUND

There is no public transport in **Maun,** but it's not a big place and most destinations are reachable on foot. Note that driving and visiting the delta on your own is not really recommended—for specific guidelines and warnings about visiting this region by car, see "Planning Your Own Trip" under "Going on Safari," above.

You can drive north from Maun to the Moremi Game Reserve. A 4×4 is definitely advisable, and can be rented through **Avis** (☎ **267/66-0039**), which has a stand opposite the airport (no street address) in Maun. To get to the reserve, take the Shorobe/South Gate Road (known as the Mababe Road nearer Maun). Eventually the road splits, with the South Gate Road going to Moremi and the other going on to Savuti. The drive takes about 3 hours, with about 2 of that on dirt roads. There are three camping sites in the reserve, offering basic facilities. Remember not to give in to the romantic appeal of sleeping under the stars—there are lions and other predators about. Keep your tent firmly closed.

## MAUN

### WHAT TO SEE & DO

As Maun operates principally as a service center for the safari industry, and not as a tourist attraction in its own right, there isn't much to do or see in the town itself. With a few hours to kill, you might consider visiting the **Nhabe Museum,** (☎ **267/66-1346**) situated on the airport road, opposite Safari South, a forum for the work of local Batswana painters, printmakers, sculptors, woodworkers, and weavers. Open weekdays 8:30am to 5pm and Saturday 9am to 4:30pm.

### WHERE TO STAY & DINE

Ideally you'll transfer directly to your wilderness camp without spending a night in Maun; but should you have to stay, the following establishments are recommended.

**Riley's Hotel.** P.O. Box 1, Maun, Botswana. ☎ **267/66-0204.** Fax 267/66-0580. 52 units. A/C TV TEL. P423 ($96.15) double, includes breakfast. AE, DC, MC, V.

Riley's, although totally rebuilt since its founding in the 1930s, harkens back to the "old Maun." Rooms are comfortable and feature basic comforts like hair dryers and tea- and coffee-making facilities. The hotel has a swimming pool, curio shop, a hair-dressing salon, and a tour operator's desk on the premises. There's good eating at Riley's Grill, and Harry's Bar is lively.

**Island Safari Lodge.** P.O. Box 116, Maun, Botswana. ☎/fax **267/66-0300.** 8 chalets and a camping site. P200 ($45.45) double. DC, MC, V. 12 kilometers outside Maun, on the way to Moremi Game Reserve.

The Island Safari Lodge is a good foretaste of what's to come in the delta for first-time visitors. The chalets are simple, but comfortable. All have private bathrooms. You can make your own food or eat in the restaurant.

## EXPLORING THE DELTA & MOREMI GAME RESERVE

Located in the northwestern corner of the country, this region is for most the highlight of a trip to Botswana, particularly during the winter months (June and July) when "the flood" turns it into an aquatic paradise. The northeastern segment of the delta has been set aside as the Moremi Game Reserve, an 1,800-square-kilometer (1,116-square-mile) expanse of wilderness extending across both wetland and dry terrain.

The delta originates in Angola, to the northwest, from where the Okavango River flows southward for 1,300 kilometers (806 miles) into the Kalahari. Thanks to the same geological activity that caused the Great African Rift Valley, the delta is more or less contained by fault lines between which the crust has sunk and filled up with sediment. It is into this bowl that the Okavango seeps, rather than making its rightful way to the sea. The annual southward flow of water is precipitated by the rainy season in the north, which begins in the Angolan uplands between January and March, and usually arrives at its southernmost point—the delta—around June or July, when the water spreads out to form innumerable pools, channels, and lagoons.

## Where to Stay & Dine

**Khwai River Lodge.** Inquiries and reservations through Gametrackers (see above). 12 en-suite units. AE, MC, V. Accessed by light aircraft to the camp's own airstrip. No children under 12 except by prior arrangement.

Overlooking the river's flood plain 8 kilometers (5 miles) northwest of the Moremi Reserve's North Gate, this is one of the region's oldest and most respected lodges. Canvas-walled luxury tents are set on raised teak platforms under thatch canopies and surrounded by old indigenous leadwood trees. The camp has hot and cold running water and electricity, and rooms have hair dryers. Hippos, elephants, and other big-game animals can be seen from the lodge and grounds, and the bird watching is excellent. Facilities include a swimming pool, book/video library, bar, laundry service, radio communications with 24-hour emergency facility, and a gift shop. Available activities include game drives, guided walks, bird-watching, and game-flights on request.

**Jedibe Island Camp.** Inquiries and reservations through Wilderness Safaris (see above). 16-bed tented camp with en-suite facilities. P1,254 ($285) per person per day, including all meals, activities, park fees, and drinks (on activities, and house wines at dinner).

Situated deep in the heart of the Okavango in the region of permanent water, Jedibe Island Camp offers water activities—mokoro trips, fishing, and bird watching on palm-fringed islands throughout the year. The river that flows past the camp joins the Boro River to form the western boundary of the Moremi Game Reserve. Guests can also go on sunset cruises on the camp's double-decker boat. The game viewing on some of the larger islands near the camp is very good. The camp is solar powered and has a thatch-roofed dining room and pub. Facilities include a plunge pool and a private airstrip.

✪ **Mombo Camp.** Inquiries and reservations through Wilderness Safaris (address and other details above). 20-bed tented camp with en-suite facilities. P2,420 ($550) per person per day, including all meals, activities, park fees, and drinks (on activities, and house wine at dinner).

Mombo is situated just off the northwestern tip of Chief's Island, deep within the Moremi Game Reserve, on the edge of a broad flood plain. Sometimes Mombo forms an island on its own, while at others it is linked to Chief's Island—the region is constantly modified by the ebb and flow of the delta's waters. One of the highlights of a trip to this camp is an afternoon game drive in a 4×4 vehicle; this is the time to spot lion, leopard, buffalo, cheetah, wild dog, elephant, hyena, giraffe, wildebeest, and zebra. Guests can also do short midday foot trails if they want to see game up close. The rustic dining room, lounge, and pub are on a raised deck under thatch. Facilities include a plunge pool and an airfield. The camp is solar powered.

**Gunn's Camp.** Private Bag 033, Maun. ☎ **267/66-0023.** Fax 267/66-0040. E-mail: gunnscamp@info.bw. P1,210 ($275) per person per night, all inclusive. 14-bed luxury camp. Also offers camping-out; safaris cost between P1,122 ($255) and P1,254 ($285) per person sharing for 4 to 6 days. MC, V. No children under 10 permitted.

Situated deep in the delta, Gunn's Camp overlooks Chief's Island and borders the Moremi Game Reserve. The camp is not accessible by road; guests are flown in. Meals are served in an elevated dining room. Rooms have en-suite bathrooms, and facilities include a swimming pool, restaurant, bar, and shop.

## Fair Game

In the delta you'll find plenty of **buffalo, hippo, crocodiles,** and a host of smaller game species like **warthogs** and **hunting dogs,** as well as more than 400 species of **birds.** Keep an eye out for the notoriously shy lechwe and sitatunga, which in southern Africa are restricted to Okavango, Chobe, and some parts of the Caprivi Strip. **Lechwe** are antelopes found near permanent water that mainly eat semi-aquatic grasses, and **sitatunga** are also water-loving antelopes (actually semi-aquatic) and can swim well. **Cheetah** are quite widespread in Botswana, but are not often seen in the delta as their preferred habitat is open savannah and light woodland. **Lions** are common, and **leopards** can often be seen at night—try to go on a night drive, where your ranger will use a spotlight to find nocturnal game. **Elephants** are also seen. For more information, see the "Where & When to See Game" chart in chapter 2.

---

**Machaba Camp.** Inquiries and reservations through Ker & Downey (address and other details above). 8 twin-bedded tents with en-suite bathrooms (hot water and flush toilets). July 1–Oct 15 P1,584 ($360) per person sharing; Mar 1–June 30 and Oct 16–Nov 30 P1,892 ($430) per person sharing. Rates include all meals and activities. Closed Dec 1–Feb 28. No children under 10.

Located on the Khwai River on the northern edge of the Moremi Game Reserve, on the easternmost edge of the delta, Machaba offers great elephant viewing and excellent birding in "the raptor capital" of Botswana. Activities include game drives in Moremi National Park, night drives, and walks. Animals that may be spotted here include lion, leopard, cheetah, wild dog, hyena, elephant, giraffe, reedbuck, and jackal.

**Pom Pom Camp.** Inquiries and reservations through Ker & Downey (address and other details above). 8 deluxe tented camps with en-suite bathrooms (hot water and flush toilets). July 1–Oct 15 P1,584 ($360) per person sharing; Mar 1–June 30 and Oct 16–Nov 30 P1,892 ($430) per person sharing. Rates include all meals and activities. Closed Dec 1–Feb 28. No children under 10.

This cozy, very comfortable tented camp is one of the more remote camps in the delta. Among its attractions are the area's superb birdlife and its fishing. From here, you can take game walks, drives, and mokoro excursions. Animals often sighted include lion, leopard, wild dog, cheetah, hyena, elephant, kudu, reedbuck, warthog, and steenbok. The lagoon in front of the camp houses crocs and hippo—bring earplugs if you're a light sleeper. There is a restaurant on site.

**Shinde Island Camp.** Inquiries and reservations through Ker & Downey (address and other details above). 8 units, consisting of 7 deluxe tented camps and 1 honeymoon suite, all with en-suite bathrooms (hot water and flush toilets). July 1–Oct 15 P1,694 ($385) per person sharing; Mar 1–June 30 and Oct 16–Nov 30 P2,024 ($460) per person sharing. Rates include all meals and activities. DC, V. Closed Dec 1–Feb 28. No children under 10.

On a lush palm island in the heart of the northern delta, Shinde is surrounded by waterways that teem with birds and game. Activities include game drives, powerboat excursions, guided walks, fishing, and mokoro safaris. Facilities include a pool and an airstrip. Elephants, lions, lechwe, cheetah, giraffe, leopard, baboon, and many bird species are commonly seen.

**Xakanaxa Camp.** Inquiries and reservations through Moremi Safaris & Tours (address and other details above). P1,210 ($275) per person per night sharing (low-season, January to June); P1,584 ($360) per person per night sharing (high-season, July to December), all inclusive. 12 luxury, twin-bed spacious safari tents set on wooden platforms with en-suite bathrooms. AE, V (both require prior authorization). No children under 12 permitted.

Situated within the Moremi Game Reserve, 50 kilometers (31 miles) to the west of Khwai in the northern sector of Moremi, Xakanaxa offers year-round boating trips and extensive nature drives into good game country. Expect to see buffalo, elephant, lion, zebra, wildebeest, giraffe, warthog, wild dog, lechwe, hippo, leopards, tsessebe, sitatunga, and sable. The bird watching is excellent. The dining room and bar overlook Xakanaxa Lagoon, and there is a gift shop.

## 4 Chobe National Park & Surrounds

The Chobe National Park covers some 11,000 square kilometers (6,820 square miles) of northern Botswana and offers extreme contrasts and a variety of wildlife experiences. It harbors a large proportion of Botswana's elephant population and more than 460 different species of birds. In the dry season, the Chobe River is the only major source of water north of the Okavango, so game gathers here from great distances. The nearby Savuti area of the west-central region, a relatively harsh landscape, was once submerged beneath an enormous inland sea. As far as game is concerned, it is at its peak at the end of the rainy season, when large numbers of zebra and wildebeest move through the area from the Linyanti farther west to the sweeter grasses on offer in the Mababe Depression to the south. Other wildlife to be seen here includes giraffe, buffalo, tsessebe, and elephant, and large prides of lion and hyena.

### ESSENTIALS

#### VISITORS INFORMATION

For information and reservations, contact the **Department of Wildlife and National Parks.** P.O. Box 17, Kasane, Botswana. ☎ **267/65-0235,** fax 267/66-1264. E-mail: dwnpbots@global.bw.

#### GETTING THERE

**BY PLANE** **Kasane International Airport** (☎ **267/65 0598**) is 3 kilometers (about 2 miles) from the entrance to Chobe National Park. **Air Botswana** (☎ **267/66-0391**) has connections to Gaborone and Maun. See "Getting There by Plane" in chapter 2 for more information on flying to Botswana.

**BY CAR** From Victoria Falls, there's a road heading southwest to Kasane.

#### GETTING AROUND

For specific guidelines, car-rental information, and warnings, see "Planning Your Own Trip" under "Going on Safari," above, and note that visiting this area on your own by car is not really recommended. That said, Chobe National Park's 35 kilometers (22 miles) of river frontage is well developed for tourism. Splendid private lodges fringe the river, and the road network is generally in good condition. However, for the rest you'll need a 4×4 and the sandy surfaces can be treacherous. There are five public campsites scattered around the park. Take everything you think you'll need as facilities are barely adequate.

### WHERE TO STAY & DINE

**Chobe Game Lodge.** P.O. Box 32, Kasane, Botswana. ☎ **267/25-0340.** Reservations through P.O. Box 130555, Bryanston 2021, South Africa. ☎ 27/11/706-0861, fax 27/11/706-0863. 44 units with en-suite bathrooms. P725 ($164.75) per person per night double, includes meals, game-viewing activities, the Chobe National Park fees, as well as transfers from/to Kasane airport. Children's rates available on request. DC, MC, V.

Overlooking the Chobe River within the Chobe National Park, this is arguably the country's most elegant hotel. It is famed for having accommodated Liz Taylor and

### Admiring Ancient Art

If you're interested in Bushman (San) culture, the **General Safari Company** can organize a visit to the **Tsodilo Hills** (in the northwest, near the panhandle), to see the over 3,000 **rock paintings** there. These paintings are known for their fine clarity and wide variety, and trips can be made by air or four-wheel drive. There is also a traditional village nestled in the foothills. Contact them at P.O. Box 41567, Craighall 2024, Johannesburg, South Africa; ☎ **27/11/990-8466,** fax 27/11/880-6136; or by e-mail at atg@igubu.saix.net.

Richard Burton on their honeymoon (after they married for the second time). Rooms have fans, and if you want to splurge on one of the four private suites, you can enjoy your own swimming pool and outside garden patio. Facilities include a wildlife reference library, gift shop, conference center, cocktail bar and lounge, and a restaurant.

**King's Pool Camp.** Inquiries and reservations through Wilderness Safaris (address and other details above). 20-bed luxury tented camp with thatched en suite bathrooms. P1,254 ($285) per person per day, including meals, activities, park fees, and drinks (on activities, and house wines at dinner). MC, V.

On a private reserve in the Linyanti/Savuti Channel area, on the western boundary of the Chobe National Park, King's Pool Camp overlooks the King's Pool Lagoon and the Linyanti River to the north, in an area noted for its elephants. Each room is built on a raised teak deck with wonderful views onto the King's Pool Lagoon—this waterway has great birdlife; and hippos, crocodiles, bushbuck, impala, elephant, and sable are all seen from the rooms on a regular basis. There is also a main lounge, swimming pool and pub, as well as a dining room under a thatched roof. There are hides from which to view game. Game viewing activities include drives in open 4×4 vehicles, night drives, walking with a professional guide, and cruising along the Linyanti River in a double-decker boat.

**Savuti Camp.** Inquiries and reservations through Wilderness Safaris (address and other details above). 8 beds in 5 large walk-in Meru tented rooms with en-suite facilities. P1,254 ($285) per person per day, including meals, activities, park fees, and drinks (on activities, and house wines at dinner). MC, V.

The dining and pub areas are under a thatched roof and facilities include a plunge pool and game-viewing hides. Built alongside the Savuti Channel, this camp is in a legendary wildlife region known for its large number of predators. Activities include game drives, night drives, and walks.

**Chobe Chilwero.** In South Africa: P.O. Box 782607, Sandton 2146. ☎ **27/11/781-1497,** fax 27/11/781-7658. In Botswana: Private Bag K46, Kasane. ☎ **267/65-1362.** E-mail: chilwero@res-centre.co.za. P1,342 ($305) per person per night sharing. 8 A-frame chalets with en-suite bathrooms. DC, MC, V.

Located near the main gates of the Chobe Reserve, this is an intimate little camp. Daily game drives and river cruises will ensure you see the widest variety of game possible. The camp is fully electrified, uses solar lighting, and has a bar, a gift shop, and a swimming pool.

## 5 The Dry South: Makgadikgadi & Nxai Pans

The Kalahari, one of the longest unbroken stretches of sand in the world, reaches across the center of Botswana, north into Zaire, and south to the Orange River in South Africa. On its northern edge are the enormous complexes of the Makgadikgadi Pans and the relatively small but no less interesting Nxai Pans. Game migrates between the two throughout the year: In the dry season (April to November), Makgadikgadi is best; while during the rains (November to March), the animals move northward to Nxai.

The Makgadikgadi Pans are a vast (12,000 square km/7,440 square miles), game-filled expanse of flat, seasonally inundated land. When they fill with water after the rains, they host countless migratory birds, most notably huge flocks of flamingoes. This is the place to go to experience space at its purest: The horizons seem endless; while at night, above the pie-crust surface of the pans, the stars shine with a vibrancy unequalled anywhere else in the world.

Ancient baobab trees are conspicuous in the Nxai Pans area. Here you can camp under large camelthorn trees and venture out to view springbok, gemsbok (oryx), red hartebeest, blackbacked jackal, and, occasionally, cheetah and lion.

## ESSENTIALS

### VISITOR INFORMATION

For campsite reservations and more information, contact the **Department of Wildlife and National Parks,** P.O. Box 131, Gaborone, Botswana; ☎ **267/37-1405.**

### GETTING THERE

**BY PLANE** Your best bet is to fly to Maun and arrange a transfer with a guided tour company or Jack's Camp.

**BY CAR** Access is by 4×4 only. The pans are best reached via the Maun-Nata Road. Gweta, a town just outside the game reserves, makes a good base.

### GETTING AROUND

**BY CAR** For specific guidelines, car-rental information, and warnings, see "Planning Your Own Trip" under "Going on Safari" above, and note that visiting this area on your own by car is not really recommended. A 4×4 is definitely recommended. Take everything you think you'll need—and more. Don't stray from the roads as the salty crust of the pans can crack and vehicles sink. Walking is not permitted. There are some campsites, which must be prebooked through the Department of Wildlife and National Parks.

**ON A GUIDED TOUR** For tailor-made tours in the pans, contact **Penstone Safaris** in Maun (☎ **267/66-1721,** fax 267/66-1722).

## ✪ WHERE TO STAY & DINE

**Jack's Camp.** Inquiries and reservations through Unchartered Africa Safari Co. In South Africa: P.O. Box 1996, Northriding 2162. ☎ **27/11/462-9448.** Fax 27/11/462-9447. E-mail: bianca@unchartedafrica.co.za. In Botswana: P.O. Box 173, Francistown. ☎ **267/21-2277.** Fax 267/21-3458. P1,804 ($410) per person per night. 8 en-suite, open air tents. MC, V.

Voted one of the top-10 honeymoon destinations in the world by the South African editions of *Elle* and *Men's Health,* as well as best safari camp by both the *London Sunday Times* and *UK Vogue,* Jack's Camp is the place to go to experience the Kalahari in style. Safari tents furnished with Persian rugs and teak and canvas furniture provide a bizarre counterpoint to the endless wild surrounds (visible from the privacy of your own verandah). And if you grow bored of lolling about on antique rugs, you can head out for one of the many activities: game drives, walking safaris, or exploring remote archeological sites and geological features. Using four-wheel drive quad bikes, guests are able to explore previously impenetrable areas in an ecologically sensitive manner. After the rains (December to April), expect to see herds of wildebeest, zebra, and springbok, as well as their predators.

# 6 The Tuli Block

This region in the eastern corner of Botswana, historically known as the Tuli enclave, is a good one to visit from South Africa if your time is very limited or if you're traveling independently. However, it doesn't have the dramatic impact of the delta. In these vast, wide-open spaces, it is rare that you'll run across another vehicle, but you'll certainly see herds of elephant and impala, as well as lion, leopard, ostrich, cheetah, hyena, impala, warthog, and hundreds of bird species.

## ESSENTIALS

### GETTING THERE

**BY CAR** From Johannesburg take the N1 north, changing to the R521 outside Pietersburg and continuing to the border post at Pont Drift. The 500-kilometer (310-mile) trip will take about 5 hours. The border-post hours are 8am to 4pm daily and the rendezvous time with the Mashatu rangers is noon (call ahead to reserve a space, or to arrive at another time). Driving time from the border post to Mashatu is about 40 minutes. Mashatu will also arrange transfers at a cost of R450 ($75) per person one-way.

**BY PLANE** From Johannesburg, you can fly a private charter from Lanseria Airport (north of Johannesburg) to Tuli airstrip. Contact Mashatu Game Reserve for flights.

## WHERE TO STAY & DINE

**Mashatu Game Reserve.** Inquiries and reservations (including air and land transfers) through ☎ **27/11/789-2677**, fax 27/11/886-4382. P.O. Box 2575, 2125 Randburg, South Africa. E-mail: jhb@malamala.com.www.malamala.com. Mashatu office in Botswana, ☎ **267/84-5321.** Main camp: 17 units includes 1 suite and 5 family rooms. A/C. R792–924 ($132–$154) per person per day sharing; children under 12 sharing 50% deduction. Tented camp: 7 twin-bed tents. R660 ($110) per person per day. No children under 12, and no reduced rate. Note that prices are quoted in rand, but may be made in any international currency accepted by South African banks. All accommodations en-suite. Rates include meals and snacks, activities, and transfers to and from the airstrip or border post. Alcoholic beverages are extra. AE, DC, MC, V.

Mashatu is very accessible from South Africa (a charter plane from Johannesburg takes just over an hour). The camp's pedigree (it is run by the same people who run MalaMala—see chapter 7) and its size (30,000 ha/75,000 acres) ensure a quality experience. There are two options at Mashatu, of which Main Camp is more appropriate for travelers who crave a shot of luxury after a long, hot game drive. The rooms here have 24-hour hot water and electricity, air-conditioning, laundry, and pool. Tented camp is more rustic, but still supremely comfortable. It's a terrific choice for those who want a real sense of being surrounded by the bush, but would rather not use a chamber pot at night. There is no air-conditioning or electricity, but the open-air showers have hot water, and at night the camp becomes incredibly romantic, lit by dozens of flickering kerosene lamps. Rooms come with solar-powered light for nighttime reading, and there is a plunge pool. All rooms at both camps have private verandahs, but don't expect to see much if you're at tented camp—the trees are great for privacy, but not for views. Activities include game drives and guided walks; the rangers are very knowledgeable, and the staff courteous and helpful. Animals are not quite as used to vehicles as they are at South Africa's private game reserves; but while I was there, we still managed to get an X-rated close-up of some rutting lions.

**Dining:** When the evening game drive ends at about 8:30pm, you'll be eager to warm yourself at the fire in the boma and tuck into the soup, salads, venison, and various vegetables that comprise dinner. (Call ahead if you have special dietary needs.)

# South Africa in Depth

People come to South Africa for its natural beauty, sunshine, and wildlife, and few leave disappointed. A vast country about twice the size of Texas, its northeastern border (formed by the Limpopo River) is some 2,000 kilometers (1,240 miles) from the Cape's craggy coastline, while the semi-arid West Coast is over 1,600 kilometers (992 miles) from the subtropical East Coast. This immensely varied terrain supports a rich diversity of animals, birds, and plants, and offers a correspondingly diverse range of experiences. Historically, too, the contrasts are great: 3.5-million-year-old hominid remains makes this one of the cradles of civilization, yet the country has only recently emerged from the dark shadow of an oppressive policy that made it the pariah of the modern world. Born with the dawning millennium, the "New South Africa," as the post-apartheid South Africa is called, has one of the most progressive constitutions in the world, yet the overwhelming majority of its people live in the most primitive conditions imaginable. Tourists who find their visit somewhat marred by the degree of poverty so many South Africans suffer can gain some comfort from the knowledge that tourism is one of the few industries that has shown real growth over the past few years, bringing in much-needed revenue. Tourism currently contributes about R53.2 billion (almost $9 billion) to the GDP. There is little doubt that this figure will increase, not least because—for many—a first visit necessitates a second.

## 1 The Natural Environment

Geographically, much of South Africa is situated on an interior plateau (referred to as the highveld), circled by a coastal belt which widens in the eastern hinterland to become bush savannah, or lowveld. It is on these undulating plains that you will find some of South Africa's most famous reserves, including Kruger National Park. A series of mountain ranges in the southwestern corner have created a unique climate and flora; while the country's most majestic range, the Drakensberg, lies in the eastern half of the country, in a south-north direction, where it creates the lip of the highveld, which overlooks the lowveld. Many species—in fact, 15% of South Africa's mammals, 30% of its reptiles, 6% of its bird species and a massive 80% of its plants—occur nowhere else in the world.

**MAMMALS** South Africa's 273 mammal species are a strong drawing card (not least of which are the increasingly large numbers of

Southern Right **whales** which migrate annually to breed off the Cape's shores). South Africa enjoys an excellent conservation history (Kruger recently celebrated its centenary), and thousands of **lions, leopards, rhinos, elephants, buffaloes, hippos, giraffes, zebras, wildebeest,** and a large variety of **antelope** live unfettered, their rituals and cycles relatively unaffected by the technology of the 21st century. Migratory behavior has been curtailed by fences and borders, however, and in the smaller parks and reserves the "natural" balance between predator and prey is something man controls. Some go as far as describing South Africa's vast wilderness tracts as large game farms; and while to some extent this is true, there is no real alternative. Hunting, or "culling," is very much part of conservation. With a government reeling from the pressure to provide housing, medical care, and schooling for the many dispossessed, the onus is now very much on the private sector to provide funding. Eco-tourism—this buzzword crops up all over South Africa—is supposed to do just that, and visitors to South Africa's wildernesses are a vital link in the protection of these pristine areas.

**BIRDS & PLANTS** South Africa also offers a huge variety of bird species—870, to be exact. Of these, 600 species breed on South African shores. This is largely due to the country's incredibly varied vegetation, consisting of over 24,000 plant species, and one-tenth of the world's flowering plants. The **Cape Floral Kingdom,** one of six floral kingdoms in the world, covers an area of some 43,200-square-kilometers (27,000 square miles), yet its plant diversity is comparable to that found in the 32-million-square-mile (20-million-square-mile) Boreal Kingdom, which covers all of Europe, North America, and northern Asia. This high concentration of unique plant species makes the Cape as important an area of conservation as the Amazon Basin; and although it is by no means as threatened, the introduction of alien, invasive species by humans during the past century has done tremendous damage.

The delicate inhabitants of the Cape Floral Kingdom are referred to as **fynbos,** or fine bush (pronounced *feign*-borse)—an evergreen vegetation characterized by the ability to thrive on nutrient-poor soil and survive the Cape's windy, baking summers and cold winters. Thought to be the oldest floral kingdom of the world, and certainly the most diverse, three-quarters of fynbos species are found nowhere else—many are so specialized, in fact, that they grow only in one valley. The most well-known groups are **proteas** (of which the King Protea is South Africa's national flower), **ericas** (which feature fine, bell-shaped flowers), and **restios** (reeds). Appearing to be a homogenous gray-green heathland from afar, the miraculously delicate, yet tough leaves and flowers are best appreciated close up. To get to know the "fine bush," you will need to explore the coast and mountains of the Western Cape on foot, and get your nose inches from the unique shapes and textures you'll find there. Book into **Grootbos Nature Reserve,** outside Hermanus (see Western Cape), or if you want a more easy-going approach, a wander through the **Kirstenbosch National Botanic Gardens** will suffice.

**MOUNTAINS** Most hikers agree that there is nothing to beat the sheer majesty of the Drakensberg. This mountain range extends northward from the Eastern Cape, reaching its highest peak in KwaZulu-Natal at Injasuti (3,408 meters/11,178 feet), before ranging through Mpumalanga and the Northern Province, where it is commonly referred to as the Escarpment. Isolated areas of indigenous forest occur in its gorges and sheltered slopes, and it is this mountain range which separates the eastern coastal belt and lowveld from the high interior plateau on which the rolling grasslands, farms, and mines of the centrally located Free State and Gauteng are situated. More famous is the flat-topped Table Mountain in Cape Town, which at a mere 1,086 meters (3,562 feet) is no giant, but is nonetheless the most climbed mountain in South Africa. Those in search of real tranquility should consider heading north for the Cedarberg Wilderness Area, a mountainous area worth exploring for its bizarre sandstone formations and rock art.

**DESERT** While South Africa has no true deserts, much of its vast hinterland is arid and, with only two major rivers (the Vaal and Orange), rapidly increasing water demands, and a decreasing water table, water is the number one problem the country will face in the next century. There are two distinct semi-desert regions. Beyond the mountains and valleys of the southwest corner of the Cape is the **Karoo,** which supports the famous **ostrich farms** and produces the delicately flavored **Karoo lamb;** and in the northwest, bordering both Botswana and Namibia, is the painterly landscape of the **Kalahari**—broad swathes of gold and red sand dunes and cobalt-blue skies. Like Namaqualand in the Northern Cape, which is famed for its daisy carpets, the Karoo also flowers in spring, but here the change is more subtle. The **Karoo National Botanical Gardens,** near Worcester in the Western Cape, offers an excellent introduction to this unique flora.

**COAST** For those who prefer a little sea with their sand, there are almost 3,200 kilometers (2,000 miles) of coast to explore; South Africa borders the **Atlantic Ocean** in the west and the **Indian Ocean** in the east. The Indian Ocean is better for swimming, due to the warm Mozambique Current that has created the world's most southerly **coral reefs** on the north coast of KwaZulu-Natal. Moving southward along the coast, the vegetation remains lush, with pockets of indigenous forest. The largest and most famous are found on the Garden Route near George and Knysna. The majestic **yellowwoods** and **stinkwoods** grow here, as do the **cycads,** often known as fossil plants as they have remained unchanged since the Jurassic era. (Examples of these also still occur in the north-eastern interior, particularly in the Magoebaskloof region). Farther south, the Indian and Atlantic oceans meet more or less at **Cape Agulhas,** the southernmost tip of Africa. Along this coast, referred to as the **Overberg,** you will find some of the best shore-based **whale watching** in the world.

Moving north up the West Coast, the coastal strip abutting the cold Atlantic Ocean is increasingly sparse and harsh. It is here, in the semi-desert called **Namaqualand,** that an annual miracle occurs—the first spring rains. When these fall in August or September, the seemingly barren earth is transformed into a dense carpet of **flowers** stretching as far as the eye can see.

Over and above these natural coastal regions are the **vineyards** and **orchards** of the Western Cape, the rolling ***mielie*** (corn) and **wheat fields** of the Free State, the **sugar cane** of KwaZulu-Natal, and the **subtropical plantations** of Mpumalanga and the Northern Province.

## 2 South Africa Today

After years of isolation and shame, South Africa has spent the better part of the last decade proving that its miraculously peaceful transformation from human rights pariah to accepted world player was no flash in the pan. Today after 300 years of white domination, South Africa enters the new Millennium with what is widely regarded as the world's most progressive constitution.

South Africa's past has been held up for close inspection by the Truth and Reconciliation Commission, the first of its kind in the world (see box). By rewriting history to accurately reflect events of the past 40 years, it is hoped that it will never repeat itself.

Augmenting these ideological achievements are those that have happened on a grassroots level: 5 years after the country's first democratic election, 750,000 houses had been built or were under construction, 3 million rural people were provided with access to running water for the first time, 2 million households were electrified and a primary school nutrition program had reached 5 million children. With 700 clinics built or modernized and free medical care provided to pregnant women and children under 6, primary health care services improved dramatically. New laws to facilitate land restitution facilitated the hand over of a tract of land to one of the last remaining San groups. Finance Minister Trevor Manual's deficit-reducing 1999 budget increased spending on social services and education, yet was applauded by the business community, balancing as it did the multi-faceted needs of the country. Simultaneously, the artistic endeavors of organizations such as the previously state-funded opera, ballet, theatre, and orchestras have found support in the private sector, as have the national parks and reserves. Sponsoring playgrounds to be enjoyed by the privileged few was obviously no longer an option for a government struggling to redress longstanding inequalities, but happily the best of these survive through private funds.

South African sports heroes, barred from competing internationally for two decades, added to the nation's growing pride, winning the Rugby World Cup in 1995 and its first gold Olympic medals in 1996. Black-owned business has grown significantly, from some 1% ($748 million) of total market capitalization of the Johannesburg Stock Exchange in 1996, to 5.5% ($9.2 billion) in 1999, and an estimated 4 million blacks now comprise more than half of the top earners in the country.

But these achievements, garnered in a mere 5 years, have not come without a price. Between 1996 and 1998, South Africa's currency lost more than 50 percent of its value against the dollar and the British pound. The incidence of violent crimes like murder, rape, assault, and armed robbery have doubled since 1994. Equally distressing is the continued divide between black and white incomes, reinforcing South Africa's strange mix of first- and third-world elements. Despite aggressive affirmative action policies, per capita white income is still 9.5 times higher than that of blacks, and 95 percent of those at or below poverty level are black.

With unemployment estimated at 38 percent and the economic growth rate ranging between 0.1 and 2 percent less, the concomitant rise in crime is hardly surprising. Since 1994, 100,000 jobs have been lost every year, and with the depression in the gold market this figure is expected to rise rapidly. According to a recent article in *Time Magazine*, AIDS is expected to cut the average life expectancy of South Africans by some 20 years and shrink economic growth by a further 2%.

If the ANC (who won the 1999 elections with a landslide victory of 66.03 percent of the vote) are to deliver on their campaign promise of a better life for all, they will have to focus on strategies to stimulate the economy, while eradicating crime and corruption. The question now is whether new president Thabo Mbeki, a man who spent his life serving the ANC in exile, can play the role that history demands.

As much as Madiba, as Mandela is affectionately known, was a force for reconciliation, Mbeki has made it quite clear that his focus will be on transformation and delivery. Many insiders feel he has the energy, wisdom, and ruthless dedication to achieve this. "Africa," Mbeki has promised, ""will prosper!" Its time has come.





## 3 A Look at the Past

Any history of South Africa depends very much on those recounting the tale. Under the apartheid regime, children were taught that during the 19th century, when the first pioneering Voortrekkers made their way north from the Cape Peninsula, southern Africa was a vast, undiscovered wilderness. At more or less the same time that whites started exploring the region, black tribes were making their way south from central Africa. Blacks and whites thus conveniently met on land which belonged to no one, and if the natives would not move aside for the trinkets and oxen on offer, everyone simply rolled up his/her sleeves and had an honest fight—which the whites, who enjoyed the protection of the Lord, almost always won. Of course, for those who pursued the truth rather than a nationalistic version of it, the past was infinitely more complex—not least because so little of it was recorded.

**FROM APES TO ARTISTS** Hundreds of hominid remains have been found in South Africa, some of which can be viewed at the **Sterkfontein Caves** in Gauteng. These suggest that the earliest known human was born here nearly 3 million years ago.

The oldest fossil evidence of Homo sapiens has also been found, this time in the Eastern Cape. This proved that man, his brain now much larger, was padding about in South Africa 50,000 to 100,000 years ago. But by far the most arresting evidence of human activity in southern Africa is the many **rock paintings** that the San hunter-gatherers (or Bushmen, as they were dubbed by Europeans) used to record events dating as far back as 30,000 years. The closest living relative of Stone Age man, a few small family units of San still survive in the Kalahari Desert; but the last San artist must have died over a hundred years ago, as the most recent rock painting dates back to the previous century.

It is from these drawings that we can deduce that Bantu-speaking Iron Age settlers were living in South Africa long before the arrival of the white colonizers. Dark skinned and technologically more sophisticated than the San,

### Dateline

- **Circa 8000 B.C.** San (Bushmen) inhabit southern Africa. They are followed by the KhoiKhoi (Hottentot), and much later Bantu-speaking people (blacks). Their history is largely undocumented.
- **A.D. 1488** Bartholomieu Dias rounds the Cape and lands at Mossel Bay.
- **1497** Vasco da Gama rounds the Cape and discovers an alternate sea route to India.
- **1652** Jan van Riebeeck is sent to set up a supply station for the Dutch East India Company. Cape Town is born.
- **1659** The first serious armed conflict against the KhoiKhoi occurs; the first wine is pressed.
- **1667–1700** First Malay slaves arrive, followed by the French Huguenots.
- **1779** The first frontier war between the Xhosa and settlers in the Eastern Cape is fought. Eight more were to follow in what is now known as the "Hundred Years War."
- **1795** The British occupy the Cape for 7 years, and then hand it back to the Dutch.
- **1806** Britain reoccupies the Cape, this time for 155 years.
- **1815** Shaka becomes the Zulu king.
- **1820** The British settlers arrive in the Eastern Cape. In KwaZulu-Natal, Shaka starts his great expansionary war more or less at the same time, decimating numbers of opposing tribes and leaving large areas depopulated in his wake.

*continues*

- **1824** Port Natal is established by British traders.
- **1828** Shaka is murdered by his half-brother Dingaan, who succeeds him as king.
- **1834** Slavery is abolished in the Cape, sparking off the Great Trek.
- **1835–1845** Over 16,000 bitter Dutch settlers head for the uncharted hinterland in ox-wagons to escape British domination.
- **1838** A party of Voortrekkers manages to vanquish the great Zulu forces at the Battle of Blood River. This, they believe, is because of the covenant they made with God.
- **1843** Natal becomes a British colony.
- **1852** Several parties of Boers move farther northeast and found the Zuid Afrikaansche Republiek (ZAR).
- **1854** The Boer Independent Republic of the Orange Free State is founded by another party of Boers.
- **1858** British defeat Xhosa after the "Great Cattle Killing."
- **1860** The first indentured Indian workers arrive in Natal.
- **1867** Diamonds are found near Kimberley in the Orange Free State.
- **1877** The British annex the ZAR.
- **1879** Anglo-Zulu War breaks out, orchestrated by the British.
- **1880–1881** First Anglo-Boer War is fought. Boers defeat British.
- **1883** Paul Kruger becomes the first president of the ZAR (Transvaal).
- **1886** Gold is discovered on the Witwatersrand.
- **1899–1902** The Second Anglo-Boer War is fought.
- **1910** The Union of South Africa proclaimed. Louis Botha becomes first premier.

*continues*

they started crossing the Limpopo about 2,000 years ago, and over the centuries four main groups of migrants settled in South Africa: the **Nguni**-speaking group, of which the Zulu and Xhosa are part, followed by the **Tsonga, Sotho-Tswana,** and **Venda**-speakers. **Trading centers** were developed, such as those at Phalaborwa, the remains of which can still be viewed in the Kruger.

By the 13th century most of South Africa's eastern flank was occupied by these African people, while the San remained concentrated in the west. In Botswana, a small number of the latter were introduced to the concept of sheep- and cattle-keeping. These agrarian groups migrated south and called themselves the KhoiKhoi (men of men), to differentiate themselves from their San relatives. It was with these indigenous people that the first seafarers came into contact. The KhoiKhoi saw themselves as a superior bunch, and it must have been infuriating to be called Hottentots by the Dutch (a term still considered degrading today).

## THE COLONIZATION OF THE CAPE

When spice was as precious as gold, the bravest men in Europe were the Portuguese crew who set off with **Bartholomieu Dias** in 1487 to drop off the edge of the world and find an alternative trade route to the Indies. Dias rounded the Cape, which he named Tormentoso (Stormy Cape), after his fleet of three tiny ships battled storms for 3 days before he tacked back to what is today known as Mossel Bay. (Interested visitors can view a replica of his caravel at the **Maritime Museum** here in Mossel Bay.) Suffering from acute scurvy, his men forced him to turn back soon after this.

It was 10 years before another group of men was foolhardy enough to follow in their footsteps. **Vasco da Gama** sailed past what had been renamed the Cape of Good Hope, making it beyond the East Coast, which he named Natal, and all the way to India.

The Portuguese opened the sea route to the East, but it was the Dutch who took advantage of the strategic port at the tip of Africa. In 1652 (30 years after the first

English settled in the United States), **Jan van Riebeeck,** who had been caught cooking the Dutch East India Company books in Malaysia, was sent to open a refreshment station as penance. The idea was not to colonize the Cape, but simply to create a halfway house for trading ships. Van Riebeeck was given strict instructions to trade with the natives and in no way enslave them. Inevitably, relations soured, as the climate and beauty of the Cape led to members of the crew and soldiers settling permanently on the land, with little recompense for the KhoiKhoi. To prevent the KhoiKhoi from seeking revenge, Van Riebeeck attempted to create a boundary along the Liesbeeck River by planting a bitter-almond hedge—the remains of this hedge still grow today in the Kirstenbosch Gardens. This, together with the advantage of firepower and the introduction of hard liquor, reduced the KhoiKhoi to no more than a nuisance. Those who didn't toe the line were imprisoned on **Robben Island,** and by the beginning of the 18th century the remaining KhoiKhoi were reduced to virtual slavery by disease and drink. Over the years their genes slowly mingled with those of slaves and burghers to create a new underclass, later known as the coloureds.

In 1666, the foundation stones for the **Castle of Good Hope** were laid and soon, still more elements were added to the melting pot of Cape culture. Van Riebeeck persuaded the company to allow the import of **slaves** from the Dutch East Indies; this was followed by the arrival of the **French Huguenots** in 1668. Fleeing religious persecution, these Protestants increased the size of the colony by 15%, and brought with them the ability to cultivate **wine.** The glorious results of their input can still be enjoyed in the valley of **Franschhoek** (French corner), where most of the Huguenots settled.

The British enter the picture in 1795, taking control of the Cape when the Dutch East India Company was liquidated. In 1803 they handed it back to the Dutch for 3 years, after which they were to rule the Cape for 155 years.

One of their first tasks was to silence the "savages" on the Eastern Frontier—these were the **Xhosa,** part of the Nguni-speaking people who migrated south from central Africa. Part of the plan was the creation of a buffer zone of

Blacks are excluded from the process.

- **1912** The South African Native National Congress is formed. After 1923 it would be known as the African National Congress (ANC).
- **1913** The Native Land Act is passed, limiting land ownership for blacks and creating homeland territories.
- **1914–1918** South Africa declares war on Germany.
- **1923** Natives (Urban Areas) Act imposes segregation in towns.
- **1939–1945** South Africa joins the Allies in fighting World War II.
- **1948** D. F. Malan's National Party wins the election; the era of apartheid is born. Races are classified, the pass book system is created, and interracial sex is made illegal.
- **1955** ANC adopts the Freedom Charter.
- **1956** Coloureds lose the right to vote.
- **1958** H. F. Verwoerd, the architect of apartheid, succeeds D. F. Malan and creates the homelands.
- **1959** Robert Sobukwe forms the Pan African National Congress (PAC).
- **1960** Police open fire on demonstrators at Sharpeville, killing 69 people. ANC and PAC banned.
- **1961** South Africa leaves the Commonwealth and becomes a republic. ANC takes up the armed struggle; Albert Luthuli awarded Nobel Peace Prize.
- **1963** Nelson Mandela and others sentenced to life imprisonment in the Rivonia sabotage trials.
- **1970s** The world begins to initiate economic and cultural boycotts in response to South Africa's human rights abuses.

*continues*

- **1976** Police open fire on unarmed children demonstrating against use of Afrikaans as a teaching medium; the Soweto riots follow.
- **1977** Black-consciousness leader Steve Biko dies in police custody.
- **1980–1984** President P. W. Botha attempts cosmetic reforms. Unrest escalates. Bishop Tutu is awarded the Nobel Peace Prize for urging sanctions.
- **1985** State of Emergency declared, gagging the press and giving security forces absolute power.
- **1989** F. W. de Klerk succeeds P. W. Botha.
- **1990** de Klerk ends the State of Emergency, lifts the ban on the ANC and frees Mandela.
- **1993** de Klerk and Mandela are jointly awarded the Nobel Peace Prize.
- **1994** The first democratic elections are held and on May 10 Mandela is sworn in as the first black president of South Africa. de Klerk and Thabo Mbeki become joint Deputy Presidents.
- **1995** Truth and Reconciliation Commission created under Archbishop Desmond Tutu.
- **1997** South Africa's new constitution, one of the world's most progressive, comes into effect on February 3.
- **1998** Truth and Reconciliation Commission ends. Mandela receives the Congressional Gold Medal from the United States.
- **1999** The second democratic elections are held. The ANC gets 66.03% of the vote and Thabo Mbeki becomes president.

English settlers. Between 1820 and 1824, thousands of artisans and soldiers were offloaded in the Eastern Cape, issued with basic implements, tents, and seeds, and sent off to deal with the Xhosa. Four frontier wars followed, but it was the extraordinary **cattle-killing incident** that crippled the Xhosa: In 1856 a young girl, Nongqawuse, prophesied that if the Xhosa killed all their cattle and destroyed their crops, the dead would rise and help vanquish the settlers. Needless to say, this did not occur, and while four more wars were to follow, the Xhosa's might was broken.

**THE RISE OF THE ZULU & AFRIKANER CONFLICTS** At the turn of the century, the **Zulus,** who lived in what is now called KwaZulu-Natal, were growing increasingly combative as their survival depended on absorbing neighbors to gain control of pasturage. A young warrior named **Shaka,** who took total despotic control of the Zulus in 1818, raised this to an art form—in addition to arming his new regiments with the short stabbing spear, Shaka was a great military tactician, and devised a strategy known as the **horns of the bull,** whereby the enemy was outflanked by highly disciplined formations that eventually engulfed them. This was used to great effect on tribes in the region, and by the middle of the decade the Zulus had formed a centralized military state with a 40,000-strong army. In a movement known as the **Mfecane,** or forced migrations, huge areas of the country were cleared. People were either killed or absorbed by the Zulus; many fled, creating new kingdoms such as **Swaziland** and **Lesotho.** In 1828 Shaka was murdered by his two brothers, one of whom, Dingaan, succeeded him as king.

On the other side of the continent, in the Cape, British interference in labor relations and their language infuriated many of the Dutch settlers, who were by now referred to as *Afrikaners* (of Africa), and later, *Boers* (farmers). The abolishing of slavery in 1834 was the last straw. Afrikaners objected to "not so much their freedom" as one wrote, "as their being placed on an equal footing with Christians, contrary to the laws of God and the natural distinction of race."

**Impressions**

*"The more of the world we inhabit, the better it is for the human race. Just fancy, those parts that are at present inhabited by the most despicable specimens of human beings, what an alteration there would be if they were brought under Anglo-Saxon influence."*

—C. J. Rhodes, British imperialist and mining magnate of the late 1800s

*"I am an African...I owe my being to the hills and valleys, the mountains and glades...to the Khoi and the San. . . . I am formed of the migrants who left Europe...of Malay slaves from the east...of warrior patriots...I am the grandchild who lays fresh flowers on Boer graves..."*

—Thabo Mbeki, President of South Africa

Some 15,000 people (10% of the Afrikaners at the Cape), set off on what is known as the Great Trek, and became known as the *Voortrekkers,* or "first movers." To their delight they found large tracts of unoccupied land, but unbeknownst to them this was due to the recent Mfecane, and it wasn't long before they clashed with the mighty Zulu nation, whom they defeated in 1838 at the **Battle of Blood River.** A century later, this "miraculous" victory was to be the greatest inspiration for Afrikaner nationalism, and a monument was built to glorify the battle. Today the **Voortrekker Monument** is still a place of pilgrimage for Afrikaner nationalists and can be seen from most places in Pretoria.

The Boer's victory was, however, short-lived. The British, not satisfied with the Cape's coast, annexed Natal in 1845. Once again the Voortrekkers headed over the mountains with their ox-wagons, looking for freedom from the British. They founded two republics: the **Orange Free State** (now the Free State); and the **South African Republic** or **Transvaal** (now Gauteng, the North-West, Mpumalanga, and the Northern Province). This time the British left them alone; with over 30 million people, the United States was of more interest than a remote colony with only 250,000 settlers. However, the 1867 discovery of **diamonds** in the Orange Free State (in modern-day Kimberley) and, 19 years later, of **gold** in the Transvaal, was to change this attitude dramatically.

**GETTING RICH & STAYING POOR** In both the diamond and the gold fields, a step-by-step amalgamation of individual claims was finally necessitated by the expense of the mining process. In Kimberley, **Cecil John Rhodes**—an ambitious young man who was to become obsessed with the cause of British imperial expansion—masterminded the creation of **De Beers Consolidated,** the mining house that to this day controls the diamond-mining industry in southern Africa. (It is worth noting that the discovery of diamonds was also the start of the labor-discrimination practices that were to set the precedent for the gold mines and the coming apartheid years.) The mining of gold did not result in the same monopoly, and the **Chamber of Mines,** established in 1887, went some way to regulate the competition. However, **Paul Kruger,** president of the South African Republic, became a spoke in the wheel. Both a staunch Calvinist preacher and survivor of the Great Trek, he did not intend to make things easy for the mostly British entrepreneurs who were by now in control of the gold mines. He created no real infrastructure to aid them, and *uitlanders* (foreigners) were not allowed to vote. Britain in turn wanted to amalgamate the South African colonies to consolidate their power in southern Africa. (British forces had in fact attempted to annex the Transvaal in 1877,

## Nothing but the Truth

*"... a commission is a necessary exercise to enable South Africans to come to terms with their past on a morally accepted basis and to advance the cause of reconciliation."*

—Mr. Dullah Omar, Minister of Justice

Following South Africa's first democratic elections in 1994, the **Truth and Reconciliation Commission (TRC)** was formed to investigate human rights abuses under apartheid rule. The many victims of apartheid were invited to voice their anger and pain before the commission, headed by Archbishop Desmond Tutu, and to confront directly the perpetrators of these abuses in a public forum. In return for full disclosure, aggressors, regardless of their political persuasion, could ask for forgiveness and amnesty from prosecution. While many white South Africans maintained their sanity by denying the truth, many more for the first time faced the realities of what apartheid meant. Wrenching images of keening relatives listening to killers, some coldly, others in tears, describing exactly how they had tortured and killed those once officially described as missing persons or accidental deaths were broadcast nationwide. Those whom the commission thought had not made a full disclosure were denied amnesty, as were those who could not prove that they were acting on behalf of or due to some political cause. However, many still think that following orders is an unacceptable excuse and yearn for a more equitable punishment than mere admission of wrongdoing. They believe that true justice can only result from retribution, and cannot forgive.

Twenty-seven months of painful confessions and $25 million later (the report and further amnesty applications took another 6 months to a year), the commission concluded its investigation. Certainly the commission has affected a more accurate rendition of recent history, but whether this will lead to true reconciliation remains to be seen.

just after the discovery of diamonds, but they had underestimated Paul Kruger; and in 1881 they restored the Boer republic's independence.) In 1899, when the British demanded full rights for the uitlanders, Kruger responded by invading the coastal colonies.

At first the Second **Anglo-Boer War** went well for the Boers, who used hitherto unheard of guerilla tactics, but the British commander **Lord Kitchener** soon found their Achilles' heel. Close to 28,000 Boer women and children died in his concentration camps, and his scorched-earth policy, whereby their farms were systematically razed to the ground, broke the Boer spirit. Ultimately Britain would pit nearly half a million men against 88,000 Boers. In 1902 the Boer republics became part of the Empire—the Afrikaner nationalism that was to sweep the country in the next century was fuelled by the resentments of a nation struggling to escape the yoke of British imperialism.

**OPPRESSION & RESISTANCE** The years following this defeat were hard on those at the bottom of the ladder. Afrikaners, many of whom had now lost their farms, streamed to the cities where they competed with blacks for unskilled jobs on equal terms and were known as poor whites. Black South

Africans had also suffered during the Anglo-Boer War, (including the loss of some 14,000 in the concentration camps), but this was neither recognized nor compensated. With the creation of the **Union of South Africa** in 1910, the country joined the British Commonwealth of Nations, and participated in both World Wars. Back home, loyalties were divided and the Afrikaners were bitter about forging allegiances with a country they had so recently been at war with. In 1934 a new "purified" **National Party (NP)** was established, offering a voice for the "poor white" Afrikaners. Under the leadership of Dr. D. F. Malan, who swore he would liberate the Afrikaner from their economic "oppression," the NP won the 1948 election by a narrow margin—46 years of white minority rule were to follow, before internal and international pressure would finally buckle the NP's resolve.

One of the first laws that created the segregationist policy named **apartheid** (literally, separateness) was the **Population Registration Act,** in which everyone was slotted into an appropriate race group. This caused the greatest problem for those of mixed descent. One of the most infamous classification tests was the pencil test, whereby a pencil was stuck into the hair of a person of uncertain racial heritage. If the pencil dropped, the person was "white"; if it stuck s/he was classified "coloured." In this way, entire communities, in some cases even families, were torn apart. This new group (coloureds) enjoyed slightly more privileges than their black counterparts—a better standard of housing, schooling, and job opportunities—no doubt an overture to their white ancestors. Interracial sexual relations, previously illicit, were now illegal, and the Group Areas Act ensured that families would never mingle on the streets. The Group Areas Act even required the destruction and relocation of total suburbs, none of which were white. The **Bantu Education Act** ensured that black South Africans could not challenge white South Africans. During this time, the majority of English speakers condemned the policies of what came to be known as the Afrikaans NP; but as they continued to dominate business in South Africa, the maintenance of a cheap labor pool was in their interests, and life was generally too comfortable for most to do anything. Change came inevitably from the non-white quarters.

By the middle of the 20th century, blacks outnumbered whites in the urban areas, but resided "unseen" in **townships** outside of the cities. Their movements were restricted by **pass laws;** they were barred from trade union activities, deprived of any political rights, and prohibited from procuring land outside of their reserves or homelands. **Homelands** were small tracts of land, about 13% of the country, where the so-called ethnically distinct black South African "tribes" (actually 42% of the population) were forced to live. This effectively divided the black majority into tribal minorities.

The **African Nationalist Congress Party (ANC)** was formed by representatives of the country's major African organizations in 1912, but it was only in 1934 that it was to find the inspired leadership of **Anton Lembede, Oliver Tambo, Walter Sisulu,** and **Nelson Mandela,** who formed the **ANC Youth League** in this year. But the ANC's hitherto passive resistance tactics were to be met with forceful suppression, and in 1960 police opened fire on unarmed

## Impressions

*"The history of the Afrikaner reveals a will and a determination which makes one feel that Afrikanerdom is not the work of men but the creation of God."*

—D. F. Malan, leader of the "Purified NP," 1948–1954

demonstrators in Sharpeville, killing 67, and wounding 200. This marked the beginning of South Africa's ostracism in world affairs, and the start of violent opposition within.

In 1963 police captured the underground leaders of the ANC—including the "Black Pimpernel" Nelson Mandela, who was by now commander-in-chief of their armed wing, **UmkhontoWe Sizwe** (Spear of the Nation). In what came to be known as the **Rivonia Trial,** Mandela and nine other leaders received life sentences for treason and were sent off to **Robben Island.** The imprisonment of key figures effectively silenced the opposition within the country for some time and allowed the NP to further entrench its segregationist policies. But a nasty surprise awaited Hendrik Verwoerd, the man who served as cabinet minister for Bantu Affairs under Malan and was named the architect of apartheid. He was stabbed to death one morning while at work in the House of Assembly (strangely, not for overtly political reasons; the murderer insisted that a tapeworm had ordered him to do it) and in 1966 B. J. Vorster became the new NP leader.

Vorster was to push for the independence of Verwoerd's black homelands, which would effectively deprive all black people of their South African citizenship, as well as enforce the use of Afrikaans as a language medium in all schools. Ironically, the latter triggered the backlash that would finally end Afrikaner dominance.

**THE BIRTH OF THE NEW SOUTH AFRICA** On June 16, 1976, thousands of black schoolchildren in **Soweto** took to the streets to demonstrate against this new law, which for the many non-Afrikaans speakers would render schooling useless. The police opened fire, killing 13-year-old **Hector Peterson,** and chaos followed, with unrest spreading throughout the country. The youth, disillusioned by their parents' compliance with apartheid laws, burned schools, libraries, vehicles, and shebeens, the informal liquor outlets that provided an opiate to the dispossessed. Many arrests followed, including that of black consciousness leader **Steve Biko** in the Eastern Cape, who became the 46th political prisoner to die during police interrogation. Young activists fled the country and joined ANC training camps. The ANC, led by Oliver Tambo, called for international sanctions—and the world responded with economic, cultural, and sports boycotts, and awarded the Nobel Peace prize to **Archbishop Desmond Tutu,** one of the strongest campaigners for sanctions. The new NP premier, **P. W. Botha,** or "die Groot Krokodil" (the great crocodile) as he came to be known, simply wagged his finger and declared South Africa capable of going it alone. The crocodile's bite proved as bad as his bark, and his response to the unrest was to simply pour an ever-increasing number of troops into townships. In 1986 he declared a **State of Emergency,** thereby giving his security forces unlimited power to track down and persecute the opposition, and effectively silencing the internal press.

The overwhelming majority of white South Africans enjoyed an excellent standard of living, a state of supreme comfort which made it difficult to

**Impressions**

*"I have cherished the ideal of a democratic and free society in which all people live together in harmony and with equal opportunities. It is an ideal which I hope to live for and achieve. But if needs be it is an ideal for which I am prepared to die."*

—Nelson Mandela at the Rivonia Trial in 1964

challenge the status quo. Many believed the state propaganda that blacks were innately inferior, or remained blissfully ignorant of the extent of the human rights violations; still others found their compassion silenced by fear. Ignorant or numbed, most white South Africans waited for what seemed to be the inevitable civil war, until 1989, when a ministerial rebellion forced the intransigent Botha to resign, and new leader **F. W. de Klerk** stepped in.

By now the economy was in serious trouble—the cost of maintaining apartheid had bled the coffers dry, the Chase Manhattan Bank had refused to roll over its loan, and sanctions and trade-union action had brought the country's economy to a virtual standstill. In February 1990, de Klerk unbanned the ANC, PAC, the Communist Party, and 33 other organizations, and released Nelson Mandela after 27 years of imprisonment.

The fragile negotiations between the various political parties were to last for a nerve-wracking 4 years. During this time, right-wingers threatened civil war, while many in the townships lived it. **Zulu nationalists,** of the **Inkatha** party, waged a low-level war against ANC supporters which was to claim the lives of thousands. Eyewitness accounts were given of security force involvement in this black-on-black violence, and accusations made of training and supplies provided to Inkatha forces by the South African Defence Force. In 1993 **Chris Hani,** the most popular ANC youth leader, was assassinated. South Africa held its breath while Mandela pleaded on nationwide television for peace—by this time, there was no doubt as to who was leading the country.

On April 27, 1994, **Nelson Mandela** cast his first vote at the age of 76, and on May 10 he was inaugurated as South Africa's first democratically elected president. Despite 18 opposition parties, the ANC took 63% of the vote and was dominant in all but two provinces—the Western Cape voted NP and KwaZulu-Natal went to Buthelezi's Zulu-based Inkatha (IFP) Party. Jubilation reigned, but the hangover was bad. Of an estimated 38 million people, 6 million were believed unemployed, and 9 million destitute. Ten million had no access to running water, and 20 million no electricity. The ANC had to launch a program of "nation-building," in an attempt to unify what the NP had spent a fortune dividing. Wealth had to be redistributed without hampering the ailing economy, and a government debt of almost R350 billion ($58 billion) repaid.

Two years after being elected, the then Deputy President **Thabo Mbeki** made his seminal "I am an African" speech, in which he stated that "Africanness cannot be determined by race, color, gender, or historical origin, but that the failure to achieve real nation-building was entrenching the existence of two separate nations, one white and affluent and the other black and poor."

That the New South African nation was born in peace was a miracle, but the ANC will need another to meet the hopes and dreams of its rainbow people.

## Impressions

*"The basic tenet of black consciousness is that the black man must reject all value systems that seek to make him a foreigner in the country of his birth and reduce his basic human dignity."*

—Steve Biko, May 3, 1976

*"Natives will be taught from childhood to realise that equality with Europeans is not for them."*

—H. Verwoerd, the "architect of apartheid," 1953

**Impressions**

*"We have triumphed in the effort to implant hope in the breasts of the millions of our people. We enter into a covenant that we shall build the society in which all South Africans, both black and white, will be able to walk tall, without any fear in their hearts, assured of their inalienable right to human dignity—a rainbow nation at peace with itself and the world."*

—Nelson Mandela's Inaugural Address, 1994

# 4 The Rainbow Nation

South African stereotypes are no simple black-and-white matter. Historically the nation was made up of a number of widely different cultural groups; and while these might under normal circumstances have amalgamated into a singular hybrid called "the South African," the deeply divisive policy of apartheid simply entrenched initial differences. While it is the ANC government's stated objective to end racial discrimination and develop a unique South African identity, the Rainbow Nation—a term coined by the ebullient Archbishop Tutu during the build-up to elections—remains difficult to define, let alone unify. Broadly speaking, approximately 76% of some 38 million people are black, 12.8% are white, 2.6% are Asian, and 8.5% are "coloured" (the South African term for those of mixed descent as well as for some 200,000 Cape Malays). Beyond these are smaller but no less significant groups, descendents of Lebanese, Italian, Portugese, Hungarian, and Greek settlers as well the 130,000-strong Jewish community. The latter, in particular, has played an enormous role in the economic and political growth of South Africa.

In an attempt to recognize this cultural diversity, the government has given official recognition to eleven languages: Zulu, Xhosa, Afrikaans, English, Sotho, Venda, Tswana, Tsona, Pedi, Shangaan and Ndebele. Television news and sports is broadcast in the four main language groups, English, Nguni (Zulu and Xhosa), Afrikaans, and Sotho. But while languages provide some clue as to the demographics of the population, particularly where a specific language user is likely to live (another apartheid legacy), they give no real idea of the complexity of attitudes within groups—for instance, urban-born Xhosa males still paint their faces white to signal their transition to manhood, but unlike their rural counterparts they may choose to be circumcised by a Western doctor. A group of Sotho women may invest their *stokvel* (an informal savings scheme), in unit trusts, while their mothers will not open a bank account. And an "ethnic" white Afrikaner living in rural Northern Cape will have very little in common with an Afrikaans-speaking coloured living in cosmopolitan Cape Town.

Common to all South Africans are worries about the economy, personal financial circumstances, and crime. But that's more or less where the common ground ends. Members of the "white tribes of Africa" are generally unhappy with the New South Africa. Many pessimists still maintain that a black government cannot rule effectively and, having ignored the findings of the Truth and Reconciliation Commission, declare that life was better in the "old" South Africa. Still, a growing percentage have cashed in on South Africa's return to the global economy and are excited by the confidence of the youth culture, evidenced in the sounds of "kwaito," the latest brand of South African music with true crosscultural appeal.

Despite continued poverty, it is the previously disadvantaged who show the most optimism for the future. Proof that life has improved for the majority of the population is not always easy to find, but in the "City of Gold" there is no doubt that the black middle class is growing, and it is the "buppies" (black-up-and-coming), that are frequenting the previously whites-only shopping malls with designer stalls. Even amongst the new elite, however, there are those who feel that the New South Africa is taking too long to deliver on its promises. "There is no black in the rainbow," an angry Winnie Madikizela-Mandela said recently. "Maybe there is no rainbow nation at all." Hardly surprising really. Years of fragmentation have rendered the nation cautious, suspicious, and critical—for a new, shared South African identity to emerge will take time; enough at least for the colors to mingle.

## 5 South African Cuisine

Visit at least one restaurant that specializes in South African cuisine and you will sample a new and truly delicious selection of dishes—for, contrary to popular belief, South Africans can cook up a storm.

The most basic African foodstuff is **corn,** most popularly eaten as *pap,* a ground maize porridge not unlike polenta, or the rougher wholegrain *samp,* and served with a vegetable or meat-based sauce. Traditionally protein was seldom provided by red meat; cows were kept as a sign of wealth and slaughtered only for special occasions; but times have changed and cheap cuts like liver, heart, and brisket are popular, as well as chicken. Popular vegetables include pumpkin, cabbage, carrots, wild spinach, and potatoes. **Roasting insects** such as locusts, flying ants, and mopani worms is a tradition that you're more likely to come across in theme restaurants than in today's townships.

Easiest on the newly initiated palate are the **Cape Malay dishes,** characterized by sweet aromatic **curries.** These include *bobotie,* a delicious baked meatloaf, mildly curried and served with chutney, and *bredie,* a tomato-based stew. Another Cape delicacy not to be missed is *waterblommetjie bredie,* or waterlily stew, cooked with lamb. They are truly mouthwatering, particularly when served with pumpkin and flavored with butter and brown sugar. Many South African menus also feature **Karoo lamb.** The theory is that the sweet and

### The Coloured Identity

Afrikaans-speaking people of mixed descent—grouped together as a new nation called "the coloureds" during the Population Registration Act—are perhaps the most affected by the policies of apartheid. Brought up to respect their white blood and deny their black roots entirely, these people were seen as second in line to whites, and received a better education and greater government support than black people. This was the apartheid state's overture to their white forefathers. The destruction of their sense of self-worth was made evident when the Nationalist Party won the 1994 election race in the Western Cape (where the majority of this group resides). Voting the selfsame racist party that created them back into power was seemingly a direct result of the false sense of hierarchy that apartheid created. Fear of "die Swart Gevaar" (a NP propaganda slogan meaning "the Black Danger") is only now, after the first 5 years of majority rule, starting to dissipate, and there are calls within the coloured ranks to stop searching for a common identity and do away with the label entirely.

aromatic herbs and grasses of this arid region flavor the animals' flesh as they graze. Another treat is the aptly named *vetkoek* (fat cake), deep-fried dough stuffed with hamburger. And to finish your typically South African meal, choose between *melktert,* a cinnamon-flavored custard tart of Dutch origin; *malvapudding,* a brandy-soaked sponge cake; or *koeksisters,* plaited doughnuts, deep-fried and dipped in syrup.

On the East Coast, Durban is famed for its **Indian curries,** whose burn potential is indicated by ingenious names such as **Honeymooners' Delight** (hot) and **Mother-in-Law Exterminator** (damn hot!). If you're looking for a delicious snack, purchase a bag of **samoosas,** layers of paper-thin pastry wrapped around a triangular-shaped ball of curried minced meat or vegetables and deep-fried; the best are crunchy, juicy, and mouth-burning hot. A cheap and filling meal, **bunnychow** is a half a loaf of white bread, scooped out and filled with spicy meat or vegetable stew.

The coastline supplies seafood in abundance: fish, abalone, mussels, oysters, crabs, squid, langoustines (a cross between shrimp and lobster), and the Cape's famous rock lobster (crayfish). Barracuda, yellowtail, shad, butterfish, kingklip, galjoen, and snoek are all fighting fish and therefore firm-fleshed and highly recommended. **Snoek** is traditionally served with *konfyt* (fruits preserved in sugar syrup, from the French confit, a legacy of the French Huguenots). Alternatively try *smoorsnoek,* a savory mixture of tomato and onion which is cooked with the fish. Visit one of the outdoor **visbraai** restaurants on the West Coast (see chapter 4, "Western Cape"), and you'll have your fill of all of the above.

Then there are the ubiquitous **braaivleis** (barbecue meat), or **tshisanyamas** (literally burn the meat). Look for the spiraling smoke trailing over suburban fences and township yards every weekend, as thousands of South Africans throughout the country enjoy the sunny weather and the excellent fresh meat cooked over coals. The best braais are made up of **lamb chops,** *ribbetjies* (ribs), *sosaties* (skewers of meat in a spicy sweet marinade), and *boerewors* (literally, farmers sausage), a spicy coarse-minced sausage made of beef and pork. A spicy tomato-and-onion sauce often accompanies this, as well as potatoes, or pap. As for vegetables, well, it's an old joke that in the Northern Cape, the only vegetable you'll find at a braai is chicken.

Game cuts of springbok, kudu, eland, impala, ostrich, or warthog are common on menus catering to tourists, but otherwise unusual, unless you're in the Northern Province (South Africa's hunting haven). Look out for *potjies* (*poy*-key—literally, little pots), named for the three-legged cast-iron pots into which ingredients are added at various crucial points and often cooked for hours over a small flame, creating wholesome filling stews.

**DRINKING** Virtually all local beers are produced by the **South African Breweries (SAB)** monopoly, and taste pretty much the same. **Mitchell's** and **Forrester's** are independent breweries based in the Western Cape, and definitely worth sampling should they appear on a menu. Namibian beers are generally better than the SAB beers, as they're produced under the strict German system of *Reinheitsgebot* (that is, without chemicals). **Windhoek** is one of the best. South African wines are terrific; for tips, see chapter 3, "Cape Town & the Winelands." The news for teetotallers is also good: South Africa has the most extensive range of unsweetened fruit juices in the world.

**SNACKS TO GO** By the time the first pilgrims had crossed the mountains dividing the Cape from the hinterland, they knew a thing or two about surviving on the move. *Biltong* (*bill*-tong), strips of meat cured with spices and salt, was the best way to carry protein, and is still the best food to take on a road trip (though beware, there are great variations in quality; it's best to go to a butcher and request beef). If you see someone pressing the biltong, this is to ascertain its ripeness—the connoisseur goes for a "wet" cut that has a slightly pink center. *Droëwors* is the sausage version. **Fruit rolls,** sugared and dried, supplied the Trekkers with Vitamin C; while **rusks,** large dry biscuits, provided carbohydrates. The latter are still a staple, and you are likely to be offered some before your early-morning game drive (dunk them in your coffee or tea.)

## 6 Suggested Reading

The first South African novel, *The Story of an African Farm* (Dover), was written in 1883 by Olive Schreiner, and her beautifully rendered account of daily life in the harsh Karoo was hailed both here and abroad. Greater escape was however to be offered by *King Solomon's Mines* (Book-of-the-Month Club), published a mere 2 years later. Written by adventure-writer H. Rider Haggard, it was to capture the imagination of the colonizers back home, and to date has been filmed five times. Another frontier tale to enjoy success for generations is Percy Fitzpatrick's *Jock of the Bushveld* (Bhb. International Inc.), a tale about a transport rider and his dog, written in 1907. You will find many references to the loyal terrier Jock throughout Mpumalanga, and even a statue erected to his honor in Barberton. The ever-popular writer Wilbur Smith provides the modern-day equivalent of these early adventure novels, with action-packed tales featuring a wild untamed landscape populated by hard-headed heroes and firm-breasted heroines. However, the best light read to combine historical elements with fiction is James Mitchener's gripping epic *Covenant* (Fawcett Books). Also often described as an adventure novelist, though his subject matter is a great deal more serious and sensitive, is the late Sir Laurens van der Post. His most famous work was *The Lost World of the Kalahari* (Harcourt Brace), written in 1958, which dealt with the cosmology of the last remaining San, a few of whom still survive in the Kalahari.

The most famous black novelist during the first half of this century is Sol Plaatje, a founder member of the ANC, who wrote *Native Life in South Africa* (Ohio University Press) in 1916, about the devastation caused by the 1913 Land Act. If the Zulu warrior, often referred to as Africa's Napoleon interests you, look out for *Chaka* (Heinemann) written by Thomas Mofolo in 1909 in Sotho. This was the first epic tale about the mercurial Zulu king and has been translated by Daniel Kunene.

As urbanization increased, the "Jim-comes-to-Jo'burg" novel evolved, a phrase coined by Nadine Gordimer to describe the plot in which a naive rural African moves into the corrupt and evil urban landscape. The most famous of these is *Cry the Beloved Country* (Addison-Wesley), written by Alan Paton in 1948. Probably the most widely read South African book, it played a major role in fueling anti-apartheid sentiment, though it has also been criticized for perpetuating the stereotype of the noble Zulu. For a more honest look at the vicious effects of apartheid, look out for any of the works by Booker Prize–winner J. M. Coetzee, as well as those by Breyten Breytenbach, and Andre Brink. Especially good are Brink's *A Dry White Season* (Penguin) and Coetzee's *Age of Iron* (Penguin). The latter was voted by the excellent weekly newspaper *Mail & Guardian* the finest South African novel of the past decade, and tells of a white woman dying of cancer who befriends the black tramp living in her garden. The semi-autobiographical *My Traitor's Heart* (Vintage),

## Afrikaans—Modern Language with a Medieval Past

Afrikaans, the world's newest language, is spoken by 15% of the South African population, making it the third-largest mother tongue (English ranks 5th). A Dutch creole that absorbed the influences of the English, French, German, and Malay, it was harshly suppressed by the British during their colonial rule, creating a strong nationalist backlash. It finally gained official recognition as a language in 1925 and, despite the fact that it has always been the mother tongue of the coloureds, it came to be thoroughly tainted by its association with the National Party (NP) and that party's apartheid policies. During the mid-1970s the NP, having learned nothing from their own history of oppression, tried to enforce Afrikaans as the sole medium of instruction in schools. This lead to the Soweto uprising of 1976, which marked the unofficial end of majority acceptance of apartheid rule.

---

written by Rian Malan, gave voice to white South Africa's primal fears in the 1980s and is essential reading for anyone who finds it hard to understand how white people could live with themselves under apartheid.

Nadine Gordimer's novels have been awarded a Nobel Prize, a Booker Prize, a Grand Aigle d'Or as well as a host of other awards, making her South Africa's most internationally illustrious writer. *The Conservationist* (Viking) is particularly good. Of her works highlighting South Africa, *The House Gun* (Penguin) is recommended, as is *Burger's Daughter* (Viking), which deals with relationships across the color bar. The latter theme is also admirably explored in *The Grass Is Singing* (Penguin), written by Doris Lessing in the 1950s.

For an excellent historical analysis, read Allister Sparkes' *The Tomorrow's Another Country* (University of Chicago Press). Political autobiography often provides the most honest and direct insights, and there is no shortage of choice here—Mandela's *Long Walk to Freedom* (Little Brown) has become an international bestseller, as no doubt will his latest, *The Parliament Years.* Mark Behr's *The Smell of Apples* (Picador) deals with the troubled psyche of the white man (from the point of view of an anti-apartheid student activist). Ronnie Kasrils, Joe Slovo, Helen Joseph, Desmond Tutu, and Albie Sachs have also all written about their struggle against apartheid. Possibly the most harrowing book to have emerged since the elections, *Country of My Skull* (Times Books), is Afrikaans poet Antjie Krog's account of her work as a journalist reporting on the TRC.

Moving beyond the political are modern writers such Sindiwe Magona and Zakes Mda. Of his two books published in 1995, Mda's *Ways of Dying* (Oxford) recounts events from the perspective of a self-styled "professional mourner," an interesting concept which provides fascinating insights into modern black culture, as does Magona's collection of short stories, *To My Children's Children* (Interlink Pub Group). For light contemporary reading, pick up a copy of Marita van der Vyfer's *Entertaining Angels* (Plume), a farce dealing with the breakdown of a marriage in white suburbia.

# Index

Index

Index

Index

## FROMMER'S® DOLLAR-A-DAY GUIDES

Australia from $50 a Day
California from $60 a Day
Caribbean from $70 a Day
England from $70 a Day
Europe from $60 a Day
Florida from $60 a Day
Hawaii from $70 a Day
Ireland from $50 a Day
Israel from $45 a Day
Italy from $70 a Day
London from $85 a Day
New York from $80 a Day
New Zealand from $50 a Day
Paris from $85 a Day
San Francisco from $60 a Day
Washington, D.C., from $60 a Day

## FROMMER'S® PORTABLE GUIDES

Acapulco, Ixtapa & Zihuatanejo
Alaska Cruises & Ports of Call
Bahamas
Baja & Los Cabos
Berlin
California Wine Country
Charleston & Savannah
Chicago
Dublin
Hawaii: The Big Island
Las Vegas
London
Maine Coast
Maui
New Orleans
New York City
Paris
Puerto Vallarta, Manzanillo & Guadalajara
San Diego
San Francisco
Sydney
Tampa & St. Petersburg
Venice
Washington, D.C.

## FROMMER'S® NATIONAL PARK GUIDES

Family Vacations in the National Parks
Grand Canyon
National Parks of the American West
Rocky Mountain
Yellowstone & Grand Teton
Yosemite & Sequoia/Kings Canyon
Zion & Bryce Canyon

## FROMMER'S® GREAT OUTDOOR GUIDES

New England
Northern California
Southern California & Baja
Washington & Oregon

## FROMMER'S® MEMORABLE WALKS

Chicago
London
New York
Paris
San Francisco
Washington D.C.

## FROMMER'S® IRREVERENT GUIDES

Amsterdam
Boston
Chicago
Las Vegas
London
Los Angeles
Manhattan
New Orleans
Paris
San Francisco
Seattle & Portland
Vancouver
Walt Disney World
Washington, D.C.

## FROMMER'S® BEST-LOVED DRIVING TOURS

America
Britain
California
Florida
France
Germany
Ireland
Italy
New England
Scotland
Spain
Western Europe

## THE UNOFFICIAL GUIDES®

Bed & Breakfast in New England
Bed & Breakfast in the Northwest
Beyond Disney
Branson, Missouri
California with Kids
Chicago
Cruises
Disneyland
Florida with Kids
The Great Smoky & Blue Ridge Mountains
Inside Disney
Las Vegas
London
Miami & the Keys
Mini Las Vegas
Mini-Mickey
New Orleans
New York City
Paris
San Francisco
Skiing in the West
Walt Disney World
Walt Disney World for Grown-ups
Walt Disney World for Kids
Washington, D.C.

## SPECIAL-INTEREST TITLES

Born to Shop: France
Born to Shop: Hong Kong
Born to Shop: Italy
Born to Shop: New York
Born to Shop: Paris
Frommer's Britain's Best Bike Rides
The Civil War Trust's Official Guide to the Civil War Discovery Trail
Frommer's Caribbean Hideaways
Frommer's Europe's Greatest Driving Tours
Frommer's Food Lover's Companion to France
Frommer's Food Lover's Companion to Italy
Frommer's Gay & Lesbian Europe
Israel Past & Present
Monks' Guide to California
Monks' Guide to New York City
The Moon
New York City with Kids
Unforgettable Weekends
Outside Magazine's Guide to Family Vacations
Places Rated Almanac
Retirement Places Rated
Road Atlas Britain
Road Atlas Europe
Washington, D.C., with Kids
Wonderful Weekends from Boston
Wonderful Weekends from New York City
Wonderful Weekends from San Francisco
Wonderful Weekends from Los Angeles